Special Edition Using

Using MICROSOFT® Exchange Server 5.5

QUE®

Special Edition

Using

Using Microsoft® Exchange Server 5.5

Written by:

Software Spectrum with Kent Joshi, Tracy Bradley, Tito Del Prado, Neil Nelmida, Richard Romo, Intekhab "Inti" Shaikh, Robert Short, Valeno Valentino, and Sal Collora, Mark Kapczynski, Ruben Perez, Ed Roberts

Special Edition Using Microsoft Exchange Server 5.5

Library of Congress Catalog No.: 97-80666

ISBN: 0-7897-1503-1

99 98 6 5 4 3 2

Interpretation of the printing code: the rightmost double-digit number is the year of the book's printing; the rightmost single-digit number, the number of the book's printing. For example, a printing code of 97-1 shows that the first printing of the book occurred in 1997.

PC screen reproductions in this book were created by using Collage Plus from Inner Media, Inc., Hollis, NH.

Contents at a Glance

Table of Contents

II Configuring and Optimizing Windows 95

Credits

SENIOR VICE PRESIDENT/PUBLISHING
Don Fowley

PUBLISHER
David Dwyer

GENERAL MANAGER
Joe Muldoon

EDITORIAL SERVICES DIRECTOR
Carla Hall

EXECUTIVE EDITOR
Al Valvano

ACQUISITIONS EDITOR
Stephanie Layton

DEVELOPMENT EDITOR
Nancy D. Warner

MANAGING EDITOR
Sarah Kearns

SENIOR EDITOR
Mike La Bonne

COPY EDITORS
Margaret Berson, Jenny Clark, Audra McFarland, Pamela Emanoil

TECHNICAL EDITOR
Bob Reinsch

TEAM COORDINATOR
Lynette Quinn

MANUFACTURING COORDINATOR
Brook Farling

EDITORIAL ASSISTANT
Lori Morgan

COVER DESIGNER
Sandra Schroeder

COVER PRODUCTION
Casey Price

BOOK DESIGNER
Ruth Harvey

DIRECTOR OF PRODUCTION
Larry Klein

PRODUCTION TEAM SUPERVISOR
Beth Lewis

GRAPHICS IMAGE SPECIALISTS
Sadie Crawford
Will Cruz
Oliver Jackson

PRODUCTION ANALYST
Erich J. Richter

PRODUCTION TEAM
Erin Danielson
Jennifer Earhart
DiMonique Ford
Laura A. Knox
Angel Perez
Heather Stephenson

INDEXER
Craig Small

Composed in *Century Old Style* and *ITC Franklin Gothic* by Que Corporation.

Acknowledgments

First, I thank **Noelani Rodriguez** and **Randy Newman** for their silent patience. Although they sacrificed sleep and consulting income to ensure the first edition of this book was done right, they were never properly recognized. Thank you, my friends. The first edition would not have been complete without your contributions. Be sure to check out Noelani's book, *Using Microsoft SMS 1.2*, published by Que.

Next, I thank **Betty Dixon** of Compaq and **Ralph Smaldino** of NEC for loaning us hubs and one incredible dual Pentium server. With the NEC server as our lab's heart and Compaq's hubs connecting to everything else, we turned a training room into a "virtual Software Spectrum." We simulated 11 Software Spectrum consulting sites across the world in one room complete with all the necessary connectors, protocols, and external mail systems.

I thank **Software Spectrum** for seeing value in this book and expending considerable time, money, and resources to ensure its success. Specifically, I thank **Michelle Hollis**, Site Manager for Software Spectrum's Technology Services Group (TSG) in Los Angeles for supporting me and helping me with my responsibilities so I could fully focus on authoring and editing. You are a great mentor and model manager. As you would say, "Thank you, thank you, thank you." I thank **Dan Gardner**, Director of Consulting West, whose warm personality and ultimate integrity continue to inspire me. I say thank you to **Link Simpson**, President of TSG. You are an outstanding example of leadership by principles. I also want to give a big Thank You to **Phillip McCollough**, Product Manager for Microsoft BackOffice Solutions who managed the marketing effort for this book from Software Spectrum's side and whose Microsoft contacts were key in taking this book to the next level. Also thank you to **Vic Clement**, Principal Consultant, TSG-LA, for assisting several authors in completing their chapters, and to **Robert Brunskill** for standing in for me to proofread and submit several chapters. Finally, I thank **Judy Sims**, Chairman, CEO, and President of Software Spectrum Inc. I have a deep respect for anyone who can successfully manage a company such as Software Spectrum.

"I would also like to thank **John Havlick** (Production Manager, Exchange Solutions) and **George Sarty** (Manager, Product Development) of Software Spectrum for their support and their creation of the Exchange Solutions Alliance, which will help companies extend the Exchange prduct beyond messaging to platform for comprehensive groupware, workflow, and collaboration business solutions. Member companies will be able to share concepts and solutions centered around Exchange. The Exchange Solutions Alliance will focus on providing its members comprehensive information on availble third-part solutions for workflow, document management, unified mesaging, disaster recovery and other areas. Other benefits will include special discounts on add-on products and bi-annual Exchange Solutions Alliance symposiums. I truly believe that all readers will find value from the Exchange Alliance."

I thank all of the Microsoft employees who helped make this book a reality. Thank you **Elaine Sharp** in Australia for all of your Exchange information and moral support, and **Brian Valentine** for letting us use your quote to kick off Chapter 1. Also, thanks to **Giuseppe Mascarella**, Total Cost of Ownership Marketing Manager, for your great assistance; **Len Wyatt** in the Exchange Group in Redmond for answering all of our late night questions on Exchange features and performance tuning; and **Marc Seifeld** for all the help with ASP.

I thank **Mario Santonastaso** and everyone else at **Campbell Hall School** for their continued support and letting the team borrow a Macintosh for a key chapter. Mario, you're one heck of a client. Thank you from the bottom of my heart.

To the **Fab Four**, thank you for your tireless work. You know who you are.

Thanks to **Mark Kapczynski** for giving me the opportunity to participate in the first edition of this book.

I extend deep and loving thanks for my Mom, **Miranda Lee**, who supported me during the earliest phases of this book. Keep the faith, Mom.

I also send a big Thank You to **Dad**, **Doe**, and **Dan** in Ohio. You guys were always on my mind throughout this book.

I also thank **Al Valvano** and **Stephanie Layton** from Que Publishing for offering this book opportunity and making sure we delivered the highest quality material on time.

A loud and powerful thank you to **Anthony Robbins**. Although we only met briefly, your wisdom, energy level, and lifestyle continue to shape my life and the relationships around me. You were the difference that made a difference. I hope one day we can extend our meeting into a lunch. Live with Passion!

And finally, I extend thanks to someone I never have the pleasure of meeting. I thank **Bill Gates** whose company gave me my first technology job at the tender age of 18. One day, I'd like to meet and personally thank you for creating the company that started all this.

As I think about the amount of teamwork it took to complete this book, I'm reminded that with every accomplishment, there are always hidden heroes. If I've left anyone out, I truly appreciate your help, and I trust the book will somehow come back to reward you over the work you've put in.

Kent Joshi
Microsoft Practice Manager

Software Spectrum, Technology Services Group (TSG), Los Angeles

kjoshi@swspectrum.com

About the Authors

Neil Nelmida is a consultant for Software Spectrum-TSG Los Angeles. He is a Microsoft Certified Systems Engineer, specializing in Exchange, Mail, TCP/IP, and Windows NT.

Before joining Software Spectrum, he co-owned a private consulting firm, which was a Microsoft Solution Provider. There he designed and installed Windows NT-based networks with Exchange Server and connectivity to the Internet. He also provided training for network administrators to maintain their systems to run at optimum performance.

He has always had a love for computers. He majored in Computer Science at UCLA, where he developed a solid foundation for problem-solving and programming. He also enjoys all multi-media games, especially golf.

Intekhab "Inti" Shaikh has more than seven years of experience in the computer industry. Starting from the DOS 3.1 days to the current NT Server 4.0, Inti has all-around experience with both Microsoft FrontOffice and BackOffice products. On the hardware side, Inti has upgraded a number of PC's, installed additional hardware components, and configured NIC cards. On the software side, Inti has a great deal of experience with Excel and Access. He has created full-service payroll software within Excel that creates a payroll, calculates the federal and state tax liability, and builds payroll reports. He has also programmed spreadsheet applications that crunch formulas, run statistics, and automatically generate useful business reports.

Inti conducts training sessions on Excel, Word, and accounting software (payroll taxes in particular) for the CPA firms and small companies in the Los Angeles area. Inti owns and manages a payroll and bookkeepinig company of his own. Additionally, Inti is a Microsoft Certified Professional and is currently pursuing the Microsoft Systems Engineer Certification. He also has multiple degrees from Cal State University and is a network consultant with Software Spectrum, INC., in Los Angeles. Currently, he is working on deploying Microsoft Systems Manager Server in a 1,000-workstation client in Long Beach, California.

His passion is spending time with his family, using Windows NT, reading technical books, keeping accounting books for his clients, and spending time with a great team of consultants he works with at Software Spectrum's Los Angeles office. His e-mail is **ishaikh@swspectrum.com**. Inti owes his networking exposure to Kent Joshi, the primary author of this book, who is a good friend, and his mentor in this industry.

Richard Romo is a principal consultant and teacher for Software Spectrum. His experience has ranged from small to large corporations, and he has worked in the Southern California area for 13 years. Richard has a BA in economics from the University of California at Santa Barbara. Richard has worked for a variety of accounts, setting up UNIX Administration and TCP/IP networks. For three years he has been setting up NT networks, Exchange, and SMS projects. Richard is an Accelerated Certified Engineer for Santa Cruz Operating System's UNIX, and a certified teacher for Santa Cruz Operation. He also is a Microsoft Certified Trainer and is a specialist for Information Internet Server. Additionally, he has worked as a

Senior Consultant for Grant Thornton, managing projects for NT and Microsoft SQL installation for Association and Professional Societies, and has served as a director of a Microsoft Authorized Training Educational Center in Orange County. He has extensive experience with Microsoft Exahange and System Management Server in some of the biggest companies in Southern California.

Tracy Bradley has been involved with Windows NT since the early BETAs of NT 3.1 in October of 1992, and the NT Inside Track Program of 1993. He has been a dedicated, avid NT and Microsoft supporter since then and travels to "Mecca" near Seattle every chance he gets. In addition to long-term experience with NT, Tracy is a Lotus Notes Certified Specialist (LCNS) since 1994 with experience in administering and developing workgroup applications for several large corporations. Since joining Software Spectrum's Dallas office in 1995, Tracy not only has completed MCSE certification, but also has been involved with Exchange almost exclusively since BETA 1 of version 4.0, with extensive work with MS Mail as well.

Currently, Tracy is the Microsoft Messaging Team leader over a thriving business in the Dallas area and has worked with literally dozens of Fortune 1000 corporations across the nation in design, implementation, and continuing development surrounding Exchange. Tracy was a presenter at the first Exchange Deployment Conference in Austin, Texas, in September 1996 and is in much demand for consulting engagements across the Software Spectrum realm.

When not jetting around the U.S. and abroad, Tracy enjoys time at home with his wife, Sheryl, and baby daughter, Rebecca, without whom "all this work would be worthless." Not bad for a Music Education major from Hardin-Simmons University in Abilene, Texas, wouldn't you say?

Robert Short has more than 12 years of experience in the industry, and his skills range from Project Management to Infrastructure design.

He is a certified engineer with Microsoft, Novell, and Banyan and has implemented large cc:Mail, Beyond Mail WordPerfect Office/GroupWise message systems. He is currently an employee of Software Spectrum and is specializing in Microsoft Windows NT 4.0, Microsoft System Management, and Microsoft Exchange Servers. He designs and implements large Banyan Networks at sites like Litton Data Systems, Warner Bros. Records, and several agencies in the Los Angeles area. Bob has also installed a number of Novell 3.x and 4x networks and has migrated Netware clients from Netware 3.x to Netware 4.x and Microsoft Windows NT. He has a strong background in System/Directory service design from his early days working with Banyan Vines StreetTalk. This knowledge makes the transition to Netware Directory Services a strong one and has helped with Microsoft Exchange designs.

Bob would like to thank his wife, Kelly, and his daughter, Shayla, for all their love and support.

Kent Joshi holds a BS in finance from the University of Utah. Currently, he is the Microsoft Practice Manager for Software Spectrum Inc.'s Technology Services Group. He is responsible for all aspects of the consulting practice including financials, resource management, employee development, and maintaining a close relationship with Microsoft.

Previously, he owned and managed The Joshi Group, a technical consulting firm specializing in the design, deployment, and tuning of large corporate networks. The Joshi Group has recently joined Software Spectrum, and Kent as well as his employees are now employed in their Los Angeles office.

Before managing his own company, he was employed at IBM Corporation, where he managed a team of consultants who installed and supported network systems for educational accounts.

Additionally, he has also worked for Microsoft Corporation, where he provided pre- and post-sales consulting for several Mzxicrosoft clients. In his role as a systems engineer, he was recognized as the Outstanding Representative in the Western Region. Kent can be reached at **kjoshi@swspectrum.com**.

Tito Del Prado has more than nine years of networking experience, having worked extensively with Novell Netware, Banyan Vines, and Microsoft BackOffice. Tito is a Microsoft Certified Systems Engineer (MCSE), specializing in the Microsoft NT 4.0 operating system. He is a certified Netframe administrator and has a diploma in Computer Technology and Electronics from Computer Learning Center of Los Angeles. Tito is a consultant at the Los Angeles office of the Technology Services Group of Software Spectrum, Inc.

Before working as a network consultant, Tito was a hardware engineer specializing in the legal arena. Having worked at most of the major law firms in the Los Angeles area, Tito has experience working with multiple platforms and applications as well as wide and local area networks. Tito also has experience working with many large government contractors such as Rockwell and TRW.

Aside from his various computer interests, Tito also enjoys spending time with his family, combing the beaches of Southern California for the perfect wave, and is an active member of his communnity, coaching and organizing youth sports and activites. His email address is **Tdelprado@swspectrum.com**.

Valeno Valentino has nine years of computer experience as a freelance programmer and five years of experience in networking infrastructure. Working for companies such as Paramount Pictures, GTE, Loma Linda Medical Center, Comp USA, and Kenneth Cole Shoes (just to name a few) has helped him become a seasoned computer professional. Database design and object-oriented programming have probably been his claim to fame. On the networking side, he has implemented Windows NT 3.51 server with Workstation 4.0 clients on the LAN/WAN environment at Lawyers Title Insurance in Glendale, California. Troubleshooting DHCP and TCP/IP problems in the Los Angeles and San Fernando areas has made him a topnotch problem solver. He is now on the Software Spectrum Consulting Team where he happily coexists in the network infrastructure and application development worlds. He gives special acknowledgment to his mother, two sisters, nephew, and his girlfriend Lisa; without their support from the very beginning none of his accomplishments would have been possible. He considers himself a dedicated and hardworking consultant who will be making his mark in the larger arena in the years to come. Drop him a line sometime at **Vvalentino@swspectrum.com**.

Michael Fawcett is a Microsoft Certified Systems Engineer (MCSE) and Microsoft Certified Trainer (MCT) specializing in Exchange. He graduated from Confederation College in Thunder Bay, Ontario from the Computer Programmer Analyst course and headed west to cut his teeth in the business in Winnipeg, Manitoba. Michael honed his Microsoft skills with Information Systems Management Corporation in Winnipeg and proceeded to make his next move due south. Michael is now working for Software Spectrum in Houston, Texas, designing and implementing Exchange solutions for oil and petrochemical companies based in South East Texas and New Orleans.

Mike would love to thank his wife, Carlene, and their three boys, Alexander, Damon, and Luke for their understanding and support.

Teresa Harmon is a consultant for the Software Spectrum-Seattle Office. She specializes in Microsoft Exchange architecting, implementation, and training. In the brief period that Teresa has been with Software Spectrum, she has completed several Exchange engagements. She spent many weeks in Anchorage, Alaska, working Exchange deployment and infrastructure issues and learning how to fish for halibut in her spare time!

Before working at Software Spectrum, Teresa was a senior analyst with King County's IT Department, and specialized in networking and Exchange.

Brent Frerck is an MCSE and member of Software Spectrum's TSG MS Messaging Team in Dallas. Brent joined Software Spectrum in April of 1997 when he entered "The Institute for Microsoft Technology." Following graduation from The Institute, Brent focused his consulting efforts on enterprise integration and deployment of Exchange Server. With over eight years of computer networking experience, he brings an array of messaging experiences and professional skills to his team.

Kristi, his wife, and Brenden and Matthew, his two sons, are Brent's greatest motivation. His most favorite activities are travelling and spending time in the great outdoors with his family. Brent thanks God and his family for their strength and love.

Wes Palmer is an MCP consultant for Software Spectrum, in Chicago. His experience includes migrating and maintaining the second largest Microsoft Mail implementation in the world to an Exchange backbone, and engineering the coexistance of Exchange with multiple mail systems with full Directory Synchronization. He also specializes in the Internet Mail Service, browser client access for mail calendar information, and the use of Publc Folders in large organizations. As a second area of expertise, Wes engineered several large Systems Management Server implementations across multiple client platforms.

Guillermo Proaño holds both a BBA and a BS in computer information science from Lamar University. A native of Lima, Peru, Guillermo has been involved in the planning and deployment of advanced Microsoft products for more than seven years. Guillermo has been a Microsoft supporter since his LAN Manager and Windows 3.0 days. Since joining Software Spectrum's Houston office, he has completed both his MCSE and MCT certifications with a focus on project management, messaging, and collaborative solutions.

Currently, Guillermo is the Messaging Team Leader for Software Spectrum's Gulf Coast Region. Together with his practice manager he has been heavily involved in the development of one of the premier messaging consulting SPs in the Texas Gulf Coast region, with a special focus on Microsoft Exchange Server.

When not working on Microsoft BackOffice projects for Fortune 1000 customers, Guillermo spends as much time as possible with his wife, Monica, and daughter, Ericka, as well as playing soccer.

Jason Roundy's core background includes Microsoft Mail, cc:Mail, Lotus Notes, & NT administration and architecture, and has helped solidify his vision of how strategic Exchange is and will continue to be. Leveraging strong people skills, Exchange integration allows him greater contact with an entire organization and that makes the consulting experience much more satisfying. Software Spectrum's Chicago office has provided a number of choice consulting engagements, including infrastructure design and enhancement for a major national association. Jason is currently developing an operational model for public folder usage in an environment that will reach 60,000 nodes.

With all this passion for consulting and Exchange, his marriage remains a focal pursuit. It takes extraordinary effort, bears the greatest rewards, and is constantly challenging, particularly when his focus is needed elsewhere. Jane Roundy, his wife of 6 years, lends a touch of the divine to their time together and Jason attributes much of his success to their "conspiracy of strength."

David A. Torres is a managing consultant for Software Spectrum. He is a Microsoft Certified Solution Developer and Microsoft Certified System Engineer. He is a speaker and author and has been featured speaker at Microsoft Developer Days and Windows World, and was a contributing author for *Special Edition Using ISAPI*, published by Que.

Zelko Kecman has been with Software Spectrum for two years as a senior consultant focusing on messaging. He is involved in the development and design of messaging architectures for corporations in Canada.

Mark Vis is a senior Software Spectrum consultant with nine years' experience as an IS Analyst and manager in Silicon Valley. A voracious sailor, he races weekly in San Francisco Bay and elsewhere. He dreams of a Microsoft-sponsored, all-MCSE team for the Whitbread around-the-world race. You can reach Mark at **mvis@softwarespectrum.com**.

Troy Vasa holds a BA degree in psychology from the University of Nebraska. Currently he is a senior consultant in Software Spectrum's Technology Services Group in their San Francisco office.

Troy is an MCSE, specializing in Microsoft Exchange and Windows NT. Along with his interests in computers, he enjoys scuba diving, sea kayaking, and other adventures that the Bay Area provides.

Introduction

In this chapter

Microsoft Exchange Server is one of the most scalable and feature-rich products from Microsoft. In a small office, it's a robust messaging and group scheduling system with Internet mail capability, so that Exchange users can reach just about anyone on the Internet. In a large corporation, it's positioned to be the messaging backbone and a versatile groupware product. Using the Forms Designer, you can build custom workflow applications, such as a personnel profiles database. (See Chapter 33, "Developing Exchange Forms" for a personnel profile form application created from scratch.) Because larger companies usually have existing mail systems, Exchange provides several connectors, gateways, and migration/extraction tools so that your current mail system can coexist with or migrate to Exchange. With the newly enhanced Lightweight Directory Access Protocol (LDAPv3) features in Exchange 5.5 and the new hooks for the forthcoming Windows NT 5.0 Active Directory Services, Exchange may also become the integrated center of a unified corporate directory service.

Plus, for any size environment, a single, intuitive Administration program manages your entire messaging environment. Exchange, in essence, becomes the heart of your messaging system.

What Are the Key Features of Exchange?

Exchange is the new reality of messaging technology to which other vendors are striving. Exchange provides revolutionary functionality and performance at a low end-user cost. Now that you have an understanding of what Exchange is and how it's positioned for different types of companies, look at some its features.

Outlook

Outlook is a feature-rich Exchange client. Positioned as an upgrade to the Microsoft Exchange Client and Schedule+ that appeared in the original Exchange 4.0, it was designed as Microsoft's premier email client for 32-bit Windows-based systems. In the latest release Exchange 5.5, versions of Outlook are now available in a 16-bit version for Windows 3.x, Macintosh, POP3/IMAP4, and for Web Browser access via Active Server Components and HTML. Outlook in all its versions is available with Exchange Server, as a stand-alone product (32-bit version), and as a component of Office97. Outlook operates as a client with Microsoft Mail and Schedule+ 7.0, Microsoft Exchange Server, POP3 / IMAP4, and other messaging systems, such as cc:Mail and Lotus Notes. The flexibility enables administrators to deploy their choice of client within a company. No matter what a company's decision, Microsoft provides a unified client architecture and logical upgrade paths from most any client currently used. Combining the features of the Exchange Client (Inbox) and Schedule+, users can still manage email, calendars, contacts, tasks, and to-do lists. Outlook, however, enhances all these previous features and adds enhanced views, journalizing capabilities, document management, and *postable* notes.

As a feature of the Internet Mail Service of Exchange when integrated with the Microsoft Internet Information Server (IIS), email functionality is also available by using a standard Web browser. Outlook Web Access (OWA) enables remote users, who either do not have access to Outlook or have limited hardware resources (RAM, hard drive space), to easily review messages and access public folders on an Exchange Server using Internet Explorer. With Exchange 5.5, the Outlook Web Access Client can also schedule calendar events and manage server-based rules. Note that you must have Microsoft's Internet Information Server (IIS) installed to provide email access to Outlook Web Access users.

Built-in Internet Standards

Exchange supports several protocols, including SMTP (Simple Mail Transfer Protocol), POP3 (Post Office Protocol), and now IMAP4 (Internet Mail Access Protocol) for email, NNTP (Network News Transfer Protocol) for Internet newsgroups retrieval, LDAPv3 (Lightweight Directory Access Protocol) for Exchange directory access (reads and writes), HTTP and HTML for Web access, and SSL for secure Internet transmission. S/MIME is added for secure encryption of MIME attachments over SMTP mail and MHTML to allow encapsulation of HTML content in MIME format. ETRN support is added to enable the Exchange server to act as both SMTP server and client for easier access to held Internet mail via dial-up.

You can use any email client that supports POP3 or IMAP4 to retrieve messages from a Microsoft Exchange Server, including the Microsoft Outlook Express Client (replacing the older Internet Explorer Mail Client). Microsoft Exchange Internet Mail Service (IMS) provides a standard SMTP server for any POP3 Client or IMAP4 Client to submit its messages.

NNTP enables a full newsfeed of Internet newsgroups into your company's public folders. Employees can post responses right into the public folder, and the response is posted back to the appropriate newsgroup on the Internet.

LDAP is an Internet protocol that enables users to access Exchange's directory information. With the proper rights, clients can read, search, and browse Exchange's directory from the Internet or corporate intranet. Even though the IETF has not completely ratified the latest LDAPv3 standard, many of the proposed functions are already included in Exchange 5.5. With LDAPv3, all 16 proposed commands—including searches, reads, and now writes—can enable updates to and from external directory services. You can grant end users the ability to update their LDAP and, thus, Exchange directory information. Referrals support has also been added to automatically forward an LDAP search to another LDAP service provider for resolution.

All of these LDAP-centric functions enable easy integration with the forthcoming NT 5.0 Active Directory Services Interface (ADSI) to dynamically update the Exchange 5.5 directory with data from ADS and vice versa.

With HTTP and HTML, along with Internet Information server (IIS) and Active Server Components, users can access their private mailboxes, calendars, and public folders using a standard Web browser, such as Internet Explorer.

SSL is a supported Internet-security protocol that protects data traveling on the Internet. Simple Authentication and Security Layer (SASL), pending ratification by the IETF, is also a supported option to force SSL authentication before the server can accept SMTP messages. This feature enables secure SMTP-based connections between Exchange servers over the Internet.

cc:Mail Connector

Exchange 5.0 offered a cc:Mail connector that provided complete email connectivity to existing cc:Mail installations. Exchange 5.5 extends these connectivity options to support additional older versions of cc:Mail. Email with attachments may be sent between both messaging platforms. Directory synchronization between Exchange and cc:Mail is also possible. By offering coexistence, the built-in connector enables you to rollout Exchange in phases instead of all at once.

Lotus Notes Connector

With the recent acquisition of the Canadian message-switching–technology company, Linkage Software, Microsoft has integrated the best of the Linkage technology into the release of Exchange 5.5, including connectivity and directory replication between Exchange and Lotus Notes. Microsoft has enhanced the acquired Linkage elements to directly use the Exchange Directory engine and to remove the previous Linkage requirement for a separate SQL server for Directory Synchronization.

PROFS and SNADS Connectors

Many of the Fortune 1000 have invested large amounts of resources in maintaining IBM's PROFS OfficeVison and SNADS messaging technologies on various flavors of big iron and mid-range systems. Microsoft Exchange 5.5 now offers Linkage technology as an integrated component to link Exchange to these legacy systems. The technology enables migration and coexistence as clients switch over to the Exchange system and clients, which cost less and have richer features.

Linkage technology also makes possible Directory Synchronization between the legacy systems. Combining all the new connectivity options makes Exchange a premier messaging switch, and many industry pundits have ironically observed that Microsoft now owns the best solution for connecting Lotus Notes to HOST-based messaging systems!

User-Definable Server or Client-based Message Rules

Exchange provides support for *server-based* rules, where users can configure rules to execute on their Exchange home servers, such as forwarding messages to particular individuals, replying with an *out of office* note to all incoming messages, and routing messages to specific folders to manage messaging flow. Because the process runs on the Exchange Server, the user doesn't need to be logged in.

The server rules can apply to applications that are using Exchange. Outside information stores, for example, have a server agent configured from the client. The next time the user logs into the system, the server agent runs to retrieve information for the user.

With several of the flavors of Outlook Client, users have the option of setting up *client-based* rules to assist in managing messages in their local folders. A useful example is to set up a client-based rule to delay sending messages from the Outbox for 15 minutes, which enables you to rethink that message you just sent to the CEO!

Integrated with Microsoft Office

Microsoft provides tight integration between Microsoft Office 97 and Exchange.

For example, you can send a document, spreadsheet, or presentation directly from any Office application to any Exchange mail user. Alternatively, you can also post any of these files or any other file directly into Exchange's public folders.

A feature available to Office and Outlook users is enabling Word as your email editor. Users who are comfortable with Word's layout and controls can have Outlook automatically use Word to create a new mail message, so you can use all the rich features of Microsoft Word.

Outlook uses Visual Basic for Applications (VBA) to enable additional integration with the Office suite. Several data interaction hooks are available from Outlook to Microsoft Access and vice versa.

Delegated Access

Managers and co-workers can delegate access to their information store, so their assistants and workgroup members can access their messages. This is useful when managers travel out of town. Their assistants can retrieve their manager's mail, forward it, send replies on behalf of the manager, and so on. Assistants can perform all these actions using their own Outlook Client and without logging on as their manager.

In workgroup scenarios, such as sales or project teams, sharing project folders, contacts, and tasks can be invaluable to improve productivity.

Integrated with Windows NT Server

Exchange and Windows NT are integrated in several areas. For example, Exchange ties directly into Windows NT Server's security. Users use a single log-in ID to access network and Exchange resources. Network administrators can create both network IDs and mailboxes for the users by using a single administrative interface program. Also, Exchange administrators can take advantage of Windows NT's log-on restrictions and password history control for tight messaging security. You can also leverage the security auditing features of Windows NT to track changes to security and access to various objects.

Exchange and Windows NT work together to support both roving and remote users. Users can move from workstation to workstation within their company and still have access to all their server-based Exchange-related information (email, calendar, journal, notes, and so on). Remote users can access their email because Windows NT's Remote Access Server (RAS) can support every standard dial-up package used by a Microsoft operating system. These dial-up packages include Shiva, used by DOS and 16-bit Windows; Dial-up Networking (DUN) used by Windows 95; RAS used by Windows for Workgroups and NT Workstation; and DUN from Windows 95 used by Internet Explorer. Note that Shiva support is bundled with Exchange and not with DOS or the 16-bit Windows operating system.

With the Outlook Web Access Client and appropriate Internet firewall considerations, users can access their Exchange mailbox resources from anywhere they can connect to the Internet.

Furthermore, the Exchange client is designed to sense line-connection speed and transfer less data over dial-up connections. This increases the efficiency of the connection. When using Remote Mail options, you can set the client software to download only mail message headers on a remote connection. You can then download full message bodies as needed, based on subject, size, and sender.

Exchange builds upon the scalability of Windows NT Enterprise Edition to enable support for both server clustering and 8-way Symmetric Multi-Processor support (SMP).

Exchange Server Information Store

One of the major perceived limitations of Exchange 4.0/5.0 was the 16 GB limit of each of the Exchange Information Store databases (Private, Public, and Directory). Microsoft has shattered the 16GB limit with new JET database technology that raises the limit to 16,000GB (16 terabytes) in each database. By combining this dramatic enhancement with the fully relational database structure and SQL-like transaction logging functions of Exchange, Microsoft opens Exchange to nearly limitless possibilities for managing very complex messaging-based applications.

Exchange makes great use of *single-instance message storage* by saving one copy of a message in its databases, and then enabling multiple users to access the message. In this way, if a 5MB message and attachment were mailed to all 1000 users on an Exchange server, the server actually would use only 5MB to store the message. When the last user deletes the message from his or her mailbox, the message is removed from the database.

Breaking the 16GB limit enables Exchange servers to support exponentially more users. With the 16GB limit of earlier versions, if the Exchange Administrator decided to limit each user to 50MB of storage space on the Exchange server, the theoretical limit on users per server was 320. With the new 16TB limit, this number can easily rise to 320000 users! (Taking into account the single-instance message storage, this number of users can rise much higher.)

Once of the most exciting, and most requested, new features of Exchange 5.5 is the capability to recover deleted messages and folders. Essentially, a tombstone/recycle bin concept has been applied to the message store, so that when you delete objects, they are not removed from the database until a specified number of days pass or a backup of the server executes.

Of course, Message Tracking has been available in Exchange from the first release to enable administrators to trace the path a message takes through the systems' various connectors, gateways, and MTAs.

Public Folders and Replication

Public folders are central repositories of common information. Exchange users can post messages, files, applications, forms, and so on. By making use of the messaging infrastructure of Exchange, you can replicate public folders throughout the Exchange enterprise. Rather than sending a mail message to many users, you can use public folders like an electronic bulletin board. A user can then post a reply into a folder and, create a thread of responses.

You can also replicate public folders down to the client PC to facilitate offline creating and reading via the process of synchronization. You also can set permissions to restrict access to certain folder contents. The public folder replication function is designed to minimize the amount of replicated data. Public folder contents are also indexed and these indexes are available across the enterprise.

To facilitate development of advanced public folder applications, Exchange 5.5 adds the Exchange Scripting Agent as a Windows NT service for managing server-executed scripts. These scripts can be time- or event-driven Visual Basic or JavaScript components that interact with messages and with the various functions of Exchange. This powerful feature enables developers to more easily build complex workflow functions and routings.

Collaboration Functions

Exchange 5.5 introduces several enhancements to enable easier online interaction and collaboration, which improves productivity. A new Exchange Chat Service has been added to enable Exchange clients to easily initiate chat sessions for virtual meetings. To further facilitate collaboration in real-time on document creation, whiteboard sessions, and so on, the Internet Locator Service (ILS) also ships with Exchange 5.5. The ILS tracks who is online and available for such interactive sessions via Microsoft NetMeeting. Users can pick meeting participants from the Exchange Global Address List. Having this single source for lookups of users reduces the need for multiple address books to track them.

Exchange's Advanced Security

With the Key Management Server (KMS), Exchange adds additional security over the C2 level security provided by Windows NT Server. Exchange offers you the ability to sign a message with a digital signature, which is used to verify that the user sending the message is really the true sender. Exchange also offers levels of message encryption to ensure that only the sender and recipient can read a message's contents. Person to Person Key Exchange (PPKE) enables users to exchange digitally signed and encrypted messages over the Internet. Previously, this was possible only between users within an Exchange Organization.

Dramatic enhancements to the KMS in Exchange 5.5 enable the bulk creation and distribution of user keys, which makes it easier to set up an entire location or corporation to use these security options. The integration of KMS setup into the Exchange Administrator program makes overall management of the KMS much easier as well. Key recovery options are also added, which enable an Exchange administrator to recover and re-issue a user's key if the user forgets the password, or if the user leaves the company without disclosing the password. Through this same mechanism, you can also revoke a user's key.

To better control an Exchange administrator's ability to affect key security, options are available to implement so-called missile silo passwords in which two different administrative passwords are required to change or disable certain security features.

Keeping in line with proposed Internet security standards, you can anticipate future support for X.509v3 (enhancing the current X.509 support in Exchange) and S/MIME certificates, such as VeriSign.

Outlook Forms Designer

Exchange's Outlook Forms Designer tool is simple enough for end users to create basic forms, and powerful enough for experienced developers to create form-based applications. The forms automate common requests, such as time-off requests or office-supply orders. Using public folders, you can multiply the effectiveness of forms by replicating the forms and their information throughout your enterprise.

Coupled with Microsoft's Visual InterDev tool, a developer can more easily convert Outlook forms into HTML forms via the new Forms Conversion Wizard. After you convert the forms, you can makes them available to Outlook Web Access clients via Active Server Pages.

Developer Tools

Exchange 5.0 added the ability to present Exchange data to the Web via Active Server Pages and components called Active Messaging. The name has been changed to reflect the unified Microsoft development strategy and is now known as Collaboration Data Objects (CDO). The included CDO library offers developers a set of pre-built objects on which they can create more powerful and complex web-based applications.

Microsoft is also bundling a single-user version of Microsoft Visual InterDev for use in creating and managing HTML forms and other Java, ActiveX, and CDO elements.

Multiple Language Support

Exchange supports more than 20 languages and provides many features for companies whose sites are spread throughout the world.

Single-seat View for Administration

The Exchange Administrator tool is the central console managing all Exchange activity within an organization. This includes all servers, users, mailboxes, connectors, gateways, public folders, and sites. As noted previously, the Administrator tool now offers you the ability to recover the deleted message objects and folders.

An enhancement for system administrators is support for Simple Network Management Protocol (SNMP) via the industry standard MADMAN MIB. You can now monitor Exchange from such tools as HP OpenView and other enterprise-monitoring solutions.

Many large corporations are composed of multiple corporate entities that are essentially separate and distinct but that want to share a common messaging backbone and directory. Exchange 5.5 introduces ***multiple organization hosting*** to enable you to break the Exchange Directory down into many virtual containers associated with each line of business unit. You can still apply all the normal Exchange security permissions, so the various users and administrators of each virtual organization can see and control only their respective components.

Online System Backup

Believe it or not, email can grow in use to become a company's most mission-critical application. Especially in international firms, Exchange must be up 24 hours a day and seven days a week for 365 days a year. Exchange enables you to perform backups of open messaging stores via appropriate Exchange-aware backup solutions without shutting down the server or having users log out.

With the new Information Store limits pushing to 16TB, backup and recovery support in Exchange have been enhanced to enable more efficient databases locks and reads, pushing backup performance to a possible 25GB per hour.

Support for 1984 and 1988 X.400 Standards

Exchange simultaneously offers Message Transfer Agent support for both 1984 and 1988 X.400 standards, which means Exchange offers you flexibility when you design an Exchange enterprise architecture. Microsoft is committed to maintaining X.400 compatibility as 199X standards are published.

Message Routing

Message routing provides multiple routes to transfer mail between sites. If one link for remote sites goes down, Exchange automatically reroutes mail using a secondary route. Exchange can also calculate the least costly route when all links are functional. Microsoft has made several to boost the capabilities of the *dynamic re-routing* feature and to force Exchange to evaluate a route based only on the cost assigned.

Migration Tools for non-Exchange Mail Systems

Microsoft realizes that many other systems are in use today. Therefore, Microsoft provides connectors, gateways, and migration/extraction tools to provide either complete coexistence with Exchange or a smooth migration path onto an Exchange platform.

Who Should Use This Book?

This book is aimed at network and system administrators as well as messaging specialists who are responsible for installing, configuring, and maintaining an Exchange system. Most of the examples in this book are geared to a large, international enterprise to draw out all Exchange's features. MIS managers can use the information in this book to make key decisions about adopting and deploying Exchange. Finally, this book touches on application-forms development. Although Exchange's Outlook Forms Designer targets novice developers who may not have a strong Visual Basic (VB) background, VB programmers can leverage their knowledge to make additional custom extensions and web-enable their forms

How to Use This Book

This book is divided into five sections. The first two sections are for a general audience, and the last three sections depend on an understanding of the previous sections.

Part I Introduction to Microsoft Exchange

Part I welcomes you into the world of Microsoft Exchange. As described briefly in the preceding sections, Exchange is a completely revolutionary client/server messaging system. Part I presents a complete overview about how Exchange integrates into your environment.

Chapter 1, "Overview of Microsoft Exchange," introduces the concepts of working with client/server messaging, groupware, document management, and the universal Inbox. This chapter also discusses many new features available with Microsoft Exchange 5.5.

In Chapter 2, "Understanding Exchange's Organization and Sites," you learn about the different tiers in Exchange's messaging hierarchy.

Chapter 3, "Exchange's Integrated Server Components," provides a more in-depth look at Exchange's core components and how they cooperate with each other.

Chapter 4, "Integrating with Microsoft Windows NT Server," identifies the integration of Exchange into Windows NT and Exchange NT dependencies.

Part II Installing and Migrating to Exchange

Part II is the core of the book. These seven chapters spells out all the planning essentials for migrating to or deploying a new Exchange architecture.

Chapter 5, "Designing Exchange Topology," introduces you to the planning process you need in order to design an Exchange architecture. In the chapter, you analyze your company's messaging needs and infrastructure, and then you design an Exchange architecture.

Chapter 6, "Installing Exchange Server," outlines the system requirements for Exchange, provides step-by-step installation instructions, and discusses adding additional Exchange servers into an existing Exchange Organization.

Chapters 7 through 11 provide information needed when you are working with non-Exchange mail systems. You are guided through connecting to or migrating from Microsoft Mail, migrating from Lotus cc:Mail, migration from PROFS/SNADS, installing Exchange in a NetWare environment, and migrating from external systems.

Part III Exchange Administration and Configuration

In Part III, you learn how to configure all the Exchange services—connectors, message transfer agents, links to external systems, public folders, and address routing. This part also focuses on the administration of Exchange.

Chapters 12 through 15 discuss how to use the Exchange Administrator program, and how to use the core components in Exchange server.

Chapter 16, "Creating and Configuring Recipients," exemplifies how to create a mailbox and Windows NT domain account for an Exchange user, which also includes distribution lists and foreign-mail system custom recipients.

Chapter 17, "Setting Up the Site Connector and Dynamic RAS Connector," discusses how to install and set up a site and RAS connector.

In Chapter 18, "Using Directory Replication and Synchronization," you learn what directory replication is and how to configure Exchange's Directory Synchronization services.

Chapters 19 and 20 walk you through using the Microsoft Mail Connector for PC and AppleTalk networks. Exchange includes several custom features to support this integration.

Chapter 21 similarly discusses configuring X.400 connections.

Chapter 22 focuses on the many features of the Internet Mail Service including SMTP mail connectivity, POP/IMAP client access, LDAP functions, and HTTP web interfacing.

In Chapter 23, "Setting Up NNTP," you learn what Network News Transfer Protocol (NNTP) is, and how to install, configure, and administer it.

The information in Chapter 24, "Exchange Performance Tuning and Capacity Planning" applies to all Exchange implementations. You learn how to use several performance-tuning tools, and to detect and tune the most common Exchange bottlenecks. You also learn the techniques that answer the burning question: How many users can one Exchange server support?

Chapters 25 through 28 discuss managing and monitoring Exchange's daily operations as well as troubleshooting Exchange when problems occur. You also learn about Exchange's advanced security features in Chapter 27.

Part IV The Exchange Client

This part discusses the Exchange client—Outlook. This includes several of Outlook's features, such as enhancing email, effective scheduling, managing tasks, journalizing your activities, organizing your contacts, and using notes to jot down important thoughts.

Chapter 29, "Installing and Configuring Outlook," describes the spectrum of setup methods and Outlook's system requirements.

Chapters 30 and 31 teach you how to use the common and advanced features of Outlook, including printing, profiles and information services, and the Outlook Web Access view.

Part V Third-Party Integration and Application Development

Part V presents some other uses for the Exchange architecture.

Chapter 32,"Leveraging Your Investment in the Exchange Platform," highlights several add-ons and enhancements from independent software vendors who are developing solutions for Exchange. The chapter also describes consulting firms that are expert in developing, piloting, and deploying Exchange.

Chapter 33, "Developing Exchange Forms," teaches you to design custom forms using Exchange's Form Designer. This chapter discusses many of the programming issues associated with developing custom forms.

Chapter 34, "Taking Exchange to the Web," covers the functions of interfacing the Active Server Pages of Microsoft's Internet Information Server with the Collaborative Data Objects (CDO) provided in Exchange to create Web-based applications and solutions.

Conventions Used in This Book

Que has over a decade of experience writing and developing the most successful computer books available. With this experience, we learned which special features help readers the most. Look for these special features throughout the book to enhance your learning experience.

Several type and font conventions are used in this book to help make your reading easier.

- *Italic type* is used to emphasize the author's points or to introduce new terms.
- Screen messages, code listings, and command samples appear in `monospace typeface`.
- Code and other information that the user is asked to type appears in **`bold monospace type`**.

Tips present brief advice on a quick or often-overlooked procedure. These tips include shortcuts that will save you time.

NOTE Notes present interesting or useful information that isn't necessarily essential to the discussion. A note is used to provide additional information that may help you avoid problems, or to offer advice that relates to the particular topic.

CAUTION

Cautions look like this and serve to warn about potential problems that a procedure may cause, unexpected results, and mistakes to avoid.

PART I

Introduction to Microsoft Exchange

CHAPTER 1

Overview of Microsoft Exchange

In this chapter

"Build the world's fastest, most scalable, most reliable, easiest to administer messaging and groupware enterprise platform that can connect to the world."

Brian Valentine, Microsoft General Manager, Exchange Group 1993

This has been Microsoft's compelling vision for Exchange since its conception in 1993.

But what exactly is Exchange? Microsoft Exchange Server is a messaging product for businesses, integrating e-mail, group scheduling, electronic forms, and common groupware applications in one product that can be easily managed via a single administrator program. Exchange facilitates collaboration within companies so teams can share the latest information obtained, internally via intranets and externally from the Internet and newsgroups. This messaging product also enables managers to schedule meetings with several people and manage resources through a common interface. Departments can set up information repositories (solution databases) for reference and discussion. Companies can create virtual knowledge bases with their business partners using an extranet. In short, Microsoft Exchange Server 5.5 is designed to help you communicate and collaborate with anyone, anywhere, anytime—easily.

This chapter provides an overview of Exchange 5.5, its new features on both the client and server side, and its positioning as an enterprise-wide messaging system.

The History of Messaging

Electronic mail has been in existence for many years. The original electronic mail systems—including PROFS, SYSM, and Memo—resided on UNIX-based host computers or IBM mainframes. The single host, whether it was a mainframe or a minicomputer, was a centralized solution. These electronic mail systems, many of which are still running today, are text-based and provide enterprise-wide messaging.

Understanding Shared-File Messaging

PCs began to grow in capability and popularity, however. As their acceptance became widespread, their cost began to drop, prompting more purchases, especially in corporate America. More and more computing was taking place at the desktop instead of within a centralized machine. The PCs began communicating with each other via small workgroups and *Local Area Networks (LANs)*, extending their reach. It wasn't long before LAN-based messaging took root and grew within the same company walls that housed the mainframe messaging solution.

LAN-based or *shared-file messaging* occurs when the client desktop initiates and controls all messaging activity. When a user composes and sends a message, the client software sends the message to the server or post office into a specific directory or file (or mailbox). A recipient retrieves his messages by accessing his specific mailbox on the server. The server is passive and primarily stores messages (see Figure 1.1).

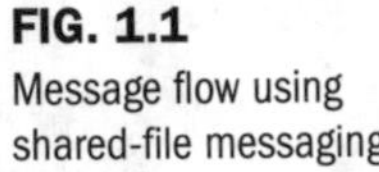

FIG. 1.1
Message flow using shared-file messaging.

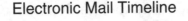

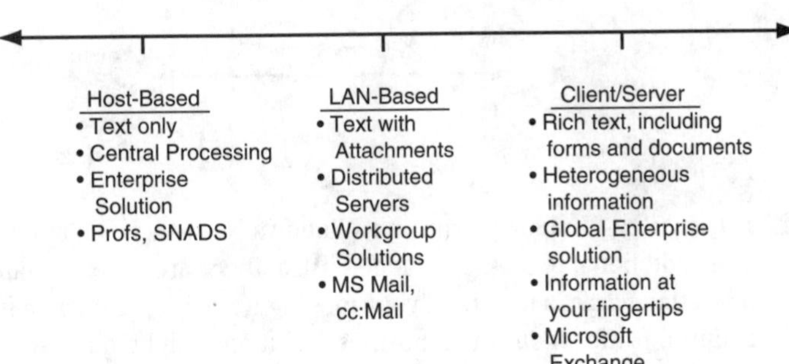

At the time, there were advantages to this architecture:

- Reduced cost—server doesn't need to be high performance
- Simple design—relatively easy setup and administration
- Increased performance in some areas—application runs locally

But there were weaknesses as well:

- Inadequate security—each user needs full control (read/write) on the entire file system, including other users's mailboxes.
- Increased network traffic—each client must constantly poll the server for new messages. In a small LAN or workgroup, the traffic can be manageable, but in a large enterprise, any traffic will grind things to a halt.
- Limited scalability—no matter how much hardware one adds to the server, there is a hard limit to the number of clients and number of messages that reasonably can be handled by the system, especially because bandwidth is the limiting factor.

Understanding Client/Server Messaging

To address these weaknesses, client/server messaging was designed to distribute messaging processing between the client and server, enabling each system to focus on tasks best suited for its role. When a user composes and sends a message, for example, the server places the message in the appropriate directory or forwards it to another server. The recipient receives the message without constantly polling the server. Microsoft Exchange was developed using client/server messaging architecture (see Figure 1.2).

Client/server messaging improves upon shared-file messaging in the following areas:

- *Better security*—Except for their own "directories" (Inboxes), users have read-only rights for other selected Exchange objects and components.
- *Decreased network traffic*—Using *Remote Procedure Calls (RPCs)*, clients connect and make messaging requests. The server processes the requests and returns only the requested information.

FIG. 1.2
Message flow using client/server messaging.

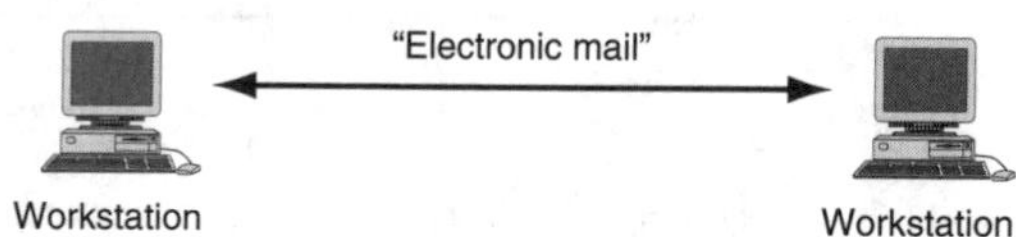

- *Extensibility*—Exchange runs on Windows NT, which easily scales when more memory or an additional processor is added. Also, there are several connectors, gateways, and migration wizards to extend your messaging reach. Exchange has evolved into a full-featured platform on which business solutions can be built, such as forms, work-flow charts, and document databases.

The Exchange client component on the recipient's PC receives information that the creator or source "pushes" to it. Exchange goes beyond the push model by providing a shared repository—*Public Folders*—for storing information that is on call for the user. This repository enables users to "pull" information down to their workstations when they need that information. Because it provides both push and pull technology, Exchange does not constrain corporations with the distribution mechanism. Exchange provides a complete solution.

Overview of Exchange's Key Features

Now that you have a historical perspective of messaging, it's time to examine Exchange's key features and how they can meet your messaging needs.

Using Key Definitions

You should become familiar with some key concepts and definitions that are used throughout this chapter:

- *Address Book*—A list of names, addresses, or other information. Names can include users, distribution lists, and public folders.
- *Custom Recipient*—A recipient outside your enterprise. For example, you would use a person's Internet SMTP address as the custom recipient when sending mail over the Internet.
- *Directory*—A hierarchical structure of objects that represent each component of the organization, such as the organization itself, containers, recipients, and more.
- *Enterprise*—A corporate environment with a large electronic messaging infrastructure. A typical enterprise will have several thousand to tens of thousands of users on the mail system.
- *Information Store*—The back-end database that contains all messages and data located on the Microsoft Windows NT server that houses the Exchange server.
- *Microsoft Exchange Client/Viewer*—The program that a client uses to read, write, and manipulate the mailbox and folders.

- *MTA*—The Message Transfer Agent, which transfers and routes mail messages and attachments between servers.
- *Recipient*—The receiver of a message or form. A recipient can be a user, distribution list, or public folder.
- *Routing Table*—A table created by Exchange and used by the MTA to move messages between servers.
- *Security Descriptor*—Permissions information attached to every object under the Windows NT server. Security descriptors tell the operating system who has access to a certain resource, whether that resource is a file, a service, or an application.

Understanding the Universal Inbox for Information and Applications

The concept of the universal inbox has been around for years, but the capability to deliver such a product is revolutionary. Microsoft learned from its research that users want an integrated desktop environment to improve their organization and control of daily activities. A ***universal inbox*** interface makes it easy to organize personal, public (shared), or online information all in one place. A user now can view information in a variety of ways, and easily find information anywhere on the desktop. Future BackOffice products and especially Windows 98 will seek to leverage this model.

The key to the Exchange inbox is the fact that Microsoft provides the gateway to all your company information. Third-party software developers are pursuing business opportunities on this foundation by building their applications on top of this technology; these applications appear as folders. The vision is to provide one standard location and interface for accessing information, regardless of the information's format. Solutions are available for integrating voice-mail systems into Exchange, for example. If you have a multimedia PC with an integrated sound system, you can access your e-mail as well as voice mail, or dial in from a telephone to "hear" your e-mail along with your voice mail.

The Exchange Outlook client interface embodies the concept of the universal inbox by providing a consistent look and feel across all the supported platforms and released versions. Exchange 5.5 now presents a "flavor" of the Outlook client for each operating system that connects to Exchange (Windows 95 and Windows NT, Windows 3.x, Macintosh, DOS, and via the Internet).

The client also enables you to place filing, printing, viewing, deleting, and other functions on convenient button bars. These button bars keep the desktop uncluttered and yet enable the desktop to contain many pieces of information.

Controlling Folder Types

When you use the Exchange Outlook client, you have control of several folders that are displayed from the Microsoft Exchange root folder tree. These folders are very similar in layout to Windows Explorer, which ships with Windows 95 and Windows NT 4.0, and to the File Manager in Windows 3.1 and Windows NT 3.x.

The three main folder types are described here:

- *Mailbox*—The Mailbox folder serves as the traditional inbox that most e-mail packages have. The main difference in Exchange, however, is that this folder holds much more than e-mail; it also can contain all the data types from several sources (for example, Dow Jones information, Word or Excel documents, JPG files, and so on). After reading the data, the user can move the data into any of several other folders or have it automatically moved to other folders based on certain rules.
- *Personal folders*—These folders enable the user great flexibility in organizing their message objects. Some people like to organize documents by author, for example; others like to organize by subject. Users also can store the information on their local hard disks for use offline. All mail in the mailbox is kept on the server until it is saved on the user's hard disk.

  Suppose that you're going on a trip. Before you leave, you log on to the Exchange server and get all your documents from the server (via replication/synchronization). You then save the documents to a private folder for reviewing offline. There you can compose your replies, and when you connect to the Exchange server the next time, those outgoing messages are sent on their way. In addition, the folder views are synchronized next time you log on to your Exchange server.
- *Public folders*—Public folders facilitate the sharing of information. Each client who has access rights can read information stored in public folders. The administrator can assign users read, write, and delete access to information contained in a public folder. Public folders also can be published to the Internet/intranet as HTML via the Active Server Pages components of Exchange and Microsoft's *Internet Information Server (IIS)*.

  In addition, the creator of the information may create a custom view to standardize the look and feel of the information. For example, in many firms there exists a document on all the bulletin boards containing what job openings exist at the company. With Exchange, you could create an Access database that would hold standard information and simply create a form that resided in a public folder. People could then browse the information in a standard way and all data would be updated whenever the database is updated.

Organizing Views

As mentioned earlier in this chapter, Exchange enables users to organize information according to their taste. Exchange provides some features to make this process much easier. Those features are described in the following paragraphs.

A *view* is simply a way to order information. Information can be sorted by author, keyword, date, or subject.

Two kinds of views are available: folder views and common views. *Folder views* order information in individual folders. If you have a private folder called Peter that contains all mail from Peter, you can define a view that sorts all the objects in the folder by date. Then you could change the view for the folder to include a secondary sort criterion, such as subject. The data then would conform to the view only in that folder. *Common views* are views that can be applied to any folder. You can define a view called Date and apply it to many folders at the same time.

In addition to providing many predefined views, Exchange is also flexible enough to enable you to create views, including custom fields from forms and even Microsoft Office documents like Word or Excel. If a public folder has a database element that contains a Boolean logical (Y or N) field, for example, you can create a view that sorts all the Yes records before all the No records.

Setting Rules and Auto-Assistants

Rules are a set of conditions that when met, organize incoming messages. For example, you can establish a rule dictating that if Sender = My Manager, to file the message in a folder called Urgent, and play a sound.

Auto-Assistants enable you to have rules in effect even when you aren't logged on. If you go away on vacation, for instance, you can have a generic message auto-replying to all messages saying you'll return in one week. If the message contains a certain keyword in the subject, you could have your mail forwarded to someone else to take care of it or to another e-mail account where you can review it.

Using Find

The *Find* feature is a powerful search engine that enables you to specify criteria for finding items in any or all of your folders. This feature is extremely useful when you remember a subject or a keyword but can't remember who sent the message or what the actual content was. You can have the Find feature look for the message in all your folders.

The Find feature runs in the background and is treated like any other running program, enabling you to continue working while the search is under way.

When you are presented with the objects that meet the specified criteria, any action you take on those objects takes effect in the actual folders the objects reside in. For example, you can use the Find feature to retrieve all messages 30 or more days old. As messages appear in the Find window, you can select all of them, and click the Delete button. They will all be removed from their respective folders.

Adding a third-party search index tool to your Outlook client can make searching even more powerful and much quicker. Options are available for search indexing on the Exchange server as well.

Using Calendar

With the proper permissions, you can view someone else's calendar or schedule to find the best time to schedule a meeting. The Calendar function, once a separate function using a Schedule+ client, is now completely integrated into one client called Outlook. Read on for more information.

Using Application Development Tools

Exchange provides the Outlook Forms Designer to extend the functionality of Exchange. Exchange now becomes a platform product upon which business messaging solutions like document databases and groupware are built. The Outlook Forms Designer is targeted for the non-developer, but experienced developers can use their Visual Basic expertise to take Exchange's forms to the next level.

Exchange provides a wizard to assist developers in converting Outlook forms into HTML format. A single seat license for Microsoft Visual InterDev is also provided to further customize and enhance the HTML code for usage with the Active Server Pages components of Exchange and Microsoft's Internet Information Server.

Outlook Forms Designer The Forms Designer enables the administrator (or any other user, if granted permission) to create custom forms that can replace paper forms. Most consulting companies have standard forms for consultants to describe their backgrounds for use in proposals. Why not create this form online, store it in a public folder, and allow the consultant to fill it out on screen and send it to you for processing? You also can create a Visual Basic program to take the data off the form and store it in an Access, FoxPro, or SQL Server database for later retrieval and manipulation. With the enhancements to the Information Store of Exchange 5.5, the data could continue to be stored in Exchange.

Imagine using an electronic form to requisition office supplies. You could quickly tally the total cost of office supplies for a month by using OLE to create an Excel table from the Exchange data.

Forms can be stored in three places: the Enterprise Forms Registry, the Personal Forms Registry, and the Folder Forms Registry. The following list describes these elements:

- *Enterprise Forms Registry.* This registry contains forms that are distributed across the enterprise—for example, office-supplies requisition forms. Most companies use a standard office-supplies vendor and a standard paper form. When you use an Exchange form, the paper form can be eliminated, and forms can be sent directly to the authorizing party or to the office-products vendor itself.
- *Personal Forms Registry.* This registry houses all the forms that the user needs to accomplish personalized tasks. If an Exchange user repeatedly needs to send out meeting summaries that follow the same format and go to the same people, he or she can use a custom form that contains all the addressees and all the appropriate fields.
- *Folder Forms Registry.* This registry contains forms that post data in public folders. This feature can be used between divisions and departments. In many organizations, a lack of communication exists between divisions. For example, production could be unprepared for some of engineering's demands due to lack of communication. By using custom forms, engineering can status the entire company about what production is working on. The form makes entering the data easy and can be customized to the user's liking and later searched by custom field criteria.

By providing a simple graphical user interface, the Outlook Forms Designer enables users to create forms without the need for complex programming.

It may be difficult to believe, but the Outlook Forms Designer is a front end to Visual Basic. Simply drawing the fields in the form sends the proper commands to Visual Basic to create the executable form. You do not have to be a Visual Basic guru to create forms and to extend the functionality of Exchange beyond the transfer of messages.

Savvy Visual Basic and C++ developers can integrate their own custom codes to extend Outlook forms to do amazing things as noted in the following sections.

CAUTION

With Outlook and Exchange 5.5, the Macintosh Outlook Client can only support the electronic forms that have been specially customized for use by the Macintosh client of Exchange because the forms are based on Visual Basic components. Forms that are not usable by the Macintosh client will display a special symbol indicating this lack of compatibility.

Custom Application Programming with MAPI Exchange Client applications aren't limited to those that ship with Exchange. Because Exchange is based on the *Messaging Application Programming Interface (MAPI)*, you can design applications that take advantage of Exchange's underlying folder architecture by accessing data via MAPI.

Custom applications can use MAPI to perform such tasks as opening a public folder and dropping in data, searching data, deleting items, and examining the contents of folders. All actions are subject to the permission that the application has for any given object. If the program is running with the permissions of a user who doesn't have the ability to delete data, the application cannot delete any data.

MAPI also can be used to add functionality to a form created with the Outlook Forms Designer. You can write a program that takes data from a custom form, imports that data into Excel, performs some calculations, sends the compiled results to the user in an e-mail message, and then faxes a copy to another recipient.

Enabling Group Information Sharing

Exchange enables the user to post information on an electronic bulletin board (public folder). For example, marketing representatives can track customer accounts from a shared contact-management database and access product information from a reference library. With Outlook, creating the folder applications can be very simple.

Understanding Internet Support

The *Internet Mail Connector (IMC)* that was first introduced in Exchange 4.0 has continued to grow in functions and protocol support. Exchange 5.0 saw the renaming of the IMC to reflect what it had evolved into—a group of "services" now called the *Internet Mail Service (IMS)*. Included here are the SMTP mail gateway between Exchange and the Internet for sending and receiving, as well as POP3 support for standard POP-based mail clients such as Eudora or the new Outlook Express client. IMAP4 support has been added in Exchange 5.5 as a dramatically enhanced upgrade to the POP standard. Web Browser support for access to a user's mailbox, calendar, and public folders is available when the HTTP protocol is configured with Active Server Pages and IIS. Any browser that supports frames can be used to log on and view dynamic HTML representations of a mailbox's content. When accessing in this method, the browser is using the Outlook Web Access components installed on the Exchange server.

To facilitate easy directory access for these POP/IMAP4 and browser clients, *Lightweight Directory Access Protocol (LDAP)* is available. Exchange 5.5 is supporting the soon-to-be-published LDAPv3 standard by offering a full set of 16 commands for LDAP usage, including reads, writes, and referrals to other LDAP servers. NNTP newsfeeds and function are supported and enhanced in 5.5, allowing for more options to configure NNTP replication to and from Internet NNTP newsfeeds.

Finally, a rich environment for interfacing Microsoft's Internet Information Server with Exchange to enable publishing and interaction with public folders within Exchange has been added, collectively called *Active Server Components*. By using*Collaboration Data Objects* (formerly called *Active Messaging*), you can easily publish Exchange public folder data and custom forms to the Web. All of these help integrate a company's messaging enterprise into a much larger messaging system—the Internet. These are described in more detail later in the chapter.

Enabling Support for Remote Users

Exchange with Outlook clients enables users to work offline. Users can use the Exchange Outlook 32- and 16-bit clients from their PCs via remote network access (dial-up connections) or while they are disconnected from the network. Exchange is designed to use RPC calls, which, when coupled with dial-up connections, are designed to sense the line speed and optimize performance.

Exchange can be used over asynchronous connections, including ISDN, PPP, PPTP, SLIP, X.25, and regular modem connections. This form of Exchange connectivity holds true for client-to-server connections as well as server-to-server connections. Additionally, security can be implemented when using NT's Remote Access Services for dial-back and challenged dial-in via NT C2 security.

Performing Administration

Microsoft Exchange Server administration is performed from a single tool capable of connecting to every site and server in your Exchange organization—Exchange Administrator. This program gives the server administrator a graphical representation of all directory objects in any site for which he or she has permission.

Exchange Administrator is used to define the hierarchical structure of the organization's messaging infrastructure. You can define and set properties for elements such as connections to other mail systems, recipients, servers, and addressing templates.

The advantage of centralized administration is that it enables you to see the entire object tree or hierarchy of information and make any addition, move, or change in an easy, straightforward manner, regardless of the location of the server. If your company merges with another company that has a Microsoft Mail messaging infrastructure in place, for example, the Exchange Administrator can add the Microsoft Mail connector, and connectivity would be available to all specified users on all specified servers. The convenience of adding functionality from a central console is apparent, in this case, in size of enterprise.

If decentralized administration is desired, you can open multiple administrative sessions and set permissions to the various objects and components of Exchange to allow different administrators to modify and control these different features. In an extremely large Exchange organization, setting specific permissions and spreading out Exchange administration responsibilities can be very advantageous.

Considering Reliability

Many companies don't consider a messaging system to be a mission-critical application. However, the reality is that e-mail is one of the few applications on everyone's desktop and that most everyone relies on. To keep your users happy, Exchange offers a number of tools and features to prevent Exchange from becoming "unavailable" (see Table 1.1).

Table 1.1 Troubleshooting Tools and Features

Tool/Feature	Function
Link Monitor	Link Monitor watches for successful message connections between two points in an Exchange organization. They also can be configured to test connections to foreign messaging systems. Use this tool to determine if an Exchange server or network link is experiencing problems. Naturally, alerts are given if the link is unresponsive.
Server Manager	Server Manager tells you whether any of a server's services has stopped and enables you to restart those services remotely, even across a wide-area network (WAN) or active telephone link. As with the Link Monitor, alerts are available to notify administrators of server problems.
Performance Monitor	NT's *Performance Monitor (PerfMon)* enables you to monitor statistics for most software and hardware components (processor utilization, available memory). Installing Exchange adds several specific counters for detailed Exchange diagnostic work. PerfMon can be set up to page you if certain thresholds are exceeded, such as a message queue that has exceeded 1,000 messages or disk space that has dropped below a preset threshold.

continues

Table 1.1 Continued

Tool/Feature	Function
Event Viewer	Event Viewer comes with Windows NT; it logs system, security, and application events (including Exchange). Not all events are errors. For example, an event is logged when Exchange finishes recalculating the routing table. Use Event Viewer to determine the source of errors from Exchange.
SNMP	RFC 1566 MADMAN MIB is supported in Exchange 5.5 to allow for monitoring of the mail connection elements of Exchange from SNMP monitoring tools such as HP OpenView.
Intelligent Rerouting	Exchange can have multiple connectors between servers to provide fault tolerance. If one connection goes down, Exchange automatically reroutes traffic through another connection. Exchange 5.5 gives the administrator the option to force Exchange to look only at route costs when considering how and when to reroute messages, making the "dynamic" element more predictable.
Directory Service (DS)	Because the DS is like Exchange's telephone book, it must be protected. Not only is the DS replicated to every server in a site and synchronized, it can recover from a catastrophic failure through the rollback features of the transacted database and distributed tree architecture.
Fault-Tolerant Store	Exchange uses a transaction-based logging system to ensure users never lose a message from the *Information Store (IS)*. All transactions are written to a transaction log, then committed to the Store. In the event of a power failure, all transactions can be completed using the transaction log.
Backup	When installing Exchange, you enhance the built-in NT backup provided as a tool of NT Server, enabling the backup of open Exchange files. Other more capable Exchange-aware third-party backup tools are available.
Auditing	NT's auditing enables an administrator to log and view the full spectrum of security events, such as someone attempting to use the Administrator ID or attempting to delete several mailboxes.

Messaging Security

As more people depend on e-mail for communication, the need for secure messaging grows. Exchange offers three levels of security and manages the user accounts and the Information Store activity. Exchange also hooks into the NT's C2 level security and incorporates several additional security mechanisms to protect the data stored on the server, the data on the client PC, and data in transit.

Exchange provides for RSA digital key encryption, which is used to authenticate the user who is sending the message. When a user "signs" a message, the signature guarantees that the name associated with the message is the actual name of the author.

In addition to the digital signature, you can enable digital encryption of messages. Exchange uses an algorithm called *CAST* developed by Northern Telecom. Security is discussed further in Chapter 27, "Exchange Security."

Understanding Connectivity and Gateway Support

Exchange offers a wide variety of connectivity features. Through its connectors and third-party gateways, Exchange enables users to exchange mail with external e-mail systems that use different messaging protocols, such as host-based mail systems using SNA, Internet mail systems using SMTP, and foreign host systems using X.400. Mail can also be exchanged between Exchange sites using TCP/IP, IPX, or NetBEUI. Exchange offers the following connectors:

- Microsoft Mail for PC Networks
- Microsoft Mail for AppleTalk Networks
- X.400
- SMTP
- cc:Mail
- Dynamic RAS (dial-up connector)
- Site Connector
- Lotus Notes
- PROFS/SNADS

In addition to the aforementioned connectors, third-party gateways for Exchange extend your reach. Exchange supports its own gateways and Microsoft Mail (PC) gateways as well. The following are just a few gateways that are available for Exchange from third parties:

- DEC All-in-One
- Fax
- CompuServe
- MHS

Regardless of the origin of a message, all message objects in a user's mailbox look exactly the same. Additionally, any installed connectors or gateways are transparent to the user. That fact is a key advantage of Exchange. A user's data is collected and consistently formatted in a universal inbox.

Like incoming mail, outgoing mail is routed through connectors and gateways that are transparent to the user. The administrator creates custom recipients that reside in address books alongside conventional Exchange recipients.

When a connector is installed to enable communication to a Microsoft Mail post office, for example, Exchange clients can immediately send and receive mail by addressing the message to the MS Mail user the same way they do when they send a message to another Exchange user. When Kent's boss says, "Please send a message to Dan Gardner at the Dallas office," Kent can start up his Exchange client and send the message directly to Dan Gardner, because Dan's name is in Kent's address book in Exchange. Likewise, because Kent shows up in the MS Mail post office and Dan's address book, Dan easily can send Kent a reply.

Understanding Migration

When a connector or gateway solution isn't available, or there is no need for coexistence because the old mail system will be retired, Exchange provides tools that are used to move data from one system to another:

- *Extraction tools.* These tools copy directory, message, and scheduling information from an existing system. For example, cc:Mail post office MLANDATA, CLANDATA, and USR files would be run through an extraction tool, dumping all the data into a file and keeping all pointers intact.
- *Migration tool.* This tool imports the data created with the extraction tools in Exchange. You run the migration tool on the file output by the extraction tools. The user information goes into the address books, and the data is moved to the Information Store. The Migration Wizard of Exchange provides the ability to perform extraction and migration together in an automated process to easily move a user's mailbox content from the old mail system directly into Exchange.
- *Administrator program.* You can use the directory import and export options in the main Administrator program in place of, or in conjunction with, the preceding tools. These options enable you to use the tools with which you are most comfortable.
- *Custom tools.* Exchange enables you to make use of custom code or command scripts that perform desired functions to extend the basic tools provided. Your custom process can be scheduled for execution with the NT Server Scheduling service to perform certain duties at certain times. If you have limited hardware capacity and want to import entries from a different messaging system over a certain number of days, you could write custom scripts that perform those tasks without overburdening your network or server. You also could write scripts that manipulate the extraction tools to feed only certain parts of the data to the migration tool.

As you can see, Exchange provides the flexibility to be suitable for large and small environments and the adaptability to import data from other messaging programs, and integration with heterogeneous environments. Exchange also provides messaging solutions for any size organization with any combination of existing mail systems.

Understanding Electronic Data Interchange

Another use of messaging is *Electronic Data Interchange (EDI)*. Most corporations use EDI applications to exchange messages that contain information about orders, sales, and inventory.

Third parties provide support for financial transactions via Exchange. Microsoft's intent is to provide support for EDI domestically (with X.12) and internationally (with EDIfac). Exchange does not provide native X.435 support, but support in MAPI will provide X.435 functionality in the client.

Exchange provides a rich architecture for use in EDI transactions. Together with the integration of Microsoft SQL Server, Microsoft Transactions Server, and other Microsoft application environments, Exchange proves to be a very solid, useful, and cost-effective EDI solution.

Additional MAPI options are available to integrate Exchange and its powerful messaging system with your Internet Commerce applications, using Microsoft Site Server and related Internet technologies.

Understanding Fax Routing

Third-party products from Right Fax, OMTOOL, Fenestrae, Cheyenne, and many others provide a gateway for DID-supported fax boards, such as Brooktrout or GammaFax Boards. Faxes can be sent to and received from a central location and routed to and from the Exchange client. This process eliminates the need to provide individual modems and phone lines at users' desktops or to print materials and walk them to a manual fax machine. Significant cost savings can result from reduced mailroom overhead and in overall reduced time for delivery. Administration of the fax solution can usually be accomplished from the Exchange Administrator tool to further reduce system administration effort.

Microsoft also supports its own fax gateway product for MS Mail 3.x. Moreover, the Exchange Outlook client for Windows 95 and Windows NT 4.0 can use the Microsoft Fax software, which is bundled with these operating systems. This way, a user can use existing aliases and contact lists in the local directory to send e-mail and faxes from one location.

Using Voice Mail

Several products are available to integrate and unify electronic mail messaging and voice mail systems into a single architecture. Octel, the leader in voice mail solutions, has invested heavily in a product known as Unified Messenger that, once installed into an Exchange site, can actually replace a traditional voice mail system, if desired, with a completely PC-based solution. Benefits of such a system include the following:

- Ease of administration of both voice mail and e-mail from the Exchange Administrator program
- Reduction of costs associated with PC hardware versus traditional proprietary voice mail systems
- Enhancement of client features, such as the capability to listen to voice mail from the e-mail client or to play back the text portion of an e-mail from traditional voice mail access

Workflow The "workflow" concept seeks to establish strict steps for a defined business process, with limited or rules-based choices presented to users. Exchange applications with workflow go beyond forms routing, and address several workflow-application issues, such as status tracking, work management, deadline management, ad-hoc initiation of workflow processes, negotiation of dates, and autonomous reassignment of work.

Workflow can be defined in two basic approaches: serial routing and rule-based workflow. Exchange offers serial routing functionality via the Messaging Application Programming Interface. A simple example of this is the creation of a document in Microsoft Office with a routing slip attached to it. Exchange takes a modular approach to rule-based workflow, providing interfaces to enable workflow developers to design solutions that run with their database engines, performing data lookups and pulls or pushes.

Exchange is an ideal platform for workflow applications because of its MAPI foundation, directory services, and Information Store. New in Exchange 5.5 is the ability to set up scripts on the Exchange server itself to be launched on a scheduled basis or upon various triggers defined by the developer.

Several third parties have developed components that can be added to Exchange to simplify the building of complex workflow applications. Leaders in this area are KeyFile (with their product KeyFlow) and Action Technologies.

Imaging Imaging expands the capability to support multiple file types and provides a strong mechanism for reading, distributing, and annotating information. In the Exchange environment, you can integrate at the information viewer level in order to access public folder data objects from the client. With *Object Linking and Embedding (OLE)* support, you can drag and drop the actual image into the message. On the server, images are stored as objects in the Information Store.

Document Management *Document management* (also referred to as *document imaging*) consists of scanning documents into a system, archiving the images, and creating full-text indexes of the content. Document management now extends into the realm of multimedia and OLE objects.

Front Office Technologies offers a tightly integrated solution built on NT, Exchange, and numerous bleeding-edge Microsoft technologies to offer document- and information-management functions that not only handle document management and archiving from a traditional PC DOCS or SAROS perspective, but also add several new twists to use the replication, security, and administration features of Exchange. Information gathering from the Internet and a "personal briefing" search-and-update agent greatly enhance the capability of Front Office to act as much more than a document-management system.

What's New in Exchange 5.5

Now that you have an overview of Exchange's features, you should learn about the specific changes and new additions in Exchange 5.5.

Ubiquitous Outlook

Outlook, based on the Universal Inbox, promotes not only communication (via e-mail_ within your enterprise), but also collaboration throughout your corporation and the Internet.

A 32-bit-only version of the Outlook client was introduced for use with Exchange 4.0 and 5.0 servers in October 1996. With Exchange 5.5, the Outlook interface is made available in a 16-bit variety for older Windows 3.x clients such as Windows 3.1 and Windows for Workgroups 3.11. A Macintosh and limited DOS flavor is being tested and is expected shortly after Exchange 5.5 ships. The Web Browser interface, making use of HTTP and dynamic HTML, also takes on the look of Outlook and is referred to as the Outlook Web Access client. The new Outlook Express client available with Microsoft Internet Explorer offers POP3 and IMAP4 support when connected to Exchange 5.5 and other supported standard servers.

The 32-bit version of Outlook is available with Exchange Server as a stand-alone product, and as a component of Office97. Outlook interoperates with Microsoft Mail, older Microsoft Exchange clients, Schedule+ 7.0, third party support cc:Mail, Lotus Notes, and a list of other messaging systems, offering companies the choice to deploy a single client interface as the right client for their enterprises.

Outlook's basic philosophy builds on Bill Gates's vision of "information at your fingertips." Today, most people experience information overload, especially with the popularity of the Internet. The quantity of information isn't necessarily the problem, but organizing it so you can find what you need is a challenge. Microsoft found that most people wanted a more integrated desktop. The company started meeting this need soon after, offering users the ability with Windows 3.0 to cut and paste a graph from DOS-based Lotus into WordPerfect 4.1.

Then, Office 4.2 was developed to work as one integrated application suite. As the Office suite evolves, Microsoft extends the original vision of organizing information. Outlook gives the Office user the ability to manage several types of information, including e-mail, calendars, contacts, tasks and to-do lists, documents or files on the hard drive, web links, voice mail, faxes, and more. Outlook also helps users share information by means of public folders on the Exchange server, electronic forms, and Internet connectivity (newsgroups). Listed below are key features in Outlook. For more information, look ahead to the following chapters: Chapter 29, "Installing and Configuring Outlook," Chapter 30, "Using Outlook," and Chapter 31, "Using Advanced Outlook Features."

Views Outlook enables users to arrange information any way they want to see it. Outlook by default supports five types of views: Table, Calendar, Card, Icon, and Timeline. Users can customize these into an unlimited number of personal or shared views. Table, Calendar, and Icon views are probably familiar to most users. The Card view resembles a list of business cards or index cards that concisely displays key information, and the Timeline view arranges items chronologically on a horizontal time line.

WWW Access Access your e-mail through HTTP over the World Wide Web. A browser such as Internet Explorer can retrieve e-mail and peruse server-based public folders via the Internet. Now, the user has more freedom to choose which operating system and platform (Internet Explorer for UNIX variants) is best suited for them. Microsoft has included calendar and scheduling into the latest incarnation of the web interface, called *Outlook Web Access (OWA)*.

Full MAPI Client Outlook is a full MAPI client application, so it can work with all e-mail systems that support MAPI. Outlook includes drivers for Microsoft Mail, Microsoft Fax, Microsoft Exchange Server, Internet Mail (SMTP/POP3/IMAP4), The Microsoft Network

(MSN), and Lotus cc:Mail. Additional third-party MAPI drivers are either available or under development for America Online, CompuServe, Lotus Notes, Novell GroupWise, Hewlett-Packard OpenMail, and Digital's All-in-One.

Backward Compatibility Outlook coexists with the original Microsoft Exchange client and Schedule+ 7.0 and works with earlier versions of Microsoft Mail, Microsoft Exchange client, or Schedule+. This allows a company to roll out Outlook in phases while enabling full communication between the old and new messaging systems.

Message Recall If a user sends a message that is inaccurate or inappropriate, they can attempt to recall the message from the recipients. Message Recall can either delete or replace the original message. Message Recall works across servers and across the Internet, but it will only recall the message if the recipient has not read or moved the message and if the recipient is also running Microsoft Outlook. If the recipients are not users of Microsoft Outlook, they will receive an e-mail message informing them that the sender would like to recall the earlier message.

NOTE If you want to replace a message, you must send a new one. If you do not send the new message, the original message is still recalled.

Meeting Planner Outlook makes it easy to schedule group meetings and invite attendees by displaying the free and busy times. Outlook will even automatically pinpoint the next available time for all attendees. See Figure 1.3 for an example.

Importing and Exporting You can import and export messaging information from several products, including Schedule+, MS Mail, ACT, ECCO, Sidekick, and Timex Data Link watches. Some of these converters are on the ValuPack CD-ROM that comes with Office97 or on the Microsoft Web site (**www.microsoft.com/outlook/**).

You can export Outlook data into comma- or tab-delimited files as well as Outlook .PST files for moving large amounts of Outlook data.

CAUTION

Be careful not to confuse the Windows Messaging System (WMS) client that currently ships with Windows 95 and NT Workstation 4.0. This client, while having many of the features of the older "full" Exchange client that shipped with Exchange 4.0 and 5.0, cannot by default connect to an Exchange server. Neither can WMS easily be upgraded to add the Exchange Server Service. Generally, an installation of the full Exchange client or Outlook is required to enable access to an Exchange server.

Using Lotus cc:Mail Connector

The *Microsoft Exchange Connector* for Lotus cc:Mail enables administrators to seamlessly integrate Microsoft Exchange into cc:Mail environments. Once installed, Exchange Server and cc:Mail systems can exchange messages and synchronize directories. The cc:Mail Connector supports both DB6 and DB8 cc:Mail post offices. By introducing Exchange Server into a cc:Mail environment, cc:Mail users benefit from Exchange Server's strong connectivity to the Internet and other systems. Also, customers can take a phased approach to migration that will cause minimal disruption with an organization. New technology acquired from Linkage Software has further enhanced the cc:Mail connector in Exchange 5.5.

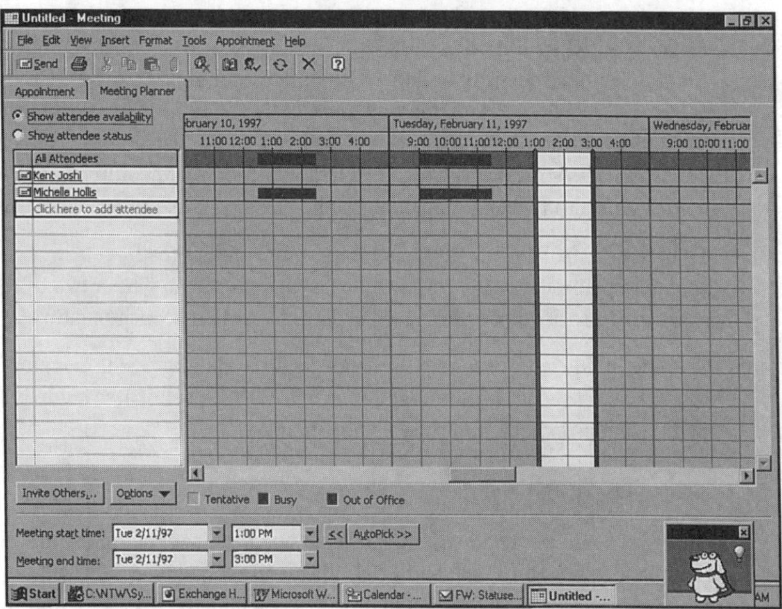

FIG. 1.3 Using the Meeting Planner in Outlook.

Using PROFS/SNADS Connectors

With the recent acquisition of Linkage Software, Microsoft has gained a world-class, proven toolset to easily facilitate connection of Exchange to a legacy HOST-based IBM PROFS *OfficeVision (OV)* or SNADS installation. Options include not only mail and attachment exchange, but also automated directory synchronization functions.

As with the cc:Mail and MS Mail connectors, migration from these older technologies offers dramatically reduced administrative and maintenance costs along with a significant increase in end-user productivity via the graphical Outlook client.

Using the Lotus Notes Connector

Also obtained with the Linkage purchase was powerful technology to connect Exchange to a Lotus Notes system for both mail and attachment exchange as well as automated directory synchronization. In an improvement over the previous versions of the Linkage product, Exchange 5.5 no longer requires an installation of Microsoft NT SQL Server to handle the directory synchronization functions. Instead, the newly enhanced databases of Exchange itself are utilized, thereby further reducing administrative overhead and increasing performance.

Understanding Messaging Security

Person to Person Key Exchange, which extended the functionality of the Key Management Server, provided in Exchange 4.0. Now, users from different organizations can exchange keys and certificates, enabling them to send signed and encrypted messages over the Internet.

Numerous updates have been made to the *Key Management Server (KMS)* to allow for the bulk creation and distribution of user keys, making it easier to enable an entire location or corporation to use these security options. The integration of KMS setup into the Exchange Administrator program makes overall management of the KMS much easier as well. Key recovery options are added, making it possible for an Exchange administrator to recover and reissue a user's key if the password is forgotten or if the user leaves the company without disclosing her password. Through this same mechanism it is also possible to revoke a user's key.

To better control an Exchange administrator's ability to affect key security, options are available to implement so called "missile silo" passwords, in which two different administrative passwords are required to change or disable certain security features.

Keeping in line with proposed Internet security standards, support for X.509v3 (enhancing the current X.509 support in Exchange) and S/MIME certificates such as VeriSign are anticipated as the standards become firmly established.

Understanding IMAP4

Post office protocol version 3 (POP3) is an open Internet standard that Exchange 5.0 offered in compliance with RFC 1939 and 1734. The *Internet Engineering Task Force (IETF)* is close to completing the standardization of new RFCs (2060, 2192, 2193, 2195) for Internet Message Access Protocol 4 revision 1 (IMAP4rev1). Actually, IMAP4 has been around since 1986, when it was originally developed at Stanford University, but its abilities have been lost due to the public's focus on POP clients. The key features of IMAP4 over POP are as follows:

- Multiple folders are allowed on the server store.
- Users have the option to keep their messages in the server store without being required to download them to the client they are working from. This enables users to access their mail messages many times from multiple client locations.
- Selective message retrieval and download options are available.
- Searching of the mailbox is offered.
- Future enhancements will include the ability to synchronize an offline IMAP store with the server and access to Public Folders.

As a result of supporting both POP3 and IMAP4, any mail client that meets these standards can access and utilize Exchange as a mail server. Exchange handles inbound and outbound mail requests from these POP3 or IMAP4 clients and then grants them access to their mailboxes on the Exchange server or routes their submitted message to appropriate Exchange users or to the Internet as SMTP mail. As support for the IMAP4 standard spreads across the industry and the Internet, users everywhere will be able to have most of the features previously only found on proprietary, non-standard mail systems.

Furthering Exchange's flexibility, it's possible to switch seamlessly between any of the suite of clients (Outlook, POP3, IMAP4, and so on). All IMAP4 messages can be stored on the Exchange server, providing a single-message store. Additionally, all POP3/IMAP4 message accesses are protected via security from clear-text authentication to NT's Challenge/Response validation. *Secure Sockets Layer (SSL)* can be used in conjunction with clear-text authentication for encryption. See Figure 1.4 for the basic flow of POP3 or IMAP4.

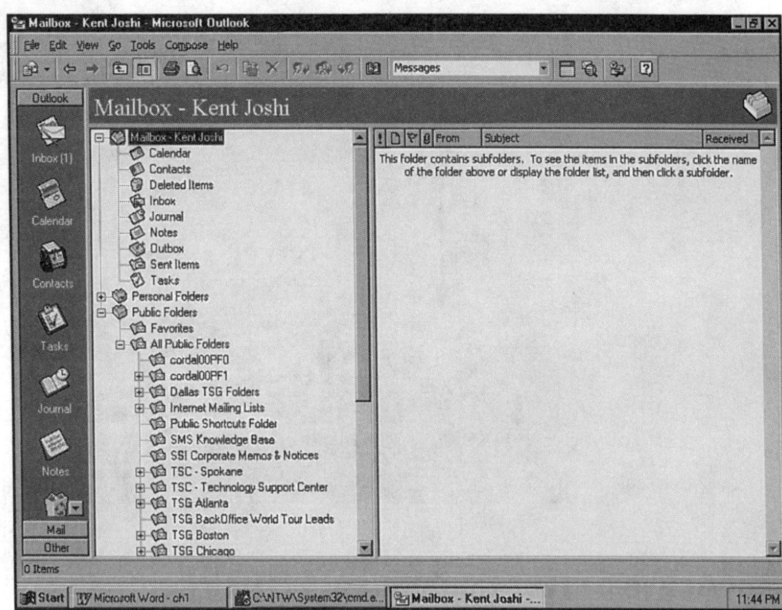

FIG. 1.4
Basic Flow of POP3.

Understanding LDAPv3

To support directory access for POP3, IMAP4 and Outlook Web Access clients along with other types of Internet-oriented applications, Exchange 5.5 enhances support for LDAP (Lightweight Directory Access Protocol) to meet the forthcoming version 3 standard. LDAP is an adapted subset of the X.500 standard that has been developed for the Internet to ease mail addressing issues between directory types that exist in various mail systems that touch the overall Internet. LDAPv3 is currently being defined by the IETF, with heavy involvement by Microsoft.

One key new feature of LDAPv3 enables mail systems to more easily participate in directory synchronization as solutions are developed to facilitate this need. A new LDAP API has been proposed to assist developers in making these directory connections. "Referrals" are also possible, allowing a corporation to link together several LDAPv3 based directory systems into one common lookup. Microsoft Exchange supports any client that implements the LDAP version 3 specification, including the latest versions of Netscape Communicator, Internet Explorer, Outlook Express, and other LDAP client providers.

The indexing associated with LDAP conventions enables users to actually search for a user in the directory based on limited criteria, such as first name and department (using wild card characters if desired), when perhaps the last name is not known. An Exchange administrator can selectively lock out certain directory attributes to non-authenticated, anonymous users (such as home addresses or other sensitive information). See Chapter 15, "Information Store Configuration," on securing directory attributes from non-authenticated, anonymous users. See Figure 1.5 for the basic operation of LDAP.

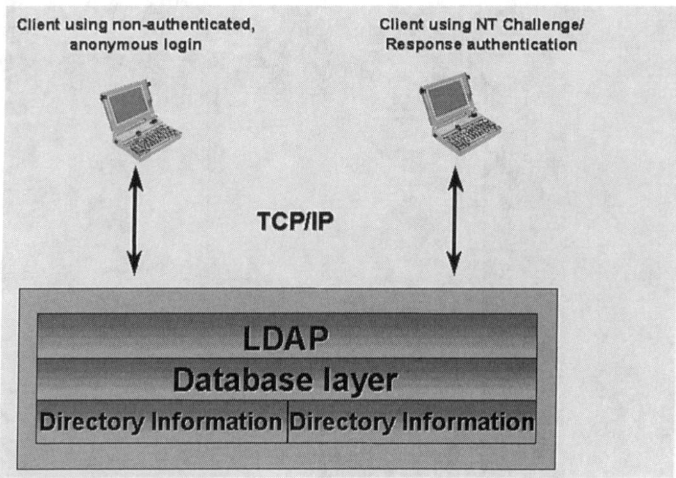

FIG. 1.5 LDAP Basic Operation.

Using Active Server Components (HTTP)

Coupled with Internet Information Server, Active Server components give developers the building blocks to enrich web sites with Exchange functionality, such as messaging, threaded discussion, and directory services. For example, Microsoft completed an Active Server application called Outlook Web Access (OWA). Web Access gives a user the ability to retrieve e-mail, access his server-based calendar, set up "rules," and of course access Exchange server-based public folders by using a standard browser running on any of a wide range of platforms, including Macintosh, OS/2, or UNIX. Web View gives users more freedom to check e-mail wherever they are. With the advent of "Internet Cafés" and Internet kiosks, users can check their e-mail from anywhere in the world by simply logging onto their companies' Web sites. Please see Figure 1.6 for a basic flow of HTTP.

Exchange 5.5 also includes several tools to make creation of Exchange public folder based web applications easier. Electronic forms can be easily created in the Outlook Forms Designer then processed by a new wizard to convert the functions into HTML and Active Server elements. This wizard output can then be opened in Microsoft's Visual InterDev tool (the code with a single license is included with Exchange 5.5 server) for further customization and then integration with Exchange's public folders and IIS. Once properly set up, it is possible for any Internet browser to access these forms and folder-based applications for usage from any client platform. Many corporations will use Exchange public folders in this fashion to create a multifaceted intranet from which users can use the standard Outlook clients or a web browser to manipulate data and collaborate in workflow.

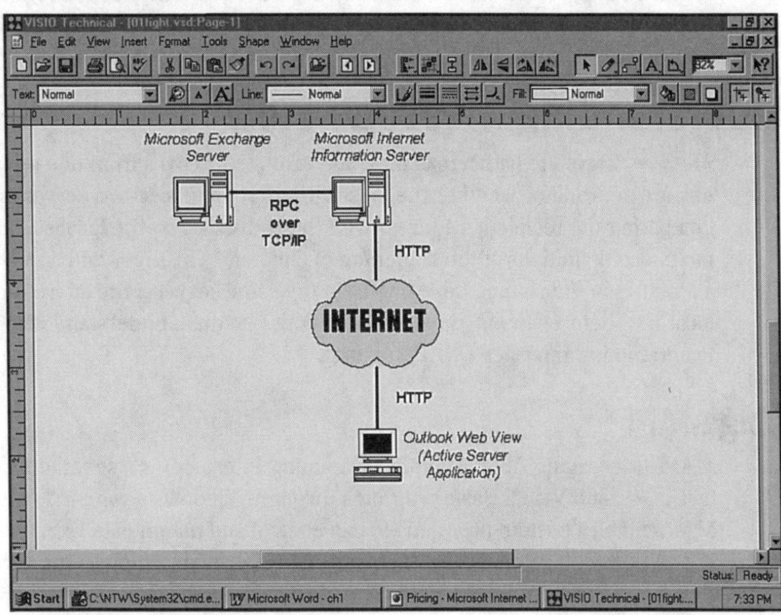

FIG. 1.6
Basic Flow of HTTP.

Additional Internet Security

Microsoft is firmly committed to supporting all Internet standards, especially those related to security. The *Simple Authentication and Security Layer (SASL)*, pending ratification by the IETF, is a supported option to force SSL authentication before SMTP messages will be accepted by the server. This feature is used to allow only secure SMTP-based connections between Exchange servers over the Internet, or to effectively restrict unauthorized access to the Exchange server via SMTP.

The Internet Mail Service's ability to connect one Exchange site to another across the Internet uses SASL and other encryption options to make the Internet a more acceptable messaging "backbone" for global corporations.

Exchange Server Information Store

Microsoft has shattered the 16 GB limit that existed in Exchange 5.0 with new JET database technology that raises the limit to 16,000 GB (16 TeraBytes) in each of Exchange 5.5's databases (PRIV, PUB, and DIR). Combining this dramatic enhancement with the fully relational database structure and SQL-like transaction-logging functions of Exchange opens Exchange to nearly limitless possibilities for managing very complex messaging-based applications.

Another exciting and much-requested new feature of Exchange 5.5 is the ability to recover deleted messages and folders. Essentially, a "tombstone"/recycle bin concept has been applied to the message store so that when objects are deleted they are not removed from the database until a specified number of days have passed or a backup of the server is made.

Understanding Message Flow

Message flow is the path a mail message takes as it moves from one recipient to another. Exchange determines whether the message will route inside of a server or between servers by comparing the recipient's address with the addresses on the local site and those in the routing table (see definitions at the beginning of chapter). Messages will flow between servers if the address is in the routing table or within the same server if the address matches those in the local site. Before jumping into message flow, you must understand what Messaging Application Programming Interface (MAPI) is, first.

Using MAPI

MAPI (Messaging Application Programming Interface) is a set of functions that can be called by C, C++, and Visual Basic programs through Windows *Dynamic Link Libraries (DLLs)*. MAPI enables custom programs to can control and manipulate Exchange objects (see Figure 1.7). A powerful extension to Exchange, MAPI provides support for developers to enhance the core functionality built into Exchange.

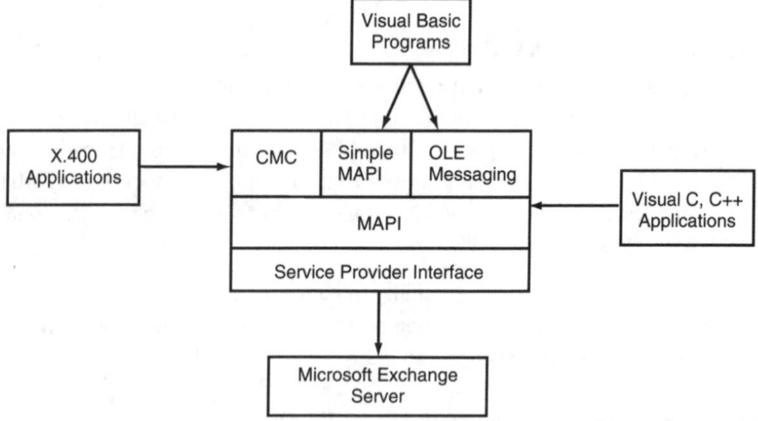

FIG. 1.7 The MAPI framework provides the map for designing Exchange applications.

MAPI has the following five components:

- Simple MAPI (sMAPI)
- Common Messaging Calls (CMC)
- OLE messaging
- MAPI
- MAPI service providers

When the client application is using a function library, messaging services are processed by sMAPI or CMC. The *CMC* interface is an API layer defined by the X.400 API Association. CMC is similar to sMAPI but is specially designed to support cross-platform development. When MAPI objects are being accessed and manipulated, client requests are serviced by OLE messaging or MAPI itself. The *OLE messaging* component enables development by using tools such as Visual C, Visual C++, and Visual Basic; MAPI itself is a powerful, object-oriented C++ interface that enables complex manipulation of folders, forms, and messages. The MAPI service providers then perform the requested actions for the client and pass back action through the MAPI subsystem to the MAPI client.

In addition to the tools and sample applications provided by Microsoft, many utilities for Exchange are available from third-party companies. These utilities, which are discussed in Chapter 31, "Using Advanced Outlook Features," consist of gateways, connectors, Visual Basic custom controls, and administrative utilities.

Many third-party developers (Lotus Development Corporation, for example) have switched from proprietary messaging standards, such as *Vendor Independent Messaging (VIM)*, to MAPI for designing messaging applications. This trend reveals the strength of the MAPI standard of the multitude of development tools that will emerge for designing MAPI applications.

MAPI is the glue that enables client applications to converse with the server to build a robust communications architecture.

Message Flow Within One Server

Here are the basic steps a message goes through when the receiver is on the same server as the sender. This process is detailed in Chapter 2, "Understanding Exchange's Organization Sites."

1. Using MAPI calls over an RPC connection, client1 connects to the server and accesses the private Information Store (IS) where all mail messages are held. Client1 sends a new message to the IS.
2. The IS queries the Directory to determine whether the recipient (client2) resides on the same server.
3. The Directory identifies that the recipient (client2) is on the same server.
4. The IS sends the recipient (client2) a notice that a new message has arrived and client2 receives the message (see Figure 1.8).

Message Flow Between Servers

Here are the basic steps a message goes through when the receiver is on a separate server. This process also is detailed in Chapter 2, "Understanding Exchange's Organization Sites."

1. Using MAPI calls over an RPC connection, client1 connects to the server and accesses the private Information Store (IS) where all mail messages are held. Client1 sends a new message to Server1.

FIG. 1.8
Message flow within one Server.

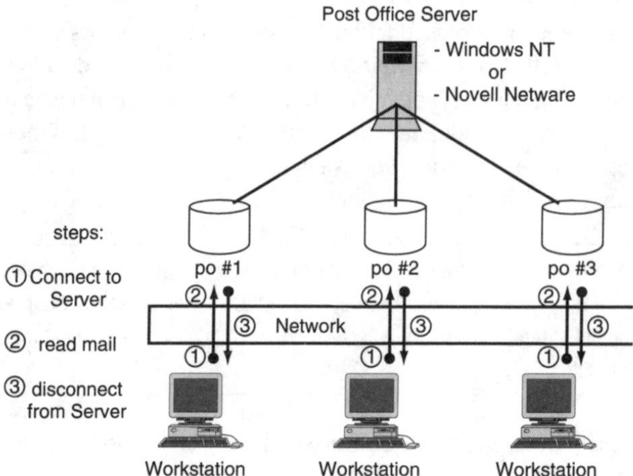

2. The IS queries the Directory and determines that the recipient (client2) resides on a different server. IS then places the message in the MTA's queue.
3. Server1's MTA sends the message to Server2's MTA.
4. Server2's MTA sends the message to its private IS.
5. The IS sends the recipient (client2) a notice that a new message has arrived; client2 receives the message (see Figure 1.9).

FIG. 1.9
Message flow between servers.

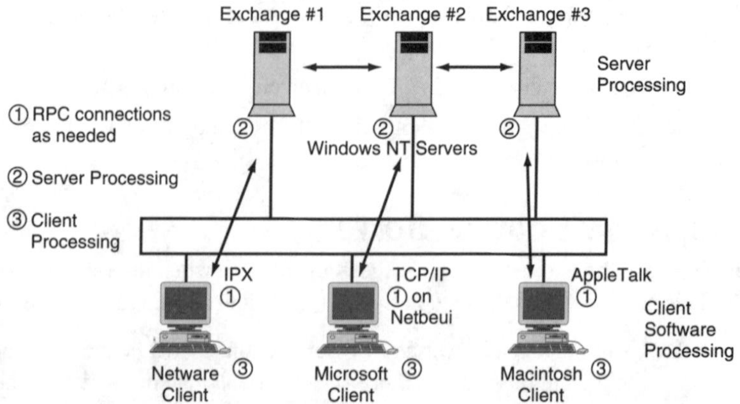

Comparing Exchange to Lotus Notes

Many critics attempt to compare Lotus Notes and Exchange, but no direct comparison can be made. Exchange has been designed from the ground up as an X.400/X.500-based enterprise messaging system. The MTA is designed to meet the exacting standards of 1984, 1988, and the proposed 1992 X.400 standards. The directory of Exchange is based on an extended version of X.500. Notes, on the other hand, began its life as a system of flat-file document databases that could replicate across multiple servers. Messaging was added as a way to enable additions to be mailed in to a database. Messaging has been enhanced in each version since Notes 4.0 to approach the needs of an enterprise messaging system. Currently, the internal mail engine of Notes 4.5 is still based on Lotus proprietary standards, but Lotus offers a series of free MTA add-ins to handle X.400 mail, SMTP mail, POP3 support with plans for LDAP and IMAP support later.

NOTE Novell's GroupWise and Netscape's SuiteSpot are the two other contenders in the ring with Lotus Notes. Due to the relatively short time SuiteSpot has been on the market, comparative information is changing daily and should be retrieved from **http://www.microsoft.com**. Novell's GroupWise version 5 has been available for nearly a year, but since it is based on older Novell server technology it has simply failed to capture a significant portion of the market mindshare.

On the other hand, Notes and Exchange have been old foes and the core differences between the two products have been the same through recent versions. Thus, a section comparing Notes to Exchange follows. Comparative information on Notes is available at the same Microsoft web address. ■

A significant limitation of Notes is the lack of a "site" concept as used in Exchange. Exchange combines servers into logical entities called *sites* for easier administration. Moving a user's mailbox from one Exchange server to another within a site is a snap, requiring no involvement of the user and especially no alteration of the user's mail address. Adding a new server to a site is also very easy, with little customization required—just point the new server at an existing server for automated configuration and integration.

The Notes directory itself is loosely based on X.500 standards and has been since Notes version 3.0. Provisions are included for all of the components of an X.500 naming scheme and most of the fields associated with extended X.500 are included.

In terms of messaging, Exchange far exceeds the functionality of Notes version 3.x. Notes version 4.x has made significant strides in providing enhancements to messaging elements. Unlike MS Mail or cc:Mail, however, Notes has no legacy in shared file system mail. Notes has been essentially client/server from the beginning. Lotus recently has stated that Notes is the upgrade path from cc:Mail to a client/server messaging system. For many cc:Mail installations this is potentially not desirable; thus, in Exchange version 5.0, Microsoft included a cc:Mail Connector and the capability to perform directory synchronization with cc:Mail. As previously noted, this technology has been enhanced in Exchange 5.5.

The two products can compete as groupware solutions, but Exchange can provide an entire messaging infrastructure to connect with legacy systems and heterogeneous environments because Exchange bases all of its "workflow" on the messaging infrastructure. Replication of data in Notes can only process by way of a direct connection of two Notes servers using a unique replicator service. Exchange, on the other hand, uses the messaging connectors across whatever paths are possible to send small messages from one site or server to a remote system. These messages are then reassembled and the data added into the remote server's applications and databases. This reliance on the mail system to move the replication messages enables a single Exchange server to easily replicate data with indirectly connected servers anywhere in the organization. Furthermore, since the replicated data is processed as small mail messages, use of the available bandwidth on the links connecting two servers can also be carefully controlled—unlike in Notes.

Both Exchange and Notes offer a "simple" forms and database development environment for basic users, and both offer several options for enhanced development with powerful programming environments. In Notes 4.x, Lotus has added a programming environment called Lotus Script, which is 95-percent compatible with Microsoft's Visual Basic. Lotus offers this tool as a way for Visual Basic programmers quickly to become productive developing Notes applications.

Exchange takes this extensibility several steps further with complete integration of Exchange with the full family of Microsoft development languages and tools. With the continuing enhancement of Internet components and web publishing via Exchange, all of the available Internet-oriented languages and environments are available for use and the Outlook forms to HTML/ASP Wizard makes it all easier than before.

NOTE Several third-party developers offer gateway solutions to give Exchange tight application connectivity with Notes. With proper implementation, Exchange and Notes applications can coexist effectively in your environment as a unified workflow system.

Understanding Notes Limitations

Probably the most limiting factor of Notes that will not be corrected in the foreseen future is the basic flat-file design of a Notes database. Notes databases are also limited to 4 GB in size. Exchange, now capable of scaling to 16 TB in size, is based on a relational database structure that lends itself to many traditional *Relational Database Management System (RDBMS)* programming concepts and features. Notes can attempt to address some of these limits with programming tricks and even replication to external SQL platforms, but the fundamental products that most clients will be working with do not take advantage of these workarounds.

Notes Advantages

Lotus Notes does have a perceived advantage over Exchange when it is used as groupware. From the market's perspective, the product is mature, and Lotus has made several enhancements in it over the years. Exchange 5.5 has been enhanced in the area of groupware development, with the addition of Exchange Server-based scripts to combat this advantage that Lotus had over it. The only actual advantage that Notes has over Exchange is in regard to "filtered replication." Notes offers administrators and developers (as well as end-users) numerous simple ways to filter data that will be replicated from one server database to another or from the server to a client. Look for Microsoft and their partners to overcome this limitation and to market Exchange very aggressively against Notes this year.

In addition to Notes's base functionality of providing groupware solutions inside any enterprise, many organizations have adopted an information distribution channel by providing Notes databases of information or direct feeds from their product support. Companies such as SAP currently use Notes as a means to support their product, but with the dramatic rise of the Internet, most companies are moving to a web-based support and information distribution-based model. Compaq and BAAN are examples of large corporations with mature installed Notes infrastructures that have recently dropped Notes and migrated to Exchange. Many more corporations are following suit and will continue to do so.

Microsoft's Use of Exchange

Interestingly, when MS Mail was in production, Microsoft internally did not use its own shared-file e-mail system. Instead they used its client interface on top of a proprietary UNIX-flavored system called Xenix mail.

To prove its commitment to the Exchange product, Microsoft has since moved all its internal mail systems to Exchange. At the time of this writing, Microsoft is on Exchange world-wide, with over 100 locations and close to 300 Exchange servers. The bulk of these servers are dedicated messaging servers, followed by nearly as many dedicated public folder servers. They have well over 15,000 public folders in use, with the majority of them used for development-tracking purposes (for build schedules, early adopter-tracking, and so on) but also used for such diverse functions as threaded discussions on almost every topic, and even online sales classifieds.

On the client side, Microsoft has moved to Outlook as the standard client browser to reinforce Microsoft's commitment to their own messaging platform.

Exchange's Momentum

Exchange has picked up considerable momentum since its first release in April 1996.

There have been over 1.25 million Exchange seats deployed to date and around 90 percent of customers use Exchange for Internet Mail connectivity. Fourty-five percent (more than one response could be marked) of those use Exchange for pieces of the company intranet. There are over 125 companies actively developing applications and over 15,000 professionals trained on the product.

Exchange migrations from MS Mail are a natural evolution and Microsoft spent a lot of marketing effort in 1996 to urge companies to make this move. Much of 1997's efforts have been focused on migrations from cc:Mail, Notes, flavors of UNIX POP/SMTP mail, and legacy HOST systems like PROFS. Software Spectrum has seen work in all of these areas with a particular focus on Notes to Exchange migrations.

With the richness of administration and development features in Exchange 5.5, even though only in its third release, expect Exchange to become a dominate force in the workflow/groupware arena to couple with its current dominance in messaging. These are exciting times for Exchange users and developers!

CHAPTER 2

Understanding Exchange's Organization and Sites

In this chapter

Exchange Server is designed on a three-tiered model. The entire collection of Exchange servers within a company is called the *organization*; i.e., the root or starting point of the Exchange Server directory hierarchy. To facilitate administration and maximize performance, the organization is separated in distinct groups of servers called *sites,* which are one or more Exchange Server computers connected together. Each site consists of *site resources,* which are the individual Exchange servers themselves and the recipients who reside on those servers. Understanding this hierarchy and the underlying network architecture that supports it is crucial to the implementation of Exchange in any company. This chapter is designed to provide an overview of these concepts for you to start thinking about how each element will apply in your specific situation.

Understanding Exchange Organizations and Sites

The largest administrative unit in Exchange is the organization. All Exchange servers in an association or company are included under the heading of organization. An Exchange organization can be a single-room office with a couple of servers, or a huge, multinational facility with dozens of servers at great geographical distances (see Figure 2.1). Regardless of the situation, often there will be other types of messaging systems with which Exchange must communicate. These systems are not considered part of the Exchange organization, though they may play an integral part in your company's overall messaging scheme.

FIG. 2.1
A Sample Exchange Organization.

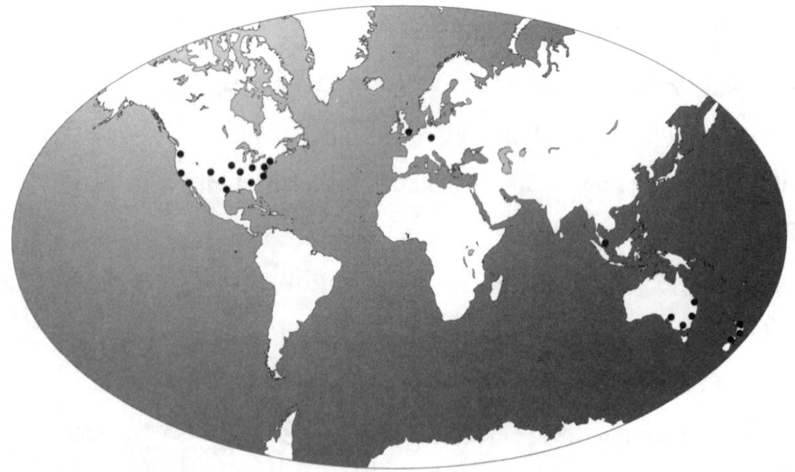

Sites are the second tier of Exchange's hierarchy. They represent a logical grouping of several Exchange Server computers. Servers in a site work together to provide messaging services to a set of users, unified administration and communication services. Within a site, all servers can easily share information and can also be managed as a collection.

There are several other advantages to having multiple servers grouped into one site:

- Centralized administration. You do not need to log on to each server in order to perform administrative functions on any of the servers in a site.
- Directory information is automatically replicated between servers in a site. No additional connectors are required for this functionality.
- A user needs only to be added once to gain user access to resources on all servers within a site.
- Easier access to information resources; a user can access a relevant bulletin board without having to know its specific server location within a site.

Defining Site Boundaries

With all of these benefits, you might be inclined to put every Exchange server in one site. For several reasons, this is not always the best solution. Therefore, defining where one site ends and one site begins is worthy of serious consideration (see Figure 2.2). Variables, such as network bandwidth, physical links, protocols, network traffic, operating systems, and, of course, cost, will affect where site lines are defined in your enterprise. Also, it is important to plan the number of sites and their boundaries because it is difficult to split or join other sites once they are created. Even moving users from one site to another is not a trivial task.

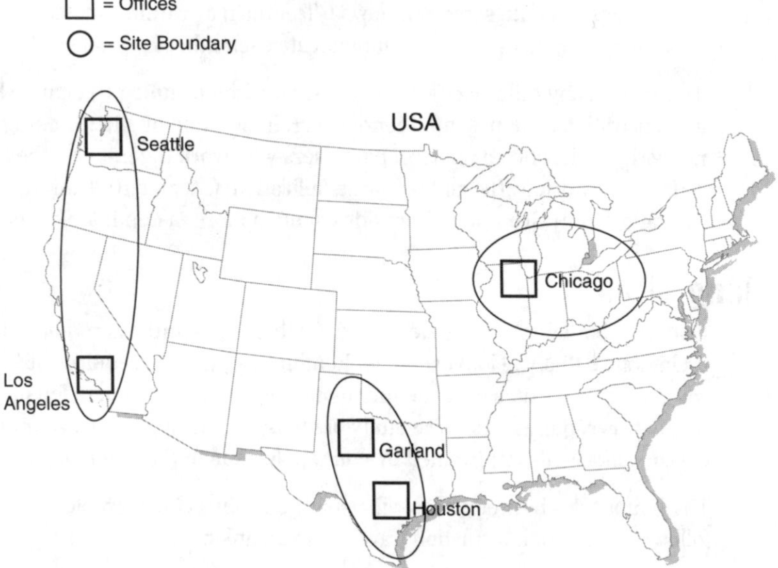

FIG. 2.2 Sample site boundaries. These are also the actual U.S. offices used as examples throughout this book.

There are some general requirements that must be met by all servers within a site:

- All servers in a site must be able to communicate via Remote Procedure Calls (RPCs). RPC is a mechanism by which servers exchange messages and directory information. RPCs can communicate over the network by using the various Microsoft Windows NT-supported protocols, including TCP/IP, IPX/SPX, and NetBEUI. Generally, this means that all the servers must be on the same LAN or WAN. But if you have a large network spanning geographical boundaries and that network connection supports communication via RPCs, you could define all those servers to be within the same site (provided the other following requirements are met).
- High bandwidth connections are required for server communication within a site. The definition of high bandwidth is somewhat arbitrary, but for our purposes we consider 128 Kb/s to be the absolute minimum bandwidth for reasonable intrasite communication. The connection must be fast enough to allow efficient RPC connections between servers as well as handle the volume data such as user messages, and Directory and Public folder replication. Of course, the bigger the pipe, the better the performance.
- The network connection must be permanent, and the links between all servers in a site must be up at all times. Permanent connections include LAN, leased line, and other WAN links. Periodic connections (connections not available at all times) such as dial-up, are not a good choice.
- All servers must exist in the same Windows NT security context. This means all servers must be in the same Windows NT domain or within a trusted domain. Exchange servers in a site must be able to authenticate each other in order to share information.

There are many other elements to consider when planning Exchange Server sites—administration schemes, number of users, integration of other messaging protocols, additional network traffic, and so on. Grouping users who work together on the same server and sites reduces network traffic and resource utilization. Chapter 10, "NetWare Considerations/Migrating from Groupwise," provides a much more in-depth look at such considerations.

Linking Sites

Once site boundaries are determined, further assessment is required to establish the network architecture that will join each one. Routing within a site requires little planning; however, routing between sites or to another e-mail system requires detailed planning and configuration. Again, this requires extensive study of messaging usage across your entire organization and any specific needs determined by your application of the technology.

The boundaries between sites will usually sustain a considerable amount of traffic due to the following types of information traversing site links:

- Standard messaging data (plus attachments)
- Directory replication data
- Public folder replication (or connections to public folders replication if not configured)

There are two primary Exchange components used to connect sites:

- Site connector
- X.400 connector

Using Site Connector This connector is designed for sites located on the same LAN. A site connector is an Exchange built-in connector used to facilitate the transfer of messages between two Exchange servers. This connector is an integrated software component to the server. The site connectors use RPC calls to communicate with the other Exchange servers. Site connectors are unlike the Internet or X.400 connectors as they will support any Microsoft networking protocol or any Exchange messaging address space or directory services. The key is that the Exchange servers have connectivity between the sites.

The site connector is the most efficient method of site interconnection, but the sites must be able to communicate at a high bandwidth using remote procedure calls. Also, because the sites must authenticate each other during communication, they must belong to the same Windows NT domain or be part of a trusted domain.

There are two major advantages to using a site connector instead of an X.400 connector:

- Efficient communication between sites because messages do not need to be converted from the Exchange internal format.
- Easy configuration since definition of a network transport is not needed (RPC communications are transport independent) and you do not have to schedule connections.

Using the X.400 Connector Conditions often mandate the use of the X.400 connector for site links. X.400 connections are used for several reasons. One reason is that your enterprise has a connection to a Value Added network provider in order to send secure messages to a business partner. X.400 is the standard protocol for the WAN connections. The other reason is if your enterprise is quite large, you may configure Exchange to use the X.400 address space as the directory service for the messaging backbone. X.400 provides a standards-based address space, ensuring the longevity of the messaging system in large enterprises. Microsoft itself uses Exchange with an X.400 backbone to support all 20,000 of its users. X.400 offers some advantages—you can define message size and schedule when connections happen, as well as see the message route. Some disadvantages include the X.400 is more complicated to configure and can be costly if there's a high volume of data. Generally, if any of the following conditions apply, you will need to opt for the X.400 connector:

- Your remote site is not on the same logical LAN. This could mean you are using an asynchronous connection, X.25, or are connecting to a site at a different enterprise.
- You want to use a public or private X.400 system as your messaging backbone.
- You want all Exchange communications to fully comply with the 1984 or 1988 X.400 standards.

Messages routed through an X.400 connector must be converted to X.400 standard for messaging interchange. However, the wide range of connectivity options provided more than makes up for the slight loss in network efficiency.

Exchange Site Resources

Site resources are the third tier in the Exchange hierarchy. This tier consists of two main elements:

- Servers—The physical hardware and software package that operates Exchange.
- Recipients—The elements toward which all messaging data is directed.

Servers

Servers may wear many hats in an Exchange environment. An Exchange server can perform any number of the following tasks:

- Hold local users' mailboxes;
- Hold public folders in a local information store;
- Be a connection or gateway to other Exchange sites, Microsoft Mail post offices, or foreign systems;
- Be a "bridgehead" server for directory replication between sites.

Also, the server might hold the following additional Windows NT supporting tasks:

- Support dial-up users via remote access lines;
- Be a Windows NT domain controller.

To avoid overloading any one server, an optimal situation would be to have a dedicated server for each of the preceding tasks. However, in real-world situations, this is often neither practical nor cost effective. A major goal in planning an Exchange hierarchy is mastering the art of load balancing across several machines. Other load balancing factors include the number of Exchange servers, the type of platform number of disks, CPU speed, amount of memory, public folder replication, and type of mailbox rules. Subsequent chapters discuss load balancing in detail.

Recipients

It is important in a discussion of Exchange hierarchy to consider the very entities of which directories are created. Recipients are the foundation of an Exchange messaging system. We are the reason that messaging technology exists in the first place. Exchange server defines the following four types of recipients:

- Mailbox—called the "inbox." It is the most common type of recipient. One is usually assigned to each user. Mailboxes are recipients within the messaging site or local post office. They contain information about users, such as where that person fits in the organization, their name, phone numbers, and e-mail addresses.
- Custom recipient—recipients outside the messaging site almost identical to mailboxes that contain information on users outside of Microsoft Exchange. One common custom recipient would be an Internet user with an SMTP e-mail address, such as **(users@domain)**.

- Distribution list—also known as aliases or groups in Microsoft Mail. This type of recipient is actually a group of other recipients (either mailboxes or custom recipients). Messages sent to a distribution list are delivered to each recipient on the list.
- Public folder—a recipient with the added functionality of allowing the received messages to be shared among many users in an enterprise. Created by the administrator with the Client interface, you can set access control and control the storage requirements.
- Hidden recipients—can send and receive mail but do not show up in the address book. Naturally, hidden recipients are not propagated in directory replication.

Exchange Server during directory replication/synchronization handles each recipient as an individual object. Each can be assigned individual trust levels (see the discussion in Chapter 7, "Planning Connections to Microsoft Mail Systems") to determine whether its directory entry will be replicated to other sites in an organization.

Each recipient has many different properties and details that can be set by the administrator, but such discussion will occur later in this book (see Chapter 16, "Creating and Configuring Recipients").

Exchange System Naming Conventions

A good naming strategy is crucial to the efficient operation of an Exchange system. Each object in an Exchange directory is identified by a unique name. This is called the Distinguished Name and it is set when the object is first built—when you create a new mail box, install a new server, add a new connector, and so on. With a good naming strategy that uses meaningful and logical names, you will be able to quickly pinpoint the object anywhere in your organization.

Good references on which to build names are traditionally:

- Geographical locations (Garland, Los Angeles)
- Company structure (manufacturing, distribution)

Other things you should consider are whether you have to be compatible with another mail system or other applications, and whether your organization may someday expand beyond the country. Cute or comical names get old quickly and generally do not provide sufficient information for the widest possible range of personnel to understand your structure.

Exchange Message Routing

A well-designed Exchange system within a reasonably large organization will reflect skillful interweaving of various messaging technologies. Message routing is the process through which a message eventually reaches its intended recipient. Because of Exchange's connector and gateway options, efficient message routing can and will be an intricate process throughout your enterprise. This section will cover basic routing concepts and start giving you a feel for how Exchange handles messages.

Fortunately for the end-user, the complex message routes are abstracted into the single inbox metaphor. As a system administrator, however, it is essential for you to understand all the possible instances of message routing in order to be able to create the most efficient routes in your Exchange Organization.

The key elements involved in a routing process are:

- Message Transfer Agent
- Directory Service
- Connectors and Gateways

Understanding Routing

To route a message correctly to an intended recipient, Exchange needs to know not only the address of the intended recipient, but also information that describes the path to that destination. This is accomplished by two crucial pieces of addressing data:

- Recipient Address—the name of the specific mailbox to which a message is intended. It must be in the standard of the recipient system, meaning a recipient on your Exchange system will be addressed following your naming standard, such as users first name and last name. An Internet SMTP address would be **(users@domain)**.
- Address Space—identifies a certain type of message that a connector is responsible for routing. Typically, these entries are a subset of a complete address, identifying the route a certain message will take. Exchange takes each address space entry as a filter to determine whether a message should be sent through a connector or gateway.

Directory Names and X.400 Originator/ Recipient Addresses

Exchange uses a subset of the X.400 Originator/Recipient (O/R) to identify individual recipients. The X.400 O/R address is comprised of attributes that define a specific recipient by country, organization, common name, and a variety of other information.

Understanding Routing

For routing of a mail message on the same Exchange Server, the Information Store is responsible for the delivery of a mail message when both the sender and receiver of a mail message are on the same Microsoft Exchange Server.

For routing of a mail message between two different Exchange Severs in the same Exchange site, the message transfer agent (MTA) is responsible for transferring a mail message when the recipient is not on the same Exchange Server as the sender. The MTA uses the recipient's distinguished name (DN) to determine the location of the server. It then routes the mail message to the other Microsoft Exchange Server's MTA.

NOTE If the recipient is a distribution list, the list is separated into its component recipients. Each recipient then enters this routing process independently. ■

If at any time an MTA encounters a connection problem with a connector, it will retry the transmission periodically until delivery is successful or until the time-out limit is met. If the time-out limit is met, then the message is returned as a non-deliverable report (NDR).

For routing between different Exchange sites or foreign systems:

1. MTA provides the engine for routing and transferring data to other servers. The routing process commences when an Exchange Server's MTA receives a message. The message can be derived from a user's mailbox, a connector, or another MTA.
2. The recipient's address is compared to the local site. If they match, the message is delivered as in the previous list.
3. If the sites do not match, MTA will match the recipient's address space to an available connector or gateway.

   For example, if the recipient has an SMTP address, the MTA knows how to route it through an Internet Mail connector.

   If more than one such connection is available, then one is selected based on routing costs.
4. The MTA sends the message through the selected gateway.
5. The message is delivered according to the process of the receiving system. If the receiving system is an Exchange site, the message will be routed as noted in the previous list. Every other messaging system will have its own delivery methods.

NOTE Often there may be multiple message routes to a particular destination. In this case, the appropriate route is chosen by the routing cost of that destination (see following section). ■

Routing Tables

Routing tables contain all the information a message transfer agent needs to determine where to send messages. Every time you make a change that affects message routing, such as removing a site connector or site, you are prompted. The routing table will be rebuilt and saved. Routing tables also can be rebuilt manually through a button on the MTA property sheet, although in most cases the routing tables are built dynamically.

Routing Attachments with Messages

Attachments are routed simultaneously with a message. All necessary file format conversions are handled by the appropriate MTAs through which the message passes. Exchange does have intelligent attachment handling when dealing with distribution lists. Only one instance of an attachment is sent to each mailbox. This eliminates wasted disk space to maintain exact duplicates of an attachment for several users in a same site.

Using Distribution Lists

Distribution Lists are groups of users that can be addressed as one by sending one message, such as sending a message addressed to a distribution list named "accounting." All members of that list would receive this message. Lists are established and modified by the administrators and can be replicated across servers and sites allowing recipients with access privileges to see the members and the messages to them.

An individual user can also join appropriate lists from within his or her Exchange Client.

From the Exchange server standpoint, lists themselves are individual directory objects. This means they can each have specific properties attached to them and are replicated by directory replication and synchronization.

A message that is sent to a distribution list is treated as a single entity until it is split into its component recipients. When configuring a distribution list's properties, you define an expansion server where the list splits into its components.

The process is as follows:

1. A user addresses and sends a message to a distribution list.
2. The message is routed as normal to its intended recipient (in this case, the distribution list).
3. The list object is routed to an Exchange server set as this list's Expansion server. At this point, the list is broken down into its component recipients.
4. Each message to the component recipients is routed individually.

Redundant Site Links, Routing Cost, and Load Balancing

For large organizations, it is often efficient and safe to establish multiple links between certain sites. This not only increases the system's fault tolerance, but also can be used to balance messaging traffic between sites. Often there will be specific links which receive an extraordinary amount of large traffic. Message routing in this situation demands establishing a priority for whatever connections will receive the traffic. This will be discussed in-depth in the site planning section of this book. Some general considerations for situations where alternative routes should be established are:

- Available Network Bandwidth—links with more robust bandwidth will generally receive the bulk of messaging data between sites. An asynchronous modem link would usually be used as a backup, for example.
- Cost of Connections—certain types of connections (such as the use of private X.400 connections) are less cost efficient and should be used only when other connections are overloaded or unavailable.

A variable called Routing Cost is assigned to each connection in its property sheet and used by Exchange message transfer agents to determine the path of a message. The cost of each route can be any number between 0 and 100. A route that costs 0 will always be used first if it is available, and a route that costs 100 will only be used if no other routes are available. Default value for all connectors is one. If two or more connections have the same routing cost, then messaging load will be roughly split equally among them.

In the Software Spectrum organization, for example, a number of connectors are set up to connect servers in site Los Angeles, California to site Garland, Texas. In the connectors' property sheets, we establish links between the following Exchange servers:

1. A site connector over a T-1 line between servers Garland01 and LosAngeles01. We assign this link a routing cost of 1.
2. A site connector over the same T-1 line between servers GARLAND02 and LOSANGELES02.

   We also assign this link a routing cost of 1.
3. An X.400 connector over a private network between server GARLAND02 and LOSANGELES02.

   We assign this link a routing cost of 2.
4. Finally, we have one last resort Dynamic RAS X.25 connection between GARLAND01, and LOSANGELES02. We assign this link a routing cost of 100 due to its inherent monetary cost of message transfer and limited bandwidth.

Messages will normally traverse the first and second site connections. Their routing cost is equal, so Exchange will attempt to distribute message load across both connectors evenly. Under heavy message loads, where message cues on both site connectors 1 and 2 are long, Exchange will utilize connector number 3 (X.400). In the rare situation where all three above connectors are disabled (e.g., the T-1 link is down and the GARLAND03 is off-line for repair), Exchange will engage connection number 4 as a last resort.

Load Balancing is the fine art of crafting your system's connections to best handle your diverse system traffic. By considering the above and many other variables, you will be able to design an efficient and fault-tolerant system for your enterprise.

Address List and Directory Management

A listing of all available recipients, such as a global address list, completes the corporate directory that contains the entire organization. Because the Global Address List is a list of individuals by name (not cryptic e-mail names), it is of great value to a user. From the standpoint of a network administrator, however, maintaining an accurate and timely address list can be one of the greatest challenges. Traditionally, Microsoft Mail has a history of difficulties in implementing such functionality, and not since the arrival of Exchange has there been a bigger push for excellence in this area.

These sections will overview the essential components of Exchange's directory architecture. Additionally, you will learn important concepts about directory synchronization that will aid in planning and implementing Exchange in your enterprise.

The Directory Service is the primary component responsible for directory manipulation in Microsoft Exchange. The Directory Service uses Directory System Agents (DSAs) that are the subprograms responsible for executing specific changes to a directory structure.

Maintaining a useful, up-to-date directory involves managing user addresses within an Exchange site, between sites, and between your enterprise and the other systems with which you pass information. If, for example, a user is added on one server, you as the administrator need to decide which other site directories should reflect that change and configure appropriate connectors to facilitate the process. By administrating a combination of system processes you will be able to detail how directory information propagates through your system.

There are two principal Exchange operations that carry out directory management tasks:

- Directory Replication
- Directory Synchronization

Directory Replication

Directory replication is the process by which all the Exchange servers in an enterprise will share directory information. To maintain a useful user directory, updates must be accurate, timely, and available to all appropriate users.

Directory Replication Within a Site Directory replication between servers in the same site is automatic (see Figure 2.3). Each server holds a local copy of the directory for that site. When you as the administrator modify a mailbox at one server, that change is automatically distributed to all servers in that site. Usually it takes about five minutes for new information to propagate across a site.

By default, all directory information is included in replication. This means an exact duplicate of each server's entire directory structure is exchanged during replication. This is efficient within a site due to the high bandwidth network connections typically found between servers. By the same token, network connections between sites are typically much lower bandwidth, so passing entire directory lists is not the most efficient method of maintaining timely address lists.

Directory Replication Between Sites Directory replication between sites is not an automatic process. For two distinct sites to share directory information, there needs to be a specific connector established. This gives you the option to filter what data is actually replicated and what remains unique to that site.

Directory replication between sites can occur if the sites are on the same logical LAN, WAN links, or public and private messaging links (see Figure 2.4). Therefore, public X.400 systems, or even the Internet, can be the transport for your directory replication information between sites.

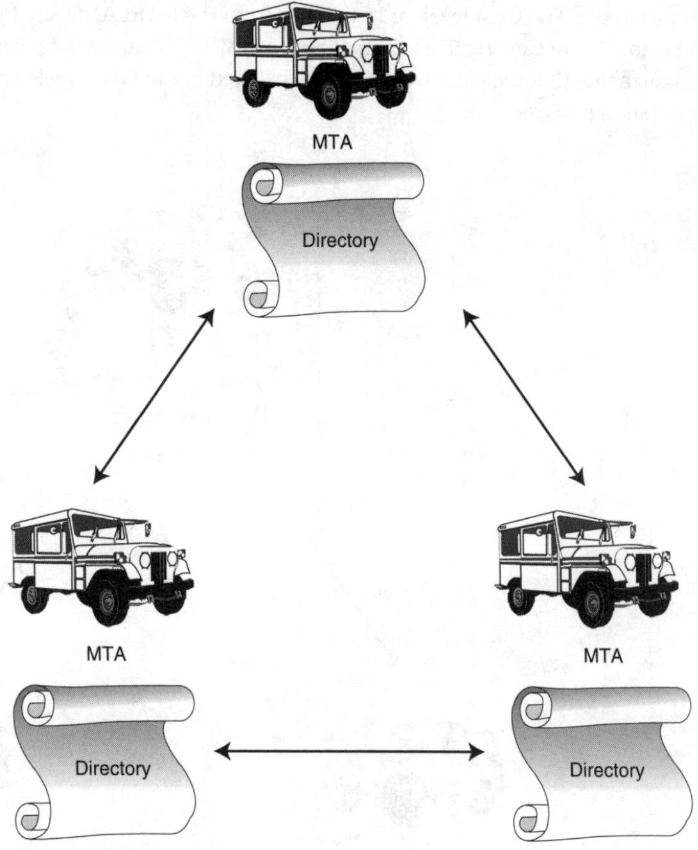

FIG. 2.3 Directory replication within a site.

Directory replication across sites occurs asynchronously and is scheduled in the administrator program. Only one server in each site can be configured to either send or receive replication information. However, one server can be set up to both send and receive the data. Servers that act as the connection boundaries for directory replication are known as the "bridgehead servers."

There are two steps to resolve before directory replication occurs across site boundaries. They are:

1. Decide what specific directory information you wish to exchange with other sites.
2. Act upon that decision and configure each site so only the desired information is replicated.

Directory Replication Trust or Sensitivity Levels Each directory object (such as mailboxes, public folders, or distribution lists) can be individually assigned a parameter called replication trust level or sensitivity level. These trust levels determine whether or not a certain object will be replicated to a certain site.

For example: The trust level for replication from the GARLAND site to the Los Angeles site is set to 50. You can create a user mailbox in GARLAND and set its trust level to 51 and information about that recipient will not be propagated to the Los Angeles site in the directory replication process.

FIG. 2.4
Directory replication between sites.

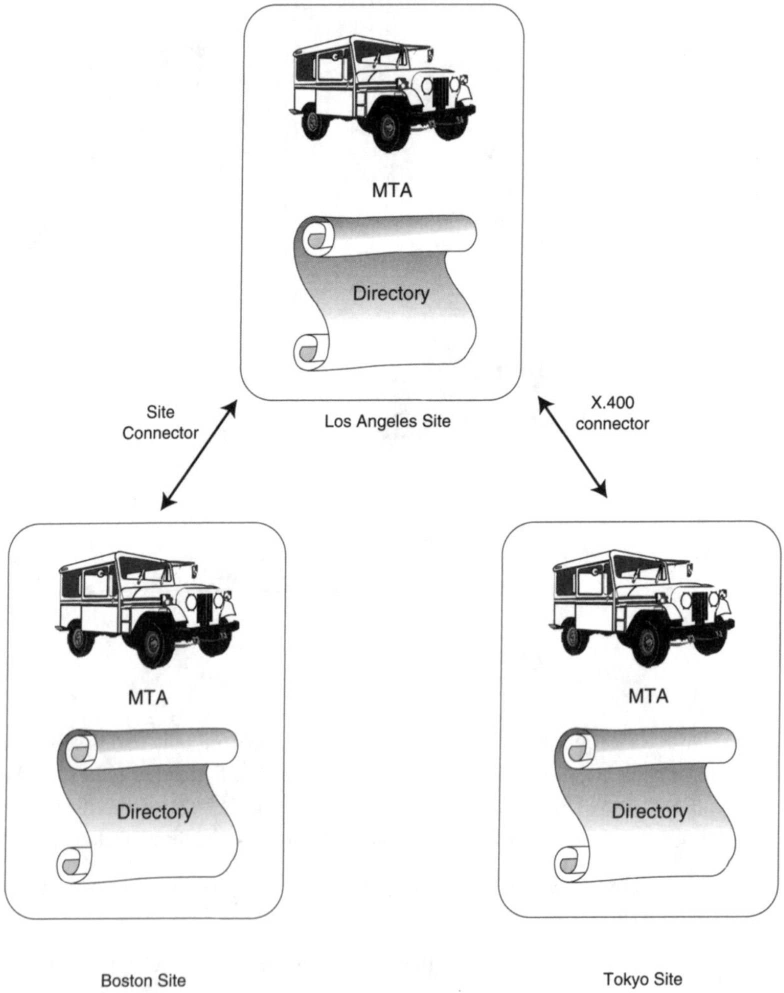

Directory Replication Tables Directory replication tables are maps that describe the replication links between servers in a site. This is useful mainly when adding new servers. For instance, you bring up Server Seattle01 in a site, and then the directory replication tables are updated to include this server. The next time replication occurs, server Seattle01 can send and receive updates to all other servers in the site.

Directory replication tables also map links between servers in a site and the bridgehead server. This server is the one machine responsible for receiving directory updates from remote sites.

Knowledge Consistency Checker

This tool is necessary for adjusting inconsistencies between the Directory and the Public Information Store. The challenge is when there is a directory entry for a particular folder in the store, yet the folder no longer exists, or the opposite situation where a folder exists, but there is no corresponding directory entry. Typically, this is due to information restored from a backup that is out of sync with current records. The Systems Administrator needs to run the knowledge consistency checker. This will adjust such irregularities.

Directory Synchronization

Perhaps a greater challenge than replicating directory data between Exchange servers is synchronizing directory data with other messaging systems. Typically, this situation arises when linking Exchange to an existing Microsoft Mail network or to a foreign system through an external gateway. Exchange Server supports synchronization with any mail system that uses the Microsoft Mail for PC Networks version 3.x directory synchronization protocol.

Directory synchronization (dir-sync) is optional and it ensures that each directory (or post office for MS Mail) has an up-to-date global or organization-wide address list. The dir-sync process is streamlined by propagating only the changes between systems and not the complete address lists.

Directory Synchronization Architecture Because Exchange's directory synchronization is based on the Microsoft Mail dir-sync protocol, let us first examine the architecture of that system before proceeding (see Figure 2.5). Microsoft Mail directory synchronization involves the following core components:

- Directory Synchronization Server—a single Microsoft Mail post office assigned to the task of synchronizing directories.
- Directory Synchronization Requestor—every other post office on the network that shares addresses with the dir-sync server.
- Server Address List—the master list of all users that is maintained on the dir-sync server.
- Dir-Sync Server—the directory synchronization server (there can be only one dir-sync server in a site) collects address list updates from requestors, updates the master directory list, and then sends out the resulting updates to each requestor.
- Dir-Sync Requestor—these systems send local directory updates to the designated dir-sync server (note: when the requestor is also a server it sends messages to itself). Requestors also obtain address updates from other requestors through the dir-sync server.

NOTE On a dir-sync server, the master address list is stored separately from local address information. Therefore, when a local address is changed on the machine operating as the dir-sync server, it will communicate that change to itself as would any other requestor.

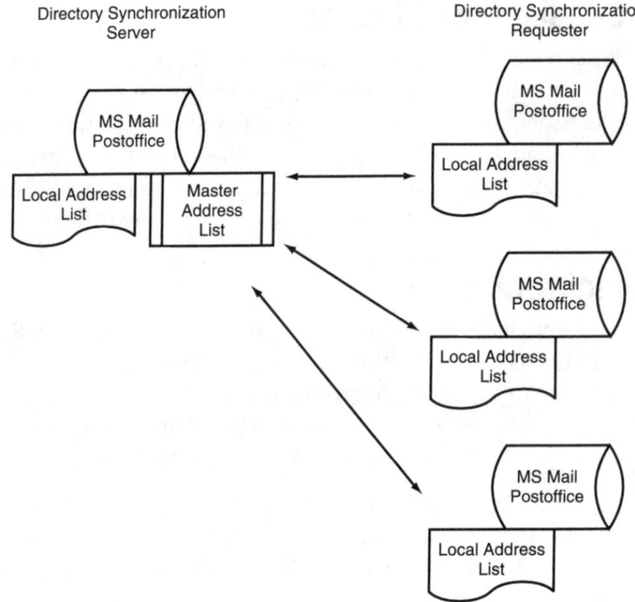

FIG. 2.5 Directory synchronization within a Microsoft Mail system.

Exchange server contains a component, the Microsoft directory synchronization agent (DXA) that can function in either the server or the requester role (see Figure 2.6). As with Microsoft Mail networks, you can set up only one directory synchronization server in each Exchange site. Instead of having a server address list, Exchange uses its standard server directory.

NOTE Microsoft Mail for AppleTalk networks can participate in directory synchronization with the Exchange Connection Gateway installed on the appropriate Microsoft Mail (AppleTalk) server. This connection includes a requester program that will function exactly as any other Microsoft Mail requester.

Directory Synchronization with Foreign Systems Foreign mail systems can also participate in directory synchronization provided they can import and export addressing information using the Microsoft Mail 3.x directory synchronization protocol.

In essence, the foreign system then becomes another requester and is seen as such by the directory synchronization server.

The following is a description of how a foreign requester participates in directory synchronization:

1. The foreign requester creates its own list of address updates and puts them into system messages.

FIG. 2.6
Exchange directory synchronization agent.

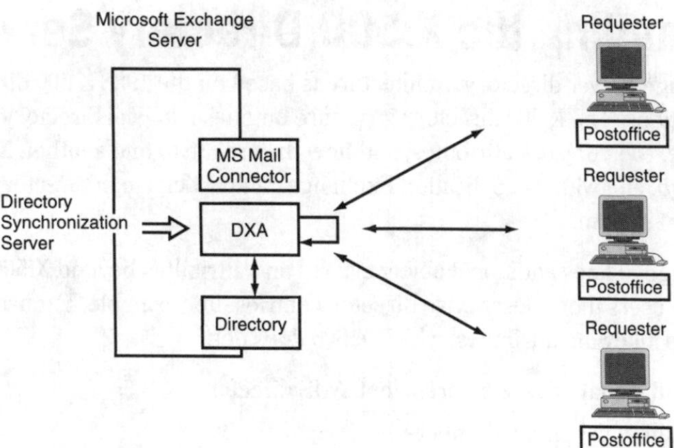

2. The address updates are submitted to the dir-sync server via the appropriate gateway or transport.
3. The DirSync server receives and incorporates the updates into its master directory list. A new message reflecting address changes is generated.
4. The message containing the updates is transmitted once again via the appropriate gateway to the foreign requester.
5. The foreign requester processes the changes into its local address list.

Microsoft Exchange as the DirSync Requestor

The DirSync Requestor will periodically query the Exchange Server directory for any changes made to mailbox recipients directory information. The DirSync component sends an update mail message and a request for MS Mail updates to the MS Mail DirSync server post office.

Exchange as the DirSync Server

The DirSync server processes the incoming update messages from all MS Mail DirSync requestor post offices. It incorporates the updates in the directory as custom recipient objects. An update is also sent for the Exchange Server recipients. This is in response to an update request generated from the MS Mail requestor postoffice. There can only be one DirSync server in a site.

NOTE The knowledge consistency checker will create a directory entry only if a folder exists in the public information store. However, never will it create an entry in the public information store if an entry exists in the directory. ■

Understanding the X.500 Directory Service

Exchange server directory architecture is based on the 1988 X.500 directory service recommendations. The X.500 directory structure outlines a logical directory object organization scheme, each object's attributes, and how they relate to one another. X.500 is a widely accepted standard, and with its application Exchange can participate in directory data sharing with many different systems.

Exchange defines additional object classes and attributes beyond X.500 standards in order to provide users more descriptive directory entries. For example, Exchange directories can support the following attributes, which X.500 does not:

- Individual titles, e.g., president, MIS director
- Additional phone numbers
- Custom attributes defined by the administrator
- Organization charting information
- Alternate recipients

Expanded Address Book Features

Exchange 5.0 introduced us to Address Book Views. An Address Book View is a customized grouping of Address Book recipients (mailboxes, custom recipients, distribution lists, and public folders) with common attributes. These customized views allow for easier and quicker access to directory information for large or specific groups of users.

With Exchange 5.5, you can still group recipients with certain matching criteria together to create an Address Book View. These groupings now appear in a sub-container under the Address Book View in the Exchange Administrator program. These views will now be displayed in the Show Names from: box in the Outlook Address Book. Whenever an Address Book View is created, you may add up to four sub-container levels. By default, these sub-containers will be grouped according to the specifications of the parent Address Book View. The grouping of the sub-containers may be changed as needed.

Permissions can be set specifying the rights that users or groups have on the Address Book Views. Assigning NT roles is how you delegate permissions to users or groups. These roles are sets of rights that define how much and what type of access a user or group has. These roles can be comprised of the default settings or they can be customized.

Use the Permissions property page to specify user and group roles, access to what users can view, and Lightweight Directory Access Protocol (LDAP) access permissions. The LDAP protocol, which only works with TCP/IP connections, enables LDAP clients to perform searches when they are connected to a directory.

The Messaging Application Programming Interface (MAPI) is the standard interface that Microsoft Exchange server and client components use to communicate with each other. Essentially, it functions as the messaging infrastructure for Microsoft Exchange. MAPI also provides an asynchronous store-and-forward messaging environment that can support a range of applications, including group scheduling and electronic mail (email).

Multiple Offline Address Books can be configured so remote users can obtain information about other users in the organization. While remotely connecting to an Exchange server, users can download offline Address Books that contain lists of recipients specified by you. They also have the option to download only the changes that occurred since the last download.

NOTE If multiple offline Address Books are required, you must set the offline Address Book server to a server running Exchange Server 5.0 or later. The offline Address Book server is the computer where the offline Address Book files are generated and stored. ■

The offline Address Books are configured from the Exchange Administrator program. While a user remotely downloads an offline Address Book to their local computer, connections are made to a hidden offline Address Book public folder from which the files are copied. The offline Address Book location can be changed so that the offline Address Book is generated and stored on a server other than the one originally specified. ●

CHAPTER 3

Exchange's Integrated Server Components

In this chapter

Exchange server comprises four fundamental system services that run under Windows NT server. Together, these services handle all basic client/server interaction, user lookups, message transmission, and storage of information in public and private folders. With these four core components, an Exchange server can function as a stand-alone unit. All other components are optional and are designed specifically to facilitate information transfer to other Exchange servers and other external information systems.

Exchange's Four Core Components

This chapter is designed to provide an overview of the Exchange server's four core components and describe how they communicate with each other and with other optional components. The following are the core integrated server components (see Figure 3.1):

- System Attendant
- Message Transfer Agent
- Information Store (public and private)
- Directory Service

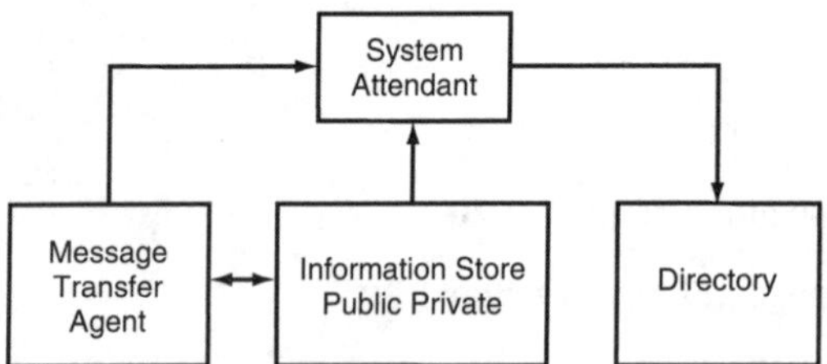

FIG. 3.1
The Integrated Exchange Server performs all the functions needed in the Exchange environment.

Introduction to System Attendant

This service performs general maintenance tasks. It functions much like the central nervous system for an Exchange server. Its operation is required in order for Exchange processes to run. The System Attendant tasks are as follows:

- Monitor status of messaging connection between servers. This includes assisting in monitoring the state of links between servers in one site, two different sites, and between different systems.
- Gather information on each server in a site (such as what services are running) to assist in running messaging monitoring tools.
- Build routing tables in a site.
- Verify directory replication information and correct inconsistencies.
- Maintain information logs about sent messages for tracking purposes.
- Generate email addresses for new message recipients you create. Default addresses created by the System Attendant are MS-Mail, X.400, and SMTP. Additionally, if you have any third-party gateways installed, the System Attendant will create appropriate addresses for those systems.

The principal reason for communication between the System Attendant and other Exchange components involves logging messaging activity. Message logs are kept for all messages arriving and departing from the Exchange server. The following are the components that make up the communication between Exchange services:

Agent	Function
Message Transfer Agent	The Message Transfer Agent notifies the System Attendant that it received or sent a message for delivery to other systems or sites.
Information Store	The Information Store communicates its messaging activity for logging by the System Attendant. This includes notice that it has received or sent a message for local delivery, i.e., on the same server.

Introduction to Message Transfer Agent

The Message Transfer Agent (MTA) comprises the foundation of Exchange server's communication infrastructure. The MTA handles message transport to other servers, other sites, or foreign systems. In addition to being the transport vehicle for messaging information, it also maps and routs addresses, and performs some message format conversion to other system's standards. (Other connectors and "gateways" installed on an Exchange server might also handle message format conversions, such as a PROFS connector.)

Being the principal message transport mechanism, the MTA communicates with all other Exchange components, as shown in the following mini-table:

Component	Communication
Directory Service	The MTA uses the directory service to look up a user address. The directory instructs the MTA to submit mail from other sites' directories (to perform directory synchronization).
System Attendant	The MTA tells the System Attendant (SA) to log each instance of a message transfer.
Administrator Program	From the Administrator Program, the MTA receives requests to manipulate messages in the queue.
Information Store	The Information Store (IS) submits messages for delivery to other systems and is notified to receive new mail by the MTA.
Microsoft Mail connector	The MTA is notified of new mail to handle.
Directory Synchronization	The MTA is directed to send directory-related component messages from foreign systems.

Introduction to the Information Store

The Information Store (IS) is the end of the line for all messaging data successfully transmitted to an Exchange server. This includes both private messages sent to individual users and public information folders intended for viewing by many users. The IS maintains data in two distinct databases—the Private Information Store and the Public Information Store.

In addition to message storage, the IS handles local delivery of messages (when both sender and recipient are on the same server), replicates public folders, and enforces storage limits. The following is a list of the principal functions of the IS. The MTAs communicate with the following Exchange components:

Component	Communication
Message Transfer Agent	The IS contacts the MTA to accept new incoming mail, to deliver new outgoing mail, and to resolve addresses intended for gateways.
Exchange Clients	To the client the IS announces the arrival of new mail. Also the IS accepts new mail submitted for delivery from the client.
Directory Service	The IS uses the directory service to look up addresses, get user mailbox information, and create directory entries for public folders.
System Attendant	When the IS either receives or sends a message, it notifies the System Attendant so a log entry is generated.
Administrator Program	The Administrator Program sends instructions to the IS to show statistics about connected users and other storage usage information, e.g., folder sizes. The Administrator Program connects to the IS to view information, logons, and resources.
Connectors/Gateways	IS communication to connectors/gateways involves the retrieval and delivery of messages to foreign systems.

Introduction to Directory Service

The Directory Service (DS) maintains all the information about users and resources in an organization. This includes a structured view of all server names, mailboxes, and distribution lists in a site. Also, the directory service keeps configuration information used by other Exchange server components when mapping addresses and routing messages.

In order to maintain consistency of addressing information across several Exchange servers, directory data is automatically replicated among all servers in a site. This replication within a site is carried out by the MTA and administered by the Directory Service. The Directory Service also manages directory replication between sites on a scheduled basis (see Chapter 7, "Planning Connections to Microsoft Mail Systems," on directory synchronization/replication.)

The directory service classifies organization information (servers, mailboxes, and so on) as objects. Being objects, through the administrator program, one can specify their characteristics as well as determine who can use or change them (see Chapter 21, "Configuring X.400 Connections," on Exchange component administration). The following is a list of components of the Directory Service and how they communicate with these Exchange services:

Component	**Communication**
Other Directories	Directories communicate with other Directory Services within the same site to replicate directory information.
Message Transfer Agent	The directory service notifies the MTA in order to send mail to and receive mail from other directories (during directory replication). The MTA looks up addresses and configuration information from the Directory Service.
Administrator Program	The administrator program commands the directory to display and modify the address book, list of recipients, user properties, and directory objects (servers, monitors, connectors, and so on). Also, the administrator program can create objects in the directory.
Exchange Clients	Client programs call upon the directory to find a specific user's address and to display the address book, resolve an e-mail name to a full alias, and modify distribution list memberships.
Information Store	The IS uses the directory to look up address and configuration information, get information about mailboxes, and create directory entries for public folders.
System Attendant	The SA uses the directory to look up address and configuration information, build routing tables, generate e-mail addresses for new recipients, and verify consistency of directory information.
Directory Synchronization	The directory synchronization component generates component requests to create, modify, and delete custom recipients. Also, it asks to look up recipients and configuration information.
Microsoft Mail Connector	The Microsoft Mail Connector looks up addresses from Microsoft Mail for PC networks and configuration information in the directory.
Connectors/Gateways	A connector/gateway uses the directory to replicate directory information and look up address and configuration information.

Understanding the Administrator Program

The Administrator Program is the primary tool for administering Exchange. Though it is not an integrated server component, it does comprise an essential part of the Exchange architecture. Further chapters will describe the multitude of functions provided by the administrator program, but this will present the basic description of its communication with a few integrated server components. The following is a list of programs controlled by the Exchange Administrator program along with their associated functions:

Program	Function
Directory	Through the administrator program, one can display the address book, the main viewer, lists of recipients, properties of a user, and directory objects. Also, the administrator program enables you to create objects in the directory.
Message Transfer Agent	The administrator program enables you to manipulate messages in the various queues of the MTA.
Information Store	The administrator program enables you to create and delete mailboxes, as well as show statistics about information storage usage such as number of users logged on. It also provides information on the private and public information stores (connections, logons, resources) and determines schedules for public folder replication.

Integrating Connectors in the Exchange Server

One of the big improvements Microsoft has made with Exchange is the integration of connectors into the server. For the most part, this feature eliminates the need for external boxes to establish connections to other mail systems. (Some exceptions might be fax or voice mail servers that may still require a dedicated machine.)

Connectors allow Exchange to swap information with various messaging systems. They provide tight integration with all the tools and utilities Exchange administrators will be using in the running of the server, such as the Performance Monitor, Link Monitor, and the Administrator Program.

This section will cover:

- What connectors and gateways are
- How connectors and gateways fit into the Exchange framework
- How gateways and connectors can be used to link sites
- What connectors and gateways are available

Using Exchange connectors is an easy transition for anyone who has configured mail gateways for other mail systems. For example, the Simple Mail Transfer Protocol (SMTP) gateway for cc:Mail has many of the same configuration parameters as the Internet Mail Service.

NOTE In Exchange 4.0, the SMTP connector was called the Internet Mail Connector (IMC). This has been renamed in Exchange 5.5 to the Internet Mail Service to reflect the enhanced features that have been added. ■

These include whether to act as inbound or outbound gateways or both; which act as the administrator, where bounced and non-deliverable messages are delivered; and whether attachments are handled via Multimedia Internet Mail Extensions (MIME) compliance or UUENCODE. Being familiar with these terms as well as with Windows NT and WIN95 properties boxes facilitates configuration. By filling out property pages in the Administrator Program, as shown in Figure 3.2, you can be up and running without a lot of hassle.

FIG. 3.2
The properties page for the Internet Mail Service gives the administrator many configuration options.

In addition, connectors can be used to link multiple mail system. For example, the Internet Mail Service can be used effectively in organizations where some departments choose to use Exchange, while others choose different platforms. Many of these organizations standardize on SMTP to transfer messages between departments because most LAN-based email packages have some form of SMTP gateway since SMTP is a non-proprietary Internet standard. These kinds of uses will be explained in more detail later in this chapter.

The following connectors will be explained in this chapter:

- Microsoft Mail
- X.400
- Internet
- cc:Mail

Understanding the Microsoft Mail Connector

Connecting existing Microsoft Mail systems with Exchange is very common in a large enterprise during a migration and coexistence phase. With an installed user base of at least four million users, it makes sense that Exchange server would strongly support compatibility with Microsoft Mail.

Primarily, this compatibility comes in the form of the Microsoft Mail Connector. This component bridges the gap between standard Microsoft Mail post offices and Exchange server. Essentially, Exchange emulates the functionality of a Microsoft Mail post office so other Microsoft Mail computers see it as just another member of the chain.

Microsoft Mail is a shared-file, LAN-based messaging system. Messages are sent to file servers hosting one or more post offices to which a user connects to retrieve messages. In order to integrate with this system, Exchange's Microsoft Mail Connector presents a post office of its own to which any other post office can connect. This enables other Microsoft Mail post offices to continue normal operation—that is, of course, until they are migrated to Exchange as well.

The Microsoft Mail Connector (PC) consists of the following components:

- Microsoft Mail Connector Interchange— a system service that handles routing and message transfer between Exchange and the Microsoft Mail connector post office.
- Microsoft Mail Connector post office (also called a shadow post office)— a temporary information store for messages in transit to and from a Microsoft Mail system. It is often called a shadow post office because despite being structured very similarly to a standard Microsoft Mail post office, it contains no local mailboxes and does not support direct installation of older Microsoft Mail gateways.
- Microsoft Mail Connector (PC) Message Transfer Agent—a system service that handles message transport between the connector post office and the Microsoft Mail post offices.

  Similarly, the Microsoft Mail connector can also establish communication with Microsoft Mail for AppleTalk systems (see Figure 3.3). For connection to Microsoft Mail for AppleTalk Networks, the Exchange Microsoft Mail connector also includes two additional components:

- Microsoft Mail Connector (AppleTalk) Message Transfer Agent—a system service that operates with the Exchange Connection gateway to handle message transfer and translation between the Microsoft Mail Connector post office and Microsoft Mail (AppleTalk) systems (see Figure 3.4).

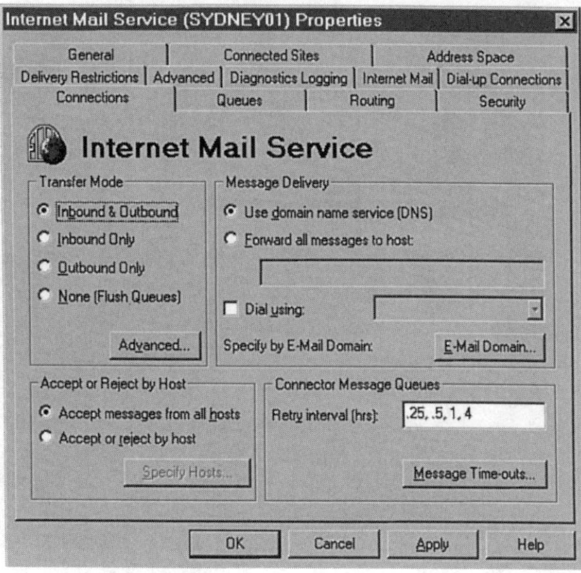

FIG. 3.3
The Microsoft Mail Connector Architecture.

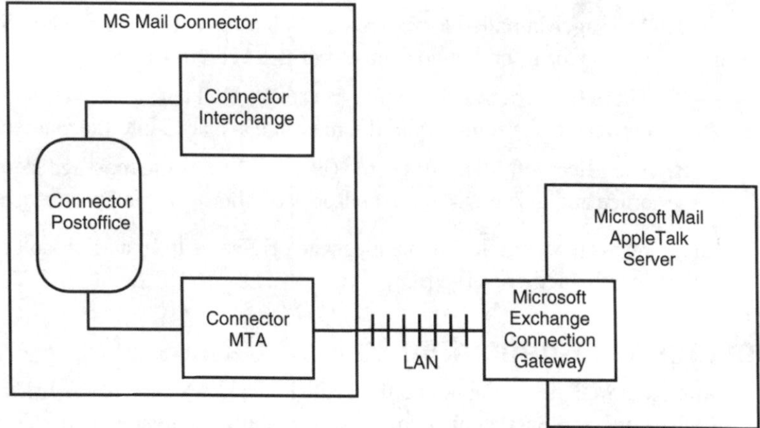

FIG. 3.4
The Microsoft Mail Connector (AppleTalk) Architecture.

- Microsoft Exchange Connection—a gateway component installed separately on a Macintosh Microsoft Mail server. It enables that server to communicate with the Microsoft Mail Connector in Exchange.

LAN Connection to Post Offices

In this scenario, an Exchange server with the Microsoft Mail Connector installed is connected to a Microsoft Mail post office (see Figure 3.5).

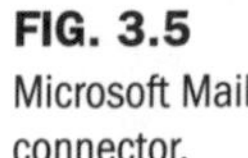

FIG. 3.5
Microsoft Mail connector.

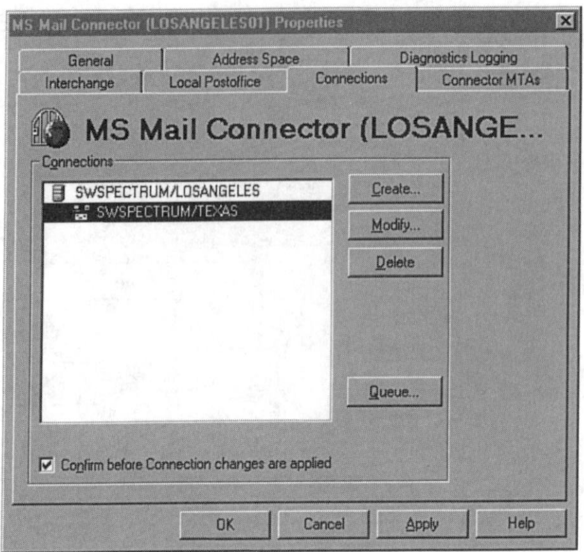

The following is a typical example of message transfer between both systems:

1. Messages intended for Microsoft Mail recipients are picked up by the Microsoft Mail Connector Interchange from either the MTA or the IS.
2. There they are translated into Microsoft Mail format; any OLE or other attachments are converted as required and the message is placed into the connector post office.
3. The Microsoft Mail Connector (PC) MTA pulls the message from the connector post office and delivers it to the appropriate Microsoft Mail post office.

In the opposite situation, when a message originates from a Microsoft Mail user, the previous sequence is exactly reversed.

Asynchronous Connection to Post Offices

Microsoft Mail networks not on the same logical LAN can also be bridged with the Microsoft Mail Connector. Such connections are commonly established by modem or wide area X.25 links. Exchange's Microsoft Mail Connector (PC) MTA can be configured to support asynchronous or X.25 connections (see Figure 3.6). However, a normal Microsoft Mail post office cannot alone handle this connection. There must be a Microsoft Mail 3.x External or Multitasking MTA program set up to provide the modem management and message transfer functions over a remote link.

Multiple MS-Mail Connector MTAs

A single Exchange server can run multiple instances of the Microsoft Mail connector MTAs (see Figure 3.7). Each MTA runs as a Windows NT system service that can be stopped and started independently of any other service. The best way to architect such connections is to create one instance of the MTA for each type of network connection. Therefore, one MTA is dedicated to an X.25 link, while another can service a modem link, and still another can connect to a local LAN.

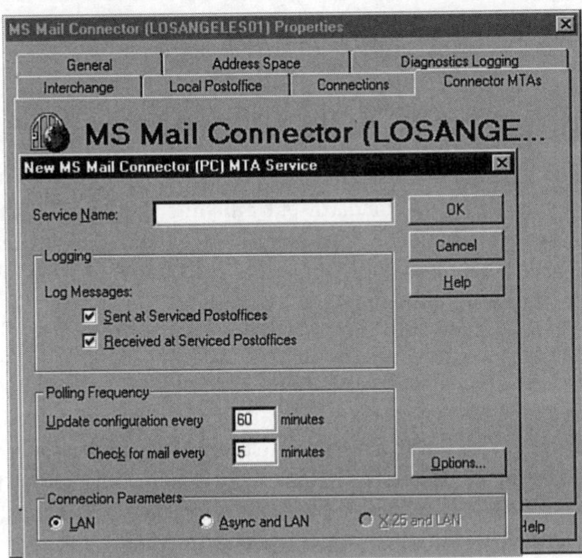

FIG. 3.6 Microsoft Mail Connector MTA.

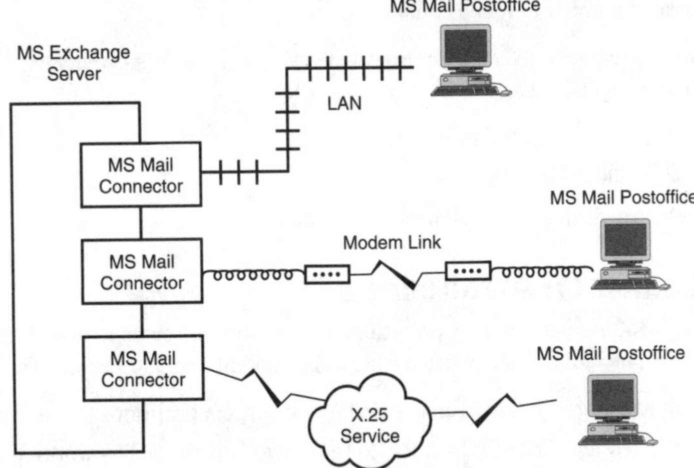

FIG. 3.7 Exchange server with multiple Microsoft Mail connectors.

If your organization uses a large number of Microsoft Mail 3.x post offices, or they are spread over a wide area, then you would perhaps want to set up multiple Microsoft Mail connectors within your organization and use Exchange as a "backbone" for these scattered post offices to ease administration and improve reliability of message transfer. It is not possible to "backbone" Exchange traffic over an Microsoft Mail network of post offices due to serial number restrictions in Exchange.

NOTE It is important to realize that all Microsoft Mail connectors in a site will use the same email address. From the Microsoft Mail perspective, each site will be seen as one large post office. As a result, it is not recommended that several Exchange servers in the same site pickup and deliver mail to a single Microsoft Mail post office in order to prevent file contention on the Microsoft Mail side. ■

Understanding the X.400 Standard

Exchange's use of the X.400 standard enables a broad interoperability with a wide range of messaging systems. X.400 is a standard set by the International Telephone Union (ITU), formerly known as the International Telegraph and Telephone Consultative Committee (CCITT). To date, there have been three iterations of the X.400 standard (1984, 1988, 1992). The initial release version of Exchange supports the 1984 and 1988 standards, with the 1992 version to be supported in later versions.

The X.400 standard defines the basic framework of a message handling system, the structure of the message and its components, and how messages are transferred. It is widely supported and used by most public email carriers and telecommunication providers. Because of its widespread acceptance, many companies have already developed gateways to bridge their messaging systems with X.400. In real-world situations, where network, hardware, and communication standards are not strictly enforced, X.400 provides a common ground for interoperability between messaging systems. Microsoft has assured Exchange's strict conformance to government X.400 standards, which means that Exchange will be a reliable solution for the widest possible number of X.400 connections.

The Exchange X.400 connector provides all essential connectivity with this standard. In this section, you will see:

- X.400 connector architecture
- X.400 Addressing
- Practical uses of X.400 with Exchange

X.400 Connector Architecture

The X.400 standard makes provisions for specific components of a Message Handling System (MHS), including a structure for message content and addressing. These components are:

- Message Transfer Agents (MTA)—transport programs that execute message delivery
- Message Transfer System (MTS) —two or more MTAs working to transfer messages (sometimes called a *Reliable Transfer System* or RTS)
- Message Stores (MS)—an intermediate message storage area between an MTA and a user agent
- User Agents (UA)—a client program designed to send and retrieve messages from an MTA and an MS
- Access Units—gateways to other messaging systems

Microsoft fulfills each element specified by the X.400 standard. In fact, the whole Message Transfer System design is the basis for Exchange's Server site and organization structure.

When referring to a Exchange X.400 connector, one is really describing the use of an Exchange MTA configured to connect to an X.400-based system. Exchange MTAs are compliant with other MTAs (in another Exchange server or an external system) that comply with the 1984 or 1988 X.400 standards. The Exchange MTA can be extensively configured to negotiate such connection over the standard X.400 network transports TP0, TP4, and TCP/IP.

The Message Store requirement is met by Exchange's public and private information stores.

The User Agents are realized as Exchange Client programs currently available on several common platforms.

The Access Units are the many gateways currently available for use with Exchange (PROFS, SNADS, Fax, pager, and so on). Each provides a route into its particular system.

X.400 Addressing in Exchange

Much like an Exchange address is identified by the user at site structure, X.400 addresses are distinguished by unique personal information and information about the system on which they receive messages. A typical X.400 address contains:

> c=US; admd=MCI; prmd=Software Spectrum; o=Garland; ou1=Consulting; s=Bradley; g=Tracy;

Each element is described in Table 3.1.

Table 3.1 X.400 Addressing Elements

Element	Description
c=US	country
admd=MCI	Administrative Management Domain. Usually the name of your X.400 service carrier.
prmd=	Primary Management Domain. Usually equates to the name of your company or your Exchange enterprise.
o=	Organization. A sub-component of the X.400 prmd that to Exchange is the name of a site.
ou1=	Organizational Unit. The X.400 attribute which helps further identify the remote site. This component is by default not utilized in auto-generated Exchange naming conventions, but could be added.
s=	Surname. Usually a user's last name.
g=	Given name. Generally a user's first name.

NOTE To appropriately route messages in a site or between sites, Exchange uses what is called the X.400 global domain identifier (GDI) of the local site. In order for messages to be routed correctly, the GDI used for an Exchange Server cannot be identical to the GDI of a connected foreign system. This will become an issue only when using Exchange to connect to foreign X.400 systems. ■

Adding Foreign X.400 Addresses into Exchange

As a system administrator, you can use Exchange's bulk import utility to merge a series of foreign addresses into Exchange's global address list. Additionally, the Exchange client's Personal or Outlook Address Book enables individual users to create user entries based on X.400 addresses via an X.400 template.

X.400 addresses for recipients on an Exchange server are automatically created when a new mailbox is created.

Application and Examples of the X.400 Connector

Connecting an Exchange Server site to a foreign X.400 system will be one of the primary uses of the X.400 connector. However, there are a number of connection possibilities afforded by the implementation of this versatile tool. Connections over X.400 between Exchange sites can be established to share directory information, replicate public folders, transmit standard messages, or all of the above. Figure 3.8 gives an example of possible usage.

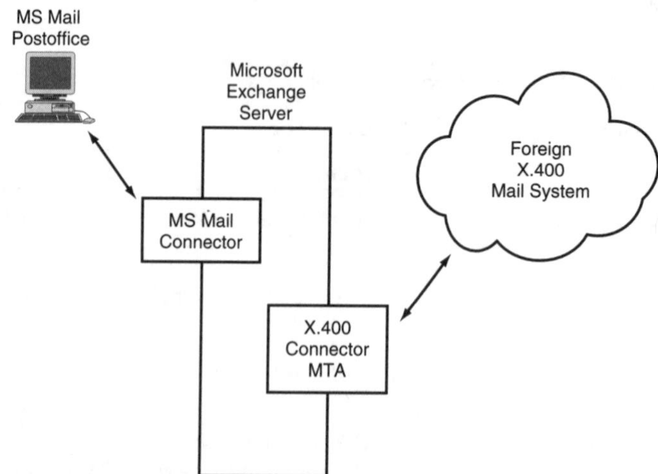

FIG. 3.8 You can connect an existing Microsoft Mail server to a foreign X.400 system (through an Exchange server).

The Exchange X.400 connector, in conjunction with the Microsoft Mail Connector, can enable users on Microsoft Mail to access X.400 systems (see Figure 3.9).

A common use of the X.400 connector in Exchange is bridging messaging systems that are geographically dispersed. In this example, an Exchange server is set up to transfer messaging data with a Microsoft Mail system using an Exchange X.400 connector on one end and a currently available Microsoft Mail X.400 gateway on the other (see Figure 3.10).

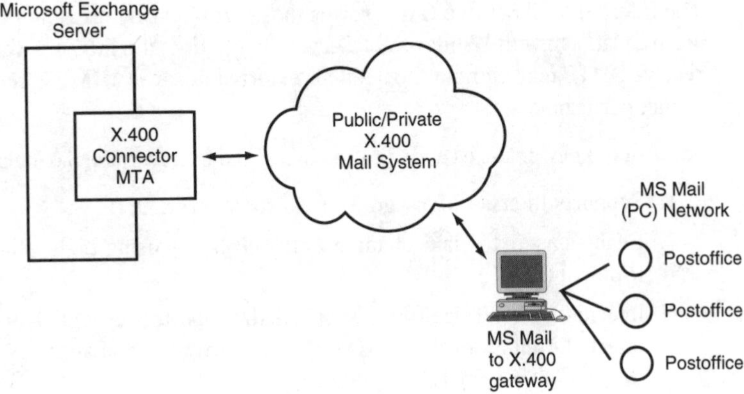

FIG. 3.9 You can connect an Exchange Server site to a Microsoft Mail post office.

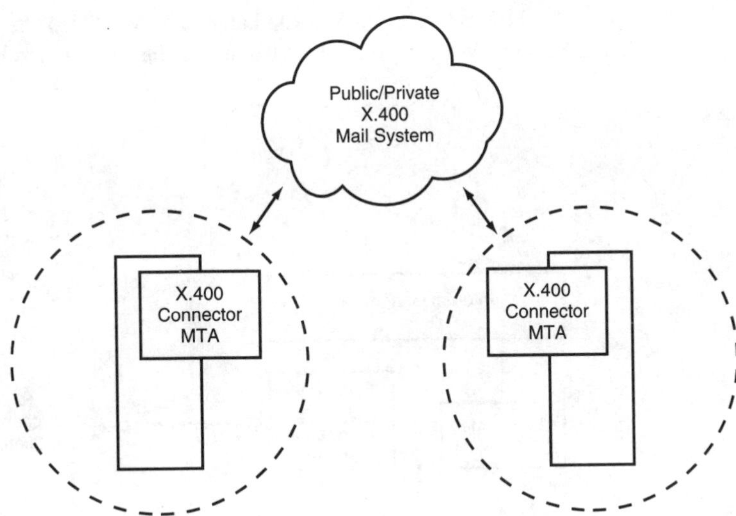

FIG. 3.10 You can connect two Exchange Server sites.

Two Exchange Server sites can be linked via a public (or private) X.400 mail system. All that is required is one properly configured message transfer agent at either end. The same technique is applicable over a TCP/IP network, either intranet or Internet and might be desirable given possible bandwidth issues that prevent the use of the Exchange Site Connector.

Understanding the Internet Mail Service

As its name implies, the Internet Mail Service (which replaced the Internet Mail Connector (IMC) in Exchange 4.0) provides integrated, native SMTP connectivity to the Exchange server along with other new features. In doing this, Microsoft has eliminated the need for the DOS-based SMTP gateway for Microsoft Mail 3.x that lacked robustness, had memory allocation problems, possessed little or no security, and needed an external HOST to send out SMTP mail.

The Internet Mail Service (IMS) solves those problems by providing a stable, proven, and secure platform with Windows NT Server. In addition, the Internet Mail Service can send and receive SMTP mail without the need for external hosts, is MIME-compliant, and provides robust performance.

Some of the new features added to Exchange 5.5 from version 5.0 include:

- Supports Internet Message Access Protocol (IMAP4)
- Enables users to make changes to the directory using Lightweight Directory Access Protocol (LDAP)
- Internet Mail Service (IMS) supports these protocols: ETRN, Secure Multipurpose Internet Mail Extensions (S/MIME), Secure Sockets Layer (SSL), and Simple Authentication and Security Layer (SASL)
- Several options of enhanced security
- Support for MIME Hypertext Markup Language (MHTML)The following diagram (see Figure 3.11) shows how the Internet Connector fits into the Exchange architecture

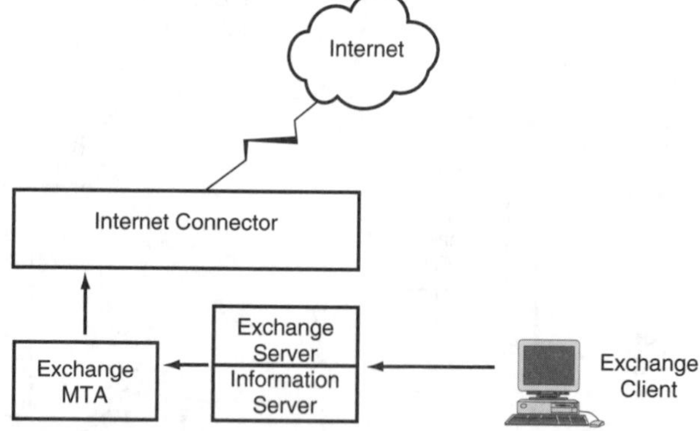

FIG. 3.11 Internet Connector Architecture.

In addition to providing Internet mail functions, the Internet Mail Service enables those users running TCP/IP over the backbone to connect Exchange sites to each other using the connector. As mentioned previously, decentralized organizations often give control of the mail system to the respective department. Many large universities and corporations operate this way. These organizations often choose SMTP as the way for disparate mail systems to communicate because it is an Internet standard. Microsoft has recognized that many companies route only TCP/IP over their WANs to maximize router throughput. A diagram showing how to link disparate Exchange sites by using the Internet Mail Service is shown in Figure 3.12.

The Internet Mail Service provides for full integration into environments where security is a big concern. Many companies configure firewalls to protect internal data from hackers on the Internet. In addition to all the security components inherent to Exchange and Windows NT Server, the Internet Mail Service provides the ability to refuse messages from any specified hosts. This provides protection from several forms of hacking or "denial of service" attacks because many hackers use the email system to carry out their work. For example, you might configure the connector to refuse mail from all hosts other than a certain mail relay. That means that a hacker could not send messages or commands directly to your Exchange server. By refusing mail from certain hosts, Exchange is flexible enough to fit into existing company security policies. Any hacker would have to compromise the firewall in order to send a message directly to the Internet Mail Service.

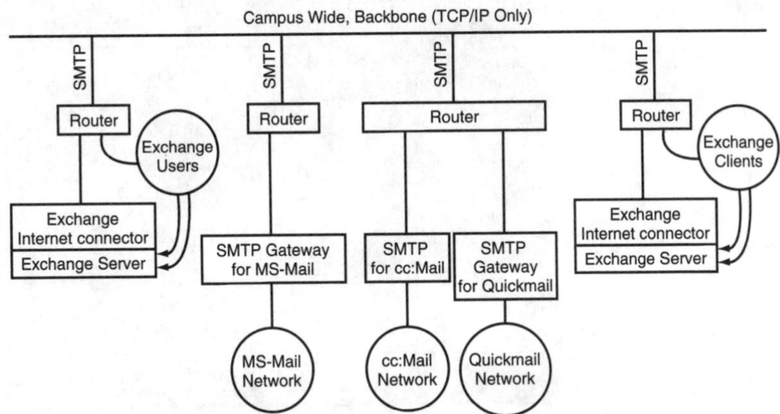

FIG. 3.12 Connecting Multiple Exchange Sites Over TCP/IP.

Exchange can also be configured to enable only incoming or outgoing traffic through the connector. This is an important feature because one Windows NT server can only do so many things and complete so many tasks without taking a performance hit. Configuring the connector to only send out mail might be a good idea for a machine that is already overloaded. This configuration should not be a cause for concern as long as there is an incoming Internet Mail Service elsewhere in the Exchange site or organization. For example, if you have the Internet Mail Service configured on two servers and configure one to receive-only and the other to send-only, the Exchange users' email addresses will still be the same. Users will not know where the mail came in. The connections are completely transparent. Figure 3.13 shows the properties screen where the administrator can configure security and transfer options.

Additional information about the functions and configuration of the Internet Mail Service can be found in Chapter 22, "Configuring the IMS."

Connecting to Lotus cc:Mail

The Exchange Connector for Lotus cc:Mail provides seamless communication between Exchange Server and Lotus' cc:Mail product. In the past year , Lotus has embraced the MAPI standard for messaging-enabled applications, switching from their previous Vendor Independent Messaging (VIM) standard. The cc:Mail Connector enables connectivity between Exchange and these cc:Mail post offices running Lotus cc:Mail Post Office Database Version 6 and cc:Mail Import version 5.15 and Export version 5.14 or Lotus cc:Mail Post Office Database version 8 and cc:Mail Import/Export Version 6.0. The cc:Mail Connector has many configuration variables enabling the use of the existing cc:Mail tools, such as Import, Export, and ADE to enable robust, hassle-free connections to cc:Mail VIM post offices.

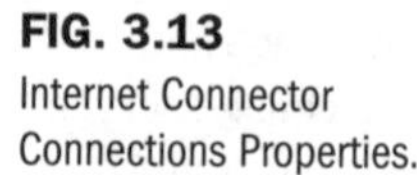

FIG. 3.13
Internet Connector Connections Properties.

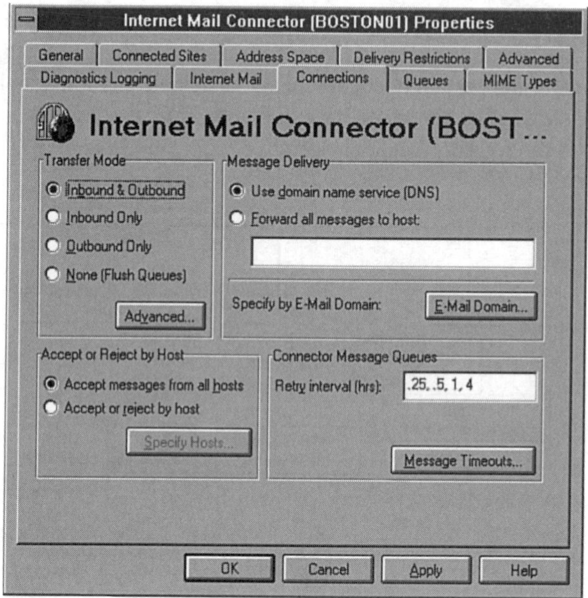

cc:Mail users are to be directly imported into the Microsoft Exchange Global Address Book and will appear just like any other Custom Recipient Exchange user.

Just as with the Microsoft Mail Connector, a cc:Mail post office is created on the Exchange server, resulting in Exchange server users appearing in the cc:Mail directory like all other cc:Mail users. This gives transparency to the cc:Mail user. As far as he or she is concerned, all users in the Global Address Book are local.

Exchange enables the administrator to set the paths to the standard Import and Export utilities that come with cc:Mail. These utilities are used to import and export directory and message data from the Exchange server to all other cc:Mail post offices in the cc:Mail network. Examples of the uses of this connector are shown in Figure 3.14.

On the cc:Mail side, Exchange looks just like any other post office; by using Automatic Directory Exchange (ADE), all cc:Mail post offices, including the Exchange cc:Mail post office, can be kept up to date as users are added on both sides. The following Figure 3.15 illustrates some of the components involved.

Microsoft realized that cc:Mail is a large player in the LAN-based messaging market. By making the cc:Mail Connector available, it has leveraged this popularity. In some organizations, many dollars have been spent on training personnel to install and maintain cc:Mail, as well as hardware resources. Using Exchange means that your organization will not have to throw away existing mail systems to roll out a new one.

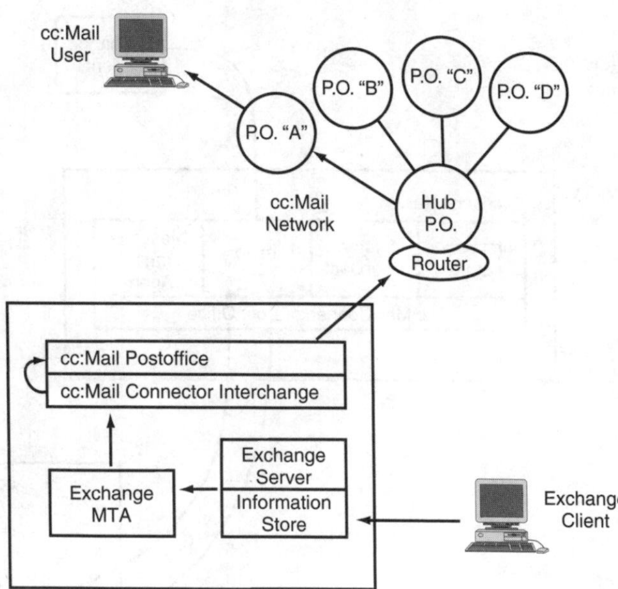

FIG. 3.14
Architecture of the cc:Mail Connector.

Understanding Gateways

Gateways provide a way for Exchange to integrate disparate information services into Microsoft's Universal Inbox, using the single Exchange Viewer to organize all types of information. These include voice mail, fax, paging, as well as email from other vendors' systems.

Despite the variety of information services that snap into Exchange, the end user sees no difference. To them, the addressee is the addressee. A user can address a message and send it, and the addressee might get a page, fax, voice mail, or Internet message. The addressee may be using cc:Mail, PROFS, SNADS, or Microsoft Mail, and the user sending the message would never know because all they need to know is the addressee's name in the Global Address Book.

Using Microsoft Mail Gateways

In addition to native Exchange gateways, Exchange can use standard Microsoft Mail 3.x gateways by using the Microsoft Mail Connector described earlier in this chapter. Each gateway uses the Microsoft Mail Connector to exchange data with foreign mail systems. This may be useful for sites with large Microsoft Mail installations that are slowly migrating to Exchange, but want to provide the core messaging functions first and add connectors and gateways later. In addition, some organizations are hesitant to sway from things that work. For example, if the Microsoft Mail gateway to PROFS has been working fine, some may be hesitant to roll out an Exchange PROFS connector or gateway because they haven't had the opportunity to test it and get their staff familiar with it. Figure 3.16 shows how Microsoft Mail gateways fit into the Exchange topology.

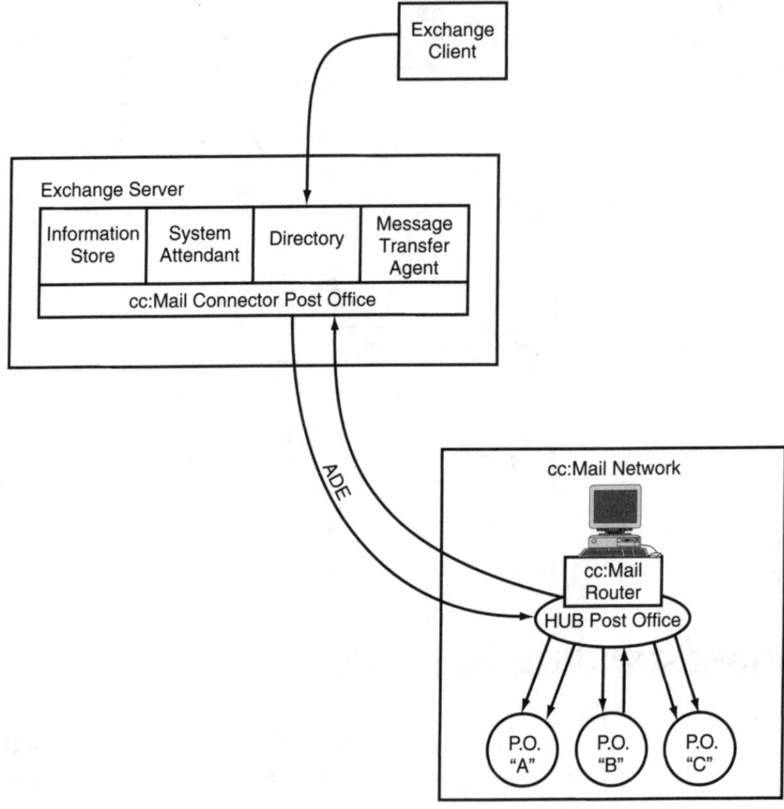

FIG. 3.15
ADE Synchronization between the cc:Mail and Exchange.

In the preceding case, the PROFS gateway for Microsoft Mail simply talks to the Microsoft Mail Connector post office. When configuring the PROFS gateway for Microsoft Mail, you simply point it at the Microsoft Mail Connector post office and the exchange of information becomes transparent.

With Exchange, Microsoft took those concerns into consideration and provided the flexibility to use legacy systems in the migration to a robust Exchange environment.

Connector for Lotus Notes

This is a new connector to Exchange 5.5. The Exchange Connector for Lotus Notes allows for the delivery of messages between Exchange and Lotus Notes to be transparent.

The Connector for Lotus Notes provides:

- The capacity for sharing rich text messages between Exchange and Lotus Notes users with very little loss of fidelity
- Support for Object Linking and Embedding (OLE)

- Support for Lotus Notes Document Links
- Support for the passing of file objects between the two systems with the attributes and the launch capability preserved
- Directory Synchronization between the two systems
- The ability to monitor and log the connector activity
- The Note Configuration Utility, this utility will automatically set permissions, create the database files required by the connector, and update several Lotus Notes settings

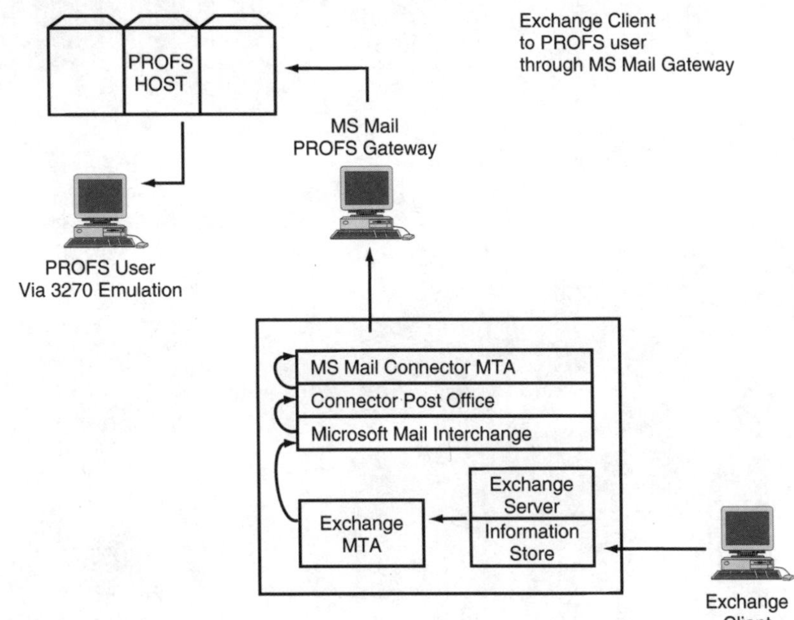

FIG. 3.16
Message flow of Exchange to PROFS using PROFS Gateway for Microsoft Mail.

The Exchange Connector for Lotus Notes is used for message transfer and directory synchronization between Exchange and Lotus Notes. Multiple instances of the connector can be used, dependent upon your organizations messaging needs. Each Exchange server in your environment can run only one instance of the connector that directly services one connection to a Lotus Notes/Domino server. Also, a connection can only be configured to service one Lotus Notes/Domino server.

The Connector for Lotus Notes and the Lotus Notes Client are installed on the Exchange Server. On the Lotus Notes Server, a user needs to be created. This will create the connector ID file, which is used by the connector. These users need to be granted appropriate permissions to the Lotus Notes Public Address Book and Exchange.box. An example of this connector is shown in Figure 3.17.

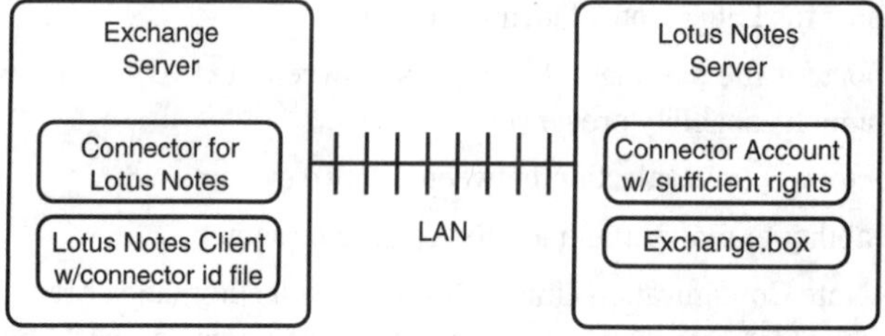

FIG. 3.17
Exchange Connector for Lotus Notes Architecture.

CHAPTER 4

Integrating with Microsoft Windows NT Server

In this chapter

Exchange Server is part of the BackOffice suite of server products that runs on top of the Windows NT operating system. Windows NT is a powerful 32-bit multithreaded, multitasking operating system. The Exchange Server can leverage this functionality by utilizing as many threads or application processes as needed to provide a robust messaging infrastructure.

You should now have an understanding of the core components and framework for the Exchange server and client. This chapter helps you understand the way Exchange integrates with the operating system. We will also discuss how Exchange can leverage the Windows NT platform to provide a robust and fault-tolerant messaging solution.

Core Functionality of Windows NT

Windows NT is a 32-bit operating system. It provides multitasking and multithreading capabilities. This means that the operating system can simultaneously process multiple requests or instances of an application.

Windows NT is more that just an operating system. It is a framework to develop fault-tolerant client server applications. To enhance the operating system, Windows NT provides a full set of Application Programming Interfaces (APIs) and Software Development Kits (SDKs). The operating system is more than a file and print server: It is an application server. Through the use of the APIs and SDKs, many applications can harness the power of the operating system.

The operating system runs on a variety of platforms, including Intel and the Alpha platform. Although Exchange 5.0 also supported Power PC and MIPS platform, Microsoft offers only limited support. This portable operating system has several key benefits. The following sections cover the benefits in detail.

Supporting Multiple Protocols

Windows NT provides native support for the following protocols: TCP/IP, IPX, NetBEUI, AppleTalk, DLC, SNA, X.25, and X.400(TP/x). This enables the operating system to support a wide array of clients. Windows NT can communicate with UNIX, Banyan Vines, DEC Pathworks, NetWare, Apple Macintosh, and of course all of the Microsoft networking clients, including MS-DOS, Windows For Workgroups, Windows 95, and Windows NT Workstation.

This feature enables Windows NT to interoperate in a heterogeneous environment. You will not be "bound" by implementing the Windows NT operating system into one of these environments. Windows NT can offer additional functionality in these situations. The alternative is providing native support that would be very costly or impossible.

For example, Windows NT can be easily added to a Novell NetWare environment to provide Remote Networking or Dial-in access. The Windows NT operating system ships with a complete remote access server component integrated with the OS. With NetWare you would have to purchase an additional product known as NetWare Connect to obtain this capability.

With Exchange, NetWare clients can easily access an Exchange server running on Windows NT with native IPX client software installed. Clients communicate with industry standards known as Remote Procedure Calls (RPC) by using the Exchange server. Windows NT supports every major communication protocol. Therefore, a client can connect to Exchange by using RPCs over TCP/IP or IPX in a NetWare environment.

In addition, Microsoft has released a standard for Remote Procedure Calls (RPCs) over AppleTalk, the Macintosh's native communications protocol. In order for a Macintosh workstation to connect to a Windows NT Exchange server, it can make RPCs over TCP/IP or AppleTalk. This functionality shows Microsoft's firm commitment to a Macintosh operating system and recognizes that the Macintosh operating system has an important share in the marketplace (see Figure 4.1).

FIG. 4.1
NT supports most industry-standard network protocols, as seen in this OSI model.

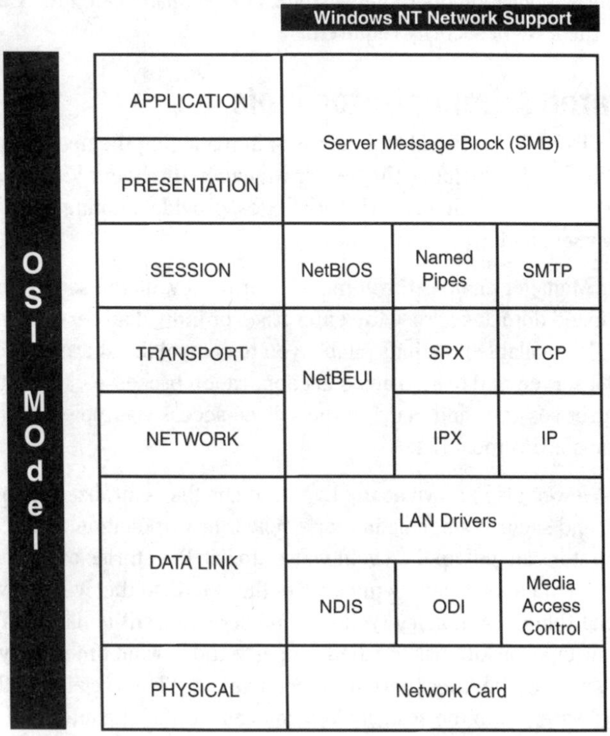

OSI Model	Windows NT Network Support		
APPLICATION	Server Message Block (SMB)		
PRESENTATION	Server Message Block (SMB)		
SESSION	NetBIOS	Named Pipes	SMTP
TRANSPORT	NetBEUI	SPX	TCP
NETWORK	NetBEUI	IPX	IP
DATA LINK	LAN Drivers		
DATA LINK	NDIS	ODI	Media Access Control
PHYSICAL	Network Card		

Using C2 Level Security

Security is a key element of any messaging system. Users want to know that their message will get to its destination without someone intercepting it. Exchange expands upon the Class C2 Level of Security, which is at the heart of the Windows NT operating system. The Department of Defense defines this level of security.

Class C2 requires a secure logon, discretionary access control, and full auditing capabilities. The secure logon requires that users identify themselves with a unique logon identifier (user ID) and password. This logon must be validated before accessing any system resources.

The discretionary access control enables the owner of a resource, whether it is a file, subdirectory, or printer, to determine who can access the resource. This also defines the level of control the user has over the resource. The owner grants rights to a user or group of users.

Auditing is the capability to log the security information of each operating system transaction to a file based on user ID. This feature provides the capability to detect and record important security-related events or instances in which security is challenged.

C2 security has several other components to its matrix of functionality. The Exchange server leverages its core features, however. Not all aspects of C2 security are required for use with Exchange. You also do not have to use every feature of C2 security when working on or creating a network application operating system. The company using the C2 security system can determine the level of security required.

Using Integrated Administrator Tools

Windows NT provides several tools to assist in managing the network as well as the operating system. Windows NT includes the Server Manager, the Event Viewer, and the User Manager to manage processes, define security privileges, provide auditing and security logging, and to create new users and groups, respectively.

The Server Manager enables the administrator to view all the servers from a single domain, multiple trusted domains across the enterprise, or individual servers and workstations inside a domain. The available functions enable you to control the share or access points to the file systems of a server, and to stop and start application processes. Using these functions, you can also close user sessions and manage specialized access via AppleTalk, NetWare Gateways, and the File Transfer Protocol (FTP).

The Event Viewer, also known as the Event Log, is the centralized repository for system, application, and security information for a server or workstation. From a remote console, an administrator can pull up the event viewer to see the etnries of a network server. All BackOffice-certified applications must write the events to the event viewer. Events can be informational (blue), cautionary (yellow), and serious (red) in nature. You will be able to tell whether your tape backup has finished properly and at what time of day it completed. From the system, you will see whether there have been any problems related to the operating system and the hardware. From the security log, you can view all the information predetermined for auditing.

The event will store information related to the Exchange server and all its gateways, connectors, and external processes. It will also store security information. Exchange itself has a security log, which extends the basic functionality provided by the event log.

The User Manager is a tool used by the security administrators or domain administrators to create the single domain logon user ID. This ID includes all the user's application profiles, the group memberships profile, and time and workstation restrictions. The User Manager helps you define trust relationships among domains, define auditing functionality, and define general domain user account functions.

From the User Menu, you can select to create a new user, a local group, or a global group. The user ID is the individual ID used in conjunction with the password to be authenticated by the domain to access network resources. Local groups are those residing within the single domain in which they were created. If the domain is referred to as "Dallas," all local groups created in this domain will be able to access resources only within the domain. Global groups, however, can be used to provide access to trusted domains. A local group can contain local user IDs, as well as global groups from both the local and trusted domains.

Exchange adds the functionality of creating a mailbox for users at the same time as the creation of their domain user account (see Figure 4.2). This gives the mail, security, and domain administrators control over the same set of user accounts. In large organizations, this is the responsibility of a Network Security Group. This one group would be responsible for creating the user Ids, as well as the appropriate mailboxes.

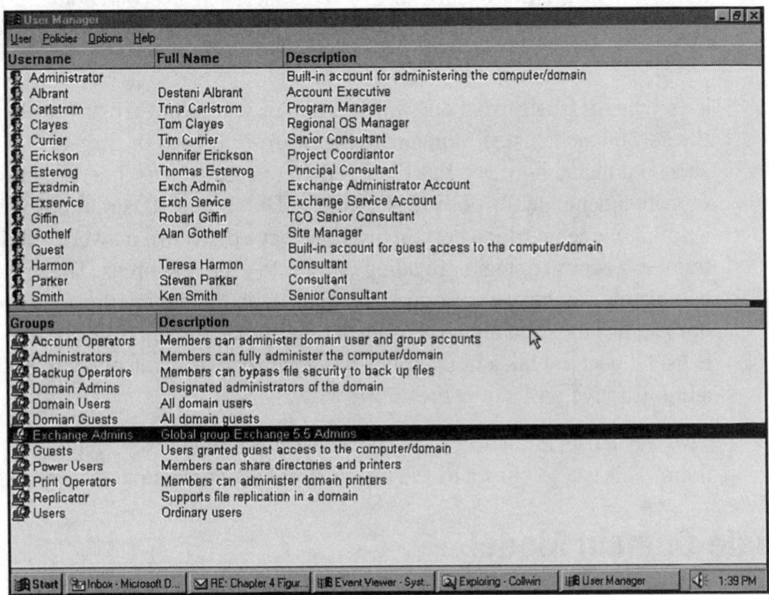

FIG. 4.2
Windows NT User Manager enables you to create domain user IDs, including the Exchange mailbox.

The functionality provided by these three tools is built into the Windows NT operating system. These tools can be run on remote machines, 16-bit workstations, and from the Internet.

Understanding the Windows NT Domain Architecture

At the heart of the Windows NT network operating system is the fundamental architecture of the domain model. A domain is a logical grouping of servers and workstations. One server in a domain must be the Primary Domain Controller (PDC) and subsequently have Backup Domain Controllers (BDCs). Windows NT provides the capability to build servers as "name servers," which belong to the domain. These servers, however, are not responsible for replicating user account and security information throughout the domain. The PDC and BDCs remain synchronized by updating each other's user and security databases at regular intervals 24 hours a day, seven days a week.

The domain architecture consists initially of a single PDC of a single domain. From there, Windows NT architecture can grow in any number of combinations that can include multiple BDCs in a single domain or a number of trusted domains with BDCs and member servers.

Trust Relationships Among Multiple Domains

Trust relationships can be created between multiple domains. Trusts enable users from one domain to be granted secure access to resources in a second domain. This maintains the concept of the single network logon. Users will see no change from a single domain to multiple domains.

Two types of trusts exist: one-way and two-way. One-way trusts are set up to enable users from the second, or "trusted" domain, to access resources of the first or "trusting" domain. The second domain, however, has the freedom to create its user accounts and manage its own domain independently of the first domain. This can be illustrated by using a distributed administration model in which certain divisions have their own network administration; however, there is a central domain providing corporate-wide resources. The divisional domains can completely administer their own domains without affecting the central domain. The central domain has the capability to enable the divisional domain to access the central resources. This is useful because full administrator privileges can be given out at the divisional level without administrative rights over the entire WAN.

Two-way trusts grant access and administrative functionality among all domains that are in them. This is also known as the Complete Trust domain model (see Figure 4.3).

Single Domain Model

A domain is a logical grouping of servers that shares the same user accounts database and provides a single logon for all users to all the servers in the domain. As a comparison, on Novell version 3.x networks, each server maintains its own user account database or "bindery." In this way, user accounts must be individually created on each server.

The concept of a domain is primarily used for centralized administration. All the servers in a domain are updated with a single action. Regardless of when the user ID is created or modified, all the servers maintain the single logon for the group of servers in the domain.

A single domain consists only of a PDC. For small organizations, additional BDCs can be added to validate user access rights. A BDC is recommended if this system is in a production environment. This second Windows NT server will provide some fault tolerance. In the single domain, there are no trust relationships. Small organizations primarily use the single domain. These organizations do not have to be interconnected with other domains. Sometimes corporations use a single domain as a development domain. In this way, they do not affect the production domain. The server in the single domain can communicate with the other domains; however, additional user IDs will be necessary (see Figure 4.4).

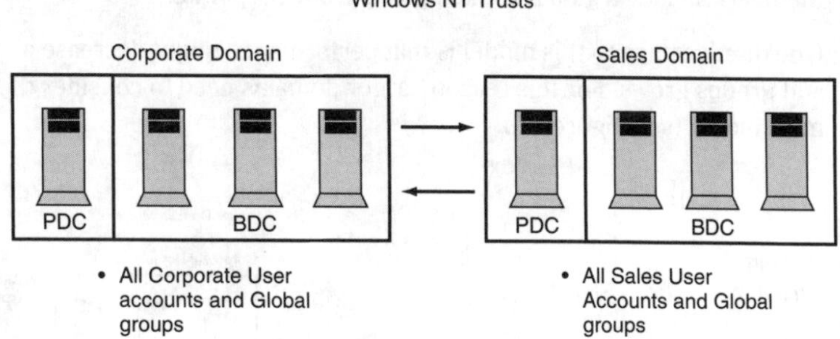

FIG. 4.3
Establishing trust relationships between domains enables one domain to access the resources of another.

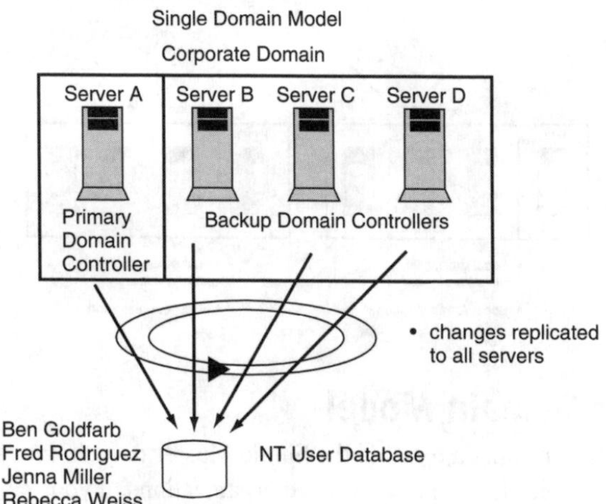

FIG. 4.4
The Single domain model represents the simplest form of a Microsoft Windows NT network.

Master Domain Model

In an environment with multiple domains, you can create trust relationships between domains. As discussed previously, domains can be interconnected via one-way or two-way trust relationships. In the master domain model, there is a one-way trust between the divisional domains and the central domain. All users and global domain groups are defined in the master domain. All other domains trust the master domain. This model ensures centralized administration for all domains. Again, this model maintains the single network logon by establishing one user account for the enterprise.

In a large organization, for example, the MIS Division manages from a central point. Therefore, the same should hold with the domain architecture. From one location, all users and security are maintained. The master domain referred to as "Corporate" houses all users and global groups. The resource domains, "Sales," "Marketing," and "Legal," only maintain local groups. When a resource is needed from the Sales domain, a local group is created in Sales, and its members include a global domain group from Corporate.

One disadvantage to this model is that performance might decrease as the number of users and groups grows. For this reason, larger domains need to consider the Multiple Master domain model (see Figure 4.5).

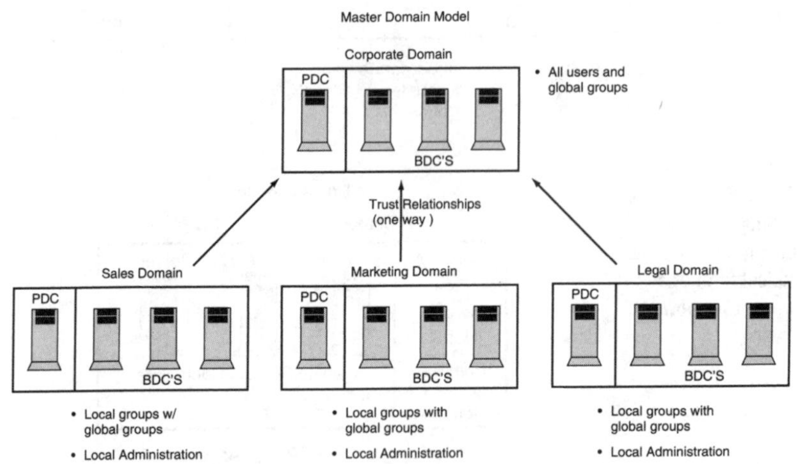

FIG. 4.5
The Master domain model puts global groups and users in the master domain. This model also places resources in separate domains.

Multiple Master Domain Model

The Multiple Master domain extends the Single Master domain into a broader scope. This domain model is typically seen in very large organizations. If your organization has two major corporate headquarters and many divisions, you might choose to implement the Multiple Master domain model.

Building on the previous example, the Multiple Master domain model has two tiers of domains (see Figure 4.6). The first tier interconnects the master domains. "Corporate" and "International" are the two domains. These two domains each house their respective users and global groups. These domains are then configured with a two-way trust. These domains trust each other; therefore, only one copy of each user ID is needed.

The second tier of domains includes all the resource domains. These domains each maintain a one-way trust to the two Master domains. This model can be scaled to networks with any number of users. You can easily have upwards of 10,000 users supported with this model. The resource domains can then be grouped logically based on function and geographic location. The resource domains also provide for local administration at the divisional level. The disadvantage to this model is that there are more trust relationships to manage. Also, not all user accounts are located in one domain.

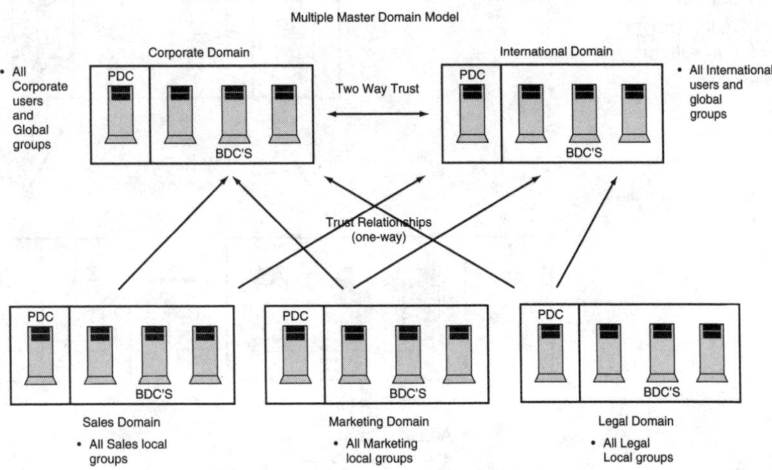

FIG. 4.6 The Multiple Master domain model provides the scaling capability needed in a large organization when the master domain model is not sufficient.

Complete Trust Domain Model

The final option available for a Windows NT domain model is the Complete Trust domain. This model is best used in companies in which management of users and groups is distributed among different departments. Rather than being centralized, this model extends the administration down to the divisional level. Every domain trusts every other domain on the network. One immediate disadvantage to this model is that an administrator of one domain has full rights over every other domain in the model. This can lead to security problems. If you are going to use this model, an auditing process could help manage who has made administrative changes on the various domains.

In this model, the resources and the user accounts are grouped into divisions (see Figure 4.7). Again, the only situation in which a Complete Trust is appropriate is when there is a lack of centralized management. This model is not practical for corporations with a large central department. The reason is that the model lacks the security needed for a large enterprise network.

Several options exist for a Windows NT domain model. In Chapter 5, "Designing Exchange Topology," you are given the criteria for selecting which domain architecture to use when planning to deploy Exchange in your environment.

Microsoft also provides a tool through its BBS and Internet site to assist with planning a domain architecture. This tool is referred to as the Domain Planner. It is a Visual Basic application that steps you through the options when choosing your domain and trust relationships.

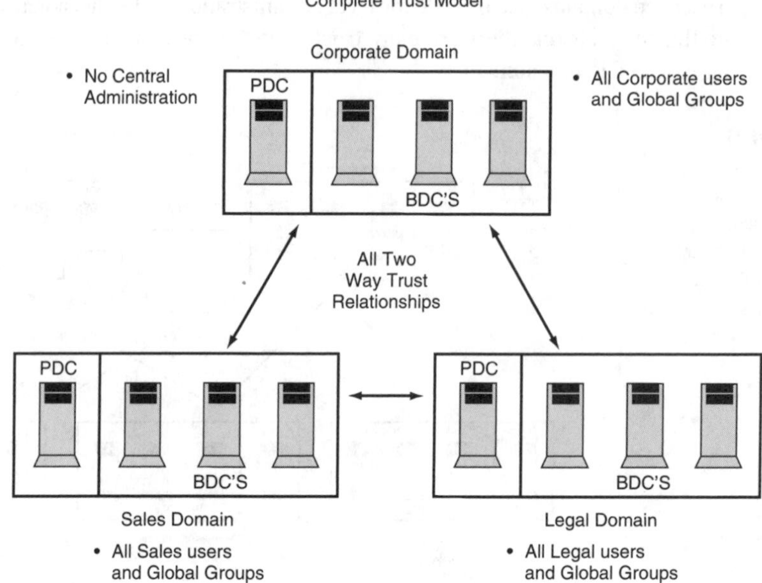

FIG. 4.7
The Complete Trust domain model is intended for decentralized management and carries many security risks for an enterprise network.

Understanding Exchange and Windows NT Operating System Integration

This section explains how Exchange leverages the Windows NT operating system. Exchange has been created to exploit all the features of Windows NT Server, including all the tools. These tools include the single logon, permissions that can be user defined, the User Manager for Domains, the Event Viewer, and the Performance Monitor.

Comparing Windows NT and Exchange Terminology

Exchange runs on top of the Windows NT OS. However, it has hooks into the OS to provide a robust, high performance messaging system. Not all of the Windows NT terminology applies or directly converts to Exchange terminology. The reason is that the messaging platform has its own architecture.

Exchange uses the concepts of Organizations and Sites, whereas Windows NT uses domains. Organizations are at the top of the Exchange hierarchy. Typically, you find only one Organization name in the entire enterprise. Sites, on the other hand, can be geographic locations, divisions, or functional areas. Sites can also map one-to-one with domains.

Sites can span across multiple domains, provided that the domains are trusted. This is necessary because a server within a site must authenticate each user.

Both the Windows NT domain model and the Exchange architecture use the term "server." Within Windows NT, a server can be a PDC, a BDC, or a domain member server. Within

Exchange, servers exist within a site. It is not necessary for the Exchange server to be either the PDC or a BDC of a domain. For performance reasons, it would be best for the Exchange server to simply be a member server. This way, the Exchange servers share the resources of a domain without having to continually replicate security information or validate user access to the network.

Utilizing Integrated Features

Following is a list of Exchange's features that help the Exchange server to closely integrate with the Windows NT Server:

- **Exchange runs as a Windows NT service.**

  Exchange is a 32-bit application written to integrate with the Windows NT Server. Therefore, all the core components and optional connectors of Exchange run as services of the Windows NT OS. This means that they will run in the background and do not require a user to manually execute their application components. A service is an application that the operating system is aware of, and manages its execution. In addition, the service will log the activity of the process to the Application Event Viewer. From the performance monitor, you can verify the impact the process has on the operating system. From the Server Manager, you can stop and start the processes.

  The 32-bit architecture of the executable enables Exchange to utilize the multithreaded, multitasking capabilities of the OS. Exchange runs in the background on the server. If a sudden burst of messages is passed to the Exchange server that needs to be forwarded, the executable can spawn more threads to effectively deal with the increased load.

  This integration is only one way in which Exchange leverages the Windows NT operating system (see Figure 4.8).

- **Additions to the User Manager for Domains.**

  Exchange adds functionality to the User Manager for Domains already discussed in this chapter. Exchange places an additional menu item with which you can administer user mailboxes from within the same consistent interface. Additionally, while you are creating users and assigning them group membership for Windows NT file access, a dialog box pops up to add the users' mailbox to Exchange. The user can be added to any Exchange server across the enterprise as long as the administrator has permission to do so.

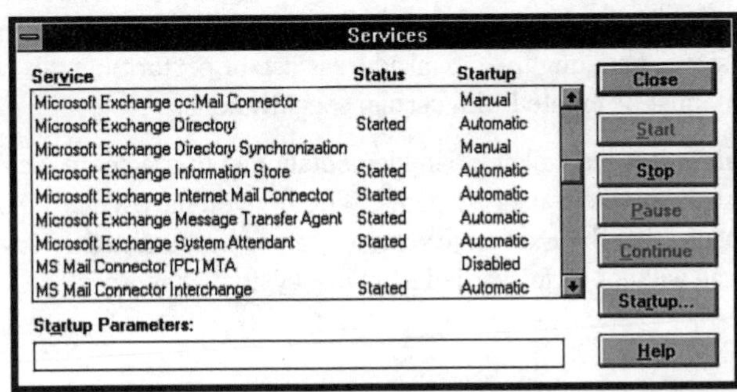

FIG. 4.8
The Windows NT Service Manager enables you to start, stop, and pause services, as well as control their startup properties.

- **Additions to the Performance Monitor.**

  Exchange extends the functionality of the Performance Monitor bundled within Windows NT. This extensive monitoring tool enables you to observe processor and disk space utilization, memory allocation, page faults, and over a thousand more counters.

  Exchange adds some specific counters to the performance monitor, which enable the administrator to view statistics of critical elements of the Exchange processes. These include the number of open tables on the message store, cache hits, I/O performance on reads and writes, RPC packets per second, number of bytes sent and received, and more.

Exchange Windows NT Dependencies

Exchange relies on the Windows NT operating system for certain functionality. The major function is that you must create a user account in the operating system for Exchange to run its services. Exchange also can import and export names from the Windows NT domain user database. This facilitates a quick migration to Exchange from your existing Windows NT Network architecture.

Exchange relies on the connectivity that Windows NT provides. Exchange enables all types of clients to connect to its servers. Novell NetWare clients, Macintosh, UNIX, and all the Windows clients can connect to Exchange using their native protocols. This is made possible through Windows NT's use of RPCs and multiple protocol support.

For remote access solutions, Exchange again relies on the Windows NT OS. Windows NT has an integrated remote access server as part of the operating system. The Windows NT server running Exchange can be configured for a user to dial directly into the server and access Exchange, as well as any other network resources. For performance reasons, it might be more appropriate to set up the remote access server on a dedicated server.

For WAN connections, Windows NT supports X.25 and ISDN without any additional software. An Exchange server can be configured to use an X.25 or ISDN connection to bridge the message route. If WAN links are already in place, these dial-up solutions provide a second level of fault tolerance, and an additional message route in an emergency.

System Service Account

The system service account enables Exchange servers to authenticate one another when transferring messages, updating the global address list, or performing directory synchronization. This account must be created with certain specifications.

It is important to carefully plan the implementation of this account. You must have a domain model that supports these user accounts. Whether you have a trusted or untrusted domain, you must ensure that the Exchange services can be authenticated between servers. If this does not occur, mail will not be forwarded from one system to another.

Security Models

Exchange relies on the C2 level security of the operating system. Any user who attempts to access the system must first be authenticated by the domain. Exchange extends the single logon ID. Therefore, the domain logon also validates users for accessing the Exchange mailbox. As mentioned previously, in the file-sharing mail systems, users had full access to the file system that comprised the post office. Exchange now manages the access to the post office based on the central domain user database.

Exchange itself provides three levels of security. The user accounts are leveraged from the Windows NT user database. From within the Exchange Administrator Program, a user account can be specified as a complete administrator, a local administrator, or a read-only administrator.

There are many issues related to using Exchange on the Windows NT operating system. Windows NT provides connectivity to almost any other operating system used in the enterprise. Windows NT should not be a point of concern when deploying Exchange. The Windows NT OS interoperates more easily with your existing network operating systems and mail environments than some proprietary systems that communicate with themselves (this is the case with PROFS or OfficeVision). Exchange leverages the Windows NT OS to provide a strong messaging backbone. ●

PART II

Installing and Migrating to Exchange

CHAPTER 5

Designing Exchange Topology

In this chapter

A successful Exchange implementation requires planning for a proper fit into your organization. This chapter outlines an iterative, ten-step process that is scalable for all company sizes. Of course, smaller companies can choose a smaller, more appropriate set of steps, while larger, international companies probably benefit from the entire process. Many of the steps, however, are valuable for all types of businesses. In addition, you may use this plan or create your own strategy based on another planning strategy.

NOTE The examples presented may not completely match your environment. Make sure that you recognize your environment's unique elements, especially when installing and naming the organization, site, primary domain, and server. You cannot change these names without reinstallation.

Step 1 Understanding Your Users

The first step in designing your enterprise is identifying your users' messaging needs. After you identify their needs, you can then match those needs to Exchange's features. This information also guides you when examining hardware purchases, training procedures, network upgrades (due to increased traffic), increased support needs, and total cost of ownership. Additionally, by understanding your users' needs, you can develop solutions on top of the Exchange platform that further leverage your organization's investment and add value to the user population. An example of this is to use Exchange as a key component of a knowledge management solution. See Table 5.1 for an example of how one company met their messaging needs with Exchange.

Table 5.1 User Needs

Company Role	Needs	Exchange Function
All departments	Connectivity to other platforms standard interface across heterogeneous desktops. Web Outlook View.	Share and organize information (email, documents, schedules, images, reports, form).
	Guarantee message confidentiality even when traveling.	Encryption and Person-to-Person key exchange. E-mail response.
	E-mail response when out of the office.	Out of Office Assistant.
	Reserve conference room.	Delegate feature.
Management	Enable secretary to respond to email received by manager.	Send on behalf; delegate access

Company Role	Needs	Exchange Function
	Distribute company report	Public folder (like an electronic bulletin board)
	Help Desk Solutions database	Custom Solutions database.
	Email connectivity to Internet.	Internet Mail Service(IMS).
Field Sales	Remote Email access.	Remote connectivity; Web Outlook View.
Legal	Connectivity to existing mail system.	MS Mail and Lotus cc: Connector.
Manufacturing	Migration from legacy mail system (e.g., PROFS).	Source extractor and migration tools.
Engineering	Research latest technical developments.	NNTP to retrieve and post to live Internet newsgroups.

The following section presents one of the many ways in which organizations of any size can take advantage of Exchange as a true solutions platform. The key point is that when planning for Exchange, you must understand your users needs, and you must leverage Exchange to provide value to your organization.

Exchange as a Component of a Knowledge Management Solution

Knowledge is the only enduring asset of an organization. The ability to capture and manage that knowledge is critical to the survival and success of any corporation. Historically, some organizations have done an effective job of capturing and managing business related data and information. When it comes to knowledge management, however, very few organizations have developed a strategy or dedicated the resources to provide an effective mechanism through which to capture and to leverage corporate knowledge, which can help a company gain a competitive advantage. Knowledge and knowledge management are quickly emerging as the next paradigm shift in computing following data processing, 1945–1965, and information management, 1966–1995.

Exchange Server provides robust functionality, which organizations can leverage as a key component of an enterprise-wide knowledge management architecture. The following sections provide definitions of knowledge and knowledge management, as well as point out how you can use Exchange as a part of a knowledge management system.

Introduction to Knowledge and Knowledge Management Before we can define knowledge management, it is important to define what is meant by knowledge. Mr. Denham Grey (a subject matter expert) defines knowledge, as follows:

> *Knowledge is the full utilization of information and data, coupled with the potential of people's skills, competencies, ideas, intuitions, commitments and motivations. In today's economy, knowledge is people, money, leverage, learning, flexibility, power, and competitive advantage. Knowledge is more relevant to sustained business than capital, labor or land. Nevertheless, it remains the most neglected asset. It is more than justified true belief and is essential for action, performance and adoption. Knowledge provides the ability to respond to novel situations. A holistic view considers knowledge to be present in ideas, judgments, talents, root causes, relationships, perspectives and concepts. Knowledge is stored in the individual brain or encoded in organizational processes, documents, products, services, facilities and systems. Knowledge is the basis for, and the driver of, our post-industrial economy. Knowledge is the result of learning, which provides the only sustainable competitive advantage. Knowledge is action, focused innovation, pooled expertise, special relationships and alliances. Knowledge is value-added behavior and activities. For knowledge to be of value it must be focused, current, tested and shared.*

The following key concepts in Mr. Denham's definition of knowledge are important to emphasize:

- Knowledge is the full utilization of people's skills.

  For organizations to develop an effective knowledge management system, they must hire and develop individuals that will leverage business information, their ideas, judgements, perspectives, talents, and concepts to generate knowledge. Organizations must then provide intuitive knowledge capture and search interfaces, so that the organization can retain and leverage this knowledge. Additionally, for organizations to truly implement a knowledge management system, which provides effective return on investment (ROI), the organization must change or adjust the corporate culture in at least one fundamental manner. Most organization's compensation and rewards programs favor individuals who are able to provide the most value to the organization based on the knowledge and experience they possess. The approach does not foster the formal sharing of knowledge, nor the motivation to effectively capture the knowledge for use throughout the enterprise. Organizations should consider changing their compensation and rewards philosophy to one that evaluates employees by the way in which they generate, capture, and share knowledge.

- Knowledge is competitive advantage.

  The effective use of knowledge in a business environment can provide a competitive advantage by enabling organizations to take effective actions in a dynamic changing global business environment, generate focused innovation, pool their expertises, and develop strategic relationships and alliances.

- Knowledge is more relevant to sustained business than capital, labor, or land.

  The effective utilization of knowledge increases competitive advantage, which in turn generates capital, labor, and land. On the other hand, the availability of capital, labor, or land does not—on its own—generate knowledge.

Understanding the Value of Knowledge Large amounts of knowledge enter and exit organizations on a daily basis. This occurs primarily by hiring new employees and through staff attrition. Many organizations may not fully appreciate the significant amounts of knowledge that the organization never uses on a regular basis. That is, many organizations do not fully understand the magnitude of the opportunity cost they incur by not leveraging existing knowledge. Before organizations consider exciting new ways to create new knowledge, they should examine the knowledge that currently exists, but they currently have not tapped. After they identify this knowledge, they should use the knowledge to achieve improved competitive advantage. After all, if a primary role of a manager is to optimize the use of resources, the manager should be very interested in a key resource that already exists and is underutilized. Many managers don't give the proper level of importance to the most important asset in the organization today—knowledge.

Many organizations, for example, invest more in managing and maintaining a fleet of cars than they invest in leveraging internal knowledge. If nothing else motivates organizations to begin planning for the implementation of a knowledge management architecture, at least they must understand that if their competitors are not currently implementing knowledge management solutions, they soon will A recent survey performed by the Delphi Group indicates that 28 percent of the companies surveyed are currently using some form of knowledge management solution, and the figure is expected to leap to 77 percent within the next two years. In fact, 85 percent of respondents see knowledge management as an important or essential new focus in their efforts to become more innovative and responsive to turbulent market forces (Source: The Delphi Group, *1997 Knowledge Management Insight Research*). In summary, the Delphi Group believes that knowledge management will define organizational IT investments over the next decade.

Knowledge Management As the term implies, knowledge management means leveraging corporate knowledge to provide a competitive edge. To truly understand the concept, you must better understand the concept of knowledge in context. "Knowledge is not the same thing as data," says Carla O'Dell, president of American Productivity & Quality Center, an industry research consortium in Houston. In late 1997, American Productivity will release a study of the "knowledge management" practices of 23 companies. American Productivity concludes that companies manage the knowledge in their organizations best by using information technology as a platform to support a combination of IT and non-IT-based information-sharing practices. Knowledge management is the process by which companies can assess, reflect on, share, and utilize individual learning and experience in order to foster enhanced individual knowledge and, thus, organizational value.

You should understand that knowledge management is inherently a collaborative activity and the opportunity for knowledge management among groups of four or more can be realized only with collaborative technologies in some form. Exchange Server can serve as a platform to enable this type of solution. These technologies may be as simple as threaded email discussions or as sophisticated as workflow knowledge bases. Additionally, collaborative technologies alone do not enable knowledge management. Knowledge must be relevant to work and overall business goals and must be accessible in the right forms and at the right time.

Principles of Knowledge Management Knowledge management is designed to support and enhance the human communication and knowledge sharing processes. Knowledge management is a team-enabling technology, which requires that organizations develop a strong and open team communications and knowledge sharing culture and support a coaching and facilitative management style. Knowledge management is the primary competence for the knowledge-based organizations today, and knowledge technology is the primary enabler. The following five knowledge management principles underpin the knowledge organization:

- Use trust as the foundation in the teamwork culture.
- Generate open communications, using the best possible technologies.
- Learn as an organization, at the fastest possible rate.
- Share and develop team and organizational knowledge.
- Enjoy the knowledge management process.

The implementation of an effective knowledge management solution within any organization depends on the existence of the following critical success factors:

- Provide top management sponsorship and support.
- Promote an aligned culture, sanction, and reward system to promote knowledge sharing.
- Utilize technology and tools to capture, distribute, update, and annotate knowledge.
- Use slack time and sufficient resources to learn, understand, appreciate, and apply knowledge management ideas involving ALL stakeholders in the paradigm shift.
- Initial knowledge management projects should be limited in scope and have clear goals and objectives.
- Initial knowledge management projects should leverage existing IT infrastructure as much as possible. This reduces initial investment and facilitates a quick ROI.

Implementing an Effective Knowledge Management System

The implementation of an effective knowledge management system requires that organizations deploy tools and procedures to provide the following functionality:

- Knowledge creation
- Knowledge retention
- Knowledge sharing
- Knowledge accounting
- Knowledge association
- Knowledge leveraging

In summary, global knowledge management possibilities now exist to transform national and international information-based organizations into global teams of knowledge-based workers. Large, dispersed, and international organizations can now make operations global and better operate as a single operation. Small organizations with global vision now have the technology available to grow their organization to trade globally—faster than ever before.

Mapping Exchange Functionality to Knowledge Management

The robust messaging and collaborative capabilities of Exchange Server make it an attractive platform on top of which organizations can implement specific components of their enterprise-wide knowledge management solution. The following are some of the specific Exchange Server features which facilitate knowledge management:

- The public folder infrastructure
- The Outlook Client and its development environment
- The implementation of Collaborative Data Objects (formerly known as active messaging)
- The implementation of server side scripting
- The robust interoperability and support for all major Internet protocols (HTML, NNTP, POP3, LDAP, SMTP, and IMAP)
- The scalability of Exchange with its support for virtually unlimited data base sizes and the performance improvements to the MTA and IMS core services.
- The security of the environment based on NT Server, encryption, and digital signatures.

If you review the key functionality components of an effective knowledge management system from the preceding list, you can identify those areas where Exchange Server can provide a solution.

Knowledge Creation You can create Exchange folder-based forms to capture corporate knowledge. The form design and functionality varies depending on the type of knowledge you need to capture. You can develop the following four main types of forms:

- Unstructured Knowledge Capture: In this scenario, you design a form to capture unstructured knowledge, such as best practices and lessons learned. The knowledge itself resides on a public folder, enabling easy secured access to the knowledge. Additionally, different users with different needs can apply views to the public folder, enabling them to view the contents in a way that is most useful for them.
- Structured Knowledge Capture: In this scenario, you develop a form to capture structured knowledge such as specific customer interaction information and marketing intelligence. This form contains controls through which to read and write data to relational databases such as SQL Server or any other ODBC compliant database.
- Document Enhancement: In this scenario, you create a form to capture additional information related to a document that you already created. This serves two purposes. The first is to provide some additional context on the nature and purpose of the document, so that when users join a team or group that needs to work with these documents, they can quickly understand the information and knowledge the document conveys. The

second purpose is to provide some keys, which are inserted into the document for the organizations' indexing purposes. Thus when users execute searches, they more quickly get at the specific information for which they are looking.

- Knowledge Replacement: In this scenario, you develop a form to enable users to update previously captured knowledge. This form documents the last modification date as well as the original author and any editors. This form is associated with or is part of the forms developed for the capture of knowledge.

Knowledge Retention Exchange Server provides a robust, secure, and scaleable data store for the retention of key organizational information. The nature of the information to be captured helps determine whether it should reside in a public folder or in a relational database.

Knowledge Sharing Exchange Server's public folders enable the easy sharing of information. Additionally, Exchange Server's capability to replicate public folders enables organizations to distribute knowledge to geographically dispersed users.

Knowledge Accounting In this area, Exchange Server's functionality provide only limited capabilities. Through the Exchange admin you can determine the amount of disk space that any given public folder utilizes. Additionally, by using Crystal Reports for BackOffice, you can define the utilization load and the frequency and rate of access to the folder. From an accounting perspective, you have no simple way to perform charge back operations.

Knowledge Association Knowledge association is perhaps one of the most complex and important aspects of creating a true knowledge management system. True knowledge is the more complex task of making connections among information. Consider how much tougher it is to create elaborate systems that contain public folder entries with links to other information sources or documents on the World Wide Web. These links form the essence of the navigation through a knowledge base, yet they also compound the problem of navigating because they significantly increase the possible interpretations of any single document. Cataloguing information previously meant searching and finding a set of documents. With knowledge links, any single document can lead to an indeterminate number of other links, making navigation nearly impossible. In addition, the links themselves must change, as must the documents, if you want to keep the knowledge base up-to-date. Not only is the job of the knowledge user made more difficult, but the maintenance of the knowledge requires additional resources. To resolve the problem, you must rely on intelligent inventory systems that catalog knowledge as it is needed and not in advance. Again, recall that you are not categorizing information that you can store in predefined categories and standard hierarchies, but you are organizing knowledge that is changing continually (excerpts from Corporate Instinct: Building a Knowing Enterprise for the 21st Century copyright 1997, Thomas M. Koulopoulos).

The knowledge association aspect of knowledge management is technically very complex and at some point requires that organizations consider the implementation of artificial intelligence technologies, such as case based reasoning (CBR). Exchange Server does not provide any tools for automating the process of information association. Artificial intelligence technologies offer a great opportunity for third party developers and integration services organizations.

Knowledge Leveraging Exchange Server's functionality provides organizations with the capability to leverage in several different ways the information contained in the system. Exchange enables users to access its data stores via the Outlook or Exchange Clients, via a web browser (HTML), or via an IMAP client. The flexibility meets most organizations' information access needs.

Step 2 Knowing Your Network

Your network topology has the greatest influence on Exchange's design. This step identifies the major characteristics of networks and maps some of Exchange's needs to your network's strengths. Contact your network administrator or architect and gather the following bulleted information regarding your network.

Each section is described in detail and summarized in a table. If you are already familiar with networking concepts, you can reference the section "Selecting Sites Based on Network Type" and Table 5.2, 5.3, and 5.4 before moving to the next step.

Network Types and Links

Several types of networks and network links exist today. After understanding the Exchange features your company needs, you can determine whether your existing network and links are sufficient. For example, one dial-up phone line probably isn't sufficient to move messages for thousands of users throughout your company.

The following bulleted items present a brief description of the most common types of communications links that you can use for connectivity of an Exchange system:

- Dial-up phone line: Phone lines are made of copper wire and mainly used for single users to remotely connect to existing LANs and WANs. They provide an inexpensive but periodic, non-permanent connection.
- X.25: X.25 lines: The lines are permanent, leased lines providing a connection between LAN segments (WANs). X.25 is an international standard for packet communication over public data networks.
- Frame Relay: Frame relay is similar to X.25, but it provides better performance than X.25 because of decreased overhead. Frame relay is a method to send packets over private and public data networks. Because frame relay can expand up to T-1 speeds, many companies use it to connect LAN segments, such asWANs.
- Fractional T-1: Because T-1 lines can be divided into 24 separate lines or channels, fractional T-1 lines make connecting LAN segments, such as WANs, more affordable than using a full T-1. You can expand bandwidth all the way to a full T-1 by adding additional channels.
- Integrated Services Digital Network (ISDN): ISDN is digital communication over dial-up lines using the ISDN standard. ISDN eliminates the need for a voice digitizer (analog to digital conversion unit) in the telephone company's central office, which enables faster

throughput than a modem over dial-up phone lines. Typically, personal computer users at home and some LAN segment connections use ISDN.

- T-1: T-1 is a digital link carrying voice or data transmissions and is usually used to connect LAN segments. You can also use T-1 to create private data and voice networks within a company.
- Satellite Communication: Satellite communication is a wireless communication scheme that provides global data access. You typically use satellite communication to interconnect LANs spread over a wide geographic area, and/or you use it to provide a redundant link when land-based lines are unavailable.
- Microwave Communication: Microwave communication is a wireless link that uses microwaves to connect LANs that are typically on a business, campus, or industrial park.
- ArcNet: ArcNet networks utilize a star or bus topology with a token-passing access scheme over coaxial cable (RG-62 or RG-59).
- T-3: T-3 is similar to T-1, but has a higher bandwidth equal to 28 T-1 lines. You can divide or group each of these channels into smaller portions. Typically, you use T-3s as high-speed WAN links.
- Thin Ethernet: Thin Ethernet uses a linear bus topology with Carrier Sense Multiple Access with Collision Detection (CSMA/CD) over thin coaxial (10Base2) or twisted-pair (10BaseT) cable.
- Thick Ethernet: The Thick Ethernet has the same topology and access method as Thin Ethernet but over thick coaxial cable (10Base5).
- Token Ring: On a Token Ring network, all the computers are connected physically as a star and electrically as a ring. Token Ring uses a token-passing access scheme over shielded or unshielded twisted pair (UTP) wire.
- 100BaseT Ethernet (Fast Ethernet): Fast Ethernet uses the CSMA-CD communication scheme and comes in two flavors (100BaseT4 and 100BaseTX) depending on the type of UTP cable in place. Stations connect to 100BaseT hubs in the same way they connect to 10BaseT hubs. Typically, Fast Ethernet is used in LANs and WANs.
- 100VG-AnyLAN: Proposed by IBM and Hewlett-Packard, 100VG-AnyLAN uses the same Ethernet frame format but replaces CSMA-CD with a deterministic protocol called the Demand Priority Access Method (DPAM). DPAM is conceptually similar to the token-passing method in Token Ring networks. You use 100VG-Any LAN in the same types of networks and linking as Fast Ethernet.
- Fiber Distributed Data Interface (FDDI): Communication over a fiber-optic cable usually uses the FDDI standard. The standard is similar to the token-passing technique of Token Ring but operates at a much higher speed. Typically, you use FDDI as a backbone to interconnect lower speed LANs, such as Ethernet or Token Ring; to connect WANs; or to provide direct, high-speed attachments for routers and hosts.

- Synchronous Optical Network (SONET): SONET is a standard for high-speed communications over fiber-optic cable. It is a network transport (like Ethernet) and has a bandwidth equivalent to 48 T-3 lines. Like T-3, you use SONET to connect WANs together.
- Asynchronous Transfer Mode (ATM): ATM, which was designed to handle voice, video, and data transmission over high-speed fiber-optic links, comes from the standardization process of International Telecommunication Union (ITU). ATM's strength is that it can transport multiple data streams on virtual circuits operating at different data rates. Initially used as a LAN backbone (like FDDI), you can also use ATM to connect WANs over fiber-optic cable. ATM can use fractional T-1, T-1, T-3, and SONET as its physical medium.

Selecting Sites Based on Network Type

Generally, links that have 64Kbps or less of bandwidth are classified by this book as class A (see Table 5.2). Class B links range up to 1.544Mbps. All links with bandwidth over the 1.544Mbps mark are considered class C.

As a rule of thumb for the average organization, you want to design sites so Exchange servers can communicate over a class B (see Table 5.3) or better (for class C see Table 5.4) network links.

Table 5.2 Class A Network Links

Type	Bandwidth
Dial-up phone lines	2.4 to 57.6 Kilobits per second (Kbps).
X.25	19.2, 56, and 64Kbps.
Frame Relay	64 to 512Kbps; newer implementations go to 1.544 Megabits per second (Mbps). At higher speeds, frame relay qualifies as a class B link.
Fractional T-1	Each channel is 64Kbps. Additional channels can be added up to 24, which equals a full T-1 line. At higher speeds, a fractional T-1 qualifies as a class B link.

Table 5.3 Class B Network Links

Type	Bandwidth
Integrated Services Digital Network (ISDN)	64 to 150Kbps
T-1	1.544Mbps
Satellite Communication	128Kbps to 1.544Mbps
Microwave Communication	1.544Mbps

Table 5.4 Class C Network Links

Type	Bandwidth
ArcNet	2.5Mbps
T-3	44.148Mbps
Thin Ethernet	10Mbps
Thick Ethernet	10Mbps
Token Ring	4 or 16Mbps
100BaseT Ethernet (Fast Ethernet)	100Mbps
100VG-AnyLAN	100Mbps
Fiber Distributed Data Interface (FDDI)	10 to 100Mbps
Synchronous Optical Network (SONET)	51.8Mbps to 2.5 Gigabits per second (Gbps)
Asynchronous Transfer Mode (ATM)	100, 200, 400Mbps up to 9.6Gbps

In certain cases, you may want to examine a smaller bandwidth link over a larger one if reliability is a factor. For example, some high (class C) bandwidth links may not be as reliable as the low (class A) links. Because Exchange Servers in the same site need a permanent link to communicate, choose the more reliable class A link if messaging volume is light.

Keep in mind, this is only one piece of information in selecting a site. You need to analyze other factors, such as the number of users per server, message traffic, the volume of public folder replication, and so on. Review the appropriate sections of this guide to gather all necessary information before making your final site selection.

Network Size

You should know the topology and size of your network. In basic terms, a small network consists of a few physical locations, one or two servers, a few clients, and a single domain or site. A large network contains multiple locations, routers, servers, clients, domains, and sites.

Second, it's important to know how quickly your network is growing and to what extent users adopt Exchange. In many organizations, email is the universal application that everyone seems to want. The need to exchange information, schedule meetings, and "to be in the loop" overcomes even the most technically stubborn user. Along the same lines, the quick adoption of email and other client/server applications sometimes forces a reluctant organization to grow its network to meet the needs of its users.

After you have a good understanding of your network topology, estimate the impact the deployment of Exchange will have on your network's bandwidth and performance. You should perform the network impact study in close partnership with the network administrator(s).

Network Bandwidth

Through careful examination of the underlying physical network, you may determine that existing network connections and bandwidths appear adequate to meet your organization's needs. For the purposes of this design guide, network bandwidth is defined as the amount of data per second that can transmit over a communication link. You must take into account the size of your links, however, and also carefully look at the link's utilization. You may find your network has very large and fast connections; however, they may already be congested with other network traffic, which impacts the overall performance of the network link. This is called Net Available Bandwidth (NAB). If your NAB falls to the same speed as a class A network link, you may need to increase bandwidth in areas of heavy network traffic.

Another area to monitor is traffic bursts. Traffic bursts are short bursts of data transmission that utilize a majority of the bandwidth for short periods of time. You may find that some network links appear to have low overall utilization; however, during peak periods of the day, these connections experience traffic bursts that reduce performance.

Knowing or predicting network traffic patterns through a network link enables you to determine whether your link has enough NAB to support additional Exchange traffic.

To predict traffic patterns and prevent them from affecting your network, you must measure the network bandwidth utilization (how close a network link is to full capacity) and the total packets per second (how close bridges and routers are to reaching full capacity) being transmitted. You can then use this baseline information to determine whether the network is operating normally or whether it is close to maximum utilization.

Monitoring network traffic requires specialized tools and dedicated network monitoring software, such as Microsoft's Network Monitor, included with System Management Server, packet sniffer, Network General's Sniffer, or Windows NT's Performance Monitor. For more information on the specific Performance Monitor counters you should monitor, please refer to Chapter 24, "Exchange Performance Tuning and Capacity Planning."

Network Protocols

For an effective Exchange design, you should know which network protocols are used on your network. Exchange offers several types of connectors, but each of them has unique requirements. For example, the X.400 connector, requires the existence of TP0/X.25, TP4/CLNP, or TCP/IP. You also must consider support for remote clients such as field sales needing remote email access, for which you can use Remote Access Server (RAS) or Dial-up Networking (DUN). Both of these support the point-to-point (PPP) protocol that enables any client to use the TCP/IP, IPX, or NetBEUI protocol.

Step 3 Determining a Windows NT Domain Model

This step describes local and global groups, trust relationships, server roles, and domain models. A domain is a grouping of computers and users that eases administration of the computers and user accounts. Windows NT Servers that are members of the same domain share a common user account and security database, which enables each user to have a single account that all servers in the domain recognize. The domain can also contain other Network Operating Systems (NOS), such as LAN Manager 2.x, and a variety of clients, such as DOS, Windows, Windows for Workgroups, Windows 95, and Windows NT Workstation.

You can review the following domain models to plan your own Windows NT domain or examine your existing one. You may choose to use Microsoft's Domain Planner Wizard, which is available in the Resource Kit or by downloading it from Microsoft's Web page.

NOTE After you create a domain, you need to reinstall Windows NT to make any changes relating to domain membership. (for example, moving a Backup Domain Controller to another domain). Be sure that you have properly planned your naming conventions and server roles before implementing them into a domain structure. ■

Local and Global Groups

Similar in structure to user accounts, groups enable you to efficiently assign access privileges to multiple users within the domain. The following are two classes of group accounts:

- Local groups are not accessible outside the home domain, but they may have global groups from the home as well as other domains as members.
- Global groups contain users from the home domain and can be assigned access to resources within the home domain as well as away domains.

Trust Relationships

Windows NT Server supports the ability for one domain to "*trust*" another domain, which gives users of the trusted (or account) domain the ability to act as authorized users on the trusting (or resource) domain. Trust also enables users in the trusted domain to access resources in the trusting domain without re-creating for a second time their user IDs and other security information. Keep in mind that no matter where network resources are located, users always log into their home (trusted) domain.

For example, you own a VCR, and your neighbor wants to borrow it to watch a video of Bill Gates speaking about Exchange and the future of messaging technologies. You "*trust*" your neighbor (a user from a trusted domain) enough to enable him or her entry into your house (resource domain) to use your VCR (a network resource) without making a second key (re-creating security information).

In addition, trust is one-way and not transitive. If domain A trusts domain B, the arrangement does not imply domain B trusts domain A. This two-way trust must be explicitly established by a domain administrator. Also, if domain A trusts domain B and domain B trusts domain C, the arrangement does not imply that domain A trusts domain C.

Trust relationships are very useful capabilities, but they also involve setup and maintenance. For best results, limit trust relationships to a number that satisfies the organization's requirements without creating unnecessary complexity.

NOTE If an Exchange site spans multiple domains, you must have a trust relationship in place so that the servers can establish synchronous Remote Procedure Call (RPC) connections. ■

Server Roles

A Windows NT Server computer can have one of the following three roles in the domain:

- Primary domain controller (PDC): The PDC maintains the original user accounts database. This database contains all the security information for the domain. The PDC should be physically attached to the most central and high-speed network segment possible. Because the PDC authenticates users and receives updates to the user accounts database, the PDC should never be on an unreliable or periodic network link, such as a wireless network or dial-up line.
- Backup domain controller (BDC): The BDCs receive a copy of the user accounts database from the PDC via replication. BDCs also authenticate users and can change their roles to a PDC in case of PDC failure.
- Member server: Member servers are not tasked with authenticating users, and thus are usually deployed as dedicated file, print, applications, such as SQL Server, communication (RAS server) or messaging (Exchange) machines. Depending on their functions, you can connect member servers over all (class A to class C) links.

You should install Exchange on a machine serving either in a BDC or a member server role. You do not want to place Exchange on your PDC, except in special circumstances, such as in extremely small networks with very light mail volume.

Domain Models

Because Exchange needs a trust relationship to communicate between sites, you want to evaluate each domain model based on its implementation of trusts. If a domain model is already in place, evaluate its current trust capacity for an Exchange rollout. To monitor the status of your domain trusts, use the following models of the Domain Monitor for Windows NT.

- Single domain model: This model doesn't use trust relationships. The model contains a single PDC and can contain multiple BDCs and member servers. Single Domain Model is the easiest model to manage because user accounts and all groups (global & local) are centralized. Unfortunately, performance may suffer as the size grows toward the domain's theoretical capacity (around 26,000 users in Windows NT Server 4.0) (see Figure 5.1).

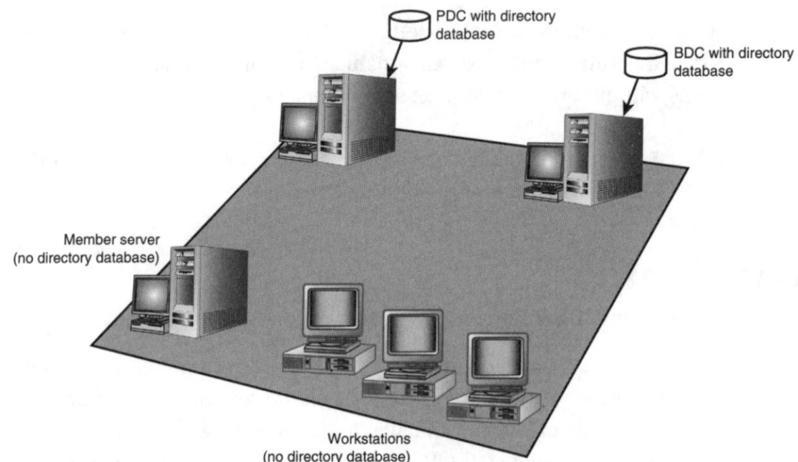

FIG. 5.1
Single domain model.

- Complete trust model:Each domain has a two-way trust relationship with every other domain in the enterprise. The total number of trust relationships that must be set up is equal to N*(N-1), where N is the number of domains. Each domain has its own user accounts and global groups.

  For organizations that use distributed management or function without a central MIS, this model provides the best fit. Each department within a domain can effectively manage its home domain as well as other domains. However, as the network grows so does the administrative burden of adding additional domains and managing multiple trusts.

  In Figure 5.2, you see that a regional office of Software Spectrum has no central MIS, which enables each functional department to manage its respective users and groups.

- Single master domain model: In this model, several domains exist, but one serves as the central or master domain. All the other domains are resource domains that trust the master domain via a one-way trust. The resource domains do not trust each other. All user accounts and global groups are contained in the master domain, and the resource domains contain file, print, communication, and SQL servers as well as local groups.

  Due to its centralized nature, this model enables a network administrator to manage all the organization's user IDs from one domain, and the local administrators of each resource domain can manage their home domains. One disadvantage is that the single master domain can theoretically support networks of up to only 26,000 users and, thus, may not support explosive growth within an organization.

  In Figure 5.3, you see that Software Spectrum centralizes its user accounts and global groups within one master domain and organizes its resource domain along geographical locations.

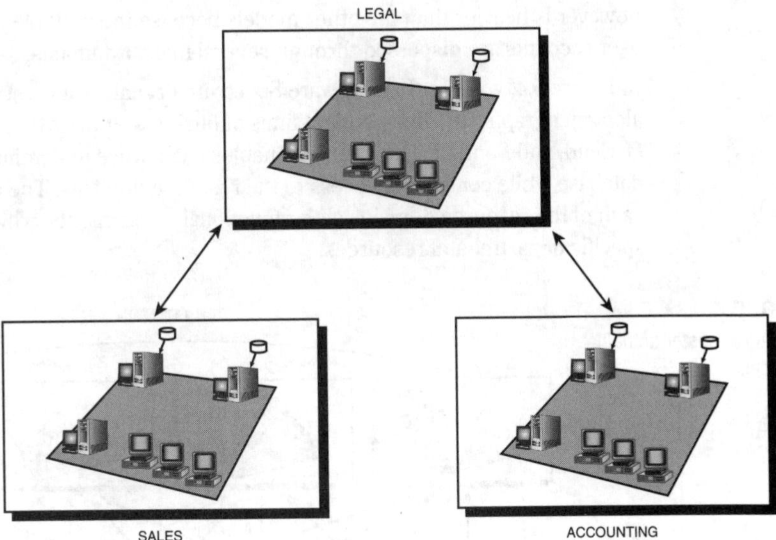

FIG. 5.2
Complete trust model.

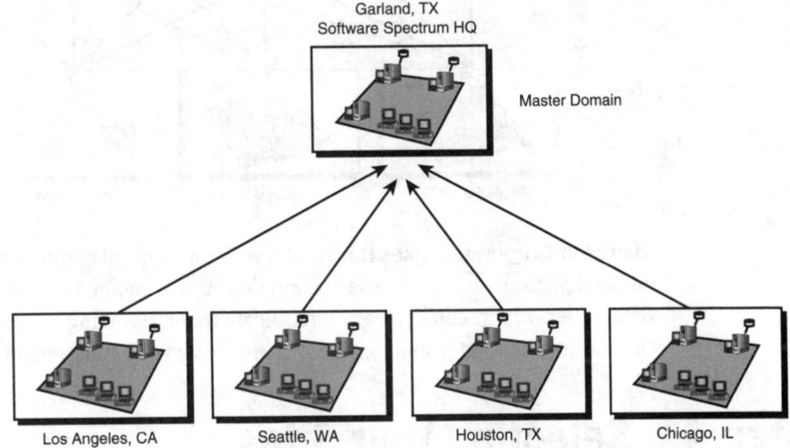

FIG. 5.3
Single master domain model.

- Multiple master domain model: This model is organized into two tiers and combines the features from the second and third domain models already mentioned. Two or more master domains are on tier one. Each master domain has a two-way trust to all other master domains. Thus, you need to define a user only once. Each resource domain on the second tier trusts all master domains with a one-way trust. The second tier domains do not trust each other.

  The multiple master domain model scales easily to an organization's growth and works well when a company has a centralized MIS department. In addition, each master domain can theoretically support up to 26,000 users each. The administrative burden, however is heavier than the other models because the multiple trust relationships and user accounts are dispersed through several master domains.

In Figure 5.4, you see that Software Spectrum organizes its first tier domain structure along geographically independent lines of business. It has offices in Tokyo, Los Angeles, Garland, and London. The strategy enables each office to administer its own security database while controlling access to the resource domains. The organization organizes each of the resource domains along functional departments, which enables access to specific departmental resources.

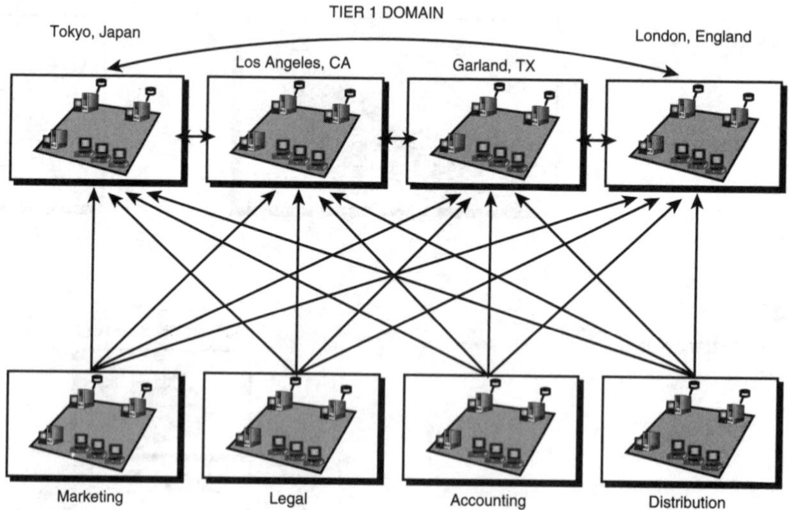

FIG. 5.4
Multiple master domain model.

Microsoft Corporation uses this model with one special addition for Exchange. A special, global domain is defined in the second tier. All Exchange servers are located in the second tier, which enables easy identification of messaging servers and provides consistently applied "global groups" to make server management easier.

Step 4 Selecting Your Sites

This step explains the difference between the critical and discretionary factors for a good Exchange site.

When determining which servers belong to which sites, you must consider two sets of qualifying factors. The first set includes permanent, RPC-compliant connections, plenty of NAB (Net Available Bandwidth), and proper security context. All these factors must be present to group servers together in one site. Please refer to Table 5.5 for details.

The second set of factors are discretionary. They include connection cost, connection performance, replication, and company organization. Please refer to Table 5.6 for details.

NOTE The following examples may not completely apply to your environment. Please carefully consider all pertinent factors before selecting a site and choosing site boundaries. Any changes require a reinstallation of Exchange Server. ■

Table 5.5 Necessary Site Factors

Factor	Requirements
Permanent, RPC-Compliant connection	Servers within a site must communicate over a permanent network link that supports synchronous RPC.
Proper security context	Within a site, all Exchange servers must run under the same security context. Because all Exchange servers' services use the service account, they must either share the same domain or belong to domains that have the proper trust relationships.
NAB (Net Available Bandwidth)	The NAB must be equal to or exceed 64Kbps. If reliability is a factor, you may want to consider a smaller bandwidth link rather than a larger one. For example, some high (class C) bandwidth links may not be as reliable as the low (class A) links. Because Exchange servers in the same site need a permanent link to communicate, you may be wise to choose the more reliable class A link if messaging volume is light.

Table 5.6 Discretionary Site Factors

Factor	Requirements
Consider large sites	Because Exchange automatically replicates all changes within a site, consider making your site as large as possible to ease the administrative burden. Remember that you can split more easily than you can merge.
Directory Replication	Network bandwidth is higher within a site than between separate sites—replication automatically occurs within sites. If you want to manually control replication, place the servers in separate sites.

continues

Table 5.6 Continued

Factor	Requirements
Performance	If you have a group of servers connected via links with 64Kbps or more bandwidth, you should consider grouping those servers together in a common site. Place servers connected via slower bandwidth connections in separate sites.
Company organization	Naturally, you want to group together users in the same department or functional unit. The grouping provides a more effective use of network and Exchange resources.
Cost	If any of your servers are connected via a link whose charges are based on the amount of data transmitted or the duration of the connection, consider placing them in separate sites.

Step 5 Selecting a Site Mapping Strategy

Now that you defined your network structure and you identified your critical site factors, you must choose a site mapping strategy. This step describes the major mapping strategies and uses several domain and network examples.

During Exchange's setup, the install program creates several services that start and run based on the context of a user account called the service account. The service account is created on the first computer within a site. The service account validates other computers within the site and gives the computers access to Exchange's services. All Exchanges computers within the same site must use the same service account.

If you have one domain and one site, the service account resides in the domain. For multiple domains within a single site, create the service account in the account domain or whichever domain handles your administrative domain functions. In a master or multiple-master domain model, the master domain contains the service account (see Figure 5.5). In a single domain with complete trust model, any domain can contain the service account because it's accessible to all the other domains (see Figure 5.6—the grayed computer contains the Exchange service account).

If two sites are in separate domains, you can use one service account for both domains if they trust each other. If they do not, you can use a site connector to serve as a link. In this case you must set up the site connector to connect to the untrusted domain's service account. For example, Exchange Site 1 uses a service account called Service1 and Exchange Site 2 uses Service2. Site 2 must connect to Site 1 with Service1's account name and password. Likewise, Site 1 connects to Site 2 with Service2's account name and password (see Figure 5.7).

When laying a site framework over your existing network foundation, consider the following mappings:

- One-to-One Mapping: For a small organization, consider a one site to one domain approach. This means one site is within every untrusted domain. A one-to-one mapping is similar to the single domain model. One advantage with the one-to-one approach is that the mapping is one of the easiest to configure and manage. In addition, everything is centralized in one site and one domain. You have a difficult time, however, increasing the number of servers per site unless you create additional domains/sites and use site connectors. Usually, as an organization grows or plans to rapidly grow, the mapping strategy moves toward a one-to-many technique.
- Many-to-One Mapping: Another mapping you may consider is mapping many sites into one domain. This is useful when you want to bring together group servers with similar bandwidth utilization. Although the mapping is easy to configure, the strategy may have more management overhead if you choose to connect the sites via one of Exchange's site connectors.
- One-to-Many Mapping: Larger organizations should consider moving to a one-site-for-many-domains mapping. This is equivalent to moving from a single domain to a single master or from a single master to a multiple master domain model. Because Exchange replicates all changes to properly trusted domains, a one-to-many mapping is fairly easy to administer and removes the overhead of managing site connectors between untrusted domains.

The following provides an overall summary of the important factors to consider:

- You do not have to map all sites to all domains.
- Consider a large site over a small one when mapping sites to domains.
- You need to map only domains containing the Exchange service account.

Review Tables 5.7 and 5.8 to determine the best mapping for your organization.

Table 5.7 Effective Site Mapping

Domain Model	Mapping Strategy	Description
Single	One-to-One	All servers within the site have access to the service account (see Figure 5.5).
Single with complete trust	One-to-One	All domains and servers can access the service account (see Figure 5.6—the grayed computer contains the Exchange service account).
Two Single	One-to-One	Servers in the single Domain Model can access the service account in domain B via a properly configured site connector (see Figure 5.7).

continues

Table 5.7 Continued

Domain Model	Mapping Strategy	Description
Single	Many-to-One	Each site can use its own service account or the service accounts in the other site via a properly configured site connector (see Figure 5.8).
Single Master	One-to-Many	With the proper trusts in place, both servers can use the service account because it's located in master domain A (see Figure 5.9).
Multiple Master	One-to-Many	As with the previous mapping, the trust relationships enable all first and second tier servers to access the service account (see Figure 5.10).
Two Single Masters	One-to-Many	The mapping enables the servers in the second tier to access the service account defined in their local master domains. With a site connector, both untrusted domains' service accounts are linked together (see Figure 5.11).

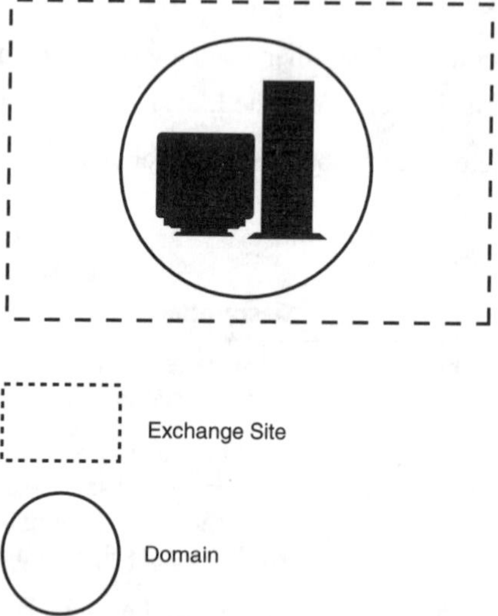

FIG. 5.5
Single domain using a one-to-one mapping.

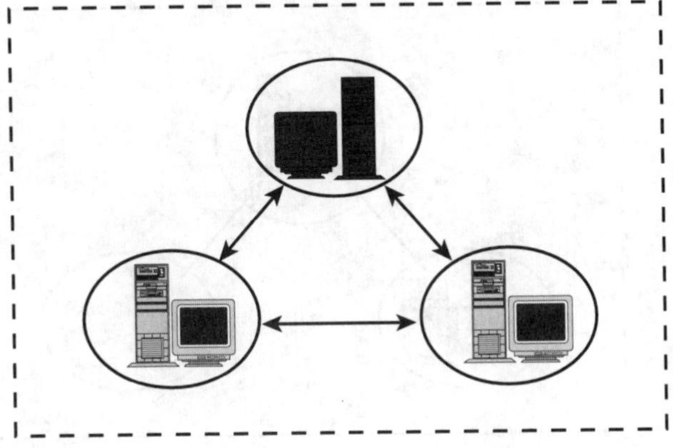

FIG. 5.6
Single domain with complete trust using a one-to-one mapping.

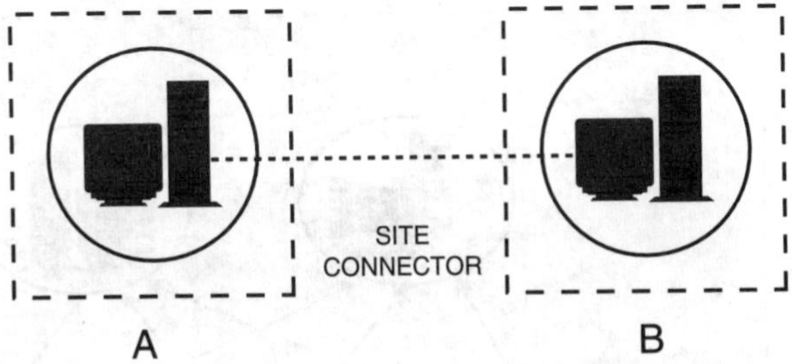

FIG. 5.7
Two single domains with no trusts using a one-to-one mapping.

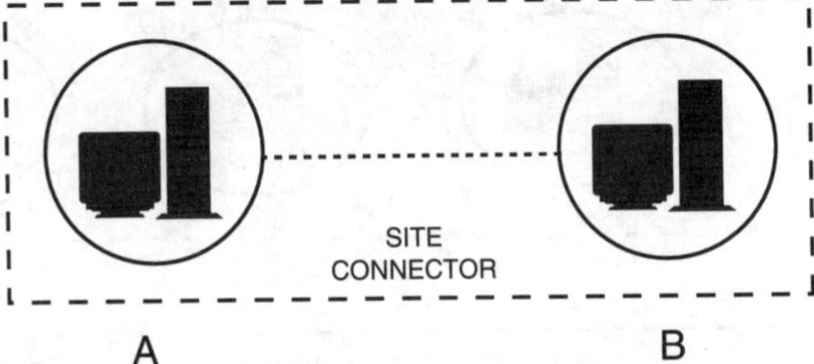

FIG. 5.8
Single domain using a many-to-one mapping.

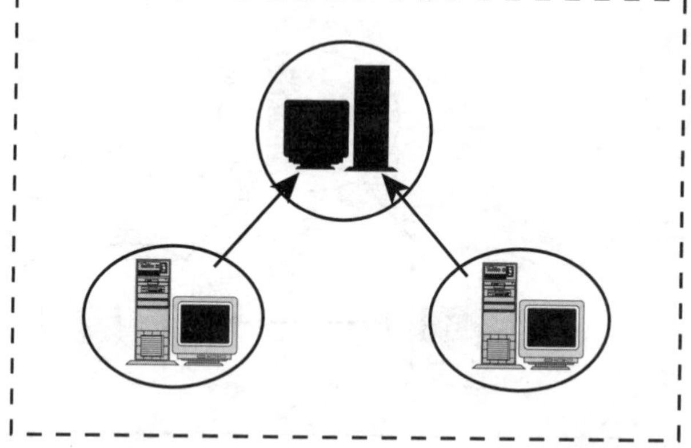

FIG. 5.9
Single master using a one-to-many mapping.

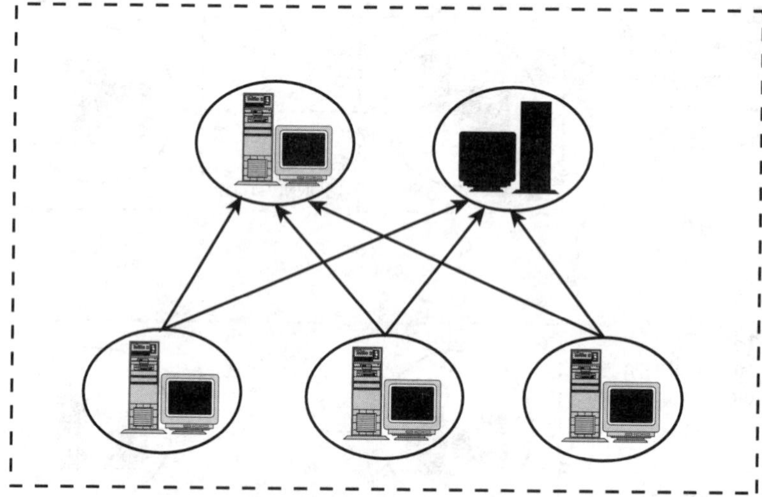

FIG. 5.10
Multiple master using a one-to-many mapping.

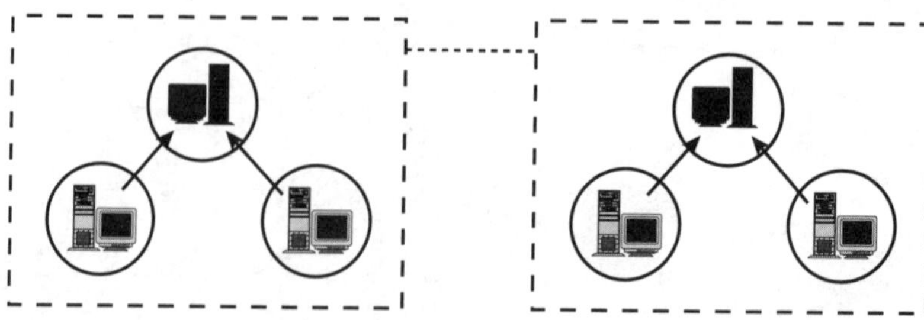

FIG. 5.11
Two single master models with no trusts using a one-to-many mapping.

Step 6 Selecting a Naming Strategy

This step describes the format, use, and restrictions of email addresses within Exchange.

External messaging standards are necessary for different mail systems to communicate and share information, and internal naming standards are just as vital to building a well run, easily administered mail system. As with many items in this chapter, you must thoroughly plan before implementing a naming strategy because some changes require reinstallation of Exchange Server.

The following are three elements of a sound naming strategy:

- The mapping strategyis not affected by a company's natural growth and reorganization. For example, base your naming conventions on geographic location, building numbers, and permanent floor locations. Avoid choosing company attributes that may change over time.
- You can easily add additional items like sites, servers, users, and other directory objects.
- You can easily use and administer the system.

Keep these elements in mind as you progress through the different mail systems and standards below.

Organization Name

An organization name should comprise your entire company and should be a part of the directory names of all directory objects, such as mailboxes, public folders, and distribution lists. Organization names can contain up to 64 characters, must be unique, and cannot be changed. When choosing an organization name, be aware that the name can be used to generate email addresses for non-Exchange systems, so it's recommended that you limit the name to 10 characters for compatibility.

Site Names

You can base a site name on function (sales, distribution), geography (countries, regions, cities), or physical location (building). Site names can contain up to 64 characters, must be unique, and cannot be changed. In addition, Exchange uses them when generating non-Exchange email addresses.

Server Names

A network uses the server name to identify a particular Windows NT machine. Server names must be unique, can contain up to 15 characters, and cannot include any of the following characters: bullet (·), currency sign ($), broken vertical bar or pipe (|), section sign (§), or end of paragraph sign (¶). In addition, do not put spaces in the server names on domain controllers if logon scripts are part of your environment.

Mailbox Names

A mailbox name should be easy to identify and similar in form to your organization's internal phone lists. Because Exchange's address book lists mailbox names, you may want to create mailbox names that sort properly when they display. Review Table 5.8 for a breakdown of mailbox names.

Table 5.8 Guidelines and Restrictions for Mailbox Names

Field	Guideline	Restrictions
First Name	User's first name	Up to 16 characters; can be changed.
Last Name	User's last name	Up to 40 characters; can be changed.
Alias Name	To route messages to non-Exchange systems, an alias name is used. Identify the external mail systems within your organization, such as PROFS, MHS, MCI Mail, AT&T Mail, and determine their unique requirements, such as PROFS can accept up to eight characters for an email address. For best results, the alias name should bear a recognizable resemblance to the original name—Kent Joshi becomes KJOSHI.	Up to 64 characters; can be changed
Display Name	Base this name on how you want to display it in the Address book and Administrator window. Be sure to consistently use the same format for all names, such as Last Name, First Name.	Up to 256 characters; can be changed.
Directory Name	Exchange uses this name to route mail messages. This is an internal name and is not displayed to users or administrators. Exchange sets this to the first alias name specified, but you can use another.	Up to 64 characters; must be unique; can't be changed.

Email Addresses

When Exchange communicates with other (or foreign) mail systems, such as the Internet, Exchange must have a valid address format the other mail system understands. A foreign messaging system user whose address exists both on a foreign mail network as well as in the Exchange directory is referred to as a custom recipient. Exchange recipients (including mailboxes, custom recipients, distribution lists, and public folders) that have addresses on foreign mail systems are known as foreign email addresses.

Exchange automatically generates an email address for the following mail systems: X.500, X.400, Microsoft Mail (PC), and the Internet (SMTP). Exchange does this to provide the widest possible compatibility with other messaging systems. Keep in mind that other addresses may be generated if you have installed a PROFS or another third-party gateway.

X.500 Addresses

X.500 was designed to provide an international standard for enterprise-wide directory service access. The 1988 X.500 directory service guidelines form the basis of Exchange's directory service. Exchange stores in the directory all X.500 object classes in an X.500 schema.

The directory objects are organized in a hierarchical structure known as the Directory Information Tree (DIT), and they are identified by a unique item called a distinguished name (see example later in this chapter).

Table 5.9 shows how the X.500 object name maps to an Exchange object.

Table 5.9 Mapping X.500 Names to Exchange Objects

X.500 Name	Attribute	Exchange Server Object
Country	c=	Country
Organization	o=	Organization
Organizational Unit	ou=	Site Name
Common Name Container	cn=	Exchange Server Recipient
Common Name	cn=	Exchange Server Recipient or directory name

For example, the distinguished name for Kent Joshi, who has a mailbox in Los Angeles within the Software Spectrum organization, is o=SWS/ou=LosAngeles/cn=recipients/cn=KJOSHI. When you remove the naming labels, you receive the form that Exchange uses: SWS/LosAngeles/recipients/KJOSHI.

Because X.500 doesn't support all object classes and attributes, Exchange also includes support for titles, organization charting information (who reports to whom in an organization), additional phone numbers, arbitrary attributes created by the administrator, and alternate recipients.

X.400 Addresses X.400 is a widely recognized and accepted international standard by the messaging industry. Exchange's compliance with the X.400 standard is important for organizations that want to use email with heterogeneous mail systems, as well as those who want to communicate with external companies via public carriers.

X.400 addresses can contain all the uppercase and lowercase letters, all numbers (0–9), a space, left and right parentheses, the plus and equal signs, the comma and the period, the hyphen and the forward slash or solidus (/), and the colon and question mark. In addition, X.400 addresses can contain the following attributes, which are listed in hierarchical order in Table 5.10.

Table 5.10 X.400 Attributes

Description	Attribute
Country	c=
Administrative Management Domain (ADMD)	a=
Private Management Domain (PRMD) (Exchange organization)	p=
Organization (Exchange server site)	o=
Organizational units	ou1=;ou2=; ou3=; and ou4=;
Common name	cn=
Generation qualifier	q=
Initials	i=
Surname (last name)	s=
Given name (first name)	g=

For example, the following is a valid X.400 address for Kent Joshi, who has a mailbox in Los Angeles within the Software Spectrum organization:

```
g=Kent;s=Joshi;o=Los-Angeles;p=SWS;a=mci;c=us;
```

This address also represents the minimum information you need to receive email from someone else.

Microsoft Mail Addresses If you connect to Microsoft Mail for PC Networks or Microsoft Mail for AppleTalk Networks systems, character restrictions are as follows:

Microsoft Mail network name	10
Post office name	8
Mailbox name	8

A valid Microsoft Mail address for Kent Joshi, who has a mailbox in Los Angeles within the Software Spectrum organization, is SWS/LSANGLES/KJOSHI. For more information on connecting to Microsoft Mail, please see Chapter 7, "Planning Connections to Microsoft Mail Systems." For information on migration from Microsoft Mail to Exchange, please see Chapter 8, "Migrating from Microsoft Mail Systems."

SMTP Addresses Exchange's SMTP connector is a dependable way to exchange mail transparently with SMTP users as well as with Mail users on other LANs over an SMTP backbone. SMTP also enables Mail users to easily access mail networks such as UUCP, BITNET, and Internet.

When communicating with the Internet or other SMTP systems, look at their particular character or addressing limitations. In general, SMTP addresses can include all uppercase and lowercase letters (A–Z), all numbers (0–9), and the hyphen (-). However, spaces are not permitted.

A valid SMTP address for Kent Joshi, who has a mailbox in Los Angeles within the Software Spectrum organization, is KJOSHI@LOS-ANGELES.SWS.COM.

External System Addresses If your organization has other mail systems (PROFS, SNADS, and so on), you want to examine any conditions they place on usable characters and addressing. This way you can properly configure the Alias Name field (see the section "Mailbox Names" earlier in this chapter) for your particular mail system.

Step 7 Linking Your Sites

Now that you have your sites laid out and the proper email address to share information, the next question is: How do I link my sites? This step explains the methods you can use to link your sites and discusses the pros and cons of different connectors and how this affects the Exchange Server.

Site Connector

The site connector is the most efficient way to connect two sites if they are on the same logical LAN. It also offers the greatest performance because it uses RPC for communication.

Listed in the Table 5.11 are the pros and cons when using the site connector.

Table 5.11 Pros and Cons of Using the Site Connector

Pros	Cons
Provides automatic load tolerance.	Requires a permanent, highbalancing and fault bandwidth connection of at least 56Kbps or higher (class B or C link).
Easiest site connection option to configure and manage because a site network transport isn't involved.	Transmits more frequently than other connection options. If you are charged for network traffic, such as frame relay or packets, you may want to examine another site connection option.
Messages don't need to be translated between sites.	Cannot control message size.
Configures both sides of the connection at the same time.	Cannot schedule connections.
Messages take fewer hops to reach their destinations.	Can overwhelm network links when multiple Exchange servers use the same link.

RAS Connector

The RAS connector is useful where no permanent LAN or WAN connection exists, but you can link up to another site remotely. This is usually the case with small branch offices where permanent links are expensive or not available.

You can also use the RAS Connector to provide a redundant connection for sites using one of the other site connection options. For example, you can configure the RAS connector to handle message routing in cases where the primary connector link becomes unavailable.

Table 5.12 reveals the pros and cons when using the RAS connector.

Table 5.12 Pros and Cons of Using the RAS Connector

Pros	Cons
You can schedule connections	Transfer is limited by speed of modem.
Can link sites over an asynchronous, periodic connection.	Link saturation is more likely because all site message traffic is flowing through one dial-up link.

X.400 Connector

The X.400 connector is useful where you are connecting to other sites via slow network links or on private or public packet networks. In addition, the X.400 connector provides compatibility with 1984, 1988, and future MTAs. This means you can communicate via X.400 with companies that are at different stages of implementing X.400 technology.

Exchange Server supports X.400 over the following OSI transports: TP0/X.25, TP4/(CLNP), and TP0/RFC 1006 to TCP/IP. After configuring to a transport, Exchange routes the message with standard X.400 messaging protocols.

Table 5.13 reveals the pros and cons when using the X.400 connector.

Table 5.13 Pros and Cons of Using the X.400 Connector

Pros	Cons
Connects to foreign, non-Exchange	Must configure network transports. systems that support X.400 standard.
You can schedule connections.	Bottlenecks may appear because all mail traffic flows through one central server.
Can determine messaging infrastructure topology.	Must verify that the existing routing through Exchange's network (bridges, routers) can support the required protocols.
You can control message size.	

Internet Mail Service

Although the Internet Mail Service can link two sites, the main purpose is to connect to the Internet using the SMTP (Simple Mail Transfer Protocol). You can also link most UNIX systems and any mail systems supporting plain text-RFC 822, MIME (Multipurpose Internet Mail Extensions)-RFC 1521, Microsoft Mail server format, or Uuencode/Uudecode standards.

Table 5.14 lists the benefits and drawbacks when using the Internet Mail Service.

Table 5.14 Pros and Cons of Using the Internet Mail Service

Pros	Cons
Can forward all mail to a single host.	Must configure a network transport (TCP/IP).
Can configure service to accept or reject host connections.	You cannot schedule connections.
Can configure service to receive inbound or outbound messages or both.	

Microsoft Mail Connector

The Microsoft Mail Connector provides seamless connectivity to Microsoft Mail for PC Networks, Microsoft Mail for AppleTalk- Networks, and Microsoft Mail for PC Networks gateways (PROFS, SNADS, Netware, MHS, and FAX). It uses a "shadow" post office that is structured like a Microsoft Mail 3.x post office.

The Microsoft Mail Connector runs over the following transports: TCP/IP, IPX/SPX, NetBEUI, X.25, Asynchronous, and Remote Access Service (RAS).

Table 5.15 lists the benefits and drawbacks when using the Microsoft Mail Connector.

Table 5.15 Pros and Cons of Using the Microsoft Mail Connector

Pros	Cons
Can connect directly to another Microsoft Mail post office, which enables you to replace it without additional software.	In most cases, you must configure a network transport.
Enables you to migrate your Microsoft Mail network in phases instead of all at once.	Must verify that the existing network infrastructure (bridges, routers) can support the required protocols.

Lotus cc:Mail Connector

The Exchange Connector for Lotus cc:Mail enables you to tightly integrate Exchange into existing cc:Mail environments. After you install the server, Exchange Server and cc:Mail systems can exchange messages and synchronize directories. The cc:Mail Connector supports both DB6 and DB8 cc:Mail post offices. Like the Microsoft Mail connector, you can take a phased approach to migration that causes minimal disruption in an organization.

Table 5.16 lists the benefits and drawbacks when using the Lotus cc:Mail connector.

Table 5.16 Pros and Cons of Using the Lotus cc:Mail Connector

Pros	Cons
Can connect directly to another cc:Mail post office, which enables you to replace it without additional software.	In most cases, you must configure a network transport.
Enables you to migrate from network in non-disruptive phases instead of all at once.	Must verify that the existing cc:Mail network infrastructure (bridges, routers) can support the required protocols.

Lotus Notes Connector

The Exchange Connector for Lotus Notes enables you to tightly integrate Exchange into existing Lotus Notes mail environments. After you install the server, Exchange Server and Notes systems can exchange messages and synchronize directories. Like the Microsoft Mail connector, you can take a phased approach to migration that causes minimal disruption among your user population.

Table 5.17 lists the benefits and drawbacks when using the Lotus Notes connector.

Table 5.17 Pros and Cons of Using the Lotus Notes Connector

Pros	Cons
Can connect directly to another Notes server, which enables you to replace it without additional software.	In most cases, you must configure a network transport.
Enables you to migrate from Notes system in non-disruptive phases instead of all at once.	Must verify that the existing network infrastructure (bridges, routers) can support the required protocols.
Can schedule connections	

Step 8 Planning Your Public Folder Infrastructure

This step provides a high-level introduction to Exchange Public Folders, an approach to the selection of tools for building information sharing solutions, and finally, an approach that organizations of any size can take to develop a public folder infrastructure for collaborative solutions.

Every organization has documentation on procedures and processes, forms for services, bulletins, business processes, and other information that needs to be available to the organization employees or specific workgroups. To aid in the collaborative use, distribution, and sharing of this information, a number of different solutions have been developed and widely implemented. These solutions primarily fall into two categories: the Intranet and Groupware.

The Intranet has quickly become a popular mechanism through which to make information easily available to users through relatively low bandwidth connections. The browser has become a ubiquitous component of the corporate and home computer. As this technology matures and addresses some of the security issues with which it is still struggling, the browser will solidify its position as a mechanism for business transactions.

Groupware enables employees to communicate, collaborate, and share information through memos and files so that they all work more effectively. Exchange provides a messaging environment along with structured tools that enable group collaboration in different ways. The main tool Exchange provides for this is Public Folders.

Introduction to Public Folders

Public folders are repositories for information that different users can share and different types of clients can access. Public folders can contain many different types of information, from simple messages to complex multimedia clips. Public folders can also contain custom forms for contributing and reviewing information and rules, and views for finding and organizing information. Public folders provide an environment for all kinds of custom applications, such as bulletin boards, discussion forums, customer tracking systems, and workflow applications. Public folders reside in the public information store (\MDBDATA\PUB.EDB) on an Exchange Server computer. You can replicate (copy) individual public folders, if you desire, to one or more additional Exchange Server computers. When a change is made in a public folder, the change copies on a scheduled basis to every replica of the folder that exists throughout the Exchange Server organization. This replication is based on a multi-master architecture. This implies that a change on any instance of the public folder immediately replicates throughout the hierarchy.

Public folders are an important part of Exchange. They provide flexibility by using a variety of forms, views, access rights, and structures. You can also use public folders to replace or compliment distribution lists, reducing storage requirements and network traffic. More importantly, instead of just reducing network traffic and hard disk requirements, public folders can hold important background information on projects, customers or other business-related activities. Some of the ways in which public folders can be leveraged to improve business processes include the following:

- People joining a virtual project team or a process in-progress can read items from the recent past and catch up on events.
- You can create a custom form and install it in a folder for employees to record information of any activities, telephone calls, or information related to customers. When a customer calls into a call center, the customer representatives can quickly review up-to-date customer-related information and provide more responsive and improved customer service.
- A help desk can maintain a folder of commonly asked questions and answers.
- You can put month-end reports into public folders for executives to track progress of projects and people.

Note that you can create, design, and view public folders only with an Exchange client. Use the Exchange Administrator program to configure public folder replication and a variety of other administrative options. In summary, folders are as follows:

- Organization-wide public information repositories
- Contain many different types of information
- Contain standard forms, custom forms, rules, and views
- Can be replicated throughout the Exchange organization as well as to users local hard drive

- Serve as the foundation for enterprise and/or departmental-wide groupware and workflow collaborative solutions

Selecting Tools for Information Sharing Solutions

As an organization plans for the implementation of managed information sharing solutions, you must realize that an effective and successful collaborative system contains elements from several different environments and technologies in order to adequately meet both the business and end-user needs.

In recent years, another popular solution to disseminate information has emerged from what was the core set of Internet technologies. The intranet (Intra-organizational network) leverages the same software as existing Internet access applications. The software—coupled with the broad availability and distribution of the browser interface—led to its popularity.

When comparing the intranet to Exchange public folders, organizations must recognize that each solution has its strengths and weaknesses. Exchange is effective at enabling users to communicate and capture their discussions into public folders. Exchange also provides a secure repository where users can submit, update or delete documents they have provided for internal consumption. Additionally, Exchange provides power users the tools with which to develop and deploy electronic forms for general use. These grassroots efforts can form the foundation for more complex workflow forms-based applications. The strengths of the World Wide Web include its ability to integrate multimedia components such as audio, video, or images, into a web page. Additionally, you can enhance the web pages by adding additional information from virtually any source through the use of hyperlinks. Unfortunately, using an intranet may present some significant challenges including security, limited document management solutions, and a limited set of standard third-party tools for integration and other administrative tasks.

When deciding which information sharing technology is best for a particular application, you must consider the following two key factors:

- The nature of the data driving the application
- The nature of the user interface (GUI) in which the data is presented

Traditional client/server applications are effective in scenarios where both the data and the user interface are well-structured. The client/server applications tend to struggle when either the data or the GUI are unstructured. In the cases where the data is unstructured, Exchange provides a good solution. In contrast, the web's unstructured interface is a good fit when the data needs is structured, such as when you publish relatively static information.

In summary, you must analyze and define the user requirements in regards to the source and nature of the information that the application uses and the nature of the GUI that best meets the user needs. After you define these two items, you can select the right technical solution or develop a hybrid solution to meet your users' needs in the most effective and efficient manner. Finally, it is recommended that you develop your organization's intranet and Exchange public folder infrastructures in conjunction—with the objective that they compliment each other.

Building a Public Folder Infrastructure

The deployment of a public folder infrastructure requires that you understand your organization's business objectives and goals as well as understand the processes and information involved in the day to day operations of your business. Only after understanding these issues are you able to develop and deploy a public folder infrastructure that adds the following values to the organization:

- Provide easy access to important information and knowledge.
- Eliminate existing "paper trails" through the development of public folder-based forms.
- Make business processes more efficient through the implementation of workflow solutions.

When defining a public folder hierarchy, you must define key design principles that serve as the foundation for any design decisions you make. These principles can include items such as:

- The first level of your public folder hierarchy should be visible to your users without a need for scrolling. If the users cannot see a folder, they probably never will use it.
- If you do not know who the folder users are, perhaps you should publish the information on another platform (such as the internet).
- The fewer the number of public folders, the simpler the hierarchy, and the easier your users can navigate the system.
- You should plan your public folders, so that any single folder does not have more that 10,000 items. You have difficulty creating a valuable user interface in a folder with more than 10,000 entries.
- If your user population does not have a client interface that provides access to the public folders, make sure that only the users with access to public folders need to use the contents of public folders.
- To ensure a positive return on investment, the contents of all public folders should in some way support a business process.

After you define the business objectives and opportunities that the Exchange public folders must address, you begin the detailed planning of the Exchange public folder infrastructure. An Exchange public folder infrastructure consists of the following components:

- The logical public folder hierarchy: You define which folders to create and how many levels deep to make the hierarchy.
- The public folder servers: You define how many servers within the Exchange organization will be public folder servers. Additionally, system architects must define whether the organization needs dedicated public folder servers, and the architects decide which public folders to replicate.
- The public folder policies and procedures: This includes defining, documenting and implementing the policies and procedures to effectively and efficiently use and manage the public folder hierarchy and contents.

Defining the Public Folder Hierarchy When planning a public folder hierarchy your primary design goal is to develop an environment that complements and enhances the day to day business tasks performed by your users. Four approaches are commonly used to develop a public folder hierarchy:

Organizational Model The organizational model is based on the way in which your organization is structured. That is, the public folder hierarchy mirrors the way the organization is divided into business units and/or functional departments. The model works well for those organizations with a highly decentralized structure based on highly independent divisions or business units. The hierarchy under this model is as follows:

- You typically name the top-level folders after the names of the divisions or business units.
- You can name second level folders after functional departments within the divisions or business units.
- Third level folders are application-specific, and you name them accordingly.

The organizational model enables you to create "*corporate*" folders, where information or automated processes, which apply to the entire organization can be located. One of the advantages of this model is that the administration of security is straightforward because the security closely resembles Windows NT user groups and/or Exchange distribution lists.

Geographical Model The geographical model is based on the geographical distribution of an organization's user population. That is, the public folder hierarchy mirrors the way your organization is distributed on a national or international basis. The model, works well for international organizations, where you encounter diverse labor and business environments. The hierarchy under this model is as follows:

- You base the top level folders you typically create on geographical regions, such as Western USA, Eastern USA, and so on., or Europe, South America, North America, Pacific Rim, and so on.
- You typically name second level folders after individual countries within the region.
- You can base the third level's naming conventions on individual office locations. The model also enables you to create "*corporate*" folders, as needed.

The geographical model enables organizations to present information that is tailored for users based on their common cultural or legal environment.

Business Process Model The business process model is based on the business processes that are the basis for the day-to-day operations of your organization. That is, the public folder hierarchy mirrors the way your organization does business. The model works well for those organizations that have well-defined business processes, which are standardized throughout the organization. The hierarchy under this model is as follows:

- You typically create the following top-level folders: one for organization-wide processes, another for business unit or department-specific processes, and a third for virtual team or user-specific processes.
- You name second level folders for the specific process they support.

- You need third level folders only if the specific business process requires it.

The model also enables you to create "*corporate*" folders for non-business process specific information, such as human resources policies and procedures. The business process model reduces the probability of redundancy with information that might be best suited for publication on your intranet.

Hybrid Model The Hybrid model is based on the combination of two or more of the previously discussed models. The following lists one example of how you can implement this model:

- Name the first level folders after the different geographical locations in which your organization has a presence.
- You can name the second level folders for the different business units or departments within each region.
- You can name third level folders after the different business processes specific to the business unit or functional department.

The main advantage of this solution is that it enables you to provide the most flexible solution to the potentially diverse needs of your user population.

Planning the Public Folder Servers When planning for your public folder servers, make sure you understand that the physical location of public folder servers and the corresponding folders on them is different from the logical hierarchy presented to users. That is, the users have no idea where the public folders are located. The only difference they might notice is the access performance between a local and a remote public folder. In order to adequately size your public folder environment, you must answer the following questions:

- Who will use the public folders?

  Understanding how many users will use specific folders. Additionally, you must ensure that all potential users can access the public folders via the Exchange Client, the Outlook Client, or a browser interface (leveraging the Microsoft Outlook web access functionality). This helps you to define the number of servers and server sizing (primarily focusing on disk space).
- Where are the users located?

  Understand the physical location of all folder users, and the network type and links across which they will connect to the public folder servers they need to access. The location of users is a critical factor in determining whether you need to replicate a specific folder to another server or not. Additionally, the information is a factor in the decision on where to place public folder servers.
- What kind and how much information will be placed in specific folders?

  Understand the kind of information (multimedia, attachments, messages, database pointers, and so on) that users will place in each folder. Additionally, for sizing purposes you must understand how much information will be retained on all folders on a per server basis at one time. These factors influence the public folder policies implemented in regards to how often you need to prune folders.

- How often will the content of the folders be updated or modified?

  Understanding the purpose of the folders and the working patterns of the designated users. The rate of change also provides a rough baseline on how much network traffic the use of these folders generates as well as the I/O load to placed on the server's I/O subsystems. You should use the estimated network and I/O load as factors to define the placement of servers, public folder replication configurations, public folder affinity configurations, and to determine whether the existing network connections will support the estimated load.

- Should dedicated public folder servers be deployed?

  The decision is based on your findings for the previous questions. If you plan to leverage public folders heavily, it is recommended that you deploy dedicated public folder servers in large user population centers (500 or more users). You should also plan to deploy dedicated public folder servers if you plan to deploy third party solutions, which leverage public folder functionality.

Defining Public Folder Policies and Procedures Historically, one of the main reasons why organizations have failed to deploy effective and manageable public folder systems is that they did not define, document, and implement the necessary policies and procedures. Additionally, for your policies and procedures to be truly effective, they must have the full support of top management and have been properly communicated to the appropriate IT (Information Technology) staff and all the user population. This is an educational process, which could potentially cause a cultural change as well.

Some of the issues you must address in defining public folder policies include the following:

- Who will be able to create folders at each of the levels defined (top level, second level, and so on)?
- Who will be assigned administrative rights for each of the different levels and/or folders of the hierarchy?
- What will be the basis on which it will be decided to replicate a public folder?
- Who will be responsible for determining whether a particular public folder will be replicated?
- How large (in megabytes) will you allow the public folders to get?
- Who will be responsible for pruning and maintaining public folders?
- How will you resolve public folder conflicts?
- Who will be given rights to install forms on folder or organization forms libraries?
- What permissions will end users need on specific public folders?

- How will end user public folder requests be submitted?
- Who will be responsible for processing end-user public folder requests?

In order for you to effectively monitor and maintain a public folder system, you must define, document, and implement administrative procedures. You should include the following procedures:

- How to create public folders
- How to set permissions on public folders
- How to configure public folder affinity between sites
- How to create public folder replicas and configure the replication schedule parameters
- How to monitor end user public folder usage
- How to monitor public folder resource usage
- How to monitor public folder replication status
- How to configure public folder age limit parameters
- How to move and delete public folders
- How to configure public folder Web Outlook view options
- How to configure diagnostic logging parameters
- How to backup and restore public folders

Step 9 Other Considerations

This step discusses other issues when planning for Exchange. This step is optional because it discusses advanced-planning items. You may want to fully complete all the other steps before beginning Step 9.

Estimating Hardware Requirements

Because Exchange is a transaction-based database, the proper server hardware is critical for a good Exchange system. The Exchange components (information store) first record a transaction, or create a message into a log file. During idle times, Exchange commits those changes into the proper component (for example, information store). If the Exchange server fails, it uses the log file to complete any missed transactions. Furthermore, Exchange heavily uses RAM to retain frequently accessed memory and address requests. A good rule of thumb is to invest in both additional memory and disk subsystem (hard drive, controller, and RAID/striping technology) for a high performance general-purpose Exchange server. Because every company has variables that may utilize hardware differently, use Performance Monitor to be certain your hardware investment provides the most value.

Also, dedicating an Exchange server (as a gateway, public folder, NNTP server, and so on) requires more testing for the best hardware mix. You also have the option of adding non-Exchange services, such as RAS, SQL, and domain controller roles onto an Exchange server. For the best performance, however, place Exchange functions onto their own servers.

For medium to large organizations, it is recommended that you define several different server hardware configurations to address the requirements of different numbers of users per location and the different roles a dedicated Exchange server has. Considering that Windows NT Server supports symetric multi-processing (SMP) systems, you can provide highly scaleable hardware configurations. Defining different Exchange server classes ensures that your are properly sizing a server for a specific role and a specific number of users. The classes assist you in planning your Exchange deployment as well as in defining an accurate project hardware budget. Finally, note that as your users' requirements grow you can increase the capacity of your systems by adding more memory (RAM) or additional processors. For specifics regarding capacity planning, please refer to Chapter 24, “”Exchange Performance Tuning and Capacity Planning.”

Remote Users

With a little planning, mobile or remote user's needs can be met with the default communication packages delivered with Exchange or the operating system.

Client requirements To connect remotely to Exchange, you need only the default communication package delivered with the Exchange Client or your particular operating system. The Exchange Client automatically detects the communication software and connects and disconnects as needed.

In Table 5.18, you find the default communication package included with different Microsoft desktop operating systems.

Table 5.18 Client requirements when connecting remotely to Exchange

Operating System or Browser	Default communication package
MS-DOS, Windows (16-bit)	Shiva—included with Exchange client
Windows for Workgroups, Windows NT Workstation	Remote Access Server (RAS)—included with operating system
Windows 95	Dial-Up Networking (DUN)—included operating System
Web Browser (Internet Explorer)	Active messaging using Internet Service Provider (ISP) or DUN

Server Requirements The Remote Access Server service (RAS) included in Windows NT Server supports all the previously mentioned communication packages, including Shiva. Furthermore, you can use a modem, null-modem cable, X.25 (via the network or using PAD), ISDN, or security hosts and switches as connection methods. Note that you need to estimate the number of users dialing in and plan phone lines accordingly.

Usage Scenarios You must define the different Exchange usage scenarios for your user population. The scenarios help you define the best Exchange client profile configuration for different groups of users. For example, a group of users who access Exchange Server only from a dial-up connection, are best served by using an offline storage file (OST), which synchronizes their local inbox with their inbox on the Exchange server. For this group of users, the client profile includes an OST file.

Step 10 Reviewing Your Plan

Congratulations! You have all the necessary pieces to build a successful Exchange design that meets your organization's needs.

Keep in mind that every time you expand your network or Exchange site, you need to enter a design phase again to create and implement a plan. Prepare for it by recording any important changes that may occur in the areas described.

Additionally, you must view the Exchange design process as an iterative process, which you optimize as the business environment around your organization's changes. ●

CHAPTER 6

Installing Exchange Server

In this chapter

Before proceeding with the Microsoft Exchange Server installation, you should make sure the machine(s) that will be used have the basic resources necessary to accomplish the task. The following lists show the minimum hardware and software requirements necessary for installing the Exchange Server.

Required Hardware: For Intel and compatible systems

Minimum:

- 486-66MHz processor
- 24 MB of RAM
- 250 MB of free hard disk space after Windows NT 4.0 Server has been installed

Recommended:

- System with an Intel Pentium 90 or faster processor; Pentium 133 recommended or supported RISC-based microprocessor, such as the Digital Alpha AXP or PowerPC
- 64 MB of RAM
- 300 MB–500 MB of available hard-disk space after Windows NT 4.0 Server has been installed

Required Software:

- Microsoft Windows NT Server version 3.51 with Service Pack 5 (SP5) or later
- Windows NT Server 4.0 with Service Pack 3 (SP3) or later
- A Network protocol (TCP/IP, NW-LINK, or NetBEUI)

Microsoft Windows NT Server is the base network operating system. You should install the appropriate Service Pack on the Windows NT Server to be used before you begin the Microsoft Exchange Server installation.

If you want access from a Novell NetWare 3.xx or 4.xx file server, the Windows NT NW-LINK and the NW-LINK NetBIOS protocol services need to be loaded on the Windows NT Server. This is a widely used protocol because, unlike NetBEUI, it is routable.

For a new or existing mail system to use the Microsoft Exchange Server to transfer messages over the Internet, the Internet Mail Service must be configured. To use the Internet Mail Service, you must have the Windows NT TCP/IP protocol installed and properly configured. For more information on SMTP connections and the Internet Mail Service, refer to Chapter 22, "Configuring the IMS."

Optional Components and Services:

- Internet Information Server (IIS) 3.0
- Windows NT Services for Macintosh (SFM)

Microsoft Internet Information Server version 3.0 is a requirement of the Active Server Components. These enable you to access mailboxes, discussion groups, public folders, and the directory on Microsoft Exchange using any Web browser.

Macintosh Services is necessary in order for MS Mail AppleTalk clients to access the Microsoft Mail Connector, which is the liaison between the AppleTalk clients and the Microsoft Exchange Server.

NOTE Microsoft Exchange Server 5.5 ships with the Outlook desktop information manager (version 8.03) and includes a MacOS-compatible version. ■

The preceding lists outline the typical requirements. To enhance the performance of the system running the Windows NT Server and the Exchange Server, you should use at least a 90MHz processor with 64 MB of RAM. For busy sites, you should use 1 GB of hard disk space. This disk space requirement does not account for user mail message stored on the server. Depending on the number of users, you will need to add additional server hard drive storage to accommodate the Information Stores.

Preparing for Server and Site Setups

Before installing the Exchange Server, you will need to gather some relevant information about the business or organization. This includes the number of users, usage patterns of e-mail, geographic locations, managerial style of the IS departments (central or distributed management), and more. You want to determine how the Exchange Servers fit into the overall company plan.

You should review these other topics before designing and installing the Exchange Server message system:

- Chapter 2, "Understanding Exchange's Organization and Sites," teaches you what is required for designing single- and multiple-site Microsoft Exchange Servers.
- Chapter 5, "Designing Exchange Topology," helps you understand the issues pertaining to the setup, connection, and migration techniques involved in planning Exchange installations.

Gathering Information Used During the Installation

During the setup process, you are asked to answer questions regarding your organization and the Exchange Server. Because some of the information can be changed only by reinstalling the Exchange Server, review the naming schemes that will be used for the message system and confirm that they are set.

You should have the following information before you begin the installation process:

- An organization name
- The Exchange Server site name
- The role the Exchange Server you are installing will play in the organization (Are you making a new site or joining an existing one?)

- The Windows NT Server Administrator account name and password
- The name of the Exchange Server Administrators Group

When designing the naming scheme for the Exchange Server Message system, use logical names with information relative to the end users and IS administrators. Because of the nature of Mail system standards, these names are case-sensitive. To avoid confusion, check each name you enter before continuing; these names are used throughout the entire message system.

Setting Up a Single Server

The first Microsoft Exchange Server to be installed in a new site is the most important. All other Exchange Server installations within the same site refer to this Exchange Server for configuration information.

These are the basic steps for installing the first or only Exchange Server in a site or organization:

1. Create the Service Account.
2. Configure the Exchange Server Administrators Group.
3. Install the Exchange Server software.
4. Grant the Exchange Server administrators permissions for the site.

The following sections break down each of these steps and cover them in detail.

Creating the Service Account

Exchange Server uses the Service Account to run its services on the given Windows NT Server. The account is granted the "Log on as a service" right. To create and join a new Exchange Server within the same site, the Service Account name and password are required. Exchange Server Setup uses this account to transfer the configuration files to the new Exchange Server. Furthermore, all Exchange Servers in the same site use this account to communicate with one another.

The following steps help you to create the Service Account:

1. Log on to the Windows NT Server as the Domain Administrator or equivalent.

NOTE You must log in to the same domain that holds the system for which you plan to create the account. ■

2. Click the Start button, select Programs, and open Administrative Tools. Then open User Manager for Domains.
3. From the User menu, choose New User.
4. In the New User dialog box (see Figure 6.1), enter the information you have listed for the Service Account.

5. Check the box titled User Cannot Change Password.
6. Check the box for Password Never Expires.
7. Remove the check from the box that says User Must Change Password at Next Logon.
8. Remove the check from the box that says Account Disabled.
9. Choose Add.
10. Choose Close.

The Service Account is created, and you are ready to create the Exchange Administrators Group.

FIG. 6.1
You can add the Service Account.

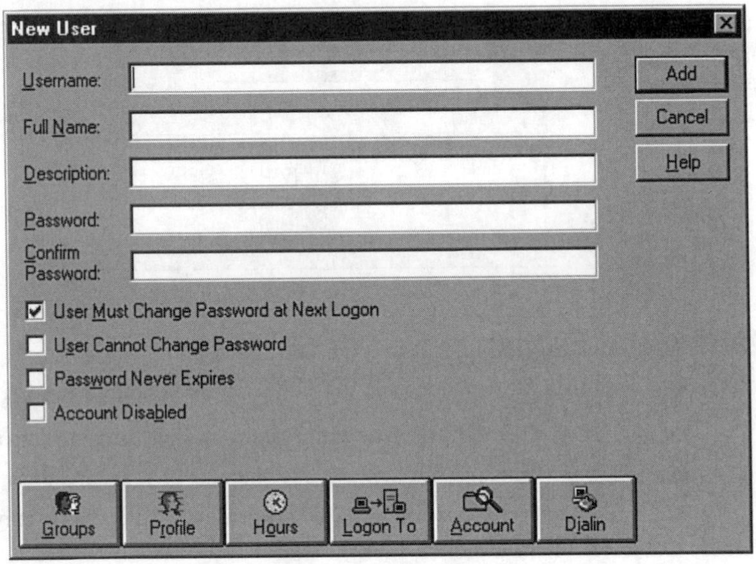

Creating the Exchange Administrators Group

The Exchange Administrators Group should consist of all the users permitted to administer Exchange. This group is a Global Group. Keep in mind that all users who become a member of this group have full control of Exchange and all of its features.

The following steps help you create the Exchange Administrators Group:

1. Log on as a Domain Administrator to the Windows NT Server that is in the same domain as the Exchange Server. This Windows NT Server will be the central location for the administrative functions of Exchange.
2. Click the Start button, select Programs, and open Administrative Tools. Then open User Manager for Domains.

3. From the User menu, choose New Global Group. The New Global Group dialog box appears (see Figure 6.2).
4. Type the name and a brief description for the newly created group.

NOTE You will be required to know this group account name later in the installation and during setup of the Microsoft Exchange Server. Refer to the section "Granting the Administrators Group Permissions for the Site." ■

The Exchange Administrators Group is created, and you are ready to install the Exchange Server software.

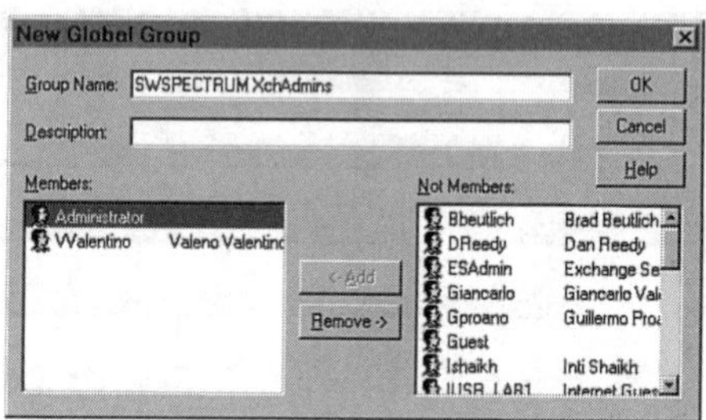

FIG. 6.2 Creating the Exchange Administrators group.

Installing the Exchange Server Software

Before beginning the actual installation, you should check the following things:

- Be sure that the PDC (Primary Domain Controller) is connected and operating.
- Review the proposed Exchange Server naming scheme and design layout.
- Verify that there is a working CD-ROM drive available as a resource on the Windows NT Server. You will use this drive during the installation process.

The following steps help you to install the Exchange Server and create the first or only Exchange Server site:

1. Log on to the Windows NT Server as the Local Administrator.
2. Load the Exchange Server CD-ROM into the CD-ROM drive.
3. Double-click the My Computer icon and then the CD-ROM icon.
4. Familiarize yourself with the directory structure on the Exchange CD-ROM.
5. Locate and change directories to the Setup directory.
6. Locate and change directories to one of the computer types. For example, to use Alpha, i386, you would type **d:\SETUP\i386**.
7. Choose SETUP.EXE. Then click Accept to continue past the Licensing dialog box.

NOTE If you plan to use Server Components (which enable you to access mailboxes, discussion groups, public folders, and the directory on Exchange using any Web browser), you must first install Internet Information Server 3.0. Then when installing Exchange, you must use the Complete/Custom install option and be sure that the Active Server Components box is checked. ■

8. An Installation Options box appears (see Figure 6.3). Select the desired type of installation and the location to which the files should be copied. The following are the installation options from which you can choose:
   - *Typical*. Exchange Server will be installed with the most common options.
   - *Complete/Custom*. Exchange Server will be installed with only the options you select.
   - *Minimum*. Exchange Server will be installed with the minimum options required to run.

NOTE One of the selections in the preceding list might not appear on-screen. The reason is that there is not enough disk space for that particular option. If that happens, choose another type of installation or a different file location on another volume that has enough disk space to handle the installation. ■

9. If you selected the Typical or Minimum installation, skip to step 10.

   If you selected the Complete/Custom installation, the next screen to appear is the Exchange Server component selection screen. You select the components you want installed by checking the box pertaining to the component; if you don't want a particular component installed, you remove the check from the box. The following list shows the components and their subcomponents available for selection during installation:
   - *Microsoft Exchange Server.* The default location for installation of component files is C:\EXCHSRVR. You can modify this by choosing Change Location of Files. To install all Server components (MS Mail Connector, cc:Mail Connector, X.400 Connector, and Microsoft Exchange Event Service), you need approximately 107 MB of disk space is required.
   - *Microsoft Exchange Administrator application.* The default directory path for installation of the Administrator components is C:\EXCHSRVR\BIN. You can change the directory path if you want to use a different location. The Administrator software component has no subcomponents. This component requires approximately 13 MB of local hard disk space.
   - *Books Online.* This installs the online documentation for Microsoft Exchange Server, and it requires 136 KB of disk space. If you have the space, install these reference materials, as they can be helpful.
   - *Internet mail.* This component is not transferred during the upgrade. If you have specific routing set up before upgrading, the routing information is not transferred from the Registry to the directory.

- *Outlook Web Access.* Installs the Outlook Web Access components needed for Web access to Microsoft Exchange Server.

Click Continue to proceed with the installation.

NOTE To perform a Complete installation, you need a minimum of 113,920 KB of disk space. This does not include disk space for user mailboxes—just the Exchange system files. ■

FIG. 6.3 Choose your preferred installation option when setting up the Exchange Server.

10. Click the check box to select Per Seat licensing, and then click OK.
11. In the Organization and Site dialog box (see Figure 6.4), choose Create a New Site. Then enter the Organization Name and Site Name (both are mandatory) and click OK.

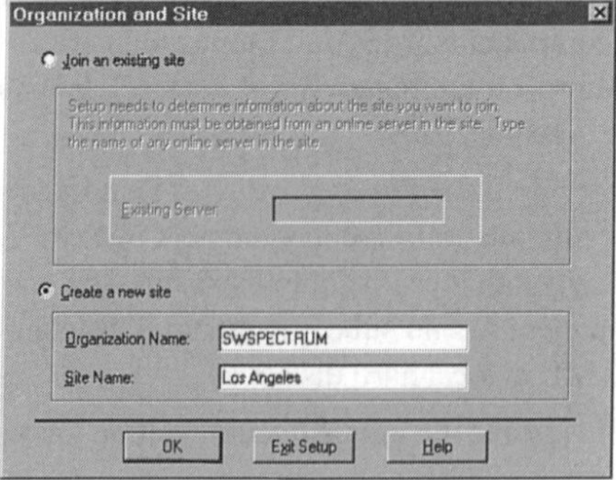

FIG. 6.4 Creating a new Exchange site.

12. A dialog box appears, asking, "Are you sure you want to create a new site?" Choose Yes.
13. Next, the Site Services Account box appears, requesting that you choose the Service Account (see Figure 6.5). Enter the Service Account name and password that you created at the beginning of this chapter.

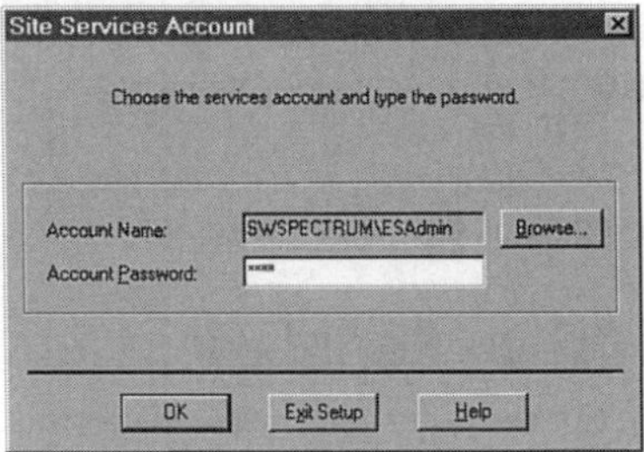

FIG. 6.5
Enter the Service Account name and the appropriate password.

Alternatively, you can click Browse and then choose the account from the list provided. Choose Add, and then click OK.

14. A dialog box appears, confirming that the rights have been granted (see Figure 6.6). Choose OK.

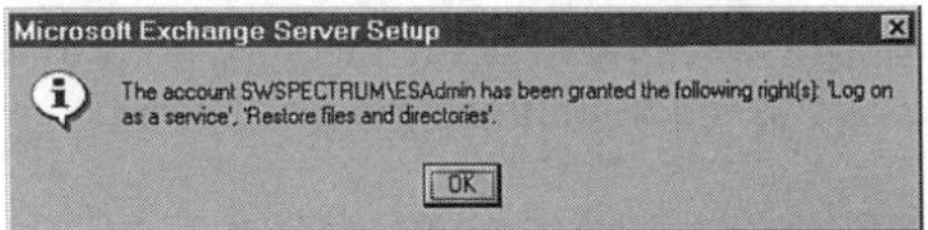

FIG. 6.6
You should verify that the proper rights have been granted.

15. To complete the installation, choose OK in the next dialog box. Exchange Server Setup copies the Exchange Server files and installs the services to the selected Windows NT Server.
16. When the installation is complete, a dialog box appears asking whether the Exchange Server Optimizer should be run (see Figure 6.7). Select Run Optimizer to have the Exchange Server Optimizer analyze your hardware configuration. The Optimizer also arranges files on the Windows NT Server for optimum performance.

NOTE Running the Optimizer is critical to the efficient operation of the Exchange Server. You do not have to run the Exchange Server Optimizer at this time; however, it should be run before Exchange is rolled out to live users. ■

Microsoft Exchange Server Setup

Microsoft Exchange Server Setup has completed successfully.

You can now optimize your Exchange Server installation for this specific machine by running the Exchange Server Optimizer. The Optimizer can also be run at a later time.

Run Optimizer | Exit Setup

FIG. 6.7
Running Setup and the Exchange Server Optimizer gets the Exchange Server up and running.

17. Although not required, it is a good idea to reboot Windows NT after the installation process is complete. This verifies that the services will start automatically and without error.

This completes the installation of the first or only Exchange Server at a single site.

Granting the Administrators Group Permissions for the Site

In order for the Microsoft Exchange Server to be administered, permissions have to be granted to the Administrators Group. The following steps provide a description of procedures for completing this task:

1. Click the Start button and select the Programs Icon. Then select the Exchange icon, followed by the Exchange Administration icon.
2. Connect to the new Exchange Server.
3. Select the File menu and choose Properties. Then choose the Permissions tab. You will see the Permissions tab of the Properties sheet(see Figure 6.8). Click the Add button, and a list of Windows NT user accounts and groups appears.

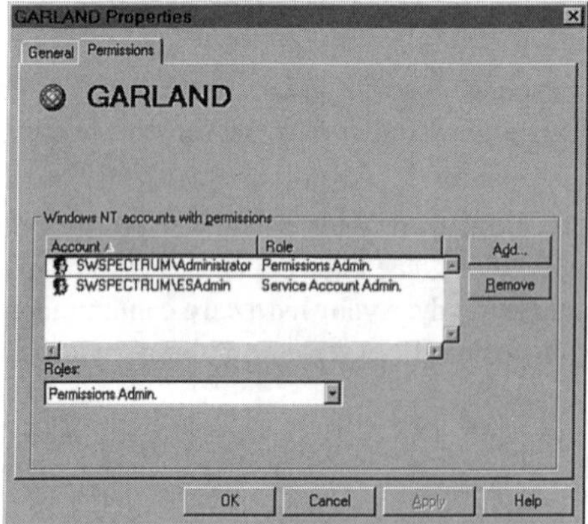

FIG. 6.8
The Permissions tab shows Windows NT user accounts for this site.

4. Select the Microsoft Windows NT domain that you want.
5. In the dialog box shown in Figure 6.9, select the user(s) or group(s) you want to add to the Administrators Group.

   Alternatively, you can manually enter the user and group names. In the Add Name box, type the domain name, followed by a backslash, followed by the user account or group name, such as **Domain1\User1**. Click Add. Then click OK to return to the Properties sheet.

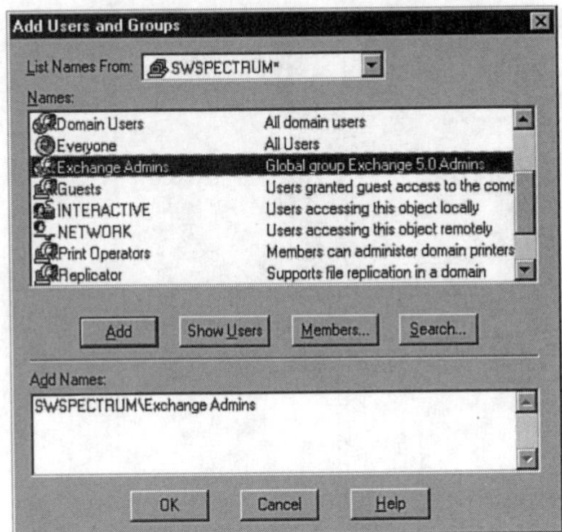

FIG. 6.9
You can choose users and groups that are to be added to the Administrators Group.

6. To continue to designate additional properties, choose Apply to activate the properties you've entered so far. If you're finished changing properties, click OK to apply the changes, close the Properties sheet, and return to the Administrators window.
7. Two other containers need to be assigned administrative privileges: the Organization container at the very top of the list and the Configuration container listed just below the Site. Repeat the preceding steps on each of these containers.

The Administrators Group has now been granted the permissions necessary for accomplishing administrative needs.

Setting Up Additional Servers at the Same Location

The procedure for setting up additional Exchange Servers at the same site are similar to the steps you used to create the first or only Exchange Server. The major difference between setting up the first Exchange Server and a second one occurs at step 11 of the directions pertaining to the creation of a new Exchange Server site.

In step 11, the Organization and Site dialog box appears. Choose the Join an Existing Site option button (see Figure 6.10). Then enter the name of an available Exchange Server and choose OK. The new server receives the site's configuration information from the specified Exchange Server and is added to the existing site. You should continue through the end of the process for creating a new Exchange Server.

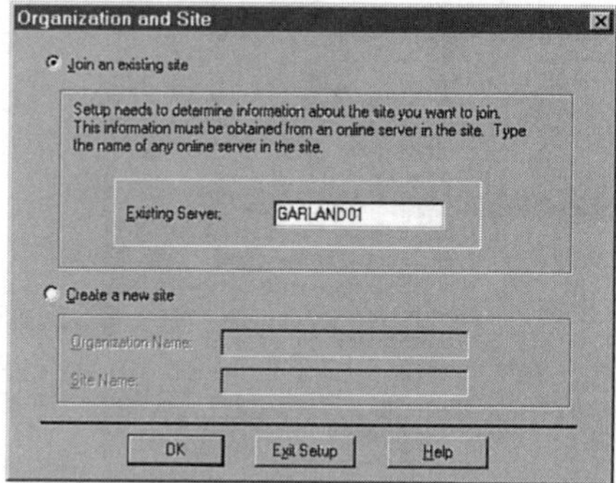

FIG. 6.10
Placing a new Exchange Server into an existing site.

CHAPTER 7

Planning Connections to Microsoft Mail Systems

In this chapter

Integration of Microsoft Mail 3.x (PC and AppleTalk) and your Exchange Server is established with the Microsoft Mail Connector, which essentially combines the functions of a Microsoft Mail gateway post office and External Message Transfer Agent. It also provides the connectivity link that ties Exchange gateways, Microsoft Mail 3.x gateways, and other Exchange connectors. The Microsoft Mail Connector allows Exchange Server to route and transfer messages to one or more Microsoft Mail 3.x (PC) systems over LAN, asynchronous, or X.25 connections.

You can configure Microsoft Mail Connector for message transfer and routing by using components provided with Exchange Server. The components built into the Microsoft Mail Connector are comparable to the components in the Microsoft Mail 3.x Post Office and External message transfer programs. The Microsoft Mail Connector comprises a temporary information store and two components that run as services on a Windows NT Server, which allows for better error logging, memory management, and performance monitoring of the entire messaging system. Integration of an existing Microsoft Mail 3.x system, using the External or the Multitasking MTA programs with Exchange Server, can be easily configured to allow a coexistence of the two messaging systems on the same LAN.

Once you establish the message route, you synchronize the Global Address List (GAL) by implementing Exchange as either a directory synchronization requestor to a Microsoft Mail 3.x directory synchronization server, or a directory synchronization server for all Microsoft Mail 3.x directory synchronization requestors. Later in this chapter, I will give you tips on when to migrate a directory synchronization server from Microsoft Mail 3.x to Exchange.

Understanding Microsoft Mail Connector Components

The following three components are located within the Microsoft Mail Connector and work together to transparently transfer and route messages to and from Microsoft Mail Post Offices (see Figure 7.1):

- Microsoft Mail Connector Interchange
- Microsoft Mail Connector Post Office
- Microsoft Mail Connector MTA (Message Transfer Agent)

Using Microsoft Mail Connector Interchange

The Microsoft Mail Connector Interchange is a Windows NT service that transfers messages between the Exchange MTA and the Microsoft Mail Connector Post Office. Outbound messages are converted to Mail 3.x format and placed into the Connector Post Office in the same file structure and format that Microsoft Mail queues messages for external post offices. Inbound messages are placed in the Connector Post Office by the Microsoft Mail Connector (PC) MTA, converted to Exchange Interpersonal Messages (IPM), and queued for the Exchange MTA. For proper configuration, make the following choices in the Microsoft Mail Connector Interchange tab:

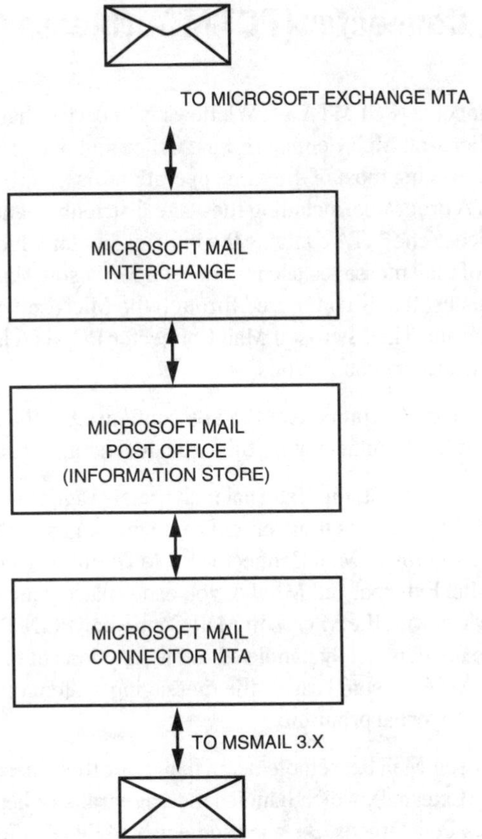

FIG. 7.1
Microsoft Mail Connector components.

- Select an Administrator Mailbox for receiving delivery status messages.
- Select a primary language used by the majority of the Post Offices using the Microsoft Mail Connector.
- Maximize the Microsoft Mail 3.x compatibility to enable Microsoft Mail 3.x clients to view or save OLE documents they receive from Exchange clients.

Using Microsoft Mail Connector Post Office

The Microsoft Mail Connector Post Office is a temporary information store for messages. It resembles the file structure of a Microsoft Mail 3.x Post Office. The Microsoft Mail Connector Post Office has enough of the file structure and support files to receive mail in a Microsoft Mail 3.x format from the Connector Interchange or the Microsoft Mail Connector PC MTA. The Connector Post Office is sometimes referred to as a *gateway Post Office* or *shadow Post Office* because it is dedicated to message transfer and has no local mailboxes.

Using Microsoft Mail Connector (PC) MTA (Message Transfer Agent)

The Microsoft Mail Connector (PC) MTA is a Windows NT service that connects to and transfers mail between the Microsoft Mail Connector Post Office and one or more Microsoft Mail (PC) Post Offices. It can execute most of the same operations as the Microsoft Mail 3.x External and Multitasking MTA programs, including message distribution and delivery to users on Microsoft Mail Post Offices. The MTA contains the information for which the direct and indirect connection routing of mail messages occurs between Microsoft Mail 3.x Post Offices. The information is read from a list that is configured through the Microsoft Mail Connector section of the Administrator program. The Microsoft Mail Connector PC MTA is configured for LAN, asynchronous, and X.25 transport connections.

Once again, all of the Connector's components can be configured in the Administrator program, under the Microsoft Mail Connector, on the individual component's tab.

In a Microsoft Mail 3.x environment, the External mail transfer agent (MTA) and the Multitasking MTA (MMTA) programs transfer and route messages between Microsoft Mail Post Offices. Because the Microsoft Mail Connector PC MTA emulates the message routing ability of the Microsoft Mail External and MMTA, you can replace your existing instances of those programs and services with the Microsoft Mail Connector PC MTA. The Microsoft Mail Connector PC MTA does not completely handle all of the functions of the Microsoft Mail 3.x External or Multitasking MTA. In some cases, the messaging system may still require some of the functions found in the External program.

For example, when Microsoft Mail 3.x remote users dial in for their messages, they dial into the Microsoft Mail MTA (External), which handles message transfer between remote users and the Microsoft Mail 3.x Post Offices. Because some users still use the Microsoft Mail Remote client program, the Microsoft Mail Connector PC MTA cannot replace the Microsoft Mail MTA (External). The continued use of the External program, as well as the Microsoft Mail Connector, must be maintained.

When both Exchange and Microsoft Mail 3.x Post Offices reside on the same LAN, you can configure the Microsoft Mail Connector to transfer route messages from the Exchange Server MTA, convert the message, and deliver the message to the correct recipient on the Microsoft Mail 3.x Post Office.

When you send a message to an Exchange Server destined for a Microsoft Mail 3.x recipient located on the same LAN, the message is received by the Exchange MTA. Then the message is routed by the Exchange MTA to the Microsoft Mail Connector Interchange, where the message and any OLE attachments are converted to Microsoft Mail 3.x format. The converted message is then sent to the Microsoft Mail Connector Post Office (Information Store), where it is held until the Microsoft Mail Connector MTA picks it up and delivers it to the appropriate Microsoft Mail 3.x Post Office (see Figure 7.2).

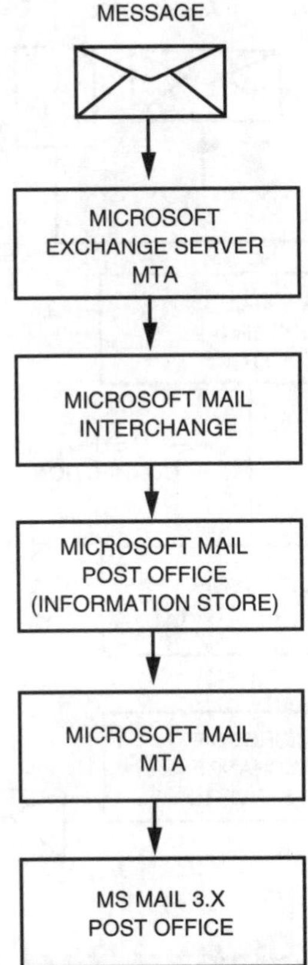

FIG. 7.2
The message transfer process from Exchange Server MTA to Microsoft Mail 3.x.

The Microsoft Mail Connector, External MTA, and Multitasking MTA determine their routing information between Exchange Server and Microsoft Mail 3.x by the information that is entered into the Address Space. The *address space* is defined as a set of Microsoft Mail 3.x Post Office names to which the Microsoft Mail Connector will rout mail messages. This entry in the address space is also known as an *Instance.*

When connecting Microsoft Mail 3.x over X.25 or asynchronous services, you have to configure the External MTA or Multitasking MTA program at the Remote Post Office location with an instance in the address space of the MTA to connect with the Microsoft Mail Connector (see Figure 7.3).

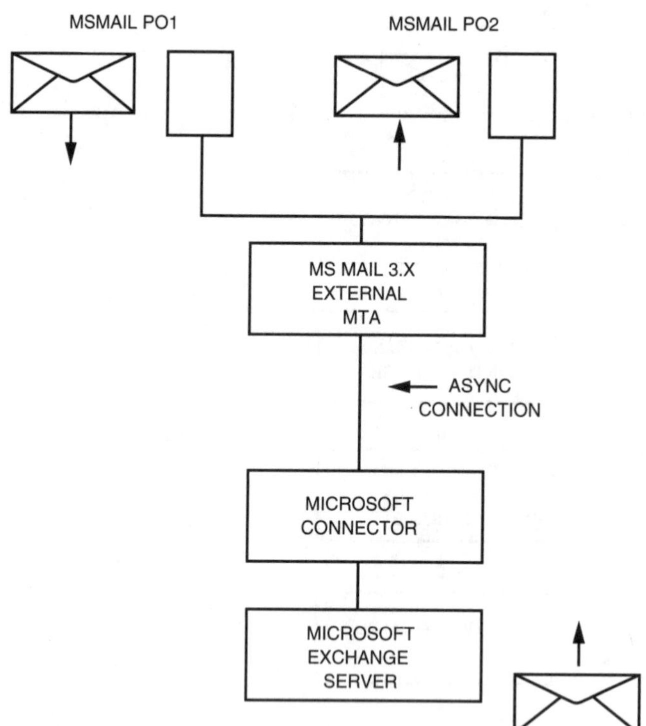

FIG. 7.3
Basic Microsoft Mail 3.x External (or Multitasking MTA) layout.

Configuring Connections to Existing Post Offices

When planning your Exchange integration with Microsoft Mail, it is important to understand your Microsoft Mail 3.x infrastructure. The Microsoft Mail 3.x infrastructure comprises network topologies and message routes. The network topology includes LAN, asynchronous, and X.25. The message routes are either direct connections between two post offices or an indirect connection via another Microsoft Mail 3.x Post Office.

Configuring LAN Connections to Existing Post Offices

The LAN connection happens to be the easiest and one of the simplest types of connections in terms of setup and administration. In this particular case, you don't have to use the External or Multitasking MTA programs at all. Instead, you can use the Administrator program in Exchange Server to configure the majority of the message routing and transfer between the Microsoft Mail Connector and the Microsoft Mail 3.x Post Offices. You can learn more about the Exchange Administration program in Chapter 12, "Using the Administrator Program."

Asynchronous and X.25 Connections for Remote Post Offices

You need two components to connect Exchange Server and a Microsoft Mail 3.x Post Office over an X.25 or asynchronous service. The first is the Microsoft Mail Connector PC MTA. The second is the Microsoft Mail 3.x External or Multitasking MTA program provided with Microsoft Mail 3.x Server. This program provides the message transfer and modem management functions necessary to communicate over a remote connection within a Microsoft Mail 3.x system. If the Microsoft Mail 3.x External MTA will reside on a DOS computer, this needs to be a dedicated computer. DOS does not allow multiple sessions, or executables, to occur at the same time.

Setting up the Multitasking MTA on a Windows NT Workstation allows multiple MTAs to reside and route messages on a single computer. The Multitasking MTA can also reside on a separate Windows NT Server if desired. I recommend using the Windows NT Workstation because it doesn't require passwords.

If a direct asynchronous or X.25 route is desired, Microsoft Mail 3.x External or Multitasking MTA must be located on the same LAN as the remote Post Office (refer to Figure 7.3).

Direct and Indirect Message Routes

As with Microsoft Mail 3.x, message routes from Exchange to Microsoft Mail 3.x can be direct or indirect.

If you have multiple Microsoft Mail 3.x Post Offices on the same LAN, one way to increase the performance of the Exchange Server is to configure a direct connection from Exchange to a Microsoft Mail 3.x Post Office. Configure the remaining Microsoft Mail Post Offices Indirect via the Direct Microsoft Mail 3.x Post Office. Once the single direct message route is established, the Exchange Server has a message route to all Microsoft Mail Post Offices as long as the Exchange infrastructure is properly configured. Performance of the Exchange Server is enhanced because the Microsoft Mail Connector PC MTA forwards and receives mail from only one Microsoft Mail 3.x Post Office. Therefore, the Exchange Server will not have to make network connections to the other Microsoft Mail 3.x Post Offices to deliver or receive mail. This configuration also reduces the complexity of the integration if the indirect post offices need asynchronous or X.25 connections to directly connect to Exchange.

As I mentioned before, it is important that you understand the Microsoft Mail 3.x infrastructure. If it is stable, you can leverage it instead of replacing it with Exchange Components (see Figure 7.4).

Microsoft Mail Connector has an integrated feature that automatically extracts indirect routing information from a Microsoft Mail 3.x Post Office. This feature eliminates the need to manually configure the routing information for each of the Microsoft Mail 3.x Post Offices connected indirectly to the Microsoft Mail Connector. The only requirement for the automatic upload of routing information is a LAN connection. Unfortunately, if the Microsoft Mail 3.x Post Office you are trying to connect to is over an asynchronous or X.25 service, the indirect routing information will have to be entered manually on the Microsoft Mail Connector Properties sheet.

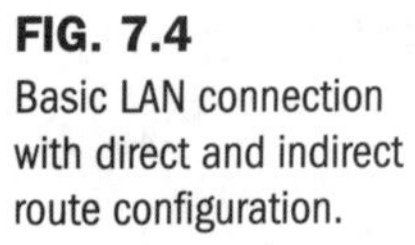

FIG. 7.4
Basic LAN connection with direct and indirect route configuration.

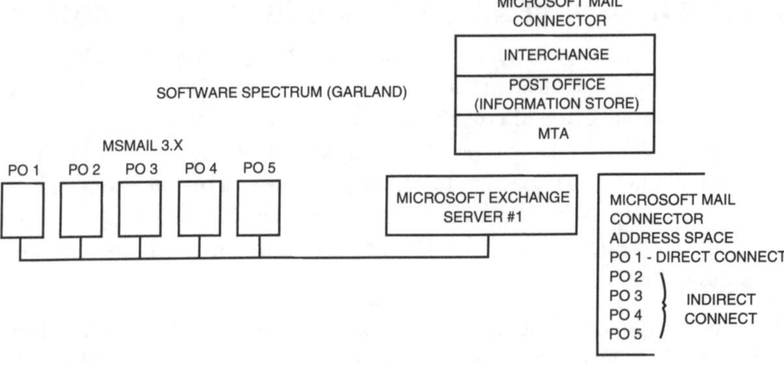

CAUTION

Use this feature with caution, I have seen invalid message routes uploaded into Exchange, which caused circular routing errors.

Optimizing the Exchange and Microsoft Mail Integration

You can optimize your Exchange and Microsoft Mail integration by adding additional Microsoft Mail PC MTAs and Microsoft Mail Connectors. Furthermore, Microsoft Mail 3.x can use Exchange's more robust infrastructure to transfer messages between Microsoft Mail 3.x Post Offices.

Using Multiple Microsoft Mail Connector (PC) MTAs

Each Microsoft Mail MTA instance will react differently depending on the type of connection it uses.

NOTE Each instance is named and registered as a Windows NT service on the Exchange Server computer on which it was created, and it can be started or stopped independently of any other service. ■

Each instance has a primary connection type, although all instances can service LAN-connected Post Offices. Depending on the number of Post Offices and their connection types, it might be more efficient to group the same connection types in the same instance. If the connection types are diverse, multiple instances should be created.

For example, if your network contains ten LAN-connected Microsoft Mail 3.x Post Offices and five asynchronous-connected Microsoft Mail 3.x Post Offices, it would be more efficient to create one instance on the Microsoft Mail Connector MTA for servicing only the LAN-connected Post Offices and another instance for connecting to and servicing the asynchron ous Post Offices.

Using Multiple Microsoft Mail Connectors

If your organization contains a large number of Microsoft Mail 3.x Post Offices, you might need multiple Microsoft Mail Connector MTAs for message connectivity between Microsoft Mail 3.x and Exchange recipients. Because every Exchange Server uses the same Microsoft Mail e-mail address in the site, Microsoft Mail essentially views each of the Exchange sites as one large Microsoft Mail Post Office. Therefore, it is recommended for routing purposes, that one Microsoft Mail Connector MTA should be used for every Exchange Server site. If your Exchange Server Organization has multiple Exchange sites and a large number of Microsoft Mail Post Offices, the post offices can be grouped into clusters much like an Exchange site. Configure each Exchange site with at least one Microsoft Mail Connector with only the address spaces of the Microsoft Mail Post Offices adjacent to the site (such as on the same LAN). Directory replication between Exchange sites makes the other sites aware of the connection to Microsoft Mail.

If you are going to use multiple Microsoft Mail Connectors, make sure each Exchange Server has its own Microsoft Mail Connector MTA. Also, you can use duplicate address entries in two or more Microsoft Mail Connectors to route messages based on cost. This is useful for redundancy and for load balancing of traffic across connections and between servers.

Using Exchange Server as a Backbone to Microsoft Mail (PC)

Because Exchange provides a more robust and stable infrastructure, you may consider replacing your existing Microsoft Mail infrastructure with an Exchange backbone. Using an Exchange Organization as a backbone enables Microsoft Mail Post Office to Post Office traffic to use Exchange messaging components such as site connectors.

To backbone Microsoft Mail over Exchange, verify the following things:

- The Microsoft Mail Connectors are properly configured to transfer mail between Exchange and Microsoft Mail Post Office clusters.
- The directory replication between Exchange sites has replicated the routing entries on each Microsoft Mail Connector.
- Your Microsoft Mail external routing definitions should use the Microsoft Mail administration program for each Microsoft Mail Post Office to be indirect via the adjacent Exchange site (see Figure 7.5).

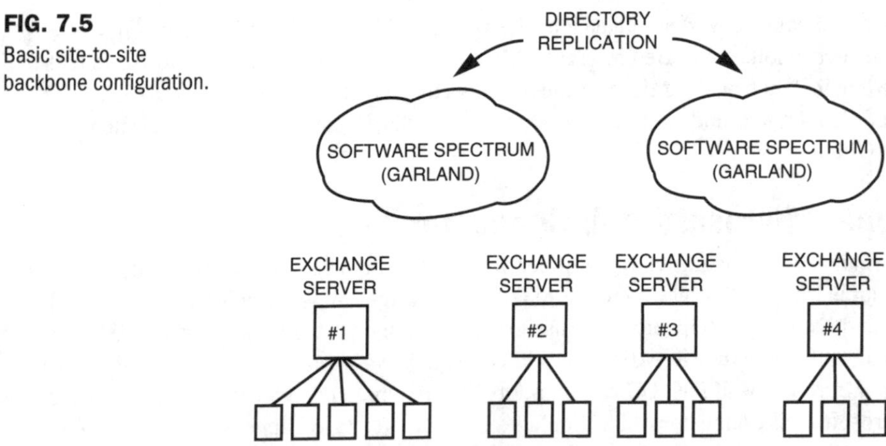

FIG. 7.5
Basic site-to-site backbone configuration.

Using Existing Microsoft Mail (PC) Gateways

Exchange Server supports a wide variety of Microsoft Mail (PC) gateways, which grant messaging services to other messaging systems. Supported Microsoft Mail (PC) gateways include the following:

- AT&T Easylink
- Fax
- IBM PROFS and OfficeVision
- MHS
- SNADS
- MCI Mail Gateway (M-Bridge for Microsoft Mail for PC Networks)

All of these gateway programs come with Microsoft Mail Server 3.x on an options disk included with the software. Each of the gateway programs requires a short installation and configuration process. They are menu driven and easy to follow.

There are two ways Exchange clients can pass information through an existing Microsoft Mail 3.x mail system gateway. First, a typical gateway scenario in an existing Microsoft Mail 3.x environment has the Microsoft Mail 3.x gateway software running on a dedicated computer. A Microsoft Mail 3.x Post Office needs to be selected as the gateway Post Office. All messages destined for the foreign mail system will pass through this gateway Post Office, and vice versa. In order for Exchange clients to access the actual gateway and pass messages to the foreign mail system, the Exchange Connector Post Office must have the Microsoft Mail 3.x gateway access component installed (see Figure 7.6). Second, if an Exchange Server is selected as the gateway Post Office, the Microsoft Mail 3.x Post Offices must have a gateway access component. Either way enables integration of an Exchange Server into an existing Microsoft Mail 3.x gateway scenario (see Figure 7.7).

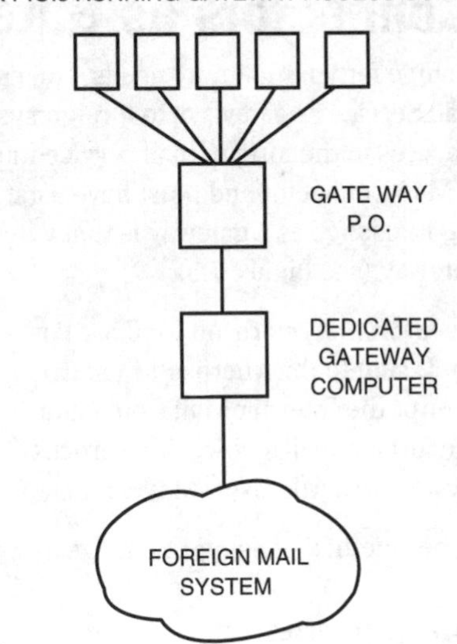

FIG. 7.6
Basic Microsoft Mail 3.x gateway layout.

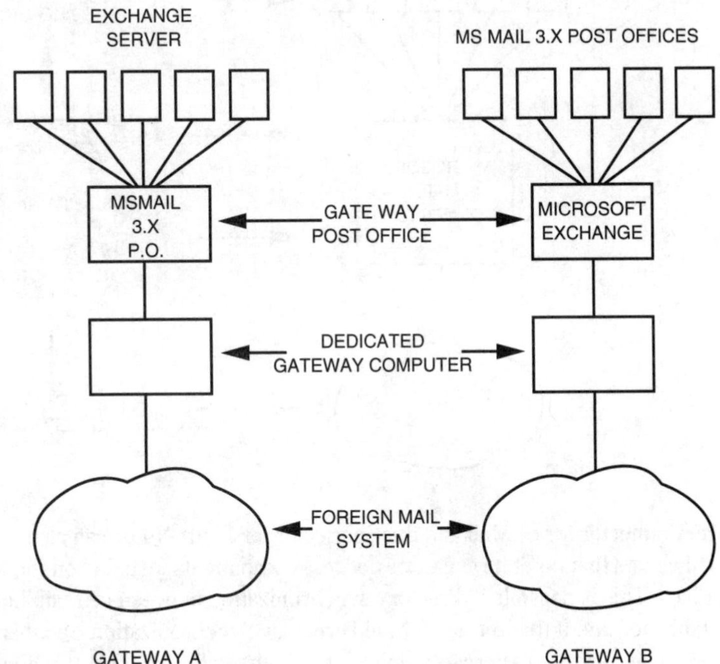

FIG. 7.7
A typical gateway scenario.

Using Exchange Connectors as Gateways

If you decide to use Exchange for your gateway needs, you can use the Exchange X.400 Connector or the Internet Mail Service as gateways to foreign systems. The Microsoft Mail 3.x Post Office that is given access to the foreign mail service must be connected to the Exchange Server via the Microsoft Mail Connector and must have a gateway access component installed on it. One benefit of using Exchange as a gateway is that you don't have to have a dedicated computer running the gateway (see Figure 7.8).

When a mail message is sent from a Microsoft Mail 3.x Post Office destined for the foreign mail service, the message is sent to the Microsoft Mail Connector, which passes it to either the Exchange X.400 Connector or the Internet Mail Connector. The selected connector then passes the message to the foreign mail service. The process is reversed for a message traveling from a foreign mail system to a Microsoft Mail 3.x Post Office.

Figure 7.8 illustrates another method of using Exchange as a gateway.

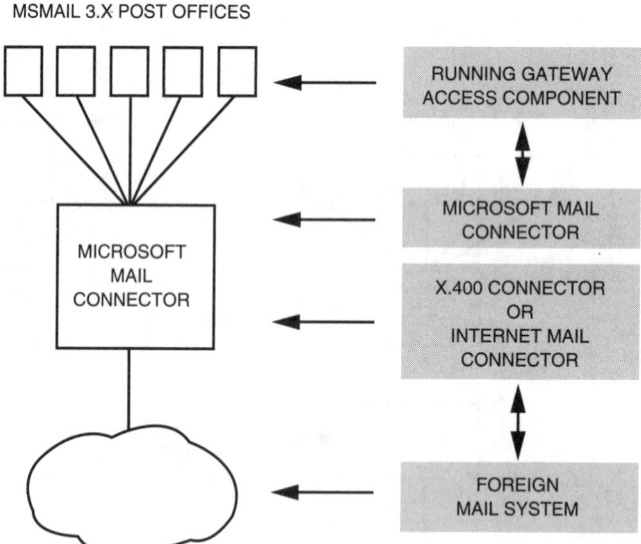

FIG. 7.8
Using Exchange as a gateway.

The Connector for cc:Mail and the Connector for Lotus Notes can also be used by Microsoft Mail clients that don't have gateway access components installed on the Microsoft Mail Post Offices. This is possible if directory synchronization between cc:Mail/Lotus Notes has been established and if the Microsoft Mail Directory Synchronization Agent is configured to export custom recipients to Microsoft Mail Global Address Books (GAL). When directory synchronization occurs between Exchange and Microsoft Mail, custom recipients of Microsoft Mail proxy addresses are synchronized with the Microsoft Mail 3.x address book. Therefore, a message composed to the cc:Mail/Lotus Notes user from Microsoft Mail will be sent to Exchange through the Microsoft Mail Connector because it has the appropriate network and post office address from the Exchange Server Microsoft Mail proxy generator. The Exchange MTA then queues the message with the appropriate connector, based on the type of custom recipient.

Directory Replication and Synchronization

It is important that you understand the difference between Exchange directory replication and directory synchronization.

Directory replication is the automatic process of updating the directories between Exchange Server and Exchange Server sites. The replicated information includes all the information available about an organization's resources and users, including mailboxes, public folders, distribution lists, servers, and more. Other components use the directory to map addresses and route messages. Replication can also be configured to automatically replicate all directory information or only the desired amount of the directory information between multiple Exchange sites.

Directory synchronization is the process of synchronizing an Exchange global address directory with post office addresses from Microsoft Mail (PC) and Microsoft Mail (AppleTalk) systems. To do this, you use the Microsoft Mail 3.x DISPATCH program included with the Microsoft Mail 3.x Server. As in directory replication between Exchange Server sites, during synchronization, only the desired information is transferred using *trust levels*.

In order for an Exchange Server to accomplish directory synchronization with a Microsoft Mail 3.x mail system, the Exchange Server must be running the Microsoft Mail 3.x Directory Synchronization Agent. The Directory Synchronization Agent on an Exchange Server plays one of two roles depending on the mail system environment: DIRSYNC Server or DIRSYNC Requester (see Figure 7.9). On an existing Microsoft Mail 3.x system, the Exchange server can be configured as either a DIRSYNC Server or Requestor (see Figure 7.10). However, the Exchange Server cannot be configured as both a Server and a Requestor simultaneously. On a Microsoft Mail 3.x mail system, there can be only one DIRSYNC Server. All of the rest of the Microsoft Mail 3.x Post Offices can be configured as DIRSYNC Requestors.

If the Exchange Server is configured as the DIRSYNC Server, it can synchronize all other Microsoft Mail 3.x Post Offices set up as DIRSYNC Requestors.

You may be tempted to migrate your directory synchronization server to Exchange Server if you are having trouble maintaining your Global Address List (GAL) on Microsoft Mail. Before migrating the directory server, it is important to understand which cycle is failing on the Microsoft Mail Directory Synchronization Protocol. The Microsoft Mail Directory Synchronization Protocol comprises three schedule events:

Time 1 (T1) is when updates are sent from directory synchronization requestors. All post offices are required to send address book updates to the directory synchronization server.

Time 2 (T2) is when the directory synchronization server takes all the updates from the requestors and processes a master transaction list that is sent back to the directory requestors.

Time 3 (T3) is when the requestors update their Global Address Lists from the update sent from the directory synchronization server.

Usually the cycle that fails on Microsoft Mail is the T3 cycle, which prohibits a proper rebuild of the Global Address List (GAL) on that Microsoft Mail Post Office, giving the impression that the directory server is not performing the T2 cycle. Migrating the directory synchronization server from Microsoft Mail to Exchange only migrates the T2 cycle, which is usually stable on Microsoft Mail. I generally do not move the directory synchronization server to Exchange unless it is necessary to decommission the Microsoft Mail Post Office that is the directory synchronization server.

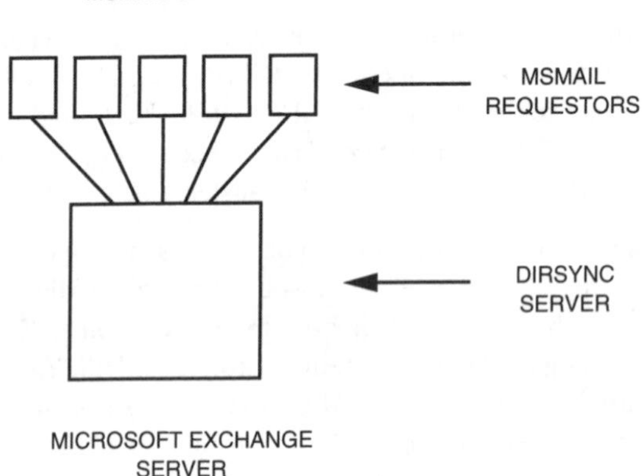

FIG. 7.9 Using Exchange as a DIRSYNC Server on an existing Microsoft Mail system.

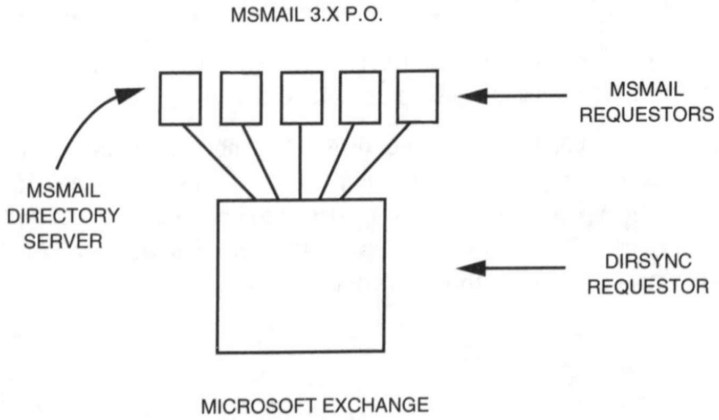

FIG. 7.10 Using Exchange as a DIRSYNC Requestor on an existing Microsoft Mail system.

CHAPTER 8

Migrating from Microsoft Mail Systems

In this chapter

Migration is the process of moving users from Microsoft Mail 3.x to Exchange. Planning the migration involves moving user mailboxes, calendars, Personal Address Books, shared folders, and connections to foreign systems.

As is true when planning the Microsoft Mail Connector, understanding your Microsoft Mail 3.x infrastructure is crucial to planning the migration to Exchange. Additionally, it is just as critical that you understand the Exchange infrastructure you are migrating to. This includes the technical infrastructure and the readiness of the support infrastructure required for maintaining users on a new messaging system.

When you are ready to migrate, you can use Exchange's many migration features that support multiple scenarios for interconnecting to other mail systems. Tools like the Migration Wizard simplify the migration process and ensure a smooth transition to Exchange.

Planning the Migration Strategy

Three strategies exist for the migration of Microsoft Mail 3.x Post Offices to Exchange Server. You will determine the appropriate strategy for your organization based on the readiness of the organization and its users to migrate mail platforms. Before you learn to identify the factors affecting your readiness to migrate, you need to understand the migration strategies available:

- *Single-Phase Migration.* Use this process when migrating all of the Microsoft Mail 3.x Post Offices at once to Exchange. This strategy eliminates the need for coexistence between the messaging systems and simplifies the migration process. This process requires the full readiness of an organization to migrate to Exchange.
- *Multi-Phase Migration/Entire Post Office.* Use this strategy when entire Microsoft Mail 3.x Post Offices are to be migrated to Exchange but not all at the same time. This strategy requires coexistence between the Microsoft Mail Post Offices and Exchange.
- *Multi-Phase Migration/Partial Post Office.* Use this strategy (the most common) when groups of users migrate from a Microsoft Mail Post Office but leave other Microsoft Mail users behind. This is common during pilot deployments and limited rollouts. This strategy also requires coexistence between Microsoft Mail Post Offices and Exchange.

Determining the Migration Strategy

Which strategy is best for your organization depends on the readiness of the organization to migrate messaging platforms.

Many factors determine the readiness of an organization for migration. To determine the level of readiness, I use a checklist made up of business and technical factors that impact the readiness of the migration. The significance of the impact varies among organizations depending on the situations they are in. For example, when Software Spectrum rolled out Outlook 97, user training was a significant factor affecting the migration date because the user community was already accustomed to messaging clients.

Use the following list to gauge your level of migration readiness:

- *Stable exchange infrastructure.* The Exchange infrastructure must be stable in order to migrate users to it. Migrating users to an infrastructure that is not reliable is dangerous. I have seen clients migrated to Exchange while servers were constantly crashing due to hardware problems. The user community lost faith in the product and in the people rolling it out.
- *Resource availability during migration.* If the number of Microsoft Mail 3.x Post Offices to be migrated is too great for your staff to migrate at once, a multi-phase migration will be required.
- *Client software.* The user community must have an Exchange client in order to access the mail from the Exchange Server. The migration rate may be dictated by the client software deployment rate.
- *Messaging gateways.* Ensure that connections to foreign systems such as the Internet and X.400 are available to Exchange users.
- *Mail-enabled applications.* Determine if the mail-enabled applications currently using Microsoft Mail 3.x as a transport work on Exchange as well.
- *Identify mail administrators.* Identifying the mail administrators and coordinating the efforts of the administrators is essential to a successful migration. This is especially true for worldwide migrations to Exchange.
- *User migration plan.* No matter which strategy you use, ensure that you have a migration plan that identifies who is migrating to which Exchange Servers and when.
- *Training.* Ensure that the users receive enough training to ensure they are self-sufficient at using Exchange. This is critical to keeping the support costs to a minimum.
- *User communication.* Much like the training, user communication regarding when users are migrated and what to expect after they have been migrated is critical to reducing the cost of support.

Using Single-Phase Migration

Depending on the size of your organization and your human resources department, you may be able to do a one-step migration. This can happen overnight, on a weekend, or during a company shutdown time. If your organization can't tolerate the downtime or doesn't have the resources to migrate everyone in one weekend, phased migration is the best choice.

Instant migration may be better for your organization if your organization meets the following criteria:

- There is little or no existing data to move from the old system.
- You have enough human resources to migrate everyone in a night, over a weekend, or during a traditional company shutdown time.
- All hardware and system software is in place.

One-step migration takes extra planning in the areas of:

- Replacing existing workflow applications
- User and help desk training
- Preparing for roll out and resource needs
- Preparing for contingencies

Should you choose to go with a single mail provider, such as the Exchange Server, the single provider option provides for these scenarios:

- Every mailbox on the post office migrates
- Only some mailboxes on a post office migrate, and their addresses change

Update the Global Address List and the directory. Mail sent to the old addresses from the Personal Address Books and personal address lists will be returned as nondeliverable (if you delete the old mailbox), or it will pile up in the old mailbox.

Using Multi-Phase Migration

If a multi-phased migration is required, you must add the following items to your list of factors that determine the readiness of the organization to migrate messaging platforms:

- *Establish reliable message transfer.* Before migrating users from Microsoft Mail 3.x to Exchange, you must ensure that the message route between Microsoft Mail and Exchange is stable. User messages, calendar free and busy times, and directory synchronization all require a stable integration.
- *Establish reliable directory synchronization.* Directory synchronization between Microsoft Mail and Exchange is critical to the success of the migration. Some organizations do not realize they have directory synchronization problems until mass changes are made to the messaging recipients. During normal operations, the address book remains relatively constant. During a migration, the Global Address Book on Microsoft Mail 3.x Post Offices must be up to date.
- *Applications coexist on different platforms.* During the phased migration, users can use mail-enabled applications on Microsoft Mail 3.x and Exchange. Ensure that the applications will not lose functionality during the migration.
- *Determine a plan for Schedule+ resources.* Exchange clients cannot directly book Schedule+ resources. To use the Schedule+ resource account, an assistant must accept incoming mail messages from Exchange clients who want to book the resource. If you are migrating to Outlook, the Schedule+ resource can migrate to Exchange before users, which allows Schedule+ and Outlook 97 users to directly book resource accounts using an automated assistant to accept incoming meeting requests.

Multi-Phase Migration/Partial Post Office Migrating everyone from an existing post office at the same time is not always possible. Some users might be waiting for hardware upgrades. Or the migration might be a pilot (test) or a limited rollout. When migrating partial post offices, consider the following facts:

- Routing to old post offices must be maintained so that the remaining users continue to receive mail.
- Mail sent to migrated mailboxes that passes through Microsoft Mail (PC) gateways will either be delivered to the Microsoft Mail (PC) mailbox or returned as undeliverable.
- Directories in Microsoft Mail (PC) and with Microsoft Mail (PC) gateways that have the old mailbox address have to be updated immediately because the old address is invalid.
- Users who are still on Microsoft Mail (PC) can reply to any mail they received in the past from a migrated user, but the reply will either be delivered to the Microsoft Mail (PC) mailbox or returned as undeliverable.
- For users who are still on Microsoft Mail (PC), any Personal Address Book or personal address list entries they have for migrated mailboxes will be invalid.

NOTE No routing changes are required or allowed during a partial post office migration. Mail must continue to be delivered to the mailboxes remaining on the post office. ■

As a part of your migration plan, you must know how many mailboxes at a time will be migrated to Exchange servers. As a general rule, migrating the entire post office (every mailbox) is easier to plan for, implement, and maintain than migrating a partial post office. However, migrating a partial post office is sometimes necessary, such as during a pilot or limited roll out when the number of users is small and the issues are easier to solve or work around. The following section explains why this is so.

Multi-Phase Migration/Whole Post Office If you migrate every mailbox on a post office, you can maintain the original Network/Post Office/Mailbox format of Microsoft Mail address for each old mailbox as one of the proxy or e-mail addresses of the new mailbox. This has many advantages:

- With limited routing changes, mail continues to be delivered without interruption.
- Mail sent to migration mailboxes that passes through Microsoft Mail (PC) gateways will be delivered.
- Directories in Microsoft Mail (PC) Post Offices and foreign systems connected to them with Microsoft Mail (PC) gateways that have the old mailbox address do not have to be updated immediately because the old address is still valid.
- Users who are still on Microsoft Mail (PC) can reply to any mail they received in the past from a migrated user.
- For users who are still on Microsoft Mail (PC), any Personal Address Book or personal address list entries they have for migrated mailboxes are still valid.

PC Mail Pass-Through Retaining the original e-mail address provides for pass-through from Microsoft Mail (PC) gateways. The Microsoft Mail Connector Post Office must have an access component for the gateway installed. Because the Microsoft Mail-type addresses for migrated mailboxes have not changed, the mail will be routed from the gateway to the Microsoft Mail Connector and from there to the Exchange mailbox.

Resolving Migration Issues

Not all of these issues will apply to your installation. For all issues that do apply, you will need to understand how they impact your organization.

Personal Address Books for Users Who Haven't Migrated

Personal Address Book (PAB) entries function similarly to replies. For Microsoft Mail (PC) users, their personal address book addresses continue to work for migrated mailboxes because the addresses are the same.

Migrated Personal Address Book entries will work for Microsoft Mail (PC) mailboxes that have not migrated. This means that if you do not update your Personal Address Book with the new Exchange e-mail addresses, some e-mail will still be directed to Microsoft Mail mailboxes that no longer exist. Mail addressed to mailboxes that have since migrated will be routed to the Microsoft Mail Connector. Because the Microsoft Mail Connector does not have a post office configured with that address, it will return the mail as undeliverable. This undeliverable mail can be re-addressed from the Exchange Server's Global Address List and can be delivered normally.

There is no tool that updates the user's Personal Address Book entries as changes are made in the Exchange Server's global address list. To avoid addressing undeliverable mail, users can remove all personal entries of the type MS from their Personal Address Books after the entries have been migrated to Exchange mailboxes.

Using Exchange Clients with the Microsoft Mail Post Office

The Exchange Windows clients can be used as clients for Microsoft Mail (PC) Post Offices. To do so, you must add the Microsoft Mail service provider to the profile. This can be done before migration. It can also be done before or during phased migration. It is important to move users to the new client while retaining the post office infrastructure.

Even if only the clients are migrated to Exchange, they will enjoy all the benefits listed at the end of the previous section. With this strategy, all users will also have a consistent user interface.

To install Exchange client, users need the Profile Wizard. The Profile Wizard is included with the client setup software. The Profile Wizard pulls default information for connecting to the post office from the MSMAIL.INI file.

NOTE To use the Microsoft Mail Post Office, also called the Microsoft Mail provider, you will need to make the Microsoft Mail (PC) provider the default for the client profile, which you do by using the Setup Editor. The Setup Editor allows complete configuration of the Exchange client prior to installation on the user's PC. This is also true for installing the Exchange provider. ■

After the client software is installed on the user's PC, the user imports the contents of the Microsoft Mail Message File (MMF) file into the Exchange inbox format. If the MMF file is in the post office, the user should move the MMF file to the local disk or a viewable network share before importing the contents. If the MMF file is left on the post office, the contents will be migrated to Exchange when the mailbox is migrated.

After a user begins using Exchange client, there is no easy way to migrate the messages he or she receives to an MMF or mailbag file. He or she can copy the messages to a shared folder and then retrieve them with the old client, but this does not guarantee privacy of the messages.

Having discussed one method for migration to Exchange, we will now discuss migrating the MMF files from Microsoft Mail into the Exchange format. In addition, we will discuss issues associated with upgrading from Schedule+ version 1.0 clients to Exchange Schedule+ version 7.0 clients.

Exchange client users must migrate their mail message files to a personal folder file. When MMFs are stored on a post office, you can use the MMFClean utility to manage their sizes and the ages of messages (how long a message will be kept on file before it is automatically deleted). Personal folder files should not be stored on the post office.

The MMF Migration tool does not delete the MMF when it creates the personal folder file. It also does not move MMF files locally or delete them after their contents are migrated to personal folder files.

Users who switch to the Exchange client must also switch from Schedule+ 1.0 to Schedule+ 7.5. When they run Schedule+ 7.5 for the first time, it migrates their CAL (Schedule+ 1.0 calendar format) file to an SCD (Schedule+ 7.5 calendar format) file.

Schedule+ 7.5 can read CAL, POF (Schedule+ 1.0 post office free/busy times), and SCD files, but Schedule+ 1.0 can read only CAL and POF files. If your users make heavy use of Schedule+, switch everyone over to the new client at the same time. If some people switch to Schedule+ 7.5, the rest will not be able to view their coworkers' calendars or act as their coworkers' delegate.

Groups and Distribution Lists

Microsoft Mail 3.x groups have many limitations once they span Microsoft Mail 3.x Post Offices. For instance, mail sent from one post office to a mixed-member group on another post office is delivered only to the local members of a group. Exchange distribution lists resolve this problem. If you have established successful integration between Microsoft Mail and Exchange, it is beneficial to consolidate the duplicated Microsoft Mail groups to single distribution lists on Exchange in order to reduce the amount of administration during a phased migration.

Shared and Group Folders to Public Folders

The Migration Wizard will migrate (copy) Microsoft Mail 3.x shared folders to Exchange public folders with the appropriate permissions assigned as specified in the wizard. Once the shared folder is migrated, there is no way to automatically replicate the contents of Exchange public folders to Microsoft Mail 3.x shared folders. Depending on the migration strategy and the use of Microsoft Mail 3.x shared folders, this could have a significant impact on the readiness of the organization to migrate.

Schedule+ Messages and Calendars

Schedule+ calendar files migrate with the user's MMF files during a migration using the Migration Wizard. When the calendar file is migrated to the Exchange Server, the calendar file password is also migrated. Prior to the migration, remind users not to forget their Schedule+ passwords because they will be required to complete the migration.

Reviewing a Sample Migration

A three-phased approach is used to simplify the task of migration. Each phase can consist of numerous individual tasks. On a high level, these three phases will apply to any organization. The following sample walks you through the migration process for an actual organization.

Software Spectrum has its headquarters in Garland, TX, and has other offices in Los Angeles, CA and London, England (see Figure 8.1). The two American offices are connected over a T1 line. The headquarters and the London office are connected over a T3 line network that uses X.400 services.

Software Spectrum's e-mail system consists of 10 Microsoft Mail Post Offices: five in Garland, two in Los Angeles, and three in London. In this example, all the PCs are using the Microsoft Mail service and the Windows 95 operating system. This enables Software Spectrum to use the Exchange client with its existing Microsoft Mail Post Offices.

Phase One: Migrating Headquarters to Exchange

Headquarters installs a Windows NT-based server with Exchange Server. Then, using the built-in Migration tool, the company migrates its Microsoft Mail Post Offices at headquarters to Exchange.

The Migration tool converts Microsoft Mail messages, Personal Address Book data, attachments, private folders, and meeting requests to the Exchange format and creates new accounts on the Exchange system.

At headquarters, they simultaneously start installing the Exchange Server driver on each of the Windows 95-based workstations to access the Exchange Server. Those still using the Microsoft Mail 3.x service can continue to communicate with other users of Microsoft Mail and Exchange, but they lack the enhanced functionality provided by Exchange. (See Table 8.1 for a comparison of Microsoft Mail client versus Exchange client functionality.)

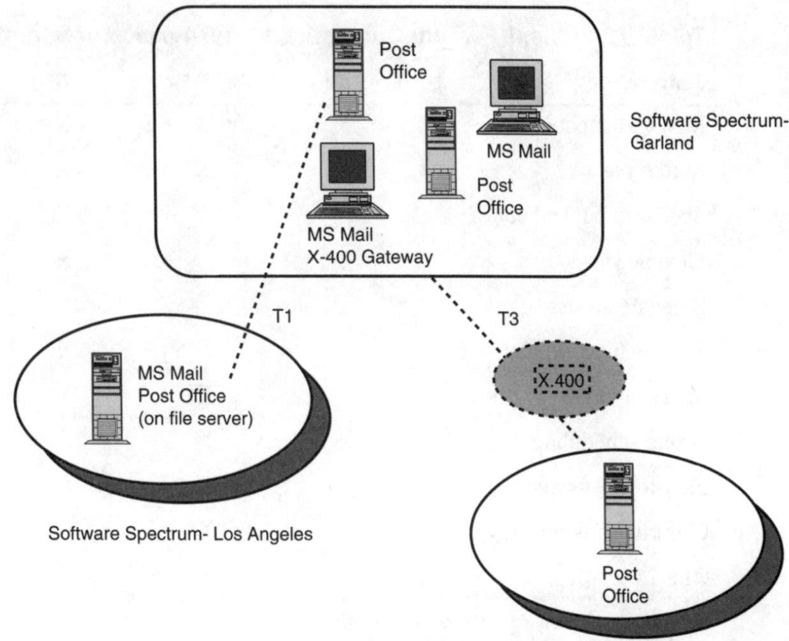

FIG. 8.1
A sample migration that uses the three-phase method.

Installing Exchange Server consolidates the functions of three machines (the two Microsoft Mail post offices and the X.400 gateway) onto one machine. It also adds single-seat administration, connection monitoring, and performance monitoring. Exchange users can use Microsoft Mail 3.x gateways, and Microsoft Mail users can use the Exchange gateways.

After the Exchange driver is installed on all workstations, users in the Garland office have access to the complete functionality of Exchange, including these features:

- The ability to send multiple messages to the same recipient
- Rich text formatting and OLE
- Information-sharing capabilities through public folders
- Flexible views
- Easy-to-use forms
- Improved group scheduling and task management
- Search tools to save time locating addresses

Exchange users in Garland can continue to communicate with their counterparts in Los Angeles and London. This enables the company to migrate in stages while still enabling all users to:

- Exchange mail messages with attached files and embedded objects
- Exchange meeting requests and free/busy information
- Take advantage of improved group scheduling and task management capabilities.

Table 8.1 Client Feature Comparison After Phases of Migration

Feature	A*	B*	C*
Rich text support	X	X	X
Auto reply		X	X
Access to public folders			X
Flexible views	X		X
Delegate access			X
Remote functionality	X	X	X
Rich searches		X	X
Group scheduling	X	X	X
Easy-to-use forms	X	X	X
Central forms registry		X	
OLE 2.0		X	X

**A—Microsoft Mail 3.x client/Microsoft Mail Post Office*
**B—Microsoft Exchange client/Microsoft Mail 3.x Post Office*
**C—Microsoft Exchange client/Microsoft Exchange Server*

Phase Two: Coexistence

Next, the company installs Exchange Server in the Los Angeles office and combines existing users of the two Microsoft Mail Post Offices on that server.

The organization still uses Microsoft Mail Post Offices at the remote locations. Using the Exchange Server as an MTA between the Exchange Servers and the Microsoft Mail Post Offices offers these advantages:

- *Auto routing.* The server automatically configures itself for efficient routing.
- *Load balancing.* If one communication link fails, the MTA automatically configures itself to balance the load over the remaining communication links.
- *Least-cost routing.* This enables administrators to assign costs to communications lines so the MTAs can intelligently route information over the line with the lowest cost. Combined with load balancing, this provides the highest availability of lines at the lowest cost.

Software Spectrum also installs Exchange clients on all PCs at the Los Angeles office to access the Exchange Server. At the end of phase two, all users in Garland and Los Angeles have access to the complete functionality of the Exchange system. They can also continue to exchange messages with users in London via the X.400 connector by way of a "pass-through gateway." The Microsoft Mail Connector manages the directory exchange between Exchange and Microsoft Mail during this coexistence phase.

Phase Three: Completing the Migration

In the final migration phase, the London office installs Windows NT Server and Exchange on both the server and the workstations. This consolidates the Microsoft Mail 3.x Post Office and the Microsoft Mail gateway onto one server. Now users across the enterprise have full use of Exchange's rich functionality and are able to share information with everyone else in their organization at any time.

The company has realized the cost savings of consolidating the functions of nine machines into three, and it has condensed the administration for all three offices onto one Windows NT-based workstation. They have a consistent enterprise-wide messaging and information-exchange system with the features listed here, and they can install additional Exchange gateways to extend these capabilities beyond the enterprise.

- AutoSignature
- Blind carbon copy (BCC)
- Universal inbox in Windows 95
- Rich text
- Views
- Schedule+ 7.5/Outlook
- Built-in remote client

By using the three-phase method, Software Spectrum was able to aggressively migrate the Microsoft Mail community one geographic site at a time to Exchange, while providing coexistence services to continue messaging interoperability.

Understanding Migration Package Elements

The following sections cover the main elements of Exchange's Migration package. This package allows you to implement Exchange into environments with legacy mail systems. Its tools assist with the extraction of e-mail addresses from the legacy systems and with importing them into Exchange.

Several tools assist with the migration from Microsoft Mail to Exchange. These tools include the functionality to extract mailbox information from the legacy system. In addition, there is a server component called a Microsoft Mail "server" post office. This post office resides on the Exchange Server and can be accessed only by the Exchange and Microsoft Mail MTAs.

Source Extractor

There is a Source Extractor for every system such as Microsoft Mail, PROFS, and the like. The Source Extractor extracts users, inboxes, folders, and address books from the source mail systems.

Components of the Source Extractor tool include the directory agent that facilitates the DIRSYNC process via the Exchange Microsoft Mail Server Post Office. Other components include the free/busy connector, which allows for group scheduling information, and the pass-through connectivity, which interconnects with Exchange. The following two components are also included:

- The Migration Assistant converts all extracted data from the source system to Exchange.
- The Migration Wizard guides administrators through migration. There is an option included for one-step migration.

Microsoft Mail Connector

The term *Connector* has taken the place of the Microsoft Mail Transfer Agent (MMTA) in Microsoft Mail. The Connector is the main link between users of Exchange and Microsoft Mail (PC), as well as Microsoft Mail gateways and Exchange gateways. Three components make up the Microsoft Mail Connector:

- *Connector PC MTA*. Connector PC MTA is a message transfer agent, similar to the MTA. It routes mail between a Microsoft Mail Post Office and the Connector Post Office or between a Microsoft Mail gateway and the Exchange Server.
- *Connector Post Office*. Connector Post Office is the data file structure used to store messages in transit between users of Exchange, Microsoft Mail, and gateways.
- *Microsoft Mail (PC) Interchange*. Microsoft Mail (PC) Interchange manages the transfer and translation of messages stored in the Connector Post Office to the Exchange MTA, and vice versa.

These components make up the Mail Connector, which allows Exchange users to transparently send and receive messages and files, meeting requests, and free/busy information with users on Microsoft Mail.

Directory Exchange Agent

The Directory Exchange Agent (DXA) in Exchange enhances directory synchronization with flexible scheduling, better time zone management, and update scheduling. Its multithreaded design improves throughput. Because the DXA includes multiple server support, the directory synchronization load is distributed across multiple DIRSYNC servers for increased reliability and faster response. This reduces address list maintenance, increases security, and assures that updates occur more promptly.

Schedule+ Free and Busy Gateway

The Schedule+ Free and Busy Gateway enables users who remain on Schedule+ version 1.0 using Microsoft Mail 3.x servers to see free/busy information in the planner view for users who are on the new release of Schedule+ on the Exchange Server computer, and vice versa. The data from each server platform is replicated across the connector and appears to users on the other platform.

Pass-Through Connectivity

Exchange Server offers group distribution list support and enables Microsoft Mail users to send messages to X.400 and SMTP environments through the Microsoft Mail Connector. Messages sent from the Microsoft Mail 3.x users through the Exchange Server computer can use the Exchange X.400 Connector and the Internet Mail Connector to interchange messages with these environments. Alternatively, Exchange users can send messages through any of the Microsoft Mail gateways by way of the Microsoft Mail Connector.

Using the Migration Wizard

You can use the Migration Wizard to migrate one or more mailboxes on a Microsoft Mail for PC Networks post office or to PST files. Using the Migration Wizard to move user mail, Personal Address Books, and schedule information to a PST file is new to Exchange 5.5. When each mailbox on the post office is migrated, you have a choice of what information to migrate.

The following is a list of available components to migrate into the Exchange environment:

- Messages, attachments, private folders, and contents of mail message files (MMF)
- Schedule+ data
- Shared and group folders
- Personal Address Book entries

The list covers the components from the actual mailbox containing data to the Schedule+ file and then the group or shared folders and the Personal Address Book entries on a user's local PC. When migrating to PST files, the group or shared folders cannot be migrated.

NOTE Make sure there is no mail activity during migration. Any mail activity can cause the senders' and recipients' mailboxes to not be up to date at the time of the migration.

Migrating Preparations

You should take the following precautionary measures before migrating in order to ensure safe migration of data:

- Make sure the Migration Wizard and necessary files are installed with the Administrator program.
- Install the Exchange Administrator program on a Windows NT computer with the Setup program.
- Compare free hard drive space on the server to the post office volume.

  The server should have plenty of available space—at least twice as much as the post office volume. If free hard disk space is less than twice the post office volume, you should watch available space with the Performance Monitor during migration. Stop migration if free space reaches less than 5 MB.

- Shut down the Exchange Server MTA, Connector, and gateway services.

  Modify or shut down any server monitors that would restart these services. If these services are running while you're using the Migration Wizard and you need to restore your Exchange Server from backup, any mail delivered during the failed migration attempt is lost.
- Shut down any MTA, External, or gateway programs that connect to this post office.

  You can restart MTA and External programs after modifying their .INI files or command line options so they do not connect to this post office. The Migration Wizard requires that no mail be delivered to mailboxes during migration.
- Disconnect the clients.

  All users on both the post office and the Exchange Server must exit and log off of their client programs. Use your network software with Microsoft Mail (PC) to check for connections to the post office share. Use the Administrator program on the Exchange Server to check the Mailbox Logons and Public Folder Logons options in the server's private and public information store properties sheets, respectively.
- If you are copying the post office to the Exchange server for migration, copy it now. When the copying is finished, you can restore MTA, External, gateway, and client connections.
- Back up the Exchange Server information store and directory.

  Back up the post office. (This is not an absolute requirement because data on the post office is read, not deleted.) You need read and write access to the post office because a date stamp is modified in each MMF as it is migrated.

Creating the User List

To create the user list from a Microsoft Mail (PC) Post Office, complete the following steps:

1. (Optional) Map a drive letter or connect to a file server where the post office resides. You will need read and write access to the share or volume, and you must have the name and password of the administrator.
2. From the taskbar, choose Programs, and then select the Exchange folder.
3. In the Exchange folder, choose Exchange Migration Wizard.
4. Select Migrate from Microsoft Mail for PC Networks, and then choose the Next button.
5. Read the informational screen and choose the Next button.
6. In the Path to Microsoft Mail Post Office box, type the path to the post office, or choose the Browse button and specify the path to the post office.
7. In the Account Name box, type the mailbox name of an administrator on the post office.
8. In the Password box, type the password for this mailbox. Then choose the Next button.
9. Select Two Step Migration and choose the Next button.

10. Select Extract a User List File. Then, in the User List to Be Created box, type the path and file name of the new user list, or choose the Browse button and specify the path and file name.
11. Choose the Next button.
12. In the Select Which Accounts You Would Like to Migrate box, choose the mailboxes you want to migrate, or choose the Select All button to select all mailboxes.
13. Choose the Next button to create the user list file.

In addition, you can make changes as needed in the user list file. If you need to change the directory name of a mailbox, do it before the mailbox is created. You can change other fields now in this text file, or you can change them later. To change them now, follow the steps in the next section. To change them later, use the Administrator program to change them one at a time, or use the Directory Import command to change them in a batch mode.

Modifying the User List

To modify the user list file, complete the following steps:

1. Make a backup copy of the user list file. You will need it later.
2. Open the user list file with a text editor.
3. Delete the first two lines that have post office information and save the file as text.
4. Open the modified user list file with a database program. The file is text, comma delimited, and the first row contains field names. Table 8.2 identifies the user fields in the user list.
5. After it is modified, export the file in CSV format.
6. Open the modified file and the backup file with a text editor. Copy the two lines from the backup file to the top of the modified file. Then save the file as text.

Table 8.2 User List Fields

Field	Contents
SFS_UserName	The mailbox name or alias of this mailbox in the post office. Do not change this.
SFS_FullName	The full or display name of this mailbox in the post office. Do not change this.
MigrateUser	"Y" if the mailbox is to be migrated or "N" if the mailbox should not be migrated.
Obj-Class	Should be "mailbox." Other valid values are "remote" for custom recipients and "dl" for distribution list.
Mode	Describes what should be done with this object; "create," "modify," and "delete" are valid options. The default is "create."

continues

Table 8.2 Continued

Field	Contents
Common-Name	The directory name of the mailbox. This can't be changed later without deleting the mailbox and re-creating it, so change it now to match your naming convention.
Display-Name	The display or friendly name that appears in the address book.
Given-Name	The first or given name of the mailbox's user.
Surname	The surname or last name of the mailbox's user.
Home-Server	The home server of the mailbox. You can move a mailbox within the site later without difficulty, but you should decide where each group of mailboxes is to be created.
Comment	The address book comment. It can be used to distinguish between two people with the same or similar names or for notes about contacts for Schedule+ resources.
Assoc Windows-NT Account*	The mailbox's associated Windows NT account that has user access. On a Schedule+ resource account, this can be a Windows NT group or account that is responsible for managing the resource, or it can be the administrator who is going to sign into the account once to set up forwarding rules and Schedule+ access permissions.

* *You can add additional directory import fields after Assoc Windows-NT Account.*

After creating the user list and modifying it, you can migrate mailboxes from the post office to your site. This does not delete the mailboxes or remove mail, it only copies the information to the Exchange Servers where the new mailboxes are created. This is covered in the next section.

Migrating from the Post Office to Your Site

To migrate mailboxes from a post office to an Exchange Server with a user list, follow these steps:

1. (Optional) Map a drive letter or connect to a file server where the post office resides. You will need read and write access to the share or volume, and you must have the name and password of the administrator.
2. From the taskbar, choose Programs, and then select the Exchange folder.
3. In the Exchange folder, choose Exchange Migration Wizard.
4. Select Migrate from Microsoft Mail for PC Networks, and then choose the Next button.
5. Read the informational screen and choose the Next button.
6. In the Path to Microsoft Mail Post Office box, type the path to the post office, or choose the Browse button and specify the path to the post office.

7. In the Account Name box, type the mailbox name of an administrator on the post office.
8. In the Password box, type the password for this mailbox. Then choose the Next button.
9. Select Two Step Migration and choose the Next button.
10. Select Use a User List File to Do a Migration. Then in the Existing User List File box, type the path and file name of the modified user list, or choose the Browse button and select the file.
11. Choose the Next button.
12. Select the import options based on your needs (see Table 8.3).

Table 8.3 Import Options

Option	Description
Information to Create Mailboxes	Create mailboxes for the selected users in the user list file.
Personal E-Mail Messages	Copy messages and folders from the selected user's mailbox and server-based MMF. You can select all messages or set a date range.
Shared Folders	Copy all shared folders to the public folder server.
Personal Address Books	Copy PAB entries in the MMFs and put into the selected user's inbox in a special message.
Schedule Information	Copy calendar files from the CAL directory on the post office to a special message in the selected user's inbox.

13. Choose the Next button.
14. In the Enter a Server Name box, type the name of the destination Exchange Server computer. Choose the Next button.
15. Select the directory container for the new mailboxes.

NOTE You cannot move a mailbox from one directory container to another after the mailbox has been created. This is a limitation of the Exchange Administration program. ■

16. If you are using a mailbox template to reduce the work of setting up new mailboxes, choose the Browse button and select the template mailbox from the address list.
17. Choose the Next button.
18. In For Users That Don't Have Windows NT Accounts, choose one of the options (see Table 8.4).

Table 8.4 Options for Users Without Windows NT Accounts

Option	Description
Create Accounts and Generate Random Passwords	Accounts are created with names that match the alias and random passwords. The passwords are written to the file BIMPORT.PSW in the working directory of the Migration Wizard. For users to log on to Windows NT, distribute these passwords to them.
Create Accounts and Use Alias as Password	Accounts are created with names and passwords that match the alias.
Don't Create Windows NT Accounts	No accounts are created, and the mailboxes cannot be used by anyone until an account is assigned later.

19. In the Choose a Windows NT Domain for New Accounts box, select the domain where the user's Windows NT accounts are located or are to be created.
20. Choose the Next button to begin the migration process.

To migrate in one step from a Microsoft Mail (PC) Post Office, follow these steps:

1. (Optional) Map a drive letter or connect to a file server where the post office resides. You will need read and write access to the share or volume, and you must have the name and password of the administrator.
2. From the taskbar, choose Programs, and then select the Exchange folder.
3. In the Exchange folder, choose Exchange Migration Wizard.
4. Select Migrate from Microsoft Mail for PC Networks, and then choose the Next button.
5. Read the informational screen and choose the Next button.
6. In the Path to Microsoft Mail Post office box, type the path to the post office, or choose the Browse button and specify the path to the post office.
7. In the Account Name box, type the mailbox name of an administrator on the post office.
8. In the Password box, type the password for this mailbox. Then choose the Next button.
9. Select the One Step Migration option and choose the Next button.
10. Select the options based on your needs (see Table 8.5).

Table 8.5 One-Step Migration Options

Option	Description
Information to Create Mailboxes	Creates mailboxes for the selected users in the user list file.
Personal E-Mail Messages	Copies all messages and folders from the selected user's mailbox and server-based MMF. You can select all or set a date range.

Option	Description
Shared Folders	Check this box to copy all shared folders to the public folder server of this server.
Personal Address Books	PAB entries in MMFs are copied and put into the selected user's inbox in a special message.
Schedule Information	Calendar files are copied from the CAL directory on the post office to a special message in the selected user's inbox.

11. Choose the Next button.
12. In the Select Which Accounts You Would Like to Migrate box, choose the mailboxes you want to migrate, or choose the Select All button to select all mailboxes.
13. Choose the Next button.
14. In the Enter a Server Name box, type the name of the destination Exchange Server computer. Choose the Next button.
15. Select the directory container for the new mailboxes.

NOTE You cannot move a mailbox from one directory container to another after the mailbox has been created. ■

16. Choose the Next button.
17. Choose one of the options in For Users That Don't Have Windows NT Accounts (see Table 8.6).
18. In the Choose a Windows NT Domain for New Accounts box, select the domain where the user's Windows NT accounts are located or are to be created.
19. Choose the Next button to begin the migration process.

Table 8.6 One-Step Migration—Options for Users Without Windows NT Accounts

Option	Description
Create Accounts and Generate Random Passwords	Accounts are created with names that match the alias and random passwords. The passwords are written to the file BIMPORT.PSW in the working directory of the Migration Wizard. For users to log on to Windows NT, you need to distribute these passwords to them.
Create Accounts and Use Alias as Password	Accounts are created with names and passwords that match the alias.
Don't Create Windows NT Accounts	No accounts are created, and the mailboxes can't be used by anyone until an account is assigned later.

Migrating MMFs

As you learned earlier, in the migration tools section of this chapter, MMFs can be migrated by the user to personal folder files or by the Administrator to the private information store (depending on the location of the MMFs). Furthermore, the Exchange 5.5 Migration Wizard allows the administrator to migrate Microsoft Mail Post Offices to PST files. This is useful when users receive the Exchange or Outlook client prior to connecting to an Exchange Server. Two things to note about MMF migration are network errors and what to do after you use the migration tool.

Network Errors If there is a network failure during MMF migration, the client or Migration Wizard retries the network connection every ten minutes to re-establish a connection. An error message is displayed during this retry time.

Any errors during client MMF migration are logged to a file in the client directory with a file name that's the same as the MMF name and an extension of .LOG. You can view them in Notepad or any other text editor.

To import an MMF file with the Windows NT or Windows 16 client, follow these steps:

1. From the File menu, choose Import.
2. In the Specify File to Import window, select the MMF file.
3. In the Import Mail Data window, type the password for this MMF file.

   Select the Import Messages check box to import all messages and folders.

   Select the Import Personal Address Book Entries check box to create an Exchange PAB file.
4. Choose OK.

After Using the Migration Tool Depending on your migration strategy, you will need to delete the Microsoft Mail (PC) mailboxes or hide the post office. Deleting the mailboxes begins the decommission process for Microsoft Mail. The old mailboxes should not be needed anymore because the mailbox has been migrated to Exchange. ●

CHAPTER 9

Migrating from Lotus cc:Mail

In this chapter

Microsoft Exchange Connector for cc:Mail enables administrators to seamlessly integrate Exchange Server and cc:Mail systems, allowing them to exchange messages and synchronize directory entries from both DB6 and DB8 environments. Customers have the flexibility to use a phased approach to migration that minimizes disruptions within an organization.

The migration process of moving users from one messaging system to another can include mailboxes and attachments, addresses, and scheduling information from your existing system. This chapter covers planning methods for interoperability and migrating users to Exchange Server. Exchange's robust migration features support multiple scenarios for interconnecting to cc:Mail. Tools like Migration Wizard greatly simplify migration and ensure a smooth transition to Exchange.

Understanding the Architecture

The minimal software version required for the Exchange cc:Mail connector with cc:Mail is Lotus cc:Mail DB6, Post Office Database version 6.0, cc:Mail Import version 5.15, and Export version 5.14. Support for cc:Mail DB8 requires Lotus cc:Mail Post Office Database version 8 and cc:Mail Import/Export version 6.0.

Connecting Exchange to Lotus cc:Mail

The Exchange Connector for Lotus cc:Mail enables administrators to integrate Exchange into cc:Mail environments. Once installed, Exchange Server and cc:Mail systems can exchange messages and synchronize directories with both DB6 and DB8 cc:Mail post offices. When you introduce Exchange Server into a cc:Mail environment, cc:Mail users will benefit from Exchange Server's strong connectivity to the Internet and other systems. Also, customers can take a phased approach to migration that will minimize disruption with an organization.

The cc:Mail connector has a lot to offer in addition to fast performance: It also can transfer messages, attachments, embedded messages, OLE attachments, and file links. The connector does not support all of the linking features in the Exchange client. An Exchange Server system enables users to embed objects into the message body, link objects to the message body, insert links to files, insert shortcuts to Exchange folders, and insert shortcuts to Internet sites.

The cc:Mail connector really enhances connectivity because you can connect cc:Mail systems to Exchange Servers and immediately take advantage of Exchange's Internet Mail Service, which provides significant performance benefits over Lotus' SMTP gateway along with MIME compatibility. You can also use any other Exchange Connector (such as Microsoft Mail) through the cc:Mail connector.

Understanding How the Connector Works

Microsoft Exchange Server uses two components to communicate with cc:Mail systems: the cc:Mail connector and the cc:Mail Import and Export programs. The connector for cc:Mail is a Windows NT Service that executes Import and Export to transfer messages between Exchange Server and cc:Mail. It also synchronizes some or all of the Exchange Global Address List (GAL) with the cc:Mail directory.

When a message is submitted to the Exchange Server message transfer agent (MTA), the MTA consults the directory service (DS) to determine where the message should be moved. In the case of cc:Mail addresses, the messages are moved to the cc:Mail connector. The connector for cc:Mail service receives the messages, converts them to ASCII file format, converts attachments as needed, and places the messages in the connector store. If the Import program can't deliver the message, a non-delivery report (NDR) is sent back to the sender. See Figure 9.1 for an overview of the components of the cc:Mail connector.

FIG. 9.1
Architectural layout of the cc:Mail connector.

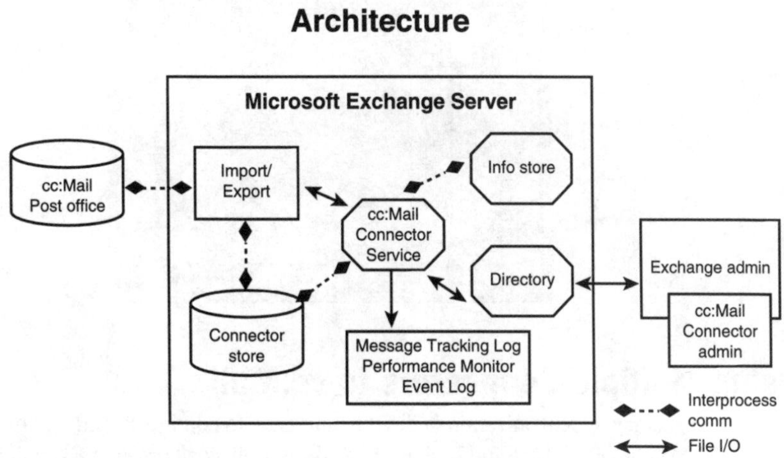

Directory synchronization in cc:Mail is a scheduled or on-demand process that performs a full synchronization of the cc:Mail directory on the connected post office with the Exchange directory. This process, like message transfer, uses the Import and Export programs provided by cc:Mail and controlled by the connector service.

From cc:Mail to Exchange, the service spawns the export process against the connected post office, which places the resulting address information file into the connector store. This file is then retrieved by the cc:Mail connector service and processed into an import container specified during the setup of the connector. The import container can be any Exchange recipient's container, including the Global Address List.

From Exchange to cc:Mail, the service spawns the import process. In order for this to succeed, there must be data to import. The cc:Mail connector service retrieves Exchange recipient information from the directory service and places that information in a file in the connector store. These addresses are then imported into the cc:Mail post office.

Figure 9.2 shows a screen shot of the connector for cc:Mail and the information required to connect to a post office. The configuration and setup for message transfer requires only a post office name, UNC path, and password. Unlike in the cc:Mail MTA, extensive drilling down in multiple screens isn't necessary to establish routing. Directory synchronization requires only basic configuration steps in which you choose what you want to export and what you want to import.

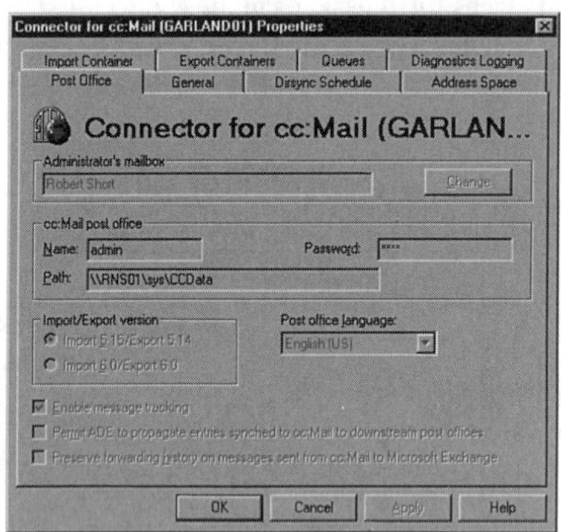

FIG. 9.2 Information required for the connection to a cc:Mail post office.

Using Multiple Connectors to cc:Mail

Directory synchronization is flexible and easy to configure, and it allows you to synchronize cc:Mail mailing lists and bulletin boards, as well as all types of Exchange recipients. You may elect to synchronize specific entries or types of entries between the two systems.

The Exchange cc:Mail connector fully integrates with Windows NT. Performance Monitor counters exhibit transfer rates, queue sizes, nondelivery occurrences, and directory synched entries. Events are logged to Windows NT Event Log in several different categories. Read receipt and nondeliverable reports are generated for both systems to use link monitors in testing connectivity between your downstream post offices.

If you have many cc:Mail post offices within your organization or multiple cc:Mail post offices spread over a large area, you can set up multiple connectors to link all cc:Mail and Exchange Servers. From the cc:Mail perspective, each Exchange Server site appears to be one large cc:Mail post office, regardless of the number of servers or recipients in that site.

When planning multiple outgoing routes to one or more connectors to cc:Mail, consider doing these things:

- Install a connector on any or all Exchange Server computers in your site, depending on your messaging traffic.
- Use identical address information in the Address Space properties sheets of two or more cc:Mail connectors to route messages.
- Install at least one Exchange Server 5.0 in every site that indirectly communicates with cc:Mail. Exchange 5.0 is required for cc:Mail address generation of Exchange Server recipients.

Lotus cc:Mail address generation enables cc:Mail users to send mail to Exchange users. (The Exchange Server users must have an address of the type CCMAIL.) Exchange Server automatically generates a cc:Mail address (*Username* at *siteproxy*) for each recipient, a public folder, a distribution list, and a custom recipient based on the site addressing. This enables cc:Mail users to send mail to any Exchange user. The administrator configures the cc:Mail e-mail address format in the Site Addressing properties sheet for the site.

Using the Migration Wizard

Once your Exchange Server and Lotus cc:Mail systems are connected, it is easy to enable them to coexist or to migrate from cc:Mail to Exchange. The cc:Mail component of the Migration Wizard enables you to upgrade custom recipients to mailboxes and retain former cc:Mail addresses so that old mail on both systems will be redirected to the new Exchange mailbox. The Migration Wizard also copies cc:Mail files to the recipient's Exchange mailbox and copies BBSs (bulletin boards) to Exchange public folders.

The Migration Wizard can create new Windows NT accounts, and you can choose from three methods how you want the Windows NT accounts for migrated users created (accounts can be created and given a random password). With the first method, you create Windows NT accounts for each mailbox and generate random passwords. The account name and passwords are written to the file ACCOUNT.PASSWORD in the working directory of the Migration wizard. The second method is to create accounts and use the Windows NT account alias as the password. The final option is to not create Windows NT accounts that match the alias of a mailbox but instead to create the mailbox without an associated Windows NT account. This means that no one will be able to access these mailboxes until a Windows NT account is associated with them.

Figure 9.3 shows the options the wizard offers for creating Windows NT accounts during migration.

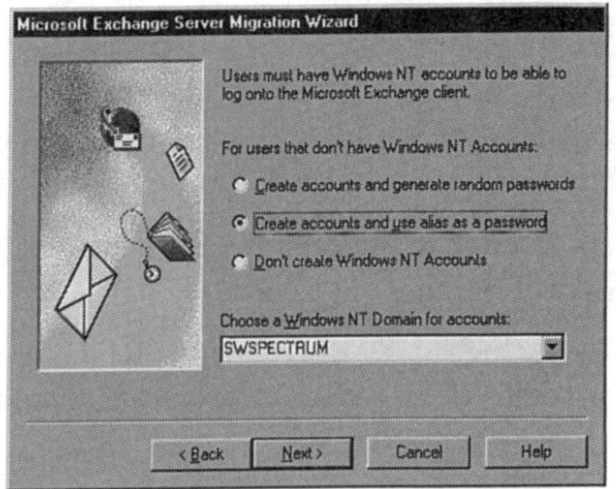

FIG. 9.3
The Migration Wizard Extracts users from cc:Mail and imports them into Exchange.

Determining Your Migration Strategy

Microsoft Exchange Server has many migration tools that can be used with Lotus cc:Mail. As you plan your migration, you will need to consider the following questions:

- What level of migration coexistence, mailbox migration, mailbox creation, or a combination of these will be best for your organization?
- Should all users be migrated, or only a subset of users?
- Do users have all the hardware necessary, or will migration occur in phases?
- What connectivity issues need to be addressed?
- Which users should migrate first?

Migration Levels from Full Migration to Coexistence

There are three levels of migration: coexistence, mailbox creation, and mailbox migration. The type you choose depends on how much data you want to move from your existing system to Exchange. Each level is described here in detail:

- *Establish coexistence with an existing system.*

  This level enables users on both cc:Mail and Exchange to exchange mail. You have a chance to test connections between the two systems because addresses are extracted from the existing system and added as custom recipients in Exchange. This provides a foundation for migrating users to Exchange, usually before the actual migration.

- *Create new Exchange Server mailboxes without data.*

  At this level, only user account information is copied from the existing system. This creates empty mailboxes and, as an option, Windows NT accounts. This approach is used to migrate users without migrating their data, with a plan to either migrate their data later or skip migrating the data altogether.

- *Migrate mailbox contents.*

At this level, mailbox contents are copied (not moved) from cc:Mail to Exchange Server mailboxes. The contents include messages and attachments. This enables the user to use Exchange without any data loss. This can follow coexistence and mailbox creation, or it can be combined with those steps for a quick migration.

You can use one of these three migration levels exclusively, or you can use all three as part of your migration plan. For example, after you install your first new Exchange server, you migrate addresses from cc:Mail. For a test run, you create new mailboxes without data. When your test is complete, you migrate the mailbox contents to the new mailboxes and have the users upgrade their clients to Exchange-based clients.

The following list outlines concerns associated with a migration from cc:Mail to Exchange:

- Migration testing shows that high volumes of data can take weeks or even months to migrate.
- Hardware used for the existing system needs to be freed up in early phases for redeployment during later phases.
- Some departments will need to use existing messaging applications until they can be replaced with Exchange public folders and custom form functionality.
- Not all departments have the budget to upgrade at the same time.
- Be sure your help desk group is able to handle the short spike of requests a quick migration is likely to create.
- Investigate to see if departments have the hardware or system software to upgrade now.
- Microsoft Exchange should be tested in a pilot with non-mission critical users.
- Keep in mind that Exchange/Outlook clients are not available for all platforms or networks.

There are three types or levels of migration from cc:Mail to Exchange. You should choose the proper phase for your organization:

- *Single-phase migration.* This gives users some of the enhanced features before migration, while you are planning and testing the enterprise design.
- *Multi-phase migration.* This gives all users a common user interface as you migrate mailboxes in stages.
- *Multi-phase migration with dual access.* This enables users to retrieve mail from their old mailboxes after their mailboxes have been migrated to Exchange Server.

Taking into consideration the previous two lists, you should be developing an idea of the migration strategy for your organization. As you plan your organization's new messaging infrastructure, you'll probably want to break down the project into steps. These are the major steps of the migration process:

1. Connect Exchange Client to existing systems.
2. Create directory and mailbox entries.
3. Extract and load accounts.
4. Set up directory synchronization.
5. Set up connectivity with gateway.
6. Migrate server contents.
7. Move users' data.
8. Update the directory.

Now that you are aware of the issues, phases, and steps involved in migrating cc:Mail to Exchange, keep in mind the effects of these items on your organization. The next three sections provide details about the three types of migration and apply them to an actual organization.

Single-Phase Migration

Depending on the size of your organization and your staff, you might be able to do a one-step migration. This can happen overnight, on a weekend, or on company shutdown time. If your organization can't tolerate the downtime or doesn't have the resources to migrate everyone in one weekend, phased migration is the best choice.

Instant migration may be better for your organization if the following statements are true:

- There is little or no existing data to move from the old system.
- You have enough people to migrate everyone in one night, over one weekend, or during a traditional downtime.
- All hardware and system software is in place.

One-step migration takes extra planning in these areas:

- Replacing existing workflow applications
- User and help desk training
- Preparing for rollout and resource needs
- Preparing for contingencies

Should you choose to go with a single mail provider, such as Exchange Server, the single provider option provides for these scenarios:

- Every mailbox on the cc:Mail post office is migrated.
- Only some mailboxes on a post office migrate, and their addresses change.

Update the Global Address List and the directory. Mail sent to the old addresses from the Personal Address Books and personal address lists will be returned as nondeliverable (if you delete the old mailbox) or will pile up in the old mailbox.

With a multi-phase migration, you have two "providers": cc:Mail post office and Exchange Server, for instance. A dual provider allows for these scenarios:

- *All mailboxes are migrated, and addresses are changed.*

  The users can still connect to the old post office and get mail that is sent to their old addresses, but as the Global Address List is updated, new messages sent to them are routed to their Exchange Server mailboxes.

- *Some mailboxes are migrated, but addresses are not changed.*

  Routing on the Microsoft cc:Mail connector is not updated, so mail sent to these users from Lotus cc:Mail users still arrives at their old mailboxes, but messages sent from Exchange Server users are delivered to the new mailbox. The users can now send mail from their Exchange Server mailboxes and can use Exchange Server public folders.

The drawback of these options is that the workstation mail profile must be edited three times: first when the client is installed, again when the Exchange Server provider is added, and again when the Lotus cc:Mail (PC) provider is removed.

When a system is configured for dual providers, the function of the Microsoft cc:Mail provider should be limited to retrieving mail from the old mailbox. Mail addressed with the cc:Mail address book will be delivered and can be replied to. However, if a user chooses the Reply to All option on a mail message addressed to both Lotus cc:Mail mailboxes (not as Exchange custom recipients) and Exchange mailboxes, the message will not reach the Exchange mailboxes. If the message is sent to Lotus cc:Mail mailboxes as custom recipients, the client transfers the message to the Exchange Server. This is because the Exchange Server updates the Exchange mailbox address when it transfers the message to the Microsoft cc:Mail connector, so the message can be replied to by Lotus cc:Mail recipients.

Multi-Phase Migration

Large organizations might consider phased migrations, concentrating on more challenging sites prior to the major Exchange rollout. In addition, large organizations require longer periods of coexistence with legacy mail. Smaller organizations, by contrast, would most likely be able to do a very quick migration—almost instantaneous.

If you belong to a large organization, your migration plan will probably take place in these three basic phases:

1. Installing Exchange Server centrally.
2. Migrating users or branch offices and coexisting with legacy systems such as cc:Mail.
3. Completing migration in remote locations.

Following a Sample Migration with Three Phases

A multi-phased approach simplifies the task of migration. Each phase can consist of numerous individual tasks. On a high level, these three phases apply to any organization. The following sample walks you through the migration process for a larger organization.

Software Spectrum has its headquarters in Garland, TX, and also has offices in Los Angeles, Seattle, and Dublin (see Figure 9.4). The three American offices are connected over T1 lines. The headquarters and the Dublin office are connected over a wide area X.25 network that uses X.400 services.

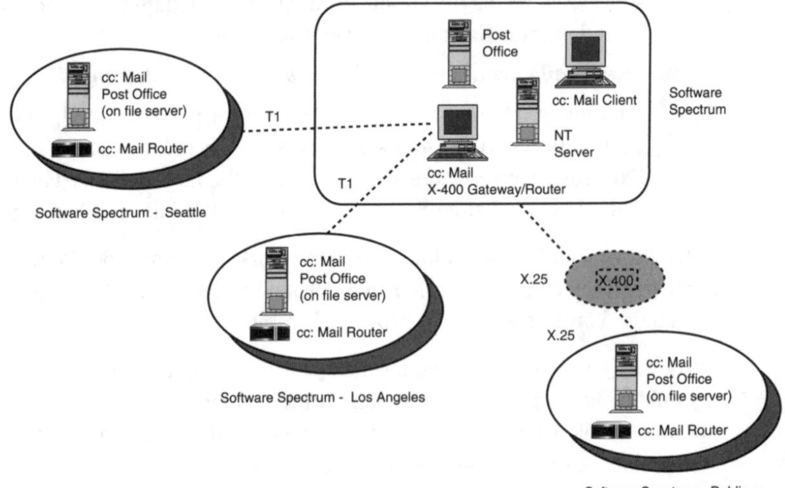

FIG. 9.4 Software Spectrum's current cc:Mail system.

Its e-mail system consists of four Lotus cc:Mail post offices, one in each office. In this example, all the PCs are using Lotus cc:Mail and Windows 95.

Phase One: Migrating Headquarters to Exchange Garland installs a Windows NT and Exchange Server on an existing Windows NT 4.0 network. Then they install the cc:Mail connector and x.400. The connector for Lotus cc:Mail transfers messages between an Exchange organization and Lotus cc:Mail systems, and it provides for directory synchronization between the two systems. An entire cc:Mail network can be connected to an Exchange organization using a single connector or multiple connectors.

You need to test each cc:Mail connector and both the cc:Mail and Exchange clients. Before you send a test message from an Exchange client to a cc:Mail recipient, you need to create a custom recipient address for the mailbox to which you are sending the test message. After the address is created, the recipient appears in your personal address list. You must know the post office name and mailbox name for the recipient, and you can use the cc:Mail Administrator program to find this information. Then to test the outbound side of the cc:Mail connector, you should send a test message from an Exchange client to a cc:Mail recipient.

Next send a test message from a cc:Mail client to an Exchange recipient to determine if the inbound side of the connector is functioning correctly. After the address is created, the recipient appears in your address list. You must know the cc:Mail address for the Exchange recipient, which can be found in the Exchange Server Administrator program. Before you send a test message from a cc:Mail client to an Exchange recipient, you need to create a recipient address for the mailbox to which you are sending the test message.

Using the built-in Migration tool, the company migrates its Lotus cc:Mail post office at headquarters to Exchange. The Migration tool converts cc:Mail messages, attachments, embedded messages, and OLE attached file links. Scheduling data is converted to text and can be imported in Schedule+. The Migration Wizard also enables users of the new system to coexist productively with existing systems during and after the migration process.

At headquarters in Garland, Texas, they simultaneously start installing the Exchange client on each of the Windows 95-based workstations and migrating mailboxes from the cc:Mail system to Exchange Server. This gives those users access to the Exchange Server. Those still using the Lotus cc:Mail client can continue to communicate with other users of Exchange, but they lack the enhanced functionality provided by Exchange.

Installing Exchange Server consolidates the functions of three machines in the Garland office (the Lotus cc:Mail post office, the cc:Mail router and the X.400 gateway) onto one machine. Exchange users can use cc:Mail gateways, and cc:Mail users can use the Exchange gateways.

It also adds one-stop administration, connection monitoring, and performance monitoring. Windows NT Server Performance Monitor, which comes with Windows NT, is a tool that can be used with Exchange Server. It provides charting, alerting, and reporting capabilities that reflect current activity, along with ongoing logging. You can also open log files at a later time for browsing and charting. Monitoring involves viewing discrete components of the system; the connector for cc:Mail has ten performance counters associated with it.

After the Exchange client is installed on all workstations, users in the Garland office have access to the complete functionality of Exchange, including these features:

- The ability to send multiple messages to the same recipient
- Rich text formatting and OLE
- Information-sharing capabilities through public folders
- Flexible views
- Easy-to-use forms
- Improved group scheduling and task management
- Search tools to save time locating addresses and the like

Microsoft Exchange users in Garland can continue to communicate with their counterparts in Los Angeles, Seattle, and Dublin. This enables the company to migrate in stages, yet maintain the ability for all users to perform the following functions:

- Exchange mail messages with attachments
- View read and undeliverable receipts
- Take advantage of improved group scheduling and task management capabilities

Phase Two: Coexistence Next, the company installs Exchange Server in the Los Angeles office. The Exchange Server will be configured with cc:Mail and Exchange site connector. The Exchange Server in Garland will be configured with a site connector to Los Angeles. Seattle and Dublin are still using cc:Mail post offices. Using the Exchange Server as an MTA between the Exchange Servers and the cc:Mail post offices offers different advantages: In the future, after all cc:Mail post offices have been migrated to Exchange Servers, load balancing can be enhanced by adding an additional site connector. The following list outlines reasons to add additional connectors.

- *Auto routing.* The server automatically configures itself for efficient routing.
- *Load balancing.* If one communication link fails, the MTA will automatically reconfigure itself to balance the load over the remaining communication links.
- *Least-cost routing.* Enables administrators to assign costs to communications lines so the MTAs can intelligently route information over the line with the lowest cost. Combined with load-balancing, this provides the highest availability of lines at the lowest cost.

Software Spectrum also installs Exchange clients on all PCs in Los Angeles to access the Exchange Server. At the end of phase two, all users in Garland and Los Angeles have access to the complete functionality of the Exchange system. They can also continue to exchange messages with users in Dublin via the X.400, and the cc:Mail connector manages the directory exchange between Exchange and cc:Mail during this coexistence phase.

Phase Three: Completing the Migration In the final migration phase, the Seattle and Dublin offices install Exchange on both the server and on the Windows 95 workstations. This consolidates the cc:Mail post office and router/gateway onto one server at each site. Now users across the enterprise have full use of Exchange's rich functionality and are able to share information with everyone else in their organization at any time. At this time, all sites exchange e-mail on Exchange Server using site connectors between sites in America and the x.400 connector to Dublin. The Lotus cc:Mail system has been completely migrated over to Exchange Server.

The company has realized the cost savings of consolidating the functions of eight machines into four and has condensed the administration for all four offices onto one Windows NT-based workstation. They have a consistent enterprise-wide messaging and information exchange system and can install additional Exchange gateways to extend these capabilities beyond the enterprise.

Implementing Exchange Client

The migration to the Exchange client will take place after Exchange Server is installed. The Exchange Server requires the appropriate site connectors and cc:Mail connectors to enable communication and directory synchronization between Exchange sites and cc:Mail systems. Once the Exchange Server and all the necessary connectors to support your environment are configured and tested, it's time to migrate your clients.

After the Exchange client is installed on the user workstation, the client's data needs to be migrated. Before migrating groups of users, you should have users delete old messages. Schedule this over a period of a week or so to allow users sufficient time to perform the task. In addition to having the clients clean up the mailbox, administrators should continue to perform normal cc:Mail post office maintenance, such as backups and reclaims.

Using the Exchange Migration Wizard

The Exchange Migration Wizard simplifies the migration process and ensures a smooth transition to Exchange. When using the Exchange Migration Wizard, you are prompted for information such as the pathname for the migration files, the Exchange Server you want the mailboxes added to, the recipient container for the new mailboxes, and the Windows NT domain you want the accounts added to. The Migration Wizard can handle large numbers of recipients; when doing so, you can select a template account that contains default restrictions and properties for created accounts.

Changing Message Storage from cc:Mail to Exchange

You now know one method for migration to Exchange. This section covers migrating the cc:Mail files from cc:Mail into the Exchange format.

Migrating cc:Mail Files to the Exchange Server Microsoft Exchange client users must migrate their mail message files to a personal folder file (.PST). Again, you should have users delete old messages, and it is a good idea to allow some time for users to perform this task. Administrators should continue to perform their normal cc:Mail post office maintenance of backups and reclaims. The Migration Wizard does not delete the cc:Mail files when it creates the personal folder file; after their contents are migrated and the client has been tested, you should delete the old files.

Migrating Partial Post Offices Migrating everyone off of a post office at the same time is not always possible. When migrating partial post offices, the following considerations are necessary:

- Routing to old post offices must be maintained so that the remaining users continue to receive mail.
- Mail sent to migrated mailboxes that passes through a Lotus cc:Mail gateway will be delivered to Lotus cc:Mail mailbox or returned as undeliverable.
- Directories in Lotus cc:Mail and with Lotus cc:Mail gateway that have the old mailbox address have to be updated immediately; the old address is invalid.
- Users who are still on Lotus cc:Mail can reply to any mail they received in the past from a migrated user, but the reply will be delivered to the Lotus cc:Mail mailbox or returned as undeliverable.
- For users who are still on Lotus cc:Mail, any Personal Address Book or personal address list entries they have for migrated mailboxes are invalid.

NOTE No routing changes are required or allowed during a partial post office migration. Mail must continue to be delivered to the mailboxes remaining on the original post office. ■

Part of your migration plan is knowing how many mailboxes at a time will migrate to Exchange Servers. As a general rule, migration of the whole post office (every mailbox) is easier to plan for, implement, and maintain than the migration of a partial post office. A partial post office migration is more likely during a pilot or limited rollout, when the number of users is small and the issues are easier to solve or work around. The following section explains why this is so.

Migrating Whole Post Offices If you migrate every mailbox on a post office, you can maintain the original Network/Post Office/Mailbox format of Lotus cc:Mail addresses for each old mailbox as one of the proxy or e-mail addresses of the new mailbox. This has many advantages:

- With limited routing changes, mail continues to be delivered without interruption.
- Mail sent to migration mailboxes that passes through Lotus cc:Mail gateways is delivered.
- Directories in Lotus cc:Mail post offices and foreign systems connected to them with Lotus cc:Mail gateways that have the old mailbox address do not have to be updated immediately; the old address is still valid.
- Users who are still on Lotus cc:Mail can reply to any mail they received in the past from a migrated user.
- For users who are still on Lotus cc:Mail, any Personal Address Book or personal address list entries they have for migrated mailboxes are still valid.

Mail Pass-Through Retaining the original e-mail address provides for pass-through from Lotus cc:Mail gateways. The Microsoft cc:Mail connector to the post office must have an access component for the gateway installed. Because the Lotus cc:Mail type addresses for migrated mailboxes have not changed, the mail will be routed from the gateway to the Microsoft cc:Mail connector and from there to the Exchange mailbox.

Personal Address Books for Users Who Haven't Migrated Personal Address Book entries function similarly to replies. For cc:Mail users, their Personal Address Book addresses continue to work for migrated mailboxes because the addresses are the same.

Migrated Personal Address Book entries will work for cc:Mail mailboxes that have not migrated. This means that if you do not update your Personal Address Book with the new Exchange e-mail addresses, some e-mail will still be directed to cc:Mail mailboxes that no longer exist. Mail addressed to mailboxes that have since migrated will be routed to the Microsoft cc:Mail connector. The Microsoft cc:Mail connector does not have a post office configured with that address and will return the mail as undeliverable. This undeliverable mail can be readdressed from the Exchange Server Global Address List and can be delivered.

There is no tool that updates the user's Personal Address Book entries as changes are made in the Exchange Server Global Address List. After the cc:Mail client is migrated to Exchange mailboxes, to avoid addressing undeliverable mail, users should remove from their Personal Address Books all entries referencing clients who have been migrated.

Migration Package Elements

The following sections cover the main elements of Exchange's Migration package. This package enables you to implement Exchange into environments with legacy mail systems. These tools assist with the extraction of e-mail addresses from the legacy systems and the importing of addresses into Exchange.

Source Extractor There is a Source Extractor for many systems such as Microsoft Mail, Lotus cc:Mail, Novell GroupWise, and PROFS. The Source Extractor extracts users, inboxes, folders, and address books from the source mail systems. One of the enhancements of Exchange 5.5 is the source extractor for DB8 post offices. The DB8 migration used to require a backwards migration to DB6 before the move to Exchange.

The following list contains the components of the source extraction tool used to convert extracted addresses into the Exchange format and provide support information for the migration process:

- The Migration Assistant converts all extracted data from the source system to Exchange.
- The Migration Wizard guides administrators through migration. There are options included for one-step migration and two-step migration.

Pass-Through Connectivity Microsoft Exchange Server offers group distribution list support and enables cc:Mail users to send messages to X.400 and SMTP environments through the Microsoft cc:Mail connector. Messages sent from the cc:Mail users through the Exchange Server computer could use the Exchange X.400 connector and the Internet Mail Connector to interchange messages with these environments. Alternatively, Exchange users can send messages through any of the Lotus cc:Mail gateways through the Microsoft cc:Mail connector.

After Using the Migration Tool

Depending on your migration strategy, you will need to delete the cc:Mail mailboxes or hide the post office. It is possible to make a full backup of the updated information store. ●

CHAPTER 10

NetWare Considerations/Migrating from GroupWise

In this chapter

There are many issues you must confront when installing Exchange in a NetWare environment, ranging from technical considerations to organizational concerns. You need to understand, support, and maintain both Microsoft's Domain Model and Novell's NetWare Directory Services, as well as determine what additional services, software, and migration tools are needed to enable both to coexist.

Understanding the History of Microsoft and Novell

Many years before Microsoft created Windows NT, their network operating system platform was a product called Microsoft LAN Manager. Without getting into the details, LAN Manager didn't sell very well, and Novell captured the networking market with its NetWare product line.

As Novell set up shop on corporate Local Area Network (LAN) servers, Microsoft chose to go after the desktop operating system market. Microsoft introduced its Windows 3.0 product. It ran on top of DOS, but was a revolutionary advance in design and function from Microsoft's Windows 286 and Windows 386 environments. Its application software for Windows consisted of Word, Excel, PowerPoint, Mail, Schedule+, and Project. Microsoft also developed Dynamic Data Exchange (DDE) and Object Linking and Embedding (OLE) technology that tied its applications to one another and provided a robust desktop platform.

The two worlds remained separate. Developers of networking technologies leveraged NetWare's popularity by designing NetWare Loadable Modules (NLMs) to run on top of NetWare servers. NetWare servers typically were purchased by individual departments in corporations, and eventually spread throughout the organization. Following this momentum, many corporations made heavy investments in NetWare because it provided the most extensible, cost-effective networking solution on the market.

As a result of these two companies' abilities in different market segments, there were many NetWare networks running with Microsoft Windows and Windows applications on the desktop. In fact, several organizations even executed Windows from the NetWare server. This enabled administrators to manage users' Windows profiles and Windows application software configurations from any workstation because all initialization files were kept on the server. Because Windows ran on top of DOS, all of the workstation network card and protocol drivers could be loaded in DOS, and a drive letter could be assigned to the NetWare volume. Once connectivity to the server was established, Windows and applications were loaded from the server.

In the past three or four years, however, things have changed. Microsoft introduced Windows NT as a network server solution, and Novell acquired WordPerfect and Borland's Quattro Pro spreadsheet. Novell then bundled these applications with its GroupWise email and scheduling package to market a suite called PerfectOffice to compete with Microsoft Office. Novell and Microsoft were now both trying to capture the piece of the business they did not have previously.

Over time, however, the Novell application suite was not accepted by a large number of companies. Novell took a lot a criticism for losing focus on NetWare and for not providing adequate support for its core product. Novell has since sold WordPerfect and Quattro Pro, and is currently out of the applications business. During the time that Novell tested the application marketplace, they were also having problems with their first release of NetWare Directory Services (NDS) NetWare 4.0. This, and the fact that NLMs were very difficult to develop, encouraged people to start testing new networking and application platforms, such as Windows NT Server. As much as NetWare was initially brought into individual departments to provide file and print services, NT servers were brought into departments to run department-specific applications. Microsoft Windows NT began to gain market acceptance, and has been gaining market share ever since.

Because of its stability, integration with Microsoft Office, open programming interfaces, and support of Internet protocols, Exchange will be successful in any environment, including those with Novell servers. The Exchange client components integrate very closely with all the Microsoft Office products. Third-party companies write applications to the standard Application Programming Interfaces (APIs) that Microsoft incorporates into its products. The underlying networking technology and protocols should not sway you from implementing Exchange. Exchange's client/server model, integration with other Microsoft applications already in use, and its open programming architecture will provide a solid foundation for your organization to build a global messaging architecture.

Exchange Installation—Server Considerations

There are several things to consider about your server when implementing Exchange. These include the following:

- Choosing a Network Protocol
- Migrating users to the NT servers
- Moving existing mail data
- NT Server expertise

Choosing a Network Protocol

The NT server that Exchange runs on can communicate over several protocols. The two most widely used protocols in the NetWare environment are IPX/SPX and TCP/IP. NT supports both of these protocols out of the box, enabling your NetWare clients to communicate seamlessly over the existing network without modifying the client workstation protocols or adding new protocols to your routers.

This leads to an important point. You must have NetBIOS support enabled on all the NT Servers that will be acting as Exchange servers. This is because clients will be looking for Exchange servers on the network based on the servers' NetBIOS names. NetBIOS is not required on the workstations, but can be used if desired.

Migrating User Accounts to NT Servers

Because most packages require you to create a separate account for email, you already have systems in place for generating new accounts. In addition, users are already familiar with the interface; and you, the administrator, are already familiar with all the back-end utilities that go along with running the mail system. You already have backup procedures in place as well. Much of this will have to change when you install Exchange. Although your clients will need minimal or no special configuration, the changes required at the server will be a bit different.

There are a few things you will have to keep in mind. One is that Exchange security is tied to Windows NT domain security. This means that an Windows NT domain account must be created for every NetWare user who will be using Exchange. This link to Windows NT security will provide the user with powerful permissions features, including the ability to delegate certain responsibilities to other users. If you wanted your secretary to be able to access your appointment book, for example, you could allow that. You may assign or deny very detailed levels of permissions to other users.

Given the preceding, the biggest job you will have is importing all the current users and data from your current email system.

Although Microsoft provides a bindery migration utility, it will import only the NetWare user names and group memberships. The problem with that is in most NetWare environments, user names are based on a first initial, last name or first name, underscore, last name standard because spaces are not allowed in NetWare user names.

In most email environments, however, the user's full name is listed in the email directory. If you import a bindery from a NetWare server, and then run the NT User List to Exchange migration utility, you will wind up with a list of first initial, last name entries rather than full names. This is unsatisfactory because you will have to go back and re-key all the user names if you want to make them easy to find in the directory.

You can overcome this by using one of the mail migration utilities that ships with Exchange, or a third-party tool. If you have Microsoft Mail post offices spread throughout your NetWare network, for example, you can run the Migration Utility and select Microsoft Mail, and that will create the Exchange users with full names while migrating data. As the Exchange users are created, you can have the utility create the Windows NT user accounts for you, thus making the transition seamless.

Moving Existing Data

When changing from a NetWare-based e-mail system to Exchange, moving data is made easier by Microsoft and third-party data migration utilities. Utilities provided by Microsoft include Gateway Services for NetWare and the Migration Wizard. Gateway Services for NetWare is a service included with NT Server. It is installed from the Services tab on the Network icon in the Control Panel. The Exchange Migration Wizard is included with Exchange and may be installed during setup.

With Gateway Service for NetWare, you can access file and print resources on NetWare servers from your computer. You can access resources on NetWare 4.x servers that use NDS and on NetWare servers that use bindery-style security. NT's Gateway Services for NetWare enables the NT server running the Gateway service to mount NetWare volumes. This feature enables users on Microsoft NT networks to access volumes on a Novell server. The administrator of the NT server logs in to the Novell server and mounts the disk as a logical drive. The NT server can then share this device with any NT server user. The same feature applies to printers on the network. You can associate a NetWare print queue with an NT print queue and provide seamless access to authorized users on the NT server. While this may seem unconventional in a predominantly NetWare environment, it does provide some very interesting functionality. This tool can prove very useful when using the Migration Wizard to move users from a Novell server-based email package such as MS Mail.

NetWare servers use the Service Advertising Protocol (SAP) to announce their available resources. To enable NT Servers to communicate with NetWare Servers, Gateway Services also uses the SAP protocol. When you install Gateway Services, you must also install the SAP Agent that comes with NT Server. The SAP Agent can be installed from the Services tab on the Network icon in the Control Panel.

If the post office exists on Novell file server NOVELL001, on volume SYS1:, you can mount it on the NT server as drive D: and just perform your import seamlessly. NT Server provides this functionality out of the box. Think of the alternative—you would have to copy all the associated post office files to a workstation and then copy them to an NT server.

NT Server Expertise

As discussed in previous chapters, Exchange integrates tightly with Microsoft Windows NT Server. Because Windows NT includes an easy-to-use graphical interface that is identical to the interface on their desktop PCs, many corporate managers assume that NT Server requires as little planning to install and implement as their desktop operating system. Do not fall into this trap. A reliable, robust email system requires a sound foundation. Like NetWare, NT Server is a fairly complex product—those installing it should understand the implications of their design decisions.

An exhaustive explanation of NetWare administrators who need to learn more about NT Server will benefit from attending training courses provided by Microsoft Authorized Technical Education Centers (ATEC). For current information on Microsoft Education, you may reference the Microsoft Training and Certification Web site at **www.microsoft.com/train_cert/**.

Exchange Installation—Client Considerations

There are many different ways a client workstation can be configured in a NetWare network. For workstations using DOS/Windows 3.1 or DOS/Windows for Workgroups, 16-bit real mode drivers are used to access the Exchange server over IPX or TCP/IP.

In an IPX configuration, the IPXODI driver provides the necessary connectivity to the Exchange server. Through the use of the NWLink protocol on the Exchange server, the IPX client can seek out the Exchange server on the network. Once a connection to the server is established by the Exchange client software, all communication is handled through Remote Procedure Calls (RPCs). These RPCs travel between the Exchange Server and the NetWare client software via the SPX protocol. If a NetWare client is having trouble connecting to an Exchange Server, one item to check is the IPXODI entry in the client's Startnet.bat file. Make sure the IPXODI entry does not include the /A switch, which disables SPX on that client. The SPX protocol is sometimes disabled because it uses additional memory on the client.

When installing the Exchange client software on a DOS, Windows 3.1, or Windows for Workgroups 3.11 machine, the installation program looks for a file called NETAPI.DLL. It then copies the appropriate RPC communication DLL based on the version of that file.

If you have TCP/IP running across your network already, and all the software is already installed on the workstation, you can have clients use TCP/IP to connect to the server. As long as the stack you use is Winsock-compliant, the connection should be seamless.

For Windows 95 clients, using Microsoft's 32-bit IPX and TCP/IP drivers for your network card will provide robust connectivity. If you have these drivers already in place to access the NetWare servers on your network, this same set of drivers will be used by the client to access the Exchange servers. If you are using the IPX protocol to communicate with Exchange, the Windows NT server will need to have the IPX protocol installed.

The client/server architecture of Exchange eliminates the need to actually mount any volumes of the server. The client communicates with the server via Remote Procedure Calls (RPCs) to provide seamless communication. In the current cc:Mail and Microsoft Mail implementations, for example, the user must provide a drive letter and path to the post office. That means they must be logged in to the server and have the proper search paths and drive mappings established to communicate with the post office. With Exchange, all you have to do is configure the client to look for a certain server on the network. RPCs take care of the rest of the communications once the Exchange server is found on the network.

Exchange Migration Considerations

There are many sites that use NetWare servers to house their shared file email system. Users have different passwords for login and email. The two systems are completely separate, with the exception of MHS-based systems such as Novell's GroupWise, which ties into the bindery or NDS. For these organizations, there are real benefits to installing Exchange.

The movement away from the shared file system to client/server is a real boon to the administrators of those email systems. Keeping database pointers in line, getting clean backups, and shutting down the system to make changes are all problems these administrators have come to know all too well.

There are several tools at your disposal to bring NetWare users into the Exchange environment. You can use the Migration Tool that ships with Exchange, or you can use the Bindery Import Tool that comes with Windows NT Server. The two solutions yield different results that will be explained in the sections that follow. In addition, Gateway Services for NetWare enables the NT server housing Exchange to access NetWare volumes.

Using the Exchange Migration Tool

When you use this tool to give NetWare users access to Exchange resources, that is all the NetWare users will have. They are not given logons to the NT domain.

Think of your current LAN-based e-mail system, be it cc:Mail, MS Mail, or POP. When you launch the client application on your PC or Macintosh, you are prompted for a login name and password, and the back-end mail engine authenticates you. This also happens when you use the Migration Tool for Exchange.

Exchange can be thought of as an upgrade to your current mail system that will provide so much extra functionality. Microsoft has provided many tools that make Exchange an easy platform to implement, regardless of your current server environment.

Although this system lacks the single logon benefit that comes along with running NT Server, it is still very manageable and very robust.

Coexistence of NetWare and Windows NT Server

Rather than migrating your existing NetWare server-based e-mail system to Exchange, you might consider coexistence. Through Exchange's wide variety of bundled connectors, you can make the most of new technology while keeping your current system up and running. Consider the following real-world example.

ABC's Information Services Department uses NetWare servers on the backbone of the campus-wide network. The system has grown to over 5,000 users, all with NetWare 3.12 accounts. ABC uses MS Mail as their messaging platform.

Recently, the MS Mail infrastructure has been showing signs of weakness because of the load being put on all the servers. The message databases have grown to over 500 megabytes, with thousands of Internet email messages going through two gateways: one for students and one for everyone else.

Meanwhile, the time and resources required to perform database maintenance were becoming unacceptable. If the utilities weren't run every night, the database would get corrupted, causing the entire system to be shut down during peak hours. Additionally, data was being lost in the process. Also, the amount of storage needed to run the utilities was getting excessive, requiring that the entire database be moved to a separate server for the utilities to be effective. Needless to say, the system was breaking down.

This scenario led ABC to explore the possibility of migrating the students to Exchange because of its client/server architecture. Rather than 3,000 students sharing one post office file on one Novell server, the company could move to the client/server model. They wanted to preserve their investment in NetWare, but at the same time wanted to move to Exchange for messaging.

To meet both objectives, ABC set up an Exchange server for students to access mail, while still using the NetWare server to load Windows 3.1 and house the Exchange client software. They used the Exchange Migration Tool to import the user data and accounts from the existing MS Mail system, so no data loss occurred.

ABC then called a Microsoft Solution Provider, who installed the MS Mail Connector and set up the proper directory synchronization in the connector properties so that any new accounts created on the MS Mail side would be reflected in the Exchange Global Address Book for the students. The Solution Provider gave ABC information on how to get hands-on Exchange training along with some basic training on Windows NT fundamentals.

Because IPX was the standard protocol loaded on the workstations, there were no workstation issues that needed to be addressed. The Exchange client software was loaded onto the Novell server, and a central program group was created and added to each user's PROGMAN.INI file by using a batch file that ran upon login to the Novell server.

The users were then provided with an online tutorial using the company's intranet. These pages helped ease the transition from MS Mail to Exchange for the users and reduced the number of calls to ABC's help desk.

By implementing this solution, the company minimized the expertise needed on the Windows NT side of the house by using the migration tools that came with Exchange. They also continued to use their Novell server as a distribution medium, as well as a file repository. The login script capabilities of NetWare were utilized in rolling out the client software to the workstations.

The one issue ABC must deal with is creating new users on the Novell server. They used to have the MS Mail user accounts automatically generated through the same script they used to create NetWare accounts. ABC edited this script to create the proper Exchange account information.

This implementation of coexisting systems can work in many environments. In addition, once the word spreads among the user community about how good the email system can be, you can leverage this demand when proposing a full migration, as well as when deliberating the use of Exchange's more advanced groupware features.

Migrating from NetWare to Windows NT Server

The introduction of Exchange by Microsoft may prompt the discussion of a complete migration from NetWare to Windows NT Server. This is because for so many organizations, email and group collaboration are the main reasons for having a network in the first place.

Combined with the introduction of Exchange are 32-Bit desktops, Windows 95, and Windows NT Workstation 4.0. As these 32-bit platforms roll out onto the desktop, migrating file and print services to Windows NT Server may be a more strategic decision. You may already have Microsoft application software. When you combine that with Exchange, and then Windows NT

Server and BackOffice, you have a completely integrated Microsoft networking solution. You should consult a Microsoft Solution Provider, such as Software Spectrum **http://www.softwarespectrum.com** or Microsoft Consulting Services **http://www.microsoft.com/Exchange**, for more information about moving your organization off NetWare and onto Windows NT Server.

Understanding the Role of Systems Integrators and Consultants

Many environments consist of nothing but NetWare for file and print services. The organizations that operate in that environment choose NetWare because it is very popular and there is a lot of third-party support for the platform. In addition, choosing one platform leverages all the staff training across the organization.

Trying to roll out Windows NT servers to implement Exchange might seem like an impossibility in these environments; however, there are several benefits to using Exchange that have been described throughout this book. Not putting this technology into place due to the lack of expertise in the organization may be shortsighted.

You can turn to the following channels to get Exchange rolled out in your environment:

- Power Users
- Newsgroups and Web Sites
- Microsoft Solution Providers
- Microsoft Consulting Services

Power Users

These are the people in the organization who experiment with different technologies on their own time. You know who they are. These people are the ones who can train the other system administrators on NT concepts and work with management to support an Exchange rollout.

Newsgroups and Web Pages

There are several newsgroups on the Internet that are related to Windows NT and groupware. They include such topics as administration, networking, hardware, services, compatibility, and advocacy. These groups are a great resource for getting in touch with people who run NT-based networks. In addition, there are Web sites solely dedicated to NT technologies that will definitely include Exchange. These sites include the following:

- **http://www.microsoft.com/Exchange**
- **http://www.softwarespectrum.com**
- **http://www.ExchangeServer.com/**

Microsoft Solution Providers

There are many consultant agencies and systems integrators that are certified by Microsoft as Solution Providers. Just as the Novell environment has the Certified NetWare Engineer (CNE) program, Solution Providers must pass tests and spend a certain number of hours using the platform to be certified by Microsoft.

You can count on these professionals to assist you with your Microsoft Windows NT and Exchange projects, as they have the expertise and can assist in one or all phases of the project. They can be used in any phase of your project, starting with development and deployment to the support and maintenance of your Exchange environment. Working with a Solution Provider delivers many benefits, including firsthand information, and most importantly, knowledge transfer. Most are also very familiar with NetWare servers and clients because many Windows NT shops migrated from NetWare with the help of Microsoft Solution Providers. Contact Microsoft to get a list of Solution Providers in your area. You can find a list of Microsoft Solution Providers on Microsoft's Web site at **http://www.microsoft.com**.

Microsoft Consulting Services

For those organizations that will settle for nothing but the real article, Microsoft has a division to help you implement Microsoft technology solutions. These professionals provide support with all the backing of Microsoft.

This group is a step up from the Solution Providers because they have access to all the resources of Microsoft including constant, up-to-date training, and experience with the product. This is especially important in the case of Exchange. Many companies have been eagerly awaiting the delivery of Exchange 5.5, and Microsoft Consulting Services has the benefit of having gone through the beta testing of the product and all the knowledge gained from that testing. The beta program for Exchange 5.5 was offered to a select group of clients. Others keep up-to-date by accessing Microsoft's Exchange Web site. Microsoft's Web sites offer the public the opportunity to participate in many of Microsoft's product evaluations, and users can acquire product support and access to online knowledge bases.

Organizational Considerations

In addition to the networking and technical considerations involved when installing Exchange in a NetWare environment, some organizations will have to undergo serious change in their IS departments, especially in those shops running NetWare servers, MS Mail, and Microsoft applications such as Excel, Word, and PowerPoint.

These organizations have made a large investment in Microsoft technologies, but the network server platform has always been NetWare. There may be great opposition in the organization to move to Exchange because it means that Windows NT server must be rolled out into the entire enterprise just to upgrade MS Mail. Some managers will be harboring resentment toward Microsoft for painting them into a corner.

Breaking the NetWare Culture

Novell, now rededicated and refocused on expanding its core technology competencies in networking, is strongly marketing and supporting its NetWare 4.1 platform with NetWare Directory Services (NDS), a global directory service, and their 32-bit Intranet Client for Windows 95 and Windows NT 3.51 and 4.0 workstations. This rededication has reassured many companies that their NetWare investments are indeed safe.

Many NetWare shops are starting to outgrow their LAN-based e-mail packages and are looking for more robust client/server solutions for e-mail and groupware. Exchange will function very well in Windows NT and NetWare shops alike. The Exchange server must be an NT server; but as long as the connectivity is provided from the client to the server, there is no problem.

Connectivity isn't the only issue, however. In many NetWare-dominated shops, Windows NT is not a welcome solution. Since it isn't a NetWare server, it takes no advantage of NDS trees already in place, although Microsoft is developing utilities that will enable Windows NT servers to be managed as NDS objects.

In addition, users must be migrated to the Exchange server; and more importantly, staff has to be trained on NT Server because Exchange is so closely tied to the Windows NT operating system. This may be the biggest barrier to entry into NetWare environments for Exchange. Many administrators might ask, "Why not use GroupWise for e-mail and groupware?"

Also, because of the IBM acquisition of Lotus, Notes is being pushed very aggressively, as Lotus Notes offers Notes mail and Groupware solutions. A Notes server can be run on a Novell server, thereby strengthening the resolve of some administrators to keep Windows NT out of their shops. It is advisable to keep in mind that Exchange will be heavily tied into the operating systems you will run on the desktop, along with the applications being run on the desktop. In the future, the server platform used to file and print services will become less important. What will become increasingly important are the applications that can be run on top of the server operating system.

Exchange ties in very closely with the Windows 95 operating system, as well as Windows NT Workstation 4.0. As your workstations change from DOS/Windows 3.1 to these newer 32-bit operating systems, NetWare's dominance as the back-end server will decline because these new Microsoft desktop operating systems make it very easy to participate in NT domains and use the resources within them.

Committing to an All-Microsoft Strategy

Many managers might be wary of committing to an all-Microsoft strategy. Not wanting to put all your eggs in one basket is a legitimate concern; however, you may want to consider the following points:

- Microsoft's products are tightly integrated via COM and MAPI.
- There is tremendous third-party support for NT and Exchange.

- Microsoft's Solution Provider program does not lock you into Microsoft for support.
- Microsoft solutions are competitively priced.

These points address many of the concerns of information technology managers. These concerns stem from the experience of IBM dominance of the mainframe market in the early days of mainframe computing. The solutions were very proprietary, very expensive, and hard to learn; however, they worked. As long as you stuck with an all-IBM solution, you felt comfortable because everything worked together, and IBM engineers were familiar with the equipment.

Microsoft's product line of today has some of the same characteristics. It is well integrated, and there are many well-trained engineers who know the software.

Unlike the old IBM, however, Microsoft has built an open architecture using the MAPI and COM/DCOM standards combined with the Win32 SDK to enable third-party vendors to extend the capabilities of the core products.

In addition, there are several channels of support previously outlined that should allay the concerns of managers. You can feel secure that although you're committing to Microsoft products, you are not dependent on Microsoft for support and extensibility.

Migrating from Novell GroupWise

Migrating users from Novell GroupWise to Microsoft Exchange requires detailed planning, and you will need to understand Windows NT and Microsoft Exchange architectures. Microsoft Exchange Server has many migration tools to be used with Novell GroupWise.

Planning the Migration

As you plan your migration, you will need to consider the following:

- What level of migration—coexistence, mailbox migration, mailbox creation, or a combination of these—will be best for your organization?
- Should all users be migrated, or only a subset of users?
- Do users have all the hardware necessary or will migration occur in phases?
- What connectivity issues need to be addressed?
- Which users should migrate first?

Tables 10.1 and 10.2 show which mappings are supported during the coexistence of both Novell GroupWise and Microsoft Exchange in an environment, and details folder mappings of migrated information.

Table 10.1 Content Mapping

GroupWise	Microsoft Exchange
MessagesRead	Note
Note Request	Read Note (Textized)
Appointment Request	Read Note (Textized)
Task Request	Read Note (Textized)
Phone Request	Read Note (Textized)
Routing Slip	Read Note (Textized)
Calendar Data	Schedule+

Table 10.2 Folder Mapping

GroupWise	Microsoft Exchange
Inbox	Inbox
Inbox\UserName	Inbox
Inbox\Username\subfolder	Inbox\subfolder
OutBox	Sent Items
OutBox\Username	Sent Items
OutBox\Username\subfolder	SentItems\subfolders
Trash	(not migrated)
Trash\Username	(not migrated)
Personal Folders	Personal Folders
Personal Folders\subfolder	Personal Folders\subfolder
Week View	Schedule+ Calendar

Migration strategies, coexistence and full migration plans are detailed in both Chapter 8, "Migrating from Microsoft Mail Systems" and Chapter 9, "Migrating from Lotus cc:Mail." These chapters detail migration strategies from Microsoft MS Mail and Lotus cc:Mail to Microsoft Exchange, and they can assist you with the planning, development, and deployment from Novell GroupWise to Windows NT and Microsoft Exchange.

Using the Migration Wizard

After your Microsoft Exchange Server and Novell GroupWise systems are connected, it is easy to enable them to coexist or migrate from Novell GroupWise to Microsoft Exchange. Microsoft Exchange Server offers a Migration Wizard to assist you with migrating. The Migration wizard assists you with the creation of new Windows NT accounts, and you can select how you want the Windows NT accounts for your migrated users created (accounts can be created and given a random password). An Exchange mailbox is not accessible until a Windows NT account is associated with it.

The Novell GroupWise migration tool is tightly integrated, and enables you to extract data from Novell GroupWise systems, create mailboxes, and import data. The Migration Wizard is the interface to the GroupWise Source Extractor, which takes information from a foreign mail system and puts it into a neutral format, which can then be imported into Microsoft Exchange (see Figure 10.1). The Novell GroupWise Source Extractor will migrate user accounts, Mail and Phone messages, Appointments, Notes and Tasks. When migrating users from Novell GroupWise to Microsoft Exchange, you have the option to migrate all Appointments, Notes and Tasks, or to select a start and ending date. There are a few prerequisites to running the Novell GroupWise Source Extractor: All users that are to be migrated must grant migration ID access to Mail and Phone messages, Appointments, Notes and Tasks before their data is exported.

FIG. 10.1
Novell's GroupWise 4.1 Source Extractor converts data to a neutral format that Exchange can see.

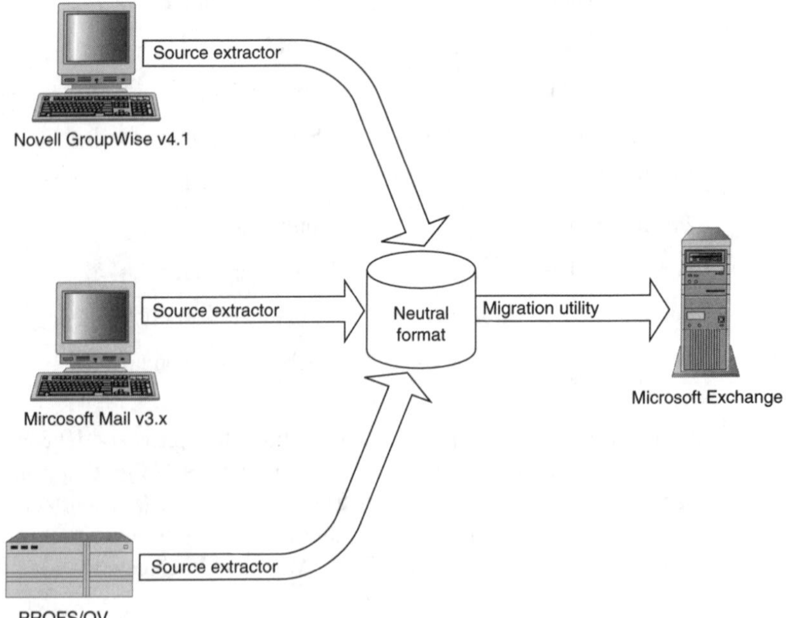

CHAPTER 11

Migrating from External Systems

In this chapter

This chapter's primary focus is on migration to Microsoft Exchange from host-based systems, but it also includes a brief overview of migration strategies from SMTP mail and foreign X.400 messaging systems. This chapter covers both the use of Exchange as gateway to these other systems and the process of transferring users to Exchange as the primary messaging system.

Migrating from a Host-Based System to Microsoft Exchange Server

The first messaging systems were proprietary. For example, PROFS was the most popular proprietary messaging system established. There are about six million PROFS users today. Proprietary messaging systems like PROFS were designed to provide messaging within organizations rather than between organizations. Today, with the advent of GUI interfaces, client/server architecture, open systems architecture, and the need for inter-LAN messaging, first-generation tools like PROFS are likely to be eclipsed by technologies such as Microsoft Exchange.

Here's a quick review of the benefits of Exchange over a legacy host system like PROFS:

- APIs—Exchange was developed to establish interoperability, allowing one client interface and transparent access to different message stores, message transports, and directory implementations. APIs are important architecturally for open architecture between disparate LAN systems. Exchange offers the recognized MAPI and CPC interface.
- X.500—Exchange is the recognized standard for distributed directory systems.
- Client/Server Architecture—Exchange partitions responsibility between client and server, using standard remote procedure calls, allowing the technology to become more efficient, and taking advantage of the price/performance benefit of using distributed PCs, such as multiprocessor RISC machines, rather than an expensive central host.
- GUI Interface—The popularity of the Windows interface, now the preference of PC users, has set the standard for user expectations, with character-based interfaces such as PROFS increasingly likely to disappear.

In addition to the preceding advantages, new Exchange clients also enjoy the advantages of group scheduling, powerful enterprise-wide workgroup applications, and one-stop enterprise-wide administration. In summary, migrating from a host-based system such as IBM PROFS to Microsoft Exchange offers several significant advantages, including the potential for enormous cost savings, communication between organizations, and freed host resources.

This chapter reviews the following for migration from host-based systems:

- Migration planning considerations
- Migration steps
- Migration elements
- Sample migration

- Client migration
- Host-to-server migration
- Single-provider versus dual-provider strategy
- Migrating partial versus whole post offices

NOTE Information that applies to IBM PROFS also applies to IBM OfficeVision/VM.

Migration Planning Considerations

The following list shows data that you can migrate from IBM PROFS by using Exchange's broad migration features:

- Calendars and reminders
- Nickname files
- Distribution lists
- Mailed documents

Introducing Migration Steps

When a large organization moves to a new messaging infrastructure, it's a good idea to break down the project into a series of steps. The major steps of migration can be divided as follows:

1. Use the MAPI driver (optional).
2. Create directory and mailbox entries.
3. Extract accounts and load accounts.
4. Set up connectivity (gateway).
5. Migrate the server contents.
6. Move the user data.
7. Set up directory synchronization.
8. Update the directory.

The Migration Elements

The following sections cover the main elements of Microsoft Exchange's Migration utilities. These tools and components of the Exchange system provide an easy and effective way to implement the system in your environment. Additionally, the migration tools are used in a similar manner for each e-mail system migrated to Exchange.

The Migration Tool

The following three tools are included with Exchange to provide an easy way for you to migrate from an existing e-mail system to Exchange. These tools extract the e-mail address information from the legacy system and guide you through the conversion and migration into Exchange.

- **The Source Extractor**—There are Source Extractors for several systems, such as Microsoft Mail Post Office, PROFS, and so on. The Source Extractor extracts users, inboxes, folders, and address books from the source mail systems.
- **The Migration Assistant**—The Migration Assistant converts all extracted data from the source system into Microsoft Exchange.
- **The Migration Wizard**—Microsoft Exchange includes a Migration Wizard to guide administrators through the process. An option is included for one-step migration.

Connectors

Connectors are the main link between users of Exchange and external systems. The Enterprise Edition of Exchange 5.5 includes two new connectors: the Connector for IBM OfficeVision/VM and the Connector for SNADS. These connectors provide coexistence for both messages and directories between Exchange and host systems.

Both connectors require the Microsoft SNA Server for host connectivity, though they do not require installation of any code on the host. Each also includes the optional ability to prevent attachments from being sent to the host mail system from Exchange. Either connector, when connected to an Exchange system that also houses an Internet Mail Service, can provide host users with access to Internet e-mail.

NOTE At the time of this writing, the author team had the most current release of the Exchange 5.5 Release Candidate 1. Unfortunately, the PROFS and SNADS Connectors were not included in that version. Check the Que Web site for more complete information on these connectors. You will find this and other updates at `www.mcp.com`. ■

Gateways

The Microsoft Exchange gateway for PROFS/OfficeVision provides seamless message transfer with Microsoft Exchange Server. The gateway supports all the features of the existing Microsoft gateway for IBM PROFS version 3.4, but with tighter calendar and directory integration. The PROFS/OfficeVision gateway encapsulates Microsoft Exchange messages sent to other Microsoft Exchange users of a PROFS backbone to maintain data integrity.

Directory Exchange Agent The Directory Exchange Agent (DXA) in Microsoft Exchange enhances directory synchronization with flexible scheduling, better time zone management, and update scheduling. Its multithreaded design improves throughput. Because the DXA includes multiple server support, the directory synchronization load is distributed across multiple "dirsync" servers for increased reliability and faster response. This setup reduces address list maintenance, increases security, and assures that updates occur more promptly. The DXA agent can function only if the proper connectivity exists between the e-mail systems. The DXA operates through the gateway to the legacy e-mail system.

Microsoft Schedule+ Free and Busy Gateway Free and busy times are the times when people are available and unavailable, respectively. The connector processes users' free and busy information from Microsoft Mail PC Post Offices and updates the information in Schedule+ Free and Busy system folders. It then sends updates on free and busy information from Microsoft Exchange for Microsoft Mail PC Post Offices.

Schedule+ 7.0 can access information from Schedule+ 1.0 users and access details about other Schedule+ 7.0 users. With the two together, Schedule+ 1 and Schedule+ 7 can do the following:

- Add specific people to the meeting organizer.
- Add people to a list of invitations and check their availability before scheduling a meeting.

However, because the file formats of Schedule+ 1.0 and Schedule+ 7.0 differ, Schedule+ 1.0 users cannot access the detailed information of Schedule+ 7.0 users.

The Microsoft Exchange gateway for PROFS/OfficeVision does not currently support integration with Outlook. However, future versions of the gateway may offer this functionality.

Passthrough Connectivity

Microsoft Exchange Server offers hardy group distribution list support and enables Microsoft Mail Post Office users to send messages to X.400 and SMTP environments through the Microsoft Mail Connector. Messages sent from the Microsoft Mail Post Office 3.x users through the Microsoft Exchange Server computer can use the Microsoft Exchange X.400 Connector and the Internet Mail Service to interchange messages with these environments. Alternatively, Microsoft Exchange users can send messages through any Microsoft Mail gateway by using the Microsoft Mail Connector.

Using the Migration Wizard

You can use the Migration Wizard to migrate one or more mailboxes on a Microsoft Mail for PC Networks post office. When each mailbox on the post office is migrated, you have a choice of the information to migrate. For more information on the Migration Wizard, see Chapter 8, "Migrating from Microsoft Mail Systems," and Chapter 10, "NetWare Considerations/Migrating from GroupWise."

Following a Sample Migration

Software Spectrum is headquartered in Garland, Texas, and has branch offices in London and Los Angeles. The headquarters has a mix of IBM PROFS and Microsoft Mail Post Office users. Both customer service and accounting departments need constant access to information on the host, communicating by way of the IBM PROFS system. Users in sales, marketing, and both consulting offices are all on Microsoft Mail post offices. Both consulting offices are connected to the headquarters by T1 lines. PROFS users are linked to Microsoft Mail users through the Microsoft Mail gateway to PROFS (see Figure 11.1). Migration will occur in three phases, as described in the following sections.

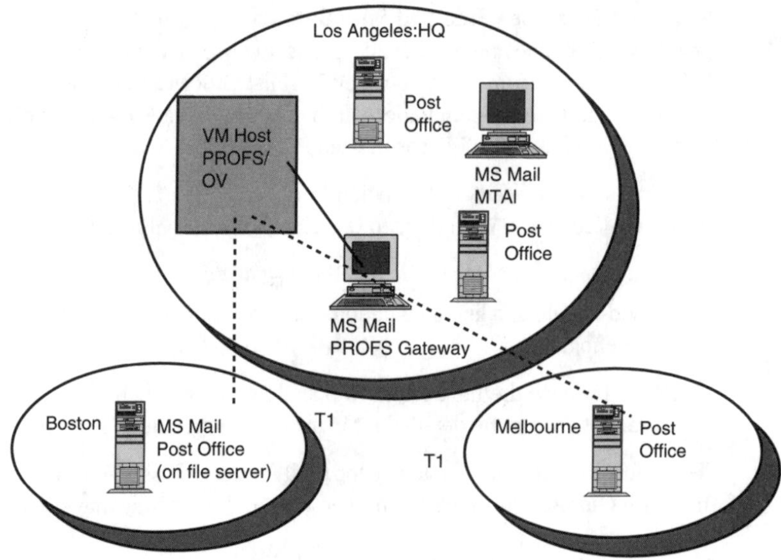

FIG. 11.1 Exchange has connector support for PROFS via the Attachmate Zip office gateways for Exchange.

Phase One—Migrating to Microsoft Exchange Clients

First, the Microsoft Exchange Client is installed on all workstations over time, both at headquarters and in the branches. Microsoft Exchange clients that work with the Microsoft Mail post offices have the rich text e-mail functionality in Microsoft Exchange and are still fully compatible with existing Mail clients.

Exchange clients talk to the PROFS host through the Microsoft Mail Post Office Connector to PROFS.

Microsoft Exchange is then installed on the Windows NT-based server at the headquarters, and both PROFS users and Microsoft Mail post offices are migrated to the Microsoft Exchange Server. This action consolidates the PROFS gateway and two Microsoft Mail post offices on one Microsoft Exchange Server, combining the functions of three machines on one (see Figure 11.2). (The customer also can continue to use the Microsoft Mail-based PROFS gateway.)

The automated Migration Tool in Microsoft Exchange works with most common host-based systems as easily as it works with LAN-based systems to automatically extract data and convert it to the Microsoft Exchange system.

The following data is migrated from a host-based system to Microsoft Exchange: notes, notelogs, calendars, reminders, and address books (nicknames).

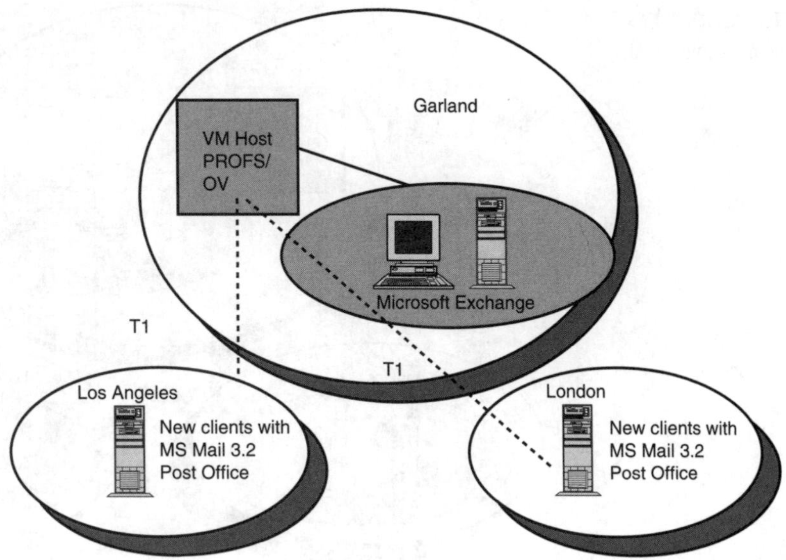

FIG. 11.2
Both PROFS users and Microsoft Mail post offices are migrated to the Microsoft Exchange Server.

The following data is not migrated: personal address information, preferences and settings, and binary file attachments. After all headquarters users are migrated, they have access to the complete functionality of Microsoft Exchange. They also can exchange messages, attachments, OLE objects, and scheduling information with Microsoft Exchange clients who are working against the Microsoft Mail 3.x post offices in the branch offices.

Phase Two—Sending Microsoft Exchange Messages Through a Microsoft Mail-Based Gateway

At the headquarters, before the Microsoft Exchange gateway to PROFS was installed, messages were routed to PROFS users from Microsoft Exchange users working against Microsoft Mail post offices through the Microsoft Mail gateway to PROFS. PROFS users also routed their messages back through the Microsoft Mail gateway.

Phase Three—Migrating the Branches to Microsoft Exchange Servers

Windows NT-based servers are added to the networks in both branches and Microsoft Exchange is installed on each server (see Figure 11.3).

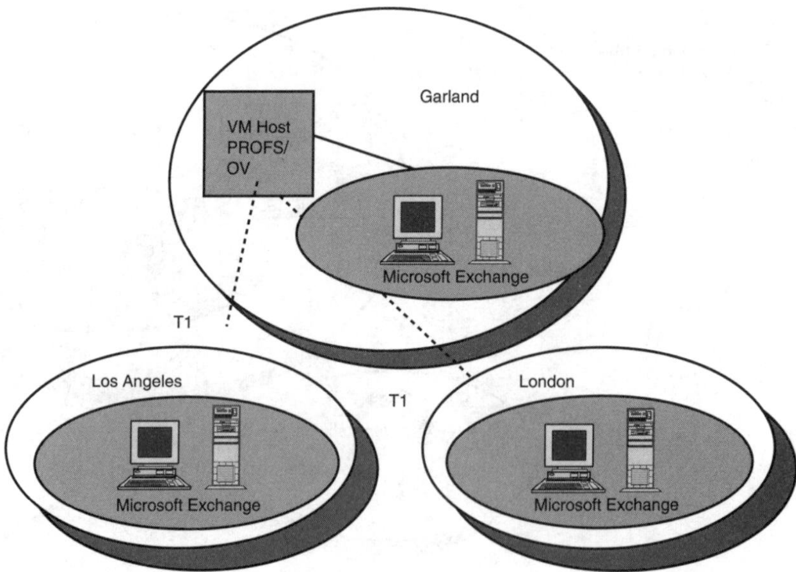

FIG. 11.3
The final configuration.

Now the power of Microsoft Exchange is unleashed across the enterprise. All users have access to rich text formatting of messages and documents, rules, public folders, forms, group scheduling, remote functionality, and more. Relevant customer service and accounting data from the host can be extracted and put in public folders that are available to all or specified users both at headquarters and at the regional offices. With immediate access to the same information, users across the enterprise can respond faster to market demands and make better-informed decisions.

In Figure 11.4, the message originates from PROFS and is routed by the PROFS gateway directly to the Connector post office in-queue, as are all other messages bound for Microsoft Exchange users.

Understanding the Role of the Microsoft Mail

It's helpful to illustrate the message flow process. When using Microsoft Mail gateways with PROFS, it's a natural development to have Microsoft Mail gateways coexist with Exchange Server.

Figure 11.4 outlines the flow of a message that originates from PROFS and is routed to the Microsoft Mail user through the Microsoft Exchange gateway to PROFS.

The message is passed through the PROFS gateway to the Microsoft Exchange Information Store. The gateway converts the PROFS message into a standard MAPI message.

When the message arrives in the Information Store, it follows the same message flow as if it originated as a Microsoft Exchange message. Going the other direction, a message from a Microsoft Mail Post Office user destined for a PROFS user takes routes through the Microsoft Mail Connector as described in the following section.

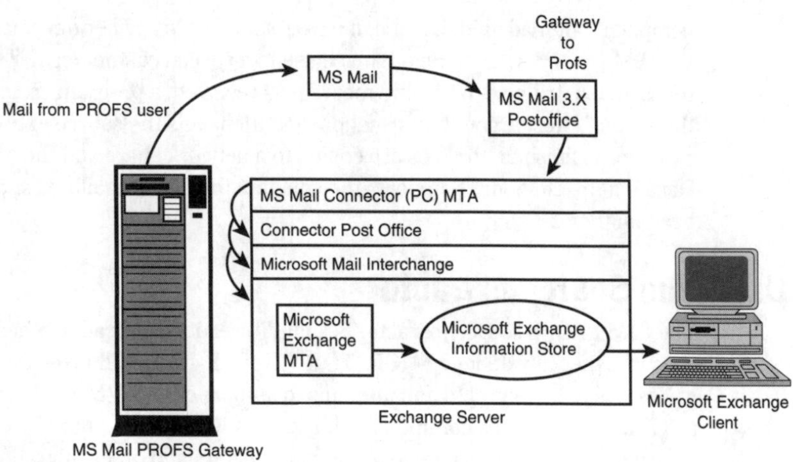

FIG. 11.4
The message flow from IBM PROFS users to Exchange users.

Message Flow from Microsoft Exchange Users to IBM PROFS Users

In the reverse situation, a message originates from Microsoft Exchange and is routed through the Microsoft Mail Connector to the Microsoft Mail post office with a PROFS gateway installed.

In this case, the message from the Microsoft Exchange user is stored in the Microsoft Exchange Information Store, and is then sent by the Information Store to the Microsoft Exchange MTA. From there, it's routed by the Microsoft Mail Interchange to the Connector post office. The message then is routed from the Connector post office to its final PROFS destination directly by the Microsoft Mail PROFS gateway.

The message from Microsoft Mail is picked up by the Microsoft Mail Connector (PC) MTA and placed in the Connector post office in-queue. Once there, the message is handled exactly the same as all other messages.

Going in the other direction, PROFS users who send messages to Microsoft Exchange users use the PROFS gateway in Microsoft Mail Post Office.

Using Client Providers for IBM PROFS

Using a PROFS MAPI client provider for the Microsoft Exchange Client is an alternative to or a variant of multiphased migration. Using Attachmate's ZIP! Office Client Connection product, the Microsoft Exchange Client can be used to connect to the IBM PROFS system, Microsoft Exchange Server, or both systems.

Having Users Drive Migration

With some programming, you can make a multiphased migration user-managed and user-driven. For example, the mailboxes for all users can be created in a Microsoft Exchange Server computer, but made hidden. When a user accesses his or her new mailbox and no longer needs the IBM PROFS system, he or she can send a special custom form. This form is already addressed to a mailbox. When the message is received, a program creates an account file with the sender's host account information, and then runs the source extractor. After the source extractor is finished, the files are copied to a network share and the Migration Wizard is started in batch mode. It imports the data into the empty mailbox, and logs that this user has been migrated.

Using the Source Extractor

The IBM PROFS source extractor is a multithreaded application when migrating messages. It runs in a specially defined MIGRATOR VM ID. Each thread takes the next VM ID from the list of VM IDs to be migrated and attempts to autolog on this VM ID. If successful, it invokes the MIGVIZ EXEC from a common minidisk. This EXEC links to the MIGRATOR's 191 minidisk, from which it can access the migration parameters and other migration programs. These programs extract the relevant data from notelogs, files, calendars, nickname files, and distribution lists and send the data to a file transfer VM ID. When it completes extracting all the data or when the maximum-wait time limit is reached, the thread goes on to the next unmigrated VM ID in the list.

Preparing to Migrate Data

Before installing the software, you need to create two VM IDs, MIGRATOR and MIGXFER, as described in the following sections. Create either a class B VM ID that can perform the autolog function or a class G VM ID that can perform this function. This ID must have the following:

- A 191 minidisk to store programs, account files, other required data tables, LOG, and STATUS files.
- A LINK to a minidisk that contains the OFSUAD FILE or a LINK to xxxDBM 191 minidisk.
- A LINK to a minidisk that contains the PROFS NICKNAME file and ADDRLIST files.
- (Optional) Pre-ESA systems may need to provide a link to the VM DIRECTORY file, unless some other means exists to perform the AUTO LOGON of VM IDs from the MIGRATOR VM ID.

The following code shows a sample directory entry for the MIGRATOR VM ID:

```
USER MIGRATOR password 4M 8M B
ACCOUNT
IPL CMS
CONSOLE 009 3215
SPOOL   00C 2540 READER *
SPOOL   00D 2540 PUNCH O
SPOOL   00E 1403 A
MDISK   191 3380 ccc 016 vvvvvv MR readpw writepw
LINK    xxxDBM   191 395 RR
MIGXFER
```

This class G VM ID may be used to receive the files generated during the migration process from the reader to a minidisk. This VM ID requires a minidisk large enough to store all notelog, calendar, mailed documents, and nickname information from the group of users participating in the migration run. Optionally, the administrator may choose to designate the MIGRATOR VM ID to receive these files, rather than creating a second VM ID. The documentation assumes that there are two VM IDs.

The following code shows a sample directory entry for the MIGXFER VM ID:

```
USER MIGXFER password 4M 8M B
ACCOUNT
IPL CMS
CONSOLE 009 3215
SPOOL   00C 2540 READER *
SPOOL   00D 2540 PUNCH O
SPOOL   00E 1403 A
MDISK   191 3380 ccc 100 vvvvvv MR readpw writepw
```

Installing the IBM PROFS Source Extractor

To install the Microsoft Exchange Server IBM PROFS source extractor with an MS-DOS 3270 Emulator, use the following procedures:

1. Log on as the MIGRATOR VM ID.
2. Insert the floppy disk with the PROFS Source extractor code into the A drive of the computer.
3. From the a:\ prompt, type **UPLOAD** ***<path to terminal emulation software>*** and press Enter. Do not include a trailing backslash on the path.
4. Move the file MIGVIZ EXEC to a common minidisk.
5. Repeat this process for the file transfer VM ID.

In addition to using a MS-DOS 3270 Emulator, you can install the Exchange Server IBM PROFS Source Extractor with a Windows 3270 Emulator. If you don't use terminal-emulation software, the files can be transferred to the MIGRATOR's 191 minidisk with the sample RUNBATCH.EBM macro.

Customizing EXECs After Installation You may need to customize the files MIGLOGON EXEC and MIGLINKP EXEC to work with your system. Before using MIGLOGON EXEC, you must change the variables `rdpass` and `vmdir`. Before using MIGLINKP, you may need to change the text for `sysadmin`.

Maintaining Directories During a Multiphase Migration, you need to keep directories in both systems current. You can use the migration tools to export and import directory information, as described in the following sections.

Creating Addresses in Your Host System

If you don't have a directory synchronization requestor for your host system, then you need to handle the following:

- Export the mailbox and foreign system addresses from Microsoft Exchange Server with directory export.
- Change the format of the file.
- Import the addresses into your host system.
- Extract Custom Recipients from PROFS.

Mail sent in Microsoft Exchange Server computers and incoming mail from Microsoft Exchange Server gateways can be routed to the PROFS addresses. You can use this rather than using directory synchronization, but you have to repeat the process on a regular basis to update the Microsoft Exchange Server directory with changes in the existing system directory.

Creating the REMADDR File To create custom recipients, extract a file of IBM PROFS addresses. Move the file to the Microsoft Exchange Server computer. Import the IBM PROFS address file into Microsoft Exchange Server with the Migration Wizard to create custom recipients. To do this, complete the following steps:

NOTE The custom recipient information is created with PROFS target addresses. If mail sent from Microsoft Exchange Server mailboxes is routed through X.400 or SMTP to reach the PROFS host, you must modify the custom recipient data before importing it to have the proper address type and address.

1. On the computer where you installed the source extractor, log on as the MIGRATOR VM ID.
2. Type **MIGWIZRD** and press Enter to start the source extractor. The screen displays the following code:

```
Source Extractor for IBM (R) PROFS (R) and OfficeVision (TM)
Microsoft Exchange Server Migration Wizard

The following parameters are specified in MIGPARMS DATA file.

You can change these parameters using this menu, or by using XEDIT.

OV/VM (PROFS) Nickname File: File name:          File type:
Accounts File:               File name:          File type:
PROFS Calendar MIGRATOR vmid (PROFS system only)
Notify VM id                                       : HOWARDS
File Transfer VM id                                : MIGXFER
Thread timeout (min)                               : 30
Spool Console required                (TRUE/FALSE) : FALSE
Number of migration threads                        : 05
Replace previously migrated accounts  (TRUE/FALSE) : TRUE

------------------------------------------------------------
```

```
<< BACK      NEXT >>         FINISH             CANCEL      HELP
F10/F22     F11/F23         F12/F24            F3/F15      F1/F13
```

3. (Optional) In the OV/VM (PROFS) Nickname File field, type the name and file type of the nickname file. If this field is not filled in, the source extractor uses OFSUAD FILE, if access to this file is available.
4. (Optional) In the Accounts File field, type the name and file type of the accounts file with a list of VM IDs for which you want to create custom recipients. If you plan to create custom recipients for all VM IDs, skip this step.

   Anywhere from one to all VM IDs can be specified in an account file. The account file has one VM ID on each line.
5. In the Notify VM ID field, type the VM ID to which alert messages are sent. This VM ID doesn't need to have administrator privileges.
6. In the File Transfer VM ID field, type the VM ID to which all the extractor data should be written.
7. Press the F11 key to continue. The screen displays the following:

```
Source Extractor for IBM (R) PROFS (R) and OfficeVision (TM)
Microsoft Exchange Server Migration Wizard

What information would you like to migrate?

Type Y to select option, or N to reject it.

Y Remote addresses creation information (REMADDR FILE)
N Mailbox creation information (MAILBOX FILE)
N Email messages (Notelogs and In-basket)
From: 1994/10/28 to 1995/10/28
N Schedule information (Calendars and Reminders)
From: 1995/10/28 to 1996/10/28
N Documents from OFSINDEX FILE
From: 1994/10/28 to 1995/10/28
N Personal Address Book (Nicknames and Distribution lists)

-------------------------------------------------------------

<< BACK      NEXT >>         FINISH             CANCEL      HELP
F10/F22     F11/F23         F12/F24            F3/F15      F1/F13
```

8. Set the Remote Addresses Creation Information to Y. Set all other options to N.
9. To continue, press the F11 key. The screen displays the remote address file.
10. Edit the remote address file as needed to remove VM IDs for which you don't want Microsoft Exchange Server custom recipients, or to change the display names. The source extractor uses XEDIT as the editor, and all XEDIT commands and subcommands are available.

11. Press F12 to complete the process.

    This procedure creates REMADDR FILE on the MIGRATOR 191 minidisk and sends REMADDR PRI and REMADDR PKL to the reader of the file transfer VM ID. The REMADDR PRI and REMADDR PKL files are in ASCII format.

Moving the REMADDR Address to the Microsoft Exchange Server To move the REMADDR address to the Microsoft Exchange Server, take these steps:

1. Log on as the MIGXFER VM ID.
2. Type **MIGXFER** and press Enter to start the transfer tool.
3. The transfer tool modifies the file named REMADDR FILE to the migration file format and transfers it from the reader to the minidisk. The MIGXFER EXEC also creates MIGXFER BAT, MIGRATOR PKL, and MIGPURGE EXEC on the minidisk.
4. Download the MIGXFER BAT file to the personal computer.
5. From the personal computer, type the following to transfer the REMADDR FILE and packing list file to the personal computer as REMADDR.PRI and MIGRATOR.PKL:

   MIGXFER ***<path to your terminal emulation software>***

6. On the host, type **MIGPURGE** to remove the files from the reader.
7. (Optional) Edit the REMADDR PRI file to remove addresses, modify display names, change the target address type, or add additional directory import fields and data. For example, if you want all the custom recipients to have telephone number data, you can add the field Telephone-Office1 to the end of the first line in the directory section, and then add telephone numbers to the end of each line of data.

The migration files now can be imported into Microsoft Exchange Server with the Migration Wizard. See the section, “Importing Migration Files,” later in the chapter for the next step.

Creating Mailboxes

The procedure for creating mailboxes is exactly the same as for creating custom recipients except that, in step 8 of the extracting process, set Mailbox Creation Information to Y. A MAILBOX file is created in place of the REMADDR file.

Migrating Data The process of migrating data creates secondary files, and autologs onto the VM IDs that are being migrated. The VM IDs to migrate cannot be in use during the extracting process.

Extracting E-Mail Data To extract e-mail data, take the following steps:

1. Log on as the MIGRATOR VM ID.
2. Type **MIGWIZRD** and press Enter to start the source extractor. The screen displays the following information:

```
Source Extractor for IBM (R) PROFS (R) and OfficeVision (TM)
Microsoft Exchange Server Migration Wizard

The following parameters are specified in MIGPARMS DATA file.

You can change these parameters using this menu, or by using XEDIT.

OV/VM (PROFS) Nickname File: File name:          File type:
Accounts File:               File name:          File type:
PROFS Calendar MIGRATOR vmid (PROFS system only)  :
Notify VM id                                      : HOWARDS
File Transfer VM id                               : MIGXFER
Thread timeout (min)                              : 30
Spool Console required              (TRUE/FALSE)  : FALSE
Number of migration threads                       : 05
Replace previously migrated accounts (TRUE/FALSE) : TRUE

-----------------------------------------------------------------

<< BACK     NEXT >>          FINISH              CANCEL       HELP
F10/F22    F11/F23          F12/F24             F3/F15       F1/F13
```

3. (Optional) In the OV/VM (PROFS) Nickname File field, type the name and file type of the nickname file. If this field is not filled in, the extractor uses OFSUAD FILE.

TIP If you are migrating only a few accounts, create an accounts or nickname file with these accounts in it and set the appropriate field to point at the file.

4. (Optional) In the Accounts File field, type the name and file type of the accounts file with a list of VM IDs for which you want to create custom recipients.
5. (Optional) If you are migrating calendars from a PROFS system, enter the corresponding VM ID in the PROFS Calendar MIGRATOR VM ID field. Ignore this step if you are migrating calendars from OfficeVision.
6. In the Notify VM ID field, type the VM ID to which error messages are sent. This VM ID doesn't need to have administrator privileges.
7. In the File Transfer VM ID field, type the VM ID to which all the extractor data should be written.
8. In the Thread Timeout field, type the maximum number of minutes it should take to migrate each VM ID. When this time runs out, the MIGWIZRD EXEC reuses the thread.
9. In the Spool Console Required field, set the value to TRUE to send console updates to the MIGRATOR VM ID to monitor progress.

   Alternatively, set the value to FALSE so that the console updates are not sent.
10. In the Number of Migration Threads, set the number of VM IDs that will be migrated simultaneously. If you set this number too high, it can affect performance and resources on the host computer.
11. In the Replace Previously Migrated Accounts field, set the value to TRUE if you want to migrate data for VM IDs that previously were migrated.

Alternatively, set the value to FALSE if you do not want to migrate previously migrated VM IDs.

12. Press the F11 key to continue. The screen displays the following information:

```
Source Extractor for IBM (R) PROFS (R) and OfficeVision (TM)
Microsoft Exchange Server Migration Wizard

What information would you like to migrate?

Type Y to select option, or N to reject it.

N Remote addresses creation information (REMADDR FILE)
N Mailbox creation information (MAILBOX FILE)
Y Email messages (Notelogs and In-basket)
From: 1994/10/28 to 1995/10/28
Y Schedule information (Calendars and Reminders)
From: 1995/10/28 to 1996/10/28
Y Documents from OFSINDEX FILE
From: 1994/10/28 to 1995/10/28
Y Personal Address Book (Nicknames and Distribution lists)

-------------------------------------------------------------------

<< BACK     NEXT >>         FINISH              CANCEL      HELP
F10/F22     F11/F23         F12/F24             F3/F15      F1/F13
```

13. Set the options to Y or N, based on the information you need to migrate. Also, update the date range for each type of information that is being migrated.

CAUTION

The date range doesn't update dynamically. To avoid not migrating recent items, set the To dates to a future date, in case you forget to update them.

14. Press F11 to continue. The screen displays the accounts file.

15. Edit the accounts file as needed to remove VM IDs that you do not want to migrate.

    The status field can have the following three possible values:

    Init—Not migrated yet but will be migrated.

    Timeout—Attempted to migrate VM ID, but reached the timeout limit before migration was finished. Will be migrated.

    Done—Exported data from this VM ID in the past. Will be migrated only if Replace Previous Migrated Accounts field is set to TRUE.

16. (Optional) If you didn't create a small nickname file or accounts file with your list of VM IDs to be migrated, pare down the full list of users to only the ones you want to migrate.

17. Press F12 to start extracting data. The screen displays the following information:

```
Source Extractor for IBM (R) PROFS (R) and OfficeVision (TM)
Migrating mailbox information...
Migrating users...
Max_threads=05. Replace=1
N_input=63
AUTO SUFINE EXEC MIGRATE MIGRATOR READ
AUTO STGRAY EXEC MIGRATE MIGRATOR READ


RUNNING  MSVM7
```

18. When the MIGWIZRD EXEC is finished, type **SHUT** to end the program.

This process creates several items in the reader of the file transfer VM ID, depending on the options selected in the second screen, which are described in the following table:

Item Name	Description
MAILBOX FILE	Information to create mailboxes
<VM ID> PKL	Packing list for the migration files of the VM ID
<VM ID> PRI	Primary intermediate file for the migration files of the VM ID
<VM ID> SEC	Secondary intermediate file for the migration files of the VM ID

These files are stored in ASCII format and should not be edited. For each VM ID there can be multiple primary intermediate files.

Migrating Files to Microsoft Exchange Server To move the migration files to Microsoft Exchange Server, follow these steps:

1. Log on as the MIGXFER VM ID.
2. Type **MIGXFER** and press Enter to start the transfer tool. The screen displays the following information:

```
Source Extractor for IBM (R) PROFS (R) and OfficeVision (TM)

There are 180 K bytes available on A disk.
Total size of selected files is 1892 K.
Select a subset of files that can be transferred by editing this file.

User ID                 File Size
00000 * * * Top of File * * *
00001 REMADDR                6080
00002 MAILBOX                4960
00003 EAST03                 1328
00004 EAST02                36628
00005 EAST01                10064
00006 CENT01                98776
00007 CENT02               309728
00008 CENT03               282512
```

```
00009 CENT05                 4344
00010 WEST01                16416
00011 WEST02                22004
00012 CENT04              1044180
----------------------------------------------------------------
FINISH                  RECALCULATE              CANCEL
F12/F24                 F10/F22                  F3/F15
====>
```

3. (Optional) Select a subset of files to transfer by editing this list. If you are limited by space on the minidisk, press F10 to recalculate the total size of selected files.
4. The transfer tool modifies the files to the migration file format and transfers them from the reader to the minidisk. The MIGXFER EXEC also creates MIGXFER BAT, <VM ID> PKL, and MIGPURGE EXEC on the minidisk.
5. Download the MIGXFER BAT file to the personal computer.
6. From the personal computer, type **MIGXFER *<path to your terminal emulation software>*** to transfer the migration files to the personal computer as *.PRI, *.SEC, and <VMID>.PKL. This step also consolidates all packing list files (PKLs) into one file.
7. On the host, type **MIGPURGE** to remove the files from the reader.
8. If you want, edit the MAILBOX.PRI file to modify information such as directory names or to add additional directory import fields and data. For example, if you want to migrate department information with each mailbox, you can add the field Department to the end of the first line of the directory header, and then add department names to the end of each line of data.

NOTE Important: If you need to change directory (common-name) names, do it before importing the migration files. After you create mailboxes, the only way to change the directory name is to delete the mailbox and create a new one. ■

Importing Migration Files

The Migration Wizard reads files created by the extractor and automates simple administrative tasks, such as creating mailboxes and custom recipients.

Import the migration files with the Migration Wizard. See Chapter 7, "Planning Connections to Microsoft Mail Systems," for steps on how to use the Migration Wizard.

Migrating from SMTP (Internet) Mail Systems

This section is relevant if your organization currently has a mail system with a proprietary gateway into the Internet or if you use an SMTP POP mail server connected directly to the Internet.

NOTE Any reference in this section about connecting to the Internet also applies to connections with other SMTP-based systems. ■

The Microsoft Exchange Internet Mail Service provides connectivity with any SMTP-based mail system. In the past, with a PC-based messaging system, it was necessary to connect a separate SMTP gateway PC to access the Internet or other SMTP system. Exchange is designed to talk to the Internet directly and, because of its other connectors and gateways, is well suited for use as a gateway for other systems.

You will encounter two types of migration when implementing Exchange in an SMTP (POP mail) environment:

- **System Migration**—Replacing existing SMTP gateways with Exchange servers
- **User Migration**—Transferring POP mail users to Exchange mailboxes

System Migration

You can use Exchange to replace the current SMTP gateways in your organization. If you currently use the MS-DOS–based SMTP gateway for Microsoft Mail, you want to do this as soon as possible. Exchange provides a far more reliable and efficient method for bridging your organization to SMTP-based systems such as the Internet.

Migrating Users from POP Mail to Exchange

If your organization uses SMTP Mail (POP) mail servers for user accounts, consider the following points about migration to Exchange.

First, POP mail provides the flexibility to check messages from any point on the Internet with several commonly available mail clients (such as Qualcomm's Eudora, or even with an advanced World Wide Web browser, such as Netscape's Navigator). In Exchange 5.0 Microsoft added a POP client giving it the same flexibility as all the other clients. This section provides some suggestions for migrating users to Exchange and beyond.

Building a Parallel SMTP System

The X.400 Connector option of sharing address spaces with a foreign system isn't an option in the SMTP world. Therefore, it's not a practical method for gradual migration from POP mail to Exchange. If you do happen to have a large number of POP mail users that you want to migrate to Exchange, the best way probably will be to build all your accounts on parallel systems. Then you have to "throw the switch" and redirect mail to your Exchange server when it's all set up.

For example, for Software Spectrum, the Internet domain `isswspectrum.com`, we can temporarily set up an offline Exchange server to receive mail at `popmail.swspectrum.com` for testing. We create all the necessary user accounts on this parallel system, and test for proper routing to this address. Then at a specified time, we modify the entry in the DNS (Domain Name Server) to route `allswspectrum.com` mail to the machine previously designated as `popmail.swspectrum.com`.

If you have users that must retain a POP mail account for some reason (for example, to check mail remotely without an Exchange Client), then you can create two profiles on their client: one pointed at their Exchange server and the other pointed at the old server, thus giving them access to both areas.

Exchange offers excellent support for remote users, so use this method when a remote user does not have access to an Exchange client while on the road.

Migrating from Foreign X.400 Messaging Systems

The X.400 Connector for Microsoft Exchange provides all the connectivity needed for replacing a foreign X.400 system in your organization. This connectivity includes gateways for connecting to any system that uses X.400 standards.

As in connecting and migrating from SMTP mail, there are two kinds of migration:

- **User Migration**—Transferring foreign X.400 system users to Exchange mailboxes
- **System Migration**—Replacing existing X.400 gateways with Exchange servers

User Migration from Foreign X.400 Systems

When switching to Exchange from a foreign X.400 system, user migration will probably be a gradual process. During migration there obviously will be some users on Exchange and others still using the foreign X.400 system simultaneously. Microsoft Exchange allows you to share the X.400 address space with a foreign system to provide coexistence during the migration process.

In the previous example, the Sydney site is connected to the Los Angeles site through a public X.400 network. Originally, the messaging system in Sydney was a foreign X.400-based system, but it is now being migrated to Exchange. Suppose that 65% of the Sydney users were migrated (using the included migration tools) to Exchange. To maintain coexistence, you set up Exchange to share an address space with the foreign X.400 system (in the Site Addressing properties page), which means that messages can arrive for users on both Exchange and the foreign X.400 at the same address.

The following list shows the message route in the preceding example:

1. A message from the public X.400 network enters through the Microsoft Exchange X.400 connector.
2. If the user is an Exchange user (or a user on another system connected to Exchange through another connector), the message is delivered normally.
3. If the user isn't on the Exchange system, it will be routed to your foreign X.400 system and delivered to the user in that mailbox.

With this system, users can be migrated to Exchange at your pace, knowing that both systems will run side by side provided that you need them to do so. This approach also reduces the amount of non-deliverable messages often encountered when switching over to a new system.

System Migration

Another common system migration scenario is to replace your current Microsoft Mail X.400 gateways with a more robust Exchange server with both the X.400 and Microsoft Mail connectors.

In this scenario, Exchange receives incoming X.400 messages through the X.400 connector, and routes them through, using the Microsoft Mail connector. Because there will not necessarily be any mail user on the Exchange servers, no user migration is needed. The next step is to migrate the users from Microsoft Mail Post Office to Microsoft Exchange, but this topic is covered in its entirety in Chapter 7, "Planning Connections to Microsoft Mail Systems." ●

PART III

Exchange Administration and Configuration

CHAPTER 12

Using the Administrator Program

In this chapter

The Administrator program will become your familiar friend as you work with Exchange. From this program, you can manage an entire Exchange organization. Because Administrator is so versatile, it is rather ominous-looking at first sight. The dozens of functions that are provided in menus and check boxes tend to be somewhat confusing initially.

The primary goal of this chapter is to familiarize you with this application and assist you in navigating it comfortably. Administrator is the most useful tool for Exchange administrators, so learning its tricks now will prevent many headaches for you in the future.

Starting the Administrator Program and Connecting to an Exchange Server

The first step is to launch the Exchange Administrator application from the taskbar in Windows NT. You'll find it under Programs, Exchange, Exchange Administrator. After the initial splash screen, if you have not yet configured a default server, the Connect to Server dialog box appears (see Figure 12.1).

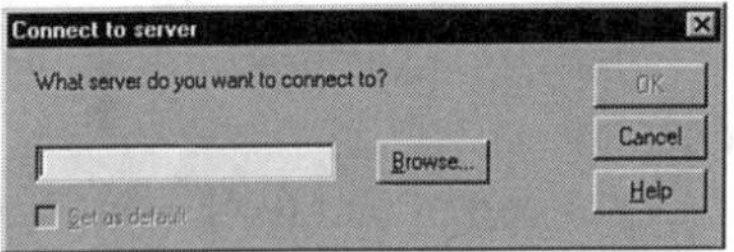

FIG. 12.1
Select your target Exchange server, and then click OK.

This dialog box appears repeatedly when you work with Exchange, so you should be familiar with it. The dialog box asks you which server you want to connect to. In the text box, type the name of the server to which you want to connect. You must type the server name accurately.

NOTE You must have local machine administrator privileges on the server to which you are trying to connect. Windows NT 4.0 requires this privilege to access the Registry, which is where Exchange Administrator writes most of its changes. Previous versions of Windows NT did not require local administrator access. ■

If you click the Browse button, you can view a graphical representation of the Exchange servers within your organization. From that window, you can choose the Exchange server you would like to administer.

The Set As Default check box enables you to designate the selected server as the default connection. The next time you launch the Administrator program, you will not be prompted to choose a server; the default Exchange server's window appears. This check box is unavailable, however, until you make an entry in the text box.

Click OK when you finish making your selections. The Administrator program attempts to connect to the server. If you typed the name of an Exchange server that does not exist, or if the selected server or its connection is down for any reason, you get an error message and the option to attempt a different connection.

If you have already configured a default server, the connection is made, and you see the Administrator interface, which is covered in the following section.

Using the Administrator Interface

The Exchange Administrator interface shows your entire Exchange organization (see Figure 12.2). Like a satellite view of the earth from space, this window presents the big picture of your Exchange hierarchy. You have the option to zoom as close as you want to view any object.

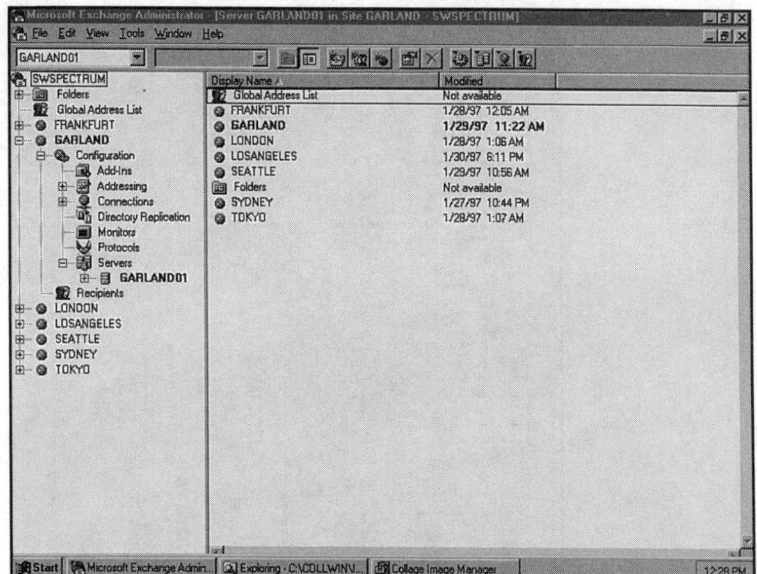

FIG. 12.2
The main Administrator window.

The left side of the window shows your Exchange hierarchy, displaying all the objects in your Exchange organization. The right side of the window displays the contents of the container object that is selected on the left side of the window. The title bar of the window identifies the server name, the site name, and name of the object that is currently selected, in the following format:

Server *name* in Site *name—Object name*

Take some time to explore the Exchange hierarchy on the left side of the window and get a feel for how the elements are organized.

Navigating the Hierarchy Tree

The Exchange site hierarchy window lists all of the components that make up your Exchange site in a treelike fashion. This includes recipients, servers, connectors, and any other Exchange component that you have installed. Navigating this window is much like navigating the directory hierarchy in File Manager or the Windows 95 Explorer. Many of the elements or objects in Exchange's hierarchy have multiple levels below them.

A plus sign (+) to the left of an object indicates that the object has branches below it. Click the plus sign to display those branches. After you display the branches, the plus sign turns into a minus sign (–). When you click the minus sign, the branches disappear. A branch that has no plus or minus sign to the left of it is at the end of the tree. When you click one of these branches, its contents appear in the right window of the Administrator window, as shown in Figure 12.3.

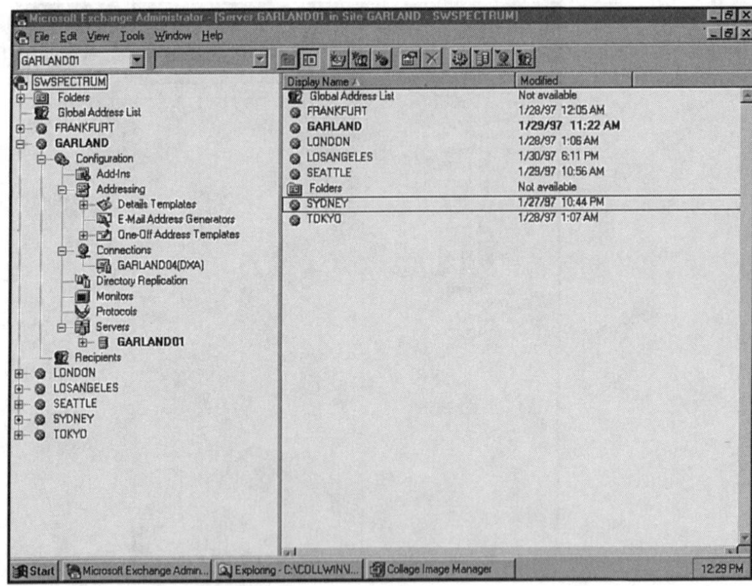

FIG. 12.3
Object hierarchy tree.

The top item of the site hierarchy tree is always the name of your organization. Double-click the name to collapse the entire tree view and start navigating from the top.

If you are setting up a new Exchange organization and have not yet established connections, you see only a small portion of the local Exchange Server elements in this default view. After new connectors and other objects are created, go through the Administrator window to see how these additional components affect the overall Exchange hierarchy.

As you navigate the Exchange hierarchy, you will notice that every object has an associated graphic icon. The following text describes and illustrates the hierarchy tree and objects that are displayed in the Exchange Administrator program (refer to Figure 12.3 for an example of this structure).

I. **Organization:** The top or starting point of the Exchange server directory. All other directory objects are subordinate to this object. This is the directory name used for addressing and cannot be changed.

A. **Folders:** The parent container for all of the folder information in an organization. Note that these components of the hierarchy are compiled across all sites.

1. **Public Folders:** Public folders hold information that can be shared by various users. When a change is made in a public folder, that change is replicated to every replica of the folder throughout the organization. Use this public folders item to view all of the public folders and public folder replicas configured for Exchange.

2. **System Folders:** The system folders include the EFORMS REGISTRY, OFFLINE ADDRESS BOOK, and SCHEDULE+ FREE BUSY folders.

   a. **EFORMS REGISTRY:** This holds all of the organization forms libraries that have been created in an organization.

      - **Organization Forms Library:** An organization forms library is a public folder that stores electronic forms. By default, any form saved to a public folder is available to all Exchange users.
      - **Events Root:** The Events Root contains folders with event configuration information for available Exchange Server computers.
      - **EventConfig_Server:** The EventConfig_SERVER folders contain event configuration information for the specific Exchange Server computers installed at your site.

   b. **OFFLINE ADDRESS BOOK:** This address book contains lists of recipients in the Exchange organization about whom remote users can get information.

      - **Offline Address Book:** There is one offline address book per site listed here. By downloading this to a laptop, a remote user can send mail to any recipient in the Exchange organization.

   c. **SCHEDULE+ FREE BUSY:** This container holds one Schedule+ Free/Busy folder for each site. Every new mailbox that is created generates an entry in the Schedule+ Free/Busy Information public folder for the associated Windows NT account.

      - **Schedule+ Free Busy:** The first time a user logs on to Schedule+, an entry is created in the appropriate site folder. Also, every change made to the user's schedule updates the appropriate folder. By setting restrictive permissions, users can prevent the publication of free/busy information and ultimately access to their schedule.

B. **Global Address List:** Lists all of the mailboxes, distribution lists, public folders, and custom recipients within your Exchange organization.

C. **Site:** The name of an Exchange Server computer's messaging site that is defined as a group of one or more Exchange servers connected together.

D. **Configuration:** Contains configuration information about the site.

1. **Add-Ins:** The Add-Ins container holds optional third-party services that don't need a mailbox (Directory exchange, PC interchange, and AppleTalk interchange, for example).

    a. **Extension:** Contains properties sheets for directory objects. Common extensions are:
    Extension for Microsoft Mail Connector
    Extension for Schedule+ Free/Busy Gateway

2. **Addressing:** The parent container for all of the directory entries pertaining to address generation in Exchange.

    a. **Details Templates:** Localized (by language/country) templates that define the details that are displayed on recipient objects.

    - **English/USA:** The default details templates for American English.

    b. **E-Mail Address Generator:** This container holds the following e-mail generators, which automatically generate email addresses for Exchange recipients:

    cc:Mail E-mail Address Generator

    Internet E-Mail Address Generator

    Microsoft Mail Address Generator

    X.400 E-Mail Address Generator

    c. **One-Off Address Templates:** Localized (by language/country) templates that are used to determine what a user should enter when he creates a new email address in his Exchange client for addressing mail messages to a mailbox not in the GAL or in his Personal Address Book. These addresses are typically used only once.

    - **English/USA:** The default one-off address templates for American English

3. **Connections:** Contains all connectors that are used to link Exchange sites with other Exchange sites, with Microsoft Mail environments, or with foreign email systems.

    a. **cc:Mail Connector:** Permits message exchange with Lotus cc:Mail networks.

   b. **Internet Mail Service:** Permits message exchange with Simple Mail Transport Protocol (SMTP) based email systems.

   c. **Microsoft Mail Connector:** Permits message exchange with Microsoft Mail (PC), Microsoft Mail (AppleTalk), and Microsoft Mail (PC) gateways.

   d. **Site Connector:** Creates a messaging bridge between two Exchange sites on the same logical LAN.

   e. **X.400 Connector:** Creates a messaging bridge between two Exchange sites over an X.400 network or to a foreign X.400 system.

   f. **Microsoft Mail Connector for AppleTalk Networks (Quarterdeck Mail):** Permits message exchange with AppleTalk networks.

   g. **Dynamic RAS Connector:** Creates a messaging bridge between two Exchange sites over a Windows NT Remote Access link.

   h. **Directory Exchange Requestor:** Sets up an Exchange server to request directory information from Microsoft Mail or other systems.

   i. **Directory Exchange Server:** Sets up an Exchange server to perform as a directory-synchronization server for external mail systems.

   j. **Dirsync Server:** Processes incoming updates from one or more directory requestors and incorporates the updates into the directory as custom recipient objects.

   k. **Remote Dirsync Requestor:** Configures the internal representations of dirsync requestors that use this server. This internal information is used to authenticate and respond to requestors during directory exchange.

4. **Directory Replication:** Contains all directory replication connectors for Exchange. These connectors are bidirectional and enable replication of directory changes from one site to others.

   a. **Directory Replication Connector:** An object that establishes recipient information sharing between sites.

5. **Monitors:** Contains monitoring tools that watch over an Exchange organization's servers and the links between them.

   a. **Server Monitor:** Watches the status of an Exchange server's services and provides warnings or alerts if errors occur (for example, if the service shuts down, if the server isn't on the network, and so on).

   b. **Link Monitor:** Watches the status of messaging connections between Exchange servers by measuring the round-trip time of ping messages and alerting the Exchange administrator if the trip takes longer than expected.

6. **Protocols (site defaults):** Holds all the Internet protocols that Exchange supports.

   a. **IMAP4:** The Internet Message Access Protocol, version 4rev1 (IMAP4rev1) enables users with any IMAP4rev1 client (that is compliant with RFC 2060) to access mail in their Exchange Server mailboxes. It can also be used to read and post messages to public folders or to access another user's mailbox to which the user has been granted access.

   b. **HTTP:** HTTP protocol (Active Server Components) enables a user to mail messages from an Exchange server using an Internet browser from a UNIX, Macintosh, or Windows-based computer.

   c. **LDAP:** Lightweight directory-access protocol (LDAP) is an Internet protocol that accesses the Exchange Server directory. Clients with security permissions can use LDAP to browse, read, and search directory listings. Use this to configure forms of authentication (clear text or SSL), gain anonymous access, perform searches, and close idle connections.

   d. **NNTP:** Network news transfer protocol (NNTP) is used to configure site defaults, message content, and time-out options.

   e. **POP3:** Post office protocol version 3 (POP3) enables users with POP3 clients to retrieve mail from their Exchange Inbox. Any third-party POP3 email client can also access messages from an Exchange server.

7. **Servers:** Contains a list of the Exchange servers in this site and each of their core components.

   a. **Private Information Store:** Stores all messaging data sent to individual mailboxes.

      - **Logons:** Displays information about users who have logged on to the information store.

      - **Mailbox Resources:** Shows resource information about mailboxes (such as the total amount of space a mailbox occupies).

   b. **Protocols:** Holds the directory objects that allow configuration of the various protocols by which Exchange can be accessed.

      - **IMAP4:** The Internet Message Access Protocol, version 4 (IMAP4) enables users with any IMAP4 client to access mail in their Exchange Server mailboxes. It can also be used to read and post messages to public folders or to access another user's mailbox to which the user has been granted access.

- **LDAP:** Lightweight directory-access protocol (LDAP) is an Internet protocol that accesses the Exchange Server directory. Clients with security permissions can use LDAP to browse, read, and search directory listings. Use this to configure forms of authentication (clear text or SSL), gain anonymous access, perform searches, and close idle connections.
- **NNTP:** Network news transfer protocol (NNTP) is used to configure site defaults, message content, and time-out options.
- **POP3:** Post office protocol version 3 (POP3) enables users with POP3 clients to retrieve mail from their Exchange Inbox. Any third-party POP3 e-mail client can also access messages from an Exchange server.

c. **Public Information Store:** Stores all messaging data posted to public folders.

- **Folder Replication Status:** Displays the status of public folder replication within a site.
- **Logons:** Shows who is currently logged on to a public folder.
- **Public Folder Resource:** Displays information on resource usage.

d. **Server Recipients:** Contains all the recipients that call this server home.

e. **Directory Service:** Controls directory handling within a site.

f. **Directory Synchronization:** Also called Exchange DXA, this object controls general properties for Exchange directory synchronization.

g. **Message Transfer Agent (MTA):** Transports messages from one server to another or to external connectors.

h. **MTA Transport Stack:** Defines the transport used with a RAS or X.400 connector.

i. **System Attendant:** A core Exchange service that manages log files and is required to start other Exchange services.

j. **DS Site Configuration:** Holds general properties for directory services in an Exchange site.

k. **Information Store Site Configuration:** Holds general properties for all the information stores in a site.

l. **MTA Site Configuration:** Holds general properties for all the MTAs in a site.

m. **Site Addressing:** Holds general site-addressing data used in message routing.

n. **Site Encryption Configuration:** You can configure advanced security features in any site in your organization by using the properties sheets in the Site Encryption Configuration object. You use these properties sheets to view and select the KM server, to assign permissions on the KM server for Windows NT accounts, and to select the type of encryption algorithms that the client will use to encrypt the contents of a message.

o. **Recipients:** Contains a list of recipients for this Exchange site.

p. **Mailbox:** A private container for messaging data.

q. **Distribution Lists:** A group of individual recipients that can be addressed as a single recipient or email address. This is similar in function to a listserver.

r. **Custom Recipients:** Foreign recipients whose mailboxes do not reside on an Exchange server.

s. **Public Folder:** Contains information that can be shared among many users.

t. **Microsoft Schedule+ Free/Busy Connector:** A connector that receives free/busy scheduling information from Schedule+ for Microsoft Mail.

Exchange Administrator Program Menu Overview

The Exchange Administrator program contains the following menus:

- *File*. Enables you to connect to other servers, create new connections and objects, and modify and view object properties.
- *Edit*. Enables you to execute standard Windows functions, such as cut, copy, paste, delete, and so on.
- *View*. Enables you to choose the type of information displayed in the Administrator window and how it is sorted; also allows you to set the aesthetic properties of the display (font, sizes, and columns).
- *Tools*. Enables you to perform various administrative tasks, such as tracking messages and importing Windows NT user lists.
- *Window*. Enables you to perform standard Windows appearance and arrangement functions, such as tiling, cascading, and switching between open windows.
- *Help*. Opens the Exchange online help system and provides Exchange version information.

The following sections describe the Exchange Administrator menus in detail.

File Menu

You will use the Administrator program's File menu (see Figure 12.4) to create the components that comprise an Exchange organization or site.

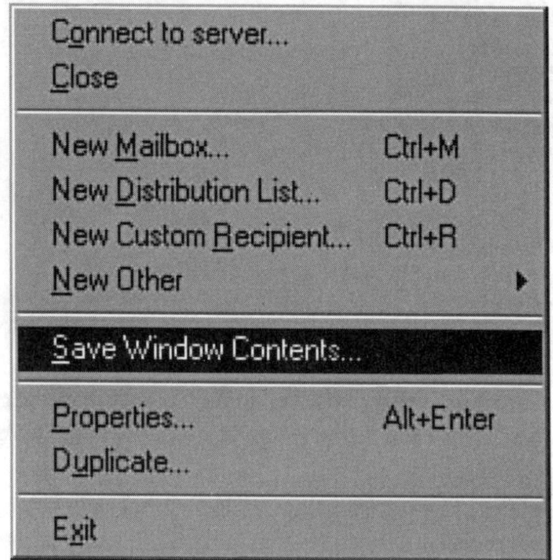

FIG. 12.4
The Administrator program's File menu.

NOTE If you have two or more Exchange Server connections open at the same time, make sure that the correct window is in the foreground when you create components. ■

Connect to Server This menu item enables you to administrate an Exchange server remotely, as though you were logged in to it directly. Although the Administrator program enables you to view all the objects in your organization hierarchy, you cannot alter site connections, mailboxes, connectors, or site servers unless you are directly connected to a server in that remote site with the Administrator program.

Close This menu item closes the active server connection window you are using.

New Mailbox This menu item creates a new user mailbox. When you select it, you must select a recipient container; otherwise, you are prompted to use the standard Exchange recipient container for that site.

New Distribution List This menu item creates a new distribution-list recipient. (You must select a recipient container first.) You must then configure the properties for the distribution list.

New Custom Recipient This menu item creates a recipient object for a mailbox located in a foreign mail system (cc:Mail, MacMail, Microsoft Mail, SMTP, X.400, or the connected gateway).

New Other This menu item displays the submenu shown in Figure 12.5, which allows you to create other types of Exchange objects.

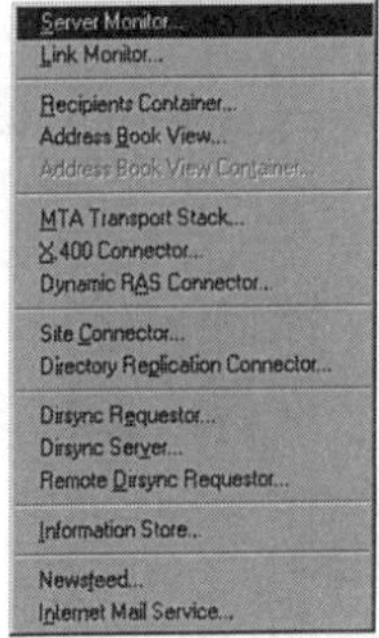

FIG. 12.5
The File, New Other submenu enables you to create one of many Exchange objects.

The items in this submenu are:

- *Server Monitor.* Creates a process that watches the operational condition of one or more servers in a site. The process can be configured to generate alerts when certain conditions (such as a stopped system service) occur.
- *Link Monitor.* Creates a process that monitors the state of messaging connections between Exchange sites and servers. The link monitors are configured to create alerts when errors occur.
- *Recipients Container.* Creates custom containers for certain object types, such as a specific Internet recipients container that holds all custom recipients with SMTP addresses.
- *Address Book View.* Configures the Address Book view.
- *Address Book View Container.* Modifies the configuration of the Address Book View Container.
- *MTA Transport Stack.* Defines underlying transport protocol for each X.400 or Dynamic RAS connector you create. Make sure that you have all necessary transport software set up properly in Windows NT (X.25 protocol); otherwise, you cannot proceed beyond this configuration point.
- *X.400 Connector.* Defines an X.400 connection to another Exchange site or foreign system. Before you select this item, you must define an MTA transport stack over which this connector is to communicate.
- *Dynamic RAS Connector.* Set up a part-time remote access link between servers. You can set up an RAS connection over a modem, ISDN, or X.25 system if you have the appropriate MTA transport stack installed.
- *Site Connector.* Sets up a connection between two Exchange Server sites (typically on the same logical LAN).
- *Directory Replication Connector.* Creates a directory-sharing relationship between two Exchange sites.
- *Dirsync Requestor.* Configures a directory-synchronization requestor that is compatible with any messaging system that supports the Microsoft Mail 3.X directory-synchronization protocol. The Dirsync Requestor is most commonly used to request

directory updates from a Microsoft Mail Post Office that is set up as a directory-synchronization server.

- *Dirsync Server.* Configures a directory-synchronization server that is compatible with any messaging system that supports the Microsoft Mail 3.X directory-synchronization protocol.
- *Remote Dirsync Requestor.* The remote Dirsync Requestor allows a foreign system's dirsync requestor to connect to an Exchange dirsync server.
- *Information Store.* Creates a public or private information store for an Exchange server. You can use this option only if a certain server does not currently have an information store of its own or if it has been deleted.
- *Newsfeed.* Use this wizard to set up an NNTP newsfeed. Be sure to have your provider's USENET site name, the names or IP addresses of your provider's host servers, the username and password your Exchange machine will use to log on to your provider's host computer (some providers do not require this), and your provider's "active file."
- *Internet Mail Service.* With this wizard, you can set up the IMS to send and receive mail from the Internet or other SMTP systems.

Save Window Contents This menu item activates a new feature in Exchange 5.5 that allows you to save the contents of an object window (the right pane) into a comma-separated (.CSV) text file.

Properties This menu item enables you to view and edit settings for particular Exchange objects or containers. Double-clicking the individual objects brings up the properties as well.

Duplicate This menu item creates a new recipient object with properties exactly like an existing one. You can select a distribution list and click Duplicate, for example, to bring up a new distribution list with a blank name that contains all the members of the original list. This option provides the copy and paste functionality of other Windows-based applications. This option is not available if you have not already highlighted or selected a recipient.

Exit This menu item closes all connections to Exchange servers and exits the Administrator program.

Edit Menu

The Exchange Administrator's Edit menu allows you to perform all the standard Windows Edit-menu functions.

Undo This command works only with property text operations (cut, paste, and delete). Because you cannot access the Edit menu while a properties sheet is open, this menu item has very little value. Press Ctrl+Z instead to undo text commands.

Cut, Copy, and Paste These menu items function as normal Windows-based commands for use with text entries. They perform the same functions that they do in Microsoft Word.

Delete This menu item removes unwanted text entries or directory objects.

CAUTION

If you delete a directory object, you cannot recover it without restoring from a backup.

Select All This command enables you to select an entire group of Exchange objects in the Administrator program.

View Menu

The View menu (see Figure 12.6) is designed to filter or sort the information displayed in the Exchange Administrator window. For example, you can choose how to view recipients, thereby making a large Global Address List a more manageable beast.

Mailboxes, Distribution Lists, Custom Recipients, Public Folders, and All These menu items all filter the view for the list of Exchange recipients. A check mark appears next to the menu item that's currently being used to filter the list you are viewing. To view only a particular subset of the recipients, select an option other than the "all" option.

Hidden Recipients This menu item is a filter that adds hidden recipients to any of the preceding viewing filters. Hidden recipients are recipients not seen in the GAL.

FIG. 12.6 The View menu filters and sorts objects displayed in the Administrator window.

Columns This menu item changes the columns of information that appear in the Administrator program's user interface. This item is available only while you are viewing a recipient container. When you click the Columns button, the dialog box shown in Figure 12.7 appears.

The left side of the dialog box shows all Exchange recipient attributes. The right column shows those that are to be displayed in the Administrator program.

To configure which columns are displayed, follow these steps:

1. From the Available Columns list, select any additional attributes that you want to display. Then click Add.
2. From the Show the Following Columns list, select any attribute that you do not want to display. Then click Remove.
3. To change the order in which columns are displayed, select an attribute from the right list (Show the Following Columns), and then click Move Up or Move Down.

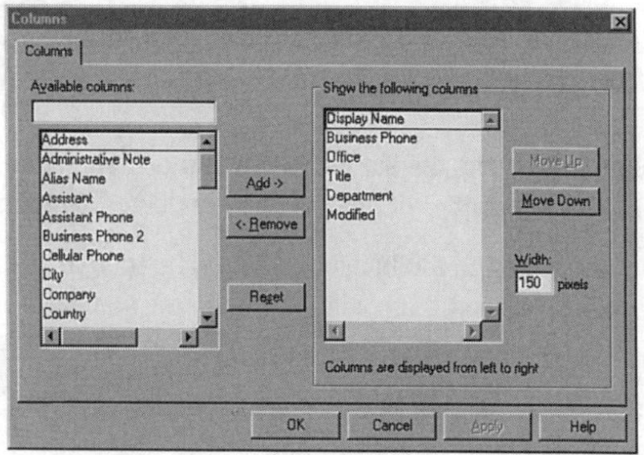

FIG. 12.7
The Columns dialog box allows you to specify which object attributes you want displayed.

NOTE Columns are displayed from left to right, even though you set their order from top to bottom. ■

4. To change the width of a particular column, select its attribute and edit the number in the Width box. This alters the number of pixels it takes up on the Administrator program's user interface window.

TIP An easier way to set column widths is to use your mouse. In the Administrator program's user interface, position the mouse pointer over the dividing line between two attribute columns. When the pointer changes to a double-headed arrow, click and drag that line to make the column the desired width.

5. Click Apply to view your changes immediately on the background window.
6. Click OK to finalize your changes.

Sort By This menu item enables you to organize what you see in the Administrator program's user interface. You can sort any Exchange object, including recipients. When you choose this menu item, a submenu appears, offering two options:

- Sort by Display Name places the objects in alphabetical order by display name.
- Sort by Last Modified Date places the objects in order of the dates (and times) they were last modified.

Microsoft Exchange remembers every view setting for each object list in the Administrator program's user interface. All at the same time, you can choose to view your Global Address List sorted by display name and your connection sorted by date last modified, and you can have your local address list filtered to show only public folders.

Font This menu item opens a Font dialog box that displays your current system fonts. Select a font, and then click OK to return to the Administrator program.

Move Split Bar This menu item selects the dividing line between the two panes of the Administrator window (the Exchange site hierarchy is on the left, and the objects corresponding to the hierarchy are on the right). You can then adjust the window's partition. Use the mouse to drag the line to the desired position, and then click to set the line.

Another way to control the split bar in the Administrator program's user interface is to position your mouse over the line, and then click and drag it to the desired position.

Status Bar This menu item turns the status bar on and off. The status bar displays useful help messages and shows the number of objects in the selected container.

Toolbar This menu item turns the toolbar on and off. The toolbar displays buttons that give you easy access to certain functions, such as creating a new mailbox.

Tools Menu

The Tools menu provides access to various administrative utilities.

Directory Import The Directory Import option allows you to read comma-delimited files and use them to create or modify recipients. These files may contain Microsoft Mail recipients, Exchange recipients, or other foreign email system recipients. The files will need to be created either by using the Exchange migration tools or by using directory export tools in the respective email systems. The files contain recipient name and email address information to be used in Exchange.

The following is a list of things you can do using the Exchange directory import function.

- Import directory information from another email system.
- Add or change personal information for existing mailboxes and other recipients.
- Add members (in bulk) to distribution lists.

Microsoft Exchange includes some useful migration tools that provide similar functionality and are easier to use. See Chapters 7 and 8 for more information on migrating from other mail systems and using the migration tools.

Directory Export This menu option creates text files of Exchange directory information that can be imported into other messaging systems.

Extract Windows NT Account List This menu item selectively copies data from the Windows NT account list of a trusted domain. Files are stored in the CSV file format, which you can use with the Directory Import command to add and create Exchange recipients.

Extract NetWare Account List This menu item selectively copies user data from a Novell NetWare account list. Files are stored in the CSV file format, which you can then use to import into Exchange to create Exchange recipients and Windows NT user accounts.

Find Recipients This menu item allows you to search for recipients anywhere in your organization, based on a variety of criteria. When you choose Find Recipients, the dialog box shown in Figure 12.8 appears.

The top half of this dialog box allows you to specify search criteria; the bottom half displays the result of your searches.

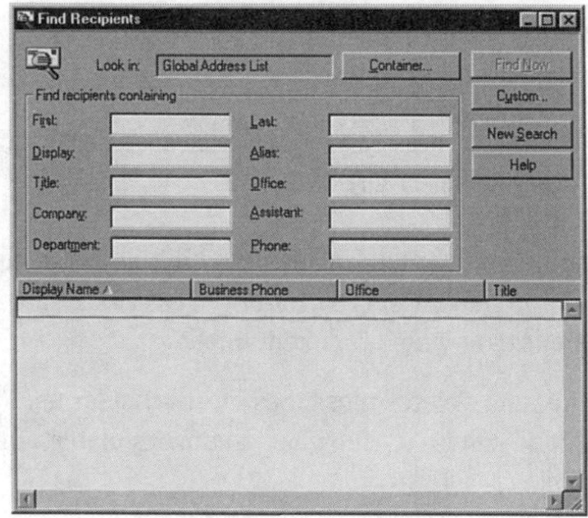

FIG. 12.8
The Find Recipients dialog box enables you to search for a recipient by any attribute.

To search for recipients, follow these steps:

1. The Look In box displays the recipient container in which a search will be executed. Click the Container button to display a global list of Exchange recipient containers in your organization. Select one, and then click OK.

   By default, the Look In box shows the primary recipients container of the server to which you are connected.
2. In the Find Recipients Containing section, enter any distinguishing search criteria for the recipient.
3. To search by custom attributes, click Custom. A dialog box opens, and you can enter your search parameters. Then click OK to return to the Find Recipients dialog box.
4. When you finish entering search parameters, click Find Now. All matches of your search criteria appear at the bottom of the Find Recipients dialog box.
5. Double-click any listed recipient to view its Exchange properties.
6. Click New Search to clear all search parameters.
7. Click Cancel to close the dialog box and return to the Administrator program.

Move Mailbox This menu item transfers a selected recipient to a different server within the same Exchange site. When you choose Move Mailbox, the dialog box shown in Figure 12.9 appears.

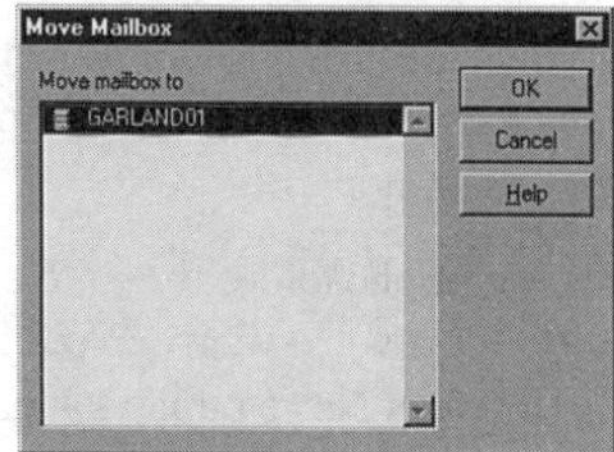

FIG. 12.9
Transfer a mailbox to another server in the site.

Select the Exchange server to which you want to move this recipient, and then click OK. The mailbox is transferred to the new server's private information store.

NOTE This menu item is unavailable unless you have selected a recipient from the recipient's container in the Exchange site hierarchy. ■

Add to Address Book View This menu item adds the highlighted recipient to an Address Book view. Remember that you must first create an Address Book view container (such as all Los Angeles Employees) before moving a recipient into it.

Clean Mailbox This menu item deletes messages in a particular user's mailbox, based on several criteria. This command can be useful when an unreasonable number of messages have piled up in a specific mailbox.

Select the criteria that you want to use to delete messages in this mailbox. A message must meet all the selected criteria to be deleted. The criteria are:

- *Age*. All mail older (in days) than the number in the All Messages Older Than (Days) box will be deleted.
- *Size*. All mail greater in size (in kilobytes) than the number in the All Messages Greater Than (K) box will be deleted.
- *Sensitivity*. All messages have a sensitivity attribute. You can select up to four sensitivity levels, and all messages that have the selected sensitivity levels will be deleted.
- *Read Items*. This option refers to the read or unread status of the messages. You must select the status of messages to be deleted: read, unread, or both.
- *Delete Folder-Associated Information*. If this is cleared, no folder-associated information is deleted. If it is checked, all information and messages associated with the selected folder are deleted.
- *Delete Items Immediately*. This item permanently removes messages from the mailbox.
- *Move Items to the Deleted Items Folder*. This item places the selected messages in that user's Deleted Items folder in the Exchange client.

Start Monitor This menu item starts the selected server monitor or link monitor. This option is unavailable if a monitor is not selected.

Track Message This option launches the Message Tracking Center, which is a tool for following the delivery of messages through an organization.

Forms Administrator This menu item displays the Organization Forms Library Administrator, which enables you to manage the various forms created using the forms designer tool in the Exchange client software to meet specific messaging needs.

News Group Hierarchies To make an existing public folder tree into a hierarchy of newsgroup public folders, you can designate a top-level newsgroup public folder as a hierarchy parent. Newsgroups that are included in the Internet News public folder by default are not listed in the newsgroup hierarchy unless you add them to the list. You can also remove public folders from the newsgroup hierarchy.

Save Connections on Exit This menu item is a toggle that can save information about your current server connections when you quit the Administrator program. The next time you open the Administrator program, it tries to reestablish the connections to those servers.

Save Connections Now The moment that you select this option, Exchange saves current Exchange Server connections. The next time you open the Administrator program, it tries to reestablish the connections to those servers.

Customize Toolbar This menu item allows you to add or remove specific function icons from the Exchange Administrator toolbar. This can be particularly useful if there are functions that you need to use during a migration period that you may not need as frequently later.

Options This menu item displays two properties sheets on which you can set options for Exchange mailboxes and other recipients. The properties sheets are:

- *Auto Naming*. Enables you to define a method for Display Name Generation and Alias Name Generation.
- *Permissions*. Enables you to set a default Windows NT domain where new mailbox accounts are to be created in addition to other object-related permissions.

To set Auto Naming options, follow these steps:

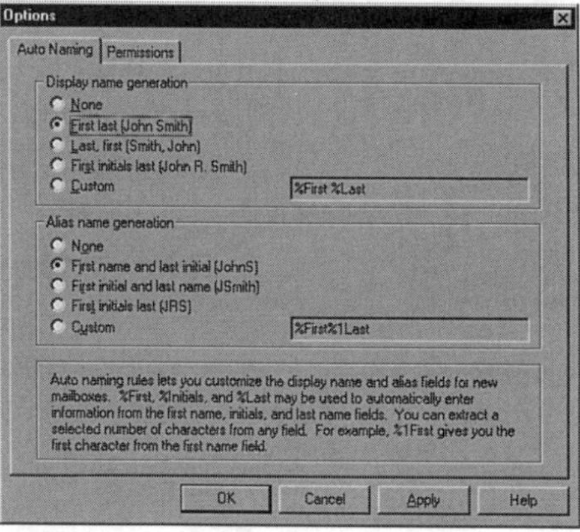

FIG. 12.10
The Auto Naming tab helps you generate mailbox display names.

1. Click the Auto Naming tab in the Options dialog box (see Figure 12.10).
2. The Display Name Generation section allows you to define how the Administrator program generates display names when the email system administrator is typing or importing new Exchange mailboxes. Choose None to always enter display names manually. Choose Custom to create a specialized entry type or template.
3. The Alias Name Generation section allows you to define how the Administrator program generates alias names when the email system administrator is typing or importing new Exchange mailboxes. Choose None to always enter alias names manually. Choose Custom to create a specialized entry type.

4. Click Apply to set these properties and continue with the other properties.
5. When you finish changing settings, click OK to return to the Administrator program.

To set Permissions options, follow these steps:

1. Click the Permissions tab in the Options dialog box.
2. Select the default Windows NT domain for all new mailboxes from the pull-down menu.
3. Choose Show Permissions Page for All Objects if you want the permissions to be displayed in all the properties sheets of the objects that have them. By default, this box is not checked, and the permissions pages are hidden.
4. Choose Display Rights for Roles on Permissions Page to display the list of rights on the permissions page. *Roles* are sets of rights that define what type of access and how much access a user or group has.
5. Choose Delete Primary Windows NT Account When Deleting Mailbox to delete the associated Windows NT account along with a mailbox. This box is not checked by default.

CAUTION

Use step 5 with caution: A deleted Windows NT user cannot log back on to the domain.

6. Choose Try to Find Matching Windows NT Account When Creating Mailbox to have the Administrator program search the Windows NT user list for the matching account name. This box is checked by default.
7. Click Apply to set these properties and continue with the other properties on the Permissions tab.
8. When you finish changing settings, click OK to return to the Administrator program.

The File Format tab defines separators and character sets for directory imports and exports.

Window Menu

This is a standard Windows menu. You can create a new display window for a particular server. The Cascade, Tile Horizontally or Vertically, and Arrange Icons menu items function as normal. The Refresh menu item requests and updates all window information from the server.

Help Menu

This is a standard Windows help menu. The menu contains three standard options:

- *Microsoft Exchange Server Help Topics.* This option allows you to view standard help information on all Exchange interface settings.
- *Books Online.* This option allows you to read the official online Exchange Server documentation and provides searchable indexes and tables of contents.

- *About Microsoft Exchange Server*. This option displays version and copyright information. It also displays a System Info button that runs Windows NT Diagnostics. Windows NT Diagnostics is very helpful for troubleshooting general-purpose problems, displaying hardware information, viewing the version of Windows NT, and viewing the version of any installed Service Packs.

CHAPTER 13

Directory and System Attendant Configuration

In this chapter

This chapter begins covering the details for configuring your Exchange server components. The steps to set up each Exchange site down to the server level are covered. This will teach you to set site configuration properties as well as general settings for the core components of each Microsoft Exchange server. Subsequent chapters cover configuring additional components and using elements together to develop a complete Exchange organization.

Configuring Directory Services

Directory site configuration allows you to set preferences on Exchange site directory functions. Settings made to this object's properties affect an entire Microsoft Exchange site.

In this section you learn to make the following changes:

- Set tombstone lifetimes
- Set garbage collection intervals
- Generate and schedule the creation of offline address books
- Define the custom attribute for all recipients within an Exchange site
- Restrict access to site directory attributes from certain LDAP (Lightweight Directory Access Protocol) users, and manage replication of directory objects between sites

The rest of this section defines some concepts essential to proper configuration of the Directory Service agent.

Setting a Tombstone Lifetime

A "tombstone" in Exchange directory terms is a marker representing a deleted directory object. At the moment when you delete a directory object, it is removed instantly from the local server only. All the other Exchange servers that participate in directory replication with this server do not become immediately aware of that object's deletion. Therefore, a "tombstone" marker is created that when replicated to other servers informs them of the original object's deletion. The tombstone lifetime dictates the number of days a tombstone marker exists before it expires and can be deleted from the system.

Here are some considerations for setting tombstone lifetimes:

Situation 1—Frequency of directory object deletion. If you set the tombstone lifetime for an excessively long period of time and you frequently delete objects, there will be a large number of tombstone markers clogging your entire directory replication system.

Situation 2—Length of time a server could be down. For example, you set the tombstone lifetime for a site at seven days. Suppose that one server in your site is down for over a week. The server that was down will not be notified of an object's deletion before the tombstone of some directory object is deleted. There will be some directory inconsistencies to correct as a result.

NOTE Tombstones cannot be used to undelete a previously deleted directory object. ■

Setting a Garbage Collection Interval

The garbage collection interval determines the number of hours between deletion of expired tombstone markers (referred to as garbage). Much like a traditional garbage collection service, this operation is a scheduled removal of expired directory "garbage." Once directory object tombstone markers have expired, they are ready (placed on the curb) for deletion at the garbage collection interval.

Creating an Offline Address Book

Remote users can take advantage of Exchange address lists by downloading a current version of the offline address book. This address list is generated from the main address list, and the process is managed through these property pages. A remote user uses the offline address book like a standard recipient directory when disconnected from the network. The offline address book contains only the recipients or recipient groups specified by the Exchange administrator. The offline address book object itself is a hidden public folder held in the public information store of a designated Exchange server. There can be only one offline address book per site.

Defining Custom Attributes

Custom attributes pertain specifically to recipients. They are added to represent any extra information you want to have entered when creating recipients. Sample standard attributes are *city*, *state*, *zip*, and *phone number*; a custom attribute can be anything from birthday, age, or hair color to favorite music or bowling average.

Restricting Access to Site Directory Attributes

The administrator can select which site directory objects are accessible to certain classes of LDAP users and which objects are to be replicated to other Exchange sites.

Configuring DS Site Property Pages

In this section, you begin to configure the DS Site property pages. You will find that a wide variety of settings affect how directory functions are carried out in your Exchange site.

The pages that will be covered are as follows:

- The General page
- The Permissions page
- The Offline Address Book Schedule page
- The Offline Address Book page
- The Custom Attributes page
- The Attributes page

The General Page

Figure 13.1 shows the General property page and the various directory settings associated with it.

You can assign a new Display name, view the Directory name, and change the Tombstone lifetime and Garbage collection intervals by going through the following steps:

1. Select the General tab of the DS Site configuration property pages. The General property page appears.

FIG. 13.1
General directory settings for a site.

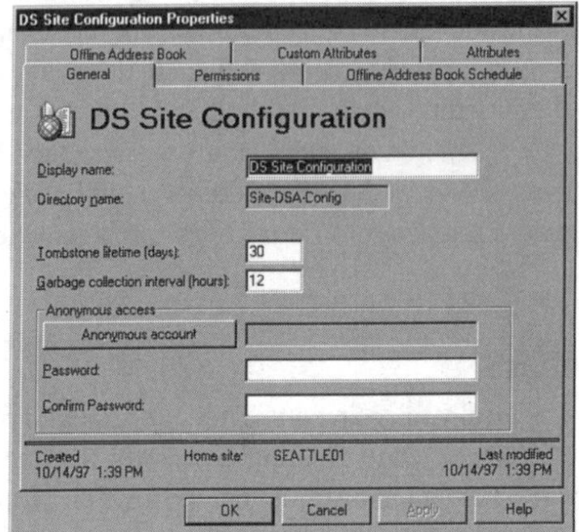

2. Enter a Display name for this object as you want it to be displayed in the Exchange Administrator program. By default, this name is DS Site Configuration. The Alias name is set to Site-DSA-Config and cannot be modified.
3. Next to Tombstone lifetime (days), enter the length of time (in days) until a directory object's tombstone marker expires. By default, this value is set to 30 days.
4. Next to Garbage collection interval (hours), enter the interval (in hours) between deletion of expired tombstone markers. See the preceding page for a more detailed description of the garbage collection interval. By default, this value is set to 12 hours.
5. Click the Anonymous account button to set up an account for use by anonymous users. You will be given the choice of using an existing Windows NT account or creating a new Windows NT account for anonymous access. This account will be used by the directory to access containers when anonymous users connect to Microsoft Exchange Server. The account is an internal account (such as the Guest account) and is used only by the directory.

NOTE The Anonymous account is different from the accounts you specify for individual containers for anonymous users. This is a single account that will be used by anonymous users (usually Web-based users) to access directories in Microsoft Exchange. ■

6. Click Apply to set these properties and continue with other properties. If you are done with all settings, click OK to return to the Administrator program.

The Permissions Page

The Permissions property page allows you to define certain Windows NT user accounts that have rights to modify this directory object.

The Offline Address Book Schedule Page

The Offline Address Book Schedule property page allows you to determine at what intervals a new offline address book will be generated. By downloading the offline address book to their computers, remote users can verify e-mail addresses as though they were online. This also makes it easier to compose mail while offline, rather than having to connect to the Exchange server to verify e-mail addresses.

To schedule a new time interval to generate the offline address book, you take the following steps:

1. Select the Offline Address Book Schedule tab of the DS Site Configuration Properties pages. The property page in Figure 13.2 appears.

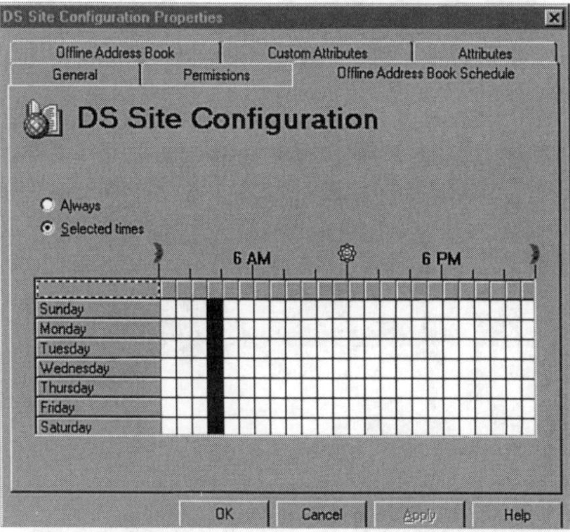

FIG. 13.2
Setting the schedule for creating an offline address book.

2. Click Always to continually regenerate updated versions of an offline address book. Once a cycle completes, a new one begins at the next system registry, defined as an "Always" interval, which by default is 15 minutes.
3. Click Selected times and use the time grid to set specific times when offline address book generation will begin.

For example: If you know that your remote users connect first thing in the morning to update their offline address books, then set the schedule to begin several hours before you expect most of them to connect. That way the whole generation cycle will be complete, and the address book they download will be as complete as possible.

4. Click Apply to set these properties and continue with other properties. If you are done with all settings, click OK to return to the Administrator program.

NOTE Generating an offline address book can often take several hours. If one cycle of offline address book generation carries into the next scheduled generation time, the generation will finish normally, then begin again at the next scheduled time after its completion. ■

The Offline Address Book Page

The Offline Address Book property page defines parameters on how the offline address book will be created. You choose what elements of the directory will be included. If you desire a highly customized list of recipients to be included in the offline address book, then consider creating a recipient container dedicated to offline address book generation.

You can take the following steps to change the offline address book server, generate the offline address book before its regular schedule, and change which recipient container is used to create the offline address book:

1. Select the Offline Address Book tab of the DS Site Configuration Properties pages. The property page in Figure 13.3 appears.

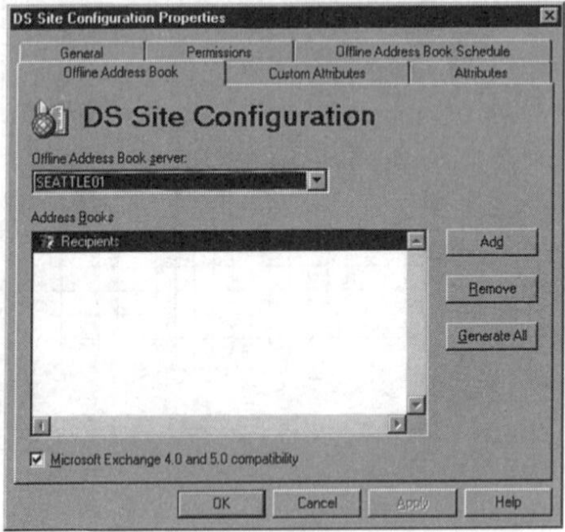

FIG. 13.3 Setting offline address book creation and location options.

2. Select the Offline Address Book server by using the drop-down menu. This is the server that will actually generate the offline address book and from which a remote user will download the information. By default, this is the Microsoft Exchange server to which you are currently connected with the Administrator program.

Because the generation of a large offline address book can be a lengthy process, select a lower-traffic, lesser-used server (if available) to perform this task.

3. Click Add to open the Offline Address Book dialog box. You can then select which recipient container you want to use to generate the offline Address Book.
4. Click the Remove button to remove selected online Address Books from the Address Books box if you no longer want them available for downloading. You may remove all offline Address Books except for the default Global Address List.
5. Click the Generate All button to manually generate an Offline Address Book. For example, if you just made numerous changes to your Organization, but the Offline Address Book generation schedule is set for once a week, you can use this button to generate the Offline Address Book immediately.
6. Check the Microsoft Exchange 4.0 and 5.0 compatibility box if any of the users in your site are running 4.0 and/or 5.0 clients. By default, Microsoft Exchange Server 5.5 generates offline address books that are incompatible with these clients. Checking this box will generate offline address books in a format that your clients support.

NOTE Before an offline address book is available to remote users, it must first be generated. Check your generation schedule to see if the next scheduled cycle falls within an acceptable time frame. If necessary, click the Generate All button to create it immediately. ■

7. Click Apply to set these properties and continue with other properties. If you are done with all settings, click OK to return to the Administrator program.

CAUTION

There must be only one offline address book per Microsoft Exchange site. Replicating the offline address book as a hidden public folder will create directory errors.

The Custom Attributes Page

The Custom Attributes property page allows you to define characteristics that will appear on the Custom Attributes property page of each recipient only in the local site. The field can be defined to display any additional information for which you want to create a space.

To create custom attribute fields, complete the following steps:

1. Select the Custom Attributes tab of the DS Site Configuration Properties page. The properties page in Figure 13.4 appears.
2. Type in the names of Custom Attributes 1-10 in the spaces provided. By default these entries are literally named "Custom Attribute 1" through "Custom Attribute 10."
3. Click Apply to set these properties and continue with other properties. If you are done with all settings, click OK to return to the Administrator program.

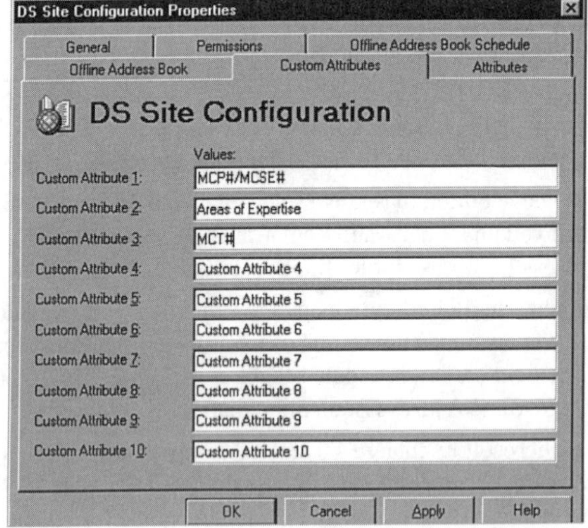

FIG. 13.4
Setting the custom attribute whose values you will set in the recipient's properties pages.

The Attributes Page

The Attributes property page assists administrators in managing access for LDAP users and in directory replication of objects in the site directory. An example would be enabling authenticated users access to most mailbox attributes, such as "direct reports" or phone numbers but denying anonymous users access to these objects.

To reduce possible network traffic and system overhead associated with directory replication, additional options are provided to control inclusion of directory objects in intersite replication. Caution should be exercised when deselecting objects under the System attributes heading because it could affect directory operation.

Modifying attribute access options requires the following steps:

1. Select the Attributes tab of the DS Site Configuration Properties page. The property page shown in Figure 13.5 appears.
2. In the left side of the Configure window, select the requestor access type you want to modify by clicking once.
3. In the right drop-down field, select the appropriate object you want to show access for in the display window immediately below.
4. As the check boxes associated with the various objects are checked or unchecked, the data values for these objects become accessible to LDAP users or are included in directory replication to other sites.

It is important to note that in the case of custom attributes, only the data associated with the custom attribute is replicated, not the new label replacing the phrase "Custom Attribute 1." This could result in one Exchange site relabeling the site's "Custom Attribute 1" to become "Cube Number" and then entering appropriate numeric values. Meanwhile, a different

Exchange site might relabel its "Custom Attribute 1" to "Favorite Color" with alpha values subsequently entered. When the two sites replicate data and the values of their respective Custom Attributes 1 are exchanged, the sites will see a mix of data types that makes no sense with the labels in their local sites!

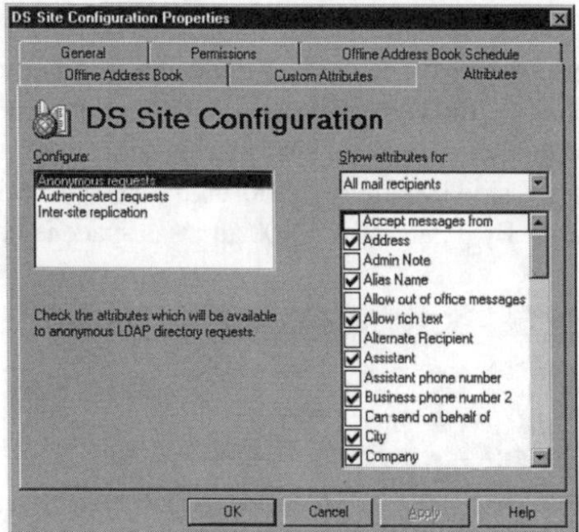

FIG. 13.5
The Attributes tab of the DS Site Configuration Properties page.

> **CAUTION**
>
> After initial installation of your Exchange site, double-check the default settings associated with anonymous requests to make sure that your site is presenting for anonymous access only the LDAP information you want to make public.

Configuring Site Addressing

These sets of property pages allow you to configure site properties that have to do with automatic creation of e-mail addresses, setting default site e-mail address values, and routing messages to their intended destination within an Exchange system. These options determine which servers will be used to calculate routing tables, and when to calculate those tables. Also, you can use these pages to get an overview of how messaging links are established in your organization.

The pages described in this section are as follows:

- The General page
- The Site Addressing page
- The Routing Calculation Schedule page
- The Routing page

The General Page

In the General property page, you can edit this object's Display name and also do the following:

1. Choose Routing calculation server. This server will be responsible for processing routing data for this server. The updated routing table will then be replicated to this server.
2. Choose Share address space with other X.400 systems (see Figure 13.6). With this option selected, if an incoming X.400 message cannot find its intended Exchange recipient, it will be routed to the system sharing this address space. This option is helpful when running Exchange side by side with a foreign X.400 system (for example, during a migration to Exchange). By default, the X.400 address space is not shared.

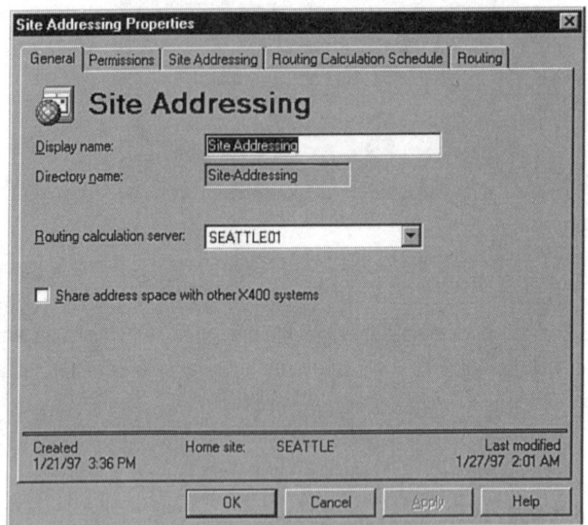

FIG. 13.6
Setting general site routing parameters.

The Site Addressing Page

E-mail addresses are used by the various Exchange gateways and connectors to identify specific directory objects to other messaging systems (see Figure 13.7). In this case, these addresses affect all messages routed to this site. There are four default addresses created each for Microsoft Mail Post Office, SMTP, X.400, and cc:Mail. If other connectors or gateways are installed, those addresses can be created by default as well.

Another feature in Exchange is the capability to select which address types will be automatically created when a new mailbox or public folder is created. This is controlled by simply checking or unchecking the box adjacent to the address type. Additionally, when a box is unchecked, the administrator is presented with the option to remove this address from all currently installed mailboxes, if desired.

Just as in Exchange version 4.0 and 5.0, the default address values are editable. A common example for editing address values might be if your corporation elected to change the root DNS value for your SMTP addresses, such as `swspectrum.com` being changed to `softwarespectrum.com`.

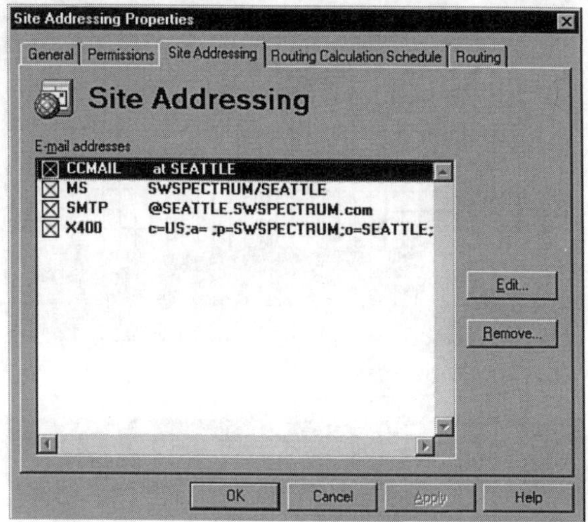

FIG. 13.7
Setting e-mail address entries for the entire site.

The Routing Calculation Schedule Page

When changes in site configuration are made, routing tables need to be rebuilt in order to maintain accurate message delivery information. By default, routing is calculated once per day at 4:00 a.m. local time (see Figure 13.8). Generally, the default settings will be more than adequate to maintain up-to-date routing tables in your site; use the manual override when immediate recalculation is necessary. If your site undergoes frequent changes in components (more servers, new connector types, and so on), you may want to increase the routing calculation frequency.

The Routing Page

The Routing page indicates the type of address space used by the Exchange routing table, shows the value for that address space, and shows the cost of sending messages to a selected site. Click on a type of message destination and click Details to view the route of such a message. The dialog boxes in Figure 13.9 and Figure 13.10 appear.

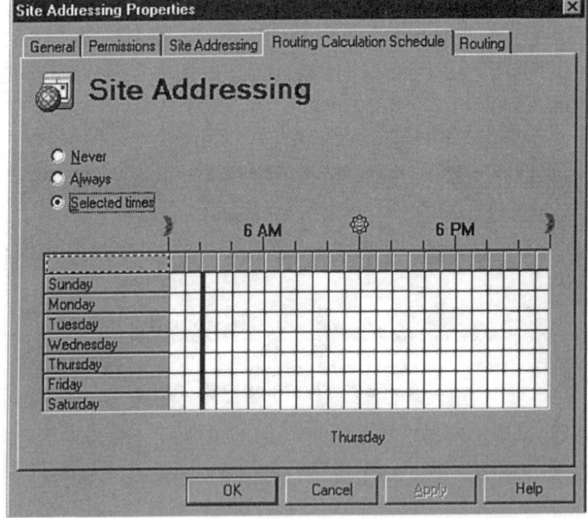

FIG. 13.8
Defining a schedule when routing table calculations occur.

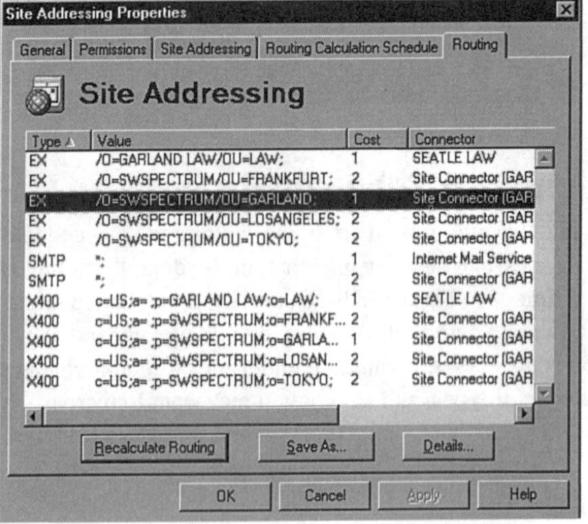

FIG. 13.9
Viewing the message routes available from this Exchange site.

FIG. 13.10
You can view routing details for connectors available from this site. Note the file extensions for this file type.

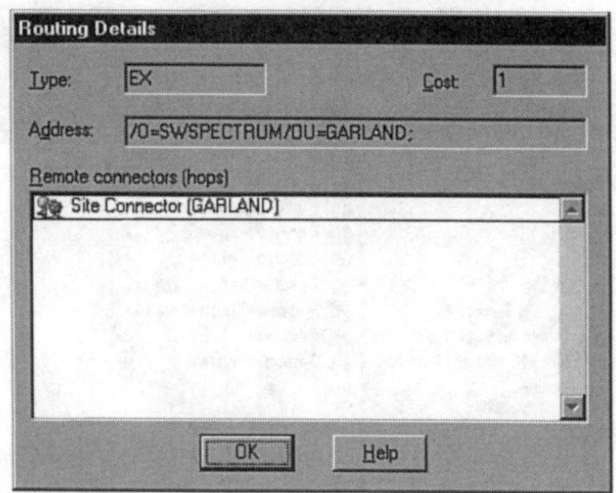

Configuring Server Property Pages

Each Microsoft Exchange server has its own set of property pages. Here, you can configure general functions that apply specifically to a single Exchange server.

The following are the property pages for server configuration:

- The General page
- The Permissions page
- The Services page
- The Locales page
- The Database Paths page
- The IS Maintenance page
- The Advanced page
- The Diagnostics Logging page

To open the Server property page, complete the following steps:

1. Navigate to your desired site with the Exchange Administrator program.
2. Click the Configuration container of the selected site. All the site configuration objects appear in the Administrator program's right window.
3. Open the Servers container. A list of Exchange servers in your site will be listed.
4. Click the server name on which is the Private Information Store you want to configure (see Figure 13.11). The list of server objects is visible on the right display window of the Microsoft Exchange Administrator program.
5. Open its property pages by selecting Properties from the Administrator program file menu or by pressing Alt+Enter.

The following sections cover configuring Exchange Server properties.

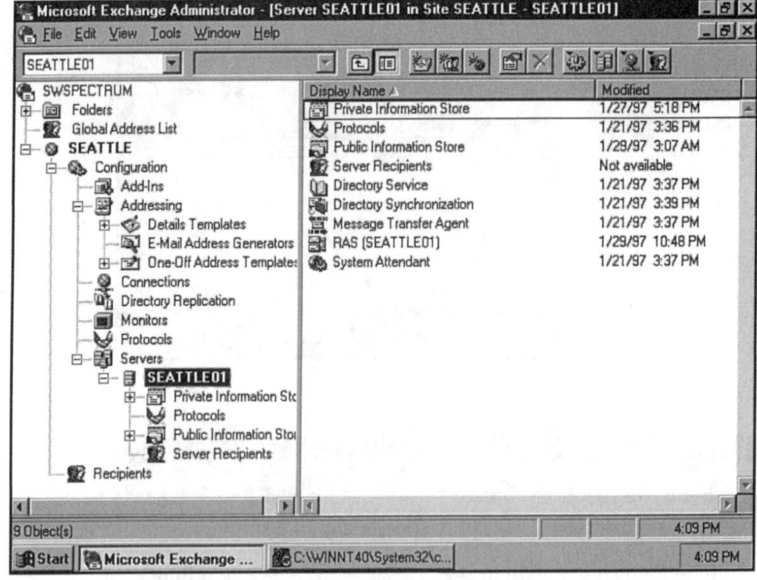

FIG. 13.11
You can select the Exchange server to edit, then open its properties.

The General Page

The General property page displays the server's Directory name and has a space for an additional administrative note (see Figure 13.12).

The server's directory name cannot be changed without reinstalling Microsoft Exchange.

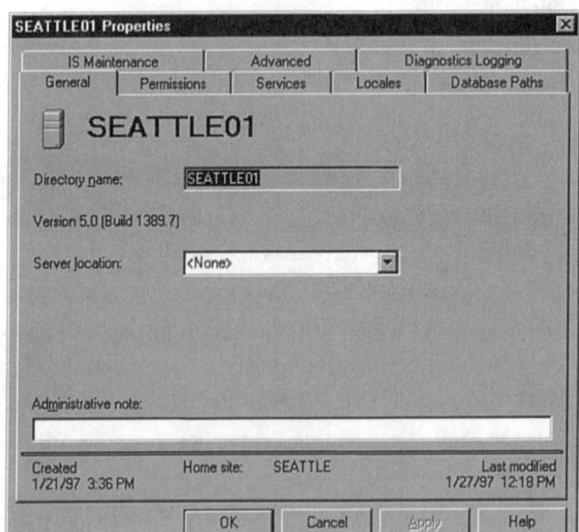

FIG. 13.12
The server name cannot be changed after Exchange has been installed.

The Permissions Page

The Permissions property page allows you to define certain Windows NT user accounts that have rights to modify this directory object. See Chapter 12, "Using the Administrator Program," for a detailed description of working with the standard Permissions property page.

The Services Page

The Services property page allows you to define what services will be checked by a Microsoft Exchange Server monitor. The top display window shows all services currently installed on this Windows NT server. The bottom display window shows all the services by default currently monitored by Exchange.

To select the service to be monitored by an Exchange Server monitor, complete the following steps:

1. Select a service from the top window and click Add to add it to the list of Monitored Services (see Figure 13.13).
2. Select a service from the bottom window and click Remove to take it off the list of Monitored Services.
3. Click Default to return to the basic services selected by Exchange Server.

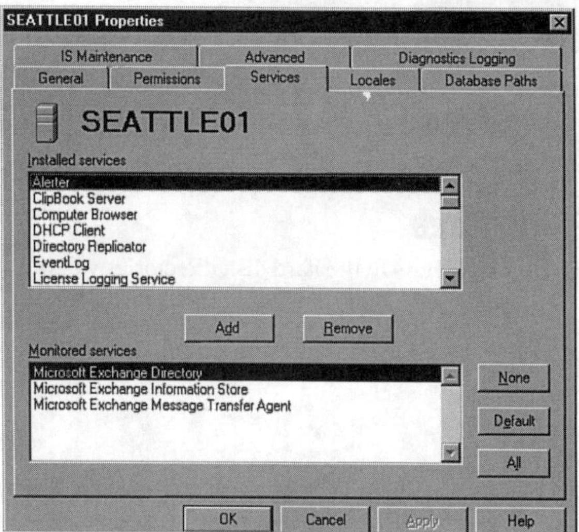

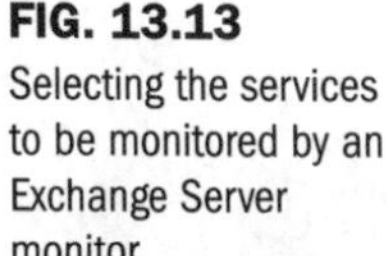
FIG. 13.13 Selecting the services to be monitored by an Exchange Server monitor.

The Locales Page

Locales determine how values (such as date or currency) are displayed in the Exchange Client. International settings are determined by the Exchange Client settings (see Chapter 30, "Using Outlook") and also affect default sorting order for lists. This property page allows you to activate certain locales from the list of installed locales.

The Installed Locales window displays all the formats currently installed on this Exchange server.

To add or remove support for various foreign-language Exchange clients, refer to the following steps:

1. Click Add or Remove to edit the list of Selected Locales.
2. The selected Locales window displays what formats are in use (see Figure 13.14).

FIG. 13.14
You can use this dialog box to add or remove support for various foreign language Exchange clients.

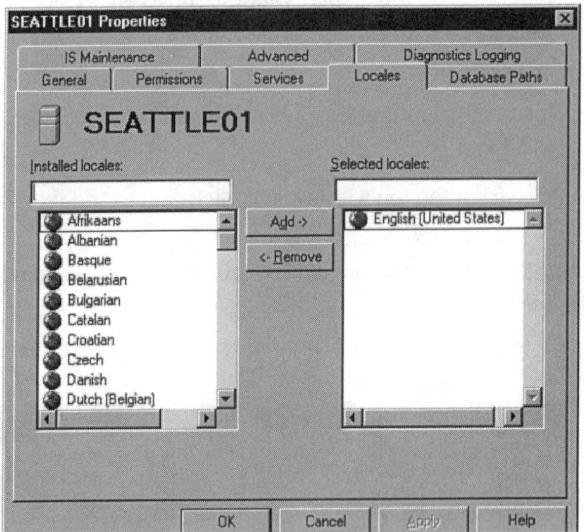

The Database Paths Page

The Database Paths are pointers to the hard disk directories where Exchange actually stores information. This property page allows you to set the paths to the directory for placement of the public and private information store files on this server. The paths are set up when you initially install Exchange Server.

> **CAUTION**
>
> It is recommended that instead of manually editing the paths to the critical databases of the Exchange server, the administrator use the Exchange Optimizer wizard to move these files and adjust the necessary directory and registry values automatically.

The three main Exchange Server databases are:

1. Directory
2. Private

3. Public Information Store

Additional information files (see Figure 13.15) store additional Exchange data such as transaction logs.

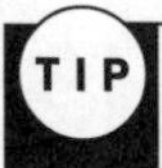

One basic way to improve Exchange performance is to spread the database files across several hard drives. The Microsoft Exchange Optimizer can assist with this process.

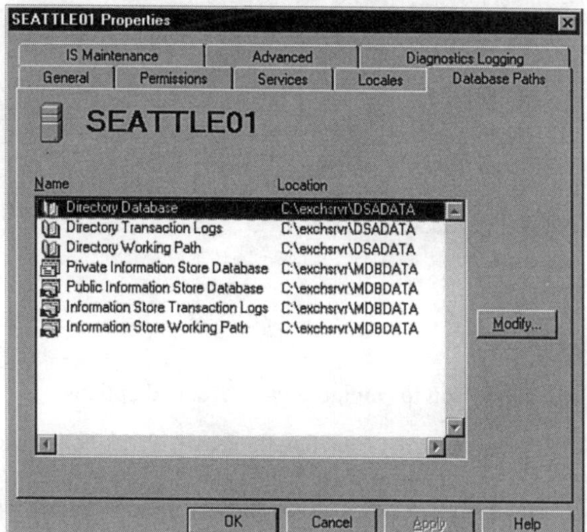

FIG. 13.15
You can use this dialog box to view the physical location.

Click the Modify button (in Figure 13.15) to bring up the dialog box that enables you to browse through your system's file structure and select a location for the database information. You can view the physical location, that is, hard disks, for the various types of Exchange data such as Directory Database, Transaction Logs, Information Store data, and so on.

The IS Maintenance Page

Information Store Maintenance optimizes an Exchange server's operating speed. Basic maintenance includes disk defragmentation for improved hard disk performance and compression of the various database files by removing excessive "white space" left by deleted data (see Figure 13.16). Use this page to schedule maintenance for each Exchange server.

Maintenance tasks are taxing on hard drive and overall server performance. Always schedule them at the server's least busy period of the day.

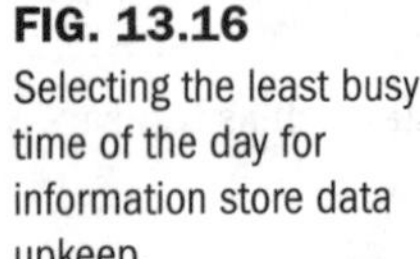

FIG. 13.16
Selecting the least busy time of the day for information store data upkeep.

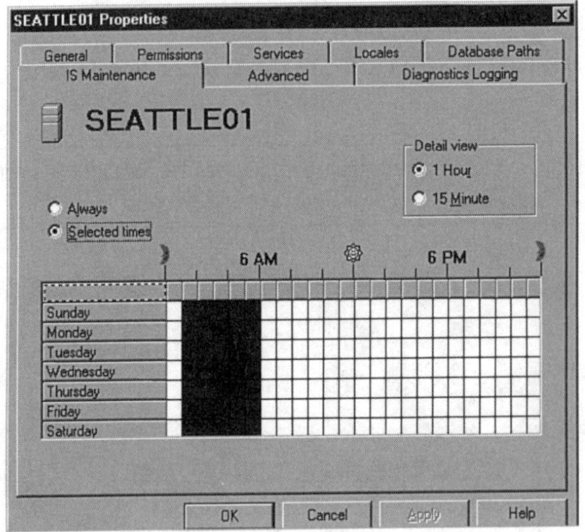

The Advanced Page

This property page allows you to configure two advanced options:

- **Database circular logging**. Enabling these two check boxes allows Exchange to write over transaction log files after their data is saved to the database. Use this option to save drive space only if storage space availability is a serious consideration.

CAUTION

If the circular logging options are enabled, you will no longer be able to perform differential and incremental backups (see Chapter 25, "Maintaining Exchange").

- **DS/IS consistency adjustment**. There are two components to each directory object saved in a server's information store: the object itself and a corresponding entry in the directory. Consistency adjustment corrects errors arising by mismatched information. This feature will either add or delete a directory entry to match the existence or absence of information store information.

This property page allows you to control at what point these inconsistencies are to be corrected.

Select All inconsistencies to correct them immediately or select Inconsistencies more than X number of days and enter the time an inconsistency can exist before it is automatically corrected (see Figure 13.17).

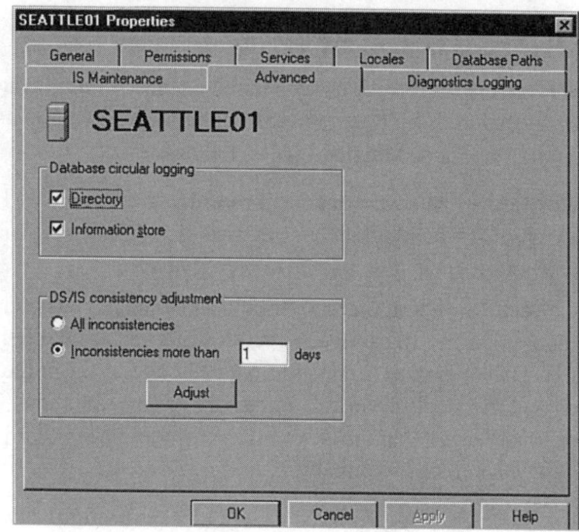

FIG. 13.17
Setting general logging and inconsistency adjustment preferences.

The Diagnostics Logging Page

This property page works in conjunction with the Windows NT Event Log to record various "events" that occur within the many Exchange services. Various levels of logging determine what constitutes an event and, therefore, what types of information are actually recorded in the event log. For troubleshooting purposes, you would want a very detailed record of occurrences and, hence, set a high logging level. However, normally you would want to log only events that are critical, so set a lower logging level for everyday operation (see Figure 13.18). Individual components (for example, Directory, MTA, and Information Store) also have diagnostic logging pages for their individual service, but all services are available through this server property page.

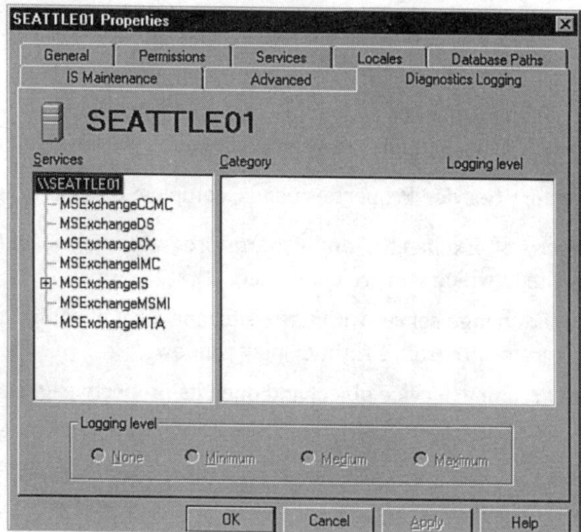

FIG. 13.18
Controlling log settings for all Exchange services running on this server.

Configuring Directory Service

The Directory Service Properties pages are mainly used for configuring diagnostics information. However, two additional functions provided by this object will be used more frequently during normal operation. These functions are as follows:

- **Manually synchronize directory information within a site**. This operation normally occurs every five minutes, but if changes have been made and you do not want to wait for automatic synchronization, use this property page.
- **Manually check knowledge consistency**. Knowledge consistency for this local server is its awareness of other Exchange servers within a site and other sites within your organization. This operation is run automatically once daily. If Exchange servers or sites were added and the local server was not aware of those changes (for example, the local server was down during that time), you may not want to wait for the automatic checking, in which case you can do it manually.

An example is as follows: Exchange Server SEATTLE01 is brought down for two hours for a memory upgrade. During the time of the upgrade, a new server, DUBLIN08, is added to the site. When SEATTLE01 is restored to proper functioning, it will not be aware of the existence of the new server until the Knowledge Consistency cycle is run at the end of the day. Knowing this, the administrator for SEATTLE01 runs the Knowledge Consistency cycle manually from the Directory Service Properties pages. SEATTLE01 is now aware of the new server's existence.

If an inconsistency is detected when checking manually, it is a good idea to manually execute all processes related to correcting inconsistencies. Use this sequence:

1. Check knowledge consistency from the Directory Service Properties pages and detect the error.
2. Manually update directory replication within the site by running Update Now also from the Directory Service Properties pages.
3. Open the Message Transfer Agent properties for this server and click Recalculate Routing from the General property page.

Although the preceding sequence is optional and will be automatically executed with a 24-hour period, performing the tasks immediately will reduce the possibility of other conflicts or errors.

To open the Directory Service Properties pages, complete the following steps:

1. Use the Microsoft Exchange Administrator program to navigate to the list of servers within the site to which you are connected.
2. Click on an Exchange server within the site, and a list of configuration objects appear in the Administrator program's right display window.
3. Select the Directory Service object and open its property pages.

The General Page

The General property page allows you to synchronize directory information manually if you have made changes to directory information on the server and don't want to wait for automatic synchronization. To update or check directory information manually, complete the following steps:

1. Select the General tab of the Directory Service Properties page (see Figure 13.19). The property page appears.
2. Click Update Now to request directory updates from all servers in the site. This process runs automatically every five minutes within an Exchange site.
3. Click Check Now to run a knowledge consistency check and detect any changes in servers in a site or sites in your organization. This process runs automatically once a day.

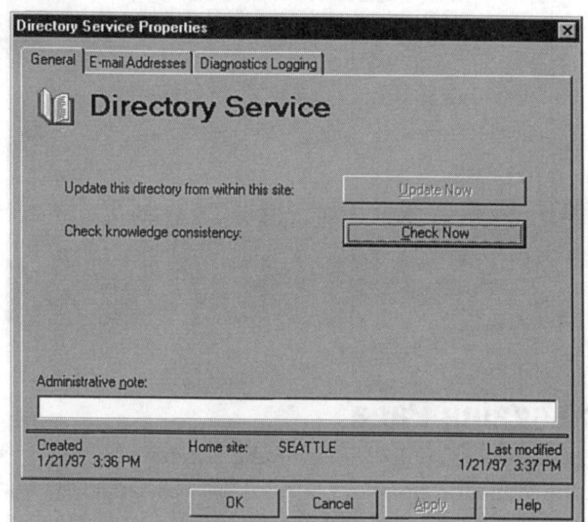

FIG. 13.19
These two controls manually update the local site directory and check knowledge consistency.

4. Enter any additional Administrative note.
5. Click Apply to set these properties and continue with other properties. If you are done with all settings, click OK to return to the Administrator program.

The E-Mail Addresses Page

E-mail addresses are used by the various Exchange gateways and connectors to identify specific directory objects to other messaging systems. There are four default addresses created each for Microsoft Mail Post Office, SMTP, X.400, and now cc:Mail.

To set public directory service e-mail addresses, complete the following steps:

1. Click the E-mail Addresses of the Directory Service Properties pages (see Figure 13.20). The dialog box appears.

The four default addresses (cc:Mail, Microsoft Mail Post Office, SMTP, and X.400) are displayed.

2. Click New to add a specific e-mail address for this directory service. Select an existing address and click Edit to modify it, or click Remove to delete it.
3. Click Apply to set these properties and continue with other properties. If you are done with all settings, click OK to return to the Administrator program.

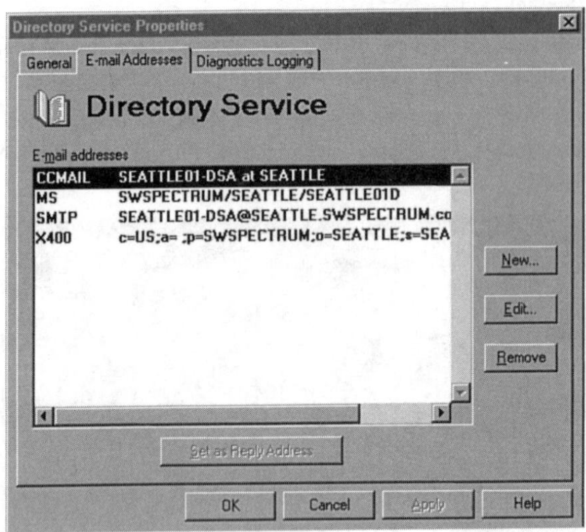

FIG. 13.20
Defining any additional e-mail addresses for this directory object.

The Diagnostics Logging Page

This property page works in conjunction with the Windows NT Event Log to record various "events" that occur within the Directory Service (MSExchangeDS). Various levels of logging determine what constitutes an event and, therefore, what types of information are actually recorded. For troubleshooting purposes, you would want a very detailed record of occurrences within the Directory Service, and hence set a high logging level. However, normally you would want to log only events that are critical, so set a lower logging level for everyday operation (see Figure 13.21).

FIG. 13.21
This page controls logging for the directory synchronization service only.

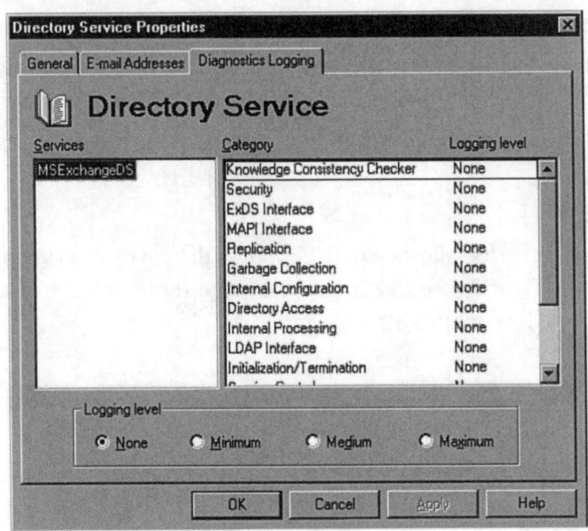

Configuring Directory Synchronization Service

These property pages allow for directory synchronization between Exchange, Microsoft Mail Post Office, and other compatible foreign systems, including direct support for cc:Mail. For further directory synchronization information, see Chapter 18, "Using Directory Replication and Synchronization."

The following are the property pages available for configuration on the directory synchronization service:

- The General page
- The E-Mail Addresses page
- The Delivery Restrictions page
- The Incoming Templates page
- The Outgoing Templates page
- The Diagnostics Logging page

To open the Directory Synchronization Service Properties pages, complete the following steps:

1. Navigate to your desired site with the Exchange Administrator program.
2. Click the Configuration container of the selected site. All the site configuration objects appear in the Administrator program's right window.

3. Open the Servers container. A list of Exchange servers in your site will be listed.
4. Click the server name for which you want to configure the directory synchronization service.
5. Click the Directory Synchronization object. Open its property pages.

The General Page

The General property page allows you to view only the current server's name and enter an administrative note (see Figure 13.22). An Exchange server's name is set when the software is installed and cannot be changed after the fact.

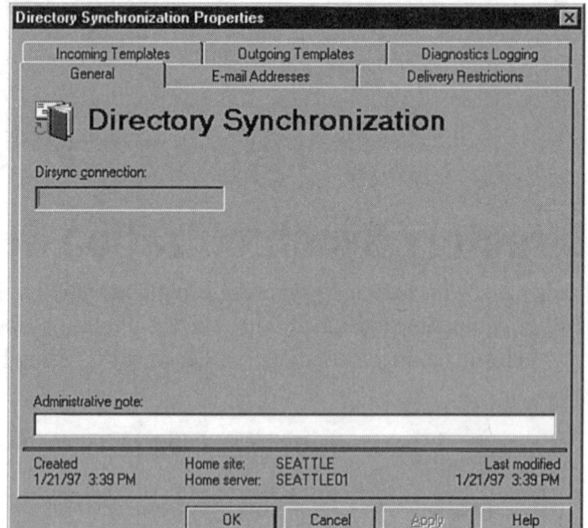

FIG. 13.22
The name of this server cannot be altered.

The E-Mail Addresses Page

E-mail addresses are used by the various Exchange gateways and connectors to identify specific directory objects to other messaging systems. The directory synchronization service receives regular update messages sent to these addresses. There are four default addresses created each for cc:Mail, Microsoft Mail Post Office, SMTP, and X.400.

The Delivery Restrictions Page

The directory synchronization service executes its functions by the transfer of messages between itself and other systems. The Delivery Restrictions property page assures that only specific users can send messages to the directory synchronization service.

To configure delivery restrictions, complete the following steps:

1. Select the Delivery Restrictions tab from the Directory Synchronization Properties pages (see Figure 13.23). The Delivery Restrictions property page appears.

2. Use the dialog box to either restrict certain senders or to permit only certain senders.
3. Click Apply to set these properties and continue with other properties. If you are done with all settings, click OK to return to the Administrator program.

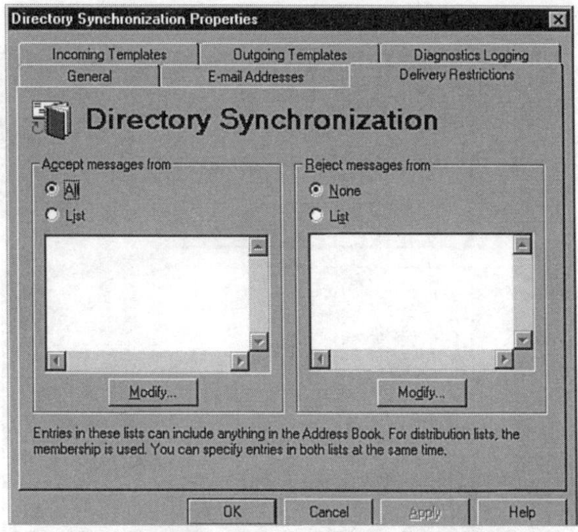

FIG. 13.23 Preventing unnecessary messages from being sent to this service.

The Incoming Templates Page

In the Incoming Templates property page you can define a template that will apply to all incoming directory synchronization messages (see Figure 13.24). See Chapter 18, "Using Directory Replication and Synchronization," for more details on this template and its use in directory synchronization.

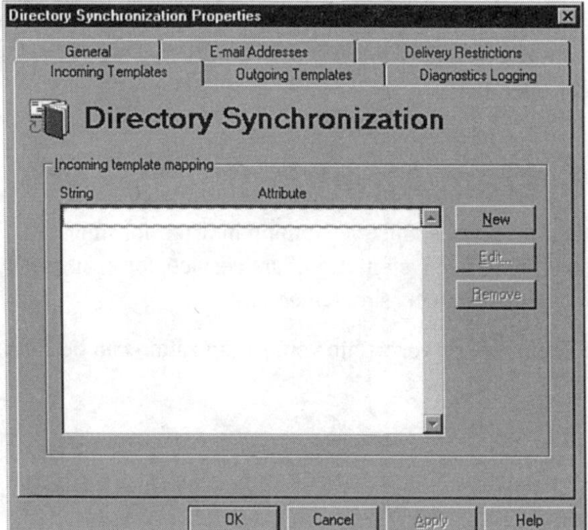

FIG. 13.24 Mapping standard Microsoft Mail Post Office attributes to Exchange Server recipients.

The Outgoing Templates Page

In the Outgoing Templates property page you can define a template that will apply to all outgoing directory synchronization messages (see Figure 13.25). See Chapter 18 for more details on this template and its use in directory synchronization.

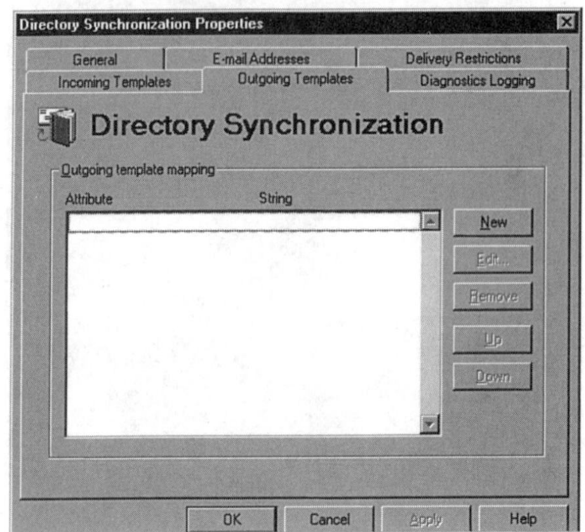

FIG. 13.25 Mapping Exchange Server recipient attributes to the standard Microsoft Mail Post Office directory template attributes.

The Diagnostics Logging Page

The Diagnostics Logging property page works in conjunction with the Windows NT Event Log to record various "events" that occur within the Directory Synchronization Service. Various levels of logging determine what constitutes an event and, therefore, what types of information are actually recorded. For troubleshooting purposes, you would want a very detailed record of occurrences within the Directory Synchronization Service, and hence set a high logging level. However, normally you would want to log only events that are critical, so set a lower logging level for everyday operation.

Configuring System Attendant

The System Attendant service must be running in order for most other Exchange system services to run. Stopping the System Attendant service, for example, will prompt the halting of several other Exchange services, simultaneously.

Each Microsoft Exchange server within your organization can be configured with different properties.

Accessing the System Attendant Property Pages

To configure the System Attendant properties, complete the following steps:

1. Use the Microsoft Exchange Administrator program to navigate to the list of servers within the site to which you are connected.
2. Click the server name whose System Attendant object you want to configure.
3. In the right display window, you will see a list of objects pertaining to that Exchange server (see Figure 13.26).

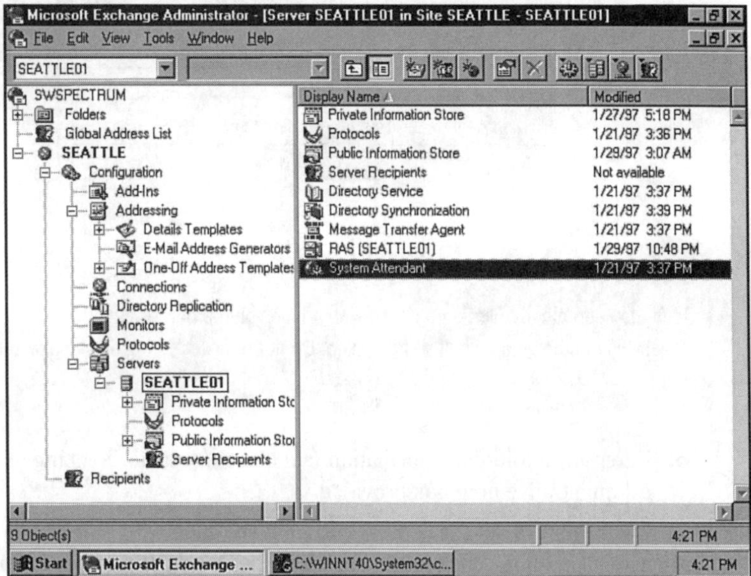

FIG. 13.26 The System Attendant is found in the individual Exchange Server container.

Click the System Attendant object and open its property pages. The property page shown in Figure 13.27 appears.

4. The General page is the first visible property page. The Display name is set as "System Attendant" by default and cannot be changed. Likewise, the Alias name for this object is set to "<server name>-SA" (for example, SEATTLE01-SA) and also cannot be changed.

   Under the Message tracking log files maintenance window: Click Do not remove old log files if you want the system attendant to keep such log files for an indefinite time.

5. Click Remove log files older than X number of days to have the System Attendant on this server delete message tracking files after a specified number of days has elapsed. Enter the number of days in the box provided. By default, this option is selected, and the log files are deleted every seven days.

FIG. 13.27
The System Attendant General property page.

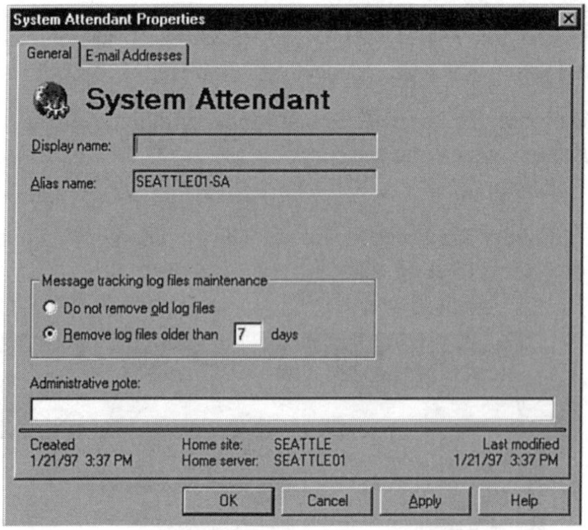

> **CAUTION**
>
> Opting to keep old log files on a server with a high volume of message traffic could easily take up many megabytes of storage space. If you do select Do not remove old log files, make sure to keep track of log file sizes!

6. Enter any additional information (such as reasons for keeping all old log files) in the Administrative note box provided.
7. Click Apply to set these properties and continue with other properties. If you are done with all settings, click OK to return to the Administrator program.

Setting E-Mail Addresses for the System Attendant

E-mail addresses are used by the various Exchange gateways and connectors to identify specific directory objects to other messaging systems. The System Attendant, though not capable of receiving messages, is a directory object just the same and has a set of e-mail addresses associated with it. There are four default addresses created each for cc:Mail, Microsoft Mail Post Office, SMTP, and X.400.

Complete the following steps to add, modify, or remove e-mail addresses from the System Attendant:

1. Click the E-mail Addresses of the System Attendant Properties page (see Figure 13.28).

   The four default addresses (cc:Mail, Microsoft Mail Post Office, SMTP, and X.400) are displayed.

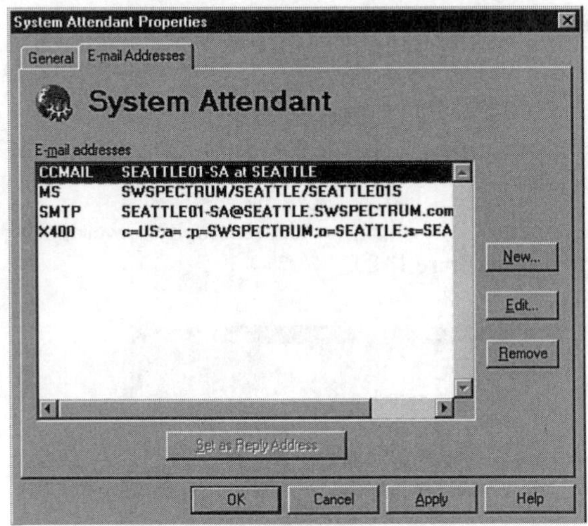

FIG. 13.28 The E-mail addresses page displays the four default addresses for this System Attendant.

2. Click New to add a specific e-mail address for this system attendant. Select an existing address and click Edit to modify it, or click Remove to delete it.
3. Click Apply to set these properties and continue with other properties. If you are done with all settings, click OK to return to the Administrator program.

All other functions of the System Attendant (such as checking directory replication inconsistencies and gathering information about other running Exchange services) are carried out without additional configuration by the administrator.

Configuring Address Book Views

The Address Book Views pages enable you to restrict what entries users are able to see in the Global Address List (GAL). This feature also allows users to create and see address book views sorted by various mailbox characteristics. You can create new Address Book Views in Exchange 5.5 by selecting File, New Other, Address Book View from the toolbar in the Exchange Administrator program.

The pages that will be covered are as follows:

- The General page
- The Group By page
- The Permissions page
- The Advanced property page

The General Page

Use the General page to specify a Display name and Directory name for your Address Book View.

Go through the following steps to change the Display name and/or the Directory name of your address book view:

1. Select the General tab of your new Address Book View property pages. You will then see a screen similar to Figure 13.29.

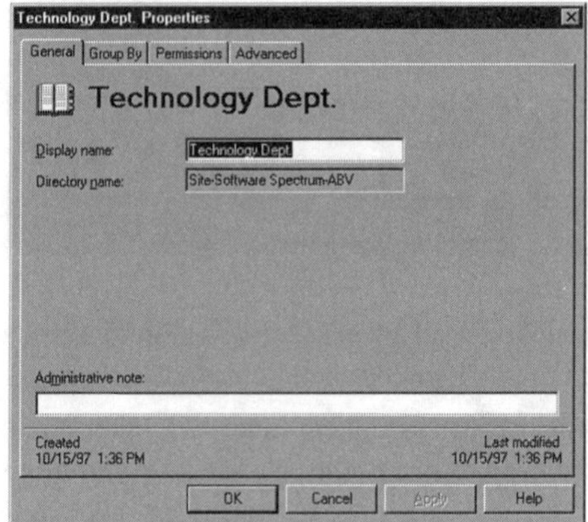

FIG. 13.29
Setting the Display Name and the Directory Name from the General page.

2. Enter a Display name for this object as you want it to be displayed in the Exchange Administrator program.
3. Enter a Directory name for this object. Once you apply your changes, you will be unable to change this directory name.
4. Enter an administrative note that pertains to this object if desired.
5. Click Apply to set these properties and continue with other properties. If you are finished setting options, click OK to return to the Administrator program.

The Group By Page

This page defines how the recipient objects in the Address Book view are grouped (see Figure 13.30).

To group recipient objects with specific attributes that appear in the Group items by box on the Group By page, complete the following steps:

1. Click on the Group By page of the Address Book View property pages.
2. Use the drop-down menu for Group items by to select an attribute you want to use to group items.
3. Use the pull-down menu for Then by to select additional attributes you want to group items.

4. Click Apply to set these properties and continue with other properties. If you are finished setting options, click OK to return to the Administrator program.

FIG. 13.30
You can have up to four grouping attributes with your Address Book View.

The Permissions Page

The Permissions property page allows you to specify the rights users will have to view the Address Book (see Figure 13.31).

To delegate permissions to a user or group, complete the following steps:

1. Click on the Permissions page of the Address Book View property pages.
2. The Windows NT accounts with inherited permissions is a read-only list box that displays all Windows NT accounts with inherited rights for this object.
3. Click the Add button to add Windows NT accounts and groups to the list of accounts and groups with permissions for this object.
4. The Remove button removes the currently selected Windows NT account or group from the list of accounts and groups with permissions for this object.
5. Use the Roles drop-down menu to assign a role to the currently selected Windows NT account or group. Roles are sets of rights that define how much or what type of access a user or group has to an object. You can define custom roles or use the default roles that come with Microsoft Exchange. For example, you can assign an account or group to the search role from this tab. The search role will restrict users or groups from viewing any other Address Book view other than the one in which they have this search role.
6. Click Apply to set these properties and continue with other properties. If you are finished setting options, click OK to return to the Administrator program.

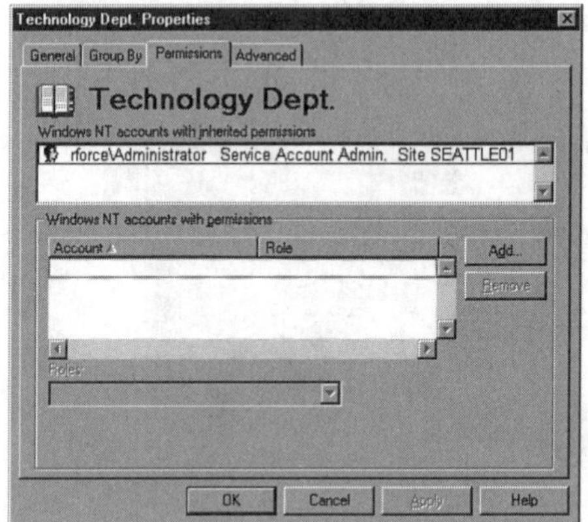

FIG. 13.31
Using the Permissions page to specify the rights users or groups have to Address Book views.

The Advanced Property Page

Use the Advanced property page to determine whether recipient objects should appear in one or more parent containers and which Address Book view containers you want to show in Microsoft Outlook. You can also delete empty containers within an Address Book view through this page (see Figure 13.32).

To configure advanced container properties, follow the steps below:

1. Select the Advanced page of the Address Book view property pages.
2. Select the Promote entries to parent containers if you want to have recipient objects included in the parent Address View Containers. For example, if you have Address Book views that group recipients by country (USA), state (Texas), and city (Dallas), you need to determine whether to include the mailbox under only the city container (Dallas), or under all of the containers (USA, Texas, Dallas).
3. If you select Show this view in the client address book, the Address Book and all of its containers appear in the Address Book.
4. If you want to remove empty containers from the Address Book view, you must do it manually. Empty containers are not removed automatically. Use the Remove Empty Containers button to remove all empty containers from the Address Book view.

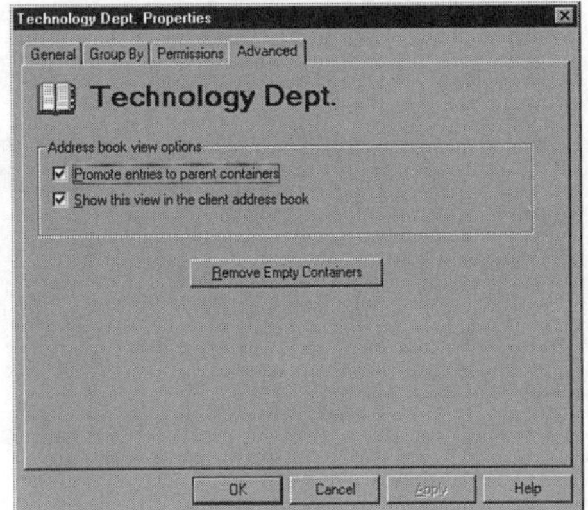

FIG. 13.32
You can configure recipient objects for parent containers, Address Book view containers for Microsoft Outlook, and delete empty containers.

CHAPTER 14

Message Transfer Configuration

In this chapter

The Microsoft Exchange Message Transfer Agent (MTA) is the key component that provides addressing, routing, and message delivery. Proper configuration of MTA settings is important to an efficient Exchange organization. As described in Chapter 3, "Exchange's Integrated Server Components," a message that originates in an Exchange mailbox reaches its destination in only two ways. The first is when a message is addressed to a user on the same Exchange server and is delivered by the information store. The second is when a message is addressed to a user on a different server or foreign system, and the MTA handles the message transfer.

Understanding the Transfer Agent Components

The Microsoft Exchange Message Transfer Agent is a Windows NT service running on each Exchange server in your organization. For connection to Microsoft Mail systems, an additional service called the Microsoft Mail Connector (PC) MTA negotiates message transfer with Microsoft Mail networks.

Configuration of the Exchange MTA is handled through two sets of properties sheets:

- *MTA Site Configuration*. Defines overall settings for message transmission within the entire Exchange site.
- *Message Transfer Agent (for a specific Exchange server)*. Defines server-specific MTA settings, such as message size limits and logging levels.

Some of the essential parameters involved in performing MTA site configurations are listed here:

Message Tracking. To keep records of Message Transfer Agent activity within a Microsoft Exchange site and enable message tracking. A daily log file is generated and stored in the EXCHSRVR\TRACKING.LOG directory. Message tracking log files are in a text format. The full file name, to use an example, might be EXCHSRVR\TRACKING\970122.LOG. The individual log files are named using this format: *YYMMDD*.log. For example, a log file for MTA activity on Jan 22, 1997 would have the name 970122.log.

Message Queues. Each server has a list of messages that are waiting to be delivered by its MTA. The queues are distinguished as being either Private or Public information store messages. Messages are held in the queue until the MTA can successfully transfer the messages by establishing a connection with the remote MTA or until the messages exceed their lifetimes (as set in the messaging defaults).

Messaging Defaults. Settings for how (and how long) to transfer a message before certain timeouts occurs are called messaging defaults. These values are set in the MTA Site Configuration properties and are used by all MTAs in the site unless a specific connection uses MTA override parameters.

MTA Overrides. Certain connectors (specifically, the dynamic RAS connector and the X.400 connector) provide for object-specific MTA settings. Use the Override property to change the default Microsoft Exchange Server MTA attributes when using a specific X.400 or dynamic RAS connector. Remember their existence when you define messaging defaults in the MTA Site Configuration properties sheet. The Override property is for developing flexibility in MTA configuration.

Performing MTA Site Configuration

To open the MTA Site Configuration properties sheet, follow these steps:

1. Navigate to your desired site with the Exchange Administrator program, and then expand the site container.
2. Highlight the Configuration container of the selected site (see Figure 14.1). All the site configuration objects appear in the right pane of the Administrator program's window.

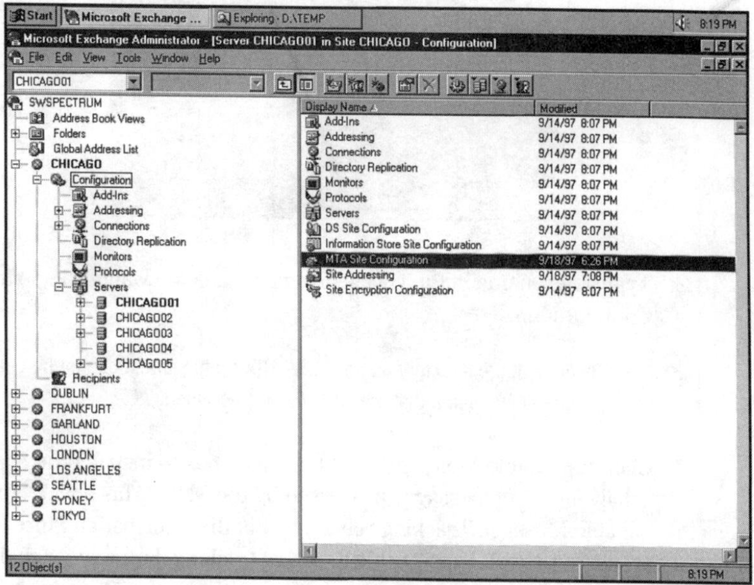

FIG. 14.1
The MTA Site Configuration is located in the Configuration container.

3. Select the MTA Site Configuration object from the list.
4. Open the MTA Site Configuration Object properties sheet by double-clicking the object.

At this point, you have three property pages to configure:

- *General.* Sets the MTA site configuration display name and the dead-letter recipient, and enables message tracking.

- *Permissions.* Sets security rights to the MTA Site Configuration object.
- *Messaging Defaults.* Defines connection and transmission parameters for the MTAs in your site.

The General Tab

To configure the General features, such as the display name of the MTA Site Configuration Object, follow these steps:

1. Click the General tab of the MTA Site Configuration properties sheet (see Figure 14.2).

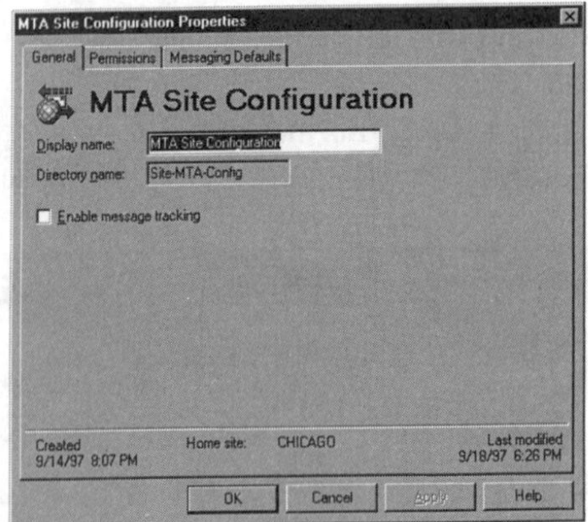

FIG. 14.2
The General page of the MTA Site Configuration properties sheet.

2. Type a new name in the Display Name box, if you want. The default name is MTA Site Configuration.

NOTE By default, the directory name is Site-MTA-Config, and it cannot be changed. This is the unique object name that the site MTA has assigned. ■

3. Click the Enable Message Tracking check box to instruct the System Attendant to keep a daily log of all messages processed by the MTA. This check box corresponds to the "Enable Message Tracking" check box in the Information Store Site Configuration properties sheet. Both enable message tracking, but only for their respective services.
4. Click Apply to set these properties and continue viewing and changing other properties.
5. When you finish changing settings, click OK to return to the Administrator program.

The Permissions Tab

This page of the properties sheet allows you to define certain Windows NT user accounts that have rights to modify this directory object. See Chapter 12, "Using the Administrator Program," for a detailed description on working with the standard Permissions properties sheet.

The Messaging Defaults Tab

To set the messaging default values for the MTA Site Configuration object, follow these steps:

1. Click the Messaging Defaults tab of the MTA Site Configuration properties sheet (see Figure 14.3).

To return to the default Message Transfer Agent settings, click the Reset Default Values button.

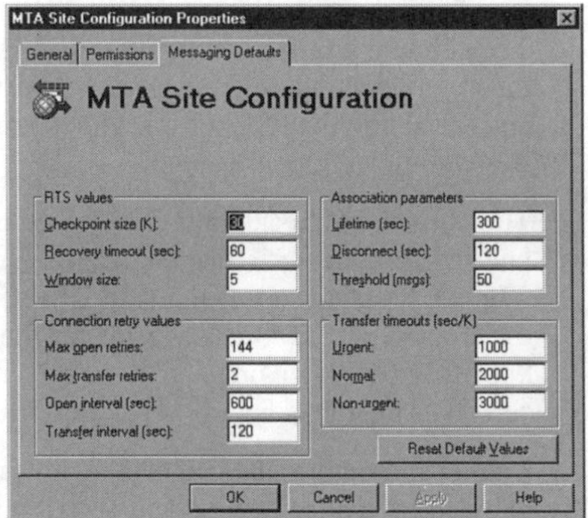

FIG. 14.3
Messaging defaults control each connection made by the MTA.

2. Enter specific MTA configuration variables, as described in Table 14.1.

   To the right of each item listed in the table is a box that contains a default numeric value. Replace any value with a number that will be used in establishing a connection through any MTA in the current site.

3. Click Apply to set these properties.
4. When you finish changing settings, click OK to return to the Administrator program.

Table 14.1 MTA Site Configuration Parameter Values

Variable	Description
RTS Values	Reliable Transfer Service (RTS) values determine how often you want to verify information as it is being transferred, how long you want to wait after an error to restart the transfer, and how often you want a verification that another system has received your transfer.
Checkpoint Size (K)	Sets the amount of data to be transferred before a checkpoint is inserted. If an error occurs and the message must be retransferred, the process restarts from the most recent checkpoint. If you specify zero, no checkpoint is set. The default is 30. Checkpointing slightly reduces transmission speed. You should decrease the checkpoint size when the link is less reliable.
Recovery Timeout (Sec)	The amount of time after an error occurs that the MTA waits for a reconnection before deleting checkpointed information and restarting the transfer from the beginning. The default is 60.
Window Size	The number of checkpoints that can go unacknowledged before data transfer is suspended. The greater the window size, the greater the transfer rate. The window size determines the amount of resources set aside for the receiving station. Specify window size only if the checkpoint size is greater than zero. The default is 5.
Connection Retry Values	Connection retry values determine how many times you want to try to open a connection and send a message and how long you want to wait to reopen a connection or resend a message after an error.
Max Open Retries	The maximum number of times the system tries to open a connection before it sends a non-delivery report (NDR). The default is 144.
Max Transfer Retries	The maximum number of times the system tries to transfer a message across an open connection. The default is 2.
Open Interval (Sec)	The delay (in seconds) between attempts to open a communication channel. By default, the delay is 600 seconds.
Transfer Interval (Sec)	The delay (in seconds) between attempts to retransmit a failed message packet. By default, this delay is 120 seconds.

Variable	Description
Association Parameters	Associations are paths that are opened to other systems. Each association is contained within a connection and is used to transfer messages to a system. You may have multiple associations in each connection. You can determine how long to keep an association, how long to wait for a response before disconnecting, and the number of messages you will let wait before you open another association.
Lifetime (Sec)	The maximum time that an idle connection between MTAs remains open. By default, an idle link is held open for 300 seconds after the last communication.
Disconnect (Sec)	The maximum time allowed for establishing or terminating a connection before the session is ended independently. By default, this time is 120 seconds.
Threshold (Msgs)	The maximum number of queued messages to a remote system. When this is exceeded, the MTA opens another association. The default is 50.
Transfer Timeouts (Sec/K)	Messages of different priorities require different levels of attention. For example, an urgent message is processed more quickly than a non-urgent message. If a transfer fails, you must determine how long to wait before sending a non-delivery report (NDR). The transfer timeout is the amount of time to wait before sending that NDR. You can assign a different amount of time for each message priority.
Urgent	The delay (in seconds per kilobyte of total message size) between retries of urgent messages. By default, this delay is 1,000 seconds. This is a timeout value before messages are sent.
Normal	The delay (in seconds per kilobyte of total message size) between retries of normal messages. By default, this delay is 2,000 seconds. The trend here is that the less important the message, the longer you wait for a transmission.
Non-Urgent	The delay (in seconds per kilobyte of total message size) between retries of non-urgent messages. By default, this delay is 3,000 seconds.

NOTE If you combine the default 144 Max Open Retries with the default 600-second Open Interval, Exchange waits 24 hours before returning a message as undeliverable. ■

The following section discusses configuring Message Transfer Agent properties for each Microsoft Exchange Server.

Configuring Local MTA Properties

Each Microsoft Exchange Server has a Message Transfer Agent. The MTA properties sheet is designed to configure and manage this service.

First, you must select the MTA from the server within your site. Follow these steps to do so:

1. Navigate to your desired site with the Exchange Administrator program, and then expand the site container.
2. Highlight the Configuration container of the selected site. All the site configuration objects appear in the right pane of the Administrator program's window.
3. Open the Servers container by double-clicking it. A list of Exchange servers in your site appears.
4. Click the name of the server that houses the MTA you want to configure (see Figure 14.4). A list of server objects appears in the right pane of the Microsoft Exchange Administrator program window.

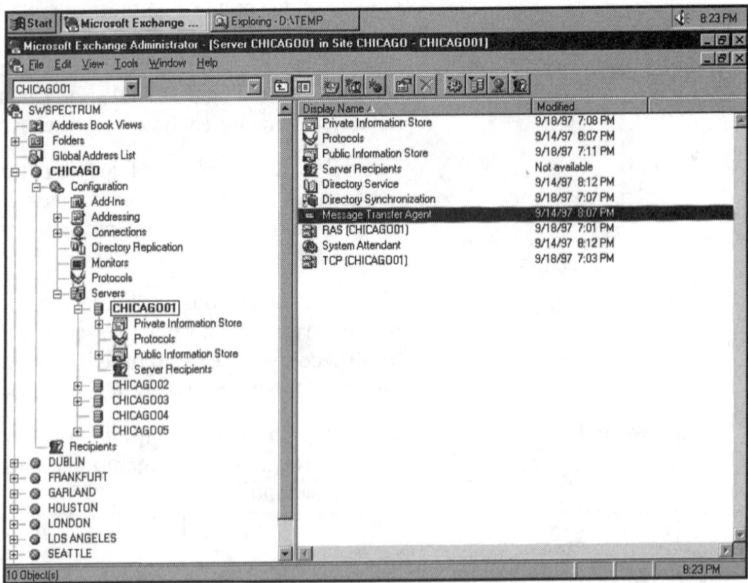

FIG. 14.4 The Message Transfer Agent directory object is located inside the server container.

5. Click the Message Transfer Agent object, and then open its properties sheet.

The following three pages become available for you to configure:

- *General.* Sets local MTA name, password, and general message transmission preferences for this server.
- *Queues.* Lists messages awaiting transmission by the local MTA.
- *Diagnostics Logging.* Sets the level of events that are entered in the Windows NT Event Log.

These pages are covered in the sections that follow.

The General Tab

To set values for the local MTA name and password and other general message transfer preferences for this server, follow these steps:

1. Click the General tab of the Message Transfer Agent properties sheet (see Figure 14.5).

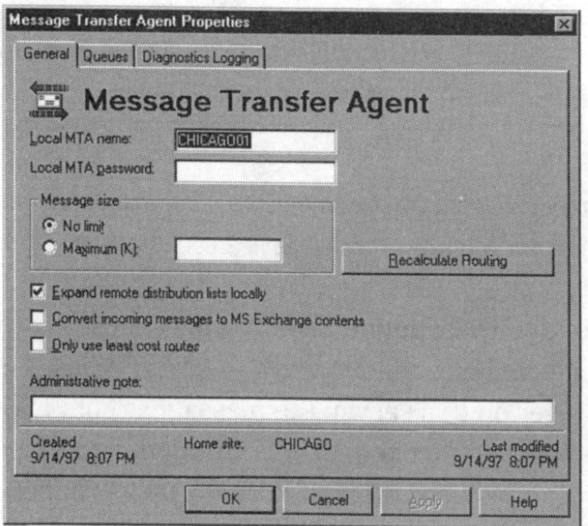

FIG. 14.5 The General page of the Message Transfer Agent properties sheet.

2. Type a name in the Local MTA Name box. This name will be used by remote MTAs (either on remote Exchange servers or foreign messaging systems) to identify this MTA. By default, this name is the name of the Exchange server on which the MTA is installed.
3. Type a password in the Local MTA Password box, if necessary. If you enter a password in this box, any remote MTA (either on remote Exchange servers or foreign messaging systems) must be configured to provide this password for authentication. By default, this box is blank, and no authentication is required of the remote MTA.

NOTE If you decide to change the Local MTA Name or to add or change the Local MTA Password, be sure to take into consideration any previously established MTA connections. All remote sites (and foreign systems, such as X.400) must be adjusted to reflect the new information. Authentication is never required between two MTAs in the same site.

4. In the Message Size section, click the option button that indicates how you want to restrict the passage of messages through this message transfer agent.

   Click the No Limit option button to allow this MTA to deliver messages of any size.

   If you want to set a size limit, click the Maximum (K) option button, and then, in the text box, type an upper limit (in kilobytes) for messages that travel through this MTA. Any message that exceeds this size limit will be returned as undeliverable.

Use these settings as a filter to manage the messaging load for all traffic to and from this server. The upper-limit settings have precedence over message-size settings in individual connectors and recipient objects.

5. Click the Recalculate Routing button to rebuild the routing tables for this MTA. (See Chapter 2, "Understanding Exchange's Organization and Sites," for more information on routing tables.) New routing information for this MTA will propagate to all Exchange servers within the site automatically.

Rebuilding routing tables sometimes takes several minutes, so it is a good idea to go through each MTA properties sheet, make all changes, and then recalculate routing.

NOTE Routing tables are rebuilt once a day automatically. The routing table will rebuild when it detects a change in a new gateway or a change in a connector configuration. ■

6. Click the Expand Remote Distribution Lists Locally check box to force distribution lists created on remote sites to be expanded on this server. When a message is sent to a distribution list by a user on this server, the message is split into its component recipients locally. If this box is not checked, the distribution list is expanded in the remote site, following the configuration in the distribution list's own properties sheet. By default, this box is checked, and distribution lists are expanded locally.

NOTE Consider both the physical location of the majority of the distribution list's recipients and the messaging load on the local server. If you choose the default settings, make certain that the local server can handle the extra messaging traffic: Expanding large distribution lists can be a considerable load on an already overburdened Exchange server. Also, if you know that the majority of the distribution list's recipients reside on Exchange servers in the remote site, consider allowing the list to be expanded there. ■

7. Click the Convert Incoming Messages to MS Exchange Contents check box to convert all messages to Exchange's MAPI-compliant format automatically. By default, this option is not selected, and messages are kept in the format in which they arrive at the MTA (such as standard X.400 format).

8. Click the Only Use Least Cost Routes check box if you don't want this MTA to reroute messages destined for an unavailable server through another possible route. This option configures an individual message transfer agent (MTA) to send messages using only least-cost routes. Only the least-cost route for each message will be attempted. This allows you to prevent messages from being routed to connectors in other sites when a connector in the local site is unavailable. If a message cannot be routed through the least-cost route, Microsoft Exchange Server generates a non-delivery report (NDR).
9. If you want, make an entry in the Administrative Note text box.
10. Click Apply to set these properties and continue with other properties.
11. When you finish changing settings, click OK to return to the Administrator program.

This page controls the functioning of local server MTA. Using this page you can limit the message size sent, how messages are routed when multiple routes are available, and where distribution lists are expanded.

The Queues Tab

The Queues tab of the Message Transfer Agent properties sheet lists messages that are awaiting delivery by the MTA. The two primary windows are Queue Name (which shows the queue that you are currently viewing) and Message List (which displays the messages in that queue). From the Message List window, you can view details about a specific message in the queue, change a message's delivery priority, or delete it.

The Message List window has three columns that contain information about a particular message:

- *Originator*: The original sender of the message.
- *Submit Time*: The time of the next transfer attempt for this message.
- *Size*: The size of the message, in kilobytes.

To configure the Queues property page, follow these steps:

1. Click the Queues tab from the Message Transfer Agent properties sheet (see Figure 14.6).
2. From the Queue Name drop-down list, select the message queue you want to display. The list shows queues for the private and public information stores, as well as for any installed gateways.

NOTE The Internet Mail Connector and Microsoft Mail connector have separate queues that you can access through their properties sheets. ■

3. Select a message, and then click Details to view additional information about it. The additional message information includes the message originator, submit time, message size, and priority. This button is dimmed if no messages are in the queue.

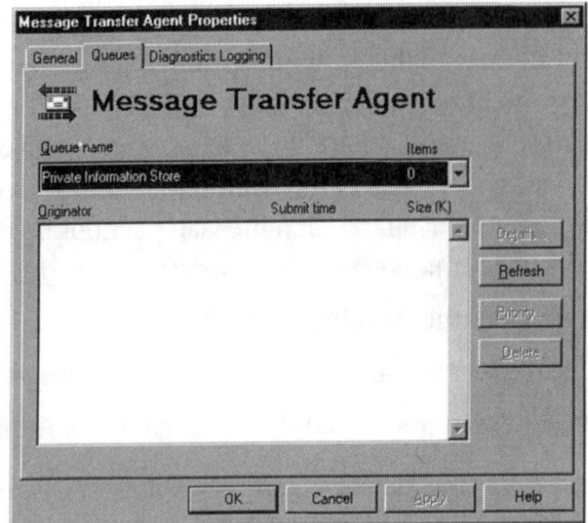

FIG. 14.6
Messages waiting to be delivered are held in the queue.

4. Click the Refresh button to update the Message List window with the latest list of messages in the MTA queue.
5. Click Priority to display the message's priority, and then change the priority of the message if you want. Priority can be low, medium, or high. Messages are sent in order of priority. A message's priority is set when a message is created.
6. To remove a message from the MTA queue, select a message and click Delete.
7. Click Apply to set these properties and continue with other properties.
8. When you finish changing settings, click OK to return to the Administrator program.

Using this page, you can monitor the messaging queues on this server. You can monitor the dynamic RAS connector, X.400 connector, Internet Mail Service, and public and private information stores.

The Diagnostics Logging Tab

This properties sheet works in conjunction with the Windows NT Event Log to record various "events" that occur within the message transfer agent.

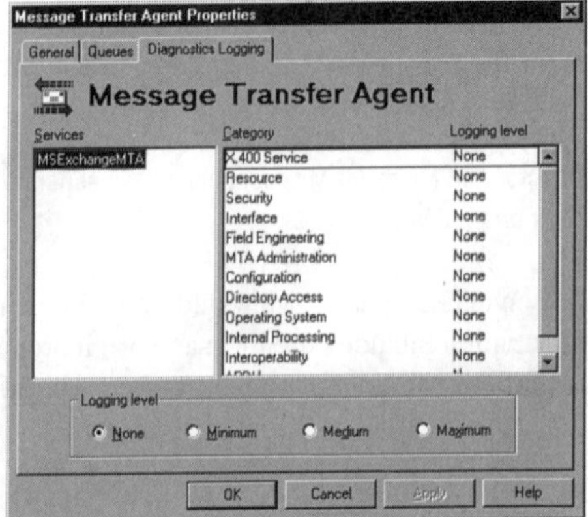

FIG. 14.7
The Diagnostics Logging page for the site MTA.

Various levels of logging determine what constitutes an event and, therefore, what types of information are actually recorded. For troubleshooting purposes, you would want a very detailed record of occurrences within the MTA; hence, you would set a high logging level. Normally, however, you want to log only critical events. So set a lower logging level for everyday operation.

CHAPTER 15

Information Store Configuration

In this chapter

The Microsoft Exchange information stores (public and private) are the databases that hold all Microsoft Exchange messaging information. In addition, the information store is the primary storage system for information relevant to users, including messages, server-based mailboxes and their contents, public folders and their contents, private folders that are stored on a server instead of on a user's computer, documents, forms, and user-defined items.

Understanding Important Information Store Concepts

Understanding the following concepts will be helpful to you as you proceed through this chapter:

- *Top-Level Folder.* A public folder created at the highest point in the public folder directory tree. Usually only certain individuals in an Exchange organization (as assigned by the Permissions Administrator) are granted the right to create folders at the top of the hierarchy.
- *Public Folder Instance.* A replica of a public folder on a site other than the one on which it was created. Users can then connect to the local site's instance of the folder instead of crossing site boundaries (and adding to network traffic) to connect to a remote site.
- *Public Folder Affinity.* When a user in a local site needs to connect to a public folder that's only available on a remote site, the choice of connection is based on the costs assigned to the site containing replicas of that folder. Users need appropriate Windows NT security rights to access the actual Windows NT server on the remote site, and of course, they need access rights to the Exchange public folder itself.
- *Information Store Message Tracking.* The information store is responsible for transferring messages between two users on the same Exchange server. To keep a record of information store message transfer activity within a Microsoft Exchange server, you enable the message tracking feature. This generates a daily log file that's stored in the EXCHSRVR\TRACKING.LOG directory. The individual log files are named using this format: *YYMMDD*.log. For example, a log file for information store activity on June 11, 1997 would have the name 970611.log.

Information Store Site Configuration

Settings made on the Information Store Site Configuration properties sheets affect all servers within an Exchange site. When first setting up an Exchange site, you should configure these properties sheets.

Open the Site Configuration properties sheets by completing the following steps:

1. Navigate to your desired site with the Exchange Administrator program, and then expand the site container.
2. Highlight the Configuration container (see Figure 15.1) of the selected site. All the site configuration objects appear in the right pane of the Administrator program window.

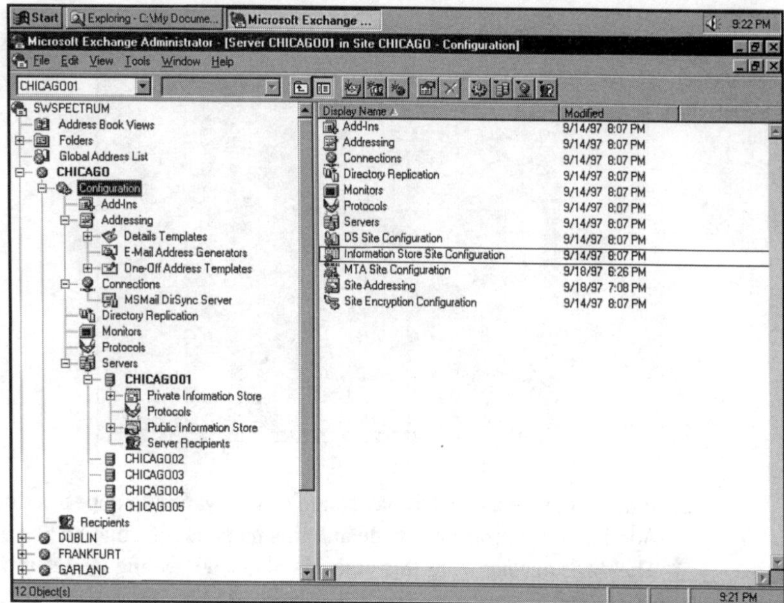

FIG. 15.1
The Configuration container holds all site configuration objects.

3. Select the Information Store Site Configuration object from the list.
4. Double-click the object to open its properties sheet.

At this point there will be five pages of the properties sheet to configure:

- *General.* Set display name, public folder container, and toggle message tracking.
- *Permissions.* Set access right to the Information Store Site Configuration directory object.
- *Top Level Folder Creation.* Define which users are allowed to create public folders at the highest level of the public folder directory tree.
- *Storage Warnings.* Schedule when notification messages about exceeded storage space are sent to those users in violation of set restraints.
- *Public Folder Affinity.* Configure connections to public folders in remote sites.

The General Page

On the General page, you can set up a default container for public folder creation, as well as enable message tracking for the entire site.

Complete the following steps to change settings on the General page:

1. Select the General tab of the Information Store Site Configuration properties sheet. The page in Figure 15.2 appears.

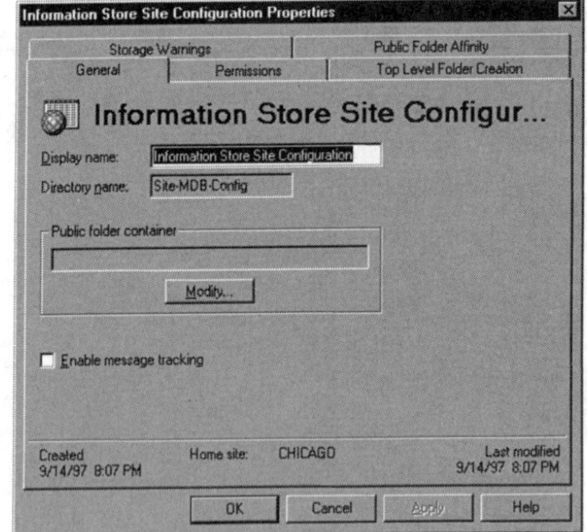

FIG. 15.2
This page controls the configuration of information stores in the site.

2. If desired, type a new Display Name as you want it to appear in the Microsoft Exchange Administrator program. By default this name is Information Store Site Configuration. The directory name for this object is Site-MDB-Config by default; it cannot be changed.
3. The Public Folder Container box displays the recipient container in which the public folders directory entries for this site are stored. By default, this box is blank, and public folders are stored in the standard recipients container. To change that, click Modify to access a dialog box with a list of all available recipient containers within this site. Then select a container and click OK.
4. Click the Enable Message Tracking check box to instruct the information store to keep a daily log file about all messages processed by the information store. All messages that are destined for a local recipient are delivered by the information store. This button corresponds with the Enable Message Tracking check box on the MTA Site Configuration properties sheet and enables use of the Message Tracking tool in the Exchange Administrator program.
5. Click Apply to set these properties and continue changing properties. If you are satisfied with all settings, click OK to return to the Administrator program.

The Permissions Page

On this page, you can define certain Windows NT user accounts that have rights to modify this directory object. See Chapter 12, "Using the Administrator Program," for details on working with the standard Permissions properties.

The Top-Level Folder Creation Page

With the settings on this page, you can either deny or allow certain users the ability to create public folders on the highest level of the public folder hierarchy.

NOTE You can also deny or allow rights to all users on a specified distribution list, and Exchange will determine top level folder creation permission based on the list's membership. As the members of the distribution list are modified, so are the permissions set here. ■

Complete the following steps to configure the Top Level Folder Creation properties:

1. Select the Top Level Folder Creation tab from the Information Store Site Configuration properties sheet. The page shown in Figure 15.3 appears.

   The Allowed to Create Top Level Folders box lists the recipients who have been given specific permission to create these folders. The Not Allowed to Create Top Level Folders box lists the recipients specifically denied permission to create these folders. By default, all users can create top level folders.

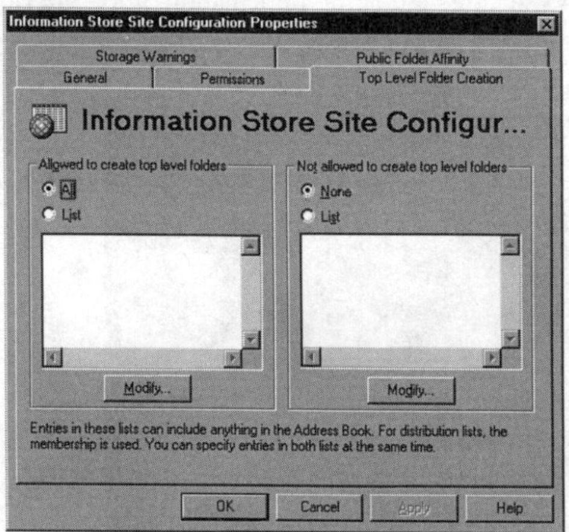

FIG. 15.3 Selectively assign top level folder creation rights from this page.

2. Click the Modify button under either box if you want to add recipients to or delete recipients from the list. A standard address list dialog box appears.
3. Click Apply to set these properties and continue changing properties. If you are satisfied with all settings, click OK to return to the Administrator program.

NOTE In most Exchange organizations, the default of allowing anyone to create top level public folders is not preferred. Most Exchange administrators limit top level creation to a select list or distribution list soon after creating a new site. ■

The Storage Warnings Page

With the controls on this page, you can schedule when information store will send out storage warnings. You set the actual storage limits in the following properties sheets for each corresponding recipient type:

- *Mailboxes.* Set limits for each individual user or set a global storage limit for all mailboxes on a particular server using the Mailbox Advanced page of the Private Information Store properties sheet.
- *Public Folders.* Set limits for each individual folder or set a global storage limit for all public folders on a particular server using the Public Folder Advanced page of the Public Information Store properties sheet.

The Storage Warnings notification schedule actually initiates an automated process that evaluates the size of each message store object in the information store on each server in the site. If a server has a high number of mailboxes and public folders, this process can take up a fair amount of system resources as it runs.

Set the Storage Warnings notification schedule by taking these steps:

1. Select the Storage Warnings tab of the Information Store Site Configuration properties sheet. The page in Figure 15.4 appears.

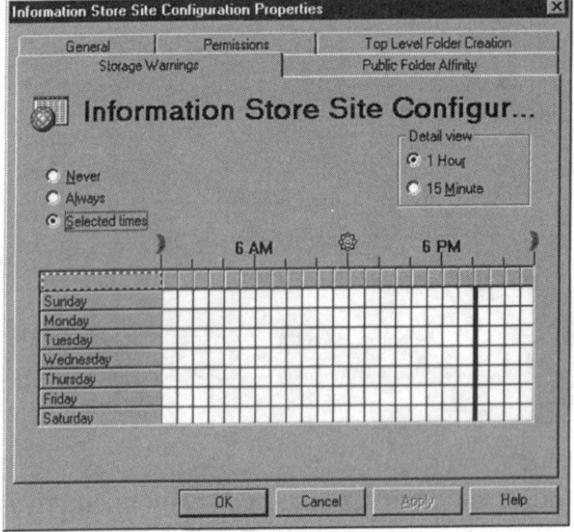

FIG. 15.4
Set the Storage Warnings notification schedule.

2. Select one of the three option buttons that determine when recipients are notified:

   Never. This effectively disables storage warning notification.

   Always. A storage warning notification is executed immediately when a storage limit is exceeded.

   Selected Times. Storage warning notifications are executed based on the time slots selected on this page.

If you are using storage limits in a large organization, it is generally not a good idea to select Always and potentially overtax your servers during high usage. It is better to schedule a time or times when the messaging load is lower and have storage warnings sent at once.

3. If you choose Selected Times, the Detail View option buttons become available. Select either the 1 Hour or 15 Minute detail view, and the time grid scale changes accordingly.
4. Also if you choose Selected Times, pick the time blocks for evaluations. By default, storage warning notifications are scheduled once per day beginning at 8 p.m.
5. Click Apply to set these properties and continue changing properties. If you are satisfied with all settings, click OK to return to the Administrator program.

The Public Folder Affinity Page

From this page, you can set up connections to public folders located in remote Exchange sites.

Complete the following steps to configure the Public Folder Affinity properties:

1. Select the Public Folder Affinity tab of the Information Store Site Configuration properties sheet. The page in Figure 15.5 appears.

   The Sites window lists all the sites in your organization. The Public Folder Affinity window lists all the sites where a connection may be established in order for a user to connect to a remote public folder. The Cost column displays the relative numeric value assigned to this site. As with message routing, the site with the lower cost will be used first.

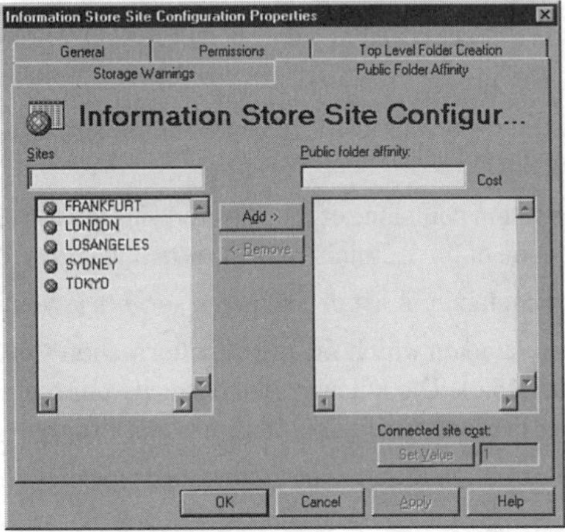

FIG. 15.5 Define the order in which a user connects to remote public folders.

2. To add a site, select it from the Sites window and click Add. To remove a site, select it from the Public Folder Affinity window and click Remove.
3. Enter the Connected Site Cost in the box in the lower-right corner. If the cost of the site is 0, this site will always be used first if it is available. The possible value for this cost field is 1–99. Sites will be used in numerical sequence with the lower valued sites used first. If the costs are equal between sites, the load will be distributed equally among those sites. If a cost of 100 is used, the site will be used only if no other site is available.

4. Click Set Value to save the cost associated with the selected site.
5. Click Apply to set these properties and continue changing properties. If you are satisfied with all settings, click OK to return to the Administrator program.

Configuring Private Information Store

Now we will move on to configuring private information store properties on an individual Microsoft Exchange server. The private information store primarily holds data posted to user mailboxes and private folders, in addition to mail associated to some Exchange connectors, such as the Internet Mail Service.

There are four separate pages you will need to configure:

- *General.* Set global mailbox storage limits for this server; designate a public folder server.
- *Logons.* View a list of users' connections to the private information store.
- *Mailbox Resources.* View mailbox settings and amount of storage space used by each mailbox.
- *Diagnostic Logging.* Set logging levels for tracking down errors and debugging your organization.

First you must select the private information store from a server within your site. Do this by completing the following steps:

1. Navigate to your desired site with the Exchange Administrator program, and then expand the site container.
2. Expand the Configuration container of the selected site. All the site configuration objects appear in the right pane of the Administrator program window.
3. Expand the Servers container. A list of Exchange servers in your site will be listed.
4. Highlight the server name on which the private information store you want to configure is located (see Figure 15.6). The following list of server objects is visible in the right pane window of the Microsoft Exchange Administrator program.
5. Click the Private Information Store object. Open its properties sheet.

The General Page

From this page, you can set global storage size limits for mailboxes on this server. Also, you can specify a different Exchange server to be responsible for the public folders created by users on this server.

Complete the following steps to configure the Private Information Store General properties:

1. Select the General tab of the Private Information Store properties sheet. The page in Figure 15.7 appears.

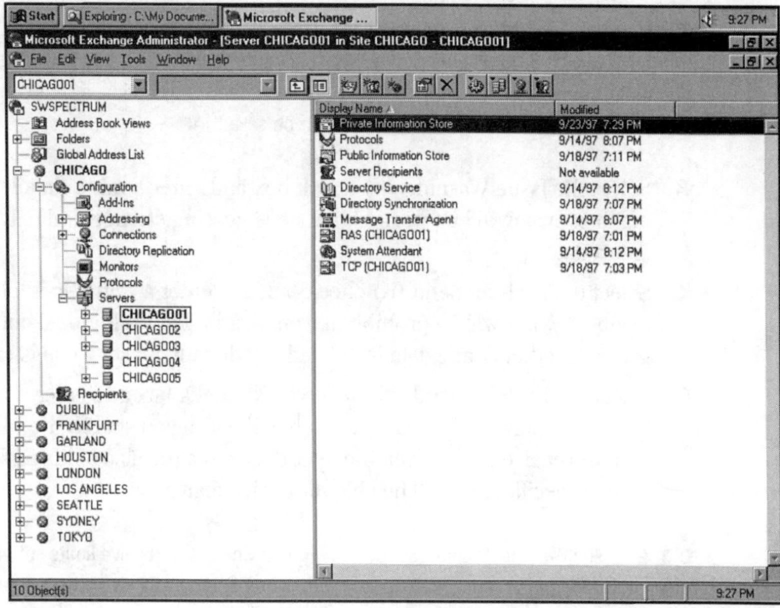

FIG. 15.6
The private information store holds all mailbox data of users on the local server.

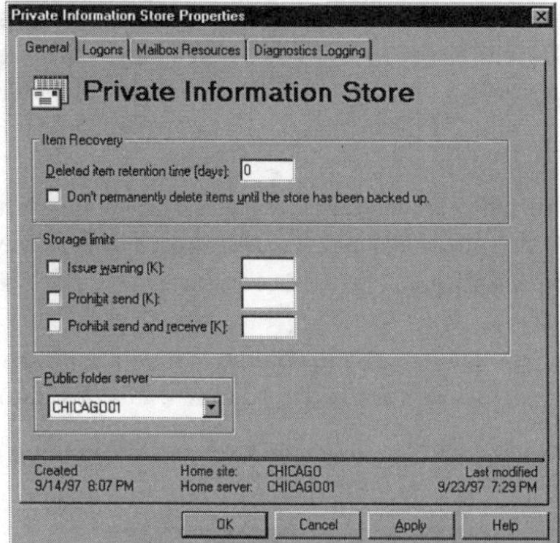

FIG. 15.7
The settings on this page apply to all mailboxes on this server.

2. Set the Deleted Item Retention Time (Days) for a period of time you would like to save deleted items. This is a new feature in Exchange 5.5. It enables you to control the period of time you want deleted mail to be saved so users can easily recover deleted mail if necessary using the Outlook client (version 8.03 and later). To save users' deleted items until the private information store is backed up, select the check box next to Don't Permanently Delete Items Until the Store Has Been Backed Up.

NOTE With Exchange 5.5, you can easily recover deleted items from within the Outlook client (version 8.03 and later). But if you configure your server not to save deleted items for a period of time, the user will not be able to recover any items. This option is set to zero days by default; it must be configured in order for deleted mail to be saved. ■

3. Select the Issue Warning (K) check box and enter a value (in kilobytes) at which a mailbox owner will be warned that he is nearing storage limits. By default, no set value is entered.
4. Select the Prohibit Send (K) check box and enter a value (in kilobytes) at which a mailbox owner will be prohibited from sending any additional outgoing messages until some stored message data is deleted. By default, no set value is entered.
5. Select the Prohibit Send and Receive (K) check box and enter a value (in kilobytes). When the individual's mailbox reaches the size you specify, he will no longer be able to send or receive mail. When the user decreases the size of his mailbox to a size below what is specified, he will be able to receive mail again.

NOTE Issue Warning, Prohibit Send, and Prohibit Send and Receive limits set on this page are overridden by individual mailbox settings on each mailbox's Advanced page. ■

6. Under Public Folder Server, select the Exchange server in your site that will store public folders created by users with mailboxes on this local server. This is especially useful if a specific, dedicated public folder server has been set up in the site or location. By default, the public folder server used is the same one on which the folder was created—the current server.

NOTE If you select a server other than the local Exchange server, you are effectively separating that server's public and private information stores. Select a different server only if this complies with your overall load balancing plan for this Exchange site. ■

7. Click Apply to set these properties and continue changing properties. If you are satisfied with all settings, click OK to return to the Administrator program.

The message shown in Figure 15.8 is an example storage size warning message.

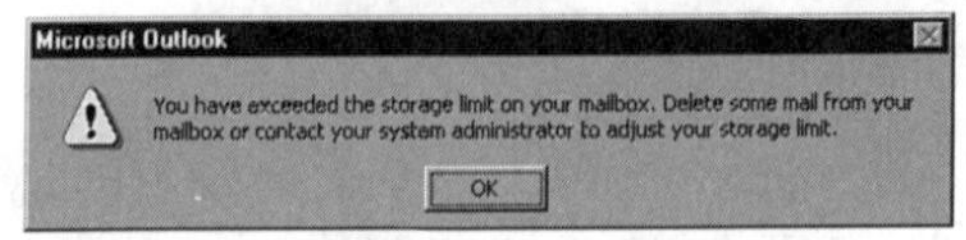

FIG. 15.8 This message appears when users exceed set storage limits for their mailboxes.

The Logons Page

This page enables you to monitor the Microsoft Exchange users currently logged into a server. It consists of one main display window that shows all currently connected users. The window is broken down into various columns of information. You can customize the columns both by the information shown and their widths on the screen.

Complete the following steps to view logon information:

1. Select the Logons tab of the Private Information Store properties sheet. The page shown in Figure 15.9 appears. The display window shows all users currently logged on to this Exchange server.

NOTE The Microsoft Exchange System Attendant is always listed in this window because the System Attendant is always logged in when the Exchanger Server is running. ■

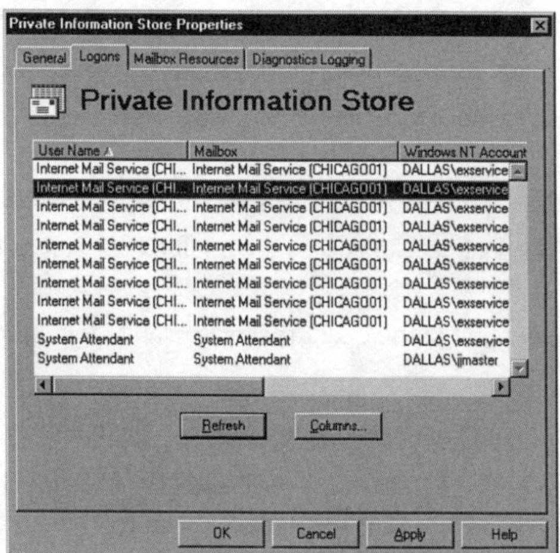

FIG. 15.9 View currently logged on users.

2. Click the Refresh button to update the display window with the latest information.
3. Click the Columns button to edit which columns are displayed and their widths in pixels (see Figure 15.10). See the list following these steps for a description of the column headings and what type of information each one can display.

NOTE Exchange 5.5 includes 12 additional measurements that can be used in the analysis of private folder use. ■

4. Click Apply to set these properties and continue changing properties. If you are satisfied with all settings, click OK to return to the Administrator program.

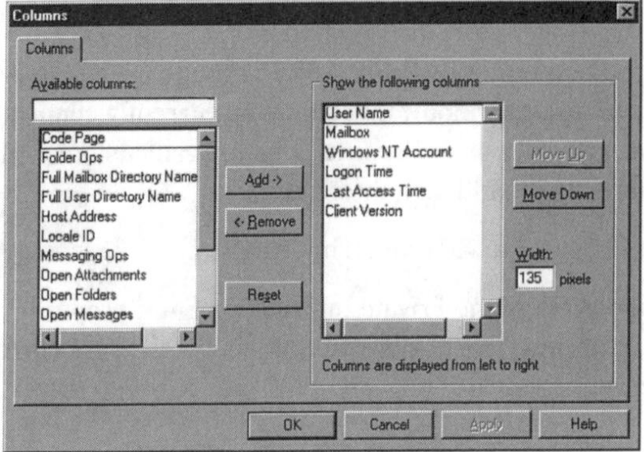

FIG. 15.10
Control the columns available for the Logons properties sheet.

The following are the default columns:

- *User Name.* The name (display name) for the user logged on to this mailbox.
- *Mailbox.* The Exchange Administrator program object's display name for this mailbox.
- *Windows NT Account.* The Windows NT account of the user currently logged on to this mailbox.
- *Logon Time.* The date and time the user logged on to Microsoft Exchange.
- *Last Access Time.* The last user to access the mailbox, as well as the time and date of the access.
- *Client Verison.* The version of the client that was used to log on to this mailbox or public folder.

Several optional columns are available. A few useful columns to note are:

- *Full Mailbox Directory Name.* The full e-mail address of the mailbox being accessed. This option is available only for the private information store.
- *Full User Directory Name.* The name of the mailbox that is accessing the private information store.
- *Host Address.* The Internet protocol (IP) address of the client.
- *Locale ID.* The locale ID for the language the client is using.
- *Messaging Ops.* The total number of messaging operations performed in the last 60 seconds, such as opening or closing a message.
- *Open Attachments.* The total number of open attachments.
- *Open Folders.* The total number of open folders.
- *Open Messages.* The total number of open messages.
- *Other Ops.* The total number of miscellaneous operations performed in the last 60 seconds.
- *Progress Ops.* The total number of progress operations performed in the last 60 seconds. Progress operations inform the user about how long it will take to complete a task.

- *Stream Ops.* The total number of stream operations performed in the last 60 seconds, such as viewing or changing an attachment.
- *Table Ops.* The total number of table operations performed in the last 60 seconds, such as viewing the contents of a folder.
- *Total Ops.* The total number of operations performed in the last 60 seconds.
- *Transfer Ops.* The total number of transfer operations performed in the last 60 seconds, such as copying or moving a message.

To save valuable time, you can quickly view logon information from the main Exchange hierarchy. Figure 15.11 shows the path you take in the left pane of the Exchange Administrator program to get to the Logons item.

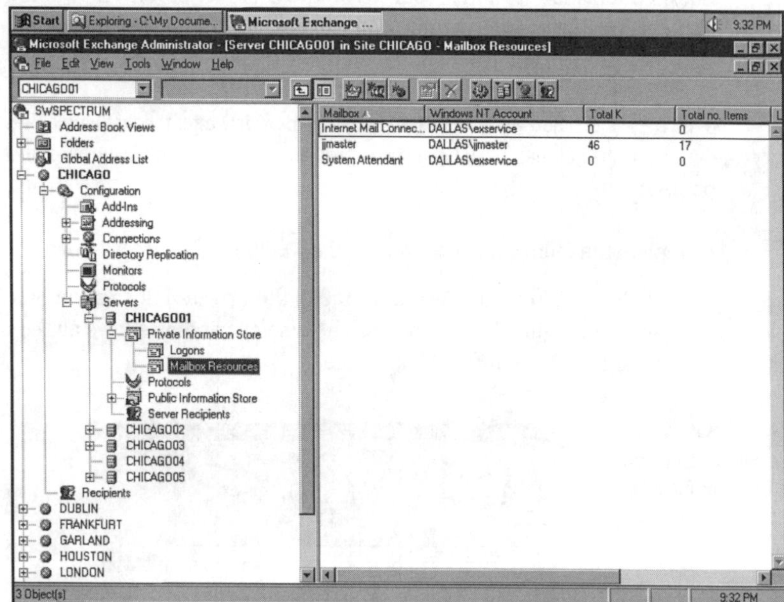

FIG. 15.11 Logon information is available in the left pane.

To access the logon information using this option, complete the following steps:

1. Navigate to your desired site with the Exchange Administrator program, and then expand the site container.
2. Click the small plus sign adjacent to the Configuration container of the selected site to further expand the hierarchy in the left pane.
3. Expand the Servers container in the left pane, and a list of Exchange servers in your site appears.
4. Click and expand the server name on which the private information store you want to configure is located.

5. The displayed server objects now visible in the left pane of the Microsoft Exchange Administrator Program are identical in name and function to similar objects displayed in the right pane. Selecting properties of either the private information store or public information store displays the same data.
6. Expand the Private Information Store object in the left pane and click the Logons object to see the Logons information in the right pane. You can add to the default columns shown in the right pane by using the View menu and the Columns command.

The Mailbox Resources Page

Using this page, you can view the physical resources (such as the hard disk storage space) used by the Exchange mailboxes on the server. It consists of one main display window that shows the mailboxes and resources on the current server. The windows are broken down into various columns of information. You can customize the specific columns both by the information they present and their widths on the screen.

NOTE A mailbox will be displayed in this window only after the first time a user logs on to it. If the mailbox has never been used, it will not appear on the Mailbox Resources properties sheet page.

Complete the following steps to view the Mailbox Resources information:

1. Select the Mailbox Resources tab of the Private Information Store properties sheet. The page in Figure 15.12 appears. The display window shows all the mailboxes on this server that have been used at least once.

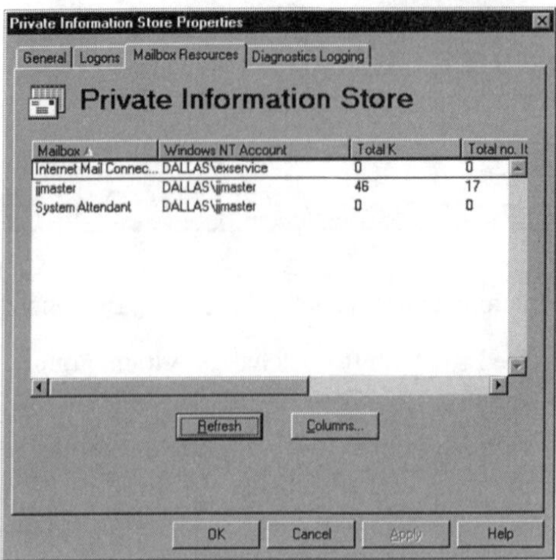

FIG. 15.12 View server resource use on a per-mailbox basis.

NOTE The Microsoft Exchange System Attendant is always listed in this window because the System Attendant is always logged in when the Exchanger Server is running.

2. Click the Refresh button to update the display window with the latest information.
3. Click the Columns button to edit which columns are displayed and their widths in pixels (see Figure 15.13). See the list following these steps for a description of the column headings and what type of information each one can display.

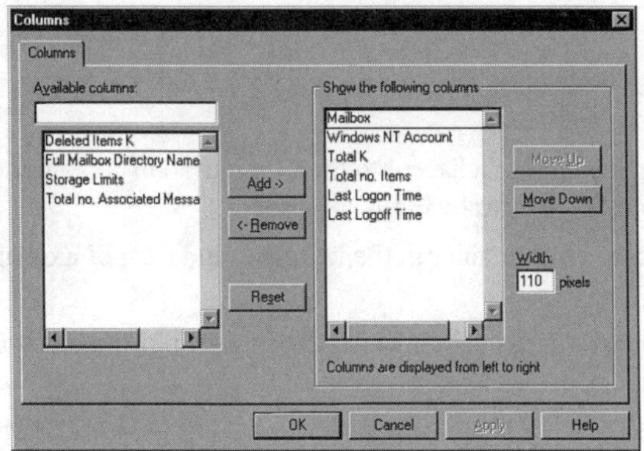

FIG. 15.13 Display columns available for the Mailbox Resources page.

4. Click Apply to set these properties and continue changing properties. If you are satisfied with all settings, click OK to return to the Administrator program.

These are the default columns:

- *Mailbox.* The Exchange Administrator program object's display name for this mailbox.
- *Windows NT Account.* The Windows NT account of the user currently logged on to this mailbox.
- *Total K.* The total amount of disk storage space (in kilobytes) taken up by the contents of this user's mailbox. This value includes message attachments.
- *Total Number of Items.* The sum of all messages and attachments stored in a mailbox.
- *Last Logon Time.* The last time a user logged on to this mailbox.
- *Last Logoff Time.* The last time a user logged off from this mailbox.

This page displays the full e-mail address for the mailbox and the total number of associated messages in this mailbox. The following are optional columns:

- *Deleted Items K.* The total amount of disk space in kilobytes occupied by retained, deleted items for this mailbox.
- *Full Mailbox Directory Name.* The entire X.400 e-mail address for this mailbox.
- *Storage Limits.* Any storage limits imposed on the mailbox (Prohibit Send, for example).
- *Total number of Associated Messages.* The sum of stored views and deferred action messages (messages scheduled to be sent/processed at a later time) in this mailbox.

As with the Logons status screen (discussed earlier), Exchange 5.0 offers the capability to quickly view Mailbox Resources information from the main Exchange hierarchy shown in the left pane. Refer to Figure 15.11 to see the path you take in the left pane of the Exchange Administrator program to get to the Mailbox Resources item.

To access the Mailbox Resources information using this new option, complete the following steps:

1. Navigate to your desired site with the Exchange Administrator program, and then expand the site container.
2. Click the small plus sign adjacent to the Configuration container of the selected site to further expand the hierarchy in the left pane.
3. Expand the Servers container in the left pane, and a list of Exchange servers in your site appears.
4. Click and expand the server on which the private information store you want to configure is located.
5. The displayed server objects now visible in the left pane of the Microsoft Exchange Administrator program window are identical in name and function to similar objects displayed in the right pane. Selecting the properties of either the private information store or public information store displays the same data.
6. Expand the Private Information Store in the left pane, and then click the Mailbox Resources object to display the Mailbox Resources information in the right pane. You can add to the default columns shown in the right pane by using the View menu and the Columns command.

The Diagnostic Logging Page

The properties on this page work in conjunction with the Windows NT Event Log to record various events that occur within the information store. This page is identical to the one found on the Public Information Store properties sheet. Figure 15.14 shows the Diagnostic Logging page of the Private Information Store sheet.

Various levels of logging determine what constitutes an event and, therefore, what types of information are actually recorded. For troubleshooting purposes, you want a very detailed record of occurrences within the information store, so you set a high logging level. However, normally you should log only events that are critical, so you set a lower logging level for everyday operation.

Public Information Store/Public Folder Replication

The Public Information Store properties sheet pages are much more extensive than those of the Private Information Store because of public folder replication. To reiterate this concept, duplicates of public folders can be created to reside on Exchange servers in remote sites. This makes it possible for users based on the remote site to connect to the local copy of the public folder instead of crossing site boundaries to access the information, which reduces network traffic between site boundaries. Replication can also be used to duplicate folders on other servers in the same local Exchange site to offer redundancy and to maintain load distribution across servers.

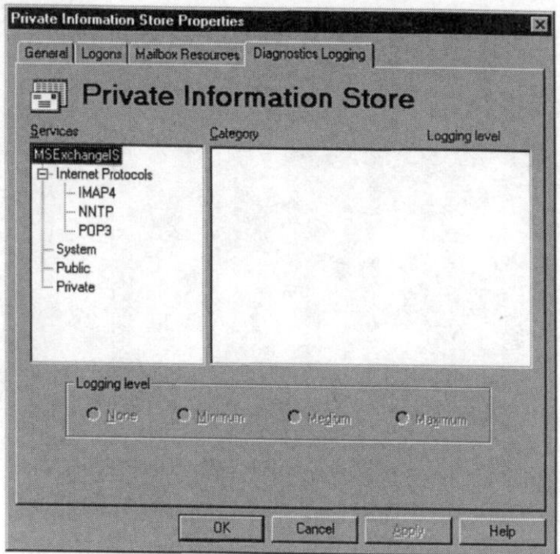

FIG. 15.14
Various events can be logged to the Windows NT Event Log.

The following are the Public Information Store properties sheet pages available on each Microsoft Exchange server:

- *General.* Impose a global storage limit warning for all folders in this public information store and set deleted item recover options.
- *Instances.* Select which public folders to replicate to the local server from remote sites.
- *Replication Schedule.* Set the times when public folders on the local server are replicated to the established remote instances.
- *Age Limits.* Set the lifetime of public folders or their contents.
- *E-Mail Addresses.* Define and modify various e-mail addresses for the public information store directory object.
- *Logons.* View data about users currently connected to a public folder.
- *Public Folder Resources.* View data about quantity of server resources consumed by a particular public folder.
- *Server Replication Status.* Monitor each server's participation in public folder replication.
- *Folder Replication Status.* Monitor the replication of individual public folders.
- *Advanced.* Define the replication cycle of public folders and define the maximum size of each individual replication message.
- *Diagnostics Logging.* Activate various levels of logging for troubleshooting purposes.

The General Page

This page has only one option: to set a global issue warning for all public folders on the local Exchange server (see Figure 15.15).

FIG. 15.15 Set the global (for all public folders on this server) public folder size warning and deleted item recovery options.

Complete the following steps to set the General properties:

1. Select the General tab of the Public Information Store properties sheet. The following page shown in Figure 15.15 appears.
2. Set the Deleted Item Retention Time (Days) for a period of time you would like to save deleted items. This is a new feature in Exchange 5.5. It enables you to control the amount of time deleted mail is saved so that users can easily recover deleted mail if necessary using the Outlook client (version 8.03 and later). To save users' deleted items until the private information store is backed up, select the check box next to Don't Permanently Delete Items Until the Store Has Been Backed Up.

NOTE With Exchange 5.5, you can easily recover deleted items from within the Outlook client (version 8.03 and later). However, if you configure your server not to save deleted items for a period of time, the user will not be able to recover any items. This option is set to zero days by default; it must be configured in order for deleted mail to be saved.

3. Click the Issue Warning (K) check box and enter a folder data size (in kilobytes) at which a folder contact will be notified. By default, this option is not checked. You can also set warnings at the individual folder level on the public folder's Advanced page, and that setting overrides this global setting for the server.
4. Click Apply to set these properties and continue changing properties. If you are satisfied with all settings, click OK to return to the Administrator program.

The Instances Page

Use this page to mark public folders from other servers for duplication to the local server. Such instances of public folders in the local site are actually created through the process of public folder replication (see Figure 15.16).

1. Select the Instances tab of the Public Information Store properties sheet. The page shown in Figure 15.16 appears.

   The Public Folders list on the left side lists all the folders in the currently selected remote site. The list on the right, Folders on this Information Store, lists both public folders on this server and other folders already designated for replication to this server.

FIG. 15.16
Create public folder replicas on the local server. These public folders will be replicated from remote servers selected from this page.

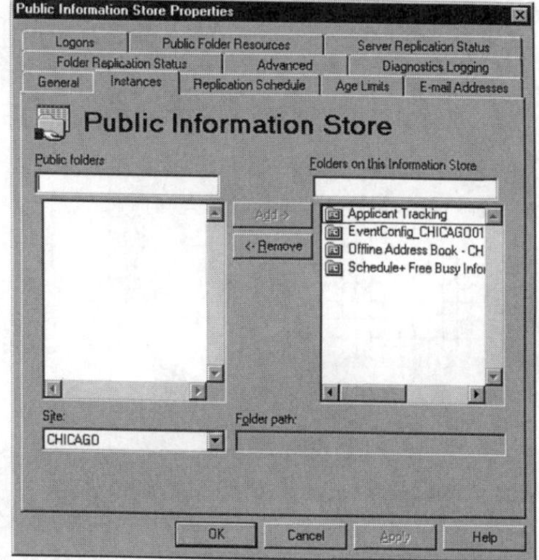

2. Use the Site pull-down menu in the lower-left corner to select a site in your organization. The public folders residing on that site appear in the list on the left.
3. Select a folder from the Public Folders list and click Add to mark that folder for replication to the local Exchange server.
4. To remove a public folder's instance from the local server, select it from the list on the right, and then click Remove.

NOTE You cannot remove a local public folder from the local Exchange server if it is the only copy of the folder in the local site. ■

5. Click Apply to set these properties and continue changing properties. If you are satisfied with all settings, click OK to return to the Administrator program.

The Replication Schedule Page

From this page, you can set times when public folder replication messages are actually transferred. Take into consideration the potentially high volume of data that may need to be transferred from a large and heavily used public folder.

Complete the following steps to set the Replication Schedule properties:

1. Select the Replication Schedule tab of the Public Information Store properties sheet. The dialog box in Figure 15.17 appears.

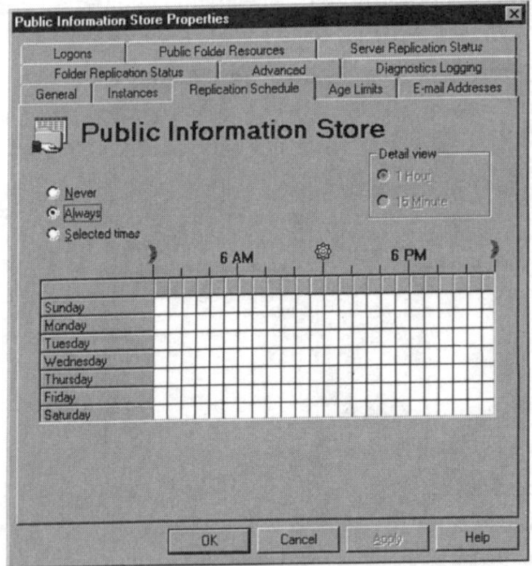

FIG. 15.17 Set public folder replication times for this server.

2. Select one of the three option buttons that determine when this server initiates public folder replication:

   Never. This effectively disables public folder replication for this server.

   Always. Folder replication messages are sent every fifteen minutes. The time delay can be changed on the Advanced page of this public information store's properties sheet. By default, Always is selected.

   Selected Times. Replication messages are transferred based upon the time grid on this page.

3. If you choose Selected times, the Detail view option buttons become available. Select either the 1 Hour or 15 Minute detail view, and the time grid scale changes accordingly.
4. Also if you choose Selected times, pick the time blocks for connection.
5. Click Apply to set these properties and continue changing properties. If you are satisfied with all settings, click OK to return to the Administrator program.

NOTE Keep in mind that replication is not the same as simple duplication or copying. Replication includes the concept of synchronization, which loosely translated means that only the changes are sent to other replica "instances" around the enterprise. Sending only the changes (as opposed to sending an entire copy of the folder) not only saves time and bandwidth, it allows changes from any instance to be added to all other instances.

The Age Limits Page

Using the Age Limits page, you can define when information in a public folder should expire and be automatically deleted. This feature prevents public folders from becoming bogged down with megabytes upon megabytes of outdated, useless information.

First, you set up a CLASSIFIEDS folder, and then you set the age limit for posting in the folder to seven days. Based on that setting, after a message sits in a folder for seven days, it expires and is automatically deleted by the information store.

Complete the following to set age limits:

1. Select the Age Limits tab of the Public Information Store properties sheet. The page shown in Figure 15.18 appears.

   The main display window shows columns of information about all the public folders on this server (including replicas). You'll learn more about the kinds of information displayed in these columns later in this chapter.

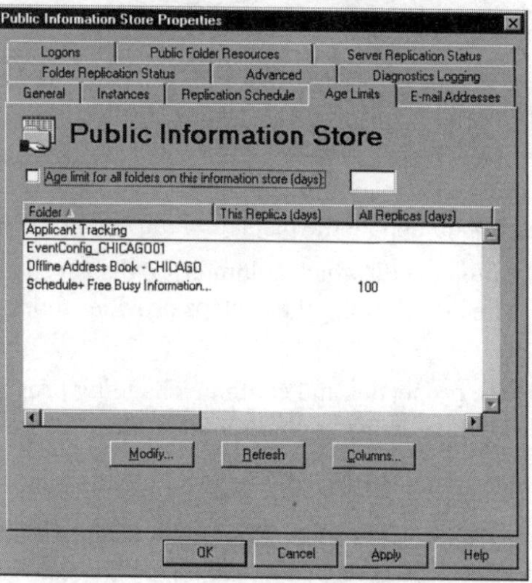

FIG. 15.18 Set the amount of time a message can exist in a public folder before it is deleted.

2. To set an overall age limit, in days, for all folders on this information store, select the Age Limit for All Folders... check box and enter a number in the text box to indicate the number of days in which messages in this server's public folders will expire.

NOTE You can override this setting for an individual public folder by changing the setting on the Advanced page of that folder's properties sheet.

3. Select a public folder from the list and click Modify to set individual age limits for this folder. The dialog box in Figure 15.19 appears.

   Click the This Replica (Days) check box to set an age limit for a public folder's instance on this server only. Click the All Replicas (Days) check box to set an age limit set for all instances of a public folder throughout your organization. Click the Remove button to delete the selected public folder *instance* from the information store. Click OK to set your choices.

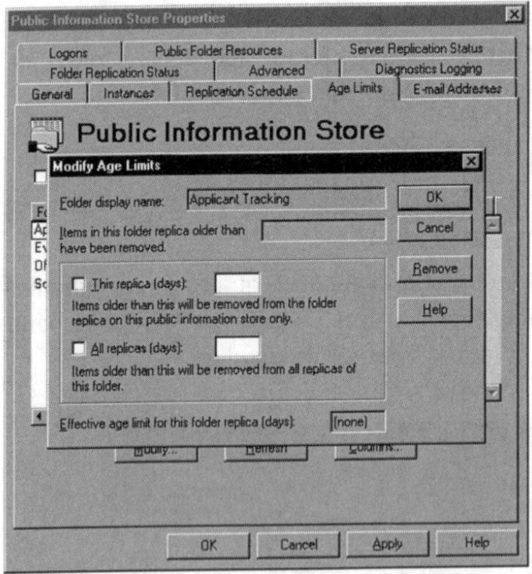

FIG. 15.19 Set age limits on an individual folder basis.

4. Click the Refresh button to update the display window with the latest information.
5. Click the Columns button to edit which columns are displayed and their widths in pixels (see Figure 15.20). The list following these steps provides more details on the available columns.
6. Click Apply to set these properties and continue changing properties. If you are satisfied with all settings, click OK to return to the Administrator program.

By default, all available columns are displayed. They include the following:

- *Folder.* The Exchange Administrator object's display name for the folder.
- *This Replica (Days).* Age limit set for a public folder's instance on this server only.
- *All Replicas (Days).* Age limit set for all instances of a public folder throughout your organization.
- *Removed Older Than.* Notification that messages older than the number of days displayed have been deleted.
- *Total K.* The sum of all messages in a public folder.

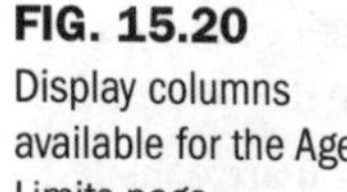

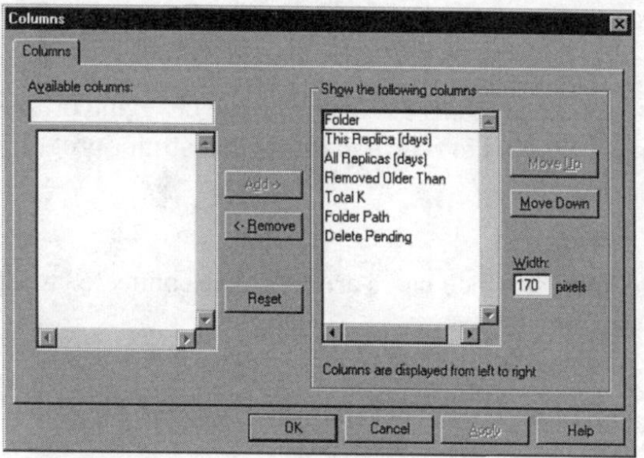

FIG. 15.20
Display columns available for the Age Limits page.

- *Folder Path.* The location of the public folder in the organization hierarchy (relative to this server or full X.400 address to another server).
- *Delete Pending.* Normally "false," this column shows "true" when a folder or messages with that folder are scheduled to be deleted.

The E-Mail Addresses Page

E-mail addresses are used by the various Exchange gateways and connectors to identify specific directory objects to other messaging systems. Four default addresses are created, one each for cc:Mail, Microsoft Mail, SMTP, and X.400.

Complete the following steps to set public folder e-mail addresses:

1. Click the E-Mail Addresses tab of the Public Information Store properties sheet. The dialog box in Figure 15.21 appears, showing the four default addresses (cc:Mail, Microsoft Mail, SMTP, and X.400).

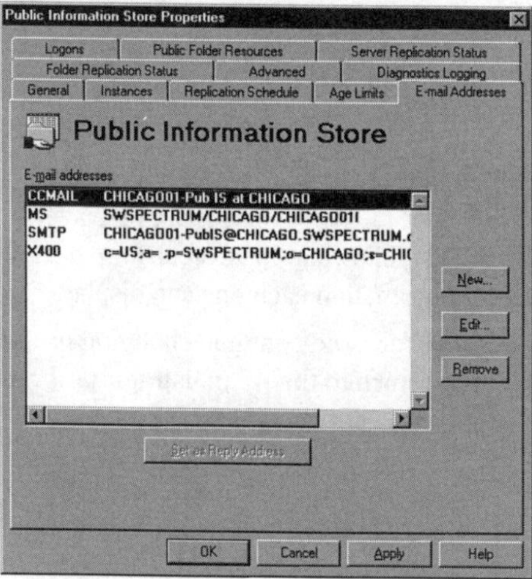

FIG. 15.21
Define e-mail addresses for this directory object.

2. Click New to add a specific e-mail address for this information store. Or, select an existing address, and then click Edit to modify it or click Remove to delete it.
3. Click Apply to set these properties and continue changing properties. If you are satisfied with all settings, click OK to return to the Administrator program.

The Logons Page

You use this page to monitor which users are currently connected to a public folder. To do so, complete the following steps:

1. Select the Logons tab of the Public Information Store properties sheet. The page shown in Figure 15.22 appears.

FIG. 15.22
View users currently connected to public folders on this server. The main display window shows columns of information about connected users.

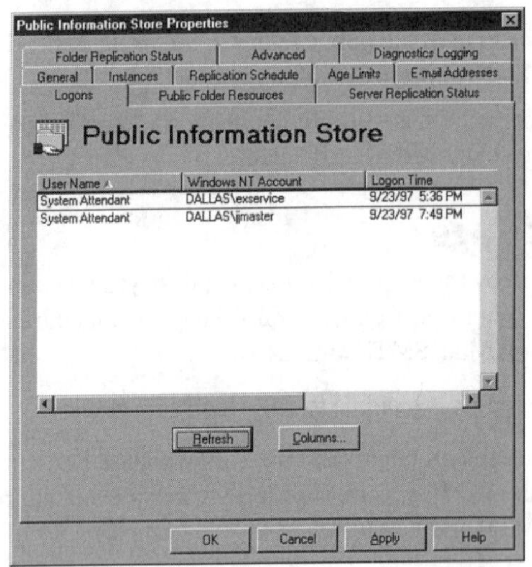

NOTE The Microsoft Exchange System Attendant is always listed in this window because the System Attendant is always logged in when the Exchanger Server is running.

2. Click the Refresh button to update the display window with the latest information.
3. Click the Columns button to edit which columns are displayed and their widths in pixels (see Figure 15.23). See the list following these steps for a description of the column headings and what type of information each one can display.
4. Click Apply to set these properties and continue changing properties. If you are satisfied with all settings, click OK to return to the Administrator program.

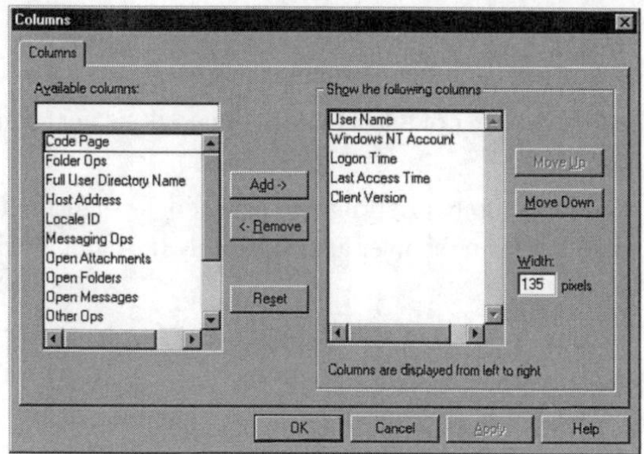

FIG. 15.23
Display columns available for the Logons page.

NOTE Exchange 5.5 includes 10 additional measurements that can be used in the analysis of public folder use. ■

The following are the default columns:

- *User Name.* The name (display name) for the user logged on to this public folder.
- *Windows NT Account.* The Windows NT account of the user currently logged on to this public folder.
- *Logon Time.* The date and time the user logged on to Microsoft Exchange.
- *Last Access Time.* The date the user last logged on and accessed the public information store.
- *Client Version.* The version number of Exchange Client used to access the server. (Of course, this does not apply to users accessing folder information via the Internet and IIS with a browser.)

Several optional columns are available. A few useful columns of note are:

- *Code Page.* The code page that the client is using.
- *Folder Ops.* The total number of folder operations (such as opening or closing a folder) performed in the last 60 seconds.
- *Full User Directory Name.* The name of the mailbox that is accessing the information store.
- *Host Address.* The Internet protocol (IP) address of the client.
- *Locale ID.* The locale ID for the language the client is using.
- *Messaging Ops.* The total number of messaging operations (such as opening or closing a message) performed in the last 60 seconds.
- *Open Attachments.* The total number of open attachments.

- *Open Folders.* The total number of open folders.
- *Open Messages.* The total number of open messages.
- *Other Ops.* The total number of miscellaneous operations performed in the last 60 seconds.
- *Progress Ops.* The total number of progress operations performed in the last 60 seconds. Progress operations inform the user approximately how long it will take to complete a task.
- *Stream Ops.* The total number of stream operations (such as viewing or changing an attachment) performed in the last 60 seconds.
- *Table Ops.* The total number of table operations (such as viewing the contents of a folder) performed in the last 60 seconds.
- *Total Ops.* The total number of operations performed in the last 60 seconds.
- *Transfer Ops.* The total number of transfer operations (such as copying or moving a message) performed in the last 60 seconds. You can quickly view logon information from the main Exchange hierarchy displayed in the left pane of the Exchange Administrator program window by following the path shown in Figure 15.24.

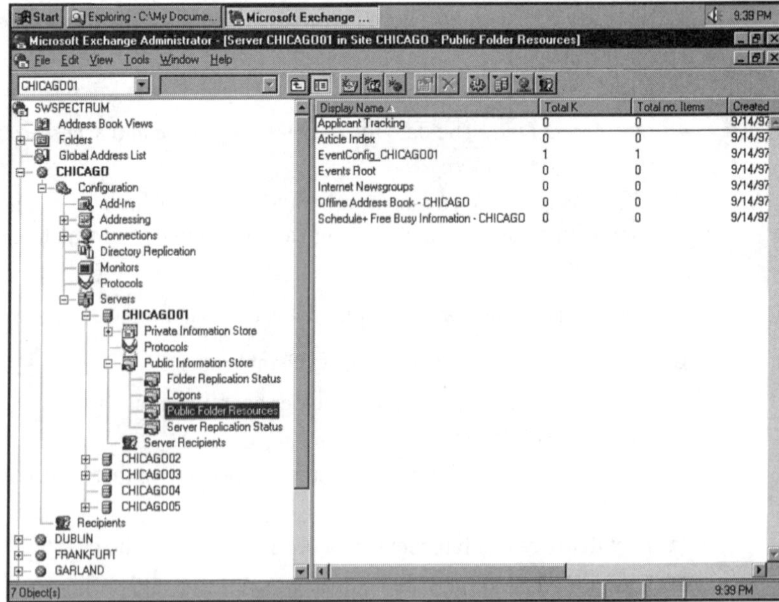

FIG. 15.24
A valuable time-saving way of viewing logon information.

To access the logon information using this timesaving method, perform the following steps:

1. Navigate to your desired site with the Exchange Administrator program, and then expand the site container.
2. Click the small plus sign adjacent to the Configuration container of the selected site to further expand the hierarchy in the left pane of the window.

3. Expand the Servers container in the left pane, and a list of Exchange servers in your site appears.
4. Click and expand the server name where the private information store you want to configure is located.
5. The displayed server objects now visible in the left pane of the Microsoft Exchange Administrator program window are identical in name and function to similar objects displayed in the right pane. Selecting properties of either the private information store or the public information store displays the same data.
6. Expand the Public Information Store item in the left pane, and then click the Logons object. The logon information appears in the right pane. You can add to the default columns shown in the right pane by using the View menu and the Columns command.

The Public Folder Resources Page

This page enables you to view the physical resources (such as hard disk storage space) used by the folders on this public information store. It consists of one main display window that shows the public folders on the current server. This window is subdivided into various columns of information. You can customize the specific columns displayed both by the information present and their widths on the screen.

Note that the Schedule+ Free Busy Information and the Offline Address Book are in essence public folders as well, and they are listed on this page of the properties sheet.

Complete the following steps to view Public Folder Resources information:

1. Select the Public Folder Resources tab of the Public Information Store properties sheet. The page shown in Figure 15.25 appears, listing all the public folders on this server.

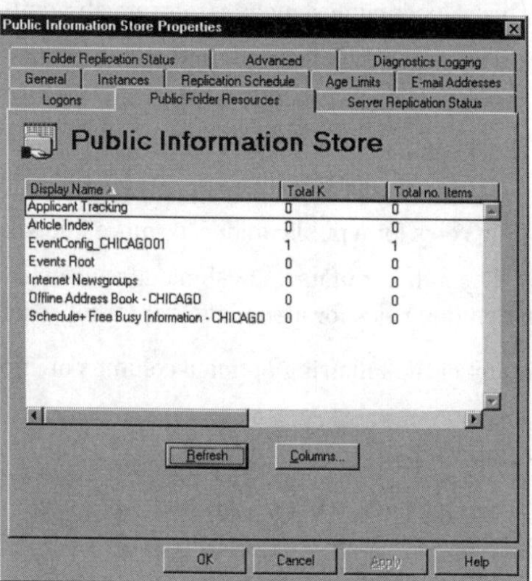

FIG. 15.25
View server resources used by each public folder on this server.

2. Click the Refresh button to update the display window with the latest information.
3. Click the Columns button to edit which columns are displayed and their widths in pixels (see Figure 15.26). See the list following these steps for a description of each column heading and what type of information that column can display.
4. Click Apply to set these properties and continue changing properties. If you are satisfied with all the settings, click OK to return to the Administrator program.

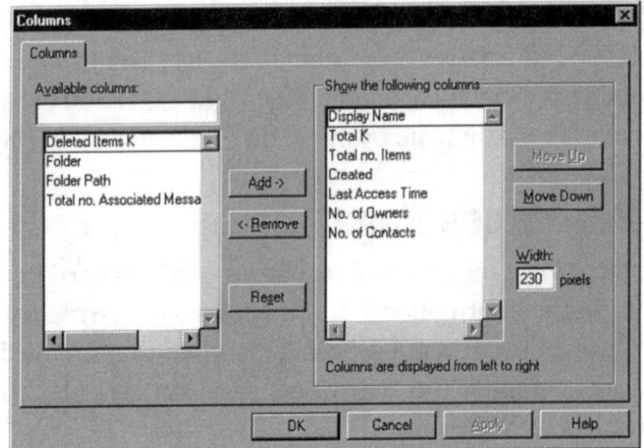

FIG. 15.26 Display columns available for the Public Folder Resources page.

You can also view/set the default columns of information that will be displayed for the public folder. These are the default columns:

- *Display Name.* The Exchange Administrator program object's display name for this public folder.
- *Total K.* The total amount of disk storage space (in kilobytes) taken up by the contents of this public folder. This value includes any message attachments.
- *Total number Items.* The sum of all messages and attachments stored in a mailbox.
- *Created.* The date and time this folder was created.
- *Last Access Time.* The last time a user logged on to this public folder.
- *Number of Owners.* The number of users designated as Owners of this public folder. (See the section on defining roles for a public folder for more information.)
- *Number of Contacts.* The number of users designated as contacts for this public folder. (See the section on defining roles for a public folder for more information.)

You can choose to display any of the following optional columns of information for the public folder:

- *Folder.* Folder name where messages are stored.
- *Folder Path.* The system file path to where this folder is stored.

- *Total Number Associated Messages.* The sum of folder views and deferred action messages.
- *Deleted Items K.* The total amount of disk space in kilobytes occupied by retained, deleted items for this public folder. You can quickly view Public Folder Resource information from the main Exchange hierarchy displayed in the left pane of the Exchange Administrator program window; the path to that information is the same as the one to the logon information (refer to Figure 15.24).

To access the Public Folder Resource information using this timesaving method, follow these steps:

1. Navigate to your desired site with the Exchange Administrator program, and then expand the site container.
2. Click the small plus sign adjacent to the Configuration container of the selected site to further expand the hierarchy in the left pane.
3. Expand the Servers container in the left pane, and a list of Exchange servers in your site appears.
4. Click and expand the server name on which the public information store you want to configure is located.
5. The displayed server objects now visible in the left pane of the Microsoft Exchange Administrator program window are identical in name and function to similar objects displayed in the right pane. Selecting properties of either the private information store or the public information store displays the same data.
6. Expand the Public Information Store in the left pane, and then click the Public Folder Resources object. The Public Folder Resources information appears in the right pane. You can add to the default columns shown in the right pane by using the View menu and the Columns command.

The Server Replication Status Page

From this page, you can monitor the status of a public folder's replication to the current public information store on the server level. Exchange servers are individually configured for transmitting updated public folder information to other replicas in remote sites. This page is primarily a single-display window with various columns of information. You can modify the columns to be displayed by using the Columns button. The information in this page is used not only to verify that the selected remote public folders are indeed being replicated to this server, but to monitor details about message transmission time.

Complete the following steps to view the Server Replication Status:

1. Select the Server Replication Status tab of the Public Information Store properties sheet. The page shown in Figure 15.27 appears. The display window shows all remote servers that replicate public folder data to this server.

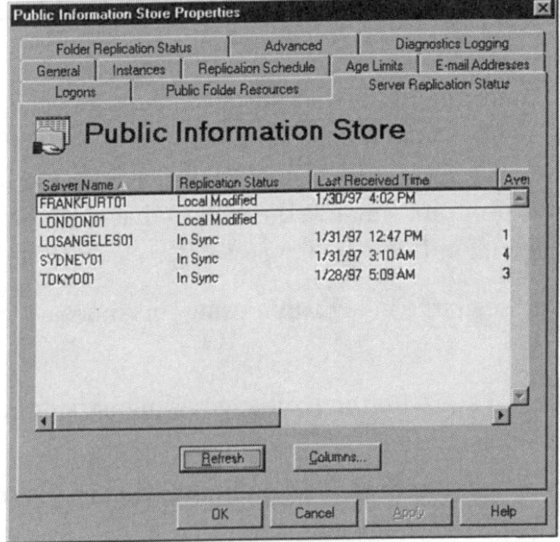

FIG. 15.27 View the status of remote servers that replicate public folders to the local server.

2. Click the Refresh button to update the display window with the latest information.
3. Click the Columns button to edit which columns are displayed and their widths in pixels (see Figure 15.28). See the list following these steps for a description of each column heading and the type of information it can display.

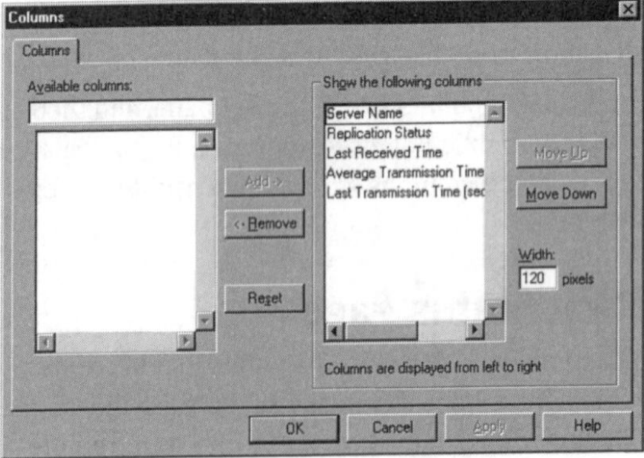

FIG. 15.28 Display columns available for the Server Replication Status property page.

4. Click Apply to set these properties and continue changing properties. If you are satisfied with all the settings, click OK to return to the Administrator program.

The following are the default columns:

- *Server Name.* Name of the Microsoft Exchange Server replicating public folder data to this server.
- *Replication Status.* Public folder replication status.
- *Last Received Time.* The last date and time this information store received an update from the remote Exchange server.

- *Average Transmission Time (Sec)*. The average length of time (in seconds) it has taken to transmit replication messages to this server.
- *Last Transmission Time (Sec)*. The length of time (in seconds) that it took to transmit the last replication message to this server.

There are no optional display columns on this page. By default, all the columns that can be displayed are displayed.

You can quickly view Server Replication Status without having to navigate too deeply into the various pages of the properties sheet. You can view Server Replication Status information from the main Exchange hierarchy displayed in the left pane of the Exchange Administrator program window; the path to that information is the same as the one to the logon information (refer to Figure 15.24).

To access the Server Replication Status information using the timesaving method, complete the following steps:

1. Navigate to your desired site with the Exchange Administrator program, and then expand the site container.
2. Click the small plus sign adjacent to the Configuration container of the selected site to further expand the hierarchy in the left pane.
3. Expand the Servers container in the left pane, and a list of Exchange servers in your site appears.
4. Click and expand the server name where the public information store you want to configure is located.
5. The displayed server objects now visible in the left pane of the Microsoft Exchange Administrator program window are identical in name and function to similar objects displayed in the right pane. Selecting properties of either the private information store or the public information store displays the same data.
6. Expand the Public Information Store in the left pane, and then click the Server Replication Status object. The status information appears in the right pane. You can add to the default columns shown in the right pane by using the View menu and the Columns command.

The Folder Replication Status Page

This page provides public information store monitoring capabilities on the individual folder level. This page contains just one main display window with information divided into columns.

Complete the following steps to view the Folder Replication Status:

1. Select the Folder Replication Status tab of the Public Information Store properties sheet. The page shown in Figure 15.29 appears. The display window shows all public folders involved in replication on this server's public information store.

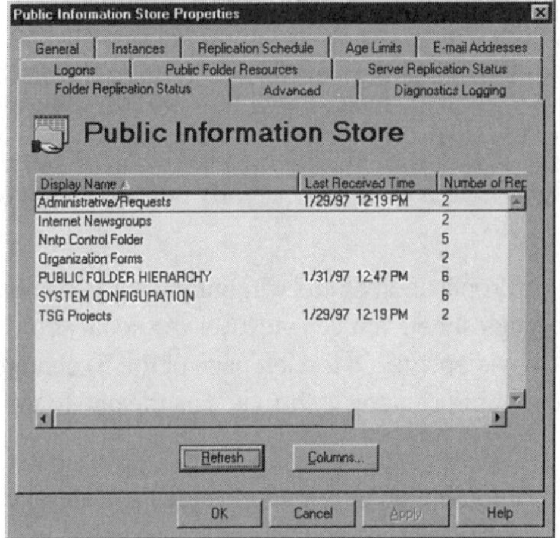

FIG. 15.29 View the status of individual folders replicated from the local server and to the local server from remote sites.

2. Click the Refresh button to update the display window with the latest information.
3. Click the Columns button to edit which columns are displayed and their widths in pixels (see Figure 15.30). See the list following these steps for a description of each column heading and the type of information it can display.
4. Click Apply to set these properties and continue changing properties. If you are satisfied with all settings, click OK to return to the Administrator program.

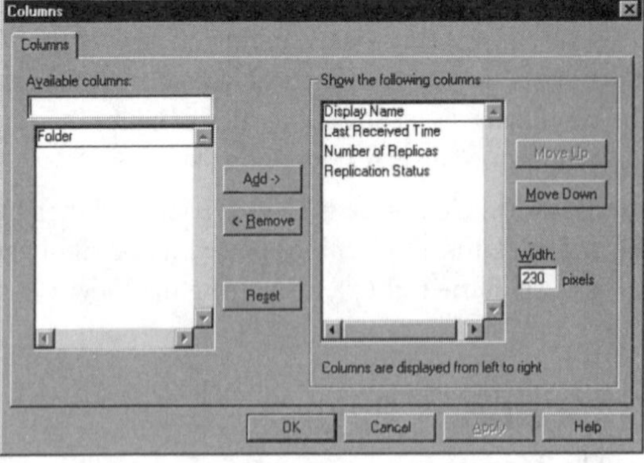

FIG. 15.30 Display columns available for the Folder Replication Status page.

The following are the default columns:

- *Display Name.* The Exchange Administrator display name for this directory object.
- *Last Received Time.* The last date and time this public folder received an updated replication message.
- *Number of Replicas.* The sum of all instances of this folder throughout the local site.
- *Replication Status.* Notification of public folder replication status.

The following is the only optional column:

- *Folder—The public folder name.*

You can quickly access the Folder Replication Status from the main Exchange hierarchy displayed in the left pane of the Exchange Administrator program window; the path to the Folder Replication Status object is the same as the one to the logon information (refer to Figure 15.24).

To access the Folder Replication Status information using the timesaving method, follow these steps:

1. Navigate to your desired site with the Exchange Administrator program, and then expand the site container.
2. Click the small plus sign adjacent to the Configuration container of the selected site to further expand the hierarchy in the left pane.
3. Expand the Servers container in the left pane, and a list of Exchange servers in your site appears.
4. Click and expand the server name on which the public information store you want to configure is located.
5. The displayed server objects now visible in the left pane of the Microsoft Exchange Administrator program window are identical in name and function to similar objects displayed in the right pane. Selecting properties of either the private information store or the public information store displays the same data.
6. Expand the Public Information Store in the left pane, and then click the Folder Replication Status object. The Folder Replication Status information appears in the right pane. You can add to the default columns shown in the right pane by using the View menu and the Columns command.

The Folder Replication Status information is a good place to start when troubleshooting public folder replication issues. The Replication Status column gives the current status of this folder. Below is a definition of each status:

- *In Sync.* Indicates that no changes have been made to the replica since the last changes were sent.
- *Local Modified.* Indicates that changes have been made to this replica that have not yet been replicated throughout the site.

The Advanced Page

Using the Advanced page, you can customize some specialized settings involving public folder replication. When a folder is replicated to a remote site, the actual replication data is broken up into messages addressed to the remote public information store. On this page, you can set the upper limit for the size of the replication messages in order to better control messaging traffic. Complete the following steps:

1. Select the Advanced tab of the Public Information Store properties sheet. The page shown in Figure 15.31 appears.

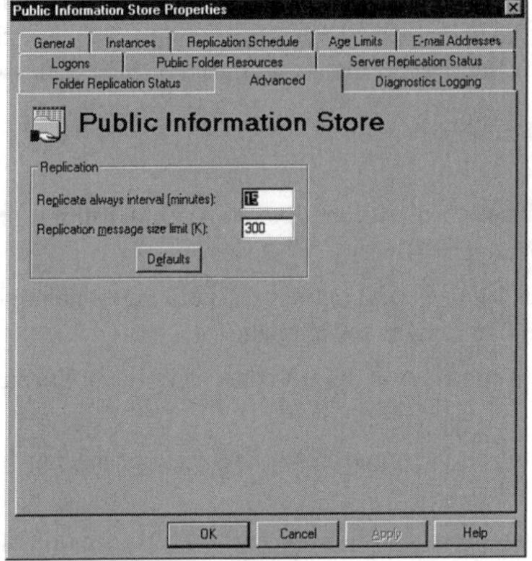

FIG. 15.31
The Advanced page of the Public Information Store properties sheet.

2. In the Replicate Always Interval (Minutes) box, enter the interval (in minutes) between outgoing replication messages, which applies when the Always option button is selected in the Replication Schedule dialog box. By default, this interval is 15 minutes.
3. In the Replication Message Size Limit (K) box, enter the maximum message size (in kilobytes) of an outgoing replication message. By default, this maximum is set at 100K. Messages are grouped together or subdivided to fit that size.
4. To reset the values of the two boxes to their default settings, click the Default button. When you're satisfied with the settings, click OK.

The Diagnostics Logging Page

This page works in conjunction with the Windows NT Event Log to record various "events" that occur within the information store. This page is identical to Advanced page of the Private Information Store properties sheet. Various levels of logging determine what constitutes an event and, therefore, what types of information are actually recorded. For troubleshooting purposes, you would want a very detailed record of occurrences within the Information Store so you would set a high logging level. However, you normally want to log only events that are critical, so you set a lower logging level for everyday operation. ●

CHAPTER 16

Creating and Configuring Recipients

In this chapter

A recipient is any directory object that is designed to receive information. This chapter explains the administrative process of creating and modifying these objects. Microsoft Exchange provides several tools to assist administrators in creating user mailboxes. The Microsoft Exchange Migration tool and the Import command in the Administrator program enable you to import directory lists in bulk from external systems, such as Novell NetWare or Lotus cc: Mail.

You manage recipients from the Administrator program. This program displays recipient objects when the users clicks their containers within the exchange hierarchy. Microsoft Exchange Server utilizes the following four types of recipients:

- *Mailbox*—A mailbox is a container for messaging data. Generally, a mailbox has only one user. However, a group of users can sometimes share a mailbox.
- *Custom Recipient*—A custom recipient defines a mail location outside of the Microsoft Exchange Server environment. Most often users on the Internet, or on other foreign messaging systems, are custom recipients.
- *Distribution List*—A distribution list is a group of recipients. A message sent to a distribution list is forwarded to all the users who are members of that list.
- *Public Folder*—A public folder is a container for information shared among Microsoft Exchange users.

Each recipient has multiple property sheets that hold its settings. This section demonstrates how to create and configure each of the four recipient types that the Microsoft Exchange Server defines.

NOTE Whenever you create a new recipient of any sort, you must first select the recipient container in which you want to store the new object. If you select none, the system notifies you that you cannot create recipients in the parent container. ■

For example, select New Mailbox from the Exchange Administrator file in the Garland site. You have not selected either the main recipients container or any other custom container; therefore, the dialog box in Figure 16.1 appears.

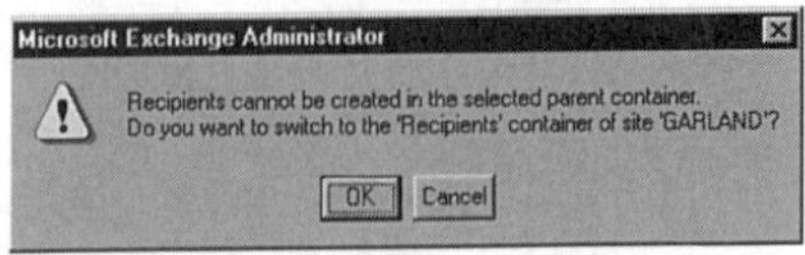

FIG. 16.1
The notice displays when you have not preselected the proper container for the object.

Creating Mailboxes

The most common type of recipient is the mailbox. As mentioned previously, each mailbox generally has one user assigned to it. Several users, however, might share one mailbox. The term *mailbox* refers specifically to a Microsoft Exchange recipient on a Windows NT Server.

You can create a new mailbox using one of the following two methods:

1. Use the Windows NT User Manager to create an NT user account along with a mailbox.
2. Use the Microsoft Exchange Administrator program to create a mailbox for either a new or existing Windows NT account.

Creating a Mailbox with User Manager

The Microsoft Exchange Server installation includes what is referred to as the Microsoft Exchange User Manager Extension (see Figure 16.2). The extension adds the menu *Exchange* to your Windows NT User Manager. The menu enables you to use the Windows NT User Manager to set up a new Windows NT account in conjunction with an Exchange mailbox.

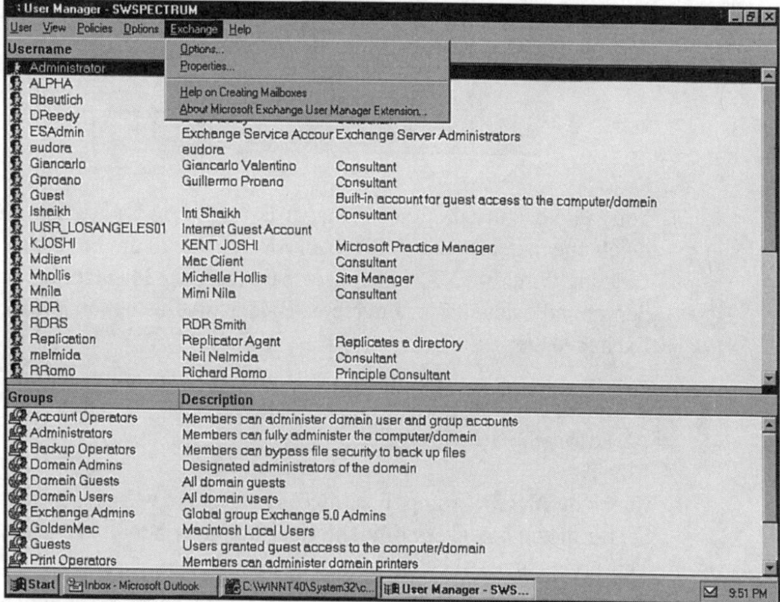

FIG. 16.2 The User Manager Extension enables you to add and delete Exchange mailboxes along with accounts in the Windows NT User Manager.

The Exchange menu enables you to view a user's mailbox properties without having to launch the Exchange Administration program. More importantly, the Exchange menu integrates the creation of new Windows NT domain users with the creation of new Exchange mailboxes. You can use the following options to configure the Exchange User Manager Extension:

1. Choose Options under the Exchange menu. The dialog box in Figure 16.3 appears.
2. You can configure the User Manager Extension to always create an Exchange mailbox when you create a new user account. The option Always Create an Exchange Mailbox when Creating Windows NT Accounts sets up the User Manager to contact your Exchange Server. The selection also makes a user mailbox every time you create a new

Windows NT user. If you check this box, immediately after you create a new user the standard Exchange mailbox property sheets appear for configuration. By default, this option is checked when you install Exchange Server.

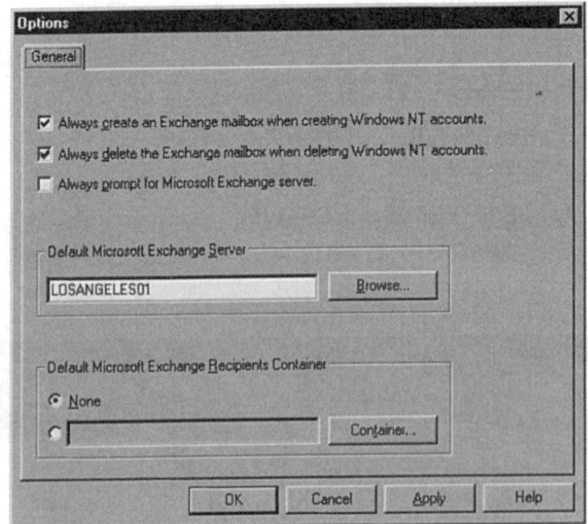

FIG. 16.3 You can select from the Options dialog box to configure the User Manager Extension.

3. You can configure the User Manager Extension to always delete the mailbox when you delete the user account. The option Always Delete the Exchange Mailbox When Deleting Windows NT Accounts sets up the User Manager to contact your Exchange Server and delete a user's mailbox. By default, this option is checked when you install Exchange Server.

NOTE For the preceding option to function properly, you must be certain that the Microsoft Exchange Server is running properly. ■

4. Checking Always Prompt For Microsoft Exchange Server brings up the Exchange Server dialog box every time the User Manager attempts a connection to Exchange. This option is not checked by default.
5. The Default Microsoft Exchange Server box displays the Exchange Server in which the User Manager Extension creates new user boxes. You can type in a new name. Alternatively, you can click Browse to select a different server.
6. Click Container to select a custom recipient container. By default, None is selected. This means that all new mailboxes become part of the general recipient's container.
7. Click Apply to set these properties and continue with other properties. If you finish all settings, click OK to return to the User Manager.

Creating Mailboxes in the Exchange Administrator

You often want to create or administer several types of recipients. Another way to do this is to create a new user mailbox from within the Exchange Administrator program.

To create a new mailbox from within the Microsoft Exchange Administrator, choose the item New Mailbox from the File menu. When the property pages for a new mailbox appear, you can proceed to the next step.

Configuring Mailbox Property Pages

No matter how you create the account, the property sheets associated with that mailbox are the same. The following is a list of property pages that are covered in the discussion of mailboxes:

- *General Information*—You use the property page to record basic mailbox information, such as name and location.
- *Organizational Information*—You use the page for optional information about, for example, a company's organization. This might include a manager or people who report to the mailbox owner.
- *Phone/Notes*—You can use the page to enter detailed telephone information and perhaps a long note about the user.
- *Distribution Lists*—The category specifies the distribution lists to which the recipient belongs.
- *Email Addresses*—This page enables you to create, modify, and delete alternate addresses for this mailbox.
- *Delivery Restrictions*—The category defines from which addresses this mailbox does or does not accept messages.
- *Delivery Options*—From here, you can give Send on Behalf permission and specify alternate recipients for messages sent to this mailbox.
- *Custom Attributes*—The category enables you to add up to ten administrator-defined fields that you may use to keep additional information about the mailbox.

NOTE You define the field names on the DS Site Configuration custom attributes page. ■

- *Advanced*—The page, changed in Exchange 5.5, contains settings relating to advanced administrator functions (trust levels, text formatting, and hidden/not hidden status). New functions enhance environments that are used NetMeeting.
- *Limits*—Limits is a new page in Exchange 5.5 that has the settings that control message size and storage size along with new functionality for deleted items.
- *Protocols*—The category specifies the available protocols to which the recipient belongs.

The General Page

The primary purpose of the General property page is to hold user information for a mailbox. In these fields, you give the mailbox the name by which it is known to the Exchange Directory and to all other users.

Display Name and Alias Name The key elements of a mailbox name are the Display Name and the Alias Name. Display Name is the name that appears in the Administrator window and in the Address Book. Alias Name is the string used to generate other addresses for this mailbox, such as the Internet address.

For example, a suitable Microsoft Exchange Display Name can be Inti Shaikh with the Alias Name ISHAIKH. The Administrator program and Address Book show the display name Inti Shaikh. The SMTP address for this account, however, is formulated as aliasname@domain or ISHAIKH@SWSPECTRUM.COM.

NOTE A mailbox is often referred to by its user name, which is the same as its Display Name.

The following explains how to set general properties for the mailbox:

1. Choose Recipients in the Exchange Server Administrator window. The list of mailboxes appears on the right side of the window. Open the mailbox you want to configure.

NOTE If you just created a new mailbox, you can omit the preceding step. The reason is that the property pages appear immediately after you create a new mailbox.

2. Select the General tab. The dialog box in Figure 16.4 appears.

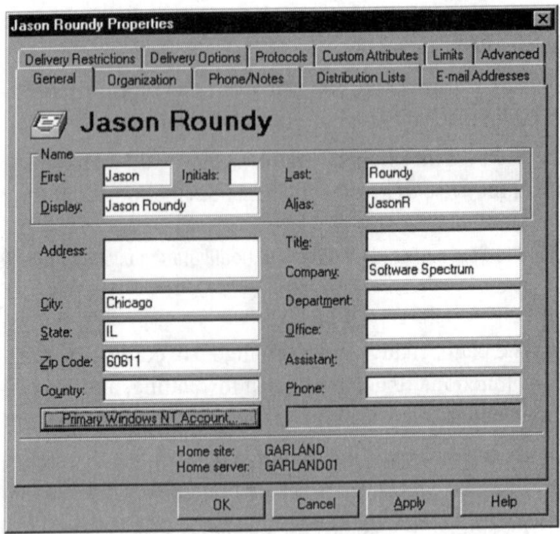

FIG. 16.4 The General page option enables you to select the mailbox you want to configure.

3. Enter the user's first name in the appropriate box.
4. Enter the user's middle initial in the Initials box.
5. Enter the user's last name in the appropriate box.

6. Type an alias that you use to generate other email addresses for this recipient.
7. Enter postal information in the available Address boxes.
8. Enter appropriate company and location (Department, Office) information for this user.
9. The Primary Windows NT Account sets the corresponding system account for this mailbox. The following section contains a more advanced description of this button.
10. Click Apply to set the properties and continue with other properties. If you finish with all settings, click OK to return to the Administrator program.

NOTE You can give a generic name to a mailbox that more than one person uses. You might name a mailbox that multiple people monitor for purposes of technical support Tech Support.

Microsoft Exchange Server can automatically generate a Display Name and Alias Name when you type the user's first and last names.

NOTE Display and Alias are the only two required fields related to the general property page.

Primary Windows NT Account Every Microsoft Exchange mailbox must have an associated Windows NT account, which is referred to as the primary Windows NT account. Logging into Windows NT gives you full access to Microsoft Exchange mailboxes for that user name/ID. If you create an Exchange mailbox in the Windows NT User Manager, the primary Windows NT account name is that new account.

The following shows how to set a primary Windows NT account from the Exchange Administrator program:

1. Select the General tab in the new mailbox property sheet.
2. Click the Primary Windows NT Account button.
3. Use Select an Existing Windows NT Account to browse through the Add Users and Groups dialog box. Select one. Then click OK.

   Alternatively, you can use Create a New Windows NT Account to bring up the Create Windows NT Account dialog box (see Figure 16.5).

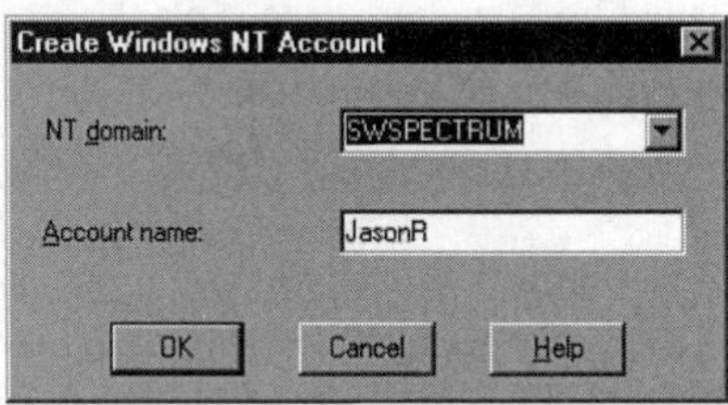

FIG. 16.5
Create a Windows NT user account for an Exchange mailbox without using the User Manager.

4. Pick the NT domain in which you want to create this account. Type a name in the Account Name box.
5. Click OK. The password for this newly created Windows NT account is the same as the mailbox's Display Name.

The Organization Page

The Organization property page records data pertinent to how your company functions. The information found in this place are names of individuals who report to this mailbox owner and the mailbox owner's manager. These individuals are all identified by their Exchange mailboxes. All the information is optional. The given space helps you to organize the information, however. The space also provides for a specific definition of your organization with Exchange.

To set the organization information, first specify the Manager of the mailbox owner:

1. Select the Organization tab. The dialog box in Figure 16.6 appears.

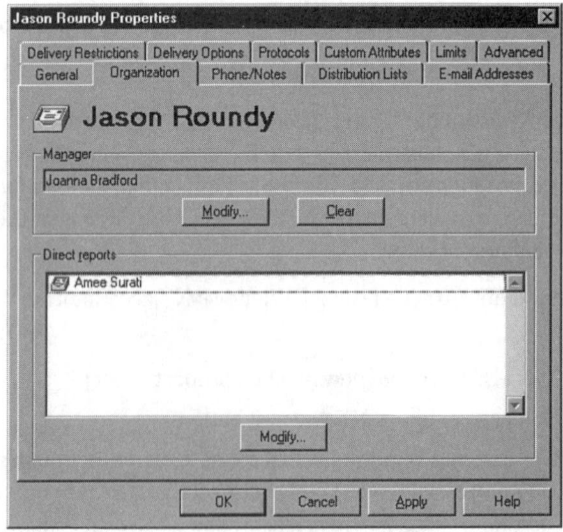

FIG. 16.6 The Organization properties page enables you to define an executive hierarchy by Exchange mailboxes.

2. Click the Modify button under the Manager box. The address book displays. Select a recipient. Click OK. By default, the Manager space is blank.
3. To clear the Manager setting, click the Clear button.

Next, specify a list of people who report to this mailbox owner, as follows:

1. Under the Direct Reports box, click Modify.
2. On the left window select the appropriate mailboxes. Click Add to create a list on the right. Manually select and delete names in the right window to remove mailboxes from the list. Click OK to return to the Organization page.

3. Click Apply to set the properties and continue with other properties. When you finish with all settings, click OK to return to the Administrator program.

The Phone/Notes Page

The Phone/Notes property page gives you plenty of room to enter detailed telephone information concerning a mailbox user. A large note space is also on the page to include any necessary comments. Once again, all these fields are optional.

The following explains how to configure the Phone/Notes property page:

1. Select the Phone/Notes tab of the Mailbox property page. The dialog box in Figure 16.7 appears.

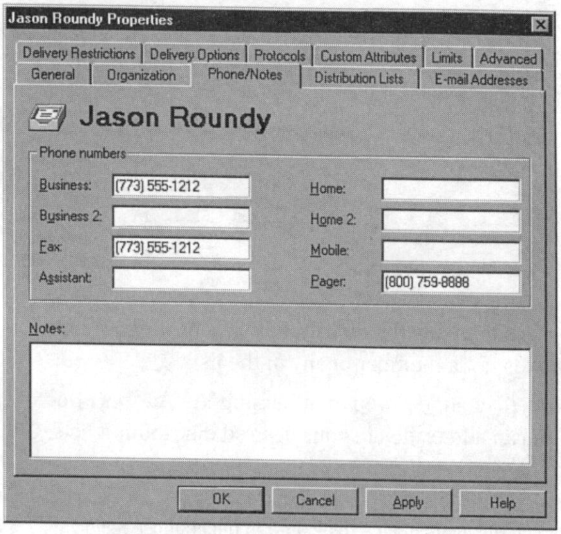

FIG. 16.7
Include any relevant telephone data or notes.

2. Enter all relevant phone numbers in their appropriate boxes.
3. If you need an administrative note, you can enter one on the page.
4. Click Apply to set the properties and continue with other properties. If you finish with all settings, click OK to return to the Administrator program.

The Distribution Lists Page

In the Distribution Lists property page, you define the mailbox's membership to various distribution lists. Distribution lists are types of recipients. The following discussion covers the lists in more detail.

You can add distribution list membership using the following steps:

1. Select the Distribution Lists tab in the user's mailbox. The dialog box in Figure 16.8 appears.

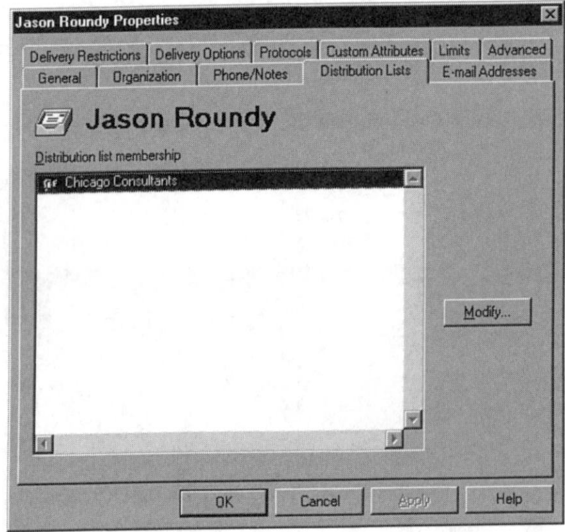

FIG. 16.8
Define distribution list membership for a mailbox.

The dialog box contains the distribution lists of which the user is a member. By default, a new mailbox is not a member of any of the lists.

2. Click Modify to change group membership. An Address Book window appears. In the window you can add or delete your desired distribution lists. Click OK.

NOTE If no lists are available, and you want to create some new lists, see the instructions later in this chapter. The instructions explain how to define those recipients.

3. Click Apply to set the properties and continue with other ones. If you finish with all settings, click OK to return to the Administrator program.

The Delivery Restrictions Page

Delivery restrictions screen incoming mail. Using the settings in the Delivery Restrictions property page, you can define specific senders from which the mailbox rejects mail. Alternatively, you can define a list of addresses from which this mailbox only accepts messages. The two options are mutually exclusive. Exchange, however, enables you to select senders in both lists.

The following explains how to set the options:

1. Select the Delivery Restrictions tab. The dialog box in Figure 16.9 appears.

   The left window lists only the senders that are permitted to send messages to the mailbox. Alternatively, the right window lists senders who are rejected if they send messages to the mailbox. By default, both windows are empty.

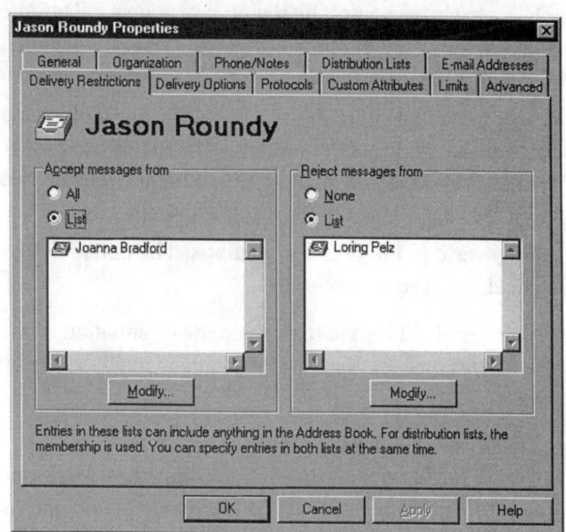

FIG. 16.9
The Delivery Restrictions page enables you to specify users who can and cannot direct messages to a mailbox.

2. Click Modify under each window to add or delete senders. The Address Book dialog box opens. Type or select senders from the list. Alternatively, you can delete them in this window. Click OK when you finish and want to return to the Delivery Restrictions property sheet.
3. Click Apply to set the properties and continue with others. When you finish with all settings, click OK to return to the Administrator program.

The Delivery Options Page

You can configure a Microsoft Exchange Mailbox with special options that provide some interesting functions. You can set the following two different delivery options on the Delivery Options property page:

- *Alternate Recipient for a Mailbox*—You can set another recipient to receive mail intended for the mailbox.
- *Send On Behalf Permissions*—Gives other users the right to send messages as if the messages originated from the primary user.

Alternate Recipient Occasionally, you need to set alternate recipients for email directed at a particular destination.

In our previous example, Jack is going on vacation for two weeks. Instead of bouncing the messages back with an auto reply, however, you can redirect them to an assistant's mailbox.

Use the following steps to set up alternate recipients:

1. Select the Delivery Options tab. The dialog box appears. The Alternate Recipient settings are in the lower-left corner of the dialog box. By default, the None option button is selected, and no entry is in the box below it.
2. Under Alternate Recipient click Modify. The Address Book dialog box appears. Select the recipient to whom you want all messages from this mailbox redirected. Click Add. Click OK to confirm your selection and return to the Delivery Option property page.
3. Select the And Alternate Recipient check box to both redirect a message to the alternate recipient and deliver it to the principal mailbox. The option delivers two messages. By default, the check box is not checked.

Send On Behalf The Send On Behalf feature creates a situation in which one or many individuals are allowed to send mail *on behalf* of the primary mailbox. Authority is distributed across several users.

The following is an example of using the Send On Behalf feature. Michael Navarro, a 3D graphics technical director in Los Angeles, has a team of animators. Michael is currently the lead on a special effects project with a major studio. The animators can communicate electronically with the effects supervisor at the studio. Each animator has the Send On Behalf privileges on the Michael Navarro mailbox. Animator Richard d'Andrea sends a message requesting information from the effects supervisor. The message received by the effects supervisor is titled as sent by Richard D'Andrea on behalf of Michael Navarro.

Use the following steps to set up Send On Behalf privileges:

1. Select the Delivery Options tab. You find the Send On Behalf settings in the top half of the property page. The Give Send On Behalf Of Permission To window displays all the users that have been granted this right.
2. Click Modify to edit the user list. The Address Book dialog box appears. In the left window, choose the user to which you want to grant the permission. Click Add to add users. You can also delete the names from the user list on the right window. Click OK to confirm your selection and return to the Delivery Options property page.
3. Click Apply to set these properties and continue with other ones. When you finish with all settings, click OK to return to the Administrator program.

The Custom Attributes Page

The Custom Attributes property page lets you define up to ten extension fields for this mailbox.

Use the following steps to set up Custom Attributes:

1. Select the Custom Attributes tab. The dialog box in Figure 16.10 appears.

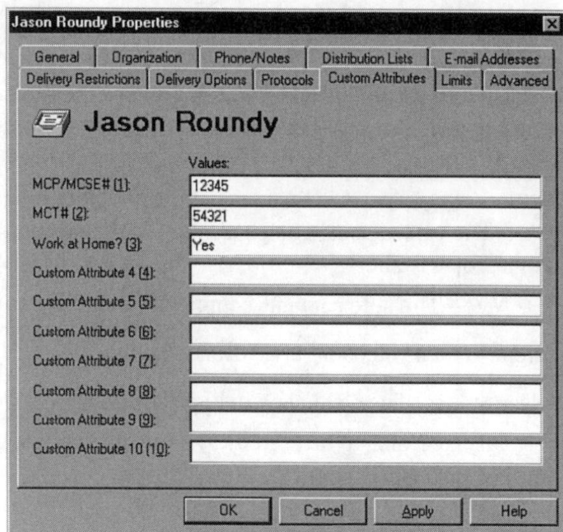

FIG. 16.10 Set values for the custom attributes designated for this site.

2. The dialog box lists all ten custom attributes on the left side of the box, and you enter the user's values on the right.
3. Type values for as many Custom Attributes as you want.
4. Click Apply to set the properties and continue with other properties. When you finish with all settings, click OK to return to the Administrator program.

The Advanced Page

Advanced properties are mainly concerned with the attribute information of a mailbox's system. The following are the advanced properties:

- *Simple Display Name*—The name is used by systems that cannot interpret all the characters, such as spaces, in a normal display name.
- *Directory Name*—The name is a read-only field and is the name by which this object is known within its context in the directory. This name shows only for information purposes, and you cannot change it in this property sheet.
- *Trust Level*—The directory replication trust level determines whether a recipient replicates to another site. If the trust level assigned to the recipient exceeds the trust level set for the connector during Directory Synchronization setup, the mailbox does not replicate. Chapter 2, "Understanding Exchange's Organization and Sites," further discusses the application of trust levels.
- *Online listings information*—The property enables you to input an ILS Server name and an ILS account. The information enables other users to find the mailbox's owner in order to set up online meetings.

- *Home Server*—The home server is the Exchange Server on which the mailbox physically resides. The user must log on to the server listed to employ its client.
- *Downgrade High Priority X.400 Mail*—You can disallow the right to send high priority X.400 messages by using the downgrade property. By default, this checkbox is unchecked.
- *Container Name*—The property is the name of the recipients container in which this mailbox resides. The value appears only for information purposes, and you cannot change it in this property sheet.
- *Administrative Note*—The note contains comments pertaining to settings on this page.

The following are steps to help you configure Advanced properties:

1. Select the Advanced tab. The dialog box in Figure 16.11 appears.
2. Enter a Simple Display Name to be used by systems that cannot interpret all the characters in a normal display name.
3. Set the mailbox's Trust Level to the desired level.

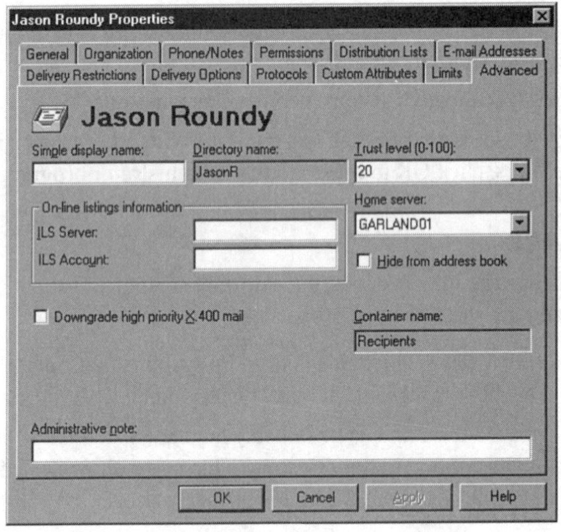

FIG. 16.11
The Advanced property page gives you control over several mailbox functions related to the system.

4. If you want to change the server on which the mailbox resides, select it from the Home Server pop-up menu. The entire contents of the mailboxes transfer to the new server's information store.

NOTE The preceding example has the same function as selecting Move Mailbox from the Administrator Tools menu. ■

5. On the Advanced property page, you can enter optional comments providing custom notes or instructions for a mailbox here (up to 1,024 characters). For example, in the comment space, you can record the reasons for overriding information store defaults.
6. Click Apply to set the properties and continue with other properties. When you finish with all settings, click OK to return to the Administrator program.

The Limits Page

The Limits page has a number of properties that were previously on the Advanced tab. You can set individualized restrictions in the Limits page for individuals who have special circumstances or may need a little more space than you have set on the Information Store. The following are the properties:

- *Deleted Item Retention Time*—The area enables you to set specific limits on how long deleted items are retained in the mailbox. The selections are exactly like those that appear in the Private Information Store properties.
- *Message Sizes*—The property sets restrictions on maximum outgoing and incoming message sizes (in kilobytes) for this mailbox. Any message above the set limits in size return as nondeliverable.
- *Information Store Storage Limits*—You can set upper storage limits for the mailbox using the Information Store Storage Limits property. By default, a mailbox uses the values set on the Private Information Store property pages.

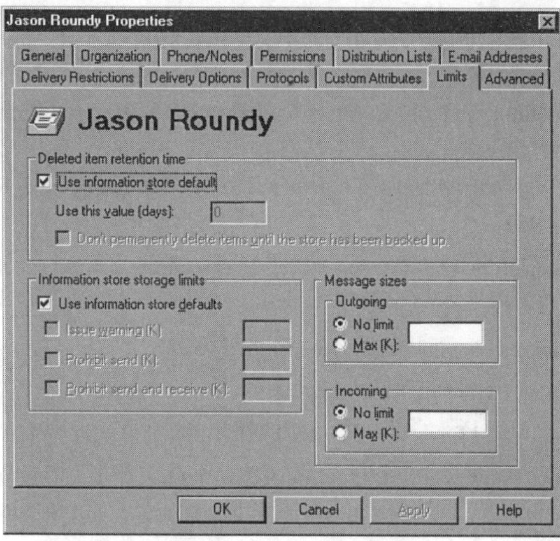

FIG 16.12
The Limits page set mailbox limits that can differ from the Information Store.

Any client newsreader can access news groups and public folders on Exchange.

Creating Custom Recipients

You can define custom recipients for sending messages to users outside the Microsoft Exchange organization global address list. Normally, the recipients are Microsoft Mail users, SMTP users (Internet), or foreign X.400 system users. You can also create custom recipients for any other third-party connector or gateway. After you create recipients, you can replicate across your organization as part of the global address list. The recipients can receive messages from and send messages to a Microsoft Exchange Server. A global icon in the Exchange Administrator program identifies custom recipient objects. Property pages for custom recipients are quite similar to those of standard Exchange mailboxes. The pages for custom recipients do not have as many advanced features as the latter.

The following steps help you to create a new custom recipient:

1. Select New Custom Recipient from the Administrator program File menu. The New Email Address dialog box in Figure 16.13 appears:

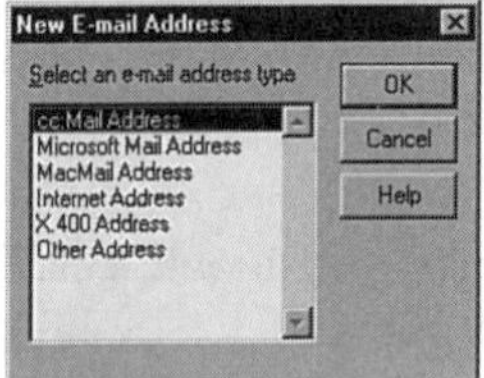

FIG. 16.13
Address types for all installed connections and gateways appear in this dialog box.

2. Select an email address type for your new custom recipient. All installed connector types are listed. Click OK.
3. In the preceding dialog box, enter the appropriate delivery information for the selected address type.
4. Click OK to set the address and proceed to the Exchange Custom Recipient Object property pages.

The following steps show you how to enter delivery addresses for specific custom recipients. Configuring a cc:Mail custom recipient is discussed later in this chapter:

1. Enter the user's Display Name (see Figure 16.14).
2. Enter the user's cc:Mail Mailbox name on the post office.
3. Enter the cc:Mail Post Office through which the user receives messages.

The following steps show you how to enter delivery addresses for specific custom recipients. Configuring a Microsoft Mail custom recipient is discussed later in this chapter:

1. Enter the correct name for the post office.
2. Enter the Microsoft Mail Network name on which this user receives messages.

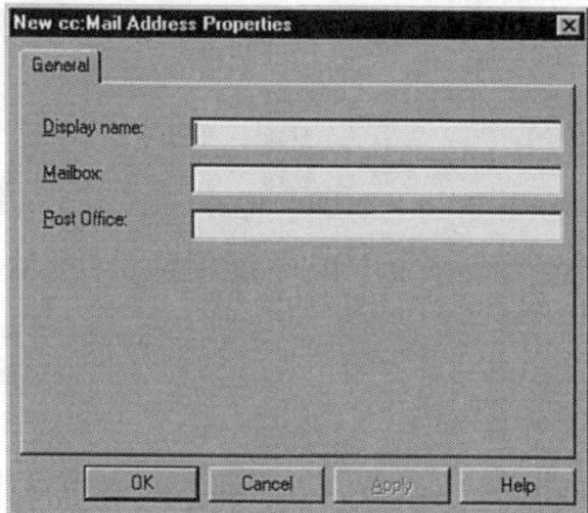

FIG. 16.14
You need to specify delivery information for a cc:Mail post office recipient.

3. Enter the Microsoft Mail Network name for the post office through which this user receives messages.
4. Enter the user's Microsoft Mail Mailbox name on the preceding post office (see Figure 16.15).

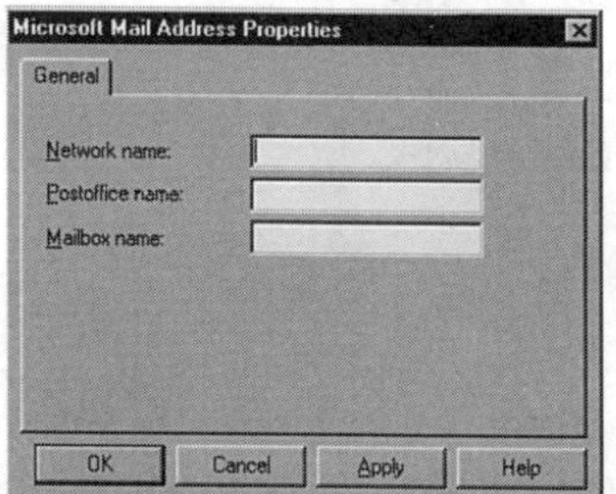

FIG. 16.15
You need to specify delivery information for a Microsoft Mail (PC) post office recipient.

5. Click OK to proceed to the Exchange Custom Recipient property pages.

The following steps explain how to enter a custom Microsoft Mail for an AppleTalk address:

1. Enter the user's Display Name (see Figure 16.16).

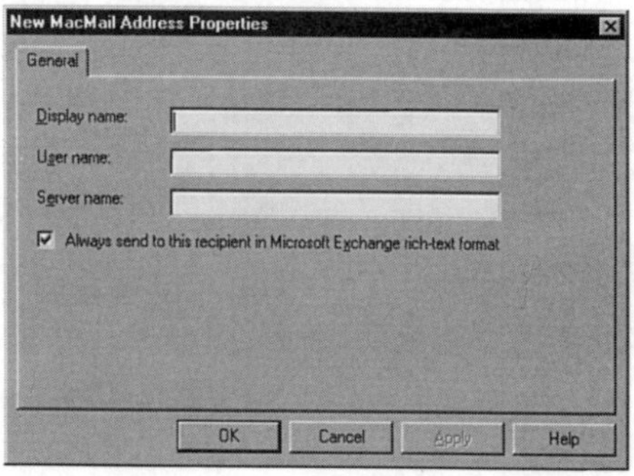

FIG. 16.16
You need to specify delivery information for a Microsoft Mail (AppleTalk) Server recipient.

2. Enter the recipient's User Name as it appears on the Macintosh Server.
3. Enter the Macintosh Server name for this recipient.
4. Click Always Send to This Recipient in Microsoft Exchange Rich-Text Format to maintain special message formatting in messages transmitted to this recipient.
5. Click OK to proceed to the Exchange Custom Recipient property pages.

Complete the following steps to enter a custom Internet or other SMTP address:

1. Enter an SMTP address in the single Email address box.
2. Click OK to proceed to the Exchange Custom Recipient property pages (see Figure 16.17).

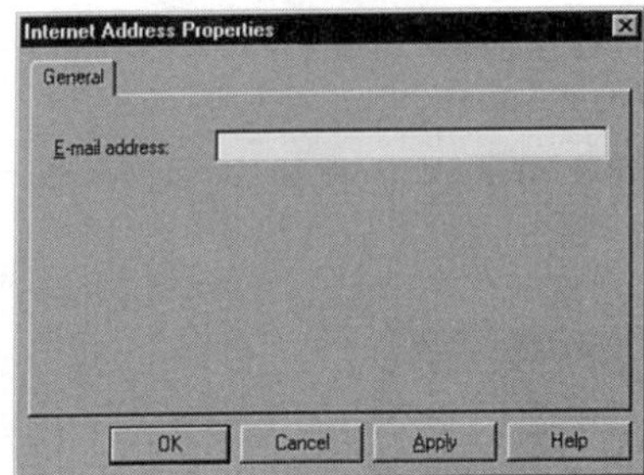

FIG. 16.17
Entering an Internet address.

You must specify an Internet or other SMTP address in the window (must be in the user@domain format).

Two property pages are available to enter an X.400 address. The General page enables you to define the specific address for a foreign X.400 recipient (see Figure 16.18). You can add more information for this recipient by using the Advanced page.

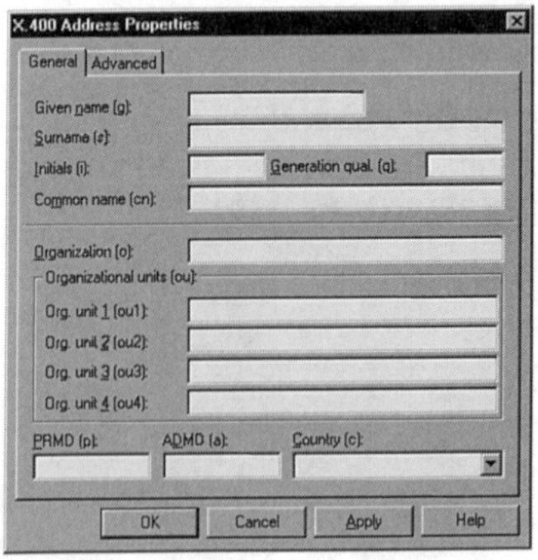

FIG. 16.18
This General property page defines a foreign X.400 recipient's delivery information.

Configuring Properties for a Custom Recipient

After selecting the address type and entering delivery information for a custom recipient, you see the Exchange property pages for this recipient. You can also use this section as a reference for modifying custom recipient property pages after you create the object.

The following explains how to complete the Exchange property pages for a recipient:

- *General Information*—Records basic recipient information, such as name, location, title, and company. The section also enables you to change the email address and its type for the custom recipient.
- *Specifics About the Organization*—You can add optional information about your company's organization, such as a manager and the people who report to the recipient.
- *Phone Number and Notes*—You can enter detailed telephone information and any additional notes about the user.
- *Distribution Lists that Include the Recipient*—The page specifies the distribution lists to which the recipient belongs.
- *Email Addresses*—The page enables you to create, modify, and delete alternate addresses for the recipient.
- *Delivery Restrictions*—The page defines from which addresses the mailbox does or does not accept messages.
- *Custom Attributes*—The page adds up to ten administrator-defined fields that you can use to keep additional information about the recipient.
- *Advanced Page*—The page contains all the settings concerned with advanced administrator functions, such as trust levels, message sizes, text formatting, and hidden/not hidden status.

The following sections explain the process of configuring custom recipient property pages. The specifics of each of the pages are discussed in depth.

The General Page

Select the General property page (see Figure 16.19). The property page is almost identical to that of an Exchange mailbox. The main difference is the Email button in the bottom-left corner of the window. When you click the button, the dialog box in Figure 16.20 appears.

NOTE Notice the globe icon denoting a custom recipient. ■

1. Select Modify Existing Email Address to edit the recipient address in the appropriate dialog box for the current address type.
2. Select Create New Email Address to create an entirely new address using the same process described previously.

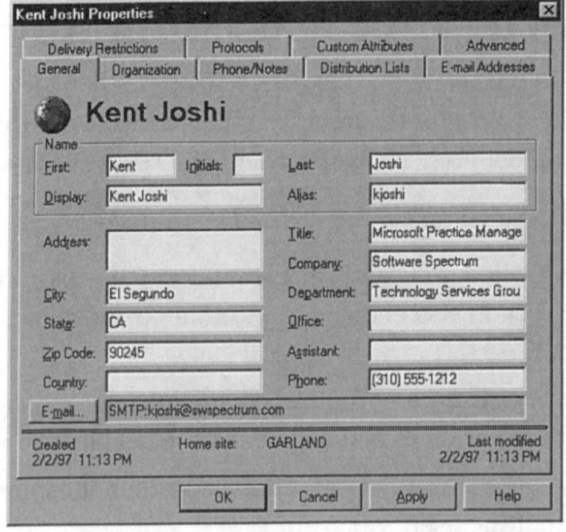

FIG. 16.19
The General property page gives you control over several system-related mailbox functions.

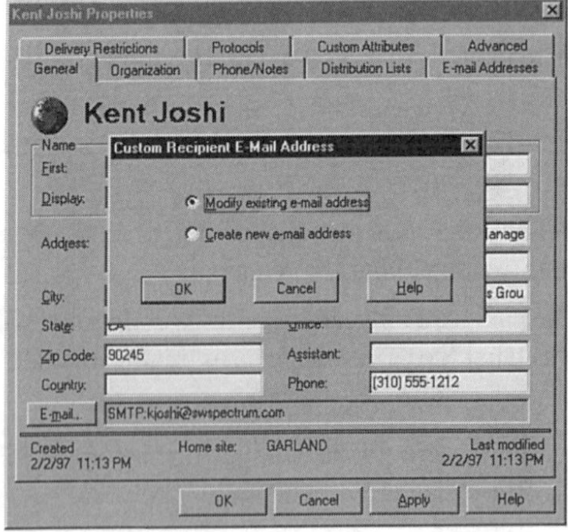

FIG. 16.20
Choose to edit the current email address or create a new one.

3. A box to the right of the Email address button shows the current address type and value of the custom recipient. Address types are abbreviated in the following way:

MS:	Microsoft Mail for PC networks
MSA:	Microsoft Mail for AppleTalk networks
SMTP:	Simple Mail Transfer Protocol addresses, such as for the Internet
X.400:	Foreign X.400 addressees

The Organization Page

If this custom recipient has one or more managers, and certain individuals must report to them, enter these names in the spaces provided. The Organization property page is functionally equivalent to a standard mailbox's Organization property page.

The Phone Number and Notes Page

On this page you can enter detailed phone number information for this custom recipient. The Phone Number and Notes property page is functionally equivalent to a standard mailbox's Phone Number and Notes property page.

The Distribution Lists Page

You can add custom recipients to distribution lists as any other recipient. The Distribution Lists property page is functionally equivalent to a standard mailbox's Distribution Lists property page.

The Email Addresses Page

The Email Addresses page holds a list of email addresses automatically created for this directory object. You can alter the recipient's principal from the window, so that it is the same as the principal on the General property page. The addresses are used when routing messages from other connected mail systems, such as Microsoft Mail. The Email Addresses property page is functionally equivalent to a standard mailbox's Email Addresses property page.

The Delivery Restrictions Page

By using the Delivery Restrictions Page, you can define other users within the Exchange organization that cannot send messages to this custom recipient. The Accept Messages From and Reject Messages From windows are functionally equivalent to a standard mailbox's Delivery Restrictions property page.

The Custom Attributes Page

Enter additional custom recipient data in the appropriate fields. The Custom Attributes property page is functionally equivalent to a standard mailbox's Custom Attributes property page.

The Advanced Page

Use the Advanced property page to create a simple display name for this recipient, if required. You also use this page to set a trust level as needed for either directory replication, synchronization, or both. Also, set an upper limit for the size of messages addressed to the recipient. Similar to a mailbox, you can select to enable rich text formatting for messages to the recipient, or you can choose to hide the formatting from displaying in the address book.

When you select the Advanced tab, the dialog box in Figure 16.21 appears.

Because a custom recipient does not use storage space in a private information store, maximum storage options are removed from this page. Also, you have no option to change the home server for the recipient. The reason is that no messages are stored locally for the recipient.

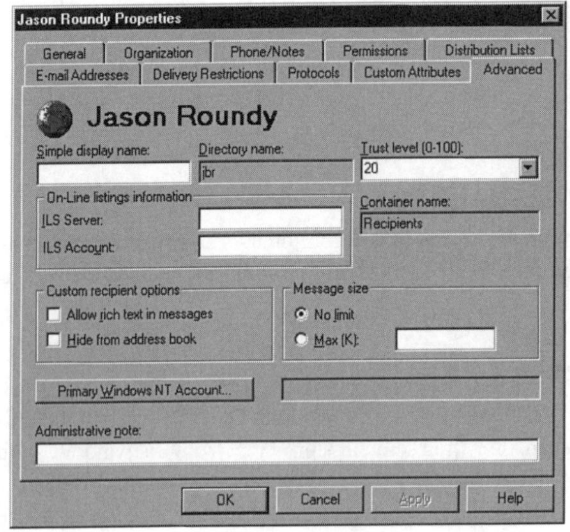

FIG. 16.21
You can set advanced properties for this recipient using the Advanced page.

The Protocols Page

Enter additional protocols data in the appropriate fields. The Protocols property page is functionally equivalent to a standard mailbox's Protocols property page.

NOTE Custom recipients do not have a Delivery Options property page. Therefore, you cannot specify alternate recipients. You also cannot give Send On Behalf privileges to that recipient. ■

Creating Distribution Lists

The following describes the function of the property pages for a Distribution List:

- *General Information*—The General Information property page records basic recipient information, such as name, owner, and members. The General Information property page also enables you to select the expansion server for the list.
- *Distribution Lists*—The Distribution Lists property page specifies the distribution lists to which the distribution list belongs. You can nest lists within each other to develop a hierarchy for message distribution.
- *Email Addresses*—The Email Addresses page enables you to create, modify, and delete alternate addresses for the distribution list.
- *Delivery Restrictions*—The page defines from which addresses this distribution list does or does not accept messages.
- *Custom Attributes*—On this page you can add up to ten administrator-defined fields that you use to keep additional information about the distribution list.

- *Advanced Page*—The page contains all the settings concerned with advanced administrator functions, such as trust levels, message sizes, reporting options, and hidden/not hidden status.

The General Page

The following describes the function of the General tab in the Distribution List property page:

1. Select the General tab in the Distribution List property page. The dialog box in Figure 16.22 appears.

FIG. 16.22 The General property page gives you control over several system-related mailbox functions.

2. Enter a Display Name for this distribution list, as you want it to appear in the address book.
3. Enter an Alias Name which you use to generate other email addresses for this distribution list.
4. The Owner box displays an Exchange user that has the right to modify a list's membership from within the Exchange client. Normally, only an administrator can modify a list's membership. Click Modify to open the Address Book dialog box. Select an owner from the list. Then click OK. Use the Clear button to remove that user as the distribution list owner.
5. The Members box lists the current distribution list membership. Click Modify to bring up an address list. You can then click ADD to put new members on the list. Members can be mailboxes, custom recipients, or other distribution lists.
6. You can also select an Expansion Server for this list. By default, Any Server In Site is selected, and the distribution list expands on the server from which the list was sent. Choose a specific server from the menu, and the distribution list will always expand on the chosen server.
7. Enter any additional notes in the Note box.

8. Click Apply to set the properties and continue with other ones. When you finish with all settings, click OK to return to the Administrator program.

The Distribution Lists Page

You can nest distribution lists by making them members of other lists. Click the Modify button to add or delete other distribution lists of which the list is a member.

The following example illustrates how you can nest one list in another: Three new distribution lists are in the SWSPECTRUM organization. The first two lists are named SWS LA and SWS Houston. Each distribution list has a membership of users, including mailboxes and custom recipients. The third address list created is named SWS Exchange Enthusiasts. This list has only five members. The members are the other distribution lists along with three additional recipients who receive messages intended for these groups. Visually, the hierarchy resembles the one in Figure 16.23.

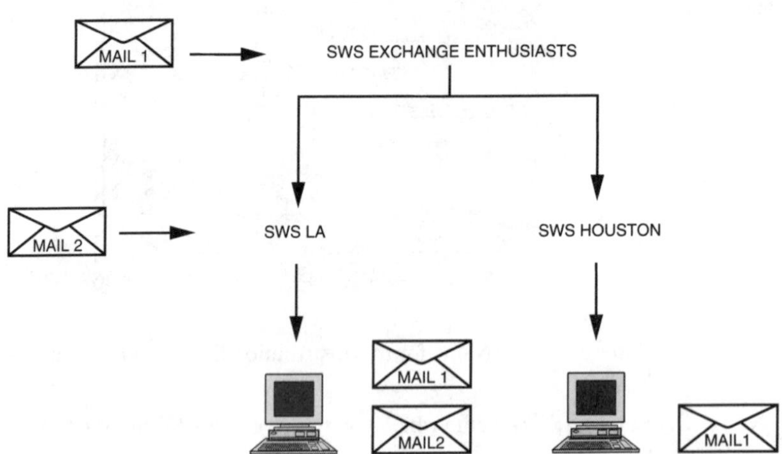

FIG. 16.23
Nested distribution lists can facilitate list management.

For comparison, examine the following three property sheets depicting this structure.

The SWS LA and SWS Houston Distribution Lists property sheets show the following membership information (see Figure 16.24).

The SWS Exchange Enthusiasts distribution list has both the SWS LA and SWS Houston and three additional recipients as its members. The property sheet for SWS Exchange Enthusiasts looks similar to Figure 16.25.

Recipients within SWS LA now receive messages addressed to the Exchange Enthusiasts as well. You can obtain a similar result by adding all the individual recipients to the Exchange Enthusiasts distribution list. However, you then have two lists in which to keep track of individual members. Nesting lists facilitates management by placing recipients into smaller, logical subdivisions.

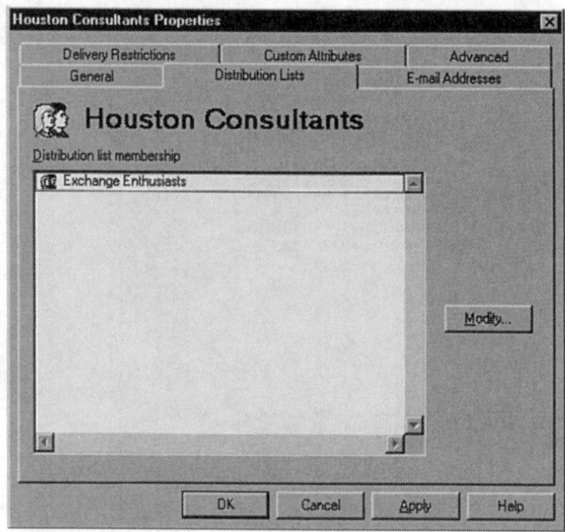

FIG. 16.24
A Distribution list can have distribution list membership as well.

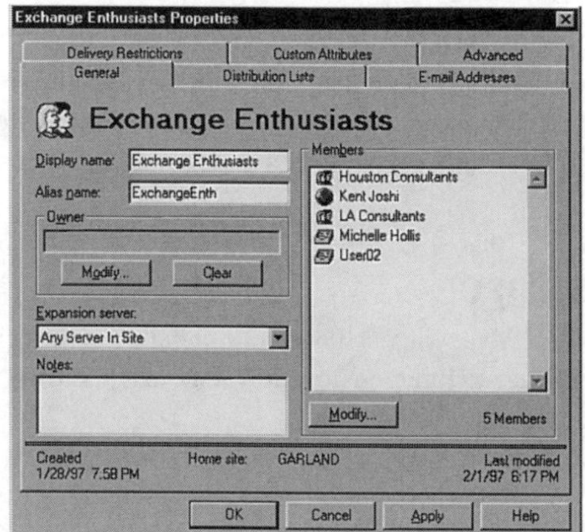

FIG. 16.25
Members of the top-level distribution list hierarchy.

The Email Addresses Page

Use the Email Addresses property page to establish alternate email addresses for the distribution list. The property page is functionally equivalent to a standard mailbox's Email Addresses property page (see Figure 16.26).

For example, jsmith@corpor.com, an Internet mail user, can address a message to ExchangeEnth@GARLAND.SWSPECTRUM.COM. In effect, the user can send the message to more than 50 members of this distribution list.

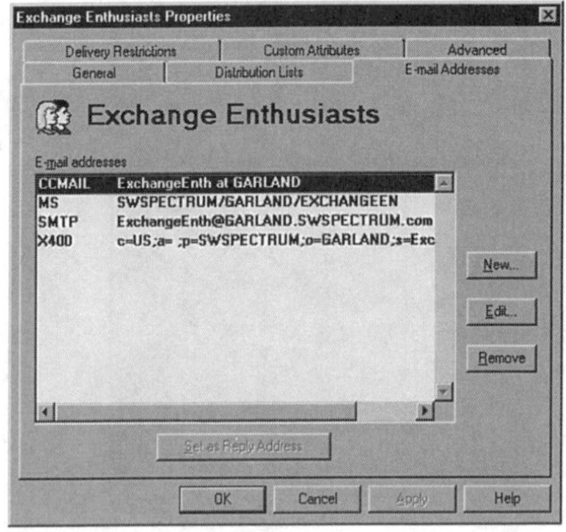

FIG. 16.26
The Email Addresses page displays alternate address data corresponding to all installed connectors and gateways.

The Delivery Restrictions Page

You can define other users within the Exchange organization who are not able to send messages to the distribution list. The Accept Messages From and Reject Messages From windows are functionally equivalent to a standard mailbox's or custom recipient's Delivery Restrictions property page.

The Custom Attributes Page

Using the Custom Attributes Page, you can enter additional custom recipient data in the appropriate fields. This property page is functionally equivalent to a standard mailbox's or custom recipient's Custom Attributes page.

The Advanced Page

The distribution list's Advanced property page (see Figure 16.27) is similar to Advanced property pages of other types of recipients. Simple display name, directory name, trust level, and message size are the same settings found on the Advanced property pages of other types of recipients. The following are options specific to the Distribution List property page:

- *Report to Distribution List Owner*—When checked, the option sends a message to the distribution list owner when a message that exceeds the specified size limit is sent to the distribution list. By default, the option is not checked.
- *Report to Message Originator*—When checked, the option sends a message back to the message originator. By default, the option is checked.
- *Enable Out of Office Messages to Originator*—When checked, the option responds with an out of office message for any registered user who is a member of the distribution. By default, the option is not checked.

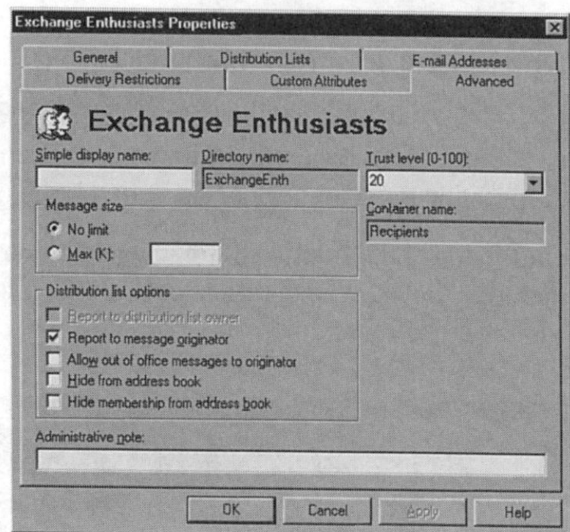

FIG. 16.27
The distribution list Advanced property page displays some settings that are similar to those of other property pages.

- *Hide Distribution List from Address Book*—As with other recipients, the option prohibits the distribution list from appearing in the address book. Users need to know the name of the list to manually address it.
- *Hide Membership from Address Book*—When checked, the distribution list name itself displays in the address book. Users can, however, view the individual members of the list.

Creating and Configuring Public Folders

You create public folders from within the Microsoft Exchange Client. Then they are copied to a public information store. You handle general configuration through the Administrator program. The following is an overview of the Public Folder property pages:

- *General Information on the Folder*—The page gives the folder's name and display name, age limits, and specific client permissions.
- *Replicas of the Folder*—Add, remove, or copies public folders on other severs within your organization.
- *Folder Replication Status*—You can view and track the folder replication process for troubleshooting purposes using the page.
- *Replication Schedule*—The page helps you specify at which times information within public folders replicate throughout your organization.
- *Distribution Lists*—A folder is a member of certain distribution lists. The page helps you specify to which lists the folder belongs. Any messages sent to the distribution list are also stored in this public folder.
- *Email Addresses*—The page enables you to create, modify, and delete alternate addresses for the public folder.

- *Custom Attributes*—The page enables you to add up to ten administrator-defined fields, which you use to keep additional information about the mailbox.
- *Limits*—Configure deleted item retention time, storage limits, and age limits on the page.
- *Advanced*—Contains all the settings concerned with advanced administrator functions, such as trust levels, replication messages importance, and hidden/not hidden status.

Public folders are listed near the top of the Administrator's object hierarchy (see Figure 16.28). To view the public folder hierarchy in your organization, click the Public Folders object in the Administrator program.

FIG. 16.28
View the public folders within your organization in the Administrator's hierarchy window.

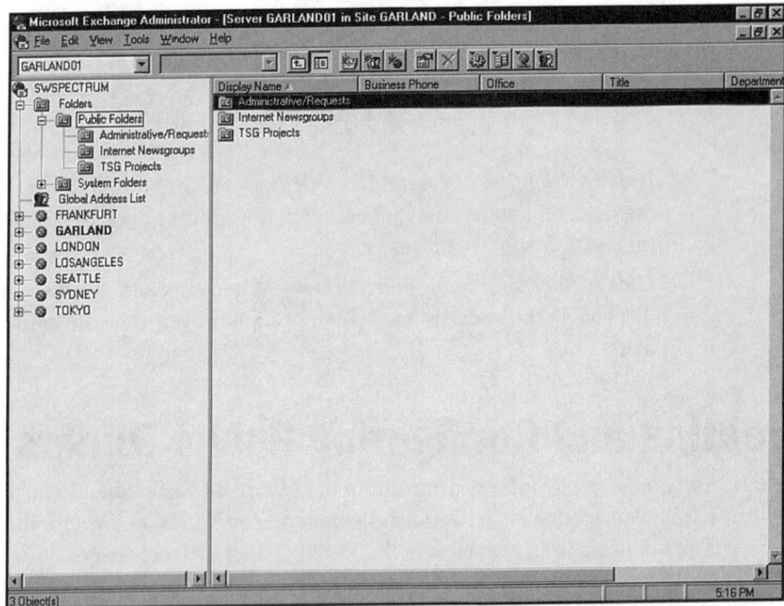

To edit a specific folder within your site, open its property pages. You can set all the options presented in the preceding list. To edit a public folder's contents, you must use the Microsoft Exchange client program and have appropriate client permissions. Another section later in the chapter discusses assigning client permissions. The next section covers the options available on the Public Folder property pages.

The General Page

The public folder is a unique recipient in that many different users can view and edit the information that it receives. As with other recipient types, the General property page enables you to set names for this object, as well as other general administrative notes. However, you have some very specific settings for this recipient type.

The following steps describe in detail how to set General properties for the public folders:

1. Select the General tab of the Public Folder property pages. The dialog box in Figure 16.29 appears.
2. You can change the Folder Name in the appropriate box. The name is first assigned when the folder is created in the Microsoft Exchange Client program.
3. If you want to give the public folder a different display name for the address book, click the option button marked Use This Name under the heading Address Book Display Name. By default, the Same As Folder Name button is selected.
4. You must enter a required Alias name used to generate additional email addresses for the public folder.

FIG. 16.29
General properties for Public Folders are somewhat different from other recipient types.

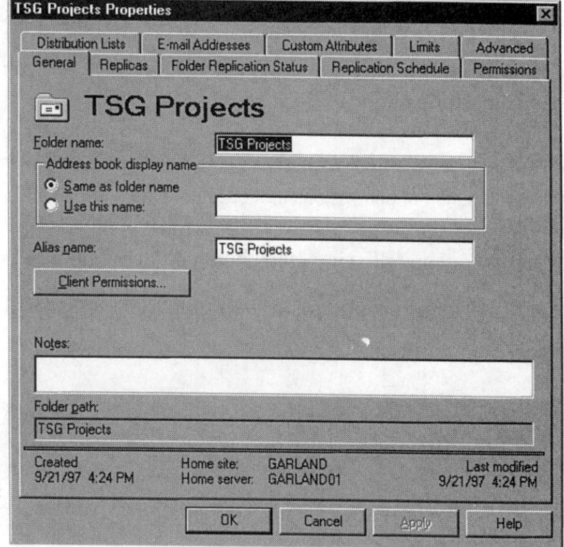

5. Enter any additional notes in the Note space provided.
6. The Folder Path box displays the hierarchy of subfolders that leads to this public folder. If this is a main level folder and not a subfolder, only the folder's name displays.
7. Click Apply to set the properties and continue with other properties. When you finish with all the settings, click OK to return to the Administrator program.

Assigning Client Permissions The Client Permissions button on the General Properties page enables an administrator to set access permissions on Public Folders without needing to use the Outlook or Exchange Client.

The following are the roles available in the pull-down menu:

- *Owner*—The owner marks the user as folder owner. The role also gives the user complete permission on the folder.
- *Publishing Editor*—The editor has all create, edit, and delete permissions on a folder. The role also gives permission to create subfolders. The permission does not, however, mark the user as the owner.
- *Editor*—The role gives all create, edit, and delete permissions.
- *Publishing Author*—The publishing author has permission to create subfolders. Also, the role gives create, edit, and delete permission only to the publishing author's items.
- *Author*—The role gives permission to create, edit, and delete only the author's items.
- *Reviewer*—The reviewer has permission to read items.
- *Contributor*—The contributor has permission to create (although not to read) items.
- *None*—No permissions are given on this folder. You often use the role as a default to limit access to a specific public folder.

NOTE The pull-down menu can also display a role of Custom. Custom indicates that you have put together a combination of permissions that does not match one of the preceding roles.

Setting Up Permissions The following steps help you to set up permissions:

1. Click the Client Permissions button on the Public Folder General property page. The dialog box in Figure 16.30 appears:

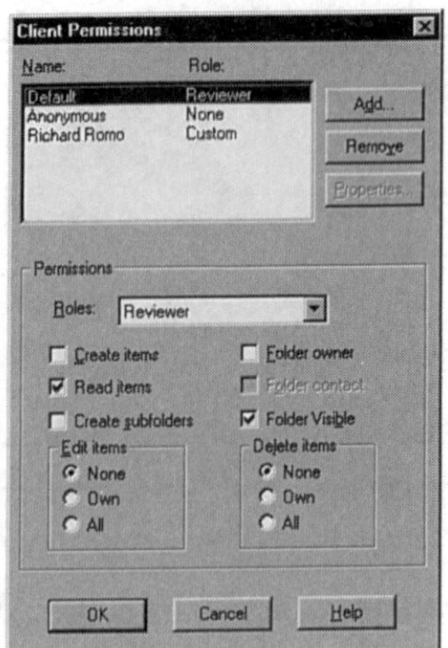

FIG. 16.30 Client permissions determine what level of access a user has on a public folder.

The Name: and Role: columns display current users and their roles (see Figure 16.31). The Default role applies to any user not shown on this list.

2. Click Add to bring up the address list and add members to the Client Permissions list. Click a name. Then click Remove to delete the name from the list. Again, click a name. Then click Properties to bring up the user's property pages.
3. The Roles pull-down menu displays preset roles for certain types of users. Clicking the menu pulls down the following list (see Figure 16.31).

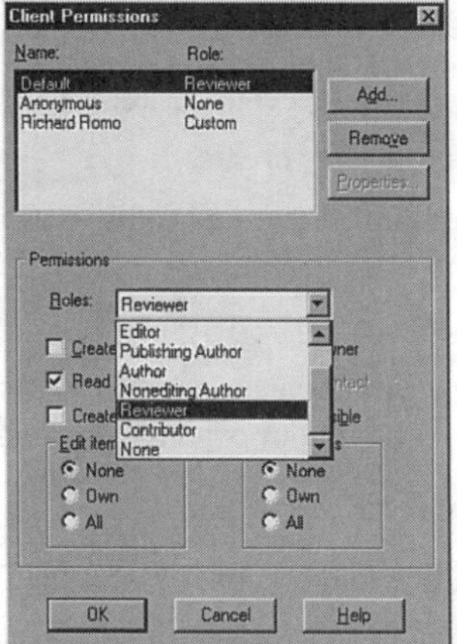

FIG. 16.31
You can use the Roles pull-down menu to give customized properties to a user.

Select a role from the menu. Note that the check boxes and option buttons reflect the change in access rights for each role.

4. Alternatively, you can customize a role by clicking the available option buttons and check boxes. If by clicking, you set a configuration that matches one of the predefined roles, the role displays in the Roles pop-up menu heading. For example, you select the Author permission from the menu. The boxes and buttons display the permissions for the user role Author. When you click the Create Sub-Folders button, the name in the Roles menu changes to Publishing Author.
5. Click OK to set the permissions and continue editing other public folder properties.

The following list details the check box definitions:

- *Create Items*—The check box gives permission to post items to the folder.
- *Read Items*—When you check the Read Items box, you give permission to open any item in a folder.
- *Create Subfolders*—Check this box to give permission to make a subfolder of the main public folder.
- *Folder Owner*—All permissions are given with respect to the folder.
- *Folder Contact*—A user with Folder Contact status receives automatic error or conflict messages from the folder, such as replication errors and oversize limit warnings. The user also receives users' requests for more access or other administrative tasks. Often, the owner and the contact are the same individual.

The following list outlines the scope of Edit permissions:

- *None*—Users cannot make any modification to existing public folder items.
- Users cannot delete any folder items, even ones they create themselves.
- *Own*—The user can edit only items that they create.
- *All*—The user can edit any folder item, regardless of its creator.

The following list details the scope of Delete permissions:

- *None*—Users cannot delete any folder item, even the items they create themselves.
- *Own*—Users can delete only items that they create.
- *All*—The user can delete any folder item, regardless of its creator.

The Replicas Page

The Replicas property page displays the destination servers to which a public folder replicates. You also can add or remove replicas throughout your organization using this window.

The following steps help you to configure replicas:

1. Select the Replicas tab from the public folder property sheets. The dialog box in Figure 16.32 appears:

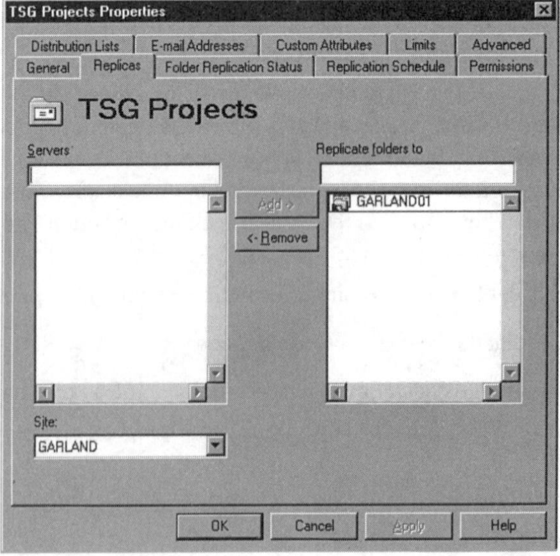

FIG. 16.32 View the public folders within your organization in the Administrator's Hierarchy window.

The left side of the screen labeled Servers lists all the public folders. The right side of the screen labeled Replicate folders lists all the servers to which the folder replicates.

2. Using the Site pull-down menu at the bottom of the property page, choose the site of the destination server. Click and highlight the desired server from the list of Exchange Servers on the left side of the window.
3. Click Add to include that server in the replication list.
4. To remove a server from the replication process, click its name on the right window. Then click Remove.
5. Click Apply to set the properties and continue with other properties. When you finish with all settings, click OK to return to the Administrator program.

The Replicate Folders To box should now list every server to which you want the particular public folder replicated. If not, repeat the preceding steps until you select all desired Exchange Servers. ●

CHAPTER 17

Setting Up the Site Connector and Dynamic RAS Connector

In this chapter

This chapter is the first in this book dedicated to the specifics of linking two or more Microsoft Exchange sites. By now, you should have learned enough to be able to select the most appropriate connector between the Exchange servers in your organization. This chapter deals with the two connectors designed to link only Microsoft Exchange severs. Other connectors, such as X.400 or Internet Mail Connector, can be used to link Exchange servers and to provide a gateway to foreign mail systems. The two connectors used only between Exchange servers are:

- Site Connector—Full-time message link over high-bandwidth network links
- Dynamic RAS Connector—Part-time scheduled message transfer over low-bandwidth lines

This chapter covers the basics of setting up a Site Connector and a Dynamic RAS Connector. Because a site can have any combination of connectors to a remote site, or even multiple connectors of a certain type, you will need to repeat the same steps outlined in this chapter each time you set up a new connector.

Understanding Site Connectors

The Microsoft Exchange Site Connector provides the most direct link between sites. Communication is handled through Remote Procedure Calls between servers in each site. Messages do not need to be converted to a different format (such as X.400) to be transmitted to a different site.

You should be familiar with the following concepts before you attempt to set up and configure a Microsoft Exchange site connector:

- *Target servers*—The list of Exchange servers in the remote site that will be involved in transferring messages to and from the local site.
- *Routing costs*—A number assigned to each connection on a relative scale from 1 to 100. Messages are first routed to connections that have the lowest cost; message transfer is distributed evenly across all connections that have the same assigned cost. You can set routing costs for a site as a whole as well as for individual Exchange servers.
- *Bridgehead server*—A specific Microsoft Exchange server in a site designated to establish communication with the remote site. Normally, the specific server that establishes this connection varies, depending on messaging traffic. Designating a bridgehead server is useful for controlling the message-transfer points between two sites.

Installing a New Site Connector

Installing a site connector to exchange messages between sites is a two-step process. First, you must set up a connector in the local site. The connector enables message traffic to the target site. Second, to receive messages from the remote site, you must install a corresponding site connector in the remote site. When you set up a new connection between sites, the Exchange Administrator program automatically prompts you to create the second site connector in the remote site. If you do not create a remote site connector (or cannot, due to access restriction in that site), you must coordinate your efforts with the remote site administrator to negotiate a successful connection between sites. The remote administrator must create a corresponding connector that links to your site.

Before you install a new site connector, make certain that the following conditions are met:

- The underlying network between two sites is properly configured and operational.
- All Microsoft Exchange services are running on both sites.
- You know the exact server at the remote site to which you want to connect.
- If you want to establish the corresponding site connector at the remote site, be sure that you have administrative access rights to the foreign Exchange server and domain if the Exchange server resides in a different domain.

To create a new Site Connector, follow these steps:

1. Navigate through the Exchange administrator program's hierarchy, and highlight the Connections object (see Figure 17.1). The right display window shows all the connections currently running within this site.

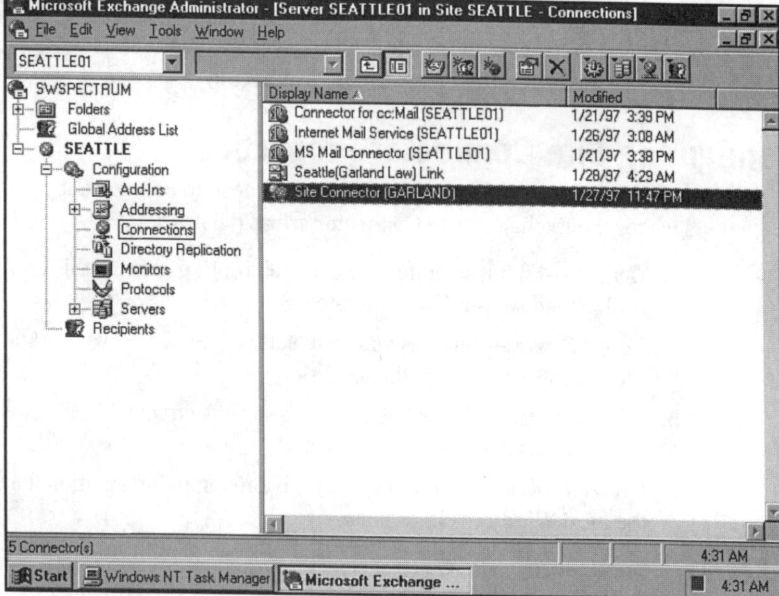

FIG. 17.1 The Exchange Administrator program's display window shows all current site connections.

2. Pull down the File menu and choose New Other; then choose Site Connector from the New Other menu. The New Site Connector dialog box appears (see Figure 17.2).
3. In the text box, type the name of a specific Microsoft Exchange server at the remote site.

NOTE The server name that you enter is used to identify the remote site and does not necessarily mean that this server is the machine that will handle message traffic between sites. Conceptually, a Site Connector resides at the site, not on any particular Exchange server.

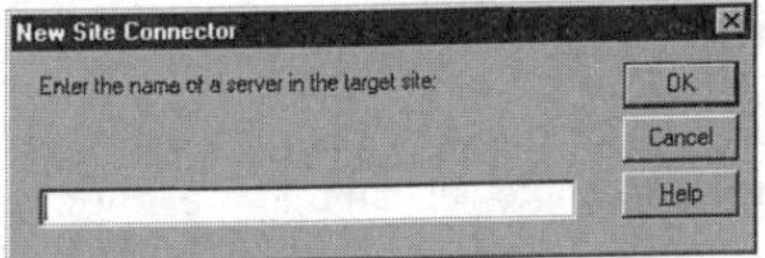

FIG. 17.2
Enter the name of an Exchange server at the remote site.

4. Click OK. The Administrator program attempts to locate and access that server on the network.

NOTE You must have a name resolution mechanism, such as WINS, DNS, HOSTS file, LMHOSTS file, or a configured browser service, to resolve the name of your Exchange server. If a name resolution mechanism is not functional, you will not be able to set up either the local or the corresponding site connector. ■

If you attempt to create a site connector to a site where such a connector already exists, you will be notified of the situation and will not be allowed to create another connector.

When creating a site connector to a server in another Windows NT domain, you need to make sure the account in which you are creating the connector not only has administrative rights to the second domain, but also administrative rights on the Exchange server in this second site. These rights are required to create the connector.

Configuring Site Connector Properties

After creating a new Site Connector, you will need to configure its properties. The property pages for the Exchange Site Connector are as follows:

- *General*—Enables you to set an overall routing cost for this connector and designate a bridgehead server, if appropriate.
- *Target Servers*—Enables you to select the specific servers in the remote site that will receive messages from the local site.
- *Address Space*—Allows you to assign various email address types and associated routing costs for this site connector object.
- *Override*—Enables you to specify custom log in information if a target server is outside the local Windows NT domain.

The General Page The General page is where you set Site Connector communication options. Primarily, you will define which site you are connecting to and which servers specifically will handle that connection. The following steps guide you through configuring the General page.

1. Click the General tab of the Site Connector property pages (see Figure 17.3).
2. If you want, type a new name for this site connector in the Display Name box. The default display name is in the format Site Connector (site name).
3. If you want, type a different directory name for this site connector in the Directory Name box. The default directory name is in the format Site Connector (site name).

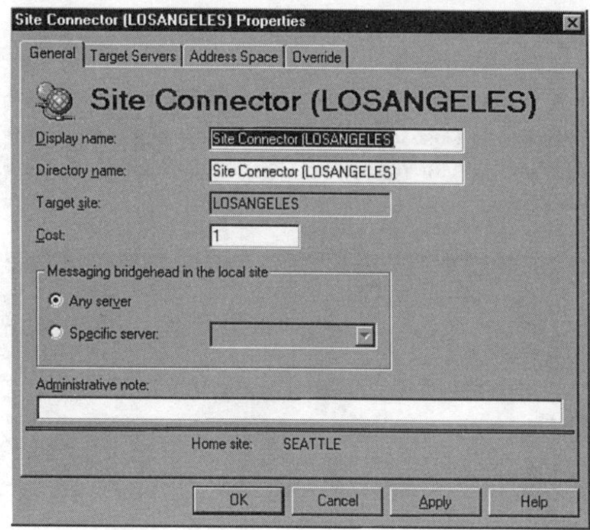

FIG. 17.3 Use the General Site Connector property page primarily to define the site to which you are linking.

4. The Target Site box shows the name of the remote site to which you are connecting. This data is provided for your information only. To change the target site at this point, you must click Cancel to exit from the property pages and create a new site connector.
5. In the Cost box, enter a routing Cost for the site connector. An Exchange server uses this cost to determine whether to use this connection over other available connections. By default, a new site connector has a routing cost of 1.
6. If you want, specify a bridgehead server that will handle communication with the remote site. By default, the Any Server option is selected, and communication will be handled by the combination of target servers specified in the remote site's connector. If you select a specific server, that one machine will process all message transfer through the site connector.
7. If you want, make an entry in the Administrative Note box.
8. Click Apply to set these properties and continue setting other properties.
9. When you finish making settings, click OK to return to the Administrator program.

The Target Servers Page Use the Target Servers page to set which remote Exchange servers will receive messages through this Site Connector. Servers that do not get listed are excluded from communication with the local site.

1. Click the Target Servers tab of the Site Connector property pages (see Figure 17.4).

   The Site Servers list on the left side of the dialog box shows all the available servers at the remote site. The Target Servers list on the right side of the dialog box shows the Exchange servers at the remote site that communicate to the local site through this site connector.

2. Select a server from the Site Servers list and then click Add to make it a target server for this site connector.

   To remove a server from the Target Servers list, select it and then click Remove.

3. The Target Server Cost section displays the routing costs for the selected target server. In the text box, type the desired routing cost for each server and then click Set Value to store that value.

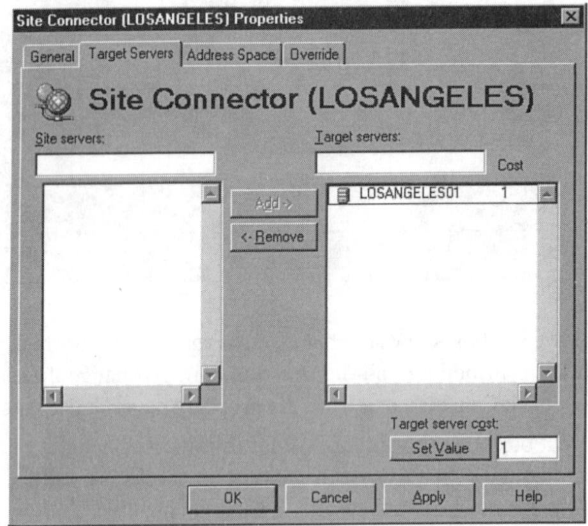

FIG. 17.4 Select the servers in the remote site to link through this Site Connector.

4. Click Apply to set these properties and continue setting other properties.
5. When you finish making settings, click OK to return to the Administrator program.

The Address Space Page The Address Space page is where you tell Exchange which messages are routed through this Site Connector. Without an appropriate entry, messages will not find their way to the remote site.

1. Click the Address Space tab of the Site Connector property pages (see Figure 17.5).
2. Click one of the New address types (General, X.400, MS Mail, Internet) to add an address space entry for this connector. Select an existing address space entry and click Edit to modify it or click Remove to delete it.
3. Click Apply to set these properties and continue setting other properties.
4. When you finish making settings, click OK to return to the Administrator program.

The Override Page If the site to which you want to connect is not within the same Windows NT domain (or within a trusted domain), you must specify logon information for this site connector. This property page allows you to enter such data. Use the following steps:

1. Click the Override tab of the Site Connector property pages (see Figure 17.6).

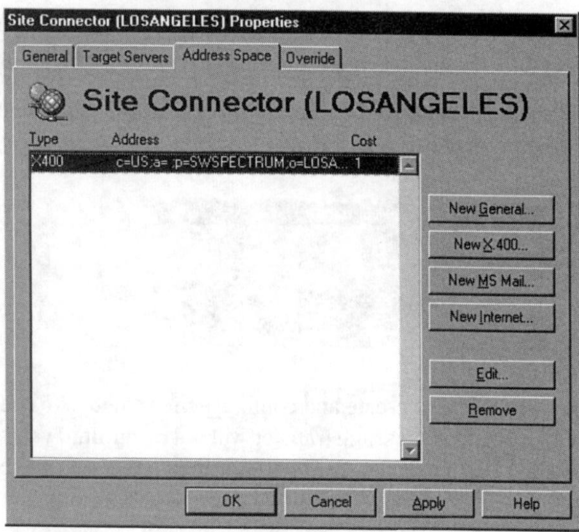

FIG. 17.5 Add or modify address-space entries to define message routing for this connector.

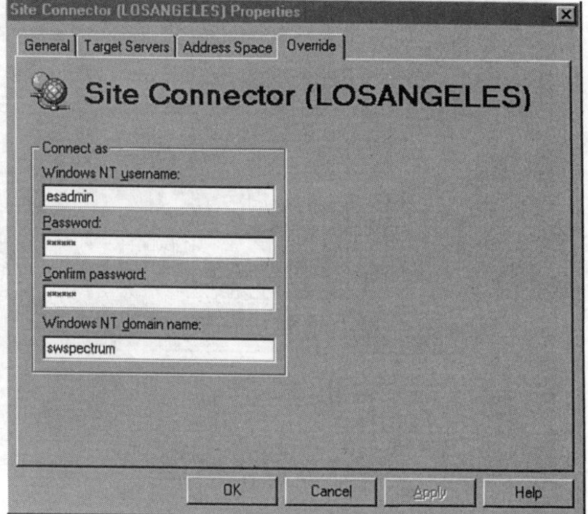

FIG. 17.6 Configure connector logon information to a remote Windows NT domain.

2. In the Windows NT Username box, type the name of the account that you want to use to log on.
3. In the Password box, type the password that is associated with that account.
4. In the Confirm Password box, type the password again.
5. In the Windows NT Domain Name box, type the domain in which the remote site resides.

6. Click Apply to set these properties and continue setting other properties.
7. When you finish making settings, click OK to return to the administrator program.

If a Site Connector is not set up in the remote site, the dialog box shown in Figure 17.7 appears. It prompts you to create one.

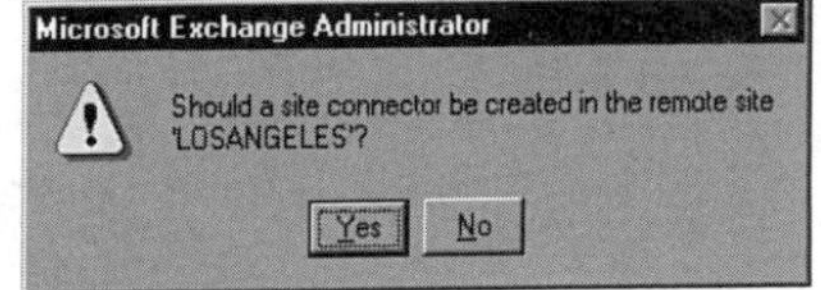

FIG. 17.7
Specify whether to create a corresponding site connector at the remote site.

Click No if you do not want to create and configure the remote site connector at this time. If you do click No, realize that message transfer will not occur until you set up that remote Site Connector at some later time. Click Yes to create and configure a site connector for the remote site at this time. The property page for the second site connector appears (see Figure 17.8).

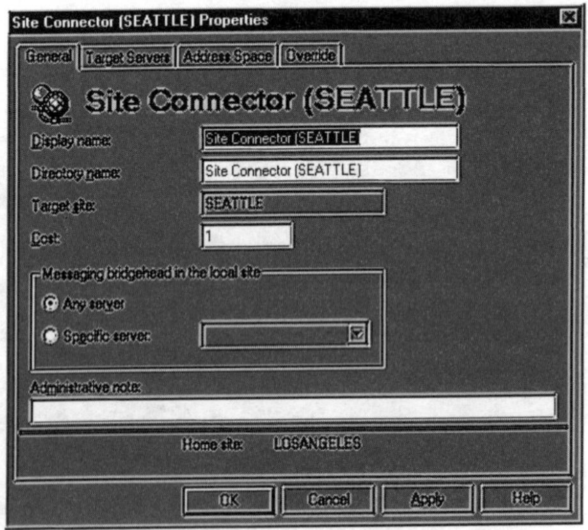

FIG. 17.8
General property page for the corresponding site connector at the remote site.

Configure this site connector following the procedure that you use to configure a local site connector. Keep in mind that the target servers now are Microsoft Exchange Servers that were the local servers in the previous connector configuration.

After you create and configure a site connector between two sites, the remote site appears in your Exchange Administrator program's hierarchy view. You can view all the Exchange objects at the remote site, but you cannot make any changes unless you log on directly to an Exchange server at that site. To share address lists with the connected site, for example, you must set up a directory replication connector to that site. See Chapter 18 for setting up directory replication between sites.

Deleting a Site Connector

If you want to remove a site connector that services message traffic between two sites, you first must determine what other services depend on the existence of that site connector. If other connections (such as a directory replication connector) rely on the site connector as the only link for message transport, you cannot delete that site connector; you first must delete any other dependent connections and then delete the site connector. If you do not want to delete the other connections, you must supply another link between sites that can service the other connections.

To delete a site connector, follow these steps:

1. Navigate through the Administrator Program's site display, and click the Connections object.
2. Select the Site Connector that you want to delete.
3. Pull down the Edit menu and choose Delete, or press the Delete key on the keyboard.

NOTE To disable all message transfers between sites, you must remove connectors from both the local and the remote sites. Log on to the remote Exchange server and then remove the site connectors, using the process described in this section. ■

Using the Dynamic Remote Access (RAS) Connector

The Microsoft Exchange Dynamic RAS Connector uses existing Windows NT Remote Access Services to facilitate temporary, low-bandwidth messaging links. The Dynamic RAS Connector establishes a temporary scheduled link to a remote Exchange server via a modem or any other RAS-compatible transport (for example, ISDN or X.25), transfers messaging data, and then disconnects. This section covers installing and configuring the Dynamic RAS Connector to link your messaging sites.

Before installing a Dynamic RAS Connector, you must do the following:

1. Install the Windows NT Remote Access service on the Exchange server that will be establishing the connection.
2. Configure the hardware required for the remote access link (for example, a modem or ISDN terminal adapter).
3. Enter a RAS phone-book entry for the remote Exchange server. Use your Windows NT documentation or online help to guide you through this process.
4. Know the name of the remote server with which you want to establish the link.

Installing a Dynamic RAS Connector involves these steps:

- Install the RAS MTA transport stack. Because the MTA will use a transport that is not supported directly through Microsoft Exchange server, you must define an external (Windows NT Remote Access Service) transport stack to use in message transfer.

- Install and configure the Dynamic RAS Connector itself. Follow the steps in the following sections.

Installing the RAS MTA Transport Stack

You add the RAS MTA Transport Stack from within the Administrator program. Follow these steps:

1. From the Administrator program, select New Other from the File menu, then select MTA Transport Stack from the submenu. The New MTA Transport Stack dialog box appears (see Figure 17.9).

   The Type section of the dialog box lists the available MTA transport stacks on this Exchange server.

NOTE Only the RAS MTA Transport Stack is used for the Dynamic RAS Connector.

The Server section of the dialog box lists all the servers at the current site.

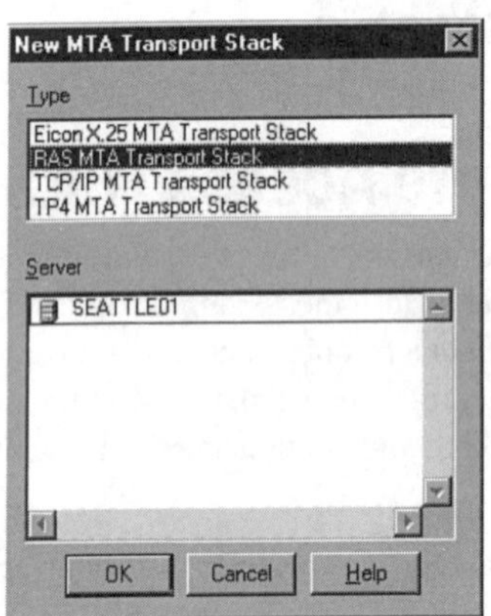

FIG. 17.9 The New MTA Transport Stack window is used by the Dynamic RAS Connector (and the X.400 connector) to select an underlying transport for message transfer.

2. Select RAS MTA Transport Stack from the list of available transports.
3. Select the server in your local site that will handle the remote-access connection. The transport stack will be installed on that server.
4. Click OK to accept the transport stack and Exchange server settings. The General page of a new Dynamic RAS Connector appears (see Figure 17.10).

   The MTA Transport Stack has only two property pages to configure: General and Connectors. Configuration usually is a one-time process unless you change the local MTA callback number. Refer to the Connector property page to view the Dynamic RAS Connectors that use this MTA Transport Stack.

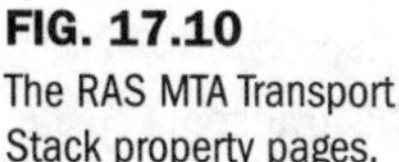

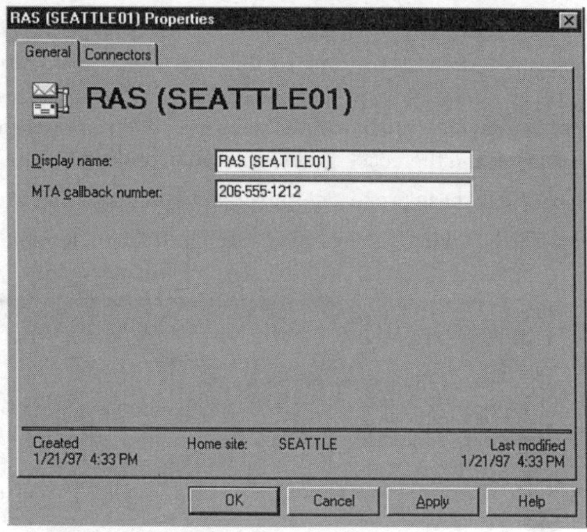

FIG. 17.10
The RAS MTA Transport Stack property pages.

Configuring MTA Transport Stack Property Pages

Settings in the MTA Transport Stack pages affect all Dynamic RAS Connectors that use it. The following section guides you through configuring the RAS Transport Stack. The process is similar to configuring MTA Transport Stack for X.25, TCP/IP, or TP4 connections as well.

The General Page The General page lets you configure a display name and callback number for this RAS MTA Transport Stack. Complete the following steps to alter the General page properties:

1. In the Name box, type the name under which you want this transport stack to appear in the Exchange Administrator object display window. You cannot modify this name after you create it. By default, the stack is named in the RAS format (*server name*).
2. In the MTA Callback Number box, enter the phone (or other device) number of the local Microsoft Exchange server.

NOTE The Windows NT Remote Access service uses a callback number as a means of authentication. The remote server receives a call, gets the callback number, hangs up, and dials the originator to establish a RAS link. It may be necessary to insert a prefix of an outside line number before the call back number when dialing out from a business phone at a company. ■

3. Click Apply to set these properties and continue setting other properties.
4. When you finish making settings, click OK to return to the Administrator program.

The Connectors Page The connectors page of the RAS Transport Stack Properties allow you to view and edit each connector that uses this Transport Stack.

1. Click the Connectors tab of the RAS MTA Transport Stack dialog box (see Figure 17.11).

   The Connectors page lists all the Dynamic RAS Connectors that use this transport stack. If you have set up the RAS MTA Transport Stack for the first time, the list is blank. After you set up at least one Dynamic RAS Connector, that connector is displayed in this page; you can select it and then click Edit to modify its properties.
2. Click Apply to set these properties and continue setting other properties.
3. When you finish making settings, click OK to return to the Administrator program.

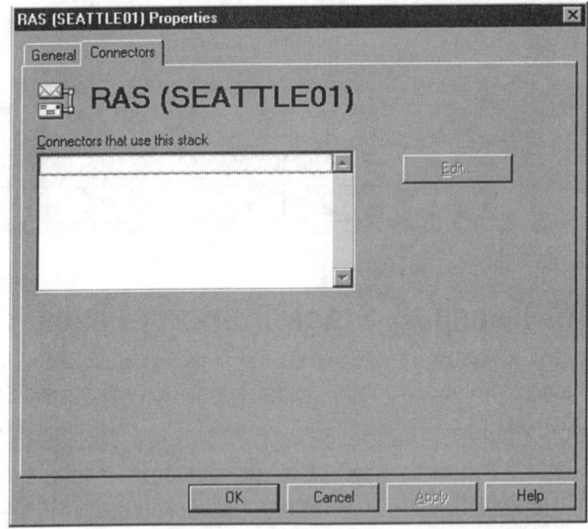

FIG. 17.11 The RAS MTA Transport Stack Connections page lists all current Dynamic RAS Connectors.

After setting up the Transport Stack you are ready to create a RAS Connector. Keep in mind that the Transport Stack is the communication layer for the RAS Connector, and is essential in its operation.

Creating a New Dynamic RAS Connector

You create a new Dynamic RAS Connector from the Microsoft Exchange Administrator program. If you have not yet installed the RAS MTA Transport Stack, you must do so before proceeding.

Installing a New Dynamic RAS Connector

Use the following steps to install a new Dynamic RAS Connector:

1. Drop down the Exchange Administrator File menu and choose New Other.
2. Choose Dynamic RAS Connector from the submenu. The pages for the new connector appear.

Configuring a New Dynamic RAS Connector

The following are the pages that you use to configure a Dynamic RAS Connector:

- *General*—Enables you to specify the name, remote server, MTA transport stack, maximum message size, and Windows NT RAS phonebook entry.
- *Schedule*—Enables you to set a connection schedule for this Dynamic RAS Connector.
- *RAS Override*—Enters alternative logon and RAS callback number information.
- *MTA Override*—Enables you to change the default MTA settings when you use this Dynamic RAS Connector.
- *Connected Sites*—Enables you to view, add, or modify addressing of the connected sites.
- *Address Space*—Enables you to define which messages pass through this connector.
- *Delivery Restrictions*—Enables you to specify which users can (and cannot) send messages to this Dynamic RAS Connector.

The General Page The General page lets you set the communication methods for this Dynamic RAS Connector. Part of this configuration will be to enter the telephone number data for the remote site, so have that information available when configuring the following options:

1. Click the General tab of the Dynamic RAS Connector property pages (see Figure 17.12).

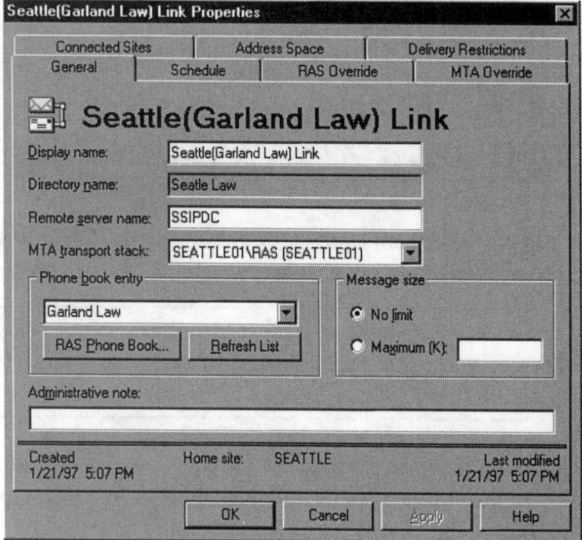

FIG. 17.12
Set general Dynamic RAS properties.

2. In the Display Name box, type the name that you want to appear in the Microsoft Exchange Administrator display window.
3. When you create a Dynamic RAS Connector, enter a name for it in the Directory Name box.

4. In the Remote Server Name box, type the name of the Microsoft Exchange server to which you are establishing a link.
5. From the MTA Transport Stack drop-down list, select the local Exchange server that will handle the remote access connection.
6. From the Dial Up Networking entry, select the entry that dials into the remote server.

   If you have not yet created an appropriate entry, complete the following:
   - Click Start at the bottom of your screen.
   - Open accessories and drag to Dial Up Networking (DUN).
   - Once you have highlighted the option of DUN, click the local Exchange server's Dial Up Network entries. In the example connector (see Figure 17.13), this brings up the Windows NT RAS entry in the Dial Up Network for GARLAND LAW.

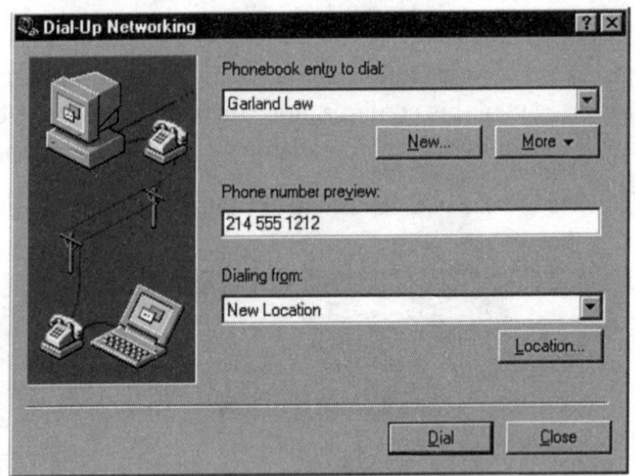

FIG. 17.13
The Windows NT remote access service Dial Up Network shows an entry set to dial into a remote Exchange server.

You can also create a phonebook entry by clicking the RAS Phone Book button, and selecting New from the Dial Up Networking window that appears.

Setting an upper limit for message sizes often is a good idea. Particularly with a low-bandwidth link (for example, a 28.8-Kbps modem), several large messages that have attachments could easily create a bottleneck through this connector.

7. If you want to set an upper limit for the size of messages that pass through this connector, click the Maximum (K) radio button, and in the text box, type the size limit (in kilobytes). A message that exceeds this maximum size will be returned as undeliverable. By default, the No Limit option is selected, and messages of any size can pass through the connector.
8. Make an entry in the Administrative Note box, if you want.
9. Click Apply to set these properties and continue setting with other properties.
10. When you finish making settings, click OK to return to the Administrator program.

The Schedule Page Use the Schedule page to control how often the Dynamic RAS Connector becomes active and initiates a connection. Follow these steps:

1. Click the Schedule tab of the Dynamic RAS Connector property pages (see Figure 17.14).

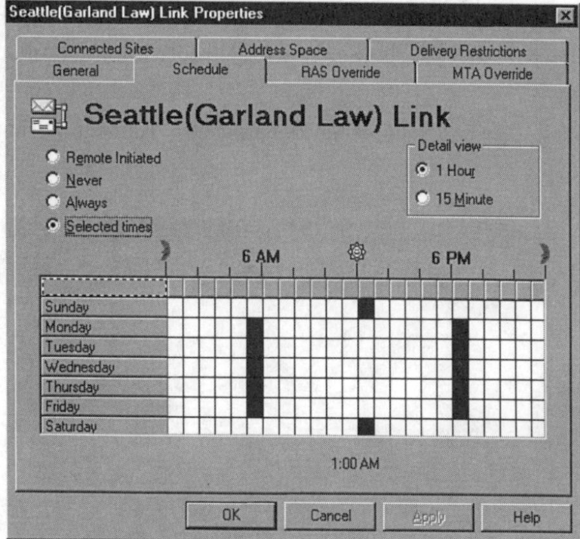

FIG. 17.14 Set connection times for this Dynamic RAS Connector.

2. Click one of the four options that determine when this Dynamic RAS Connector connects:

   - *Remote Initiated*—This option sends messages only when the remote MTA connects to this MTA. Both MTAs must have the two-way alternative option selected.

CAUTION

Only one MTA can be configured to be remote-initiated. Otherwise, if both MTAs are waiting for the other to initiate the connection, the messages will never be delivered.

   - *Never*—This option effectively disables this Dynamic RAS Connector.
   - *Always*—This option provides a remote access connection whenever messages need to be transferred. By default, this option is selected.
   - *Selected Times*—This option enables the Dynamic RAS Connector to initiate communication, based on the time grid.

3. If you chose Selected Times in step 2, the Detail View option buttons become available. Choose either 1 Hour or 15 Minute; the time grid changes its scale accordingly.

4. If you chose Selected Times in step 2, choose the time blocks that you want to use for the connection. In Figure 17.14, the Dynamic RAS Connector is set to initiate connections at 6 a.m. and 6 p.m. on weekdays, and at noon on weekends.
5. Click Apply to set these properties and continue setting other properties.
6. When you finish making settings, click OK to return to the Administrator program.

The RAS Override Page The RAS Override page is designed to supersede RAS settings for both logon information and callback numbers. The following steps guide you through these settings.

1. Click the RAS Override tab of the Dynamic RAS Connector property pages (see Figure 17.15).

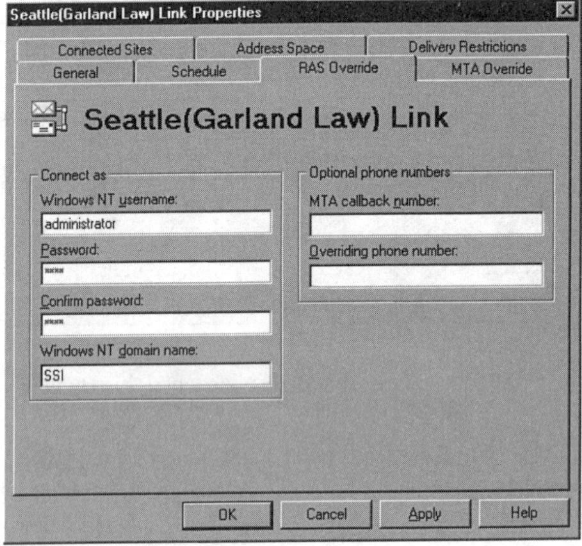

FIG. 17.15 RAS Override allows you to configure custom logon information from this page.

2. In the Windows NT Username box, type the name that you want to use to authenticate this Dynamic RAS Connector.
3. In the Password box, type the password.
4. In the Confirm Password box, type the password again.
5. In the Windows NT Domain Name box, type the name of the domain where the remote server resides.
6. In the Optional Phone Numbers section, type a phone number in the MTA Callback Number box.
7. Enter a different phone number in the Overriding Phone Number box.
8. Click Apply to set these properties and continue setting other properties.
9. When you finish making settings, click OK to return to the Administrator program.

The MTA Override Page Because of the typically low-bandwidth links associated with a remote access connection, it often is a good idea to set a different MTA configuration specifically for messages transmitted through this Dynamic RAS Connector. You set the MTA default configuration through the Site MTA property pages. Any setting in the MTA Override property page supersedes default MTA settings when the Dynamic RAS Connector negotiates a connection (see Figure 17.16).

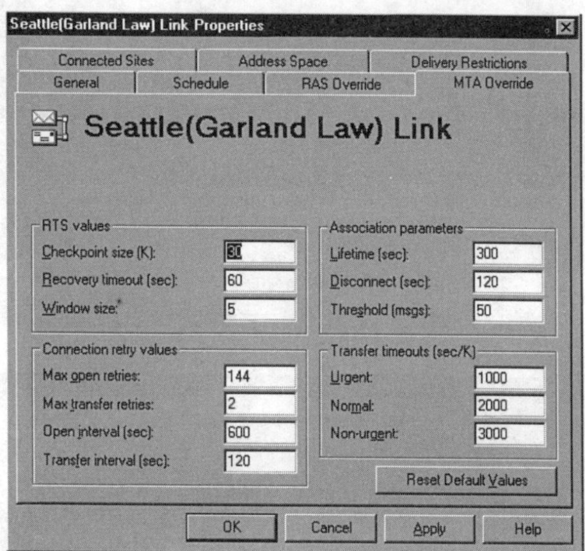

FIG. 17.16
Set specific override properties for the Message Transfer Agent.

The Connected Sites Page This property page lets you view which sites are linked via the current RAS Connector. Figure 17.17 shows a Connected Sites property page listing linked sites (blank if none).

Sites listed in the Connected Sites page can receive messages from the local site via the current connector. If a site is not listed it may be available to view other links established via other connectors.

The Address Space Page The Address Space page (see Figure 17.18) defines which recipients can be reached through this connector. Only enough addressing data is provided to distinguish messages that should be sent through this connector.

Routing costs are entered along with each Address Space entry.

The Delivery Restrictions Page The Delivery Restrictions page specifies which users can and cannot send messages through this connector.

- Accept Messages From. Creates an exclusive list of recipients who have permission to send messages through this Dynamic RAS Connector.
- Reject Messages From. Lists specific recipients who are denied permission to send messages through this Dynamic RAS connector.

FIG. 17.17 View directly and indirectly connected Exchange sites.

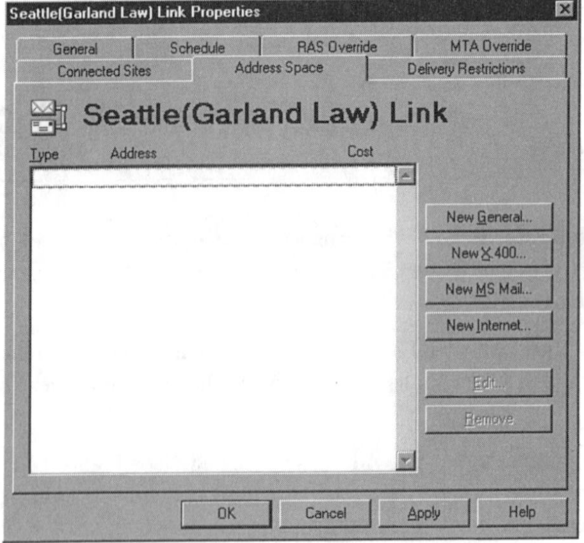

FIG. 17.18 Identify routes to this connector by using Address Space entries.

To set delivery restrictions, follow these steps:

1. Click the Delivery Restrictions tab of the Dynamic RAS Connector property pages (see Figure 17.19).
2. In the Accept Messages From or Reject Messages From section, click the List option button.
3. Click the Modify button below each list to display the Microsoft Exchange address list.

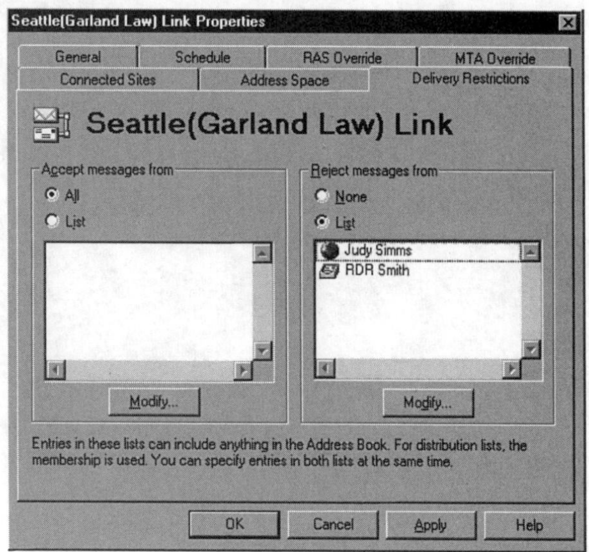

FIG. 17.19 Delivery restrictions allow you to specify who can access the Dynamic RAS Connector.

4. Select the desired senders to include or exclude as per the above lists and then click OK.
5. Click Apply to set these properties and continue setting other properties.
6. When you finish making settings, click OK to return to the Administrator program.

CHAPTER 18

Using Directory Replication and Synchronization

In this chapter

This chapter assumes you have a basic understanding of Exchange's directory architecture; Exchange Server is installed and running on at least two sites; and that the external system is functional (you can send and receive messages).

Just for a quick review, each Exchange Server retains a copy of the organization's directory. This directory is an X.500-based directory of Exchange objects including addresses, mailboxes, public folders, distribution lists, and configuration information about sites. Directory replication is the process by which Exchange Servers insure that they have a current copy of the stored directory information. This process occurs between servers in an Exchange site, as well as between servers in different sites throughout your organization. The following sections describe the steps you will use to set up replication between your Exchange servers.

Directory Replication Within a Site

Directory replication within an Exchange Server site is automatic. The replication function is handled by the directory service and is always in operation while that service is running. This process requires no maintenance other than making certain that the servers in a site can exchange standard messaging information.

Mean time between replication requests is approximately five minutes, depending on when you made your last change. When a change has been made to the directory, the directory service waits five minutes from the last change before sending a notification, so that changes can be replicated in batches.

The following is an example of how a directory change propagates through an Exchange site:

- An administrator creates a new mailbox recipient, Ron Elliott, on the server SEATTLE01.
- Upon creation of the user, the new directory object is a legitimate candidate for directory replication.
- Within five minutes, users on Exchange Server SEATTLE02 (a server at the same site as SEATTLE01) can address Ron Elliott as a recipient, and see his name in the Global Address List.

  Directory replication within a site is automatic. If you do not want Ron Elliott's name to appear in the Global Address List (GAL), you must make the mailbox hidden. This does not stop the object from replicating. The hidden mailbox will replicate to the other server to maintain an updated directory information store.

Directory Replication Between Sites

Replicating directory information between two Exchange sites is the second logical step in maintaining a cohesive directory structure within your organization. This section covers replication between the following:

- Exchange sites on the same network (LAN)
- Exchange sites on different networks

Using the Directory Replication Connector

The principal tool used to set up directory replication is the directory replication connector. The replication connector does not transfer directory information to other sites; it only defines a logical path for the directory replication topology. One of the intersite connectors is required between sites to transfer mail messages unless two sites are connected via another site. A directory replication connector could be established between sites that are not directly connected, therefore, as long as they are connected indirectly. As the administrator, you need only provide the site names and the names of the appropriate bridgehead servers to establish a replication connector.

Setting up replication between two Exchange sites involves four steps:

1. Ensure that messages can be transferred between sites.
2. Create a directory replication connector for both sites.
3. Identify the bridgehead server at each site that is responsible for transferring directory updates.
4. Establish a replication schedule to determine how often directory updates will traverse a site link.

The following sections provide details about configuration for specific situations; however, the general steps for setting up directory replication are the same for all types of networks.

Using Directory Replication Between Sites on the Same Network

This section describes the procedure for using directory replication between two Exchange sites physically connected on the same local area network. Typically, this means high-bandwidth links between groups of servers in close geographical proximity. In the real world, this can be two distinct corporate divisions in the same building. Whatever the case, your Exchange servers will be able to communicate with each other over your standard network connections and will not require the use of any additional transport mechanism.

The following is a list of requirements to meet before setting up replication between sites on the same network:

- The messaging link between both servers is fully functional (sending and receiving messages). Usually, you use a site connector to establish such a link between sites on the same network.
- You have administrator permissions on each server with which you will be establishing a directory-replication relationship.

To set up directory replication between sites on the same network, follow these steps:

1. Open a New Directory Replication Connector from the Administrator program's File menu under New Other. The New Directory Replication Connector dialog box appears (see Figure 18.1).
2. From the Remote Site Name drop-down list, select the site to which you want to connect.

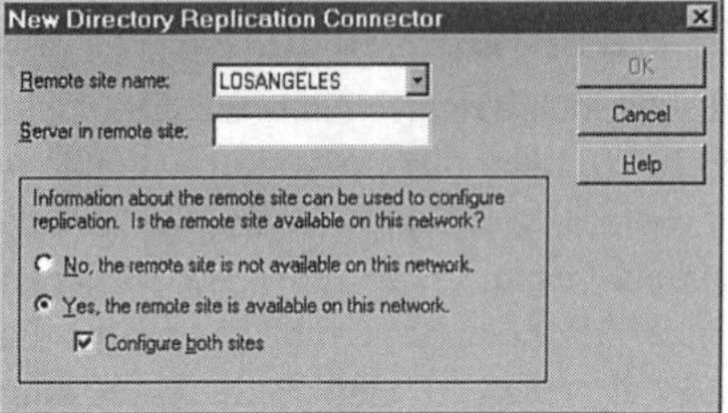

FIG. 18.1 Use this dialog box to set New Directory Replication Connector options.

3. In the Server in Remote Site dialog box, type the name of the remote server.
4. Click the radio button labeled Yes, the Remote Site Is Available on This Network.

You almost always choose this option when both sites are on the same LAN because the option saves you time and reduces configuration errors. Only external situations, such as administrative security restriction within a company, might require separate configuration of such directory replication connectors. For example, an Administrator on one site may not be given sufficient administrative privileges of the remote site to establish a connection alone.

5. Click the Configure Both Sites check box. This option automatically creates and configures a corresponding directory connector at the remote site.
6. Click OK to proceed to the Directory Replication Connector property pages.

NOTE Because both servers are on the same LAN, Exchange can locate the site and communicate with the remote server via remote procedure calls. You need to specify only the remote site's name in the New Site Connector dialog box.

To facilitate the interchange of directory data between sites, you must designate replication bridgehead servers. These servers process directory update requests from other bridgehead servers and also generate their own requests for updates. A one-to-one relationship must exist between bridgehead servers for sites that exchange directory information.

Following are a few example situations:

Example 1: You want to establish directory replication between the sites GARLAND and SEATTLE. GARLAND01 and SEATTLE01 are the selected bridgehead servers. These servers will be the only replication point for Exchange directory information between the Garland and Seattle sites. You make no allowances for the use of multiple directory replication connectors to balance server load, link traffic, and so on.

In directory replication, you must designate a local bridgehead server and a remote bridgehead server when you set up a directory replication connector. Local and remote are relative terms. When you configure a directory replication connector between sites, the General page of each connector shows different information for each end of the connection.

The GARLAND Directory Replication Connector's General page displays the following information:

Local bridgehead server GARLAND01

Remote bridgehead server SEATTLE01

The SEATTLE Directory Replication Connector's General page displays the following information:

Local bridgehead server SEATTLE01

Remote bridgehead server GARLAND01

Example 2: This example discusses the use of multiple directory replication connectors in a site. In this case, GARLAND is the site that has multiple connectors. The Seattle bridgehead server (SEATTLE01) replicates directory information with the bridgehead server GARLAND01 (see Figure 18.2).

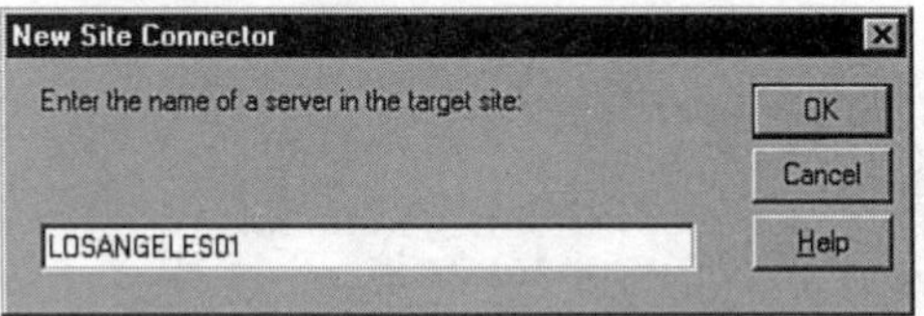

FIG. 18.2 Directory replication across multiple bridgehead servers.

Simultaneously, the LOSANGELES site replicates information to the GARLAND site. LOSANGELES01 is the bridgehead server for the LOSANGELES site. LOSANGELES01 links to a second bridgehead server at the GARLAND site: GARLAND02.

A smaller organization could manage by setting up multiple directory replication connectors on one server. This procedure is not generally recommended but is an option for sites that have few users, infrequent directory updates, or a limited number of servers. In this case, both SEATTLE01 and LOSANGELES01 can be bridgehead servers linked to GARLAND01 (see Figure 18.3).

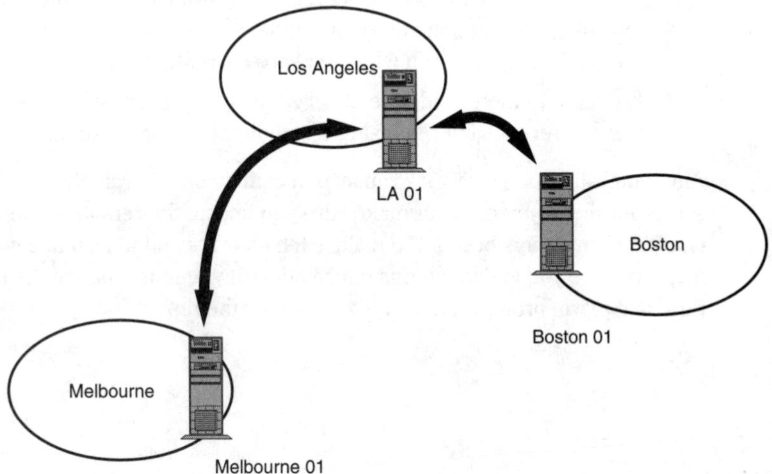

FIG. 18.3 Setting up multiple directory replication connectors.

In the preceding examples, directory information between the SEATTLE and LOSANGELES sites is synchronized automatically by the sites' common link, GARLAND. When three sites are joined with a connector and directory replication is configured between them, connections between the two distant sites (Los Angeles and Seattle) becomes transitive. Therefore, a directory replication connector is not required between the Los Angeles site and the Seattle site since changes made in either Exchange site will be replicated via the Garland site. Microsoft Exchange will not enable you to create a directory replication connector between sites when the connection is already transitive.

You set up bridgehead servers in the Exchange Administrator program. To designate bridgehead servers, follow these steps:

1. Click the General tab of the Directory Replication Connector Properties page (see Figure 18.4).

FIG. 18.4
The General page of the Directory Replication Connector Properties page.

2. From the Local Bridgehead Server drop-down list, select the local server that will handle incoming and outgoing directory update requests. The default selection is the name of the Exchange server on which you are currently logged in.
3. From the Remote Bridgehead Server drop-down list, select the server at the remote site that will receive and request updated directory information.

After you establish a directory replication connector, you can change the local bridgehead server for that connector, but make sure you update the remote connector to reflect the change. Usually, it is best not to make such changes and to plan in advance for a situation that might require you to change this information. If you must change the local bridgehead server, this change will prompt Exchange to reinitiate the replication cycle.

Setting Up Directory Replication Between Sites on Different Networks

Sites located on different logical LANs can share directory information almost as easily as sites on the same LAN. You cannot use a site connector to link bridgehead servers; however, you must configure a custom connector to that site.

The following conditions must exist before you set up directory replication between sites on different LANs:

- The messaging link between both servers is fully functional (sending and receiving messages). This link can be set up with any available connector (Site, X.400, or Internet) that supports message transfer between sites.
- You know the e-mail address of the remote site bridgehead server's directory. The Exchange directory replication connector needs this address so that it knows where to direct replication messages. You must enter this information manually.

To set up directory replication between sites on different networks, follow these steps:

1. Open a New Directory Replication Connector from the Administrator program's File menu under New Other. The New Directory Replication Connector dialog box appears.
2. Click the radio button labeled No, the Remote Site Is Not Available on This Network. This will highlight the two input boxes below it.
3. In the Remote Site Name box, type the name of the remote site with which you are establishing replication.
4. In the Server in Remote Site, type the name of the remote bridgehead server.
5. Click OK to proceed to the Directory Replication Connector property pages.

The following sections define the contents of the property pages for the directory replication connector required when connecting sites on different networks.

The Addressing Page When you configure replication between two sites that are not on the same network, you must supply the e-mail address of the bridgehead's server directory. Follow these steps:

1. Click the Addressing tab of the Directory Replication Connector Properties page. The Addressing dialog box appears.
2. In a new connector, you see a blank address space for the remote bridgehead server's directory.
3. Click the Modify button. The New Entry dialog box appears.
4. Select the address type you want to create. This type should be identical to the type of connector used to transmit normal messaging data between sites. GARLAND and

SEATTLE, for example, are linked via a private X.400 link, so the address selection in the New Entry box should be X.400.

5. The next dialog box will be different depending on what address type you selected in the preceding step.

The Schedule Page Directory updates transmitted between bridgehead servers are executed according to an administrator-defined schedule. You need to evaluate the following elements before you decide on an appropriate replication schedule:

- Expected replication traffic
- Network bandwidth between sites
- Server load on bridgehead servers
- Any scheduling constraints created by the type of messaging link

The first three items are related. If replication traffic is heavy between the two sites (if directory objects are frequently added, deleted, or modified, for example), this will affect available bandwidth. Sometimes you must have a frequent replication schedule to maintain an accurate global address list.

Scheduling constraints arise due to the type of site link used. This is especially the case when using part-time connections.

The site link between GARLAND and GARLAND LAW, for example, is established by a Dynamic RAS Connection. Three times a day, a modem connection to the GARLAND01 site is established; the connection is maintained for 30 minutes and then closed. You must configure the directory replication connector to transmit data when the network connection is up; otherwise, the connector may attempt to transfer directory updates through a nonexistent link.

To configure the replication schedule, follow these steps:

1. Click the Schedule tab of the Directory Replication Connector Properties page (see Figure 18.5).

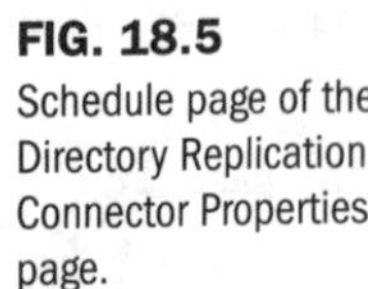

FIG. 18.5
Schedule page of the Directory Replication Connector Properties page.

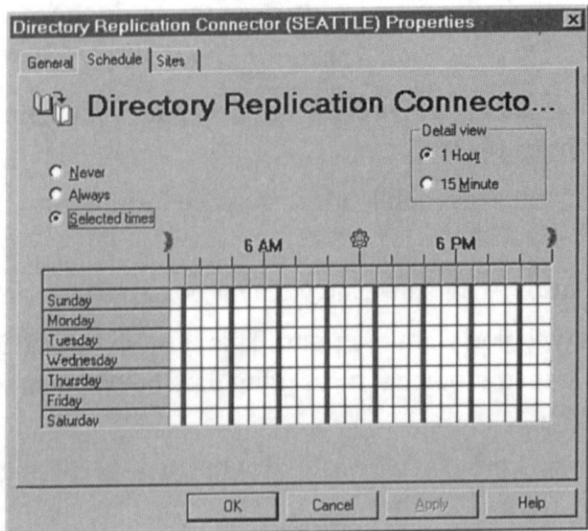

2. Click one of the three radio buttons in the top-left corner of the dialog box:

   Never disables directory replication.

   Always updates the replication schedule every 15 minutes.

   Selected Times enables you to specify the replication schedule manually.
3. If you chose Selected Times in step 2, click one of the Detail View radio buttons (1 Hour or 15 Minute) to view the time grid in different increments.
4. Select the block(s) of time during which you want replication to occur by clicking the schedule grid.
5. If you are done configuring all other pages for this connector, click OK. Otherwise, click another tab to continue making adjustments.

Following are two general recommendations on scheduling replication time:

- For international replication links, be sure to take into account the various time zones in which your site will operate. Off-peak hours for a server in London, for example, could fall in the middle of a high message-volume time in Chicago.
- For sites that have a large number of frequent directory updates, you should opt for frequent replication, keeping in mind that increased message traffic affects network performance.

Viewing a Site's Directory Data

After you configure both directory replication connectors and establish directory replication between two sites, you can view all sites with which you are exchanging directory data. This is the case because the local site receives directory updates from the immediately connected remote site, as well as from every other remote site with which that site is replicating data.

To view inbound and outbound sites, click the Sites tab of the Directory Replication Connector dialog box. Inbound sites are those from which the local site receives directory updates. Outbound sites are those to which directory updates are sent.

Earlier we created, as an example, a directory replication connector from SEATTLE to GARLAND, from FRANKFURT to GARLAND, and TOYKO to GARLAND. After the first successful replication request, you see the site names displayed in the Sites page on the GARLAND replication connector to SEATTLE, as shown in Figure 18.6.

SEATTLE is displayed in the Inbound Sites list. The Outbound Sites list displays FRANKFURT, GARLAND, and TOKYO, since directory changes made in SEATTLE will be sent to those sites.

You also can use the Sites page to request directory updates from selected inbound sites. You might need to request a directory update in the following situations:

- Your replication schedule is set to occur nightly, but you are aware that many changes were made at a specific site (perhaps a new Exchange server was created with several new users), and you need to update the system immediately.

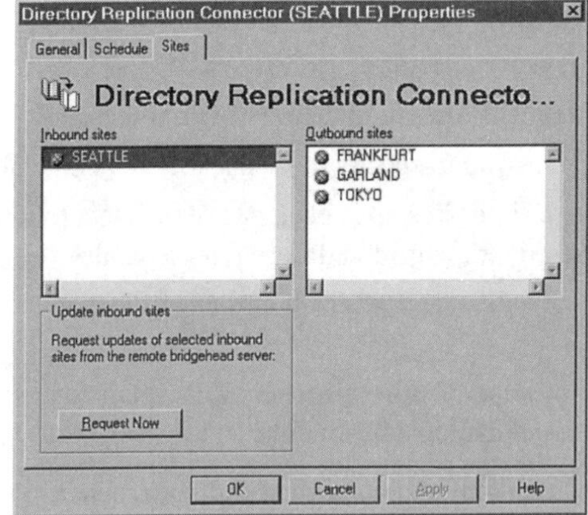

FIG. 18.6 The Directory Replication Connector Sites Properties page shows which sites are sharing directory information.

- A remote server was down during its scheduled replication time, and you need to force replication to maintain an accurate address list.

To request a directory update, follow these steps:

1. Click the Sites tab of the Directory Replication Connector dialog box.
2. Select the site from which you want to request directory updates. (You can select multiple sites by Shift+clicking them.)
3. Click Request Now.

Understanding Directory Synchronization

Directory synchronization is the process by which an Exchange server shares address information with foreign messaging systems. Dirsync in Exchange is based on the Microsoft Mail directory synchronization protocol, which is widely supported by many messaging systems.

This section covers the setup and configuration of dirsync between Exchange and Microsoft Mail, as well as between Exchange and foreign systems that support the Microsoft Mail dirsync protocol.

Before you begin, you must verify the following information about your Exchange setup:

- All services that are required to run the Administrator program are up and running.
- A functional messaging link exists between your site and the systems with which you want to establish dirsync. A link is usually established by the Microsoft Mail connector or by another specialized connector or gateway.

Following is a brief review of how directory synchronization works and of the tools that you use to set up dirsync in Exchange.

The Microsoft Mail dirsync protocol has two principal elements:

- Directory Synchronization Requestor is an agent that sends directory updates to and receives updates from a directory synchronization server.
- Directory Synchronization Server is an agent that collects local address updates from requestors, compiles the updates into a master list, and sends the resulting modifications back to the requestors.

Exchange Server includes one principal component—the Directory Synchronization Agent (DXA)—that operates directory synchronization. The Exchange DXA can act as either a dirsync server or requestor. In standard Microsoft Mail dirsync, the dirsync server maintains a server address list. Exchange uses the Global Address List to replace the server address list.

NOTE When Exchange receives external addresses that are imported during synchronization, the addresses are stored in the directory as custom recipients. ■

Setting Up the Directory Synchronization Requestor

Generally, there is just one directory synchronization server that receives directory updates from multiple requestors. Because directory replication maintains the Microsoft Mail addresses for all users in the Exchange organization, only one directory synchronization requestor is required for the entire Exchange organization.

Follow these steps to create a connection to Microsoft Mail:

1. In the Administration Window, select a site in your organization.
2. Click the connections icon. Your list of current connection objects appears.
3. Double-click Microsoft Mail Connector in the Interchange page and select Administrator's MailBox.
4. Click the Connection tab.
5. On the right side of the window, there is a Create button. Click this button to create a connection to your Microsoft Mail PO.
6. Fill in Organization, Postoffice, and full UNC to Maildata. Make sure before you do this that the Maildata directory has been shared.

Follow these steps to create an Exchange requestor:

1. In the Administrator window, select a site in your organization.
2. Click the Connections icon. Your list of current connection objects appears.
3. Choose File, New Other, Directory Exchange Requestor. The New Requestor dialog box appears (see Figure 18.7).
4. From the list of post offices defined in the Microsoft Mail connector, choose the dirsync server that you will use. If you are setting up a requestor for a non-Microsoft Mail

system, select <Non Microsoft Mail Dirsync Server> (this procedure will be detailed in the section "Requestor Configuration").

5. Click OK. The Properties page for your new requestor appears.

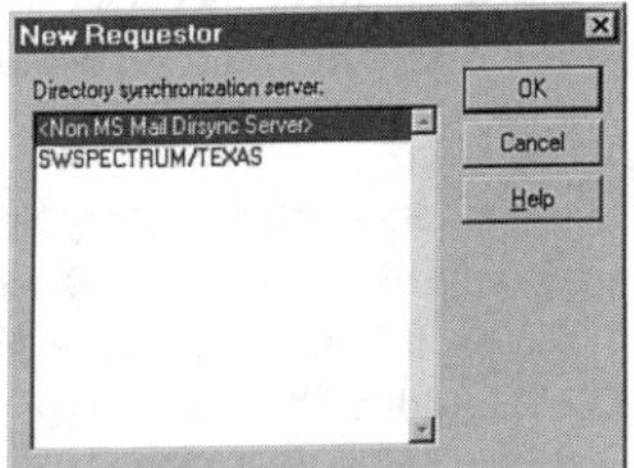

FIG. 18.7 This is the new Directory Exchange Requestor dialog box.

Now you must set up properties in each of the available pages, as described in the following sections.

The General Page The General page enables you to name and configure the basic dirsync requestor properties. Follow these steps to configure the location from which to request directory updates and select the address types supported by this requestor:

1. Type the name of the requestor. You have 255 characters to give this requestor a name that should also identify the Exchange server site (see Figure 18.8). Check the Append to imported Users' Display Name box to add the requestor name to each custom recipient that is created in the DXA process.

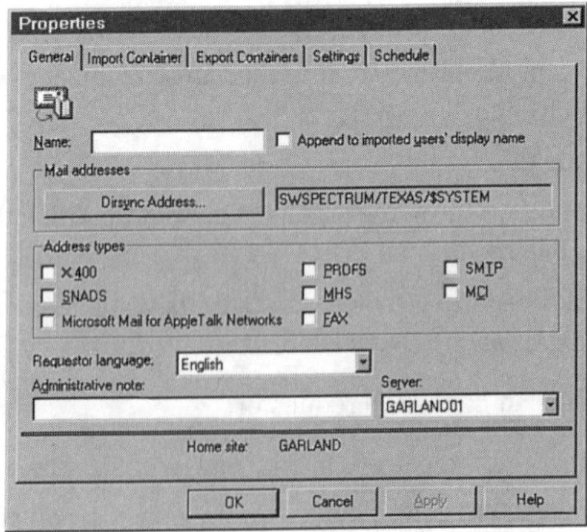

FIG. 18.8 The Dirsync Requestor General Properties page lets you set the basic options for a dirsync requestor.

2. Click the Dirsync Address button to bring up the Exchange address list. From that list select the custom recipient that pertains to your dirsync server.

NOTE The $SYSTEM Microsoft Mail account should already be in the Dirsync Address field if the directory synchronization server is a Microsoft Mail Post Office. If the directory synchronization server is not a Microsoft Mail Post Office, you must first create a Custom Recipient for the dirsync server with which this requestor will be exchanging dirsync messages. That custom recipient can be any Microsoft Mail or compatible directory synchronization server in your organization. See Chapter 15, "Information Store Configuration," for information about creating custom recipients. ■

3. In the Address Types section, check all the types that you want this requestor to obtain from the dirsync server. By default, Microsoft Mail addresses are sent and received. If you choose an address type that the server cannot provide, the Microsoft Mail default format (proxy) address is extracted instead.
4. The Requestor Language pull-down menu enables you to select the default address language template. Use the pull-down menu to choose a language template.
5. In the Administrative Note box, type any comments (up to 1,024 characters) that you feel are pertinent to this situation. The note is visible only in this page.
6. The Server pull-down menu enables you to change the server at the local site that will handle this directory synchronization requestor. The default selection is the current server. Choose an Exchange server from the pull-down menu. A single Exchange server can be either a dirsync server or requestor, but not both. Also, only one requestor can be set up per Exchange server.
7. Click Apply to set these properties and continue setting other properties.
8. When you finish making settings, click OK to return to the Administrator program.

The Import Container Page An import container is the recipient container that receives imported information from a dirsync server. This page enables you to assign trust levels to the imported directory objects.

Because trust levels are exclusive to Exchange Server, any imported recipients will not have trust levels assigned by the foreign system. The import container setting gives that object a trust level that Exchange uses to determine synchronization security. As in any other case of trust level use, only objects that have a trust level equal to or lower to the trust level of the next site are synchronized.

Suppose that you are using Exchange servers GARLAND01 and GARLAND02 as requestors to two Microsoft Mail network dirsync servers and that you do not want the Microsoft Mail networks to share recipient information. You set each requestor to import to a different recipient container in the GARLAND site, each with different trust levels. When synchronization occurs, each list of recipients is imported into its own container (with its own trust level). The information is not mixed and is not synchronized to the other Microsoft Mail server because of the trust level settings.

The following steps describe how to configure the Import Container page:

1. Click the Import Container tab of dirsync requestor property pages (see Figure 18.9).

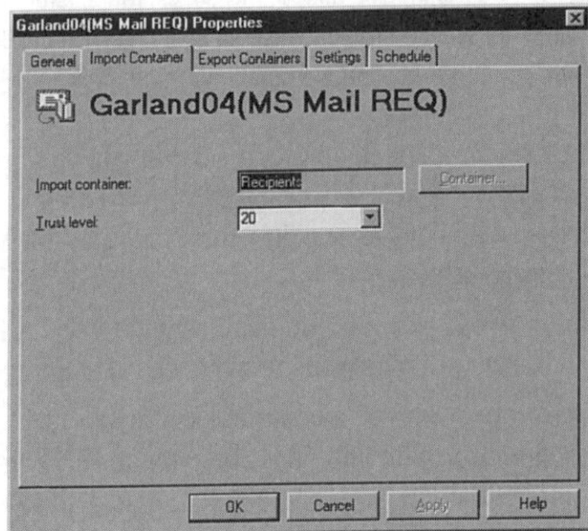

FIG. 18.9 The Import Container page.

2. The Import Container page shows the current selected recipient. (The page is blank for a new setup.)
3. Click the Container button to display all container recipients. The Import Container Properties page appears (see Figure 18.10).
4. Select the recipient container in which you want all the custom recipients to be imported.
5. Click OK to return to the Import Container page.
6. Enter a number in the Trust Level box. The default is 20.
7. Click Apply to set these properties and continue setting other properties.
8. When you finish making settings, click OK to return to the Administrator program.

CAUTION

After you choose a directory import container, you are stuck with it. The only way to alter where directory information is stored is to delete the requestor and set up a new one.

The Export Containers Page An export container holds the directory data that an Exchange requestor sends out during synchronization. By default, a requestor does not send out any containers. If you need to export directory information via a requestor, follow this procedure:

1. Click the Export Containers tab of the dirsync requestor's Properties page (see Figure 18.11).
2. To start exporting from a container, select it in the Recipient Containers list and then click Add.

   To remove an exported container, select it in the Export These Recipients list and then click Remove.

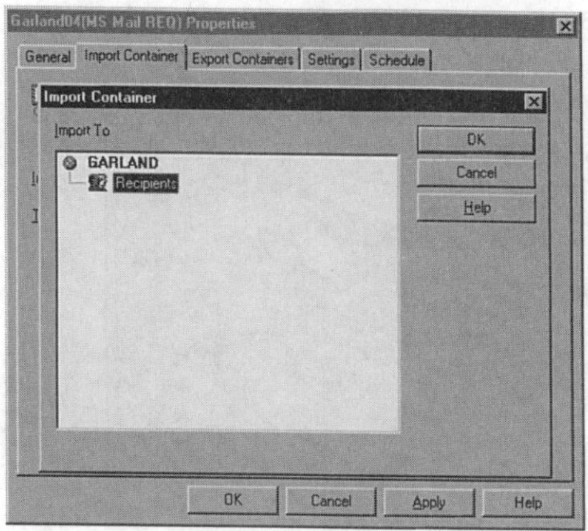

FIG. 18.10
Specify where you want incoming recipients to be stored.

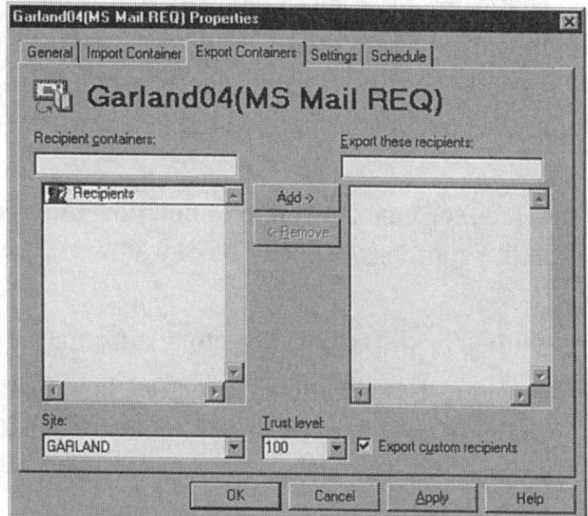

FIG. 18.11
The Export Containers page.

3. Use the Site pull-down menu to view recipient containers from other sites and select those for export (optional).
4. In the Trust Level box, set a general trust level for this export function. Individual objects within the selected container(s) are exported only if their trust level settings are equal to or less than the settings in this box.
5. If you do not want to include custom Exchange recipients in the export procedure, click the Export Custom Recipients check box to clear it.
6. Click Apply to set these properties and continue setting other properties.
7. When you finish making settings, click OK to return to the Administrator program.

The Settings Page The Settings page enables you to set advanced properties for a directory-synchronization connector.

To configure the Settings page, follow these steps:

1. Click the Settings tab of the Directory Exchange Requestor Properties page (see Figure 18.12).

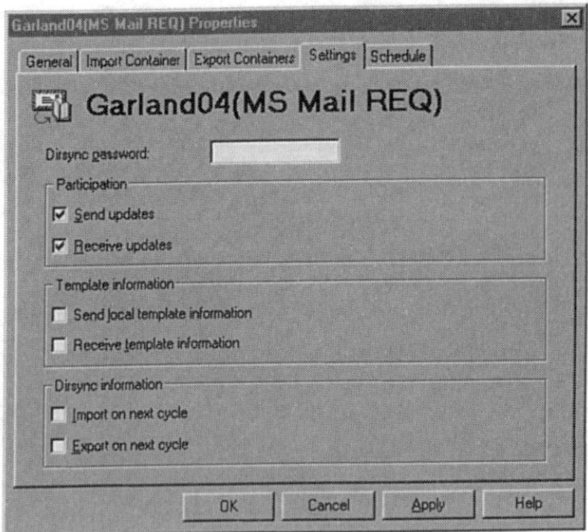

FIG. 18.12
The Settings page.

2. The Dirsync Password box enables you to give this requestor a password to use when it sends directory updates to a dirsync server. Enter a password if one is needed to access the desired dirsync server. The password is selected when you set up the dirsync server on the remote system. If a password is not needed to access the dirsync server, leave this space blank.
3. The Participation check boxes enables you to define how this requestor is involved in synchronization. Click the appropriate check box for how you want this requestor to function:

   Send Updates—The requestor will export directory information to a dirsync server.

   Receive Updates—The requestor will import directory information from a dirsync server. By default both boxes are checked. If neither is checked, the requestor will not operate.
4. Choose one of the following Template Information options (optional):

   Send Local Template Information exports address templates to the dirsync server.

   Receive Template Information imports address templates from the dirsync server.
5. Choose one of the following Dirsync Information options, which forces the connector to import or export (or both) all appropriate information to the dirsync sever:

   Import on Next Cycle requests every entry of the selected address type at the next dirsync sequence.

   Export on Next Cycle sends addresses from the specified export containers to the dirsync server.
6. Click Apply to set these properties and continue setting other properties.
7. When you finish making settings, click OK to return to the Administrator program.

The Schedule Page The Schedule page enables you to set the time when update messages are transmitted to the directory synchronization server.

NOTE The verification messages or updates from the dirsync server are handled automatically. ■

To set the requestor's schedule, follow these steps:

1. Click the Schedule tab of the dirsync requestor's Properties page (see Figure 18.13).

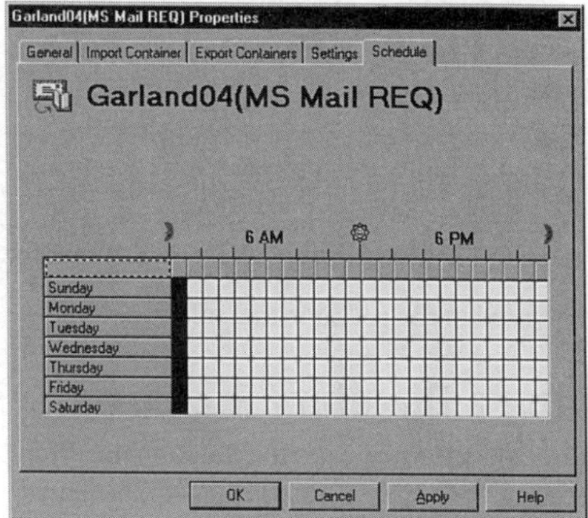

FIG. 18.13
The Schedule page.

2. In the grid, click the boxes to select the time when you want directory update messages to be exchanged with the dirsync server. Update messages are sent at the beginning of the selected time. By default (if you don't select a specific time), dirsync messages are automatically scheduled for transmission at midnight.
3. Click Apply to set these properties and continue setting other properties.
4. When you finish making settings, click OK to return to the Administrator program.

So far, this chapter has covered all the available options for configuring a Directory Exchange Requestor. You must now configure the Microsoft Mail dirsync server to accept your new Exchange requestor. There are two primary settings to configure:

- *Password.* You must configure the Microsoft Mail Directory Exchange server to recognize your new Exchange requestor. If you selected a password in the Settings page, remember to include it in your configuration. Your Microsoft Mail for PC documentation will guide you through this process.
- *E-mail address.* When you configure your Microsoft Mail dirsync server to recognize your new Exchange requestor, you need the Microsoft Mail network and post office e-mail address of the local site. The local site's Site Addressing property pages contain this information.

Using Exchange as a Directory-synchronization Server

Another way to integrate Exchange into directory synchronization with Microsoft Mail-compatible networks is to set up a directory synchronization server (also called a dirsync server) on Exchange. Then you can use standard Microsoft Mail requestors on remote machines to participate in directory synchronization.

Following are the general steps for setting up Exchange as a dirsync server:

1. In the Administrator program, create a directory synchronization server for the local Exchange server site. Configure its properties.

NOTE Although you can have multiple Exchange dirsync servers in your organization, you can have only one for each Exchange site. ■

2. In the directory, define a remote directory exchange requestor object that corresponds to each requestor that will link to this server.
3. Configure each requestor on other systems that will use this server.

Each of the steps will be covered in the sections that follow.

Creating and Configuring a Directory Exchange Server

When you create a new directory exchange server, it automatically gets an e-mail address based on the Microsoft Mail address type for the local site. Because you can have only one directory exchange server per site, no addressing conflicts can exist.

To create a new directory exchange server in the Administrator program, choose File, New Other, Dirsync Server. If you have already set up another directory synchronization server in this site, the new Dirsync Server option is not available.

To configure an existing server from the Administrator program, follow these steps:

1. Click the Connections icon under the desired Exchange site.
2. From the list of connections icons, click the icon of your current dirsync server. By default, the name for this object is *DXA server*.
3. Choose File, Properties to open the dirsync server property pages.

The following sections cover configuration of the dirsync server's property pages.

The General Page The general property page enables the administrator to name the DXA, select a DXA administrator account, view synchronization messages, and select the Exchange Server that will run the Exchange directory synchronization service.

To set general properties, follow this procedure:

1. Click the General tab of the dirsync server's Properties page (see Figure 18.14).
2. In the Name box, type a unique name for this dirsync server. (You can use only 64 characters.)
3. Select a dirsync administrator that will receive dirsync status and error messages and click the Dirsync Administrator button (optional). The Exchange address List dialog box appears. Type or select a name (a user, public folder, or distribution list) and click OK. You return to the General page.
4. To send a copy of each outgoing update to the administrator, click the Copy Administrator on Outgoing Messages check box.

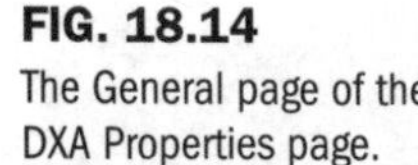

FIG. 18.14
The General page of the DXA Properties page.

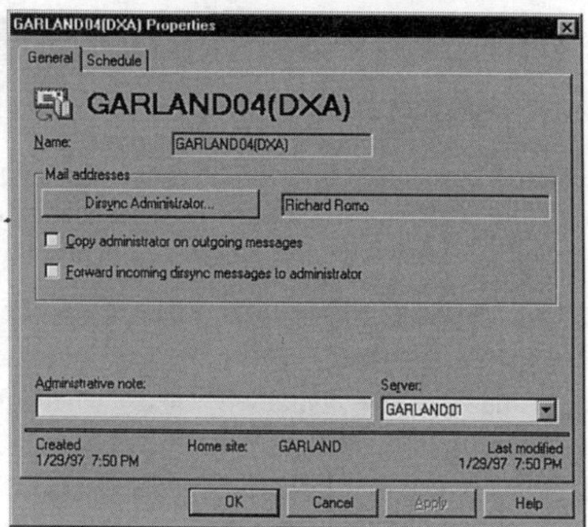

5. To view each incoming update message from each requestor, click the Forward Incoming Dirsync Messages to Administrator check box.

NOTE By default, neither Copy Administrator on Outgoing Messages nor Forward Incoming Dirsync Messages to Administrator is selected. Typically, you would choose these options only for troubleshooting purposes. ■

6. If you want, enter comments (up to 1,024 characters) in the Administrative Note box. The comments will be visible only in this page.
7. Use the Server pull-down menu to select the Exchange server computer that will host the directory synchronization process. By default, the current Exchange server is selected.
8. Click Apply to set these properties and continue setting other properties.
9. When you finish making settings, click OK to return to the Administrator program.

The Schedule Page The Schedule page defines when the directory synchronization server sends updates to its requestors. Server updates are independent of the schedule under which the requestors send their updates to the server. Directory updates are sent to requestors at the beginning of the scheduled hour.

To set the schedule, follow these steps:

1. Click the Schedule tab in the dirsync server property pages.
2. In the time grid, select the times when you want this dirsync server to send update messages to its requestors.
3. Click Apply to set these properties and continue setting other properties.
4. When you finish making settings, click OK to return to the Administrator program.

Defining Remote Directory Synchronization Requestors

Just as you do with a standard Microsoft Mail directory synchronization server, you must identify and define each remote requestor that will be communicating updates to the local Exchange dirsync server. Setting up each remote requestor involves two steps:

1. Define a remote dirsync requestor object in the Exchange Server Administrator program.
2. Establish the permissions that these containers will use when importing and exporting addressing data.

These two steps make your Exchange directory synchronization server aware of its requestors. Review the following section to verify that a remote requestor is properly configured and able to communicate with the local Exchange dirsync server.

Creating a Remote Directory Synchronization Requestor

To create a new remote dirsync requestor, follow these steps:

1. In the Administrator program, choose File, New Other, Remote Dirsync Requestor. The property pages for a new remote dirsync requestor appear.

NOTE The New Remote Dirsync Requestor command is unavailable until you set up an Exchange directory synchronization server. ■

Configuring a Remote Directory Synchronization Requestor

The following sections describe the pages that you configure for a remote dirsync requestor.

The General Page The general property page enables the administrator to name the DXA, select the directory synchronization address and password on the foreign system, and export all Exchange addresses to the foreign system.

To set general properties, follow these steps:

1. Click the General tab of the Remote Dirsync Requestor Properties page.
2. Type a display name (up to 255 characters) for this remote dirsync requestor. This name is displayed as the directory exchange server object name in the Administrator program.
3. Check the Append to Created Users' Display Name check box to add the name of this requestor to each recipient created when synchronizing addresses with this requestor. This is useful for keeping track of a recipient's origin.
4. Click the Dirsync Address button to bring up the Exchange address list. From that list select the custom recipient that pertains to the remote dirsync requestor.

NOTE You must first create a custom recipient for each remote dirsync requestor to provide address information about the requestor. ■

5. Enter a password in the password box if your Exchange dirsync server requests one during synchronization. By default, this box is blank. If you do use a password for security, remember to set the same password on the remote Microsoft Mail requestor to avoid authentication errors.
6. The Request Address Type box specifies the format in which address updates are set. MS (the default) is used by Microsoft Mail (PC) and other compatible directory exchange requestors. Select MSA if you are synchronizing directories with a Microsoft Mail for AppleTalk network.
7. The Requestor Language pull-down menu enables you to change the default language template.
8. Click the Export On Next Cycle check box to send all address information to the remote requestor during the next synchronization session. By default, this option is not selected. Keep in mind that all directory information is exported automatically when you first configure a remote requestor.
9. If you want, enter comments (up to 1,024 characters) in the Administrative Note box. These comments will be visible only in this page.
10. Click Apply to set these properties and continue setting other properties.
11. When you finish making settings, click OK to return to the Administrator program.

The Import Container Page Much as you do in setting up directory exchange requestors, you use import containers to assign trust levels to objects that are being imported.

Because trust levels are exclusive to Exchange Server, any imported recipients will not have trust levels assigned by the foreign system. The import container gives that object a trust level that you set in the Import Container page. As in any other case of trust level use, only objects that have a trust level equal to or lower than the next site's trust level are replicated. The following steps cover Import Container page configuration:

1. Click the Import Container tab of the Remote Dirsync Requestor Properties page (see Figure 18.15).

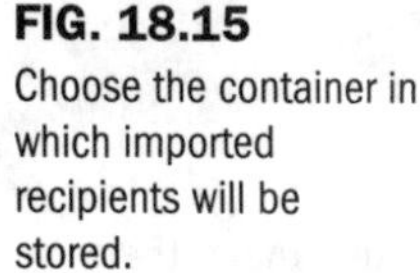

FIG. 18.15
Choose the container in which imported recipients will be stored.

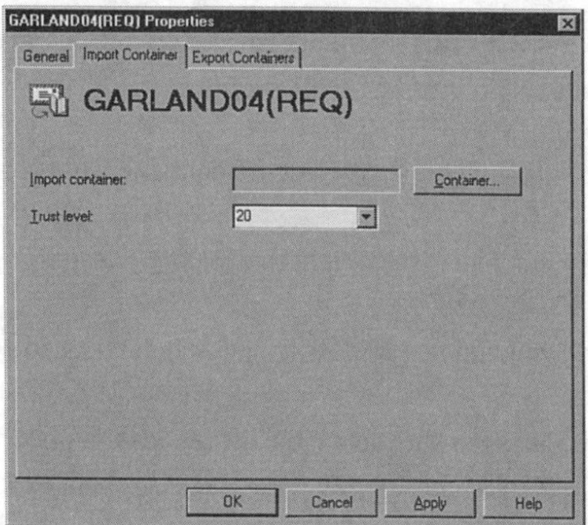

2. The Import Container box shows the name of the recipient container that stores the imported addresses. By default, this box is blank. Click the Container button to select a recipient container. All current recipient containers appear in a dialog box. Select one container to hold directory imports and click OK to return to the Import Container page.
3. In the Trust Level box, assign a trust level to the import container (the default setting is 20). Remember that only objects that have a trust level equal to or lower than the setting in this box will be updated during synchronization.
4. Click Apply to set these properties and continue setting other properties.
5. When you finish making settings, click OK to return to the Administrator program.

NOTE You cannot modify import containers after you create them. If you must change where information is placed, you must delete the existing container and create a new one.

The Export Containers Page The Export Containers page specifies what information is sent out to the remote requestor during directory synchronization. By default, no information from the local site is exported. To configure data export, follow these steps:

1. Click the Export Containers tab in the Remote Dirsync Requestor Properties page (see Figure 18.16).

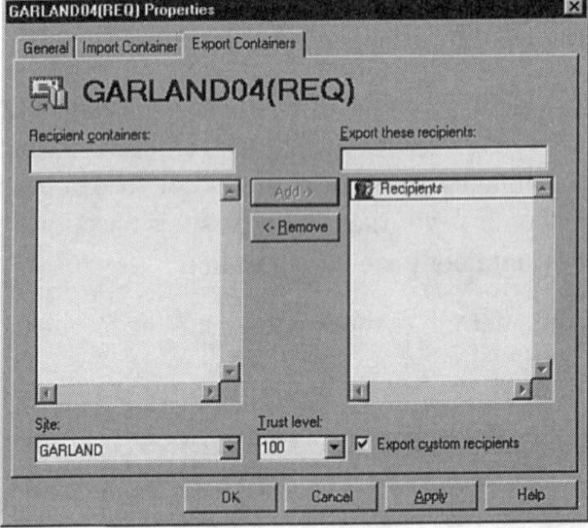

FIG. 18.16
The Export Containers page.

2. In the Export These Recipients list, select the container that you want to export, then click Add.

   To stop exporting a container, select it in the Export These Recipients list, then click Remove.
3. Use the Site pull-down menu to view other sites' containers, to which you can export recipients.
4. In the Trust Level box, set a trust level to limit replication of certain objects in the containers that you selected to export.

5. Click the Export Custom Recipients check box to include those recipients in synchronization. By default, this option is selected.
6. Click Apply to set these properties and continue setting other properties.
7. When you finish making settings, click OK to return to the Administrator program.

Configuring Remote Requestors

The final step in establishing directory synchronization between an Exchange directory synchronization server and remote requestors is configuring the remote requestors on Microsoft Mail or compatible systems.

The following sections provide general recommendations on configuring directory synchronization requestors on the following types of remote systems:

- Microsoft Mail for PC networks
- Microsoft Mail for AppleTalk networks
- Other foreign mail systems

Directory Synchronization Requestor for Microsoft Mail for PC Networks The requestor that you are most likely to set up is one for a Microsoft Mail for PC network. Standard Microsoft Mail requestor programs connect to Exchange directory synchronization servers through the Microsoft Mail connector as though the requestor were of the standard Microsoft Mail type. You need to configure the requestor from within your Microsoft Mail Administrator program. Consult your Microsoft documentation for the procedure.

You can test the operation of a Microsoft Mail connection by entering the address of your recipient manually in the *to* line of the Exchange client.

Before you configure the requestor, make sure that you have met all of the following conditions:

- Exchange and the Microsoft Mail connector are properly configured and running.
- The Exchange directory synchronization server is installed and running.
- Microsoft Mail for PC Networks is set up and running correctly on its own.
- If your Exchange server and the Microsoft Mail post office are not on the same logical network, the Microsoft Mail external or multitasking MTA program must be set up and running correctly.

Directory Synchronization Requestor for Microsoft Mail for AppleTalk Networks This section is dedicated to a discussion on address list sharing between Exchange and a Microsoft Mail for AppleTalk network. These solutions, though functional, are a poor substitute for the direct use of a Macintosh Exchange client. Primarily, these solutions will be used as a stopgap in preparation for an eventual complete migration to Exchange. Existing Microsoft Mail AppleTalk servers can act as requestors to standard Microsoft Mail (PC) dirsync servers. By pointing the Macintosh dirsync requestor to an Exchange dirsync server, your Mac servers can begin sharing address lists with your Exchange organization.

The Exchange Client for MAC 5.0 can act as a direct client to Exchange Server 5.0. Strategies are now different for the migration of MAC clients. It is important, however, to understand how Exchange and Microsoft Mail for AppleTalk networks behave and are configured. Microsoft will continue to support the Macintosh Gateway by loading it onto the client CD that is MAC friendly.

The first part of this section covers the set up of a Directory Exchange Requestor in a Microsoft Mail for AppleTalk network.

The directory synchronization requestor for Microsoft Mail AppleTalk is installed with the Exchange connection gateway.

Before you configure the Microsoft Mail AppleTalk requestor, confirm the following situations:

- Exchange and the Microsoft Mail connector are properly configured and running.
- Microsoft Mail AppleTalk (MSA) is selected in the appropriate Exchange Remote Dirsync Requestor property pages. This setting is found in the General page of this dirsync requestor.

CAUTION

If you do not set the requestor to receive messages in MSA format, duplicate entries are created in the Microsoft Mail AppleTalk address list.

- The Exchange Connection gateway software is properly configured and running on the Microsoft Mail AppleTalk server.

If you have met all the preceding conditions, you are ready to continue setting up the directory synchronization requestor. If you have been looking at a Windows screen layout all day, the following steps could be a nice change of pace.

Requestor Configuration

When you set up directory synchronization, you need to configure three principal requestor options. You must log in as the network manager on your Microsoft Mail AppleTalk server to make all configuration and administrative functions available. The following sections describe how to make these settings:

- Install General Requestor settings
- Identify the appropriate gateway
- Request the correct address types

General Requestor Settings Complete the following steps to configure the Macintosh Microsoft Mail Server directory requestor to exchange addresses with Exchange:

1. Open the Exchange Connection folder on the Macintosh Microsoft Mail server.
2. Click the Exchange Connection Directory Exchange Requestor icon.

3. The first time you open a new requestor, a dialog box appears. Type your network manager password and click OK.
4. The first time you set up a requestor, a configure dialog box appears. Subsequently, you must select Application from the Configure menu.
5. The Send Directory at box enables you to enter the time when directory updates were sent to the Exchange dirsync server. Use the 24-hour format hh:mm. By default, this time is set to 4 a.m.
6. The Receive Updates at box enables you to enter the time when the requestor scans the Network Manager's inbox for directory updates.
7. In the Exchange Network box, enter the network name of the Microsoft Mail connector.
8. In the Exchange PO box, enter the post office name of the Microsoft Mail connector. This information is available on the Exchange Microsoft Mail connector's Local Postoffice property page.
9. Use the Exchange Password box if you have also set a password in the corresponding Exchange server remote dirsync requestor object. By default, this box is blank.
10. DXA Mailbox specifies the Exchange server mailbox to which the requestor will send update messages. By default, this is $SYSTEM. Normally you do not want to change this setting.
11. The Network Manager box defines the Microsoft Mail AppleTalk account to receive address list updates from the Exchange dirsync server. By default, this mailbox is Network Manager. The Password field is for the account specified in the Network Manager box.
12. Requestor Name refers to the corresponding remote directory exchange requestor as set in the Exchange server directory.
13. The Fault Tolerance check box enables tracking of address updates. Synchronization numbers are created and used to recover addresses when an error occurs. This will avoid having to do manual directory import and export. By default, this is checked.
14. Include Server In Friendly Name sets all Microsoft Mail AppleTalk addresses to display as user@servername. By default, this is checked.
15. The Export World List check box when not checked will cease all updates being sent to the Exchange dirsync server. By default this is checked.
16. Click OK to save new settings and close the Configure dialog box. Click revert to keep previous settings.

If you are configuring this requestor for the first time, the Gateway dialog box appears.

NOTE If this is not your first time configuring this requestor, then choose Select Gateway from the Configure menu. ■

In this dialog box, you must select a gateway. This is the passage through which messaging data will reach the Exchange server. By default, this is the connection gateway. Choose your preferred gateway and then click the Select button.

Address Filters Address filters enable you to specify the address types that you want to receive from the Exchange server.

To configure address filtering, follow these steps:

1. Open the Address filtering dialog box. If you just proceeded from the gateway dialog box, this is already open.
2. Check each address type you want to request from the Exchange dirsync server.
3. Click OK to save your settings and move on, or click Revert to return to the previous settings.

Starting and Stopping the Requestor

Complete the following steps to start and stop the directory requestor on the Macintosh Microsoft Mail Server:

1. Open the Exchange Connection folder in Macintosh Finder.
2. Double-click the Microsoft Mail AppleTalk directory exchange requestor icon to start it. The requestor starts, and a status dialog box appears.

NOTE The status display refreshes when the system receives directory update messages. ■

If the requestor is not given the network manager name and password, or if you are not currently logged in as a Network Manager, then the request will run as a foreground application, locking the desktop and preventing you from running other applications. If you have given the password or are logged in as the Network Manager, however, then the application runs in the background.

To stop the requestor, choose File, Quit.

It is convenient to make the Macintosh dirsync requestor a startup item so you do not need to manually launch the application every time you restart the system. To make the requestor a startup item, follow these steps:

1. Make an alias of the directory exchange requestor. Do this by highlighting the requestor icon, then choose File, Make Alias.
2. Move the alias to the Startup Items folder inside the Macintosh System Folder.

Microsoft Mail AppleTalk Requestor

As network manager, you may want to execute a few maintenance tasks as part of administrating Exchange directory synchronization from the Microsoft Mail AppleTalk end. Those tasks are importing a complete list of addresses, exporting a complete local address list, and re-synchronizing that information.

To import a complete list of known addresses, follow these steps:

1. Start the Exchange Connection Directory Exchange Requestor by double-clicking its icon in the Macintosh Finder.
2. Choose File, Import Directory. The Import Directory dialog box appears.
3. Choose Changes Since Last Update Only to immediately request the addresses that have changed since the last directory synchronization cycle.

   Alternatively, click the Complete Directory radio button and then click OK to import all available addresses of the selected type.
4. Click OK to finalize your settings.

NOTE To verify that imports have proceeded correctly, you need to start Microsoft Mail AppleTalk manually and choose Mail, Gateway Recipient. A dialog box appears that lists the new recipients. All requested information should be available in this list after you receive an import confirmation message from the dirsync server. ■

Exporting Directory Information to Exchange Server

The previous section described how to get Microsoft Mail AppleTalk to receive addresses from Exchange. The following section describes how to update the Exchange address list with changes made on the Microsoft Mail AppleTalk server. You will do this by telling the Exchange Connection software to export its contents to the Exchange dirsync server. The following steps describe the steps necessary to accomplish this:

1. Start the Exchange Connection Directory Exchange requestor by double-clicking its icon in the Macintosh Finder.
2. Choose File, Export Directory.
3. Choose Changes Since Last Update Only to immediately request the addresses that have changed since the last directory synchronization cycle.

   Alternatively, click the Complete Directory radio button to import all available addresses of the selected type.
4. Click OK to commence directory export.

After the Exchange server processes these update requests, it sends a confirmation message and a status report to the network manager's mailbox.

Another option is to export the local Microsoft Mail AppleTalk addresses into a text-file format that the Microsoft Mail (PC) import utility can read. Use this alternative when other methods are not operational.

To export the addresses (also called the word list) manually, follow these steps:

1. Start the Exchange Connection Directory Exchange Requestor by double-clicking its icon in the Macintosh Finder.

2. Choose Save to File from the File menu. A dialog box appears asking you for a location in which to save your exported information.
3. Select the folder in which you want to save your file.
4. In the Dump Work List Into box, type a file name. A unique identifiable name is recommended (perhaps including the date of the export for future reference).
5. Click OK to complete the export.

You can open the exported file with any text editor. All your addresses should be in that file, displayed in the following format:

A 30_character_alias MSMAIL:address

Microsoft Mail is the address type of this entry.

Microsoft Mail AppleTalk or Exchange Server Addresses

Sometimes you need to remove all Microsoft Mail for AppleTalk recipients from the Exchange address list, and vice versa. This situation occurs when Microsoft Mail AppleTalk users become full-fledged Exchange clients.

To remove Microsoft Mail AppleTalk recipients from the Exchange server address list, follow this procedure:

1. Start the Exchange Connection Directory Exchange Requestor by double-clicking its icon in the Macintosh Finder.
2. Choose Remove Mac Names from Exchange from the File menu. A confirmation dialog box appears to verify that you actually want to do this.
3. Click OK. Every Microsoft Mail AppleTalk and gateway recipient is removed from the Exchange global address list.

NOTE If you suddenly realize that you really need the addresses, you must import them to restore the entries. Subsequent directory synchronization cycles do not replace deleted entries. ■

Removing Exchange Recipients from the Microsoft Mail AppleTalk Local Address List

Follow this procedure to delete Exchange recipients from Microsoft Mail AppleTalk:

1. Start the Exchange Connection Directory Exchange Requestor by double-clicking its icon in the Macintosh Finder.
2. Choose Remove Exchange Names from Mac from the File menu. A confirmation dialog box appears to verify that you actually want to do this.

3. Click OK. Every Exchange recipient in the local directory is deleted from the Microsoft Mail AppleTalk word list.

Re-synchronizing Address Information

As directory synchronization occurs, updates are exchanged, and the network manager receives periodic messages confirming that the process is operational and that changes have been incorporated.

Sometimes this process does not operate smoothly. In such cases, the requestor gives you the option of forcing re-synchronization of the entire system manually.

If you believe that your system is out of sync, follow these steps:

1. Log in as network manager.
2. Start the Exchange connection directory exchange requestor by double-clicking its icon in the Macintosh Finder.
3. Choose Resync Cycle from the File menu. The Directory Exchange Requestor proceeds to restart its synchronization cycle.

The requestor receives the global address list from the Exchange server and resets the send/receive cycle.

If you get a message stating that the directory synchronization cycle is out of phase, you should initiate a complete directory refresh (import and export) between both systems. As described in the preceding sections, you should import the Exchange global address list and export the local address list to the Exchange dirsync server.

The Microsoft Mail AppleTalk directory exchange requestor keeps a log of all its activities. This log is a text file stored inside the Preferences folder (in the System folder). Any standard text editor displays this file.

NOTE This file logs all directory Exchange requestor activities, so the file could be very large if it is heavily used. Make sure that you delete or clear the file on a periodic basis. Confirming that synchronization is functional before you delete any log entries is a good idea. ■

Configuring Foreign Directory Exchange Requestors

Any foreign system that conforms to the Microsoft Mail 3.x directory synchronization protocol can connect to an Exchange dirsync server. You probably need to consult your appropriate documentation for the process, but here are some general recommendations to follow before you configure synchronization with foreign systems:

- Make sure that all Exchange server operations are working correctly.
- Install and configure the correct gateway for Exchange communication with the foreign system.

- Properly configure the Exchange directory synchronization server and the appropriate remote requestor.
- Install whatever gateway the foreign mail system requires to communicate with Exchange.
- Test to see whether standard messages can be transferred between systems. Because directories are not in sync, you must enter the addresses manually.

Configuring Microsoft Directory Exchange Agent (DXA) Settings

The DXA is the Exchange component that actually runs the dirsync server and requestor. By default, the DXA is configured to enable both server and requestor processes to run. You can modify general settings for the DXA, as described in the following sections. The DXA is configured through an object named Directory Synchronization on each Exchange server in your site.

See Chapter 12, "Using the Administrator Program," for more information on configuring all directory services on Exchange.

Choosing a Server to Carry Out the DXA Functions

The Directory Synchronization General page enables you to choose the server that carries out the DXA functions. Any server at the site is eligible, but always take into consideration other functions that a server is performing. To choose a server, follow these steps:

1. In the Administrator program, select a site in your organization.
2. Click the Servers icon to list the Exchange servers in this site.
3. Select the Exchange server that you want to configure.
4. Select the Directory Synchronization object.
5. Click the General tab in the Microsoft Directory Synchronization object.
6. Type any additional comments you may want to add in the Administrator Note box.
7. Click Apply to set these properties and continue setting other properties.
8. When you finish making settings, click OK to return to the Administrator program.

Modifying DXA Addresses

The e-mail addresses are used to send and receive synchronization update messages. You will need the E-mail Addresses Properties page to create, modify, or delete these addresses. By default, Exchange server automatically generates Microsoft Mail (PC), X.400, and SMTP addresses for each DXA. Several services, such as dirsync requestors and servers, use these addresses for communication with the DXA.

To create or modify Microsoft DXA addresses, follow these steps:

1. Click the E-Mail Addresses tab.
2. To change an existing address, select it and then click Edit. The dialog box for its particular address type appears.
3. To create a new address for this DXA, click New. Select what type of e-mail address you want to add, then type in all necessary addressing information. Click OK to return to the E-Mail Addresses page.
4. To delete an existing address, select it, click Remove, and click OK to confirm the deletion.
5. Click Apply to set these properties and continue setting other properties.
6. When you finish making settings, click OK to return to the Administrator program.

CAUTION

Many other Exchange services use these addresses. If you plan to change or delete them without appropriate consideration of such services, directory synchronization will fail.

Setting Delivery Restrictions

This page is useful because it prevents messages that are unrelated to directory synchronization from being sent to the DXA. You also can set up delivery restrictions to allow messages to be sent only by specified senders. In the Delivery Restriction page, you select specific addresses from which the DXA will reject or allow messages. By default, the DXA accepts messages from all senders. Such an open door could cause errors and delays in proper directory synchronization.

To set delivery restrictions, follow these steps:

1. Click the Delivery Restrictions tab of the Microsoft DXA.

   The left side of the page lists the specific senders who have permission to send messages to the DXA. The right side lists senders who are not allowed to send messages to this DXA.

Entering specific accepted senders is the most fault-tolerant approach to this setup. Be aware, however, that if you set up a new requestor without modifying the page, all of that requestor's messages will be rejected.

2. To accept messages only from specific senders or to reject messages from specific senders (the settings are mutually exclusive), select List and click Modify. The Exchange Address Book appears.
3. Select the specific container from which you want to view recipients in the Show Names From The: Menu. The corresponding recipients are shown in the Type Name Or Select From List box.

4. Type **select** or a name from the list. If you can't see or remember the name you are looking for, you can use the Find button. The Properties button will display standard recipient properties for your selection.
5. Once you have selected a name or multiple names on the left, click Add.
6. Click OK to return to the Delivery Restrictions property page.
7. Click Apply to set these properties and continue setting other properties. If you are done with all settings, click OK to return to the Administrator program.

Mapping Templates to Exchange Server Attributes

Incoming Templates are Address templates that take incoming address information and map it for specified Exchange server directory recipient attributes.

An address imported through synchronization with a Microsoft Mail network, for example, could have the occupation and telephone attributes. For consistency, you would want to map the occupation tag to the Exchange Title attribute.

To map templates to Exchange server attributes, follow these steps:

1. Click the Incoming Templates tab of the Directory Synchronization Properties page (see Figure 18.17).
2. To modify an existing mapping, select it from the list and then click Edit. The Incoming Template Mapping dialog box appears.

   In the Map the String box, edit the template identifier string that Microsoft Mail uses. In the To the Attribute box, edit the recipient attribute in which you want to store the incoming information. When you finish, click OK to return to the Incoming Templates page.

NOTE All mapping strings must match the incoming strings.

3. To create a new mapping, click the New button. The Incoming Template Mapping dialog box appears. Type a string found in the incoming address information. Use the To The Attribute pull-down menu to select which Exchange attribute you want to associate with that string. Click OK to return to the Incoming Templates page.
4. To delete an existing mapping, select it and then click Remove.
5. Click Apply to set these properties and continue setting other properties.
6. When you finish making settings, click OK to return to the Administrator program.

Mapping Exchange Server Attributes to a Microsoft Mail Template

Outgoing template mappings are the inverse of the preceding function. You can map Exchange server directory recipient attributes to outgoing Microsoft Mail-compatible template information.

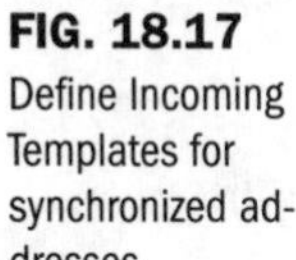

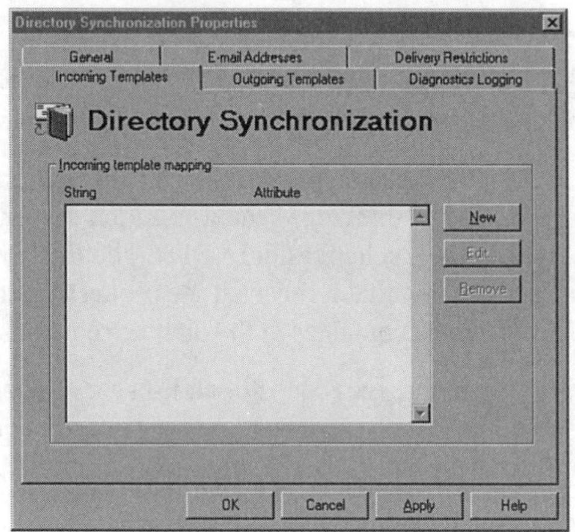

FIG. 18.17 Define Incoming Templates for synchronized addresses.

To map Exchange server attributes to a Microsoft Mail template, follow these steps:

1. Click the Outgoing Templates tab of the Directory Synchronization Properties page (see Figure 18.18).
2. To modify an existing mapping, select it in the list and then click Edit. The Outgoing Template Mapping dialog box appears. In the Map the Attribute box, edit the recipient attribute that you want to map to the Microsoft Mail template. In the To the String box, edit the Microsoft Mail template identifier string in which you want to place outgoing-attribute information. When you finish, click OK to return to the Outgoing Templates page.
3. To create a new mapping, click the New button. The Outgoing Template Mapping dialog box appears. Use the Map The Attribute pull-down menu to select which Exchange attribute you want to map to a string on the remote system. Type that string in the To The String box. Click OK to return to the Outgoing Templates page.

FIG. 18.18 Outgoing Template Mappings translate Exchange attributes to a user-defined string.

4. To delete an existing mapping, select it and then click Remove.
5. Click Apply to set these properties and continue setting other properties.
6. When you finish making settings, click OK to return to the Administrator program.

As soon as you activate the directory exchange requestor for the first time, it exports a complete local address list to its Exchange directory synchronization server. Also, the requestor sends out a request for entries in the Exchange address list. The Exchange dirsync server returns a confirmation message saying that it received the requestor's transmission; then that server sends all the data in the export container to the dirsync requestor.

Subsequent transmissions between dirsync requestor and server consist only of updates to the address lists. You can force the import or export of directory information manually, as well as from the appropriate connector pages.

Be aware that directory synchronization updates sent by the Exchange dirsync server are in the form of messages sent to the network manager's mailbox. From that mailbox, the messages are picked up by the Exchange connection and synchronized into the local address list. These messages should not be modified or deleted; altering those messages interrupts the synchronization process and could produce data loss.

NOTE Large imports (several thousand entries) from the directory exchange server are known to take up to several hours. Be aware of such time requirements. Also be aware that during that time, no other messages will pass the Exchange connection gateway.

Starting Directory Synchronization

After you meet the preceding requirements, you can start the directory synchronization service. Follow these steps:

1. Open the Windows NT services control panel for the server on which you want to begin synchronization (see Figure 18.19).

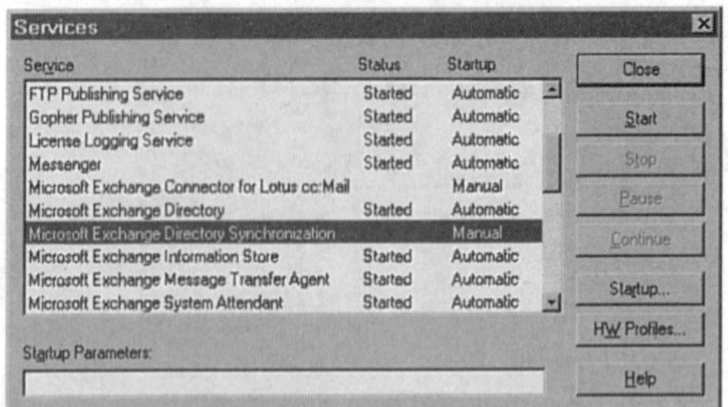

FIG. 18.19
Exchange services running under Windows NT.

2. Select the service name Exchange Directory Synchronization.
3. Click Start. The service starts, and synchronization begins.

4. Close the Services window.

NOTE If you set a specific time for directory synchronization that occurred while the service was stopped, a delay may occur until the first sync cycle actually begins. You can force immediate execution of a replication cycle in the property pages of the appropriate connector supporting synchronization. ■

Stopping Synchronization Services

To stop the synchronization services, complete the following steps:

1. Open the Windows NT services control panel.
2. Select the service name Exchange Directory Synchronization.
3. Click `Stop`. The service and synchronization stop.
4. Close the Services window.

NOTE Remember from earlier discussions that when the synchronization is shut off, there are no updates and changes of Exchange Servers Directory Services. It is a good idea to notify fellow administrators and users that the synchronization services have stopped. ■

CHAPTER 19

Using the Microsoft Mail Connector for PC Networks

In this chapter

Microsoft Mail, as discussed previously, is a shared file messaging system that includes an active client and a passive server. The client initiates messaging activity, and the passive file server (usually referred to as a post office) acts as a storage location for the messages.

Exchange Server is a client-server messaging system that provides distributed processing between the client and the server to provide for messaging functionality.

To enable Microsoft Mail and Exchange Server to communicate and exchange messages, the Microsoft Mail Connector must be configured to provide connectivity for the Exchange Server to either coexist in a Microsoft Mail environment or to act as backbone support for a Microsoft Mail environment.

In this section, we will discuss the main components and the configuration of the Microsoft Mail Connector, as well as audit the Microsoft Mail Connector to assist with debugging and routing between Microsoft Mail and Microsoft Exchange.

Understanding the Microsoft Mail Connector

In Chapter 7, "Planning Connections to the Microsoft Mail Systems," you were introduced to the main components of the Microsoft Mail Connector that enables connectivity between the Microsoft Mail System and Microsoft Exchange. Recall that the messaging functionality in Microsoft Mail (responsible for the transfer and routing of messages) is provided by the Microsoft Mail External. Microsoft Mail External is the MTA for Microsoft Mail, which is available in three modes. The first mode of operation is the Microsoft Mail External, which is a legacy MTA application that runs in single threaded DOS mode. The other two modes include the OS/2 MMTA and NT MMTA, which are the multitasking External applications.

Figures 19.1 and 19.2 illustrate a visual comparison of the two message transfer agents.

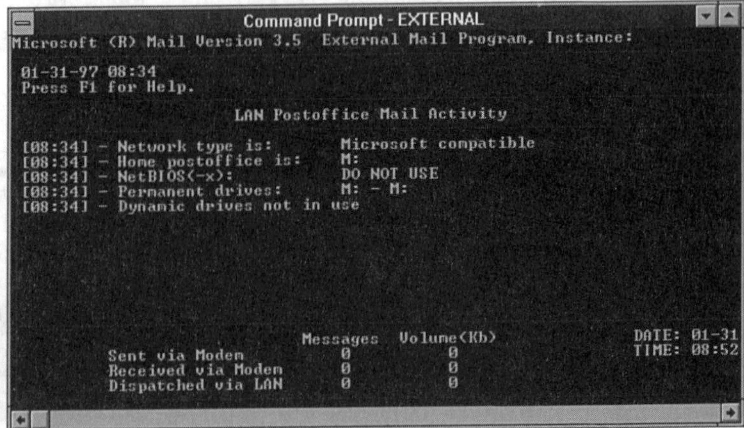

FIG. 19.1
The External application running on DOS.

NOTE In contrast to the External Application running on DOS, the Exchange Microsoft Mail Connector has a rich GUI interface that provides many new features and more functionality. ■

FIG. 19.2
The Exchange MS Mail Connector.

To connect to a Microsoft Mail post office from any messaging system on the same WAN/LAN, the MTA must be configured to do the following:

- Send and receive messages
- Convert the messages to the native format
- Deliver the messages to the destination post office and recipient

In Microsoft Exchange, you configure the Microsoft Mail Connector to receive messages from the Microsoft Exchange MTA, convert the messages into the Microsoft Mail format (MMF), and then deliver the messages to the target post office diagrammed in Figure 19.3.

Exchange creates a local, or virtual, post office on the Exchange server. This post office models the Microsoft Mail 3.x post office architecture and emulates a shared file messaging system under the Exchange hierarchy. The components of the Exchange server include the Information Store, Directory Services, System Attendant, and the Message Transfer Agent. These services coupled with the components of Microsoft Mail Connector are instrumental in the exchange of information between the messaging systems.

The core component of the connection from Exchange to Microsoft Mail (PC) is the Microsoft Mail Connector. It is used for the information transfer between Exchange and Microsoft Mail sites and post offices. Once the Exchange server processes the data interchange, the Microsoft Mail (PC) MTA can route the information to the Microsoft Mail downstream post offices. Exchange serves as the hub post office for several clusters, or spokes, of Microsoft Mail Post Offices.

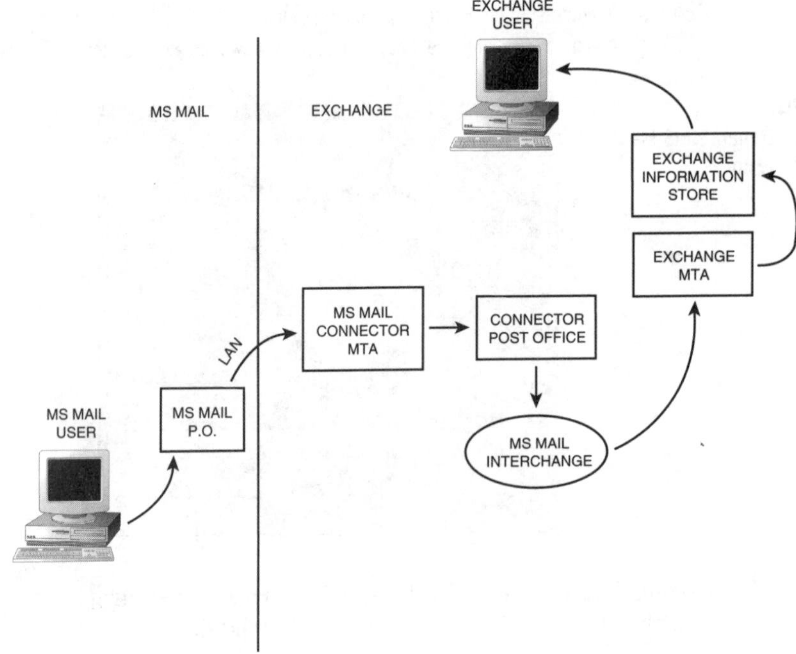

FIG. 19.3
The Exchange to Microsoft Mail Architecture.

NOTE Once you migrate the hub and spoke architecture of Microsoft Mail to Exchange, the Exchange servers become the mail hubs. The key benefit is that the same server that processes local mail or the information store can be the MTA for the existing Microsoft Mail Post Offices. Exchange can easily incorporate into existing mail architectures. This includes existing Microsoft Mail Post Offices running on Novell NetWare file servers. ■

The Exchange MS Mail Connector marries the functionality of a hub or gateway post office and the External application. The Microsoft Mail Connector (PC) MTA component of the Microsoft Mail Connector provides the functions of the Microsoft Mail External and Multitasking MTA application. These include the following:

- Message delivery between Microsoft Mail Post Offices and gateways
- Distribution of messages to recipients on Microsoft Mail Post Offices on the same WAN/LAN

As you migrate from existing Microsoft Mail shared file post offices, you may need to continue operating MS External or the Multitasking MTAs at the same time as the Microsoft Mail Connector of Exchange. These older MTA applications do not provide the same rich feature set as the Microsoft Mail Connector. The Microsoft Mail Connector enables you to integrate Exchange into any Microsoft Mail environment using existing External or Multitasking MTA applications.

This example applies to all MTA connections including asynchronous modem connections or X.25 service.

NOTE With the Exchange server running on Windows NT, you can take advantage of the built-in remote access services of the operating system. This way you can create a WAN environment without separate asynchronous connections. All the servers are networked together via a WAN/LAN. ■

Now that we have reviewed how Microsoft Mail integrates with Microsoft Exchange, we will re-introduce the components and the configuration requirements of the Microsoft Mail Connector. As identified in previous sections, the components of the Microsoft Mail Connector include:

- Microsoft Mail Connector Interchange is a Windows NT service that transfers and routes information between the Microsoft Exchange MTA and the Microsoft Mail Connector Post Office.
- Microsoft Mail Connector Post Office emulates a Microsoft Mail post office that resides on the Exchange server to provide the translation between the native Microsoft Mail message store and the native Exchange information store. This is a temporary information store for messages.
- Microsoft Mail Connector (PC) Message Transfer Agent (MTA) is a Windows NT service that connects to and transfers the Microsoft Mail Connector Post Office with one or more Microsoft Mail Post Offices. This MTA also handles the mail transfer between post offices.

These components are configured in the Administrator program.

The message route from Exchange to Microsoft Mail (PC) is as follows:

1. The Microsoft Exchange user creates a message addressed to a Microsoft Mail (PC) recipient and submits it.
2. The Microsoft Exchange Information Store forwards the message to the Exchange MTA.
3. The Microsoft Mail Connector Interchange scans the Microsoft Exchange Server MTA and converts the message to Microsoft Mail format including attachments, OLE objects, and rich text formatting. It then places the message into the Microsoft Mail Connector Post Office, as well as queues for any messages within the Microsoft Mail Connector Post Office for delivery to the Microsoft Exchange MTA.
4. The Microsoft Mail Connector (PC) MTA scans the Microsoft Mail Connector Post Office for messages, and then queues the message in the Microsoft Mail (PC) Post Office.

Configuring the Microsoft Mail Connector

There are six key steps required to configure the Microsoft Mail Connector within Microsoft Exchange. The pages provided in the GUI interface will guide you through the procedure. The steps are as follows:

1. Define the Microsoft Mail Connector administrator mailbox within the Interchange page of the Microsoft Mail Connector.
2. Configure the Microsoft Mail Connector settings in the General page.
3. Using the Connection page, connect to each Microsoft Mail Post Office.
4. Configure the Microsoft Mail Connector (PC) MTA for each post office communication (asynchronous, LAN, or X.25 within the Connectors page).
5. Launch the Microsoft Mail Connector services in the Services applet of Control Panel or Services in the Computer menu of Server Manager.
6. Configure the Directory Services to include Microsoft Mail Post Office recipients.

The following are step-by-step procedures to assist in configuring the Microsoft Mail Connector within the Microsoft Exchange Administrator program:

1. Open the Exchange Administrator Program. This can be performed from the console on the Microsoft Exchange server or from a workstation with connectivity to both the Microsoft Exchange server and the Microsoft Mail Post Office.
2. Choose the site from the organization list, the server name from the site, and the Microsoft Mail Connector from the Connections list (see Figure 19.4).

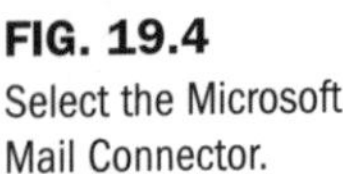

FIG. 19.4
Select the Microsoft Mail Connector.

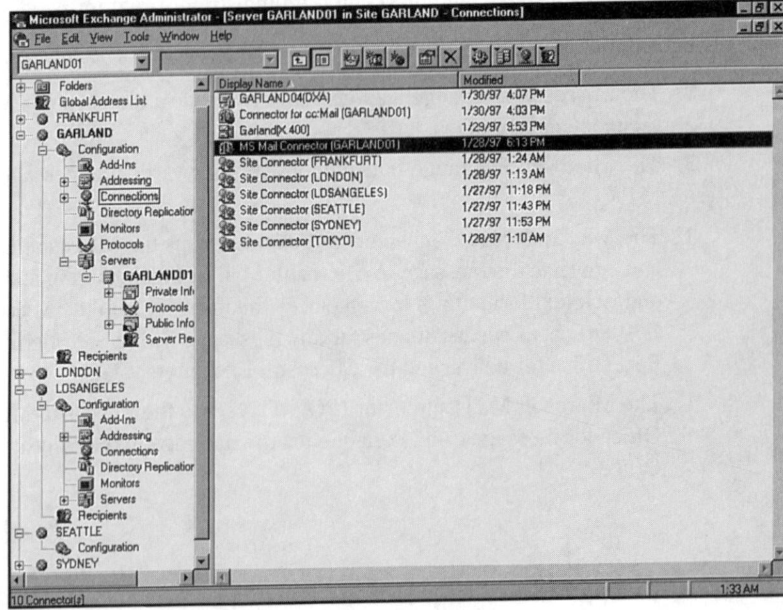

3. Open the Microsoft Mail Connector to configure the properties for the initial post office connection (see Figure 19.5).

FIG. 19.5 The Microsoft Mail Connector dialog box for (GARLAND01) with the Interchange page selected.

The Interchange page is the first tab that is displayed, which enables you to select the Administrator's mailbox. The mailbox you select will receive system information and alert messages from the Connector. These messages are typically due to non-delivery of mail (bounced mail) and failed messages.

4. Select the Administrator account. This account can be a user, group, distribution list, or public folder (see Figure 19.6).

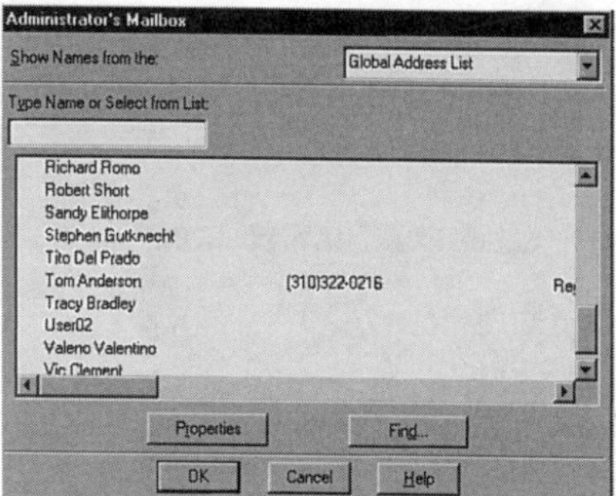

FIG. 19.6 Configuring the Administrator Account for the Connector.

5. Select OK to return to the Interchange page.
6. From the Interchange page, select the primary language for the recipients. The selected primary language is used for interoperability with Microsoft Mail clients using an alternate language. This is useful for International users of Exchange. The default value is prompted from the Exchange server.

7. Select the Maximize MS Mail 3.x Compatibility check box. This option is used for OLE compatibility in messages transferred between the older version used in MS Mail clients and the new version of Exchange Clients.

   By selecting Maximize MS Mail 3.x Compatibility, two versions of each OLE object are created. This option will increase or double the size of any OLE messages. If this option is not selected, MS Mail 3.x clients will not be able to view or save embedded objects originating from an Exchange client.

   If you want to enable Message Tracking for the Microsoft Mail Connector, select Enable Message Tracking. This option will record message information into the tracking logs. It can also debug problems when messages do not appear to be routing properly, or it can be used to locate potential lost messages. The default for this option is *disabled*. For more information on message tracking, see Chapter 28, "Troubleshooting Exchange with Diagnostic Tools."

8. Click Apply to set these properties prior to defining the additional properties of the remaining page menus.

NOTE The AppleTalk MTA Connector is discussed in Chapter 20, "Using the Microsoft Mail Connector for AppleTalk Networks."

Configuring the Microsoft Mail Connector (continued)

The following are steps to configure the Microsoft Mail Connector General page:

1. Select the General tab.

   This page shows the server name (GARLAND01). The server name cannot be modified (see Figure 19.7).

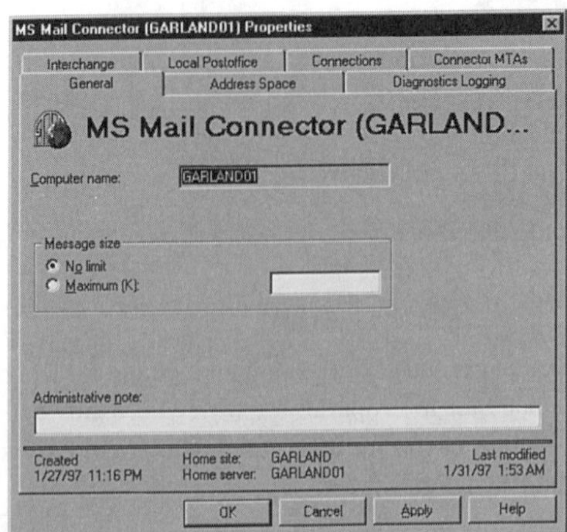

FIG. 19.7 Use the General page to set basic properties of the Microsoft Mail Connector.

2. Define the Maximum Message Size.

   You can define an upper limit for messages transferred through the Connector or accept the default value of No Limit. This option is useful if you want to restrict the size of the message transferred between systems (attachments included within the message can easily reach megabytes of data in size).

   To limit the size, enter a maximum value between 0 and 9999999 kilobytes.
3. Type an administrative note or comment with respect to the MS Mail Connector. Include the initials of the technician working on the service. This comment can only be viewed from this Property page.
4. Click Apply to set the properties and configure the remaining Property pages.

Defining Post Office Connections

If you will recall from Chapter 7, "Planning Connections to Microsoft Mail Systems," there are two primary ways to connect Exchange to existing Microsoft Mail Post Offices: LAN connectivity or remote connectivity, which includes asynchronous and X.25 connections. LAN connectivity is the easiest to maintain in terms of setup and administration by virtue of configuring the message routing and transfer between the Microsoft Mail Connector and the Microsoft Mail 3.x Post Offices. Remote connectivity requires two components to connect the Exchange Server and the Microsoft Mail 3.x Post Office over the X.25 or the asynchronous service. The first is the Microsoft Mail Connector (PC) MTA. The second is the Microsoft Mail 3.x External or Multitasking MTA program at the remote Post Office location configured with an instance in the address space of the MTA to connect with the Microsoft Mail Connector.

If you have remote post offices with this configuration, you may want to either use NT Remote Access service to perform LAN-based connections or migrate these post offices to Exchange ahead of other post offices.

The following steps are used to set up the connections for Microsoft Mail (PC) Post Offices over LAN, asynchronous, or X.25 connections. Each connection method is described individually.

Creating a LAN Connection Use the Connections page and Property page to create a LAN connection from Exchange to a Microsoft Mail post office.

The following are steps to perform a LAN connection to a Microsoft Mail post office:

1. Select the Connections tab.

   This page shows the organization and site name, which is actively being configured (see Figure 19.8).

NOTE You may want to clear the Confirm Before Connection Changes Are Applied check box if you do not want to have additional confirmation messages displayed before changes are set. ■

FIG. 19.8 The Connections page is used to define LAN connections.

2. Click the Create button to configure a new LAN connection post office (see Figure 19.9).

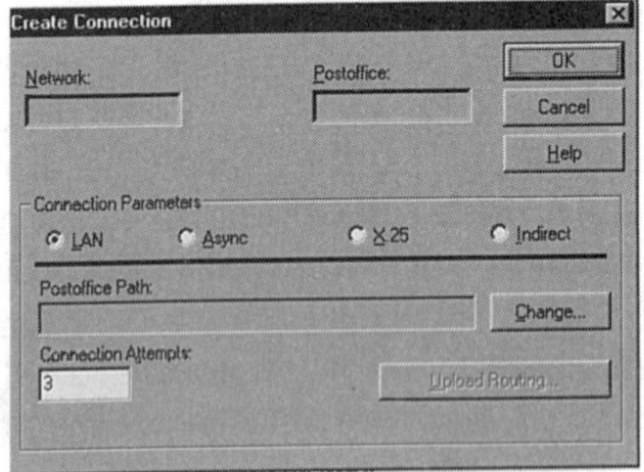

FIG. 19.9 Create a connection to a Microsoft Mail Post Office.

3. Select LAN under the Connection Parameters window.
4. Click the Change button to specify the path to the LAN-based Microsoft Mail Post Office.
5. In the Post Office Path dialog box, enter the complete path to the server, file share, and directory containing the Microsoft Mail Post Office in the Path box. Use the following format:

   Microsoft Networking: \\server\share\path

   Novell Networking: \\server\volume\path

6. Specify a Network or Domain login name and password in the Connect As and Password fields. You only need to complete these entries if any one of the following are true:
   - The post office is on a server with share-level security and no domain security.
   - The post office is in an untrusted domain, outside the domain model for the Exchange rollout.
   - The Exchange service account is not a valid user on the target server.
7. Click OK to confirm entries. If the connection is valid, the network and post office names will be entered into the appropriate fields in the Create Connection dialog box.
8. Define the number of connection retries for messages being sent to this post office. If this value is exceeded, the message is returned to the sender with an undelivered notification. The default value is 3.

An optional setting is to configure the routing information about the downstream post office from the one created. To import this information, follow these steps:

1. Click the Upload Routing button.

   A Downstream Post Offices Summary dialog box appears with the routing information of any post office or gateway indirectly connected through this post office. If this post office is a hub for other post offices, this information should be uploaded. If the post office is a downstream post office, you may want to skip over these steps.
2. Select any downstream post office you do not want to have uploaded. Choose the post office and click Delete.
3. Click OK to set the routing changes.

NOTE The information upload from this selection does not affect the configuration of the external options on the MS Mail Post Offices. ■

4. Click OK and return to the Connections Property page.
5. Click Apply to set the changes for the connection.

Creating an Asynchronous Connection Use the Connections page and Property page to create an asynchronous connection from Exchange to an External MTA for an MS Mail Post Office (see Figure 19.10).

Do the following to perform an asynchronous connection to a Microsoft Mail Post Office:

1. Select the Connections tab.
2. Click the Create button to configure a new asynchronous connection (see Figure 19.11).
3. Select the Asynchronous radio button (see Figure 19.12).

FIG. 19.10
The Connections page is used to define asynchronous connections.

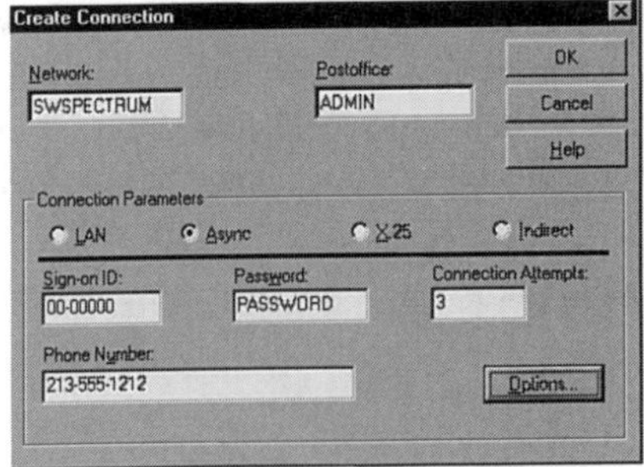

FIG. 19.11
The New Connections dialog box with Asynchronous selected.

4. Type in the Network name and post office in the respective field for the asynchronous connection post office.

NOTE Unlike the LAN connection, you must enter the information for these values.

5. In the Sign on ID field, enter the serial number for the remote post office. The Sign on ID format is ##-#####.
6. Enter the remote post office site password in the Password field.
7. Enter a value for the Connections Attempts box. The range is from 0 to 99. This value determines how many connection attempts Exchange will make to try to communicate with the remote post office before returning the message to the original sender. The default value is 3.

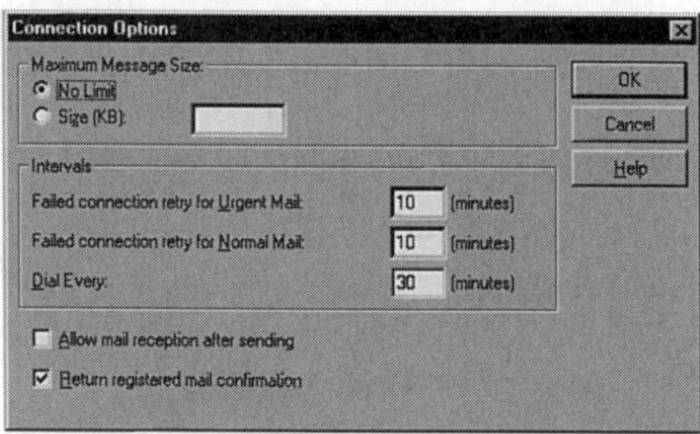

FIG. 19.12
Advanced options for the asynchronous connections.

8. Enter a phone number in the respective field. Make sure to add an area code and any additional dialing prefixes. If you must dial a special digit (9, for example) to get an outside line, this must be included in the configuration. The phone number entered is the phone number for the remote post office MTA running the External application.

NOTE Make sure that the phone number you enter contains all prefixes. In addition, this number should direct Exchange to the remote MTA running the External application. ■

9. Click the Options button to enter additional configurations for asynchronous connections.
10. Enter a value for Maximum Message Size. The default is set to No Limit (see Figure 19.12). If you want to limit the message size to be transferred over an asynchronous connection, enter a value between 0 and 9999 kilobytes in the respective field. This limits the size of attachment data without limiting routing data.
11. Enter a value for Failed Connection Retry For Urgent Mail. The value ranges from 1 to 99 minutes between connection attempts for messages defined as urgent. The default value is 10 minutes.
12. Enter a value for Failed Connection Retry for Normal Mail. This value ranges from 1 to 999 minutes between attempts to reconnect for messages defined as normal. The default is 10 minutes.
13. Enter a value for Dial Every. This value ranges from 1 to 999 minutes between connections for regular calls.
14. Check the box in order to select Allow Mail Reception After Sending. This enables messages to be transferred in a bi-directional single connection. This option offers faster and more efficient message delivery. If this selection is not made, connections are made on an individual basis for sending and receiving messages.
15. Check the box to select Return Registered Mail Confirmation. This will enable message confirmations to be transferred over the connection and between mail systems.
16. Click OK to set changes.

Creating an X.25 Connection Use the Connections page and Property page to create an X.25 connection from Exchange to an External MTA for a Microsoft Mail Post Office. This connection is very similar to the asynchronous connection. This section assumes that the X.25 protocol is already configured and running on this Windows NT server.

Do the following steps to perform an X.25 connection to a Microsoft Mail Post Office:

1. Select the Connections page (see Figure 19.13).
2. Click the Create button to configure a new X.25 connection (see Figure 19.14).

FIG. 19.13 The Connections page is used to define X.25 connections.

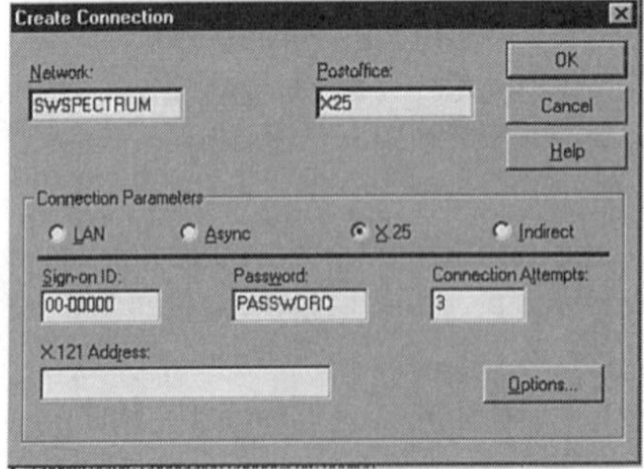

FIG. 19.14 The New Connection dialog box with X.25 selected.

3. Select the X.25 radio button. This brings up the additional configuration for the X.25 parameters.
4. Enter the Network and Post Office names in their respective fields.
5. Enter the sign-on serial ID in the format ##-#####.
6. Enter the remote post office password.

7. Define the number of connection attempts. The default is 3.
8. Define the X.121 address. This value should include the entire X.121 address, consisting of up to 16 digits. The format should be as follows:

   [Area] [DNIC] [DTE Address] [sub-address]

   For more information on Exchange and X.25 support, refer to Chapter 21, "Configuring X.400 Connections."
9. Click Apply to set the specifications.

NOTE The Options dialog box for X.25 is identical to that for the asynchronous connection. ■

Creating an Indirect Connection You can use the Microsoft Mail Connector to act as a hub post office. The hub post office can be specified to feed various spokes or indirect post offices.

Indirect connections are supported over LAN, asynchronous, or X.25 connections. They can be used to replace the External application running to service multiple downstream post offices.

Do the following steps to perform an indirect connection to a Microsoft Mail Post Office:

1. Select the Connections tab.
2. Select the hub post office and then click Create to configure the indirect post office.
3. From the Connection Configuration dialog box, select the hub post office from the Indirect Via drop-down list (see Figure 19.15).

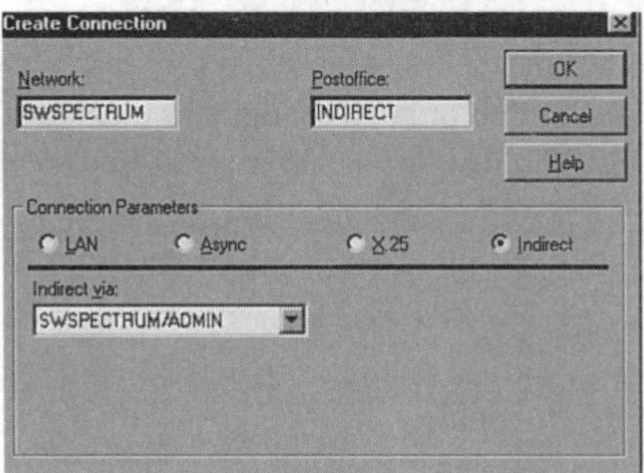

FIG. 19.15 The Connection page is used to define indirect connections.

4. Click OK to set the configuration.

The message queue is the final component of the Connections page menu. The queue lists messages awaiting delivery by the Microsoft Mail Connector. Figure 19.16 shows an empty queue after all pending messages were delivered. Normally, you would use the queue window to monitor the message load passing through your Microsoft Mail Connector.

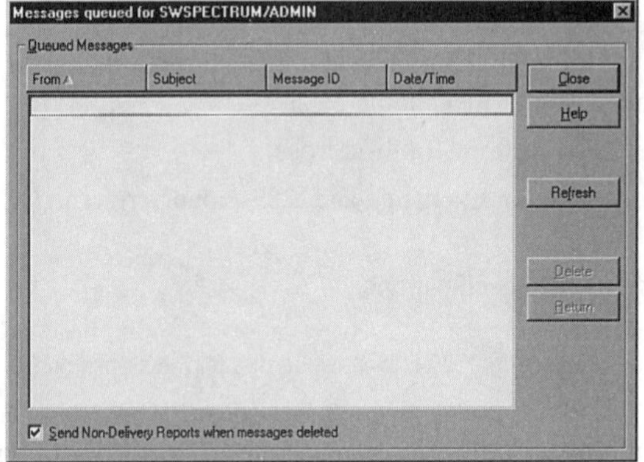

FIG. 19.16 The Microsoft Mail Connector message queue.

Configuring the Message Transfer Agent

The following steps are used to create the Message Transfer Agent services for connections over LAN, asynchronous, or X.25. Each connection method will be described individually.

Creating a Microsoft Mail Connector (PC) MTA Use the Connector MTA's page to create the MTA services required to transfer messages from Exchange to a Microsoft Mail Post Office. Follow these steps:

1. Select the Connector MTA's tab (see Figure 19.17).
2. Click New to create a new MTA service (see Figure 19.18).
3. Enter a name for the MTA service. This name is used by the Windows NT operating system to register the MTA Connector as a system service. Once the service is defined, you cannot modify the name. You would have to remove the service and re-create it.

   Because the MTA runs as a system service, there are several character string limitations:

   - up to 30 characters, maximum
   - letters a–z in lowercase format
   - letters A–Z in uppercase format
   - numbers 0–9
   - the <space bar>

   If you use any other character string, the service will not be able to register with the operating system.

NOTE The naming convention is important with services. If you preface the MTAs with "MS Mail Connector," they will interfere with the integrated Exchange Mail Windows NT services listed in the Control Panel Services.

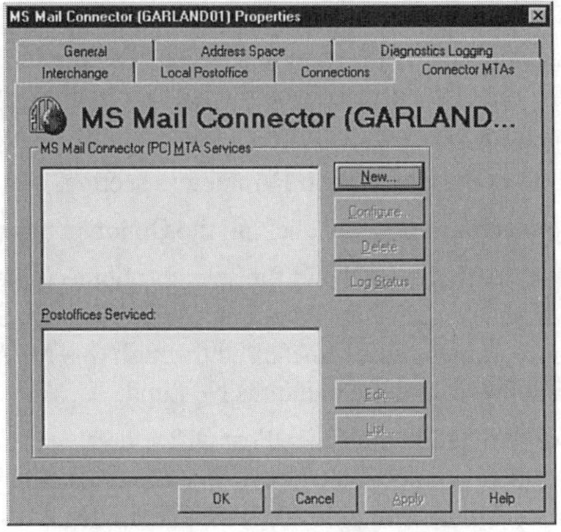

FIG. 19.17
The Microsoft Mail Connector MTA's page menu.

New MS Mail Connector (PC) MTA Service

Service Name:

OK

Cancel

Help

Logging

Log Messages:

Sent at Serviced Postoffices

Received at Serviced Postoffices

Polling Frequency

Update configuration every 60 minutes

Check for mail every 5 minutes

Options...

Connection Parameters

LAN Async and LAN X.25 and LAN

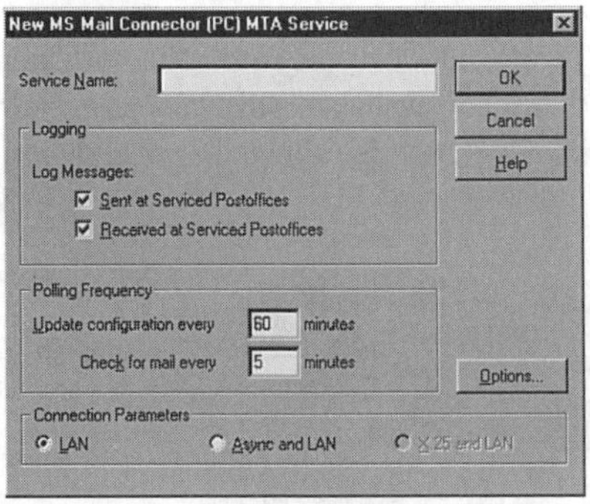

FIG. 19.18
The Microsoft Mail Connector MTA's page menu–New Service.

4. Select the Log Messages Sent At Serviced Post Offices check box. This option will set up logging in order to record each message transferred to the Microsoft Mail Post Office environment.

5. Select the Log Messages Received At Serviced Post Offices check box. This option will set up logging in order to record each message transferred from the Microsoft Mail Post Office environment.

6. Enter values for the Update Configuration field in minutes. This scans for updated information based on the interval minutes entered into this field. The default is 60 minutes.

NOTE If you enter a 0 in this field, you will stop the configuration from checking for messages.

7. Enter a value for the Check For Mail Every field. This field accepts values from 0 to 999 minutes. This is the polling interval for how long the MTA waits before rechecking for mail coming to the MS Mail Connector post office. The default value is five minutes.

If you have multiple instances of the MTA service-to-service multiple Microsoft Mail Post Offices and gateways, you may want to stagger this time interval so that each instance does not overlap. One service would check for mail every five minutes, and the next service would check every six minutes.

8. Select the LAN option in the Connection Parameters section.
9. Define the MTA Connector options by clicking the Options button (see Figure 19.18).

   These options apply to both the LAN and the asynchronous connection methods (see Figure 19.19). The first selection is for Maximum LAN Message Size. You can set an upper limit for the size of messages transferred through this MTA. The values range from 0 to 9999999 kilobytes, and the default is No Limit.

   The next entry is used to define the Close Post Office If value. This value is used to close the destination post office connection when disk space utilization has reached whichever threshold point you designate from 0 to 999999999 kilobytes. Messages will queue up on the MTA until they are timed out or additional disk space is added on the destination post office.

   In addition to closing the connection, you can set a value for Open Post Office If disk space that has been added or made available. This value ranges from 0 to 999999999 kilobytes. Disk space availability must rise above this value in order for message transfer to restart.

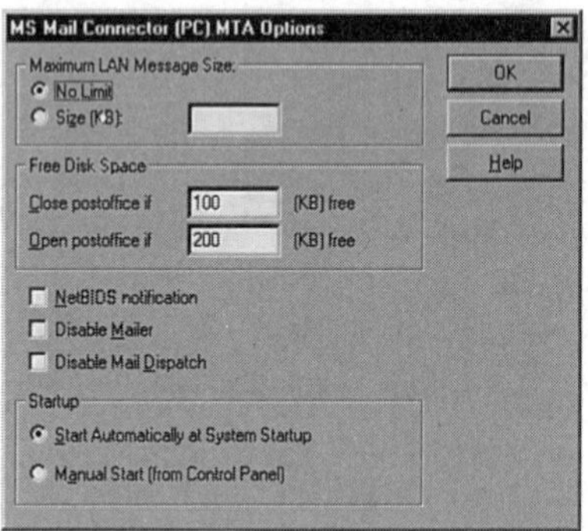

FIG. 19.19 The Microsoft Mail Connector MTA's page menu–New Service, Options dialog box.

The next three check boxes are used for administrative notifications to the Microsoft Mail LAN post office users. These have no impact for Exchange users. The first option is to check the NetBIOS Notification in order to have the MTA send a NetBIOS broadcast message.

The NetBIOS Broadcast will only work if the server and clients are running the NetBIOS protocol. In addition, you must start all the NT service MTAs prior to launching the External application on the destination post office for NetBIOS broadcasts to function properly. For more information, see the user manuals for the respective operating system to learn how to install NetBIOS.

Select Disable Mailer and Disable Mail Dispatch to stop mail notifications from being distributed via the External and Dispatch applications associated with the destination Microsoft Mail Post Offices. These do not impact the Exchange users. For more information on the application, refer to your Microsoft Mail Administrator's Guide.

Select the Startup box to define the method that this NT MTA service will launch. You have the option to have the MTA start automatically or manually.

Click OK to set these configurations.

10. Click OK followed by Apply to set all the configurations for this MTA service. If you modify these options for this service at a later point, you will need to stop and start the NT service in order to have the changes take effect.

Defining the Post Offices Service by the MTA To complete the MTA service, you need to define the post offices service by the MTA services. Complete the following steps:

1. From the Microsoft Mail Connector property sheet, click the List button. The Serviced LAN Post Offices dialog box appears.
2. In the Serviced LAN Post Offices dialog box, select the post office to be serviced from the right panel of Available LAN Post Offices.
3. Click the Add button in the middle and the selection becomes a Serviced LAN Post Office.
4. Click OK to set the configurations.

If you need an additional service for an asynchronous connection, you will need to modify an existing MTA or create a new service. Following are the configuration differences for the asynchronous connection:

1. Click Create to create a new MTA service, or click Edit to modify an existing MTA.
2. On the Property page, select the Async And LAN option (see Figure 19.20).

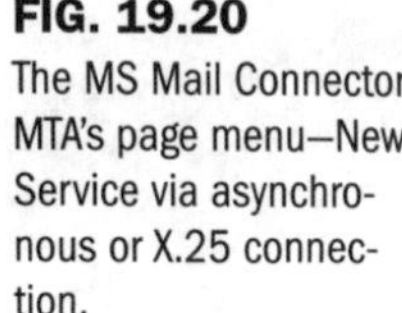

FIG. 19.20
The MS Mail Connector MTA's page menu—New Service via asynchronous or X.25 connection.

3. Enter the appropriate values for the following:

   Communication port is the server communication port to be used for the MTA service. The default value is COM1.

   Modem script is used to define the initialization string for your particular modem.

NOTE If you have an existing modem that requires a customized script file, you can copy this script to the following path on the Exchange server:

<UX.NO>%Exchangeroot%\connect\msmcom\maildata\glb ■

   Modem Time-out is the value for the number of minutes the MTA will wait for a connection with the destination post office.

   Communication Mode is the value that defines whether the MTA will send and receive messages or handle only one-way message transfers.

4. Click OK to set the configuration settings.

   If this MTA has been modified, it will need to be stopped and restarted from the services control panel.

Starting the MTA NT Services After you have configured all your MTA services and defined which post offices are serviced, you need to start the MTA NT services in order to begin message transfer. Do the following steps to start these services:

1. Open the control panel for the server services.
2. Locate the MTA service to be started, select the service, and click Start (see Figure 19.21). The service starts, and you can begin transferring messages between mail systems.

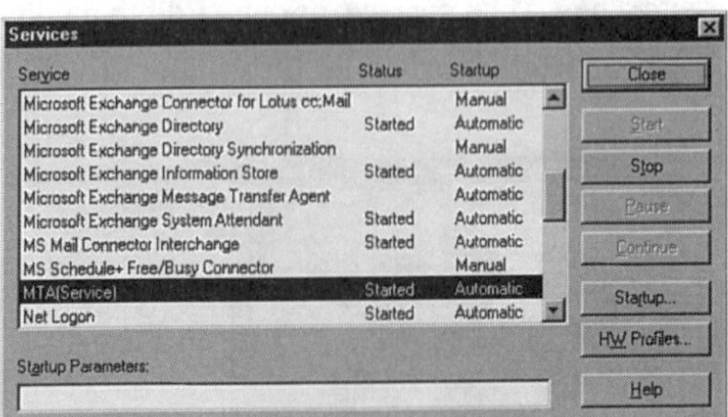

FIG. 19.21
The Microsoft Mail Connector MTA Windows NT service.

Microsoft Mail Connector Address Space

The following steps are utilized to create the address space for the Microsoft Mail Post Offices to be serviced by the Microsoft Mail Connector.

Configuring the Address Space

Configuring the address space is used to properly route messages throughout the organization. If you have additional gateways installed, configuring the address space is important to ensure the proper message route. Complete the following steps:

1. Select the Address Space tab (see Figure 19.22).
2. Select the address space to be created. Your selection will depend on the type of gateway used to receive these message transfers. The address spaces are associated with a specific template for each connector. The template assists with entering the destination mail address. The options are as follows:
   - New General is a blank template for creating a destination address when a template is not available. Typically, each connector provides an address template.
   - New Internet is a blank template to enter SMTP or Internet message routes.
   - New X.400 is a blank template for creating an X.400 message route.
   - New MS Mail is a blank template to create a Microsoft Mail message route. After the Microsoft Mail Connector is configured to transfer messages through the associated MTA service, a message route is automatically generated in the Microsoft Mail address space.

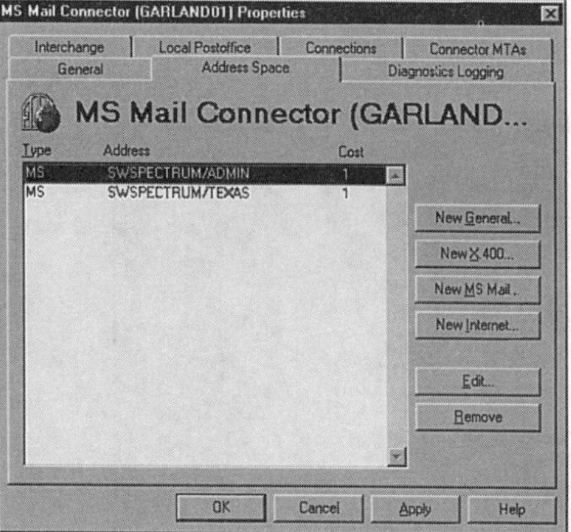

FIG. 19.22 The Microsoft Mail Address Space page menu.

The following describes how to configure the Microsoft Mail Address Space access property pages on the Microsoft Mail Connector:

1. To create or edit the Microsoft Mail address space, select the address space in the connection window.
2. In the Property page for the Microsoft Mail address space, you must enter the network and post office of the destination Microsoft Mail Post Office.

NOTE When you enter values for the address spaces, you can use wildcards, as in the following example:

MS:SWSPECTRUM\ADMIN*

This address routes messages to all users on the destination post office.

3. All address spaces will create a message route from this Microsoft Mail Connector to the destination or foreign mail systems. For more information on routing and addressing, see Chapter 25, "Maintaining Exchange."

Configuring the Local Exchange Post Office

When you use the Microsoft Mail Connector for Microsoft Mail (PC), Exchange must emulate a Microsoft Mail Post Office. This is known as the local post office, which is created automatically when you install the Microsoft Mail Connector. It is first configured when you set up the Microsoft Mail Post Office interchange, as discussed earlier in the chapter.

The local post office is a working Microsoft Mail Post Office. Exchange uses this post office to transfer messages to Microsoft Mail Post Offices. The message is first placed into the MTA and is then transferred and converted into the local post office before being transferred out to the destination post office.

To configure the local post office, follow these steps:

1. Select the Local Postoffice tab (see Figure 19.23).

FIG. 19.23 The Microsoft Mail Connector local post office configuration.

2. Enter the network and post office names for the local Microsoft Exchange MS Mail post office interchange. These values can be changed. By default, Exchange enters the organization and site name into these fields.
3. Enter the password to be used by External MTA applications when you are connecting to and signing on to this local post office to transfer messages.

NOTE This is a good time to note the local post office Sign on Serial ID. You will need this information when you are configuring External to communicate with this local post office. ■

4. Click the Regenerate button under the Microsoft Mail Connector Addresses heading. This selection will generate the proper addressing scheme to be used in routing messages through this local post office.

   If any changes are made to this local post office, you must execute the address regeneration. You will need to update the information on the remote External MTA, gateway, or post office as well. Additionally, if you change this information, you must stop and restart the NT MTA service and Microsoft Mail Connector Interchange.

   A warning will appear to require you to confirm this action.

5. Click OK to accept configuration settings and apply them to the Microsoft Mail Connector.

Microsoft Mail Connector Post Offices and Gateways in PC Mail

Once you have completed configuring the Exchange Microsoft Mail Connector, you must then configure each Microsoft Mail PC post office to work with the settings in Exchange. Refer to the Microsoft Mail Connector's local post office settings to create an External post office site in Microsoft Mail 3.x.

To configure the Microsoft Mail Post Office, follow these steps:

1. Attach your Exchange server to the Microsoft Mail Post Office with a network connection.
2. Launch the Microsoft Mail Administration utility to configure the post office settings.

NOTE Once you have used the Exchange GUI interface, the DOS character-based administration utility of Microsoft Mail v3.x seems antiquated. ■

3. Toggle to the External-Admin Configuration menu item (see Figure 19.24).
4. Select Create and define the network, post office, and route for the Exchange MS Mail Connector local post office.

   In this example, the Microsoft Mail Post Office is called ADMIN on the SWSPECTRUM network. An External route has been added to the Exchange local post office named TEXAS on the same SWSPECTRUM network. The connection type is direct. The only time you would use indirect is if you were routing Microsoft Mail through another Microsoft Mail hub post office prior to transferring the message to Exchange.

5. Select Yes to create the route and then exit the Administration application.

If you have other Microsoft Mail 3.x gateways, you will need to modify the settings for those post offices as well. Because there are many different types of Microsoft Mail gateways, you will be unable to define the process for each one. The key components to modify are the network and post office names, the sign-on ID, and the post office password. Refer to your user's manual for more information on how to configure the gateway.

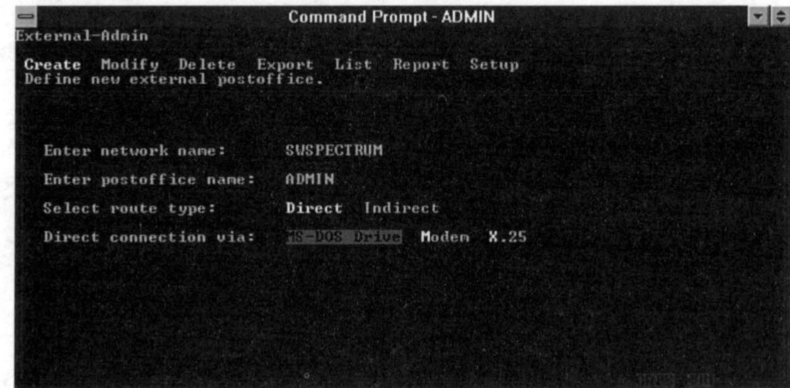

FIG. 19.24 Use the Microsoft Mail Administration utility to configure the post office.

Managing the NT Service for the Microsoft Mail Connector

Now that the Microsoft Mail Connector is completely configured, you must start the connection service to begin transferring messages between Exchange and Microsoft Mail.

To start the Microsoft Mail connection services, follow these steps:

1. Open the Windows NT Control Panel or Windows NT Server Manager and select the Services option.
2. Select the Microsoft Mail Connector Interchange service (see Figure 19.25).
3. Click Start to launch the service.

NOTE The Microsoft Mail Connector (PC) MTA is set to *disabled* because it is only used in the configuration of individual Microsoft Mail MTA services. This service cannot be started. ■

4. Close the Services window.

Testing the Connection Between Exchange and MS Mail

Now that all the services are running and messages are configured to route between Exchange and Microsoft Mail, you should test the connection.

To test the message routing between Exchange and Microsoft Mail, follow these steps:

1. Using the Microsoft Exchange client software, create and send a message to a recipient with a destination on the Microsoft Mail Post Office.
2. Verify in the Microsoft Mail 3.x client software that the message has arrived.
3. Reverse this process to verify message routing from Microsoft Mail to Exchange.
4. If the messages do not arrive, the first place to begin diagnosis is in the Windows NT Server Event log for the Exchange server.

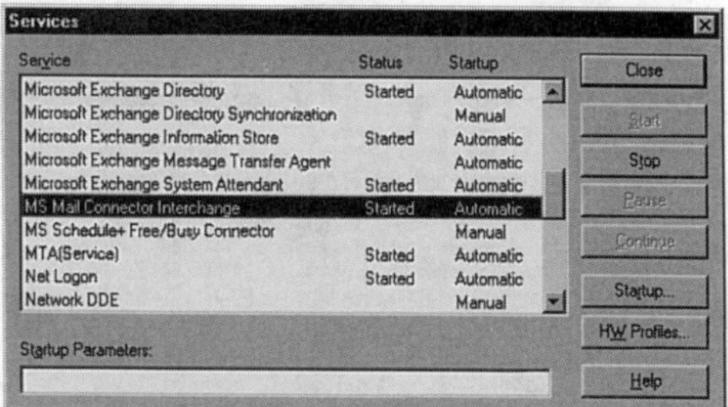

FIG. 19.25
To start the MS Mail Connection, select the MS Mail Connector Interchange service.

The Microsoft Mail Connector interchange events are logged as "MSExchangeMSMI" for mail transfer between the Exchange Information Store and the Microsoft Mail Connector local post office.

The Microsoft Mail Connector (PC) MTA events are logged under the associated Microsoft Mail MTA services names.

In this figure, you can see that the MTA has created a system message on the Exchange local post office with the respective name (see Figure 19.26).

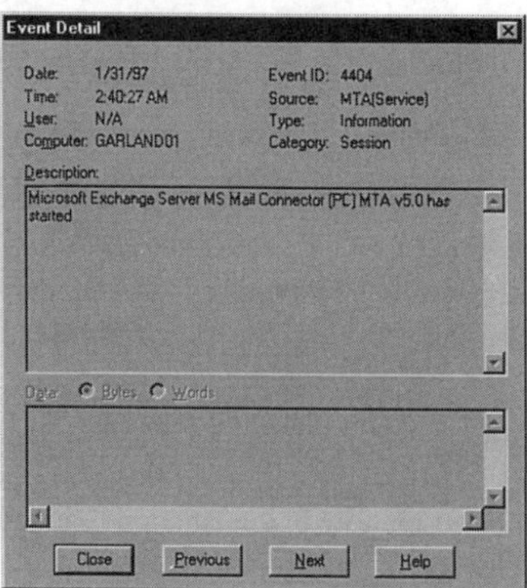

FIG. 19.26
The Windows NT event log for Microsoft Mail Connector entries.

In this example, the MTA service is called "MTA(service)," and the event would be logged with this name (see Figure 19.27). As you can see, the MTA server, ADMIN, has successfully started. When the MTA begins, we can use our Event Viewer to permeate through the event detail.

As you can see, Exchange provides numerous messages to the event log. If you have trouble with communication between Exchange and the Microsoft Mail Post Office, you can adjust the sensitivity of the auditing levels.

Event Viewer - Application Log on \\GARLAND01

Log View Options Help

Date	Time	Source	Category	Event	User	Co
1/31/97	2:40:27 AM	MTA(Service)	Session	4404	N/A	
1/31/97	2:39:57 AM	MSExchangeIS Priv	Transport	2000	N/A	
1/31/97	2:39:50 AM	MSExchangeIS Priv	Transport	2000	N/A	
1/31/97	2:36:03 AM	MSExchangeIS Pub	Transport	2000	N/A	
1/31/97	2:35:57 AM	MSExchangeIS Pub	Transport	2000	N/A	
1/31/97	2:34:12 AM	MSExchangeMSMI	Session Error	2383	N/A	
1/31/97	2:34:05 AM	MSExchangeMSMI	Session Error	2305	N/A	
1/31/97	2:00:42 AM	MSExchangeSA	General	5000	N/A	
1/31/97	1:33:10 AM	MSExchangeIS Priv	Transport	2000	N/A	
1/31/97	1:33:03 AM	MSExchangeIS Priv	Transport	2000	N/A	
1/31/97	1:29:16 AM	MSExchangeIS Pub	Transport	2000	N/A	
1/31/97	1:29:10 AM	MSExchangeIS Pub	Transport	2000	N/A	
1/31/97	1:08:37 AM	MSExchangeMSMI	Session Error	2383	N/A	
1/31/97	1:08:28 AM	MSExchangeMSMI	Session Error	2305	N/A	
1/31/97	12:24:08 AM	MSExchangeIS Priv	Transport	2000	N/A	
1/31/97	12:24:01 AM	MSExchangeIS Priv	Transport	2000	N/A	
1/31/97	12:20:28 AM	MSExchangeIS Pub	Transport	2000	N/A	
1/31/97	12:20:08 AM	MSExchangeIS Pub	Transport	2000	N/A	
1/31/97	12:06:58 AM	MSExchangeMig	None	10004	N/A	
1/31/97	12:04:25 AM	MSExchangeMig	None	10002	N/A	
1/30/97	11:39:35 PM	MSExchangeMSMI	Session Error	2383	N/A	
1/30/97	11:39:24 PM	MSExchangeMSMI	Session Error	2305	N/A	
1/30/97	11:26:44 PM	MSExchangeMig	None	10004	N/A	

FIG. 19.27
The Windows NT event log will store a significant amount of events from the Exchange server. Each process has a unique service ID.

Adjusting the Auditing Levels for the Microsoft Mail Connector

To assist with debugging and routing problems between Exchange and Microsoft Mail, you may want to increase the level of auditing for the Microsoft Mail Connector.

To adjust the audit levels, follow these steps:

1. Open the MS Mail Connector Property page and select the tab for Diagnostics Logging (see Figure 19.28).
2. The left panel displays the services to be monitored, and the right panel displays the categories and logging levels. The service is the Microsoft Mail Interchange Connector. The categories to adjust are the MS Mail Interchange Connector, the MS Mail PC MTA, and the MS Mail AppleTalk MTA. (Note that the AppleTalk MTA is discussed in the next chapter.)

   The levels indicate the level of granularity of information that you would like logged in to the event viewer. The levels for the MS Mail Connector are None, Minimum, Medium, and Maximum. Typically, you will have Minimum selected for the categories of the service that you are using. If you are not going to use the AppleTalk MTA, there is no need to turn logging on.

   If problems do arise with the connections between Exchange and Microsoft Mail, you can increase the logging levels while you are in the debug mode. Realize that increasing the logging levels can potentially overload your event logs with an abundance of information as well as the system itself. The increase in logging should only be set while you are debugging a problem. Once the connection has been stabilized, it is a good idea to reduce the logging levels.

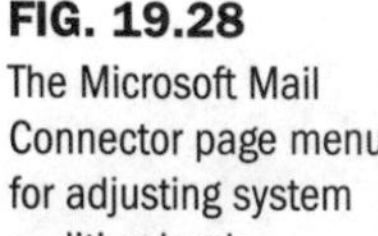

FIG. 19.28
The Microsoft Mail Connector page menu for adjusting system auditing levels.

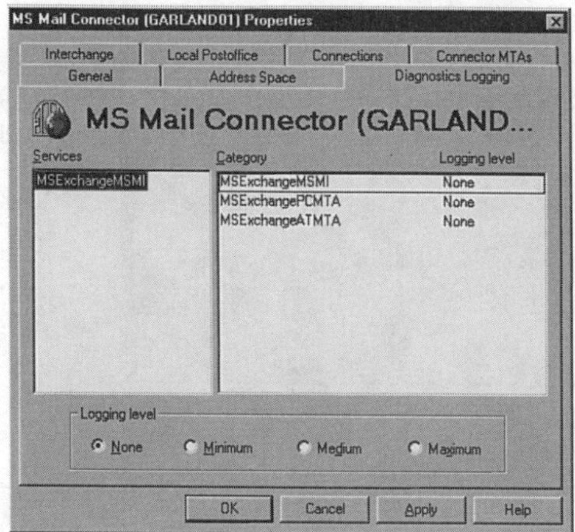

If you are still having problems with Microsoft Mail message routing and the event logs are not providing the information necessary to solve the problem, try the following:

- Delete and then re-add the MS Mail Connector, including all the MTA services.
- See Chapter 28, "Troubleshooting Exchange with Diagnostic Tools."
- Contact Microsoft Product Support Services. Support for Microsoft products can be found on the Internet at **http://www.microsoft.com/support/**.

Configuring Directory Synchronization

The final component to configure is the Directory Synchronization between the Exchange server and Microsoft Mail.

This section will assume that the Directory Synchronization server is already set up and running on Exchange. Each site can only run one Directory Synchronization server. Each server, however, can support numerous directory requestors and remote directory requestors. In addition, this section will assume that Exchange and the Microsoft Mail Post Office can both send and receive messages via the Microsoft Mail Interchange Connector and the PC MTA. Directory Synchronization was explained in detail in Chapter 18, "Using Directory Replication and Synchronization."

Once the Directory Synchronization server is set up and configured on the Exchange server, there are a few steps needed to ensure that the MS Mail post offices are included in the synchronization process.

1. Make sure that the Exchange Site Directory Synchronization Service is installed and running (see Figure 19.29). Check your Windows NT Services applet to confirm this.

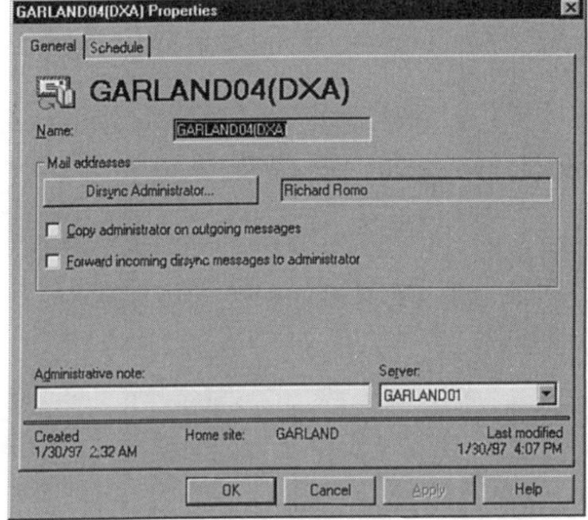

FIG. 19.29 The Exchange Directory Synchronization server properties.

2. Install and configure a remote directory requestor to synchronize the Exchange Global Address List (GAL) with the GAL on the Microsoft Mail 3.x post office network (see Figure 19.30).

   The remote directory requestor has complete information necessary to communicate with the Exchange local post office prior to synchronizing with the connected Microsoft Mail Post Office.

3. Open the Microsoft Mail 3.x administration application and select the post office configuration options (see Figure 19.31).

   From this panel you can configure the directory synchronization options, as well as the use of the global address for the local post office.

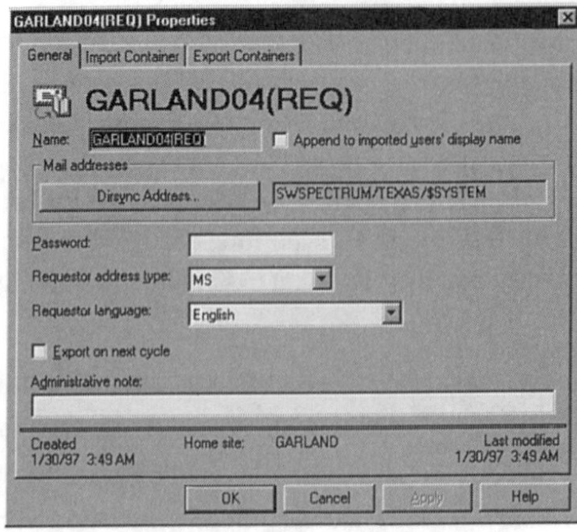

FIG. 19.30 The Exchange remote directory requestor used to synchronize with foreign systems, including Microsoft Mail 3.x.

4. From the Dir-sync menu, toggle to the Registration menu to configure the Directory Synchronization server information.

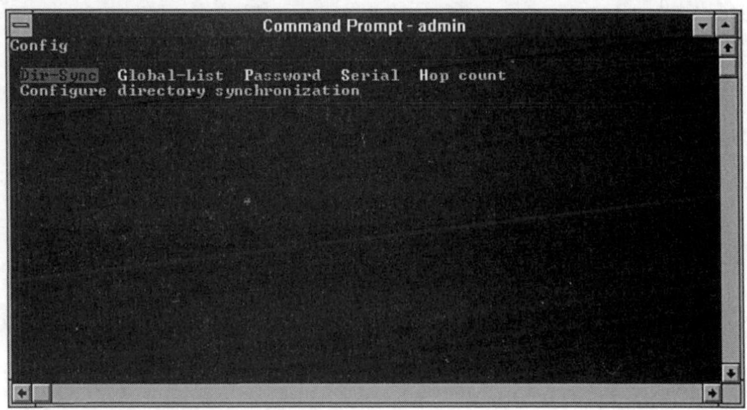

FIG. 19.31 Configuration options in the Microsoft Mail Administration program.

The information for the Directory Synchronization server will be the same as the Exchange MS Mail local post office. From this panel, enter the network, post office, and password for the server (see Figure 19.32).

5. From the Global Address menu in the post office configuration options, you will need to specify for the MS Mail 3.x post office to use the global address list.

Once the Microsoft Mail administration configuration is completed, stop and restart the Exchange Directory Synchronization Server service. Stop and restart the Microsoft Mail Connector Interchange as well.

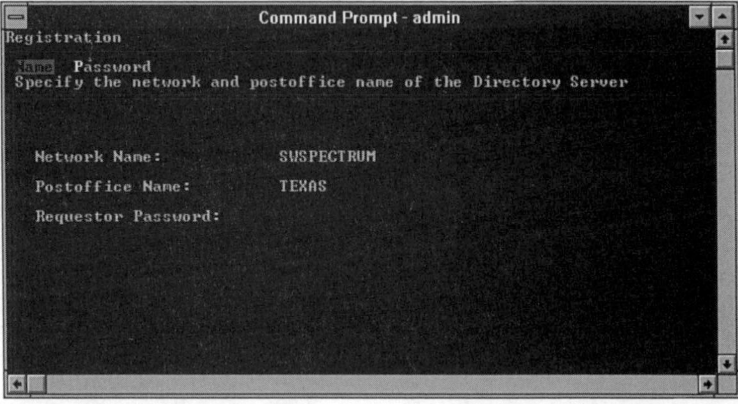

FIG. 19.32 Creating a Directory Synchronization requestor in MS Mail.

In summary, there are many components required to connect Exchange with Microsoft Mail (PC) post offices. Each component of the Microsoft Mail Connector is tightly integrated with the components and services of Exchange to provide messaging functionality between the two mail systems.

CHAPTER 20

Using the Microsoft Mail Connector for AppleTalk Networks

In this chapter

This chapter delineates how to establish a messaging link between Microsoft Exchange and a Macintosh Server running Microsoft Mail for AppleTalk networks. Unlike a Microsoft Mail for PC network, Microsoft Mail (AppleTalk) does not use the Post Office paradigm. Therefore, the process of connecting to a Microsoft Exchange Server is more complex. The Macintosh Server believes it is communicating with a standard Microsoft Mail (PC) Post Office. Microsoft Mail for AppleTalk uses a special gateway component to communicate with the Microsoft Exchange Microsoft Mail Connector. Respectively, the Microsoft Exchange Microsoft Mail Connector has specific configuration settings and a message queue for Microsoft Mail (AppleTalk) connections as well. Any configuration pertaining to Microsoft Exchange communicating with Microsoft Mail Post Offices is not applicable.

Introduction to the Microsoft Mail Connector

This section describes how you use connectors to establish a link between Microsoft Exchange and Microsoft Mail (AppleTalk) Servers.

The two core Exchange Microsoft Mail Connector components are the following:

- Microsoft Mail Connector Interchange: The interchange is the Microsoft Exchange service that routes messages between the Microsoft Exchange Server and the Microsoft Mail Connector Post Office.
- Microsoft Mail Connector Post Office: This component is a Microsoft Exchange emulation of a Microsoft Mail Post Office. The post office stores messages in transit to and from Microsoft Mail (PC and AppleTalk).

Microsoft Exchange also includes one additional component for communication with Microsoft Mail (AppleTalk) Servers:

- Microsoft Mail Connector (AppleTalk) Message Transfer Agent: This is a Windows NT service that routes messages between the Microsoft Mail Connector Post Office and the Microsoft Mail (AppleTalk) Server.

The following explains the procedure for connecting Microsoft Exchange to a Microsoft Mail for AppleTalk network:

1. Set up all necessary network connections between the systems.
2. Install and set up the Exchange Microsoft Mail Connector.
3. Place the Connector Post Office on a Macintosh-accessible NTFS volume.
4. Configure the Exchange Microsoft Mail Connector to communicate with Microsoft Mail (AppleTalk) Servers. This includes starting the Microsoft Mail (AppleTalk) MTA service.
5. Install and configure the Microsoft Exchange Connection software on the Microsoft Mail (AppleTalk) gateway server.
6. Enter address space entries for the Microsoft (AppleTalk) Server. Test the configurations for correct message routing between systems.

7. If you want additional Microsoft Mail (AppleTalk) Servers to communicate indirectly with the Exchange Server, install and configure the gateway access component on each Macintosh Server.
8. Test the transfer of messages to indirectly connected Microsoft Mail (AppleTalk) Servers, if applicable.
9. After messages route properly to all servers, set up directory synchronization to maintain up-to-date address lists among systems.

The preceding steps conclude the introduction to connecting Microsoft Exchange to a Microsoft Mail for AppleTalk network. In the next section, you take a closer look at Exchange by starting with installing Services for Macintosh.

Installing Services for Macintosh

The following procedures define the configuration of the Microsoft Exchange Server to support Microsoft Mail for AppleTalk networks. Windows NT Services for Macintosh enables your server to communicate over Apple's native AppleTalk protocol. The requirements for installing Services for Macintosh include 2M of hard disk space and an NTFS Macintosh-Accessible Volume to enable Macintosh Clients to access resources on the Windows NT Server.

The following steps offer a quick guideline for installing Windows NT Services for Macintosh:

1. Open the Control Panel and double-click the Networking icon (see Figure 20.1).

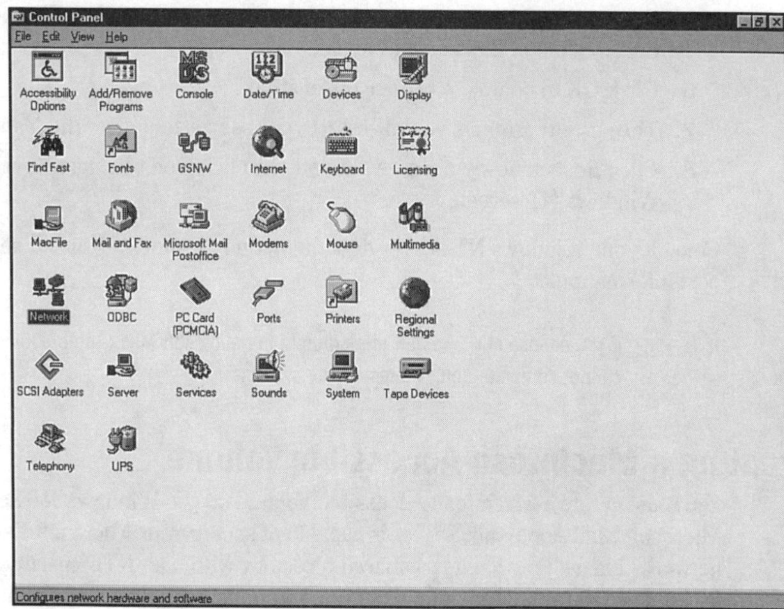

FIG. 20.1
The Windows NT Network is part of your Windows NT Server.

2. If Services for Macintosh is not listed in the Installed Network Software scroll box, it is not installed. Click Add Software. The Network dialog box appears (see Figure 20.2).

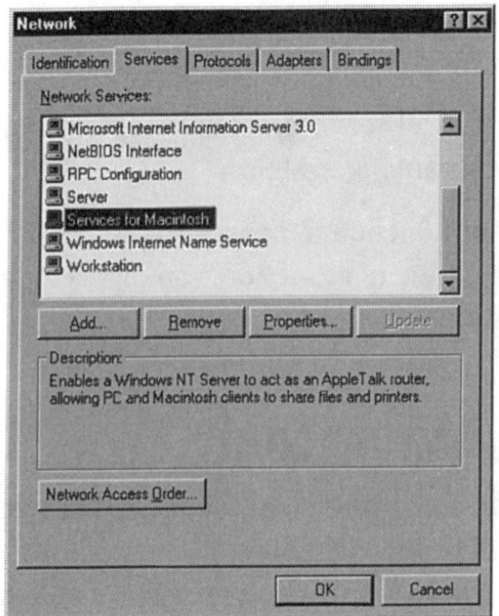

FIG. 20.2
Select Services for Macintosh in the list of available components.

3. Select Services for Macintosh from the list of available network software. Click Continue.
4. Type the directory path to your Windows NT Server source files, such as CD-ROM, floppy disk, or server volume. Click Continue.
5. After the services are installed, the program returns to the Network Services dialog box. Services for Macintosh should now appear in the Installed Network Software list on the Services tab of the Network applet.
6. Click OK to complete service installation.
7. The system prompts you to restart your server to update the Network settings.
8. Click Restart now. Alternatively, you can click Don't Restart Now to return to the Windows NT screen.

Consult your Windows NT Server documentation for more advanced configuration and support information.

NOTE If you choose not to restart immediately, the Microsoft Mail (AppleTalk) configuration cannot complete until you restart the system. ■

Creating a Macintosh-Accessible Volume

You must create a Macintosh-Accessible Volume on the Windows NT Server, so that your Microsoft Mail AppleTalk Server is capable of seeing your Microsoft Exchange Server on the network. The volume itself is a shared directory within an NTFS partition, which is configured for connection from a Macintosh Server. You must configure the Macintosh Server to automatically log on to this volume upon initialization.

The following steps demonstrate how to create and configure a Macintosh-Accessible Volume:

NOTE For more information on Macintosh-Accessible Volumes, refer to your Windows NT Server documentation.

1. Open the Windows NT Explorer.
2. From Windows NT Explorer, find the following folder.

   <Drive Letter where Microsoft Exchange is installed>:
   \EXCHSRVR\CONNECT\MSCON\MAILDATA

NOTE This assumes that you named the main Exchange directory EXCHSRVR during installation.

3. From the MacFile menu, choose Create Volume. Recall that a Macintosh-Accessible Volume is nothing more than a shared directory. The Create Macintosh-Accessible Volume dialog box appears (see Figure 20.3).

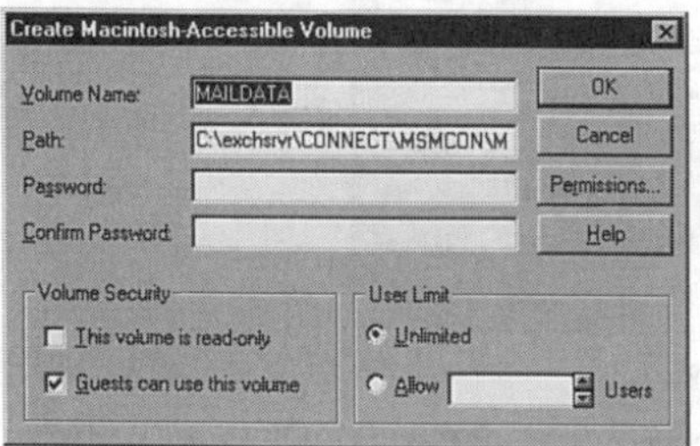

FIG. 20.3 Create a New Macintosh-Accessible Volume from the MacFile menu.

4. The Volume Name should be MAILDATA.
5. Enter a password. Users connecting from Macintosh workstations must enter a password to access the volume. The password applies only to Macintosh users. Non-Macintosh users are not required to provide a password when accessing the same directory structure through a share name. Enter confirm password.
6. For enhanced security, clear the Guests Can Use This Volume checkbox.
7. Confirm that This Volume is a Read-only remains deselected.
8. Be sure that the Unlimited User Limit option button is selected.
9. At this time, you may click the Permissions button to assign permission to those users that you want to access this volume or click OK to return to the MacFile dialog box.

Configuring Macintosh-Accessible Volume Permissions

After creating a Macintosh-Accessible Volume, you must define what users and groups will have permission to access the volume. If you do not complete this step when creating the Macintosh-Accessible Volume, you can complete the configuration in the Macintosh-Accessible

Volume Permissions dialog box. This dialog box is almost identical to the Macintosh File Sharing dialog box. In this box, select the users or groups that have access rights to the volume. The following steps guide you through assigning access rights to the Macintosh-Accessible Volume:

1. You can use two methods to open the permissions for a Macintosh-Accessible Volume. You can click Permissions from the Create Macintosh-Accessible Volume dialog box. Alternatively, you can choose the volume from the Explorer. Then choose Permissions from the MacFile menu. The Macintosh View of Directory Permissions dialog box appears (see Figure 20.4).
2. Use the (ellipses) buttons to configure an Owner and Primary Group for this volume. The configurations determine who is able to connect to the volume through the Macintosh Chooser.

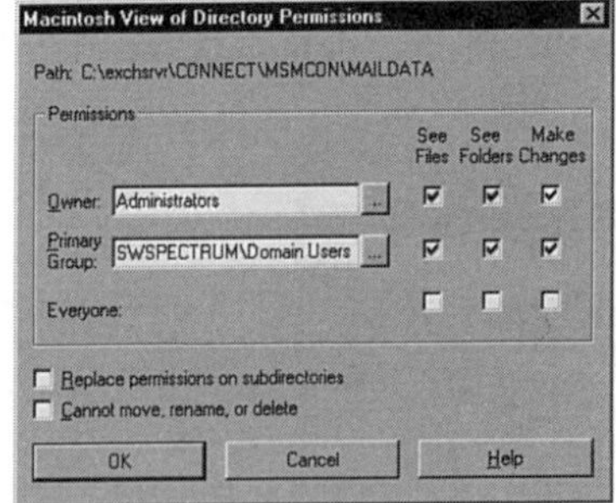

FIG. 20.4
You can set access permission for this volume.

3. Confirm that See Files, See Folders, and Make Changes permissions remain checked for the Owner and Primary Group.
4. Clear the check boxes pertaining to Everyone. This prevents anyone, except those users contained in Owner and Primary Group, from using this volume. By default, the Everyone permissions are checked.
5. Select the Replace Permissions on Subdirectories check box. This permission gives all directories within the current one permission settings identical to the ones on this page. By default, this box is not checked.
6. Click OK to set the permissions and return to the explorer.

After setting permissions on the Macintosh-Accessible Volume, the next logical step is to test the connection.

Testing Connection to the Macintosh-Accessible Volume

Upon completion of the Macintosh-Accessible Volume, the directory is now available for connection through the Macintosh Chooser. To confirm accessibility, you can test a manual connection by using the following steps:

1. Open the Chooser application from your Macintosh's Apple menu.
2. Click the AppleShare icon in the Chooser. Then select the AppleTalk Zone, if applicable, in which your Microsoft Exchange Server is located.

   The Microsoft Exchange Server should now be listed in the Select a File Server display window.
3. Click the Microsoft Exchange Server's name. Then click OK.
4. On the Connect dialog box, make sure the Registered User option button is selected. Enter the user Name and Password for this server. Then click OK.
5. After authentication, a list of available Macintosh-Accessible Volumes displays in the Select the Items You Want to Use: window.

   Your newly created MAILDATA (or whatever customized name you chose) volume should appear on the list.

If the Microsoft Exchange volume does not appear, repeat the preceding steps for creating and configuring a Macintosh-Accessible Volume. Otherwise, proceed to the following section.

Configuring the Microsoft Mail Connector for Use

After configuring the network link between the Macintosh Server and Microsoft Exchange, the next step is to configure the Microsoft Exchange Microsoft Mail Connector to send and receive messages with the Microsoft Mail (AppleTalk) Server.

The following explains the property pages for the Microsoft Exchange Microsoft Mail Connector, as well as how you should configure the connector to work with AppleTalk networks:

- Interchange: Use to configure the Microsoft Mail Connector (AppleTalk) MTA.
- Local Post Office: Sets the local information that a Microsoft Mail (AppleTalk) Server uses to identify and connect to the Microsoft Mail Connector. Any standard Microsoft Mail (PC) Post Office uses this data to connect.
- Connections: Enables viewing of the AppleTalk MTA's message queue.
- Connector MTAs: This page is not used with respect to connecting to Microsoft Mail for AppleTalk networks. Normally, this page defines which Microsoft Mail (PC) Post offices are serviced by a Microsoft Exchange Server.
- General: Use this page for both PC and AppleTalk Microsoft Mail connections to set an upper limit for message sizes.
- Address Space: Define which messages will be routed through this Microsoft Mail Connector to either type of Microsoft Mail system.
- Diagnostics Logging: Define logging levels for the Microsoft Mail (AppleTalk) MTA service. Also, configure on this tab the logging for the Interchange activity and the Microsoft Mail (PC) MTA.

Configuring Exchange Microsoft Mail Connector Properties

This section covers the installation of Microsoft Mail Connector properties primarily corresponding to communication with Microsoft Mail (AppleTalk) Servers. For a complete guide to the Microsoft Mail Connector, see Chapter 19, "Using the Microsoft Mail Connector for PC Networks."

The Interchange Page

Use the Interchange page to configure the Microsoft Mail Connector (AppleTalk) MTA. The following steps guide you through the Interchange configuration:

1. Open the Microsoft Exchange Administrator program. Select the site from the Organization list and the Microsoft Exchange Server name from the site. Select Connections from the list and click the Microsoft Mail Connector. The Microsoft Mail Connector property pages appear.
2. Select the Interchange tab. The Microsoft Mail Connector (GARLAND01) Properties page appears (see Figure 20.5).

FIG. 20.5
In the Microsoft Mail Connector Interchange property page, you can designate mailboxes.

3. From the Interchange tab, identify the administrator account for the Administrator's mailbox. This account receives system information and alert messages from the Connector in the case of nondelivery of mail and failed messages.

For larger organizations, create a POSTMASTER account to receive the potentially large volume of status messages. This way, one administrator mailbox is not burdened with an extra message load. In addition, other administrators can view the delivery messages without logging on to a general administrator mailbox or any recipient's personal mail.

4. Next, select the Primary Language for the recipients from the pull-down menu. Use the primary language for interoperability with Microsoft Mail Clients using an alternate language.
5. Check the Maximize Microsoft Mail 3.x Compatibility box to provide for OLE compatibility in messages transferred between older version applications used in Microsoft Mail Clients and the new version applications of Exchange Clients.
6. Ensure the Enable Message Tracking check box is cleared. You should select this option only for message tracking for troubleshooting purposes. For more information on message tracking for troubleshooting purposes, see Chapter 28, "Troubleshooting Exchange with Diagnostic Tools."

After configuring the Interchange property page, the AppleTalk MTA settings should be configured. The following section discusses these settings.

The Mail Connector AppleTalk MTA Dialog Box

To open a messaging link between Microsoft Exchange and Microsoft Mail (AppleTalk), you must configure the Microsoft Mail Connector AppleTalk Message Transfer Agent (MTA). Complete the following required steps:

1. Click the Configure button under the Microsoft Mail Connector (AppleTalk) MTA. The Microsoft Mail Connector (Apple Talk) MTA Options dialog box appears (see Figure 20.6).
2. Select the Enable Microsoft Mail Connector AppleTalk MTA option button under the Set Status window.

NOTE Enabling the AppleTalk MTA adds the property to the list of services in the Services applet of the Control Panel. ■

3. Select the Start Automatically at System Startup option button to configure this option. Subsequently, by default, this option will be selected. Click OK to return to the Interchange property page.

NOTE Typically, the automatic startup should remain selected. If you have a situation that requires troubleshooting in which you require manual control of the Microsoft Mail (AppleTalk) MTA, select the Manual Start option button. ■

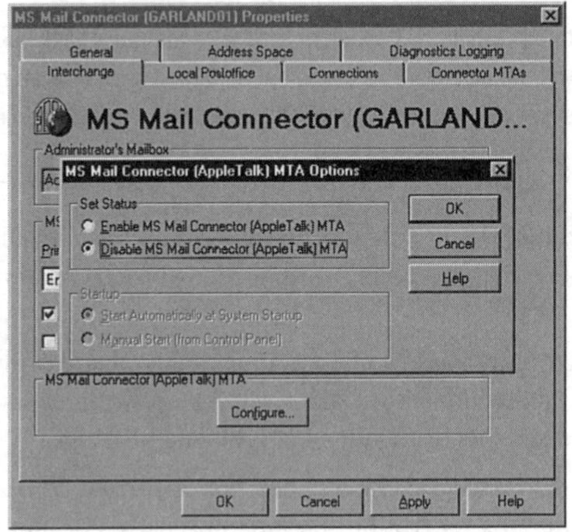

FIG. 20.6
You can view and set Microsoft Mail (AppleTalk) MTA service status.

4. Click Apply to set the properties and continue with the remaining configuration of the Microsoft Mail AppleTalk Connector.

The preceding steps conclude the configuration of the Microsoft Mail Connector AppleTalk Message Transfer Agent (MTA).

The Local Postoffice Page

The Local Postoffice information identifies the Microsoft Mail Connector Post Office to the Macintosh Microsoft Mail (AppleTalk) Servers and any Microsoft Mail Post Offices on the network. The following steps outline the configuration of the Local Postoffice page:

1. Select the Local Postoffice tab from the Microsoft Mail Connector property pages. The Microsoft Mail Connector (GARLAND01) Properties page appears (see Figure 20.7).
2. Enter the Microsoft Mail Network name for this post office. By default, the name is the Microsoft Exchange organization name.
3. Enter a post office used to identify this connector to other Microsoft Mail Servers. By default, the name is the Microsoft Exchange Server's name.
4. Enter a Sign-on Password used to authenticate other mail systems. By default, this is set to PASSWORD. You should change it for security reasons.
5. If you make any changes to post office settings, click Regenerate to rebuild addressing data.

NOTE To make Local Postoffice information changes take effect immediately, you must restart the Connector Interchange service as well as the Microsoft Mail MTAs. ■

6. Click Apply to set the properties and continue with other properties.
7. When you finish with all settings, click OK to set them and return to the Administrator program.

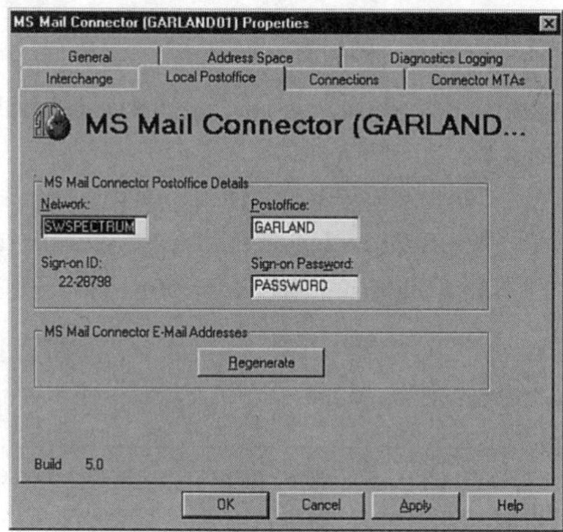

FIG. 20.7 You can configure the local Microsoft Mail Connector Postoffice information.

The Connections Page

The Connections property page enables you to view the Microsoft Mail (AppleTalk) MTA message queue. Options such as Modify, Delete, and Create, are available only for Microsoft Mail (PC) connections. The MTA queue lists all outgoing messages awaiting transmission by the Microsoft Mail AppleTalk message transfer agent.

To view the Microsoft Mail (AppleTalk) MTA message queue, complete the following steps:

1. Select the Connections tab from the Microsoft Mail Connector Properties page. The Microsoft Mail Connector (GARLAND01) Properties page appears (see Figure 20.8).

FIG. 20.8 The Connections tab enables you to view the Microsoft Mail Connector AppleTalk message queue.

2. The Connections dialog box displays all current Microsoft Mail connections.
3. Click the AppleTalk Mail entry in the window. Note that the Modify and Delete buttons are dimmed.

4. Click the Queue button to view the Queued Messages dialog box for AppleTalk Mail. (see Figure 20.9).
5. The Queued Messages window shows the current messages awaiting delivery by this MTA.

From	The message sender
Subject	The information on the message's Subject line
Message ID	The Microsoft Exchange *message* identification code
Date/Time	The date and time the message entered the queue

6. Click Refresh to update the message list.

The queued message window is a listing of messages awaiting delivery at that moment. To get a more dynamic view of messages passing through the connector, you must repeatedly click the Refresh button. Clicking this button also gives you the latest updates.

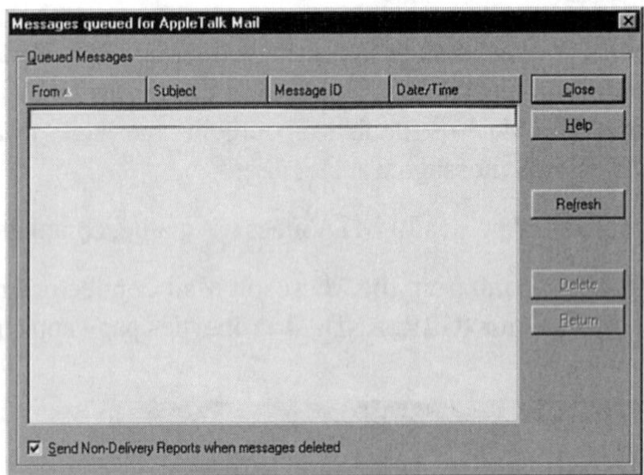

FIG. 20.9 The Microsoft Mail (AppleTalk) message queue displays the pertinent information on current messages.

7. Select a message. The Delete tab enables you to remove a message for the message queue. If Send Non-Delivery Reports When Messages Deleted is checked, the message sender is notified of the deletion.
8. Select a message. The Return tab removes the message from the queue and returns it to the sender.
9. After viewing the Microsoft Mail Connector AppleTalk message queue, click Close to return to the Connections property page.

Configuring Macintosh Microsoft Mail (AppleTalk)

This section describes the configuration required on the Macintosh side of the Microsoft Exchange/Microsoft Mail (AppleTalk) connection.

The following are the Macintosh Server configuration elements:

- Log in to the connector Post Office (Maildata volume).
- Log in to the Local Microsoft Mail (AppleTalk) Server as Network Manager.
- Install the Microsoft Exchange Connection Gateway.
- Configure the gateway with the Microsoft Mail Client.
- Install the Macintosh Directory Exchange Requestor (DER) (optional).

Complete the following steps to log in to the connector Post Office:

1. Open the Chooser application from your Macintosh Apple menu and click the AppleShare icon.
2. Then select the AppleTalk Zone in which your Microsoft Exchange Server is located.

   The Microsoft Exchange Server should now be listed in the Select a File Server display window.
3. Click the Microsoft Exchange Server's name. Then click OK.
4. On the Connect dialog box, make sure the Registered User option button is selected. Enter the user Name and Password required to access this volume. Click OK.
5. After you are authenticated, a list of available Macintosh-Accessible Volumes displays in the Select the Items You Want to Use: window.

   The MAILDATA, or the customized name volume should appear on the list.
6. Select Maildata volume.
7. Select the check box to the right of the Maildata volume to have this volume automatically mounted every time the Macintosh Server starts up.

   Select the Save My Name Only option button to request your password when the volume attempts to mount at startup.

   Select Save My Name and Password to store your logon data, and then automatically authenticate your connection when the Macintosh starts up.
8. Click OK to mount the volume.

After following these steps, the Maildata volume mounts.

Installing the Microsoft Exchange Connection Gateway

The Microsoft Exchange Connection Gateway is provided with your Microsoft Mail Connector software. Install the Microsoft Exchange Connection Gateway on your Macintosh Microsoft Mail Server to enable connectivity to the Microsoft Exchange Connector Post Office.

The following section assumes that you have installed Microsoft Mail for AppleTalk Networks, and it is properly running on your Macintosh Server.

The following steps guide you through installing the Connection Gateway on your Macintosh Server:

1. Log on to your Microsoft Mail (AppleTalk) Server as Network Manager.
2. Load the disk containing the Exchange Connection Installer. Open the installer application. The Connection Installer dialog box appears.

   If no previous gateways have been installed, the Gateways Installed on This Server: window appears blank.
3. Choose Install Gateway from the Gateway menu.
4. Select the GW icon from the dialog box and click Install. The dialog box appears.
5. Enter a unique Gateway ID. The Microsoft Mail (AppleTalk) Server uses this identifier to distinguish each gateway. By default, the ID for this gateway is NC.
6. Enter a Gateway name as you want it to display in the gateway list. Click OK. The dialog box appears.
7. Select which gateway templates to install for this gateway. Choose only those that you can access through this gateway or those typically used in your Microsoft Exchange organization. Click OK.

NOTE A gateway template becomes available in your Microsoft Mail (AppleTalk) Client, so you can create custom recipients for other messaging systems. ■

8. The Gateway is installed. Now, switch to your Microsoft Mail (AppleTalk) Client still logged in as Network Manager.

Configuring the Exchange Connection

With the Microsoft Mail (AppleTalk) Client, you may proceed to configure various gateway and post office connection options.

NOTE You must be logged in as Network Manager to administer a Microsoft Mail (AppleTalk) Server. ■

Specify the post office location and general gateway configuration by following these steps:

1. Select Gateway. Then choose Configuration from the Mail menu.
2. A dialog box prompts you to locate the Connection Store (MacGate) directory. Click OK.
3. Scroll through the MAILDATA volume and locate the MACGATE folder. Click Open.
4. Enter a Blocking Factor value. This value limits the number of messages that can transfer with each gateway cycle.
5. Enter an Aging Factor value. This is the amount of time, in minutes, that a message can remain in the Microsoft Mail Connector Post Office before a notification message is sent to the Network Manager.

NOTE Setting the Aging Factor to zero turns off notification. ■

6. Set the Max Size value. Messages exceeding this size (including attachments) cannot pass through this gateway. By default, this size is 100 kilobytes.
7. Select a logging level for this gateway. Select one of the three option buttons: Critical, Errors, or Details.

The gateway is now configured. Follow the next section to schedule gateway connections.

Scheduling Gateway Connections

The schedule screen is functionally similar to Microsoft Exchange's schedule property pages. Use this dialog box to configure at what times during the day the gateway connects to the Microsoft Mail Connector Post Office. You should base your decision for the time of the day the gateway connects to the Microsoft Mail Connector Post Office on factors particular to your environment. For most, bandwidth, server loads, and connection costs (for example, over leased lines or ISDN) are the limiting factors in the decision. If bandwidth or line costs are not an issue in your case, set the connection times as frequently as you want.

To set connection times, follow these steps:

1. Select Gateway. Then choose Connect Times from the Mail menu. A schedule grid appears for you to set connection times.
2. Select the option button that determines how frequently you want this gateway to initiate connection.

   The Never button effectively deactivates the gateway.

   The Always button connects at the interval (in minutes) set at the bottom of this dialog box.

   The At the Times Selected in the Chart Below button defines connection times by those that are highlighted in the time grid.
3. Select the Connect Immediately When There is Outgoing Mail check box to initiate a gateway connection as soon as a message is sent to the gateway.
4. If you chose the Selected Times option, use the time grid to mark the specific time you want the gateway to connect and transfer messages.

The connection schedule has now been set.

Installing an Access Gateway

After you have installed and configured the Connection Gateway, you can install additional access gateways on your Microsoft Mail (AppleTalk) system. This enables other Macintosh Microsoft Mail Servers to communicate with Microsoft Exchange and all its gateways and connectors.

You install an Access Connection Gateway by completing the following two steps:

1. Extract the Access gateway from the Microsoft Exchange Connection Gateway.
2. Install the Access gateway on another Microsoft Mail (AppleTalk) Server.

For step-by-step procedures for additional gateway installations, consult your gateway documentation. ●

CHAPTER 21

Configuring X.400 Connections

In this chapter

The Microsoft Exchange X.400 Connector is used to create a message route between two Exchange servers or between one Exchange server and another messaging system that complies with the X.400 standard. An X.400 connector is flexible due to its variety of available transport protocols. An Exchange site can utilize several X.400 connectors over various transport stacks, simultaneously providing multiple message routes as well as load balancing.

X.400 Supported Transport Protocols

The X.400 Connector can communicate over several network transport protocols. Out of the box, Exchange supports the use of the X.400 Connector with the following transport stacks:

- **TCP/IP**—Transmission Control Protocol/Internet Protocol. Uses the Windows NT TCP/IP services to establish communication over TCP/IP networks.
- **X.25 with the Eicon port adapter**—Transport Protocol 0/X.25. Both dial-up and direct connection over X.25 networks using the Eicon software or hardware solution. You may use multiple X.25 port adapters on each server, and each must have its own MTA Transport Stack (and appropriate hardware).
- **TP4**—Transport Class 4/Connectionless Network Protocol. Exchange includes a setup driver that enables it to work with the TP4 interface on Windows NT.

Before you can install a new X.400 connection, you must do the following:

- Make sure that the Exchange server has a necessary network transport protocol. For example, you must have the Windows NT TCP/IP protocols running and configured to successfully set up an X.400 connector with a TCP/IP Transport Stack.
- Configure and test all necessary networking hardware to confirm that a link exists. In the TCP/IP example, you can use the PING IP ADDRESS statement from the Windows NT command line to test this link.
- Know the exact X.400 address of the remote site or foreign system.

X.400 Connector Installation and Configuration

Whether you are installing an X.400 connection to another Microsoft Exchange server or foreign system, there are four primary steps to follow:

1. Install an appropriate MTA transport stack.
2. Install and configure a local X.400 connector.
3. Configure the X.400 connection on the remote Exchange site or foreign system.
4. Test the connection for message receipt and formatting consistency.

These steps summarize the overall process involved in configuring the X.400 connector. The following section delves more deeply into each of the steps involved.

Installing an MTA Transport Stack

When you are certain that all applicable network software and hardware is installed on the Windows NT server that will be handling the connection, you are ready to proceed with installing an MTA Transport Stack. This section first covers how to install the MTA Transport Stack and then how to configure the property pages for each one.

The installation procedure is as follows:

1. From the Exchange Administrator program File menu, select New Other, then select MTA Transport Stack. The New MTA Transport Stack dialog box appears (see Figure 21.1).

   The Type section of the dialog box lists the available MTA Transport Stacks on this Exchange server.

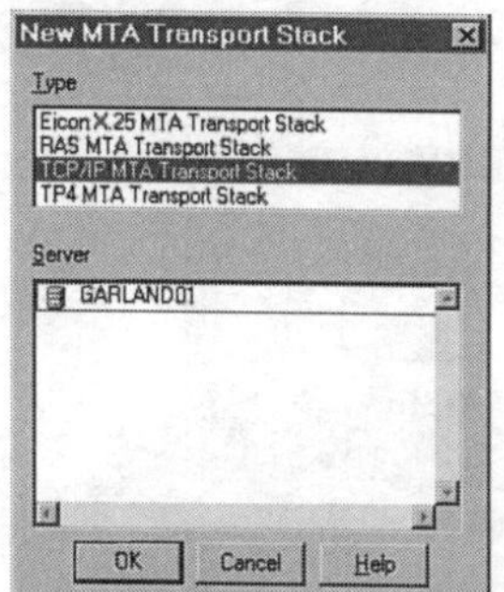

FIG. 21.1 The New MTA Transport Stack is used by the X.400 Connector (and also the Dynamic RAS Connector) to select an underlying transport for message transfer.

NOTE The RAS MTA Transport Stack is not used for X.400 connections. ■

   The Server section of the dialog box lists all the servers in the current site.

2. Click MTA Transport Stack. Select the server in your local site that will handle that type of connection. The transport stack will be installed on that server.
3. Click OK to accept the transport stack and Exchange Server settings. The properties page for the appropriate transport stack appears.

NOTE If all the necessary hardware/software for the network transport is not installed, you will get an error message stating that the required components are not ready. The MTA Transport Stack cannot be installed until these conditions are met. ■

A critical factor to remember is that the underlying network installation must support the transport. Once the X.400 connector is successfully added to Microsoft Exchange Server, you must then configure it for the specific protocol chosen as described in the following section.

Configuring MTA Transport Stack Property Pages

Each MTA Transport Stack has two corresponding property pages: a General page that identifies specific local addressing data, and a Connections page that lists all the X.400 connectors using this transport stack for communication.

This section includes steps to set up a new TCP/IP transport stack. If you are not using TCP/IP as a network transport, you can skip this section.

The General Page The General tab fulfills two functions for a new TCP/IP MTA Transport Stack. First, you can give it a name for display in the Administrator program. Second, you can enter specific OSI address information if your network environment requires that you distinguish between applications that use the TCP/IP network transport. Complete the following steps:

1. Select the General tab in the TCP/IP MTA Transport Stack Properties page (see Figure 21.2).

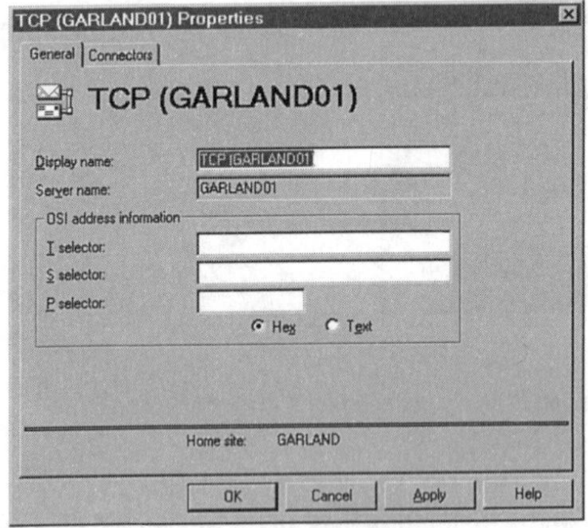

FIG. 21.2 Setting the name and local transport information in this property page.

2. Enter a Name for this MTA Transport Stack as you want it to appear, in the Administrator program's display window. By default, this transport is named as TCP (*server name*). You can change it only when you are creating a new transport stack.
3. The Server Name box displays the Exchange server on which this MTA Transport Stack is installed. The server cannot be changed at this point. To use a different server, you must cancel out of these property pages and install a new MTA Transport Stack.
4. Under OSI Address Information, enter numbers required to distinguish Exchange from other services or applications using the TCP/IP Transport Stack. There is one box for each of the following three network layers:

   T selector: Transport Service Access Point (TSAP)
   S selector: Session Service Access Point (SSAP)
   P selector: Presentation Service Access Point (PSAP)

5. Select either the Hex or Text option button, depending on the type of data you enter in the preceding boxes.
6. Click Apply to set these properties and continue with other properties. If you have completed all the settings, click OK to return to the Administrator program.

The preceding steps, which are part of the General page, involve the information that will be required when communicating with any X.400 system.

The Connectors Page The Connectors Property page displays a list of every Microsoft Exchange X.400 connector that uses this TCP/IP MTA Transport Stack. You can open the property pages for each listed X.400 connector from this page as well.

The following is only a quick overview of the steps for configuring the connectors. Each step is described in more detail following this section.

1. Select the Connectors tab on the TCP/IP MTA Transport's Properties page (see Figure 21.3). All X.400 connectors using this MTA Transport Stack are listed in the Connectors that use this stack window.

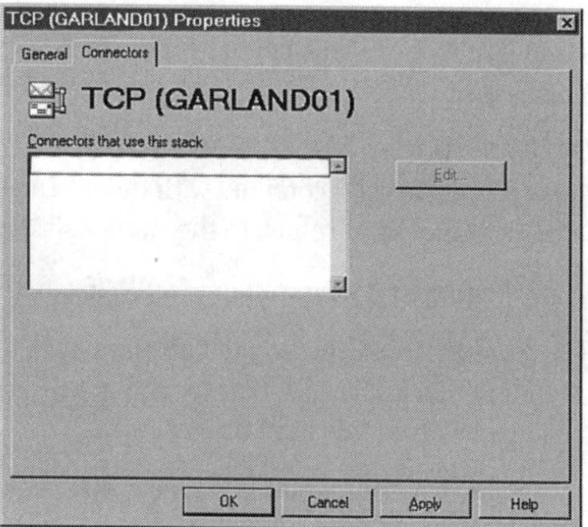

FIG. 21.3 A listing of X.400 connectors using this MTA Transport Stack (blank if no connectors are set up).

2. Select an X.400 connector name from the list (if any are available), then click Edit so that its properties page appears.
3. Click Apply to set these properties and continue with other properties. If you have completed all the settings, click OK to return to the Administrator program.

Setting Up a New X.25 Transport Stack

This section includes steps to set up a new X.25 transport stack. If you are not using X.25 as a network transport, you can skip this section.

The General Page The General tab fulfills two functions for a new X.25 MTA Transport Stack. First, you can give it a name for display in the Administrator program. Second, you can enter specific OSI address information if your network environment requires that you distinguish between applications that use the X.25 network transport. Complete the following steps:

1. Select the General tab in the X.25 MTA Transport Stack Properties page.
2. Enter a Name for this MTA Transport Stack as you want it to appear in the Administrator program's display window. By default, this transport stack is named as Eicon X.25 (*server name*). This name can be changed only when creating a new transport stack.
3. Enter the Call User Data as provided by your X.25 network provider. This can be up to 256 characters.
4. Enter the local X.121 Address as specified in the X.25 network set up under Windows NT.
5. Under OSI Address Information, enter numbers required to distinguish Exchange from other services or applications by using the X.25 Transport Stack. There is one box for each of the following three network layers:

   T selector: Transport Service Access Point (TSAP)
   S selector: Session Service Access Point (SSAP)
   P selector: Presentation Service Access Point (PSAP)

6. Select either the Hex or Text option button, depending on the type of data you enter in the preceding boxes.
7. Select the option button that corresponds to your type of X.25 connection—Async Phone Line (Dial-Up X.25) or Leased Line.
8. If you select Leased Line, enter the I/O port on which your Eicon adapter is installed.
9. Click Apply to set these properties and continue with other properties. If you have completed all the settings, click OK to return to the Administrator program.

The preceding steps allow for the proper configuration of an X.25 connection.

The Connectors Page The Connectors Property page displays a list of every Microsoft Exchange X.400 Connector that uses this X.25 MTA Transport Stack. You can open the properties page for each listed X.400 connector from this page as well.

Use this properties page to view which Microsoft Exchange X.400 connectors use this X.25 MTA Transport Stack. Follow these steps to view the list of connectors and open the properties page for connectors on the list.

1. Select the Connectors tab on the X.25 MTA Transport's Properties page.

   All X.400 connectors using this MTA Transport Stack are listed in the Connectors That Use This Stack window.
2. Select an X.400 connector name from the list (if any are available), then click Edit so that its properties page appears.
3. Click Apply to set these properties and continue with other properties. If you have completed all the settings, click OK to return to the Administrator program.

The preceding steps will ensure that the appropriate connector is used in conjunction with the X.25 transport.

Setting Up a New TP4 Transport Stack

This section includes steps to set up a new TP4 transport stack. If you are not using TP4 as a network transport, you can skip this section.

The General Page The General tab fulfills two functions for a new TP4 MTA Transport Stack. First, you can give it a name for display in the Administrator program. Second, you can enter specific OSI address information if your network environment requires that you distinguish between applications that use the TP4 network transport.

To configure the TP4 Transport for communications to a network, complete the following steps:

1. Select the General tab in the TP4 MTA Transport Stack Properties page.
2. Enter a Name for this MTA Transport Stack as you want it to appear in the Administrator program's display window. By default, this transport stack is named as TP4 (server name). You can change this name only when you are creating a new transport stack.
3. Under OSI Address Information, enter numbers required to distinguish Exchange from other services or applications using the TP4 Transport Stack. There is one box for each of the following three network layers:

   T selector: Transport Service Access Point (TSAP)
   S selector: Session Service Access Point (SSAP)
   P selector: Presentation Service Access Point (PSAP)

4. Select either the Hex or Text option button, depending on the type of data you enter in the preceding boxes.
5. Click Apply to set these properties and continue with other properties. If you have completed all the settings, click OK to return to the Administrator program.

The Connectors Page The Connectors Properties page displays a list of every Microsoft Exchange X.400 connector that uses this TP4 MTA Transport Stack. You can open the properties page for each listed X.400 connector from this page as well.

To select the appropriate connector with the TP4 transport stack, complete the following steps:

1. Select the Connectors tab on the TP4 MTA Transport's Properties page.

   All X.400 connectors using this MTA Transport Stack are listed in the Connectors that use this stack window.
2. Select an X.400 connector name from the list (if any are available), then click Edit so that its properties page appears.
3. Click Apply to set these properties and continue with other properties. If you have completed all the settings, click OK to return to the Administrator program.

The preceding steps ensure that the appropriate connector is used with the TP4 transport.

Because there are many variations in configuring the X.400 connector with various transports, it is important to verify each page. The order of which side is configured first (Exchange or

Remote) will determine which one becomes the baseline for the opposing connector. In most cases, unless you are connecting two Exchange sites, it will be an external X.400 connector that you will need to determine the settings to enter into the pages.

Installing and Configuring an X.400 Connector

When you have properly installed all the needed MTA Transport Stacks, you can create the actual X.400 connector that will transfer messages over that transport. You must have the following information in order to proceed in setting up a new X.400 connector:

- **A unique name for this connector:** For identification in the Exchange Administrator program.
- **Remote MTA name:** String identifying the Message Transfer Agent on the remote Exchange site or foreign system.
- **Remote MTA password:** String used to authenticate an X.400 messaging link (needed only if the remote MTA requires password authentication).
- **Stack address:** The unique identifying address for the local X.400 connector.
- **Address space:** Any address entry that will uniquely identify a message's route through this X.400 connector to a remote site or foreign system.

NOTE For an X.400 connection to be established, a connector must be set up on both sides of the link. For a Microsoft Exchange server, this means setting up a corresponding Exchange X.400 connector. For a foreign X.400 system, this involves using that system's administrative tools and entering appropriate addressing data for the Exchange server. (See guidelines near the end of this chapter.)

Creating a New X.400 Connector

From the Administrator program File menu, select New Other, then select X.400 Connector. The New X.400 Connector dialog box is displayed (see Figure 21.4).

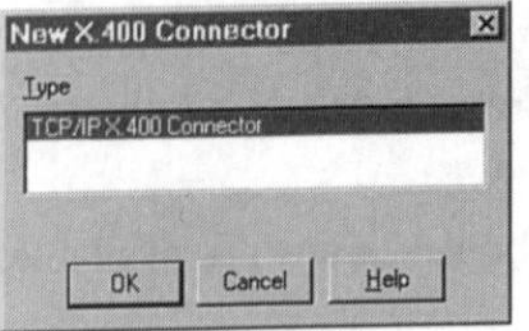

FIG. 21.4 Selecting an MTA Transport Stack for this X.400 connector.

The New X.400 Connector Type dialog box lists all the currently installed MTA Transport Stacks. Select one from the list and click OK. The X.400 property sheets open.

NOTE If you have not yet configured an MTA Transport Stack, you cannot continue from this point. Follow the instructions in the previous section to set up the underlying transport stack.

Configuring an X.400 Connector

The X.400 Connector property pages allow you to configure any X.400 connection, whether it is between two Exchange sites, or to a foreign X.400 system. The following is an overview of the X.400 property pages and the functions of each:

- General
- Schedule
- Stack
- Override
- Connected sites
- Address space
- Delivery restrictions
- Advanced

The General Page Use the X.400 General tab to set the principal communication options for a new connector. The following steps guide you through configuring the X.400 connector General tab:

1. Select the General tab of the X.400 Connector Properties page (see Figure 21.5).
2. Enter a Display Name for this connector as you want it to appear in the Exchange Administrator display window.

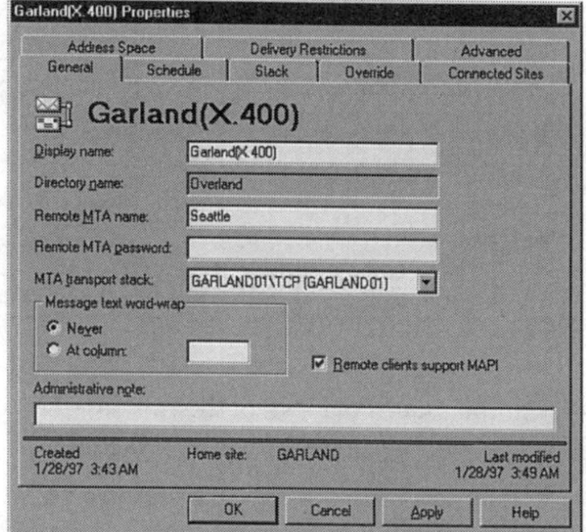

FIG. 21.5 Selecting an MTA Transport Stack for this X.400 connector.

3. Enter a Directory Name used for addressing purposes.
4. Enter the Remote MTA Name in the box provided.
5. If required, enter a Remote MTA Password for the preceding remote MTA.
6. The MTA Transport Stack displays the currently selected transport for this X.400 connector. You can change the MTA Transport Stack with the drop-down menu.

7. Under Message Text Word-Wrap, you can force a carriage return in all the outgoing messages by clicking the At Column button and entering the column number. By default, this is set to Never.
8. If your X.400 connection is to a foreign messaging system that does not support MAPI, clear the Remote Clients Support MAPI check box. All rich text and other MAPI characteristics are removed from outgoing messages.
9. Enter any additional administrative note.

The preceding steps allow for configuring the general information on how the X.400 connector appears to other systems and to ensure that non-MAPI clients can format messages properly.

The Schedule Page Use the Schedule Properties page to control how often the X.400 Connector becomes active and initiates a connection.

The following steps are required to ensure that the connection is utilized effectively:

1. Select the Schedule tab in the X.400 Connector Properties page (see Figure 21.6).
2. Select one of the four option buttons that determine when this X.400 Connector connects.

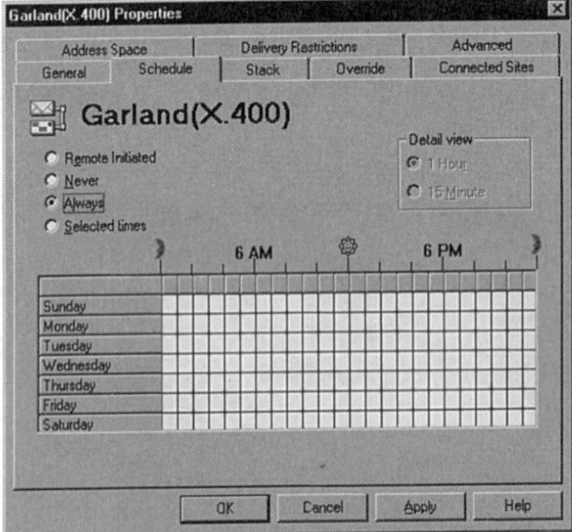

FIG. 21.6
Setting connection times for this connector.

Remote Initiated—Send messages only when the remote MTA connects to this MTA. Both MTAs must have the two-way alternate option selected in the Advanced property page.

CAUTION

Only one MTA can be configured to be remote-initiated. Otherwise, if both MTAs are waiting for the other to initiate the connection, the messages will never be delivered.

Never—A connection is never established. This option effectively disables this X.400 Connector.

Always—An MTA connection is established whenever messages need to be transferred. By default, this option is selected.

Selected Times—The X.400 Connector initiates communication based on the time grid on this properties page.

3. If you choose Selected Times, the Detail View option buttons become available. Select either the 1 hour or 15 Minute detail view and the time grid will change its scale accordingly.
4. If you choose Selected Times, pick the time blocks for connection.
5. Click Apply to set these properties and continue with other properties. If you have completed all the settings, click OK to return to the Administrator program.

The ability to schedule the X.400 connector is probably the most desired feature insetting up a site-to-site connection within Exchange Server. This is an important feature to remember when there is a low bandwidth situation that will assist in better utilization of the connection.

The Stack Page Each MTA Transport Stack has a different Stack page, primarily because each transport uses different addressing conventions. This section first covers the top section of the Stack Properties page, which is unique to each transport. The second part of the page covers entering OSI information to identify a particular X.400 connector with the transport stack. The OSI information is common to all Stack properties pages and is covered only once following the address information section.

In most cases, TCP/IP will be utilized as the transport stack to communicate with remote systems. The steps that follow describe the configuration:

1. Select the Stack tab in the X.400 Connector Properties page (see Figure 21.7).

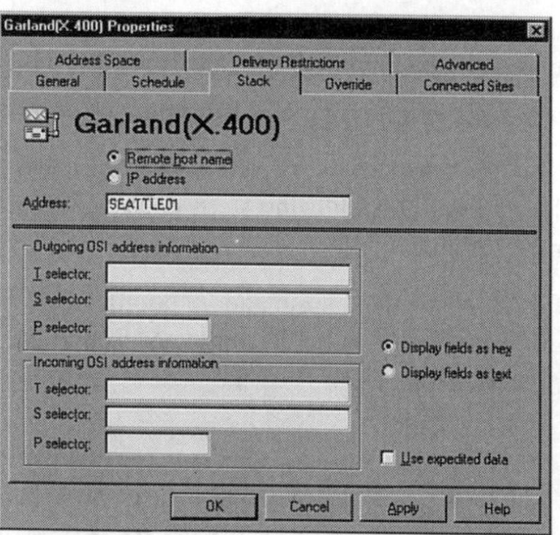

FIG. 21.7 Entering the TCP/IP addressing data for the remote MTA.

2. Select the appropriate option button for the remote site's address. Use Remote Host Name if the remote server can be identified either through the Domain Name Service (DNS) or the Windows Internet Naming Service (WINS). Use IP Address if a host name is not available.

Using an IP address will make for a slightly faster connection time to the remote system. However, using the IP address numbers may be too cryptic for administration purposes (that is, more difficult to remember and identify at first glance).

3. Enter the host name or IP address in the Address box.
4. Proceed to the "Outgoing and Incoming OSI Information" section later in this chapter.

If the TCP/IP transport is not utilized to communicate with the remote system, it will be necessary to configure either the X.25 or TP4 stack properties described as follows.

To configure the X.25 Stack Properties page, complete the following steps:

1. Select the Stack tab in the X.400 Connector Properties page. The X.25 Transport version of the Stack Properties page appears.
2. Enter your Call User Data as given by your X.25 provider.
3. Enter Facilities Data as specified by your X.25 provider. This contains a comma-delimited list of additional connection parameters.
4. Enter the X.121 Address of the remote server. This information can be obtained from the remote server's X.25 transport information.
5. Proceed to the "Outgoing and Incoming OSI Information" section later in this chapter.

To configure the TP4 Stack Properties page, complete the following steps:

1. Select the Stack tab in the X.400 Connector Properties page.

   The TP4 Transport version of the Stack Properties page appears.
2. Enter the network service access point (NSAP) or the address of the remote X.40 system.
3. Proceed to the "Incoming and Outgoing OSI Data" section later in the chapter.
4. Proceed to the "Outgoing and Incoming OSI Information" section that follows.

The Outgoing and Incoming OSI information, shown in Figure 21.7, is the same for all transports that were previously covered. The following steps cover how to configure the various outgoing and incoming information:

1. Under Outgoing OSI Address Information and Incoming OSI Address Information, enter numbers required to distinguish this X.400 connector from other services or applications using this transport stack. There is one box for each of the following three network layers:

   T selector: Transport Service Access Point (TSAP)
   S selector: Session Service Access Point (SSAP)
   P selector: Presentation Service Access Point (PSAP)
2. Select either the Display fields as hex or display fields as text option button depending on the type of data you enter in the preceding boxes.

3. Select the Use expedited data check box if your network recognizes data packets identified for accelerated transfer. Some networks require the use of expedited data. Refer to your transport and network documentation for more information.
4. Click Apply to set these properties and continue with other properties. If you have completed all the settings, click OK to return to the Administrator program.

The Override Page With the Override Properties page, shown in Figure 21.8, you can set the connector-specific MTA. These settings affect only MTA links established through this X.400 connector.

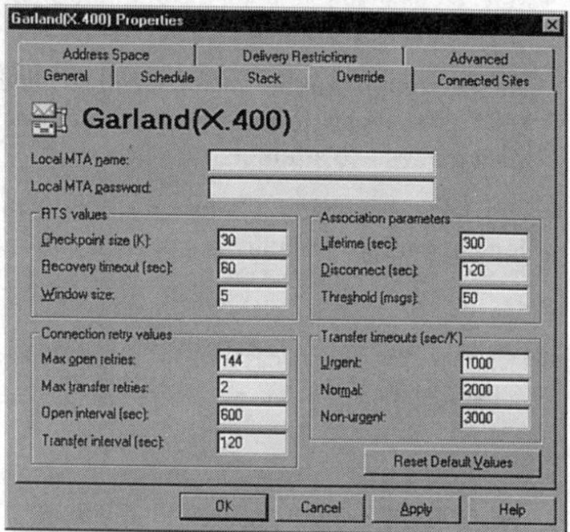

FIG. 21.8
Entering MTA override settings for this connector.

Enter a different Local MTA Name if the foreign X.400 system cannot accept the Microsoft Exchange server name. Sometimes the server name may be too long or contain characters (for example, spaces) that a foreign X.400 MTA cannot accept.

Enter Local MTA Password to require authentication when establishing communication from a remote system.

Enter specific MTA configuration variables. Table 21.1 lists each variable and its function within the MTA.

Table 21.1 MTA Variables and Functions

Variable	Function
	?RTS Values
Checkpoint size (K):	The value used to verify packet transmission with returned checkpoints. By default, this is 30 kilobytes.
Recovery timeout (sec):	The time delay before retrying a broken transmission. By default, the delay is 60 seconds.

continues

Table 21.1 Continued

Variable	Function
	?RTS Values
Window size:	The maximum number of checkpoints that can be transmitted without acknowledgment. By default, this value is 5 kilobytes.
	Connection Retry Values
Max open retries:	The maximum number of consecutive failed attempts before the MTA stops trying to open a communication channel with a remote MTA. By default, an MTA makes 144 attempts.
Max transfer retries:	The maximum number of consecutive failed attempts before the MTA stops trying to transfer a message packet. By default, the MTA makes two attempts.
Open interval (sec):	The delay (in seconds) between attempts to open a communication channel. By default, this delay is 600 seconds.

NOTE If you combine the default "144 Max open retries" with the default "600 second Open interval," it adds up to a total of 24 hours before a message is returned as undeliverable.

Variable	Function
Transfer interval (sec):	The delay (in seconds) between attempts to retransmit a failed message packet. By default, this delay is 120 seconds.
	Association Parameters
Lifetime (sec):	The maximum time that an idle connection between MTAs remains open. By default, an idle link is held open for 300 seconds after the last communication.
Disconnect (sec):	The maximum time allowed when establishing or terminating a connection before the session is ended independently. By default, this is 120 seconds.
Threshold (msgs):	The number of messages that must be queued at this MTA for it to initiate a link to a remote MTA. By default, 50 messages must be awaiting transmission.
	Transfer Timeouts(sec/K)
Urgent:	The delay (in seconds per kilobyte of total message size) between retries of urgent messages. By default, this delay is 1,000 seconds. This is the timeout value before messages are sent. An Urgent message is set by the user when composing a message.

Variable	Function
Normal:	The delay (in seconds per kilobyte of total message size) between retries of normal messages. By default, this delay is 2,000 seconds. The trend here is the less important the message, the longer the wait in sending the message again.
Non-urgent:	The delay (in seconds per kilobyte of total message size) between retries of nonurgent messages. By default, this delay is 3,000 seconds.

Each item has a box to its right with a default numeric value. Replace any value with a number that will be used when establishing a connection through this X.400 connector. To return to the default Message Transfer Agent settings, click Reset Default Values.

The Connected Sites Page The Connected Sites Properties page lists other Microsoft Exchange sites that are available through this X.400 connector. This includes sites that are indirectly linked through this connector.

Here is an example of when to use this feature. Exchange site SEATTLE is linked to site FRANKFORT through a public X.400 network. SEATTLE, in turn, is linked to GARLAND through a high bandwidth line by using a site connector.

When data replication between sites occurs, information about indirectly connected sites appears in the Connected Sites window.

In this case, the indirectly connected sites are GARLAND and LOS ANGELES. A message sent from FRANKFORT to LOS ANGELES is sent to the first site it is connected to and then forwarded to the next site, and so on, until LOS ANGELES is reached (see Figure 21.9).

Manually Modifying Indirectly Connected Sites

You may also manually insert an address entry for an indirectly connected site. This is done from the Connected Sites Properties page as well. This page may also be used to modify an existing route.

NOTE If you are using an X.400 connector to link to a foreign X.400 system, you can skip this section. ■

The following steps are used to add or modify connected site entries:

1. To create a new entry, click the New button on the Connected Sites Properties page. To change an existing entry, select it from the list and click Edit on the Connected Sites Properties page. The properties page in Figure 21.10 appears. The General page appears first.
2. Enter the Organization name in which the remote Exchange server exists. By default, your current organization is displayed.
3. Enter the name of the Microsoft Exchange Site in which the remote server exists. By default, this entry is left blank.

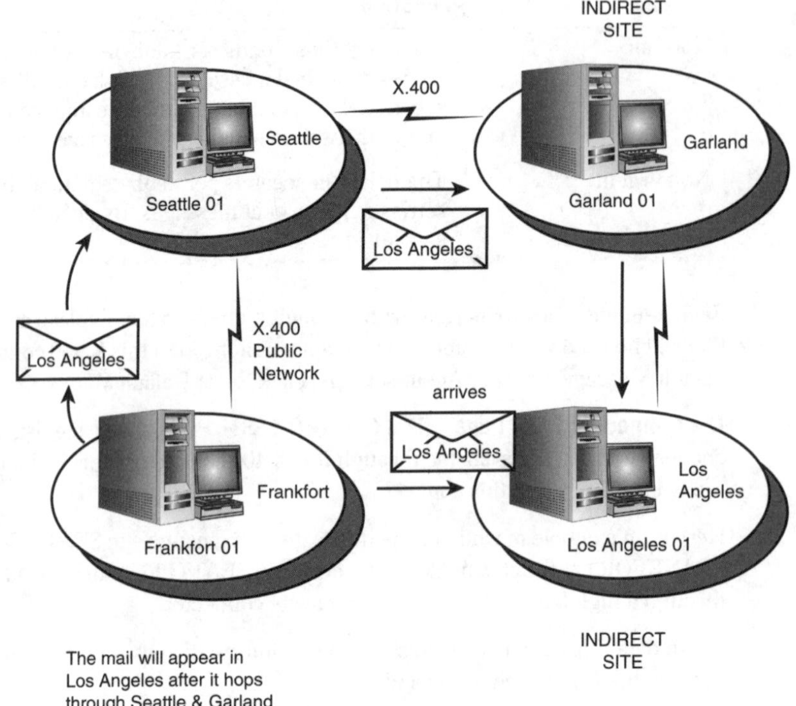

FIG. 21.9
Indirect link sites: The mail will appear in Los Angeles after the hops through Seattle and Garland.

The following steps are to specify a routing address for an indirectly connected site.

1. Click the Routing Address tab (see Figure 21.10).
2. By default, the Organization name displayed is the site name you entered in the preceding General Properties page.
3. Enter X.400 routing information needed to connect to the remote server. The following is a list and description of the routing information required:

Organizational Units	Identify the Exchange servers via their valid X.400 names.
Private Management	Enter the PRMD of the remote Domain Name (PMDN) server.
Administrative	Enter the PRMD of the remote Management Domain server. Name (ARMD)
Country	An X.400 value that identifies the country of the server.
Cost	Standard Microsoft Exchange routing cost value. By default, this cost is 1.

To delete a connected site entry, select the site address entry from the Connected Sites Properties page. Click Remove. That remote site will no longer be available through this X.400 connector.

FIG. 21.10
Entering connected site information manually.

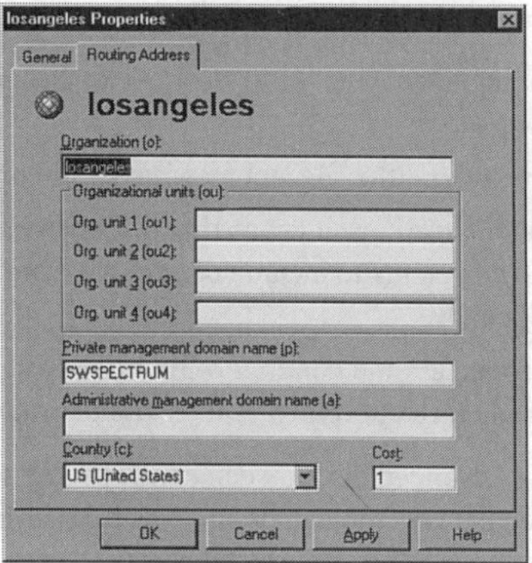

The Address Space Page The Address Space Properties page defines the messages that are routed through this connector. Only enough addressing data is provided to distinguish messages that should be sent through this connector.

Routing costs are also entered along with each address space entry.

The Delivery Restrictions Page The Delivery Restrictions Properties page filters the individuals that can or cannot send messages through this connector. There are two easy-to-understand delivery options (see Figure 21.11):

FIG. 21.11
Delivery restrictions limit who can access this X.400 connector.

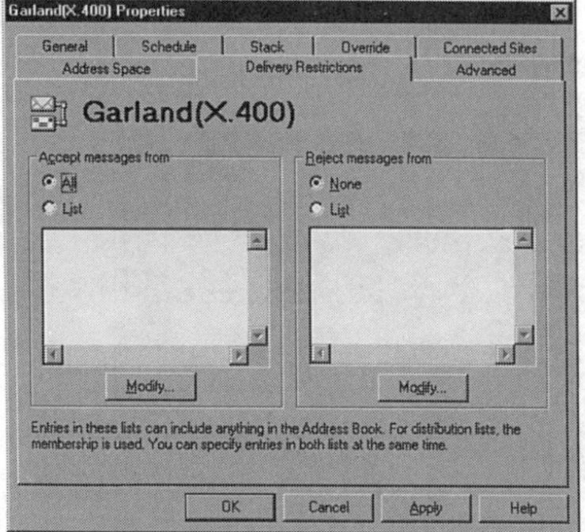

- Accept Messages From: Creates an exclusive list of recipients with permission to send messages through this X.400 connector.
- Reject Messages From: Lists specific recipients that are denied permission to send messages through this X.400 connector.

The following steps show how to set up the different delivery options:

1. Select the Delivery Restrictions tab in the X.400 Connector Properties page (see Figure 21.11).
2. Click the List option button under either Accept messages from or Reject messages from.
3. Click the Modify button underneath each list so that the Microsoft Exchange address list appears. Select the desired recipients to include or exclude from X.400 message transfer through this connector. Click OK.
4. Click Apply to set these properties and continue with other properties. If you have completed all the settings, click OK to return to the Administrator program.

The Advanced Page Under the Advanced tab, you can control some of the finer points of X.400 connectivity with Exchange Server. You can define which X.400 standard to utilize, and how various elements of the messages are transferred through the system.

In most cases, configuring the Advanced properties is not required if communicating to standard X.400 systems. However, if there are any communications failures with the remote system, you should review it to verify accuracy. Complete the following steps:

1. Select the Advanced tab from the X.400 Properties page (see Figure 21.12).
2. Under MTA Conformance, select the option button pertaining to the correct X.400 standard you will be using. Exchange supports all the latest X.400 standards, but you must select the setting that conforms to what your provider uses. These are your three options:

   1984
   1988 X.410 mode
   1988 normal mode

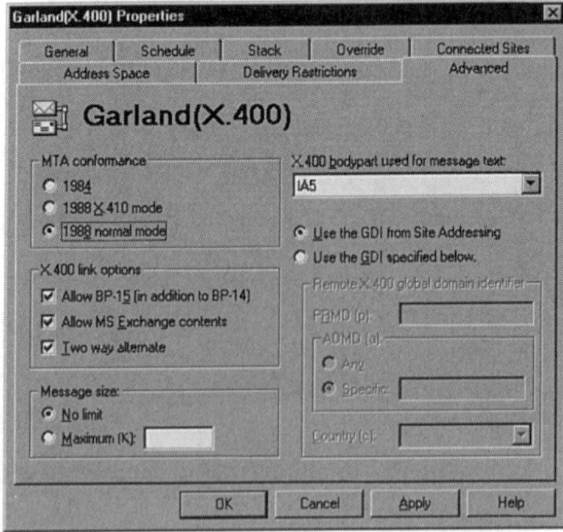

FIG. 21.12
Entering a routing address for the indirectly connected site.

CAUTION

To avoid message transmission errors, be sure to select the standard supported by your X.400 carrier and the remote X.400 system.

3. Under X.400 Link Options, select all the check boxes pertaining to features you want in this link.

   Enable BP-15 (in addition to BP-14) (available only if 1988 MTA conformance is selected). Use the BP-15 extension standard for message attachments.

   Enable MS Exchange Contents (use only when the remote system is a Microsoft Exchange server). Permits the transmission of MAPI message properties as an object of the X.400 message using the Message Database Encoding Format (MDBEF). Two-Way Alternate Permits both to take turns sending and receiving message data. Use when the remote MTA supports this functionality.
4. Under Message Size, click Maximum (K) and enter a value (in kilobytes) if you want to set a maximum for message transmission. By default, No Limit is selected and messages of any size can pass through this connector.
5. Under X.400 Body part Used for Message Text, use the drop-down menu to select the body part type used for the content of an outbound message. It must be supported by the foreign system. These settings do not affect inbound messages.
6. Select the Use the GDI from Site Addressing to use the Global Domain Identifier from the Site Addressing page to prevent message transfer loops.
7. Select Use the GDI Specified Below and enter the foreign system's GDI in the space provided. Obtain this information from the foreign system's configuration settings.
8. Click Apply to set these properties and continue with other properties. If you have completed all the settings, click OK to return to the Administrator program.

Configuring a Foreign X.400 System

The specifics to configuring a foreign X.400 system vary from system to system. This section will provide you with general guidelines to follow when setting up a foreign X.400 system to communicate with a Microsoft Exchange Server X.400 connector.

To ensure that messages are properly processed and interpreted on both sides of the X.400 connection, follow these guidelines described:

- Microsoft Exchange Server supports a wide variety of X.400 content and body part types. It is a good idea to attempt to match X.400 capabilities exactly with a foreign system's settings whenever possible.
- If the local Microsoft Exchange X.400 connector is configured first, use the settings in the Administrator program X.400 Properties page to retrieve settings for the foreign system.

- If the foreign system is configured first, obtain all the necessary settings for the local Exchange server.

Verifying Connections

When both ends of an X.400 link are configured, you must proceed to test the connection. Because X.400 performs message format conversions during transmission, you must not only make sure that a message is properly received, but that its contents are correctly formatted.

Messages sent to a remote Exchange site through an X.400 connector should be received in the exact same format as they were transmitted. This includes the transmission of all the attachments as well. All MAPI information should be preserved in the conversion and transmission process.

Here is a sequence you can use to test your X.400 link between sites:

1. Create and send a message to a remote site using the Exchange client. Include the following in the message:

   Rich text formatting (various colors, font sizes, and so on); an attached file (of any sort); or an embedded OLE object (word processing document, spreadsheet, and so on).
2. Verify that the intended recipient receives the message in his or her inbox.
3. Check the message contents (including attachments and embedded objects) for data integrity.
4. If required, on the Advanced tab for the mailbox, select the Downgrade High Priority X.400 Mail so all X.400 mail delivery will be at normal mode for that mailbox.
5. Repeat the preceding steps by sending a message from the remote site to the local site.

When testing message transmissions to foreign X.400 systems, here are some important test steps to follow:

1. Create a message as previously described, with rich text formatting and attachments.
2. Verify that the message is delivered to the intended recipient.
3. Check that message for data integrity.
4. A foreign system with a MAPI-based client should preserve all rich text formatting and attachments.
5. A foreign system with a non-MAPI-based client should receive the message in plain text. Any attachments should be preserved, and there should be an additional attachment that contains all the information this client cannot display.
6. Create and send a message from within the foreign system's X.400 client, addressed to a local Microsoft Exchange mailbox.
7. Ensure that the Remote Host Name option in the TCP connector stack is selected, and a fully qualified domain name is entered. If only a partial name exists, it may produce an event id of 9215.
8. Verify that the local user receives all messaging data (including attachments).

CHAPTER 22

Configuring the IMS

In this chapter

Exchange provides Internet electronic mail through the use of a robust Simple Mail Transfer Protocol (SMTP) connector service. The Internet Mail Wizard in Exchange 5.5 automates the Internet Mail Service configuration and enables Exchange clients to send and receive messages to and from people across the Internet. Clients do not need to be directly connected to the Internet to use this functionality.

This IMS is one of the core components of Exchange Server; it integrates directly with the rest of the mail services. You can configure the IMS as a standalone solution or use it as the backbone connectivity protocol.

Learning the Internet Mail Service Wizard

The Internet Mail Wizard helps you to navigate graphically through the configuration of the Internet Mail Service (IMS) that relies on industry standards to enable seamless integration with Exchange and existing SMTP mail systems. The IMS provides message transferring with any other system that uses the SMTP protocol. When you first start the Internet Mail Wizard (IMS), you must have DNS set up already on your computer. The components of DNS (Domain Name Service) are Hostname, Domain name, Domain Name, Computer's IP Address. It is also good to put the domain name (that is, `softwarespectrum.com`) into the domain suffix search order.

When this is complete and you have rebooted the computer, you must configure the A record and the MX record in the DNS Manager. The A record stands for Authority Record, which is an IP starting point of navigation through the vast Internet pathways. The MX record is a pointer to your Exchange server so that you can be found by your ISP for mail delivery from the Internet. You can obtain the exact configurations for these components from your ISP. Once you have these items set up correctly, you can continue with the installation of the IMS through the Internet Mail Wizard.

NOTE If you have two WINS servers in your environment, then set each of the WINS servers to point to their own IP Address for the primary as well the secondary addresses. The reason for doing this is that if one WINS server is faster than the other on your network, it will try to register itself with the faster WINS server. This will cause an endless loop to occur, which in turn could cause other unknown problems. ■

Learning the Internet Mail Service (IMS)

The IMS is very versatile. It relies on industry standards to allow seamless integration with Exchange and existing SMTP mail systems. The IMS provides message transferring with any other system that uses the SMTP protocol.

Internet Standards on the Internet Mail IMS

Users from single or multiple Exchange or Microsoft Mail 3.x sites can communicate with the Internet through the IMS.

NOTE Client workstations do not need to have an Internet connection to use the IMS. ■

The functionality provided with the IMS complies with Internet standards. The IMS relies on a set of standards that have been ratified over the past 30 years. These standards are a set of published documents known as Requests for Comment (RFCs). These are the guidebooks for developing applications to be used on the Internet. Following is a list of the key standards to which the Internet Mail IMS adheres:

- RFC 821. This RFC is the Simple Mail Transfer Protocol (SMTP) standard. RFC 821 describes the message definitions for passing or transferring mail from one computer system to another.
- RFC 822. This RFC, which is the continuation of RFC 821, describes the message format and structure of the data in the message. The standard covers the header information (To, From, Subject, and message body data). This RFC deals with non-text attachments by decoding the data with uuencode and uudecode encoding. If you have an attachment, the IMS converts the attachment to text and populates the body of the message with the encoded data.
- RFC 1521. This RFC, which defines the standard for sending attachments over the SMTP protocol, is called Multipurpose Internet Mail Extensions (MIME). This RFC breaks down the components of a message and allows different portions to be sent in separate fields. With MIME, you can attach a variety of data types (such as Microsoft Word documents, video clips, and audio files) and transmit the data without conversion. This provides ease of use for sending data between sites.
- RFC 1554. This RFC defines the protocol used by the legacy Microsoft SMTP gateway for Microsoft Mail 3.x. RFC 1554 defines the message format that is created when a message is transferred through the MS SMTP gateway. This RFC is similar to RFC 822, which provides for encoding attachments into the body of the message as text.
- RFC 1939. This RFC defines the POP3 (Post Office Protocol v3) protocol for the retrieval of messages from a mailstop. It enables POP3 clients to connect directly to the Exchange Server information store, listening to PORT 110.
- RFC 1777. This RFC defines a method of allowing LDAP clients to find, add, delete, and modify the directory with Exchange Server. The RFC provides Exchange 5.0 read-only access to the directory. Exchange 5.5 incorporates version 3.0 of LDAP, which allows for Bind, Unbind, Search, Add, Modify, and Delete to the directory. Exchange Server 5.5 listens to port 389 for communications.

- RFC 2060. This RFC defines a method for IMAP4 clients to access multiple folders and mailboxes on the Exchange Server. It utilizes SMTP for sending mail.

These RFCs allow for seamless integration with other SMTP mail systems across public and private Internet networks.

Understanding IMS Uses

Exchange supports a variety of connection methods, using IMS as the message connector.

The following are different ways to use IMS in a production environment:

- SMTP gateway to a Microsoft Mail Network of post offices (see Figure 22.1).

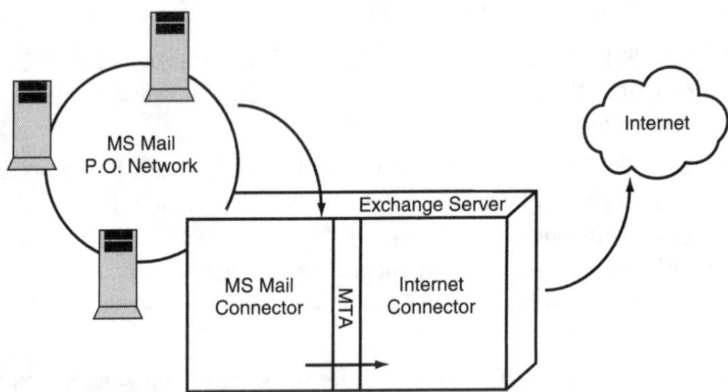

FIG. 22.1 Microsoft Mail users can leverage the gateway in Exchange to provide Internet connectivity.

As described in Chapter 19, "Using the Microsoft Mail Connector for PC Networks," Microsoft Mail 3.x users can send and receive Internet messages through the Microsoft Mail Connector on Exchange. In this example, Exchange acts as an Internet SMTP gateway. Exchange converts the messages to Microsoft Mail 3.x format, using the Microsoft Mail Connector interchange, and then transfers the messages to the Microsoft Mail 3.x post offices with the MS Exchange MTA services.

- SMTP connector to an Exchange Network of post offices (see Figure 22.2).

  This example is similar to Microsoft Mail 3.x use of the IMS, providing SMTP connectivity from the native mail-system client to the remote SMTP mail-system recipient. This functionality is seamless to users. The advantage of having all Exchange clients using the IMS is the fact that this architecture reduces the need for data-format conversions. At the same time the IMS services Exchange clients, it can service existing Microsoft Mail clients. This example extends the preceding example by providing additional support for Exchange clients.

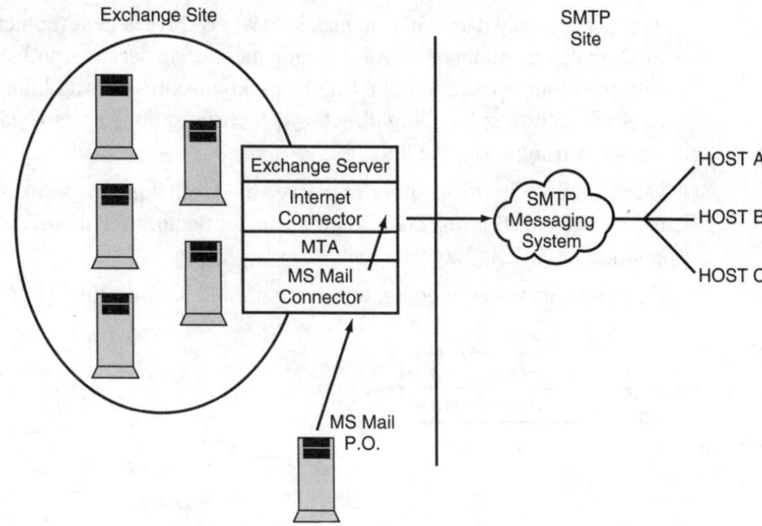

FIG. 22.2 The IMS integrates directly with the Exchange Server.

The following is how to utilize the IMS within an organization:

- Allow POP3 and IMAP4 clients to send and receive mail through the Exchange Server. This feature enables any POP3 or IMAP4 client to connect to an Exchange server for mail retrieval. This capability extends the reach of Exchange into areas where the Outlook client cannot be utilized.
- Using the IMS to link Exchange sites (backbone) (see Figure 22.3).

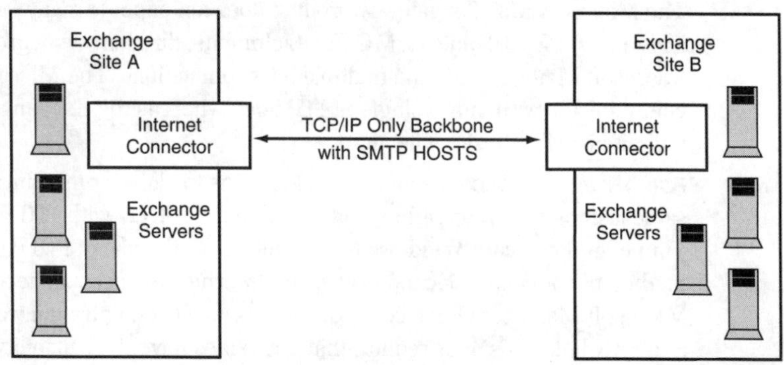

FIG. 22.3 The IMS can be used to link multiple Exchange sites.

In this example, the IMS is used to link two Exchange sites. SMTP messaging is the backbone between the sites. Both Exchange sites need to be running the IMS locally. The IMS then communicates with the destination IMS.

This is especially useful in organizations where MIS is geographically distributed. Each location can maintain its own Exchange messaging services and still provide connectivity with the other sites. Using the IMS to backbone sites puts additional overhead on the IMS, which now is handling directory synchronization, folder replication, and message transfer through a single link.

Using the IMS in this manner preserves the Exchange functionality of rich text formatted messages, OLE objects, and public folder postings. This solution is a manageable solution for linking Exchange sites.

- Exchange Server connecting to Microsoft Mail 3.x with the IMS (see Figure 22.4).

FIG. 22.4
The IMS can be used to enable Microsoft Mail 3.x to communicate with Exchange sites.

This example follows the backbone model. Instead of connecting with another Exchange site, however, the IMS is used to create a backbone with a Microsoft Mail site. The Microsoft Mail site will be using the Microsoft SMTP gateway.

This solution permits immediate transmission of messages between Exchange and Microsoft Mail sites. You do not have to configure the Microsoft Mail Connector interchange, configure MTA IMSs, or set up remote directory synchronization.

The Microsoft Mail 3.x gateway product does not support many Exchange features, including OLE v2.0 objects, MIME attachments, directory synchronization through the Microsoft Mail gateway, and multiple-host connections. The Microsoft Mail gateway can communicate with only a single SMTP host, whereas the Exchange IMS can have unlimited SMTP-host connections.

Another method of connecting these locations to allow communications to occur in the same fashion that you might if connected to the LAN is with PPTP (Point-To-Point Tunneling Protocol). Windows NT 4.0 allows for the use of PPTP (a standard and secure method of connecting locations over the Internet) to encapsulate all Exchange and Microsoft Mail Post Office communications so all configuration would remain the same as a LAN link. This does require that both sides have the capability of running PPTP.

In some situations, if the Internet Service Provider (ISP) supports PPTP, only one side would require PPTP capability. In this scenario, it is possible to support a legacy system that does not support PPTP to communicate with an Exchange server over a secured line through the ISP.

- Windows 95 client connecting to Exchange Server over the Internet (see Figure 22.5). This example focuses on the client connection with Exchange. A Windows 95 client with Exchange Client software installed can access the Internet through a local service provider. After getting connected to the Internet, the client can transmit and receive messages through an Exchange IMS.

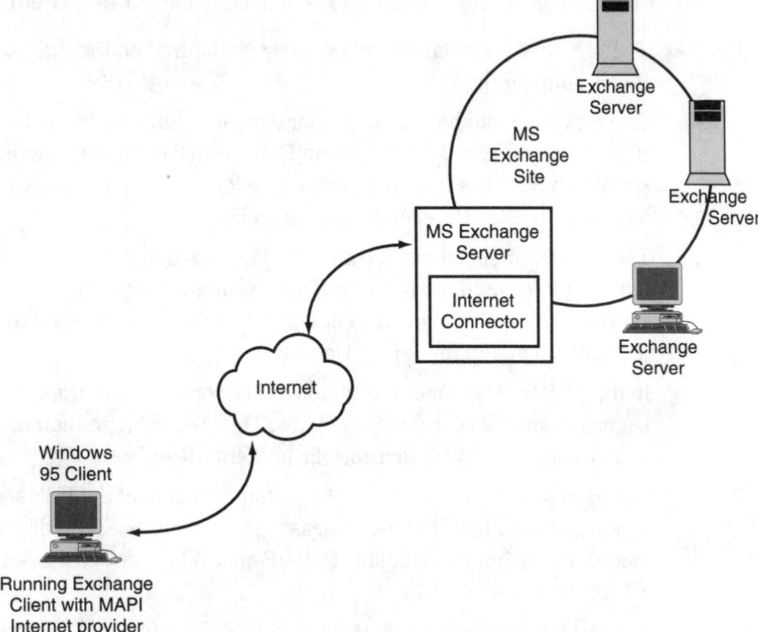

FIG. 22.5 The IMS can send and receive messages to Windows 95 client workstations.

These examples provide suggestions and solutions that companies can utilize for communications through the IMS.

Understanding the Internet Mail IMS Components

The IMS has many features that are not available in the Microsoft Mail 3.x SMTP gateway. These new features offer a balance of power and flexibility to route messages over SMTP networks. As described in the preceding section, you can use the IMS's rich feature set in many ways.

After it is configured, the IMS transfers messages to remote SMTP mail systems by initiating a connection. When the connection is made, the messages are transferred across systems.

For incoming messages, the IMS listens to a TCP/IP port for connection requests. In similar fashion, once the remote system establishes its connection with IMS, messages and data are transferred into Exchange.

Inside the Exchange site, the IMS converts the message to an Exchange-format message and routes it to the Exchange recipient. The user will not notice any difference between an SMTP message and a normal Exchange message.

Setting Up IMS Components

Before you configure and run the IMS, you need to meet these requirements:

- TCP/IP must be installed and properly configured on the Exchange Windows NT server that is running the IMS.

  The server should have a static (nondynamic) Internet Protocol (IP) address. If you are using Dynamic Host Configuration Protocol (DHCP), you should exclude the IMS server's IP address from the pool of IP addresses used by DHCP. DHCP assigns IP addresses to TCP/IP clients automatically.

  The reason for specifying a static IP address is that you are required to have a fully qualified Internet domain name. These values do not change dynamically with IP addresses; they are manually configured, and you would need to update them daily for the name to match the server's address.

- In the TCP/IP section of the Windows NT server configuration, you need to enable Domain Name Server (DNS) lookups. The DNS matches common domain names (such as `yourcompany.com`) into a specific numeric IP address.

  You need to enter the host name and domain name of the IMS server (see Figure 22.6). In addition, you have to enter at least one value for the IP address of the DNS server. For more information on installing TCP/IP on a Windows NT server, refer to your Windows NT user manual.

- Add the IP address, host, domain, and Mail Exchange (MX) entries in the DNS server.

  Use the IP address and the host and domain information from the Windows NT TCP/IP configuration to enter into the DNS. Adding these values to the DNS allows for name resolution. The DNS provides the function of mapping a "friendly" name to an IP address. This way, when a user enters a friendly name, such as `LosAngeles01.softwarespectrum.com`, the DNS maps this name to its actual numeric IP address.

  Figure 22.7 shows an entry for a server name and then an associated IP address. In addition to the host name and IP address, add an address space entry in the IMS configuration for Internet-bound Exchange messages to pass through the IMS. This entry is called the Mail Exchange entry, or MX.

  MX records associate SMTP mail messages with a routed destination host name and IP address. In Figure 22.7, you see an MX record for mail destined for `msmail.softwarespectrum.com` to be routed to server `LosAngeles01.swsspectrum.com`. This way, when remote SMTP systems need to know where to send messages, they can look in the DNS records for the destination IP address of the mail messages. For more information on DNS entries and configuration, consult any related documentation for those products. A wealth of information is also available on Internet Web sites and newsgroups to assist you in learning more.

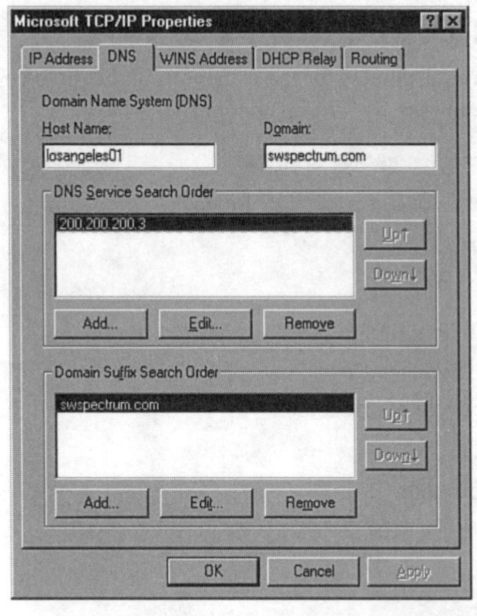

FIG. 22.6 These are the TCP/IP settings that enable DNS lookups on the Exchange server running the IMS.

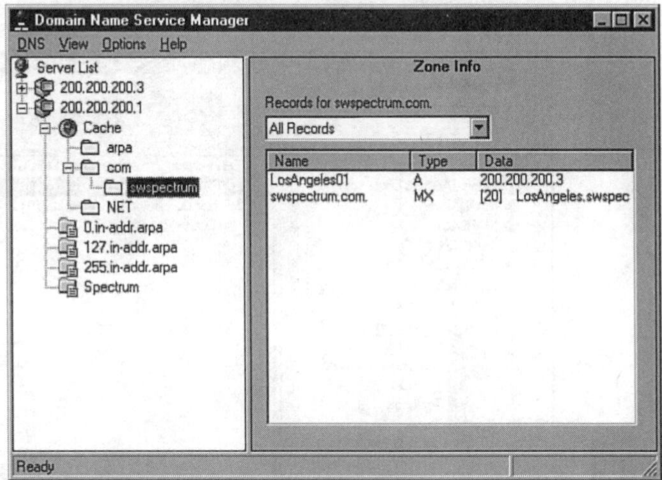

FIG. 22.7 The DNS entries for server LosAngeles01 in the domain `swsspectrum.com`.

It is very important to ensure that these recommendations are followed for the proper configuration of DNS records to enable mail delivery to occur.

Administrators should be careful not to create message loops, and to ensure that all mail domains that will be serviced by the IMS are defined. Aliases can be used to allow multiple domains to be serviced by one IMS.

Setting Up the Internet Mail Service

After you meet the initial requirements for the IMS, you can begin to configure the IMS. The following is a list of procedures to use as you configure the IMS:

- Define an administrative message account
- Configure the address space serviced by the IMS
- Specify the site address
- Configure connection options
- Define message-content options
- Set interoperability options
- Set specific IMS message restrictions
- Management of SMTP messages
- Security access restrictions
- Additional features of the IMS
- Test the IMS

You can configure all options from the Exchange Administrator program; select the Internet Mail IMS from the Connections section of the site hierarchy (see Figure 22.8).

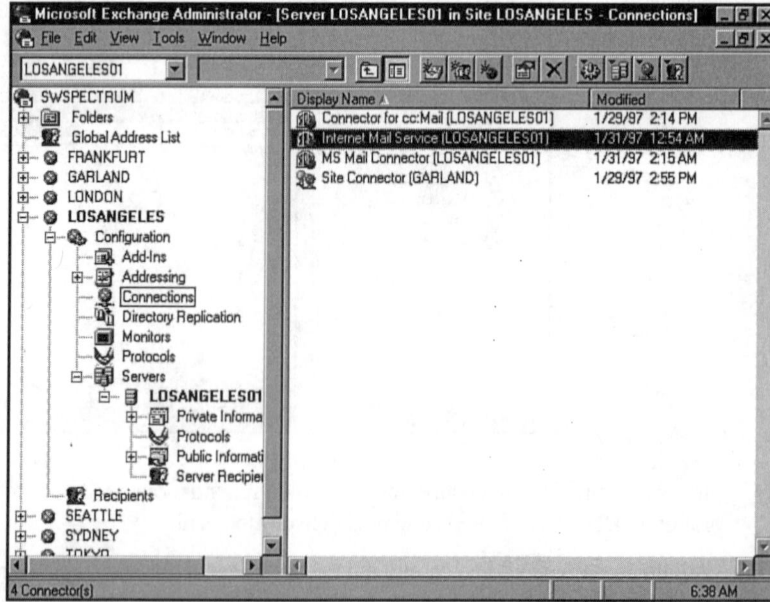

FIG. 22.8
Selecting the Internet Mail IMS from the Exchange Administrator program.

NOTE The IMS is very complicated and has a multitude of options. Prepare yourself by setting aside a few solid hours to set up the IMS. ■

Defining an Administrative Message Account

You must select an Exchange mailbox that will receive notification regarding the function of the Internet Mail IMS. This mailbox can be an administrator's one or a special account created for this purpose. Whichever option you choose, just make sure that the mailbox is checked periodically to catch important notification messages sent by the IMS.

To configure the IMS to send administrative messages to an account, complete the following steps:

1. Open the IMS property pages (see Figure 22.9) for the server that you want to configure.
2. Click the Change button to the right of the Administrator's Mailbox box. The dialog box shown in Figure 22.10 appears.

FIG. 22.9
A blank IMS tab.

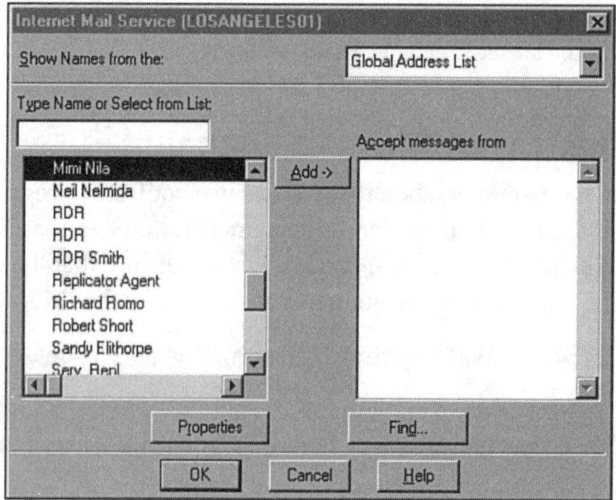

FIG. 22.10
Selecting the administrator message account.

The administrator message account is used to send notices of events associated with the IMS and is similar to the postmaster account on the sendmail system for UNIX. This account is the default account for message errors, bounced mail, problems with the IMS, and other administrative notifications.

3. Define the notices to be sent to the administrator message account (see Figure 22.11).

   From an administrative standpoint, selecting all the notifications is beneficial. If the volume of the notices is too excessive, change the administrator account to a public folder for the Exchange administrator group's use, or try to troubleshoot the cause for the notices before decreasing the notification settings.

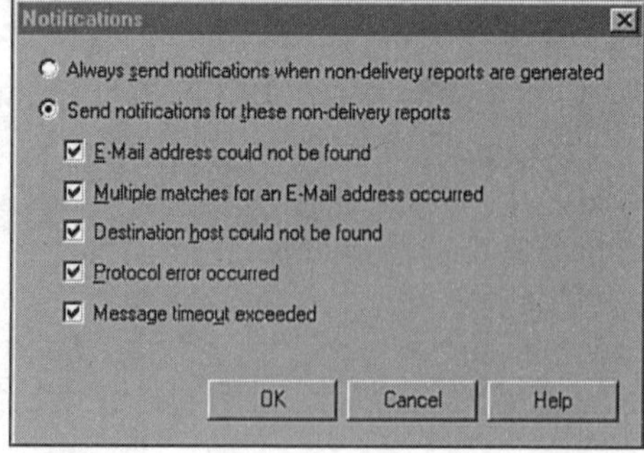

FIG. 22.11
Defining the notices to be sent to the administrator message account.

The preceding steps ensure that any messages that need to be addressed by administrators are delivered to the proper account. In most cases, administrators will utilize this feature for troubleshooting purposes.

Configuring the Address Space Serviced by the IMS

The address space entries for the Internet Mail IMS define which messages are routed through it. You must make at least one entry in this page to activate message routing through the IMS.

The following steps guide you through creating and editing address space entries:

1. From the IMS property page, select the Address Space tab (see Figure 22.12).

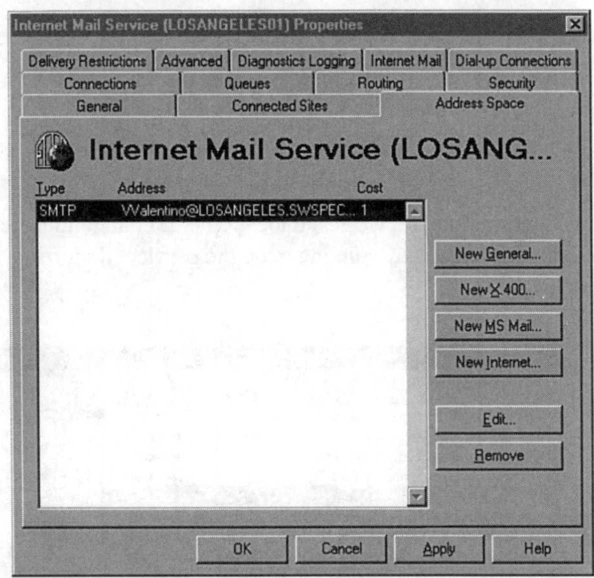

FIG. 22.12 This Properties page displays Address Space entries for the IMS.

2. Click the New Internet address space button. The dialog box in Figure 22.13 appears.

   In the Address Space property page, you can enter multiple Internet domain names, Microsoft Mail server names, X.400 names, or other IMS names to route messages through this IMS.

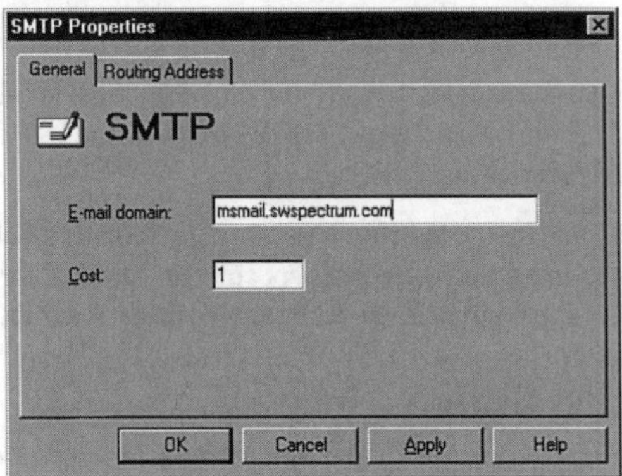

FIG. 22.13 Creating a new Internet address space for the IMS.

3. A third property page available in Exchange 5.5 is the Restrictions page. On this page, you can restrict the access to usage of the server to either individuals that are from the Organization, Site, or This Location only.

4. Click OK to set the configuration.

The preceding information describes the main steps in configuring how the IMS is to be used.

Specifying the Site Address

To configure how Internet Mail addresses will be generated for the site, complete the following steps:

1. From the IMS property sheet, click Apply to set all the configuration settings. You see a reminder that you have to stop and restart the IMS.
2. Open the Control Panel services and locate the Exchange Internet Mail IMS (see Figure 22.14). If the IMS is already running, stop the service, then restart it for your new setting to take effect.

FIG. 22.14
NT service for the IMS.

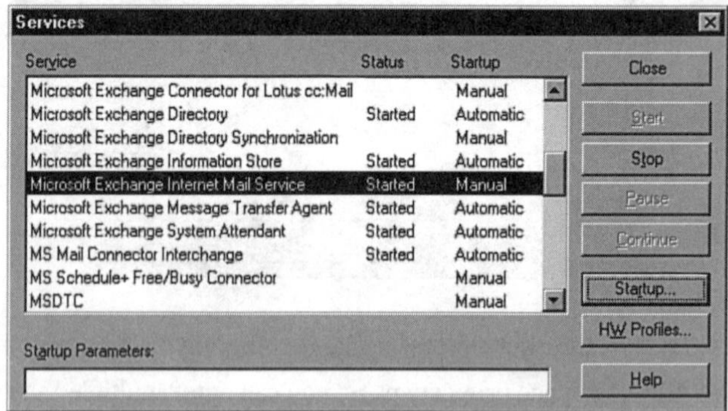

3. Select the Site Addressing icon in the Administrator program's display window and open its property pages.
4. Click the Site Addressing tab. The IMS dialog box appears (see Figure 22.15).
5. The addresses in the IMS dialog box are the global settings for all recipients at this particular site. Make sure that the recipient address for the IMS is the same as what is entered in the MX record of the DNS.

At this point, the IMS should be up and running. The IMS should be listening to port 25 of the TCP/IP protocol stack on the server—the port specified in RFC 822 for SMTP mail transferring. Now you can proceed to configure the additional options of the IMS.

Configuring Connection Options

You can modify the settings for inbound and outbound transfer modes, connection limitations, delivery options, and message queues. Follow these steps:

1. From the IMS property pages, select the Connections tab (see Figure 22.16).

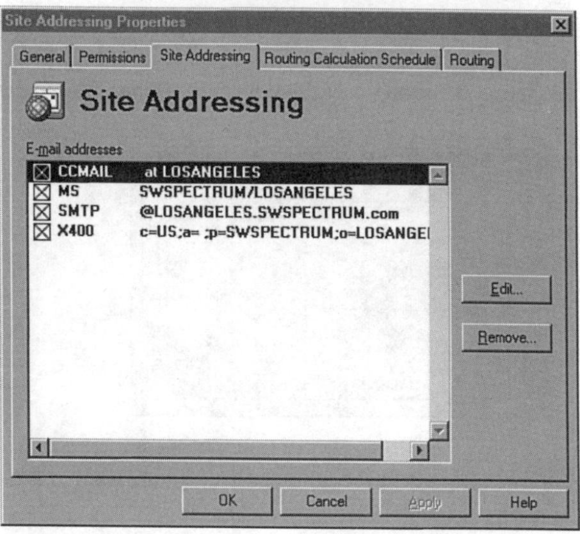

FIG. 22.15
Global site-addressing properties.

FIG. 22.16
Configuring the IMS connections properties.

NOTE The None option is a great tool to use in debugging the IMS. When this option is selected, you can keep the IMS running but restrict messages from being transferred from the site. Users will not notice any difference in their work because messages will just queue up on the server until the transfer mode is reestablished. ■

2. In the Transfer Mode section, click an option button to indicate whether messages will be incoming, outgoing, both, or neither.
3. Click the Advanced button to set the following options (see Figure 22.17).

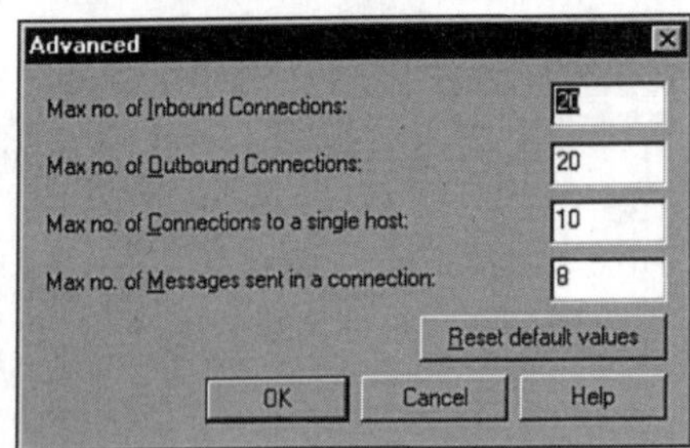

FIG. 22.17 Configuring the advanced settings for the Transfer mode.

These options can be set based on the resources in your environment.

4. Configure the message delivery settings.

The IMS allows you to use the DNS to resolve SMTP Mail message routes or use a single SMTP relay host. If you choose the DNS option, the IMS attempts to connect with the various destination SMTP mail systems directly. If you do not want to have Exchange perform the actual message transfer to the remote hosts for performance or security reasons, you can specify an SMTP relay host. Exchange is not a relay host. A ***relay host*** has the capability to receive SMTP mail, look at the header destination information, and then perform the message transfer to the remote host. Typically, the smart host functionality is run on a UNIX server. The process is known as ***sendmail.***

The DNS option removes the need to have a UNIX server running sendmail just to relay messages to remote hosts.

An additional option is to configure the message-delivery options based on domain. Message delivery can be based on Domain Name Service (DNS) lookup. The IMS can perform a DNS request before forwarding messages to the appropriate destination. With the Microsoft Mail 3.x SMTP gateway, you were forced to point the gateway to an existing SMTP relay host, which would actually deliver the mail to the final destination. The Microsoft Mail 3.x SMTP gateway forced users to manage two servers to transfer Internet mail (see Figure 22.18).

One new feature enables administrators to choose a variation on queuing of messages. Click the E-Mail Domain button to select the ETERN option. ETERN is an alternative method of queuing messages based on the responses from the Host. If the host either initiates a specific command (for example, PING), or issues a "ready to receive" message, Exchange will wait to send or receive mail.

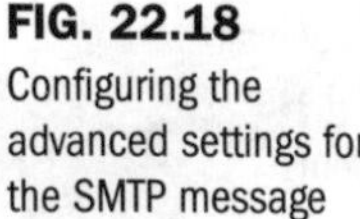

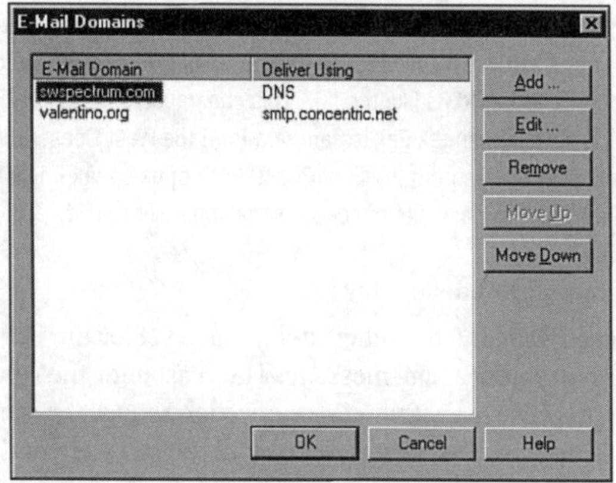

FIG. 22.18 Configuring the advanced settings for the SMTP message delivery.

This is useful if it appears that the IMS is having a difficult time transferring messages to a particular remote host. You can configure an individual entry for that specific domain causing message transfer problems. Entries can be in the form of domain, subdomains, and IP addresses. You can use wild cards as well.

5. Define inbound connections.

   You can configure the IMS to receive messages from all incoming hosts or reject remote hosts based on your input (see Figure 22.19).

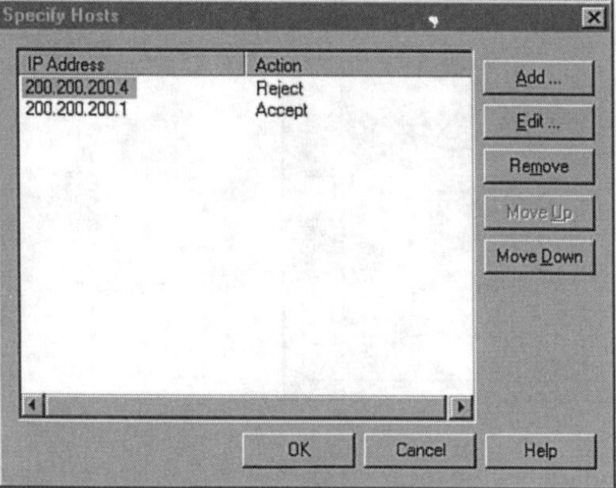

FIG. 22.19 Configuring the incoming connection to be accepted by the IMS.

   You can specify entries only in the form of IP addresses and subnet mask of the remote host to be rejected or accepted. This is useful when remote hosts are having a difficult time communicating with the IMS or when a particular remote host has a history of transferring junk messages or corrupt data.

NOTE Typically, as your users subscribe to Internet listserv mailing groups, a wide variety of mail systems will attempt to communicate and transfer mail into the system. Some of these remote systems do not adhere to the RFCs like the IMS. This can cause communication problems between the systems. Suppose that I speak English and am from the West Coast, and that my business partner speaks English and is from the East Coast. Both of us speak English, but we may not always be able to communicate if our accents affect our speaking abilities.

6. Define the IMS message queue retry intervals.

   This option is used to define the retry attempt interval for the IMS, if it encounters a host to which it cannot transfer a mail message. The reason for the retry is that the remote host is too busy to process another communication request or is otherwise unavailable. The IMS queues up the message and waits until the retry interval expires before trying to transfer the message to the remote host. The default setting retries the first time in 60 minutes; the subsequent retries are made at 150 percent of the set time interval.

   If you use the default setting—the initial retry at 60 minutes—subsequent retries occur at 1 hour, 1.5 hours, 2.25 hours, 3.4 hours, 5 hours, 7.5 hours, and so on, for a total of 8 retries over 72 hours.

   Select the Message Time-Outs button to configure more specific retry intervals (see Figure 22.20).

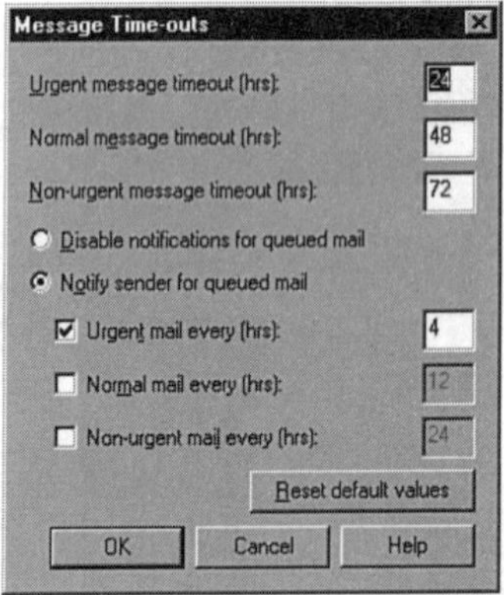

FIG. 22.20 Configuring the message time-out settings to drop remote connections from the IMS.

   Notice the granularity of the message queue retries. You can configure a specific retry interval based on the priority level of the mail message.

   Make sure to apply your configuration changes before you move to another configuration tab. Remember that you have to stop and restart the IMS after you complete your configurations.

These steps are used to ensure that messages are delivered in a timely and secure manner. In some cases, the administrator may want to modify the retry values to decrease the resolution time-out to provide quicker notification if the connection is reliable.

Defining Message Content Options

This section explains how to configure the default message content format, Exchange rich text formatting options, and message formats for individual domains.

To configure the options for inbound and outbound messages, follow these steps:

1. From the IMS property page, select the Internet Mail tab.
2. The first option is to select the message content type for attachments. You have the option of configuring the IMS to send and receive message by MIME or uuencode. MIME provides support for a variety of file formats, which do not get broken up or encoded into the mail message as in uuencode. MIME support separates the attachments from the text portion of the message, retaining the original format.
3. Choose the MIME character set translation standard (see Figure 22.21). The default option is to use the ISO 8859-1 standard for MIME outbound mail messages.

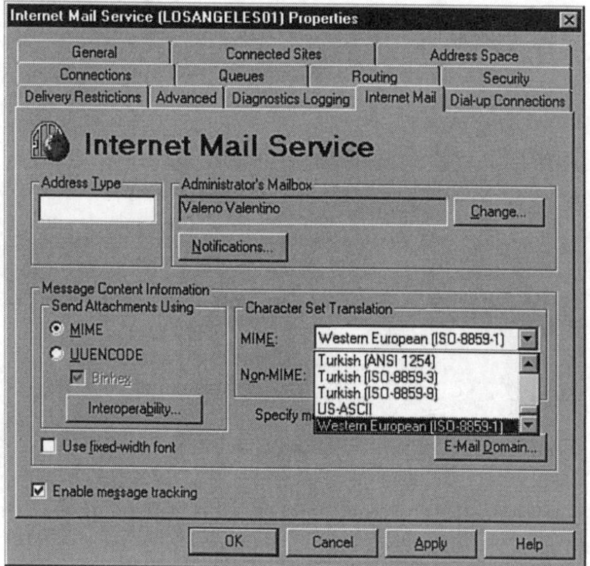

FIG. 22.21 Configuring the MIME character set translation.

4. Use the drop-down menu to select the Non-MIME character set translation. The default option for uuencode messages is US ASCII for both inbound and outbound messages.

NOTE To send message content to the Microsoft Mail 3.x SMTP gateway, make sure that you are using uuencode. The Microsoft Mail 3.x gateway does not support MIME attachments.

5. Click the E-Mail Domain button. The E-Mail Domains dialog box appears (see Figure 22.22).

   This dialog box enables you to configure specific character sets, message content formats, and maximum message size for messages transferred through the IMS.

6. Click Add to create additional e-mail domain entries, Edit to change an existing one, or Remove to delete one. When you are done with these settings, click OK to return to the Internet Mail property pages. Figure 22.23 shows the Add e-Mail domain dialog box after you click the Add button.

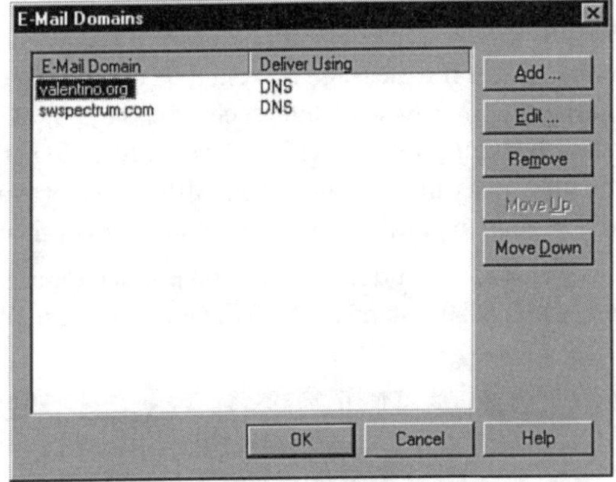

FIG. 22.22 You can use this dialog box to specify message content by e-mail domain.

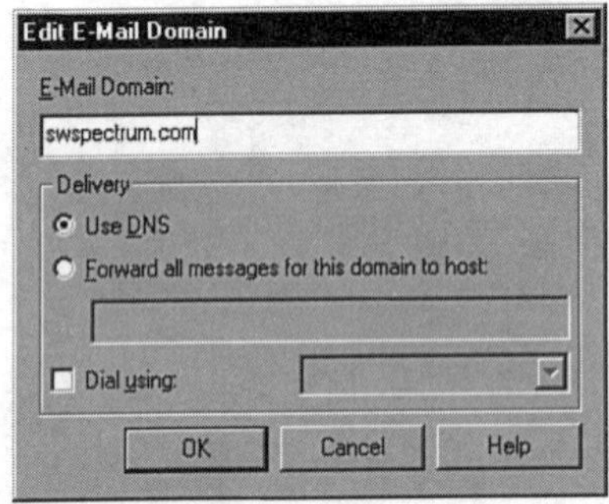

FIG. 22.23 Dialog box for creating a new e-mail domain configuration with message content options.

7. Click a site, then click the plus symbol beside the icon for servers, then click the server's icon for that site. From the menu, select properties and the MIME Types tab to define attachment formats.

   From this property page, you can configure the MIME types (see Figure 22.24). MIME types include support for Microsoft Word documents, video files, audio files, HTML documents, binary executables, and other format types.

8. Click the New button to create an additional MIME type. The New MIME Type dialog box appears.

   For the Microsoft Word Application, enter the MIME content type and the associated extension in the dialog box (see Figure 22.25). The Microsoft Word MIME type is application/msword and the associated extension is `.doc`. When done, click OK to set the change and activate this new content type.

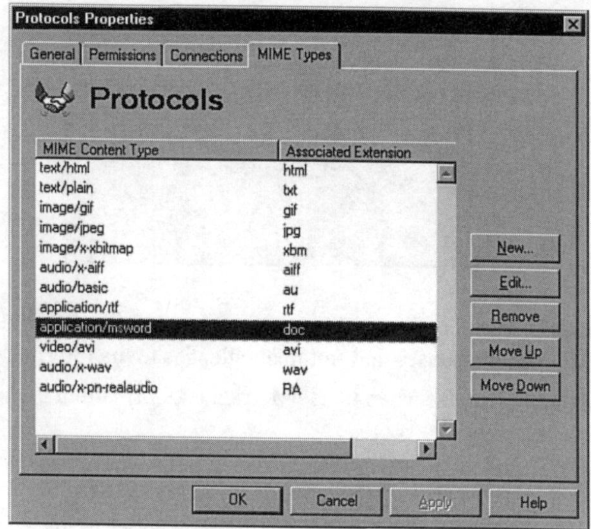

FIG. 22.24
Configuring MIME attachment formats.

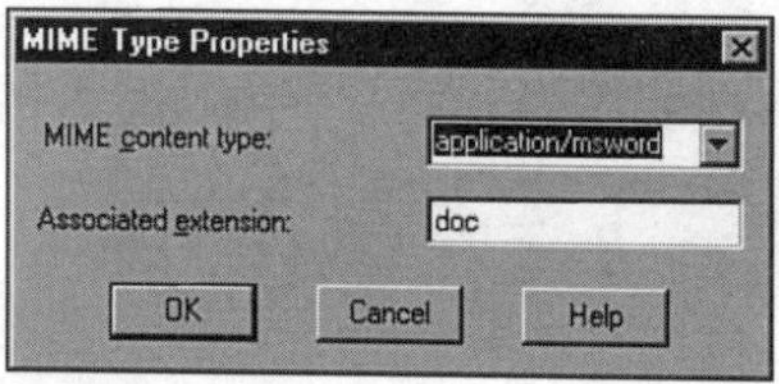

FIG. 22.25
Creating a new MIME type or edit an existing type. You can configure for document formats, multimedia formats, or even application binary formats.

Message content, like MIME, may need to be configured differently depending on the applications utilized within the organization. If organizations have custom applications that are used to view documents or multimedia files, this can be changed to fit their needs.

Setting Advanced Options

To configure the advanced options for the IMS, follow these steps:

1. From the IMS property page, select the Internet Mail tab.
2. Click the Advanced button; the Advanced Options dialog box will appear (see Figure 22.26).

   The IMS sends outbound messages with the display name of the sender/creator and the sender's alias. The display name typically is the sender's full name, first and last. If you have a user named Fred Rodriguez, for example, his alias might be fredro and his display name, Fred Rodriguez. You can choose to disable sending the display name over the Internet from the Advanced dialog box.

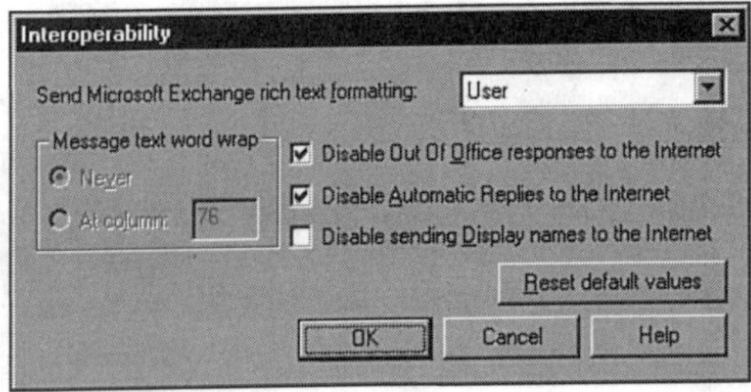

FIG. 22.26
Defining the interoperability options for the IMS.

In addition to disabling display names, the IMS can be configured to disable Out Of Office Message responses and Automatic Replies to the Internet.

In addition, you choose when to use MS rich text formatting in messages (see Figure 22.27).

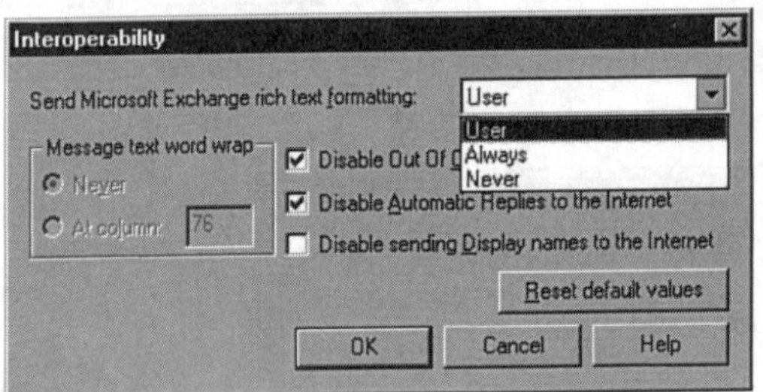

FIG. 22.27
Listed are the options of when to send RTF formatting in outbound messages.

The three options allow the users to select when they want to send RTF data, always send RTF data, or never send RTF data. If this IMS communicates only with a Microsoft Mail 3.x SMTP gateway, you should select the option to never send RTF data because the Microsoft Mail SMTP gateway will not be able to understand this information.

3. Define the Message size limit.
4. Open the General tab (see Figure 22.28).

   This option enables you to configure message limitations for the IMS.

The Advanced page for most organizations will not need to be changed. However, in certain situations where Internet mail is sent to specific clients or organizations, administrators may agree to allow RTF messages and increase or decrease limits on message sizes. The message size limits can be configured to minimize the impact on Exchange servers for having to convert large messages.

Defining IMS Message Restrictions

These settings deal with the actual message settings for the IMS.

To configure message-specific properties for delivery through IMS, complete the following steps:

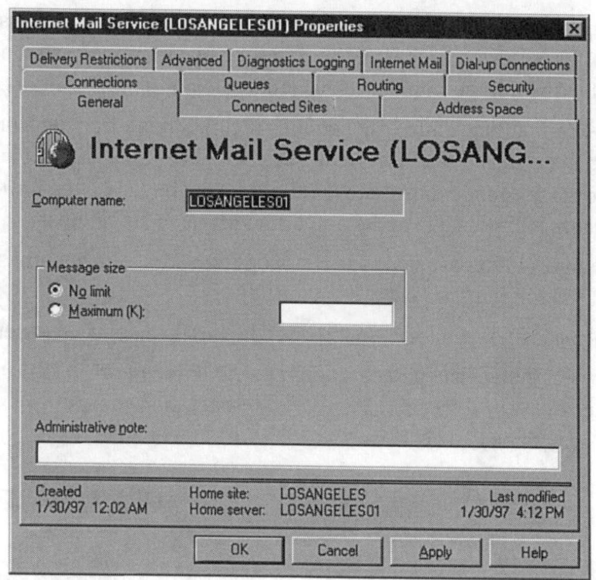

FIG. 22.28
The General tab enables you to set the maximum message size.

1. From the IMS property page, select the Advanced button on the Connections tab, as well as the Time-Outs button for message delivery options (see Figure 22.29). From the Advanced and Time-Outs dialog boxes, you can define the message parameters, maximum message transfer times, and the message transfer quotas.

FIG. 22.29
The Advanced tab enables you to configure message transfer parameters.

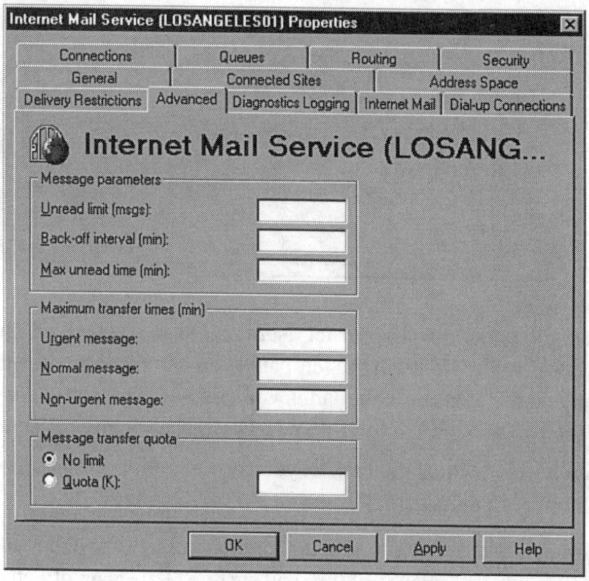

Message parameters are used to limit the number of unread messages, to set the time to back off from message transfer, and to set a maximum unread message time. The values are set in the number of messages, and in the number of minutes.

The second button, Time-Outs, defines the maximum transfer times broken down by urgent, normal, and non-urgent messages. These values are set in minutes and can be used to close connections that would otherwise be held open for long periods of time. This quota helps to reduce the amount of traffic to single hosts.

The last set of values is used to set upper limits for the size of messages transferred from the IMS to the remote hosts.

2. Click Apply when you have finished modifying these entries to set your new values.
3. Next select the Delivery Restrictions tab menu (see Figure 22.30). Use this tab to restrict message delivery to certain users or to restrict those users from sending outbound SMTP mail through this IMS.

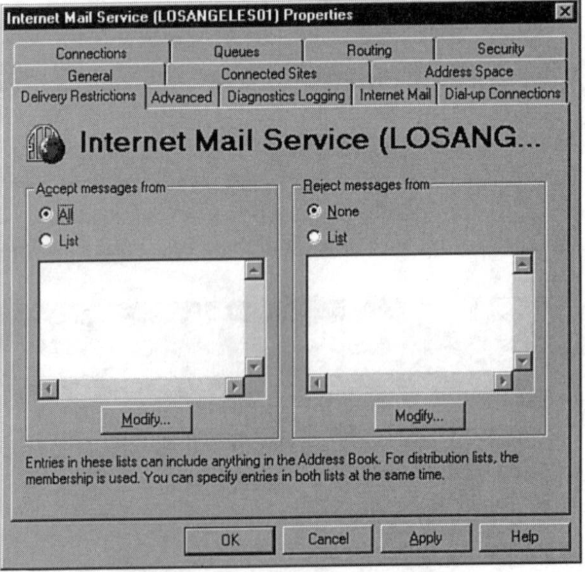

FIG. 22.30
Users can be granted access rights to use the IMS or restricted access to the IMS.

You have the option to either grant users access to the IMS or, on the flip side, deny users access to the IMS. On the left panel you can manage the usage by adding users who can connect. On the right panel, you choose who cannot connect. Figure 22.31 shows the two windows of the IMS's Delivery Restrictions Property page.

In addition to individual mailboxes, you can set delivery restrictions to distribution lists and custom recipients as well.

Of the topics mentioned in this section, the ability to restrict which mailboxes can be sent to and from can help prevent misuse of the mail system. This is an effective way of managing who has the ability to send and receive e-mail (such as temporary employees, or new employees).

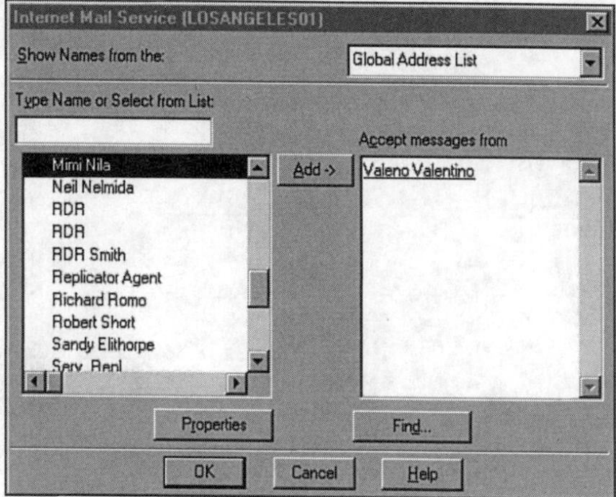

FIG. 22.31
You can manage access down to the user level.

Setting Security Options

Exchange Server 5.5 has extended the security capabilities to support a wider range of security standards.

Exchange 5.5 offers enhanced security to ensure reliable message delivery. One selection that is available is to enable S/MIME capabilities. You can do this from the Internet Mail tab by checking the option box (see Figure 22.32).

This option, however, should be selected only if the clients that will be connecting support S/MIME. S/MIME is an addition to the MIME standard, which allows for secure message delivery. A client that currently supports S/MIME is Outlook Express, which enables clients to sign and encrypt messages being delivered over the Internet.

A second option that is now available is the Security tab.

The security tab allows for a per-domain configuration depending on the servers you will be connecting to. If the message communications occurs between two Exchange servers, all information will be encrypted across the wire.

An administrator may choose no validation between servers, SASL/AUTH (clear text), or SSL. The final option for security between domains would be Windows NT Challenge/Response encryption. With these options, an administrator can secure channels between multiple Exchange servers, or no security with other domain communications.

Supporting Other Protocols

To ensure that Exchange Server can support a variety of clients for connectivity, Microsoft has included support for IMAP4 and POP3.

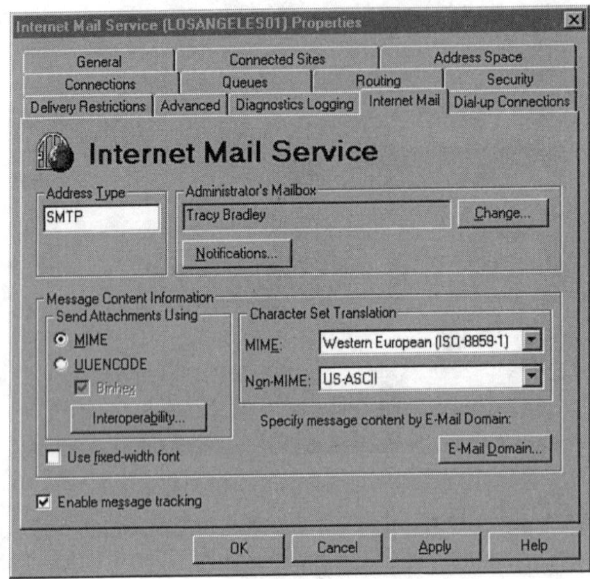

FIG. 22.32
Configuring S/MIME on the server side.

IMAP4 (Internet Message Access Protocol), and POP3 (Post Office Protocol) are similar in the sense that they provide a convenient method of accessing mailboxes on an Exchange server without using the Exchange Client or Outlook. With this support, Microsoft has made it possible for an organization to allow all types of workstations to connect as long as they support the specifications.

POP3, which Exchange 5.0 began to support, is also available in Exchange 5.5. With a simple mail client that supports POP3, a client may retrieve and send mail through the Exchange server. POP3 clients communicate directly with the Information Store. The configuration of the POP3 services can be configured on a per-site or per-user basis.

You need to add security to POP3 connections to ensure the correct clients are connecting and have access to only the information the company wants to present.

IMAP4 allows for similar connectivity to the Exchange Server; however, it expands on the capabilities. IMAP4 clients may connect to multiple mailboxes, as well as access public folders. IMAP4 can be enabled on a per-site per-user level. Two features that are not currently supported within Exchange IMAP4 are RFC 2086 (ACLs) and RFC 2087 (Quotas).

To make certain that these clients can receive mail through the Exchange IMS, ensure that the routing of messages is properly configured.

Accessing the Directory Through LDAP

With Exchange Server 5.0, Microsoft extended the capabilities to allow clients to get direct access to the Directory within Exchange. With the adoption of new standards in version 5.0, Exchange 5.5 updates the LDAP support to version 3, which unlike 2.0 allows Modifies to the directory.

This support allows LDAP clients to search for information in the Exchange directory without the need of the Outlook or Exchange client.

To ensure that the client sees only what the organization wants the client to see, the administrator may configure LDAP to present only certain pieces of the directory.

Because of the direct access to the directory, and with the future considerations of ADS (Active Directory Services), developers are able to begin scripting ADSI through LDAP.

Managing SMTP Messages

After you configure the IMS and have the Windows NT service running, you can configure the following additional features to assist you in managing the IMS.

To configure and monitor message tracking, complete the following steps:

1. From the IMS property page, select the Internet Mail tab.
2. Your first option is to check the Enable message tracking field. This will log information about the daily IMS transactions to a common log, which can be browsed to find transmission data on a particular message.
3. Your next option is on the Queues tab (see Figure 22.33). In this tab, you can get real-time statistics on the current processing of IMS data.

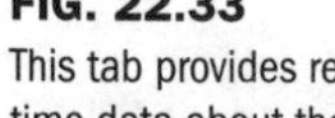

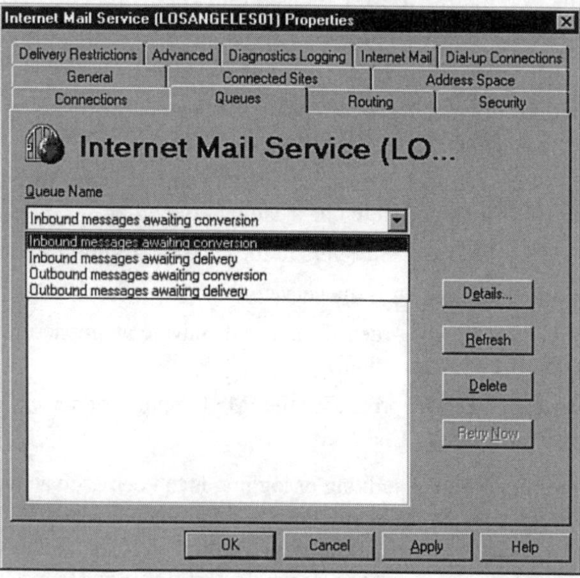

FIG. 22.33 This tab provides real-time data about the status of messages in the IMS queue.

If you check the queue and see that several messages are waiting to be processed or transferred to another system, you can begin to diagnose where you may have a problem.

4. Select the Diagnostics Logging tab (see Figure 22.34).

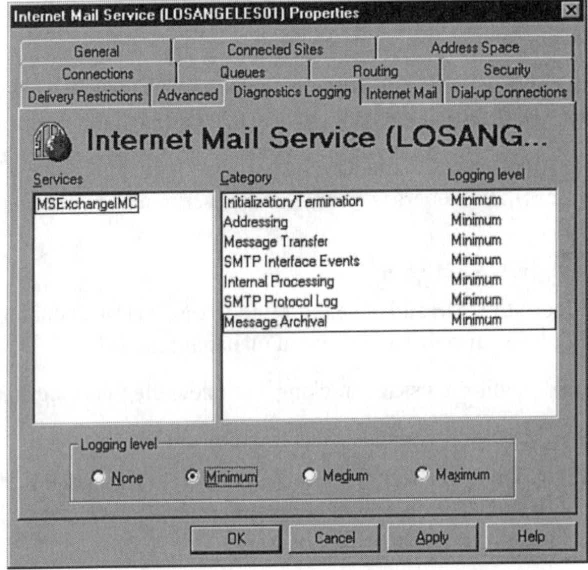

FIG. 22.34 From this tab, you can specify what level of service logging you need for the IMS.

Logged information gets written to the common Windows NT event logs. On the left panel, the IMS (known as MSExchangeIMS in the event log) is listed. The right panel lists the actual log category options. These include:

- Initialization/Termination monitors that the IMS starts and stops.
- Addressing monitors the resolution of e-mail addresses with display names and foreign names.
- Message Transfer is the process that communicates with the remote hosts and transfers message from one system to the other.
- SMTP Interface event refers to the core application IMS operation.
- Internal processing is the service that routes the data inside of the IMS.
- SMTP protocol log records all events having an impact from the protocol stack or network communication.
- Message Archival processes the IMS temporary data while connections are being restored.

Typical configuration of auditing or logging is to keep each active process set to the minimum log level. In the event that the IMS queue begins to back up, you may want to increase the logging level. Turning the logging on to maximum will flood the event log with many additional messages for you to sort through. Once you have solved the problem, I suggest returning your logging levels back to the minimum level.

5. Select the Connected Sites tab for the option to view the Exchange sites reached through this IMS. To configure routing to an additional site, click the New button at the bottom of the tab (see Figure 22.35).

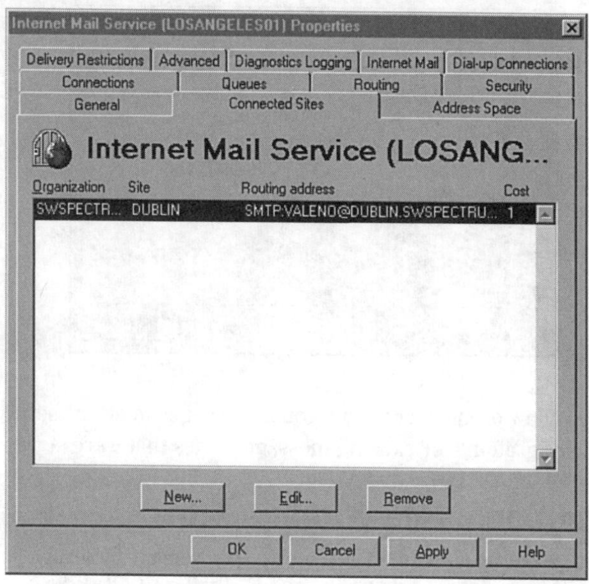

FIG. 22.35 This option shows the additional sites connected to the IMS.

Adding a connected site creates additional routes for messages. Additional Exchange sites, as well as Microsoft Mail 3.x post offices, can be routed to take advantage of the IMS.

6. Enter the organization and site of the additional routed post offices when adding a connected site (see Figure 22.36).

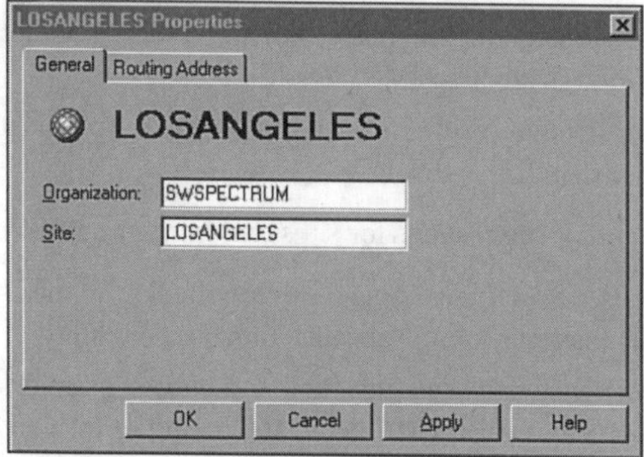

FIG. 22.36 Entering a value for the organization and the site.

7. After you enter the site name, click the routing address tab to complete the new message route. The Properties dialog box, shown in Figure 22.37, appears.
8. Enter a type of mail connection. You can add an SMTP type and include the destination mailbox address.

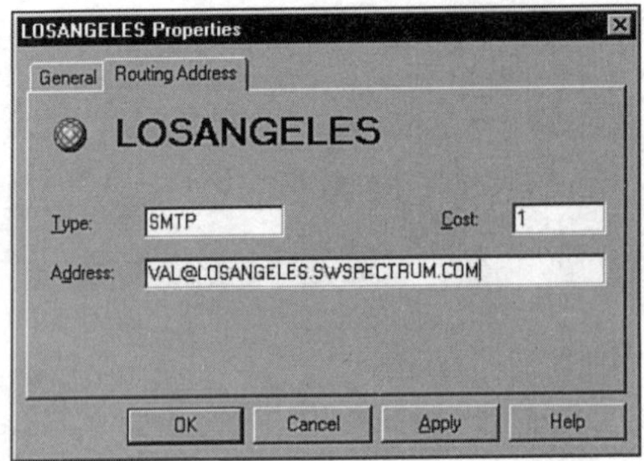

FIG. 22.37
Completing the message route with a message type and post office.

These features allow organizations to reroute messages to other mail systems. This can be utilized during migrations for existing message routes that were serviced by sendmail servers.

Defining an Additional IMS Within a Site

The IMS runs as a single Windows NT service per server. Typically, you have one IMS per organization to service the public Internet connection. Additional connections may be needed if you are going to use an SMTP backbone to move messages throughout the organization. The IMS is robust and can handle several thousand users. To balance the load, you can set up additional IMSs to distribute the processing.

To allow coexistence between two or more IMSs, you must perform the following adjustments:

1. In the Address Space tab, modify the entries for existing IMS to accommodate the address space of the new IMS.
2. In the Connections tab, modify the maximum inbound and outbound sessions, along with what is specified in any new IMS.
3. Finally, for the new IMS to resolve properly in the DNS, you must modify the DNS or host file to reflect a new IMS's IP address.

Following are special routing suggestions for sites that have multiple IMSs:

- If your organization has multiple domains within the SMTP mail system, consider having each IMS handle messages for one specific domain.
- If your site has relatively balanced incoming and outgoing SMTP messages, consider configuring one IMS to receive SMTP mail and the other to send SMTP mail.

Testing the IMS

When the configuration of the service is complete, the last thing to do (after you stop and restart the service) is test the connection. Use the following steps to test your Internet mail connection.

First, send a message from an Exchange client on your site to a remote SMTP server. Verify that the message was properly received.

Examine the body of the message to make sure that any attachments came through without a problem.

From the remote host, send a message back to the IMS. Verify that the message was properly routed to the appropriate mailbox. If the message is delayed or does not reach the destination mailbox, you must track it down by using Exchange's troubleshooting tools. Refer to Chapter 24,"Exchange Performance Tuning and Capacity Planning," for more information on such tools. A good place to start to verify the working state of the IMS is first the IMS Queues tab and then the Windows NT Event Viewer for any alert messages. ●

CHAPTER 23

Setting Up NNTP

In this chapter

As you may already know, Exchange has robust Internet e-mail connectivity that enables any Exchange client to communicate with just about anyone on the Internet. But sometimes e-mail isn't enough. Sometimes people need to communicate in an electronic discussion, like an online meeting or group discussion. Other times, people just want to get information out to thousands of people. Using e-mail for these tasks can be difficult. Thus, Internet newsgroups were created to do this task. In the 5.5 release of Exchange, users are able to participate in these newsgroups by using the Exchange Internet News Service (INS). INS uses a special application protocol called Network News Transfer Protocol (NNTP). NNTP was created for the purpose of working in conjunction with the Internet newsgroups. In Exchange, the INS and NNTP technologies are so closely tied together that their terms will be used interchangeably. When necessary for clarity, any differences will be highlighted in this chapter.

To help provide a better understanding of this Internet capability, this chapter goes over the history of newsgroups before moving into the actual configuration of the NNTP and INS functions in Exchange.

Historical Overview

Tom Truscott and James Ellis invented a system to pass information between UNIX systems. This system, called UNIX-to-UNIX CoPy or UUCP, was used to pass files from a server at Duke to a server at the University of North Carolina and the reverse. As the technology matured, the software was rewritten to handle a larger volume of data. The original version was limited in the number of articles per newsgroup each day it could manage. Today, the system is called UseNet and is estimated at over 250,000 sites worldwide hosting over 18,000 newsgroups. However, UseNet had its share of problems. Luckily, several systems and solutions were created to address these problems.

First, there was a need to develop an efficient way to distribute the news to non-UNIX clients. Many people began to realize there was valuable information in the newsgroups, and they wanted to access them from non-UNIX desktops. Other users needed a newsreader that would help format the screen and take care of SMTP-like transmissions for the newsfeed. Still other users found the current versions of the newsreader software too cryptic to use. Also, this system needed more intelligence. It needed a built-in method that knew what to send and when to send it, the ability to record the condition of the server's last transmission, and everything necessary to run on top of a streaming protocol like TCP/IP. In February of 1986, an RFC appeared that established a higher-level internetwork protocol that would fulfill the needed requirements. It was called NNTP, and it became the natural choice for sites using the Internet to transfer data in the form of articles. NNTP has also been chosen by Microsoft to run its Exchange 5.5 Internet News Service.

NOTE An Exchange Server site is not the same as a UseNet site. A UseNet site is either a Backbone Server or an Intermediate server organized into an internetwork to pass data from one site to the next. ■

Understanding Newsgroups

The basic building block of UseNet is a newsgroup. As mentioned earlier, newsgroups are an online discussion group that are a many-to-many communication whereas e-mail is one-to-one.

These newsgroups are organized by subject into directories and subdirectories on the Backbone Sites (a key UseNet site that processes a large amount of UseNet traffic). These newsgroups (directories) are categorized by subject, area, and place. Examples of this follow.

Examples of Subject:

- Comp. Computers
- Sci. Science and technology
- Rec. Recreation Arts and Leisure
- News. News on the UseNet itself
- Soc. Society, social issue

Examples of Area:

- na. North America
- ca. State (California)
- ba. Local (San Francisco)

Examples of Place:

- Att. AT&T
- Well. Site-specific (The WELL conference)

Each category of the newsgroup has one or more subcategories. A fictitious example may be the category cartoons, which may be called *cart*. The cartoon area could have several categories under it. One category may be loon (short for Looneytunes). Under the loon category, there may be a subject called Rat. The newsgroup name would be `cart.loon.Rat`. It could be broken down even further specifically into different interests. At the leaf node, people can send messages and start strings of conversations about their favorite topics by using newsreader software. A leaf node is a UseNet site that originates and reads UseNet news. It does not relay any UseNet traffic like a backbone site. The newsreader software will aid in pulling these articles from the leaf node machine. It is important to note that you could send and read the newsgroup articles from Backbone and Intermediate sites, but this may not be practical considering the design of these sites.

Understanding UseNet's Flow

When you post an article, it is spooled into a specific area where it is stored until another server contacts this server and queries for newsgroups. Then it is passed to the requesting server. This happens with all servers sharing newsgroups until all machines on UseNet are updated. This is automatically done many, many times a day at predetermined times. Finally, the last server that receives information sends a message back to the parent server that it will not pass news. There are three categories of servers that participate in this flow:

- Backbone Site servers that are the core of the UseNet system.
- Intermediate servers that pass news to leaf nodes and are usually the large ISPs and universities.
- Leaf node servers that do not have the ability to send information forward.

See Figure 23.1 for more information.

FIG. 23.1
The flow of Information within UseNet.

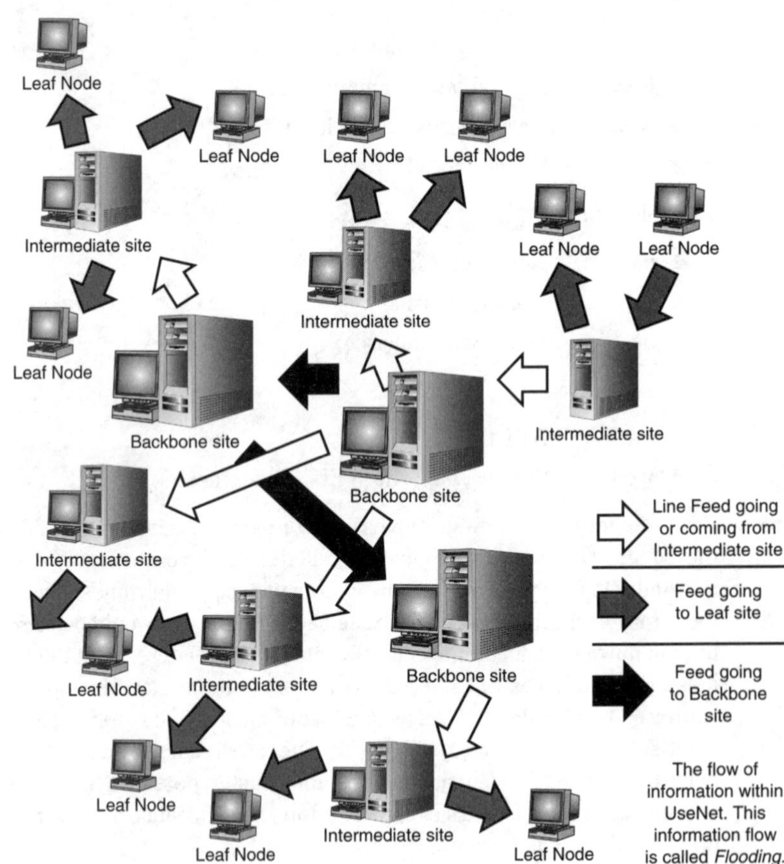

Understanding Newsfeeds

The flow from one UseNet site to another is called *newsfeed*. Each UseNet site receiving a newsfeed can be configured to accept and generate an NNTP connection and newsfeed to an outside source like Exchange Server running the INS. The INS processes this flow of information and converts it into a usable Exchange format to be accessed by a compatible Exchange client. To participate in the UseNet, you will connect your Exchange server to an Internet Service Provider (ISP) or Internet host machine offering newsfeeds and NNTP connection.

Keep in mind that once you configure Exchange to participate in UseNet newsfeeds by allowing inbound and outbound posting, you are effectively including your Exchange Server site *in the UseNet loop*. It is important to understand Internet firewall issues as well as the type of newsgroups that newsfeeds are being established to access. Also, multiple newsfeeds can be established from different providers, so be careful not to overlap or duplicate the information (two feeds from different sources streaming in the same information) supplied by the newsfeed to your Exchange server.

Two types of newsfeeds can be used in Exchange, push and pull. The basic difference is who initiates the newsfeed. With a push feed, your provider initiates the newsfeed and essentially controls which newgroups you receive. Obviously, you will want to tell your provider which newsgroups your company needs, but from a configuration standpoint, the provider is in the driver's seat. The advantage of the push feed is the capability of better handling of large newsfeeds.

The pull feed works well for smaller newsfeeds and for UseNet sources that are not compatible with an Exchange push feed. Here, you configure the connection and choose which newsgroups your company needs. Then, Exchange initiates the newsfeed and retrieves any new messages. This feed allows more control of the flow of information to and from your Exchange server.

Two more terms need to be defined before a discussion of inbound and outbound newsfeeds. Typically, a UseNet provider will have two hosts in one of two roles: an inbound host and an outbound host. These names can be somewhat confusing because the flow of information is the reverse compared to the host type. An inbound host is the host that provides a newsfeed into Exchange. An outbound host is the host that accepts a newsfeed from your Exchange server. The inbound and outbound host roles can be on the same machine, but for the purposes of example, this discussion places the roles on separate machines.

So to put everything together, you can use a pull feed to pull messages from your provider's inbound host. Using a push feed, the inbound host initiates the connection and pushes the newsfeed messages to your Exchange server. Both of these transfers are called *inbound* newsfeeds.

Alternatively, you can use a push feed to send or push messages from Exchange to your provider's outbound host. You can also use a pull feed where the outbound host will receive messages from Exchange. Both of these transfers are called *outbound* newsfeeds.

The NNTP protocol works with either push or pull feeds to get or receive a newsgroup. The communication between servers is governed by a set of rules built into the NNTP protocol. So, while the push and pull feeds are dynamically working, the NNTP protocol is communicating on a different level of the internetwork protocol stack in achieving control of the desired amount of the message flow, coming in or out of the servers.

Planning for the Internet News Service (INS)

When planning the roll-out of INS in your organization, you must consider the large amount of resources that newsgroups can require. Unless you are installing a dedicated Exchange News Server or resources (such as server processing and storage and Internet connection bandwidth) are not an issue, it is recommended to first establish an INS newsfeed to a few limited newsgroups. When resources are limited, it is critical to understand the effects newsfeeds can have on overall network and Exchange Server performance. There are many options in Exchange when configuring INS that allow complete control of how resources are utilized.

Having answers for the following questions will make the initial installation and configuration of NNTP much easier.

What is your Fully Qualified Domain Name or Internet Protocol (IP) address of the Microsoft Exchange Server computer that is running the Internet News Service? Do you plan to use a pull or push newsfeed for inbound messages or outbound messages?

How are you connecting to your provider? Will you use a dial-up (through DUN) or direct LAN connection to communicate with the host computer?

For a push newsfeed, do you want a secured inbound newsfeed? You will need to supply your ISP providing the newsfeed service with an inbound host account and password.

Which newsgroups will be downloaded by INS to the Exchange Public Folders, who has permission to access them, how long are inbound postings retained, and do you allow outbound posting? Have a plan on the organization of newsgroups on your Exchange server.

The following are questions that you will need to ask the ISP provider with the subscribed UseNet host that you are establishing a newsfeed with:

Specifically, ask your UseNet or Internet site administrator for your FQDN (Fully Qualified Domain Name).

How will you receive your active file? There are several ways to obtain this file from your provider. It can be e-mailed or sent by FTP (File Transfer Protocol) to you or downloaded directly from the host through the INS connection.

Who is responsible for the list of newsgroups you need to subscribe to? If you are planning to use push feeds, a list of newsgroups that you need to subscribe to must be sent to your newsfeed provider.

Establishing NNTP Connectivity Phases

To install an NNTP connection to another Microsoft Exchange server or foreign system, there are five primary steps to follow:

1. Gather the necessary information from your newsfeed provider. Using the questions mentioned in the preceding section should make this easier. Be prepared to give your provider the appropriate technical information about your site.

2. Install the appropriate networking equipment and protocols. This equipment could include modems, CSU/DSU, and so on.
3. Install and configure a local NNTP connector.
4. Configure the NNTP connection at the remote Exchange or Host site with necessary information of local NNTP connector.
5. Test the connection for message receipt and formatting consistency.

The information provided in the following sections will allow you to achieve these goals.

Installing an NNTP Newsfeed

When the appropriate software and hardware is installed (including Inter/intranet connectivity) on the Windows NT/Exchange server that will be handling the NNTP connection, you are ready to proceed with running the Newsfeed Configuration Wizard. The Newsfeed Configuration Wizard makes installing the INS easy. All you must do is supply the answers to several questions that were covered earlier in this section. Here are some of the items the wizard will ask you for:

- The UseNet site name of the newsfeed provider that is supplying the newsfeed. Newsfeed is similar to mail messages in that there is a path header for newsgroup messages. This could be helpful in understanding the origin of your feed. Typically, the name is the Fully Qualified Domain Name (FQDN) of your Backbone Site that has the UseNet feed (for example, `server.ginco.com`).
- The name of the Newsfeed Administrator who will receive status notifications related to the newsfeed and will own and control all the Internet Newsgroup public folders. This is someone who should have administrative rights within Exchange so as to act on any alerts related to an NNTP newsfeed or administer the Newsgroup public folders.
- The name and location of the active file if it is not going to be downloaded.

The Configuration procedure for the NNTP connection runs through a series of setup wizard screens that will guide you.

To run the Newsfeed Configuration Wizard, from the Exchange Administrator program, select the File menu, then New Other, and then Newsfeed. The NNTP Configuration Wizard appears (see Figure 23.2).

The first screen reminds you to contact your NNTP newsfeed service provider for the information needed in configuring NNTP.

NOTE If you are using Dial-Up Networking, the Dial-Up Network has to have an entry for the NNTP remote site's phone number to answer the wizard's question on who is your UseNet provider.

With the information you have collected, you are ready to proceed with the NNTP installation by choosing Next on the first wizard screen.

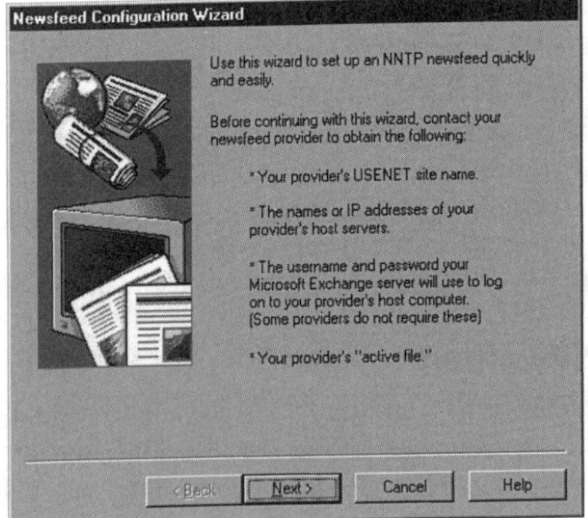

FIG. 23.2
The Newsfeed Configuration Wizard will take you through NNTP connector setup.

The next wizard screen requires you to fill in the UseNet site name with a Fully Qualified Domain Name (FQDN). The Server To Install On is automatically selected. You can choose to install this connector on any server in the organization providing that there are proper permissions and administrative rights. Choose the Next button on the bottom of the screen.

It is important to remember that you are configuring a newsfeed that will transfer through a connection that has been configured with NNTP. Note that NNTP is a component that moves data (news) across an internetwork, between sites, and into Exchange public folders. Then a client is used to read and post news messages as well as to post replies into the public folders. Those messages eventually are posted to the appropriate newsgroup (see Figure 23.3).

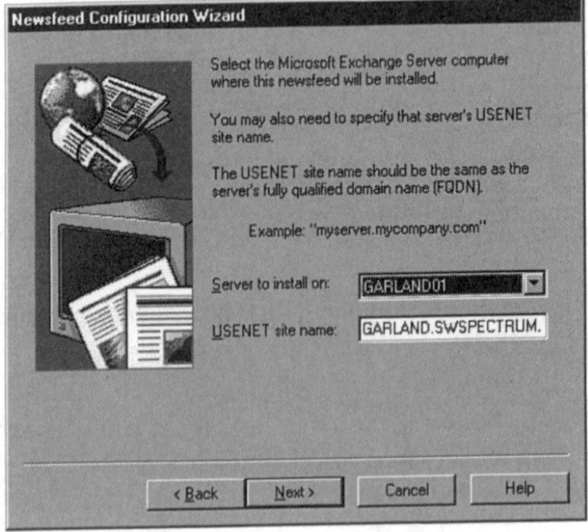

FIG. 23.3
You need to have FQDN for your Newsfeed server.

It is necessary to configure whether you are going to pull or push with a newsfeed from the UseNet provider. A pull newsfeed is associated with inbound newsfeed or an upstream newsfeed. An inbound pull newsfeed refers to the Exchange server initiating the call to the newsfeed provider.

NNTP controls the conversation, which ends when the sender hangs up. The news articles that NNTP distributes on the Exchange server will be handled in public folders.

Push feeds are associated with inbound and outbound newsfeeds. When a push inbound connection is established, the host initiates the call to the Exchange server. Then the Exchange server is configured to accept the inbound push newsfeed. The newsfeed is filtered through an active file. Further, you must establish a push outbound newsfeed at your newsfeed provider and establish the security issues that go with the outbound feed.

The NNTP Configuration Wizard provides three choices of newsfeeds:

- Inbound and outbound (typical)
- Inbound only
- Outbound only

The NNTP Configuration Wizard also provides the choice of the type of inbound newsfeed:

- Accept incoming messages (typical)
- Pull incoming messages (see Figure 23.4)

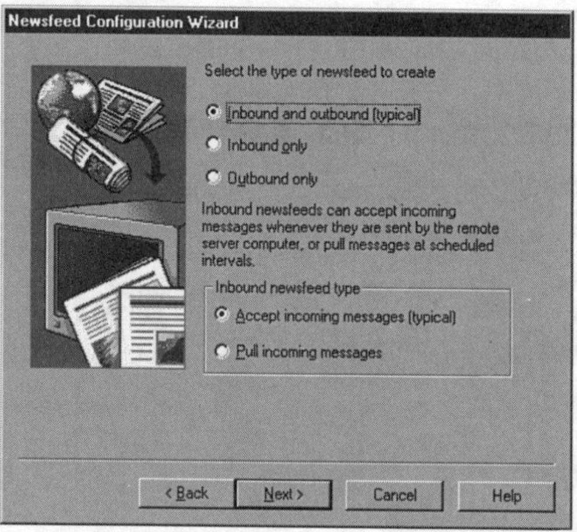

FIG. 23.4 Deciding what type of newsfeed to create.

The Newsfeed Configuration Wizard begins to check on your network protocol. The network is either a LAN or Dial-Up Networking (DUN). The network should be configured before using the wizard. The phone book should have an entry for the Newsfeed Service provider. If there are no DUN phone book entries, the wizard will flash a warning message informing the user that there are no phone book entries. After clearing the warning message, you are returned to the wizard and the connection using DUN option will be grayed out. If there is a phone book entry, it will appear in the box and you can select the appropriate site. If there is further authentication needed for your UseNet host, there are entries for Account and Password (see Figure 23.5).

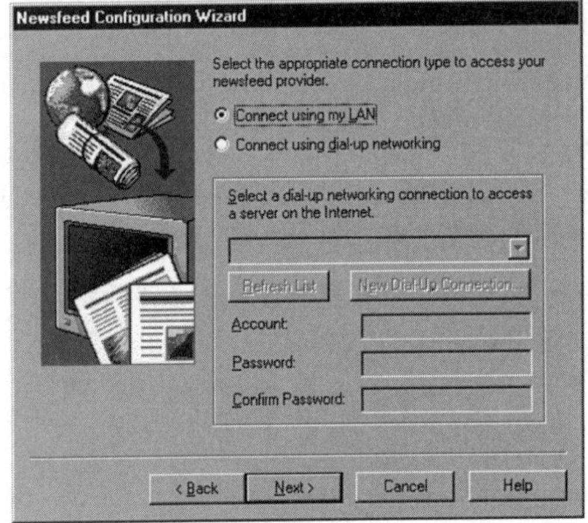

FIG. 23.5
Deciding on the network type. If necessary, enter UseNet Host Account and Password.

On this screen the wizard program sets up a connection schedule, which specifies how often the Microsoft Exchange Server computer will connect to your newsfeed provider. The drop-down menu has intervals of 15 minutes, 1 hour, 3 hours, 6 hours, 12 hours, and 24 hours. From the Exchange Wizard program, choose Next (see Figure 23.6).

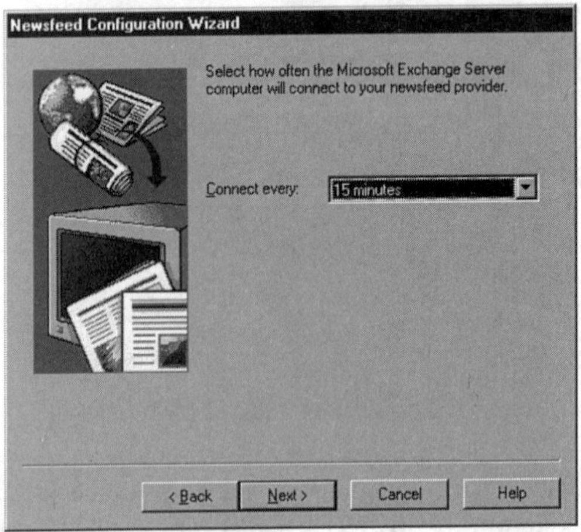

FIG. 23.6
Setting up the time intervals for the newsfeed connection.

The UseNet site name is entered in this box (see Figure 23.7).

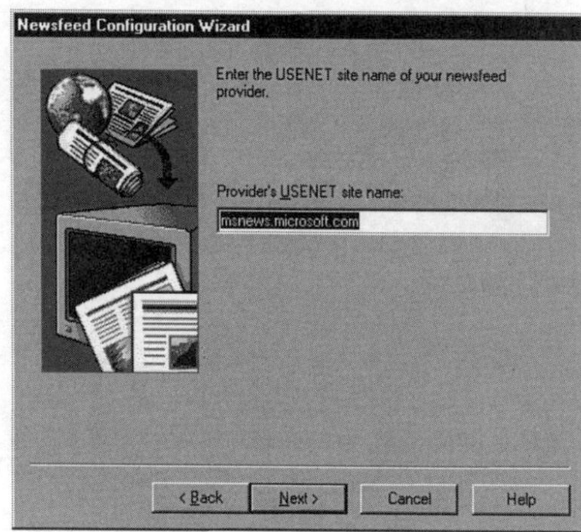

FIG. 23.7
Entering your site name for your newsfeed provider.

The wizard provides space to enter the host's name or IP address. There is also a box in which a host name or IP address may be added for additional host computers (see Figure 23.8).

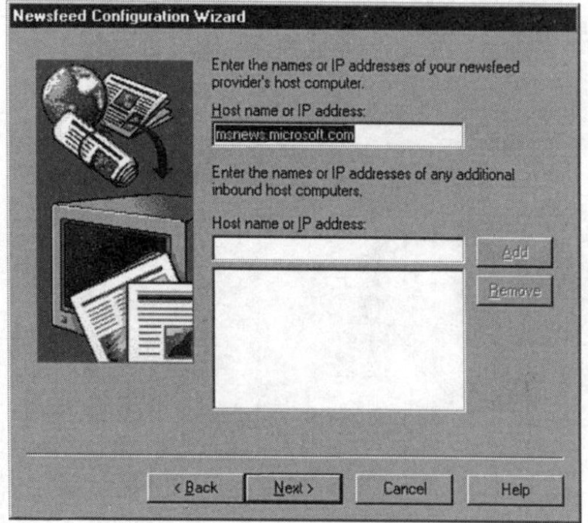

FIG. 23.8
An IP address or host name of the inbound host computer.

The next screen in the wizard allows the options for a secure connection to the provider. Ask the newsfeed provider if a Login and password are required. With Exchange 5.5 NNTP, there is now Secure Socket Layer (SSL) support. If your host provider supports SSL, you can select this. If your provider does not require any of this security, you can skip it. By choosing the Next button, you will be ready to install your NNTP Internet News Service (see Figure 23.9).

You will need to provide the Exchange Service account password to install the INS for the first time (see Figure 23.10).

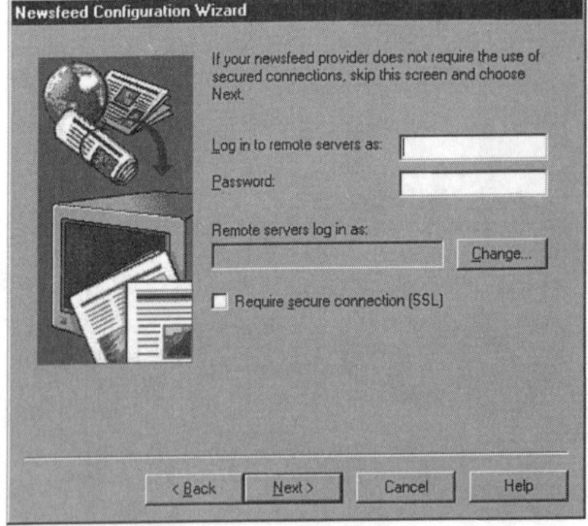

FIG. 23.9 Security for your Internet provider if it is required.

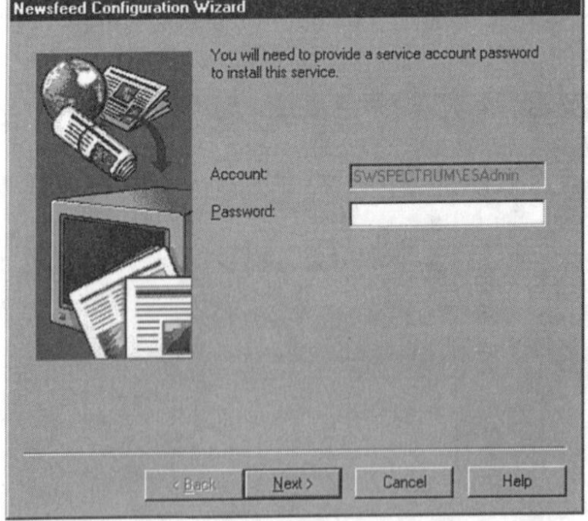

FIG. 23.10 Providing an Exchange Service account password.

At this point, the Internet Newsfeed Service is installed and started. However, no newsgroups have been selected for the newsfeed. The wizard indicates that there still must be a newsgroup selected. One reason that the wizard hasn't asked for a newsgroup up to this point is that it needs the road map to all News Groups, which is called the Active File. However, the Newsfeed needs to connect to the host so that it can download this file (see Figure 23.11).

The administrator will delete and create all the Internet Newsgroup public folders and receive INS alert notifications. Choose a person with administrator rights in Exchange for these tasks (see Figure 23.12).

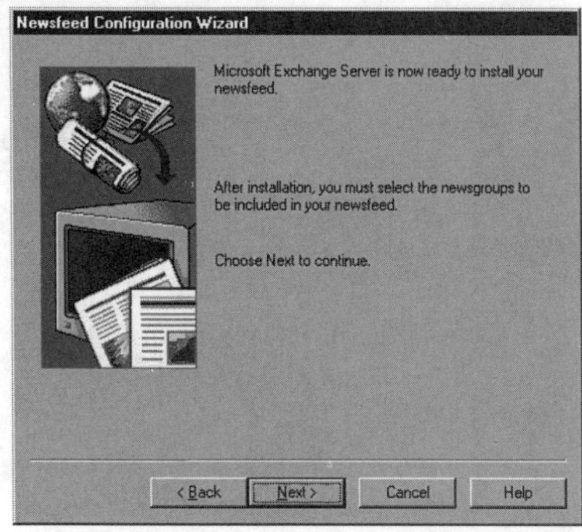

FIG. 23.11
The wizard needs to connect before downloading the active file.

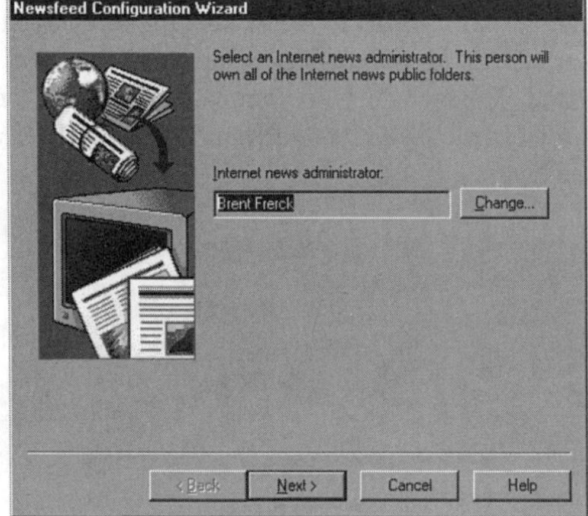

FIG. 23.12
You should choose a Newsgroup administrator with Exchange administrator rights.

Exchange Server has made the connection with the host computer through NNTP. The wizard wants to download the active file, which is a road map to Newsgroups or conversations throughout the world. The wizard gives three options:

- To import a new active file (local browse)
- Download the file from provider
- Configure newsfeed later (see Figure 23.13)

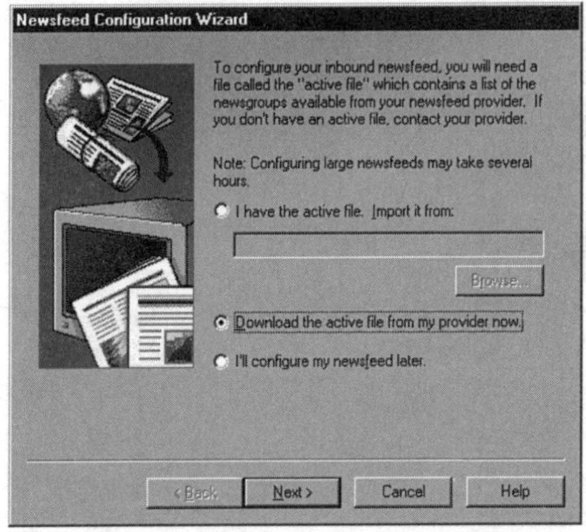

FIG. 23.13
For inbound connections the Active file is a road map to the world's newsgroups.

After the Active File is loaded and you have proceeded to the next screen,. you can select the newsgroups that you want to subscribe to. If you expand the root directory of the news server shown in the box, the various newsgroups will be displayed. To subscribe to a specific newsgroup, highlight it and click Include. Once you have selected all the newsgroups you want, click the Next button and all the Exchange public folders will be created for those subscribed newsgroups (see Figure 23.14).

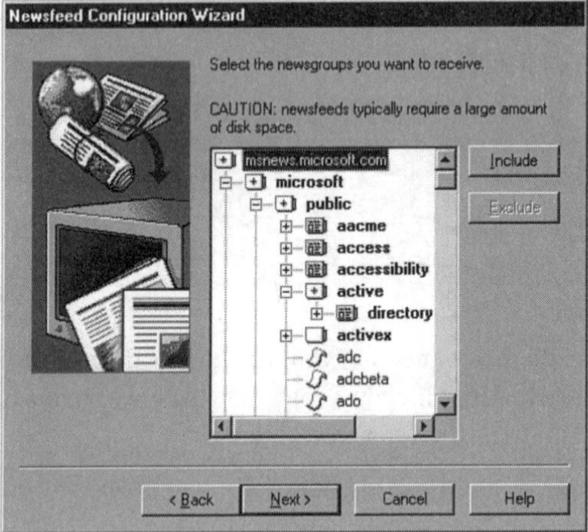

FIG. 23.14
Selecting the newsgroups you want to subscribe to.

The wizard is completed. The INS is running and by default has enabled the newsfeed you just installed. However, if you have installed a push newsfeed, it is now time to call your provider to coordinate the newsgroups you have subscribed to and have them activate the push from their host server. Clicking the Finish button completes the installation process (see Figure 23.15).

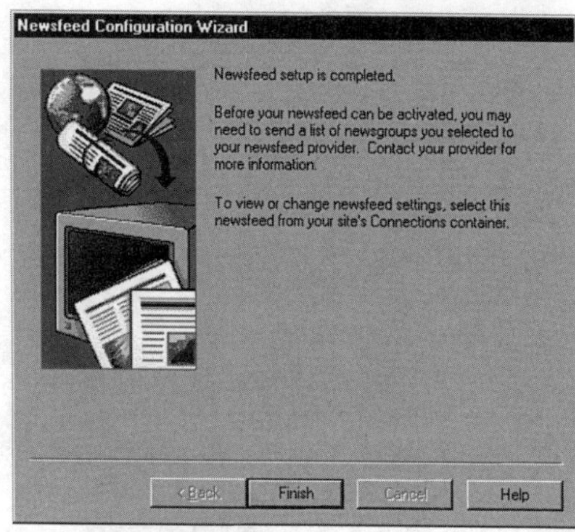

FIG. 23.15
The wizard has completed installing the Microsoft Internet News Service.

Configuring an NNTP Connection

The NNTP Connector property pages allow you to make configuration changes to any installed NNTP newsfeed. Each NNTP Newsfeed property page is covered in the following sections.

The General Page Use the NNTP General page to change the basic communication options for a selected newsfeed. The following steps guide you through configuring the NNTP Newsfeed General page:

1. Select the General tab of the NNTP Newsfeed Properties page (see Figure 23.16).
2. Enter a Display Name for the Newsfeed as you want it to appear in the Exchange Administrator display window.
3. The Directory Name is defined during installation and can't be changed.
4. (Optional) Change the name of the administrator mailbox that was entered during original installation with the wizard.
5. Choose to enable or disable newsfeed by clicking the box to place or remove the check. By default, the newsfeed is enabled when first installed.

The Messages Page Use the Messages Properties page to specify the maximum incoming and outgoing and message size in your newsfeed. Complete the following steps:

1. Select the Message tab in the NNTP Newsfeed Properties page (see Figure 23.17).
2. Under Outgoing message size or Incoming message size, select an option.

No limit	There isn't a size limit for the message.
Maximum (K)	Select and type a number representing the largest size of message that can be sent.

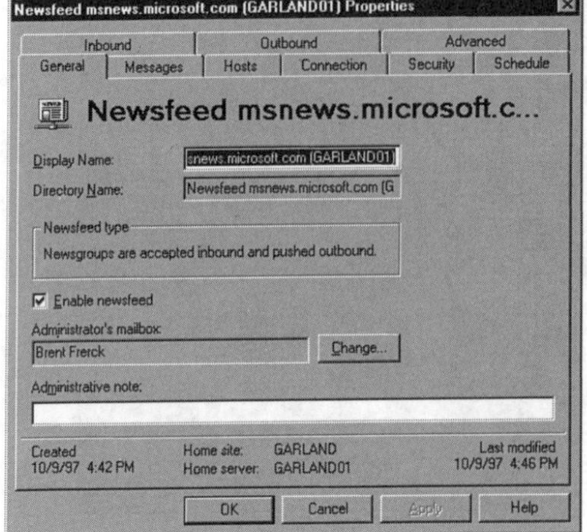

FIG. 23.16
The General tab.

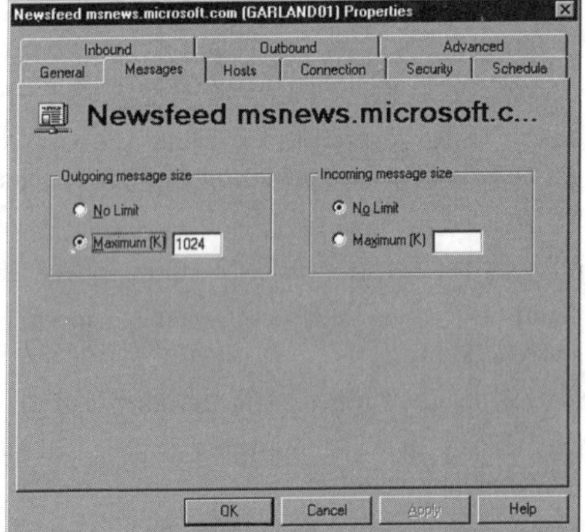

FIG. 23.17
Entering the size limit of incoming and outgoing messages.

The Hosts Page Set Site and Host name or IP address for establishing a connection to the remote newsfeed Hosts server. Additional inbound hosts are set here:

1. Select the Hosts tab on the NNTP Newsfeed Properties page (see Figure 23.18).
2. Enter your UseNet site name if your server initiates connections. You must connect the newsfeed to your remote UseNet site by specifying the node name.
3. Enter the IP address or UseNet Host computer name of the server that is providing the newsfeed. This name must be a Fully Qualified Domain Name for use on the Internet.
4. Enter any additional inbound host computers. This depends on your UseNet site and whether they have additional servers. Always make sure that there isn't any overlap of newsgroups or messages.

5. When you want to remove an inbound connection, select the remote host name or IP address you want to remove and choose Remove.

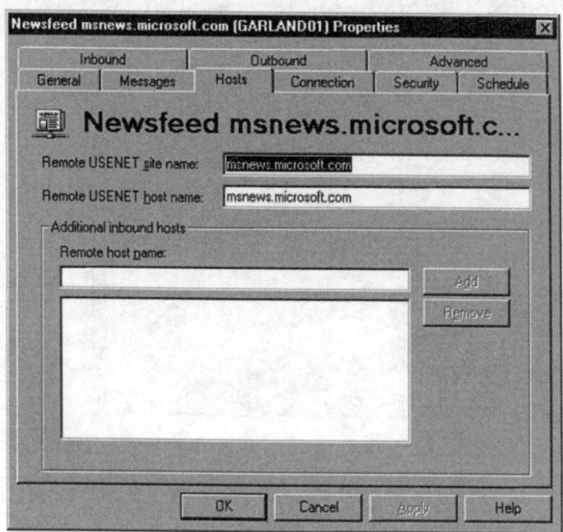

FIG. 23.18
Entering the remote site and host name.

The Connection Page Set the connection type, LAN or dial-up connections to your hosts, by completing the following steps:

1. Select the Connection tab on the NNTP Newsfeed Properties page (see Figure 23.19).
2. Select the connection type using either Local Area network (LAN) or Dial-Up Networking. Options for Dial-Up Networking are:

Refresh List	Updates current connections.
New Connections	To add a new dial-up connection to the list of connections, you must Refresh to update list.
Connection	Select from the list of available Dial-Up Networking connections.
Account	Account name of dial-up connections.
Password	The password for the dial-up connection if necessary. Confirm password. Verify that the password is correct.

The Security Page The Security page applies to both inbound and outbound feeds. Unless required for connection to the host computer, this page is optional (see Figure 23.20).

An inbound feed is a push to the newsfeed server. An outbound feed is a pull to the newsfeed server or the reverse. Security is set up in consideration of newsfeed server calling an Exchange server or Exchange server calling your newsfeed provider. Complete the following steps:

1. Select Login Authentication for use with inbound, outbound, or both newsfeed connections.

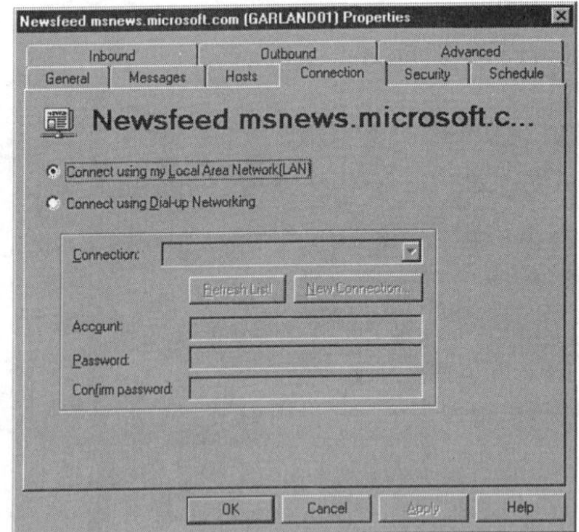

FIG. 23.19
You can select either Local Area Network or Dial-Up Networking.

2. Set security for outbound connections by selecting Log In To Remote Servers As. Here you are setting up a pull feed and need information from a remote host. If you are connecting to a host server, that requires a login to make the connection. The Exchange server must supply the account and password for the host server to establish that connection. That login information will be entered into the respective Account and Password fields.
3. Set security for inbound connection by selecting Remote Servers Log In As. Here you are setting up a push feed and you need to supply information to the remote host so that your newsfeed provider can log on and push the newsfeed to the Exchange server. You must supply your newsfeed provider with the information for the account entered in this field.
4. If supported by the host server, the Secure Socket Layer secured connection option can be selected. All data transfer will be encrypted. As an option, login account and password can be used for additional security (account and password will be encrypted as well).

The Schedule Page Use the Schedule properties page to control how often the NNTP newsfeed initiates a connection to the host server to update the newsgroups that you subscribed to. Scheduling specific times for newsfeed sending and receiving newsgroup updates can be an excellent way to limit the effects on network and server resources during peak production hours. Complete the following steps:

1. Select the Schedule tab on the NNTP Newsfeed Properties page (see Figure 23.21).
2. Select one of the three option buttons that determine when this NNTP Newsfeed connects.

Never	In effect, disables newsfeed.
Always	Starts connections every five minutes.
Selected Times	Assigns specific connections times in the Schedule grid.

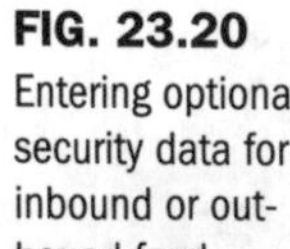

FIG. 23.20
Entering optional security data for inbound or out-bound feed.

3. If you chose Selected Times, under the Detail view you can select a schedule grid for:

1 Hour	Displays the schedule grid in one-hour increments.
15 Min.	Displays the schedule grid in 15-minute increments.

FIG. 23.21
Scheduling connection times for newsgroup updates.

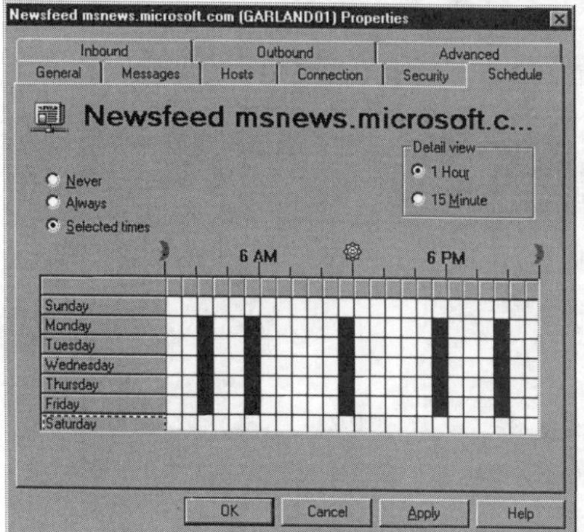

The Inbound Page Inbound newsfeeds are typically a push feed from your UseNet host. The inbound newsfeed can also be installed as a pull feed. The type of inbound newsfeed is selected during initial newsfeed installation with the configuration wizard. Consequently, you cannot change the type of inbound feed once the newsfeed is installed. To change the type of inbound newsfeed, you must delete the newsfeed and rerun the wizard. You can select which news-groups you want to subscribe to on this property page. The list of available newsgroup servers reflects the active file that was downloaded during the configuration wizard process. Configure as follows:

1. Select Inbound tab from property page of the Newsfeed property page (see Figures 23.22 and 23.23).

For pull-type newsfeeds:

2. Select the newsgroups that you want to subscribe to and click on the Include button to subscribe.
3. You can unsubscribe a newsgroup by highlighting it and pressing the Exclude button.
4. When you click the New Active List button, the New Active List menu appears. To update the Active List on the Exchange server, select Download.Via NNTP or Import From A File.

For push-type newsfeeds:

2. Select the newsgroups that you want to subscribe to and click the Accept button to subscribe.
3. You can unsubscribe from a newsgroup by highlighting it and clicking the Reject button.
4. The Inbound properties page has the option button to Create Newsgroup Folders. This feature will create the Exchange public folders for selected newsgroups.

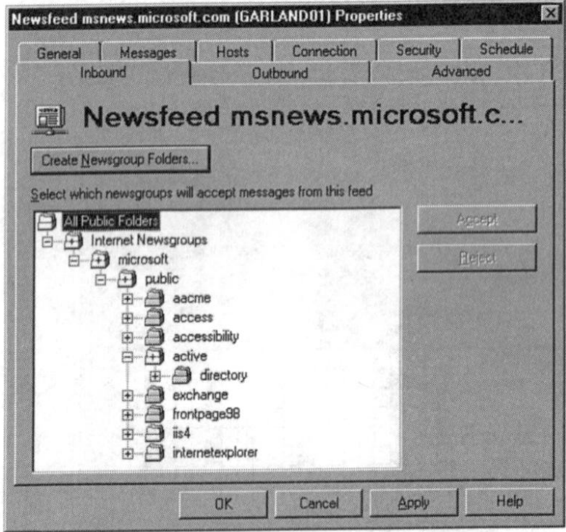

FIG. 23.22
A push inbound newsfeed.

The Outbound Page The Outbound Newsfeed is responsible for sending or posting messages on a newsgroup. If the News host computer needs to pull messages from your Exchange server, you need only configure NNTP client support on your computer. The host computer can then pull messages off your Exchange server acting as though it was an NNTP newsreader. Configure your outbound newsfeed (see Figure 23.24) as follows:

1. Select the Outbound tab.
2. Select the Exchange public folder that corresponds to the newsgroup you want to post messages to and add it to your list of Newsgroups To Include In Your Outbound Newsfeed by highlighting it and clicking the Include button.

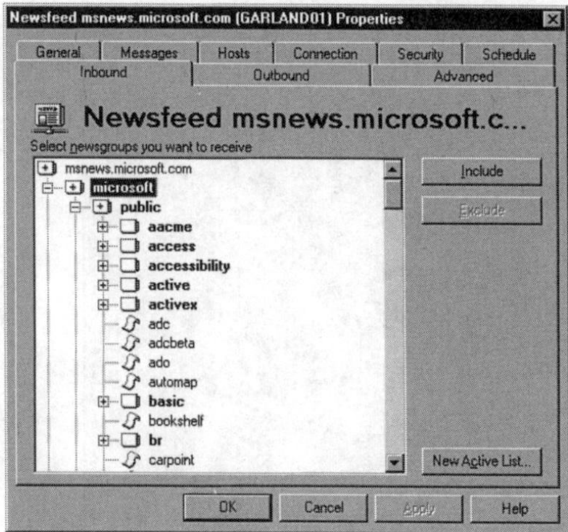

FIG. 23.23
A pull inbound newsfeed.

3. Removing a newsgroup from an outbound newsfeed is very straightforward.
4. Select the public folder from the list of Newsgroups To Include In Your Outbound Newsfeed that you no longer want to be able to post and click the Exclude button.

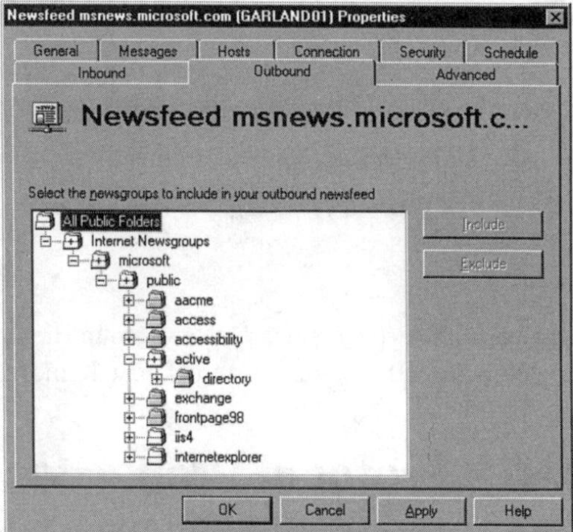

FIG. 23.24
Configuring outbound newsfeed.

The Advanced Page Use the Mark All Newsgroup Messages As Already Delivered option to mark all queued messages as delivered. This *flushes* the queue of messages waiting to be processed, allowing the Exchange server or another host computer to catch up to the most recent newsgroup postings (see Figure 23.25).

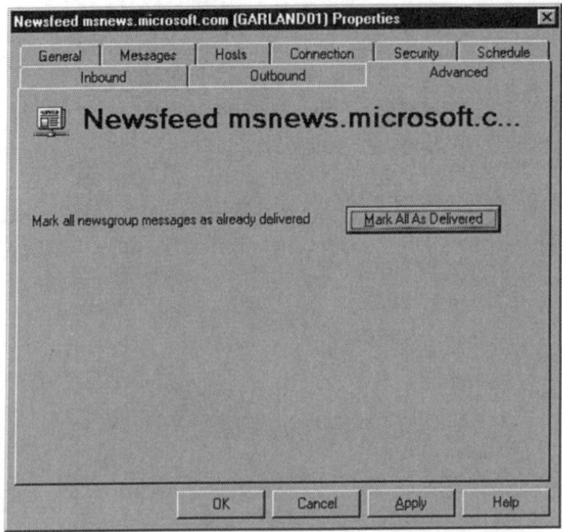

FIG. 23.25
Flushing the newsgroup queue of all messages.

Understanding Newsgroup Hierarchies

Newsgroup hierarchies are folders built with UseNet public folders from newsfeed. Selecting a parent folder from an existing public folder enables you to rearrange this folder by user preference. Exchange 5.5 enables the organization to build their own order of folders from their newsfeed (see Figure 23.26).

Complete the following steps to add and remove public folders to a newsgroup hierarchy:

1. From the Tools menu, choose Newsgroup Hierarchies.
2. Select the public folder that you want to designate as a hierarchy parent newsgroup public folder.
3. Click OK.
4. You can remove the parent folder by choosing Newsgroup Hierarchies. Select the public folder you want to delete from the hierarchy and choose Remove.

Understanding NNTP Protocol Properties

This section covers the Network News Transfer Protocol (NNTP). You can adjust a few settings from the NNTP protocol property page. These property settings can be configured to affect the Protocols NNTP object at both the site and server level. Default settings are set at the site level; you can use site defaults or change the settings at the server level for a specific server. Here's an overview of some key pages (see Figures 23.27 and 23.28):

- General Properties: Define display name and Directory name.
- Permissions: Specify the rights that users or groups have on this protocol.
- Anonymous: The Anonymous tabs allow you to assign this right for NNTP protocol.

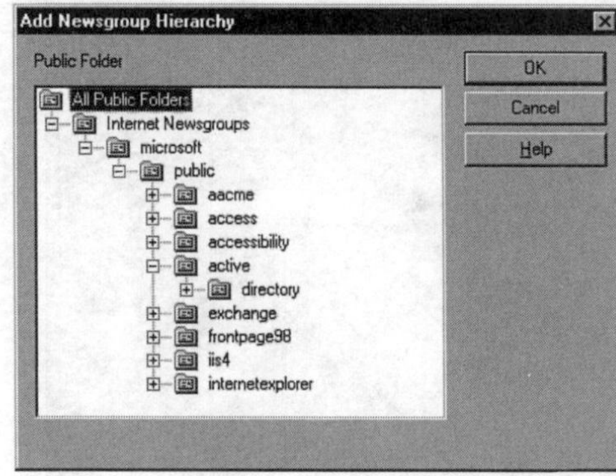

FIG. 23.26 You can add or remove public folders to create newsgroup hierarchies.

- Newsfeed: View newsfeed property pages.
- Diagnostics Logging: For troubleshooting or tracking, logging can be set to provide information in varying levels of details. (This tab is available only at the server object level.)
- Control Messages: Choose to accept or delete queued Control Messages. (This tab is available only at the site object level.)

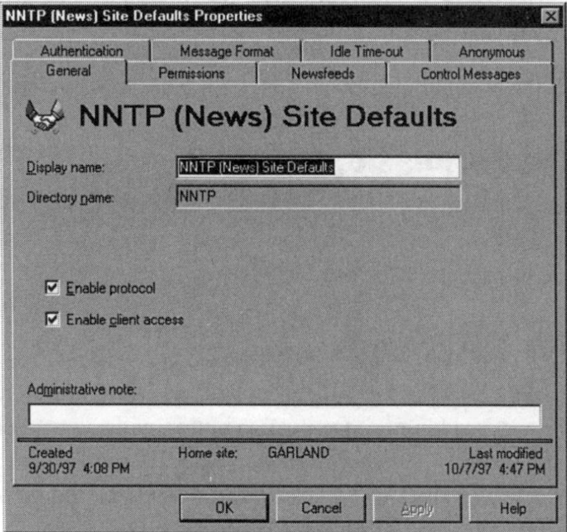

FIG. 23.27 Setting the Exchange site-level defaults.

Use the General page to set the defaults for your site or server NNTP object. Complete the following steps:

1. In the Administrator window, choose the site or server object level, and then choose Protocols.

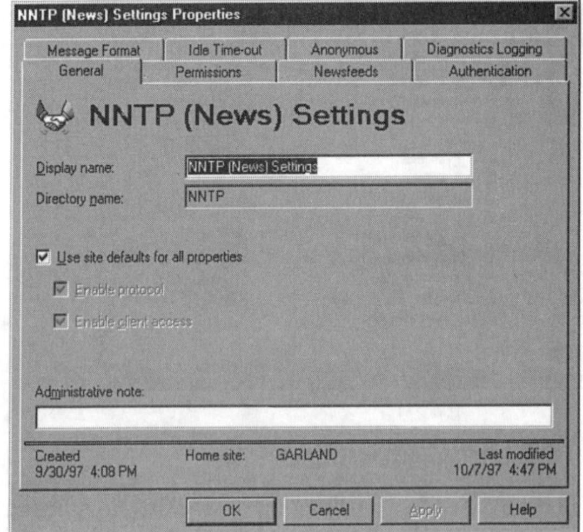

FIG. 23.28
Setting the Exchange server-level settings.

2. Double-click NNTP(News) Site Defaults for the site level and NNTP(News) Settings for the server level.
3. Select the General tab.
4. Display name is a name that can be 256 characters long. This display name is not provided for by the system.

Note that the Directory is not adjustable and is named during installation.

Using Properties for Permissions

Use the Permissions property page (see Figure 23.29) to specify the rights that users or groups have on this protocol. Permissions can be used to delegate roles. *Roles* are sets of rights that define what type of access a user has.

Using Properties for Newsfeeds

The Newsfeed page allows you to view the properties of newsfeeds that have been configured by the Newsfeed Wizard. Clicking the Properties button will show you the properties for the highlighted newsfeed. The Properties button is a fast and easy way to reference your newsfeed configurations. At the server level, there is a Create Active File option button to allow you to update the server active file (see Figure 23.30).

Using Authentication

Authentication occurs when a client logs on to the server and password and account information are compared and authenticated. The authentication process provides a user with certain permissions that provide access to resources. The problem with authentication is that people can intercept the password and account. After they have access to your accounts, they have access to your computer. With Exchange Server, six options are available for authentication:

Basic Clear-Text, Windows NT Challenge/Response, MCIS Membership System, and then each of those choices using SSL Encryption.

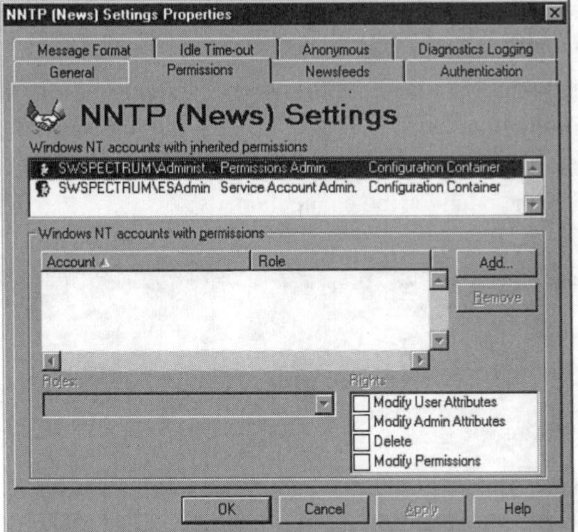

FIG. 23.29
The Permissions tab.

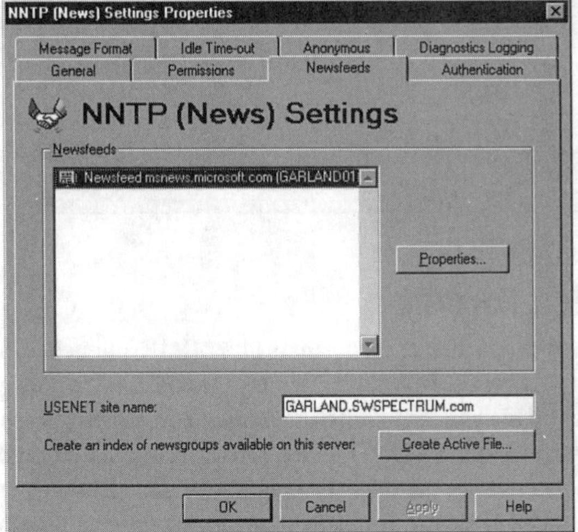

FIG. 23.30
You can highlight the newsfeed and choose Properties.

Use the following steps to configure Authentication:

1. In the Administrative window, choose site or server and select protocols.
2. Double-click NNTP(News) Site Defaults to configure site NNTP default or NNTP(News) Setting to configure server NNTP setting.
3. Select Authentication tab (see Figure 23.31). NNTP client uses authentication to log on to access the server. The client computer needs to authenticate one of the security methods:

Basic Clear-Text—A user name and password sent through the line without any encryption.

NT Challenge/Response—Enable authentication through Windows NT. The Challenge and Response is through the NT accounts. The Internet News Clients Mailbox or custom recipient cannot be used for this type of security.

MCIS Membership System—Enable authentication using Windows NT to occur through Microsoft Commercial Internet Server (MCIS) Membership System.

SSL Encryption—This open Internet security standard is supported by Exchange. It adds the SSL encryption for the connection.

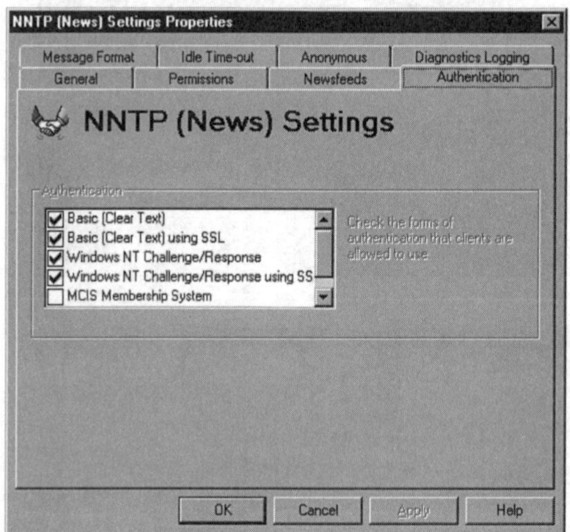

FIG. 23.31 Choosing the authentication you need.

Converting Message Format

The Message Format properties cover formats like MIME, uuencode, and Multipart forms. Messages come into Exchange in foreign formats that need to be converted at the NNTP site or server object level. This applies to both incoming and outgoing messages. Exchange Server messages are converted when an NNTP client retrieves them. Messages that are sent by an Internet user are not converted, and NNTP clients retrieve messages in the format that they were originally sent. The Message Format Properties pages can be set to convert these message formats. There are also ways to control the message queue. Topics to be covered are

- Message Format: MIME, uuencode, and Multipart forms
- Control Message: Controlling the queues for news feed

NNTP Messages coming from the Internet are often retrieved by NNTP clients and are unreadable. This applies to NNTP messages arriving and leaving. On the NNTP object protocol, you can set encoding methods to convert the newsfeed into a readable format:

1. In the Administrator window, choose a site or server and then choose Protocols.
2. Double-click NNTP(News) Site Defaults for the site or NNTP(News) Setting for the server.
3. Select Message format options (see Figure 23.32). Select any of the message formats that apply to your needs:
    - Initialization/Termination monitors that the IMS starts and stops.
    - MIME: A standard that will help translate a message coming from the Internet. It complies with RFC 1521 and 1522. It will allow for multiple attachments like plain text, binary file data, graphics image data, and video data. If a non-MIME-aware client gets a MIME message, the message will not be readable.
    - Send message body as plain text: A MIME body part is generated for the messages, because it is plain text. If HTML text is selected, a multipart plain text is generated.
    - Send message body as HTML: An HTML MIME body part is generated for the message. If sent, the message body part is plain text and is also selected, an HTML MIME body part is generated. HTML is an Internet standard that enables rich text formatting, such as bold, italic, or color, to appear in the message. If the HTML text is selected, then a multipart plain text is generated because HTML is an Internet standard that uses plain text containing special codes called tags, which make the text appear bold, italic, or in color when read by a program that can interpret HTML.
    - uuencode: The uuencode format is a simple 7-bit ASCII format that encodes a binary file along with control information to assist in decoding the file.
    - Binhex (for Macintosh attachments): Takes the message body as text with any attachments encoded by the BinHex method. This is a common method used by the Macintosh operating system.

Control Message Properties

Microsoft Exchange Server has a way it can control messages. Exchange can queue messages until you decide to use the messages. This can be helpful in many different ways. One possible use is that NNTP host computers use a control message to communicate with one another. Control messages are used to create and delete newsgroups and cancel messages that have already been posted through an inbound newsfeed. When Microsoft Exchange Server receives a control message to delete or add a newsgroup, it queues the control messages until you decide to reject or accept these new newsgroups. Exchange can control these messages through the Control Message page (see Figure 23.33):

1. Select the Control Message tab.
2. Select the queued control message you want to process.
3. Select Accept or Delete.

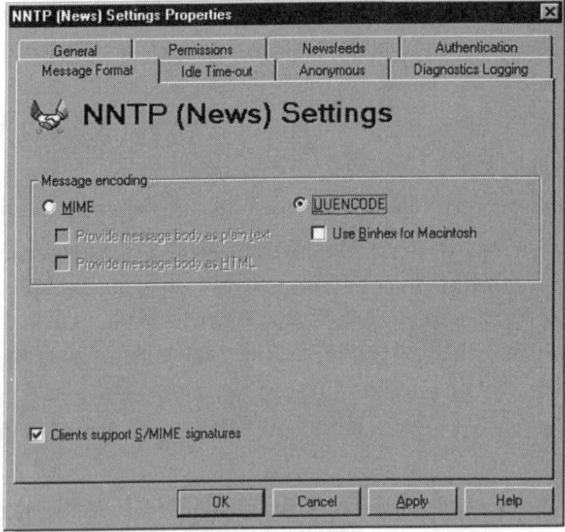

FIG. 23.32 The Select Message Format page.

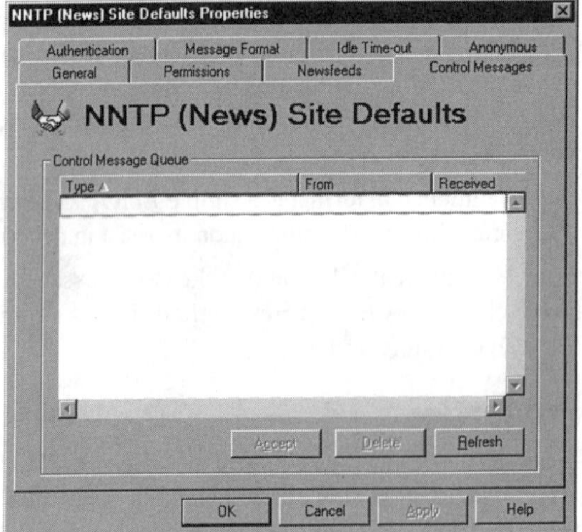

FIG. 23.33 You can delete or accept control messages.

Enabling Anonymous Access

A user can be given permissions to an NNTP object. You can give permissions for anonymous access so a user doesn't have to provide a unique login ID. The permissions limit the access that this type of user has on that object. Complete the following steps:

1. Select the Anonymous tab on the NNTP property page (see Figure 23.34).
2. Select the box Allow Anonymous Access.

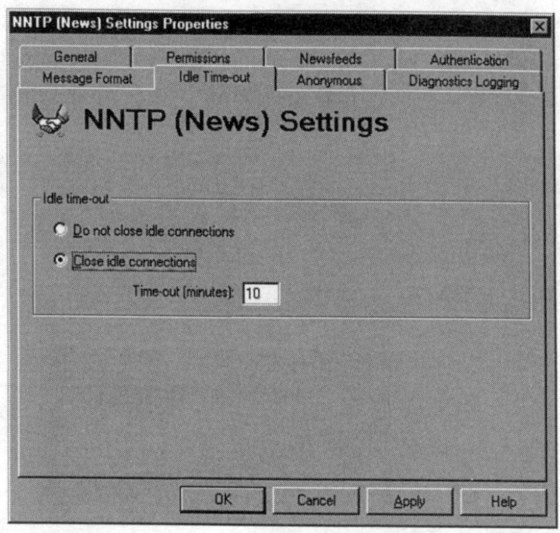

FIG. 23.34
The Anonymous tab.

Setting Idle Time-Out

This is the setting for how your Exchange server handles NNTP intervals of inactivity (see Figure 23.35).

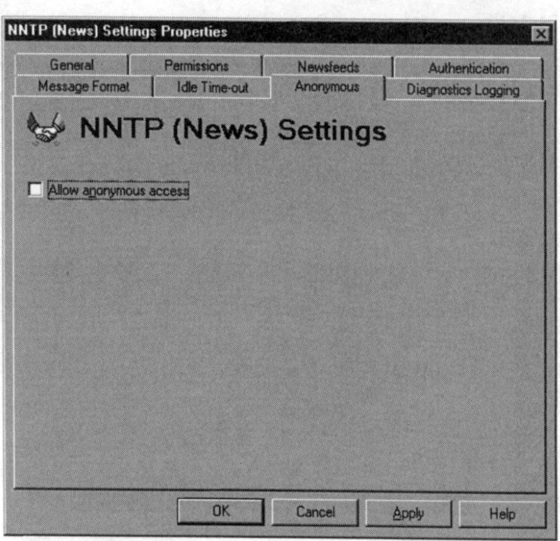

FIG. 23.35
Idle time-out is set to control how your server handles intervals of inactivity.

Setting Diagnostics Logging

Diagnostics logging levels determine which Exchange Server events are written to the Windows NT application event log. You can set logging levels to provide information in varying levels of detail (see Figure 23.36). Events can range from significant events (application failures), to moderately important events (receipt message across gateway), to events relevant only to debugging. Usually you log only critical events. When you are not troubleshooting NNTP, it is recommended that you turn off logging because large log files can be generated rapidly depending on log level and NNTP activity.

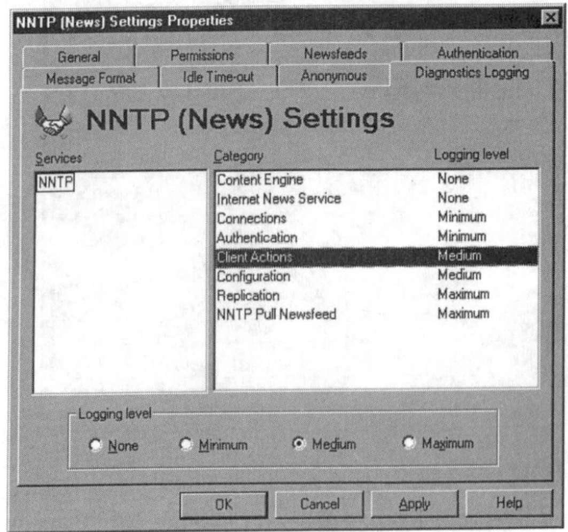

FIG. 23.36 You can use diagnostics logging for NNTP troubleshooting.

Configuring the Client

No client/server discussion would be complete without touching on the client. You can configure the client through the user mailbox or Custom Recipient Address. Authentication must be enabled at the server, the mailbox, or a custom recipient. The client cannot connect if NNTP has been disabled. Set NNTP client options from a mailbox or custom recipient properties (see Figure 23.37).

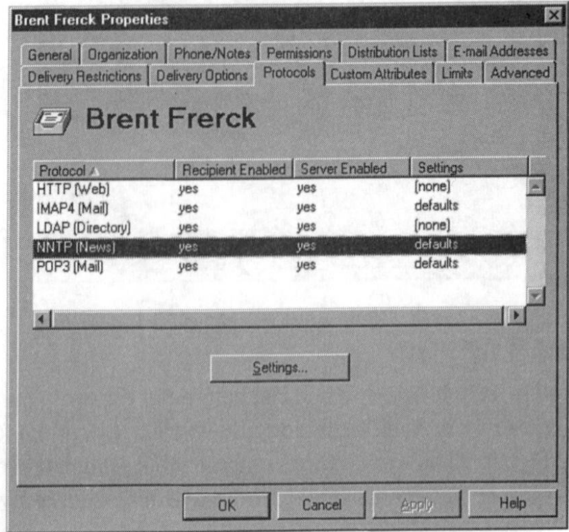

FIG. 23.37 Enabling NNTP for a recipient.

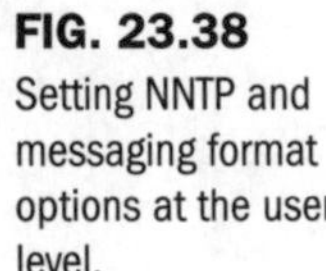

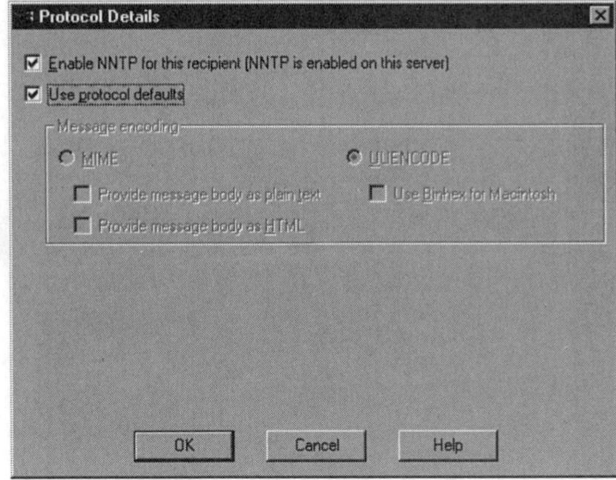

FIG. 23.38
Setting NNTP and messaging format options at the user level.

Configuring Internet Newsgroup Public Folders

Internet News options can be configured on the Internet Newsgroup public folders properties page when accessed from an Outlook client (see Figures 23.39 and 23.40).

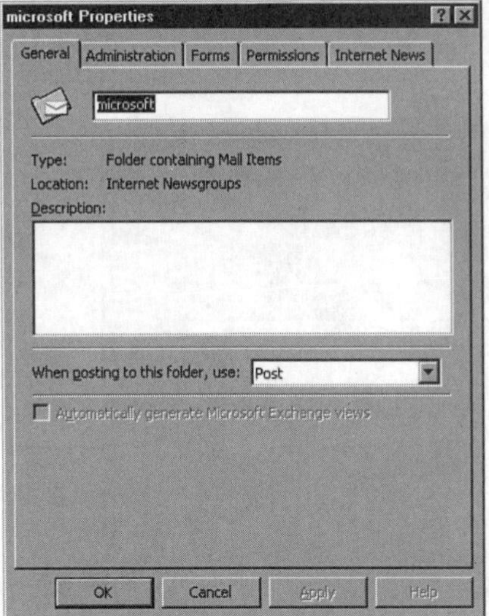

FIG. 23.39
Configuring properties for Internet Newsgroup Public Folders.

NNTP options can be set for individual subfolders in the Internet Newsgroup public folder on the specific folder's properties page when accessed in the Exchange Administration program (see Figure 23.41).

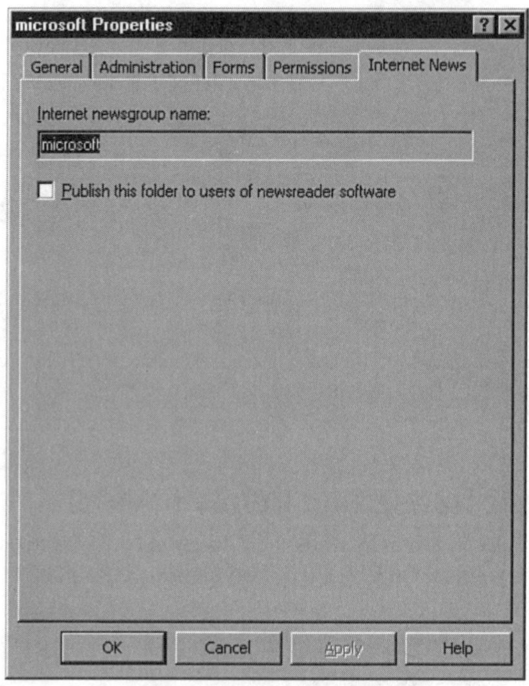

FIG. 23.40
Public folders for users with newsreader software.

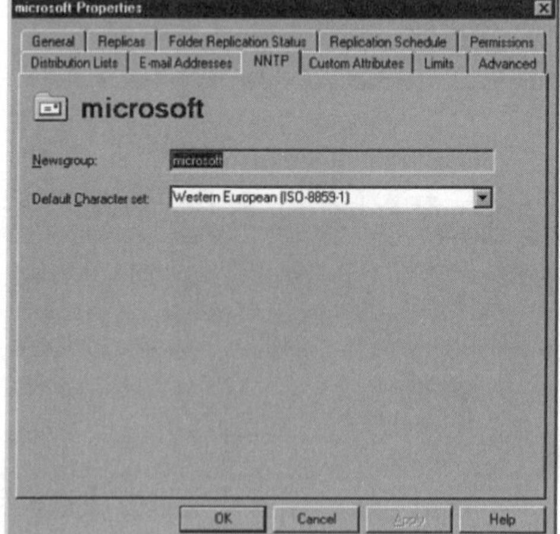

FIG. 23.41
You can make property changes for individual Internet Newsgroup Public Folders.

CHAPTER 24

Exchange Performance Tuning and Capacity Planning

In this chapter

I'm sure every system administrator has had the temptation to launch the network server from the company's roof in order to make it go faster. Likewise, I'm sure you find your temptation increasing when users stop you in the hall to complain about poor performance. However, you can find an alternative to the preceding dramatic option by discovering why Exchange is slow and then taking more positive action to fix the problem.

In particular, this chapter discusses what situations can cause Exchange to operate sluggishly. This is important to know because poor performance costs money in terms of lost time and productivity. The sections in this chapter give you tools to solve your problems. You also learn some answers to that simple question, "How many users can Exchange support?" This chapter also touches on capacity planning, which you need to consider in order to ensure that your server and network can stay ahead of their workload.

NOTE The examples presented in this chapter might not completely match your environment. It is extremely important that you recognize your environment's unique elements and move forward with the most appropriate tuning strategy.

The Art of Performance Tuning

As you may have heard before, tuning is more of an art than a science. There are no mystic techniques that detect and tune all Exchange servers in all situations. A majority of the time, you'll find yourself learning how individual system components work together to produce a result. Then you must consider the tradeoff between the different results. For example, you may want to adjust your system components to provide more stability at the cost of slower performance.

Defining Users

Before you can answer the question, "How many users can an Exchange server support?," you need to understand the types of Exchange users in your organization.

Usage patterns show that users read and generate anywhere from a few messages each week to hundreds of messages every day. A small percentage of the user population, therefore, can be responsible for a majority of usage. It's a bit like driving in the left lane on the highway and encountering some traffic: There's always one slowpoke that seems to cause the traffic to slow down.

Overall, you must understand the different types of users (light, medium, or heavy) within your organization, as well as their daily tasks.

Defining Servers

Obviously, each organization will purchase hardware specifically for its business needs. Take, for example, a centralized company with one main location and several warehouses and sales offices distributed throughout the country. The firm might house most of its computing power in corporate headquarters in the form of high-end servers. The company then places cheaper low-end machines in the remote offices. The high-end servers meet the needs of power users in headquarters, while remote field personnel are satisfied with low-end machines to dial into and receive e-mail.

Another company might have several independent business units throughout the country. In this firm, mid-range servers are used to provide computing power as close to the customer as possible. Therefore, each business unit can provide the fastest service.

You need to understand your company's use of server resources, as well as distinguish between low- and high-end machines (CPU speed and RAM) as defined by your organization.

Defining Load

When monitoring a server, you will notice its workload rising as more users connect and begin to work on it. In addition, you might notice other remote servers connecting to the server (through Exchange's connectors), thereby generating even more load. The remote servers have users connecting and asking their local servers to perform remote tasks. These remote user requests ultimately are generating some load on your local server.

All server load, therefore, is ultimately generated by users' requests.

Direct versus Background Requests

When a user asks the server to open an unread message, the server performs that task as a direct result of the users' request. As such, a server's workload rises in direct proportion to the number of users working directly with it. On an Exchange server that is serving only users, *direct* requests such as these make up most of the load. Direct requests are also synchronous in nature.

Background requests occur when a server is performing a task related to or on behalf of a user's request. Some examples of these tasks include replicating public folders and directory service information, expanding distribution lists, performing background maintenance, and transferring and delivering mail messages. As with direct requests, the load resulting from background requests is also proportional to the number of users directly connected. However, background requests occur asynchronously. Therefore, users do not need to be directly connected to initiate this work.

In the context of background requests, delivering mail places most of the load on the server. The resources consumed for message delivery are directly proportional to the volume of mail generated by your users. Therefore, accurately determining what types of "users" are within your organization is key to tuning Exchange.

Remember, direct and background requests create different types of load on the server. You can measure this with the tools that this chapter describes.

How Many Users Can Exchange Support?

When a user initiates a request, the server uses one or more of its hardware resources to complete the task. The main resources are the CPU, memory, mass storage (disk drives), and the network card. Suppose a request requires one second of CPU time and two seconds of disk time—and that these cannot overlap. Assume also there is no other process that will interfere with this request's execution. The disk, therefore, is the "bottleneck" of the operation, as it is the resource that expends the most time during a request's execution.

For example, two users issue the same request. Requests arrive at the server spaced three seconds apart. Each request will be serviced, and the users will not notice any unusual delays (other than the typical three-second response time).

However, if the second request arrives one second earlier, a bottleneck momentarily forms as the server is placed under a slightly heavier load and begins to form a queue. Consequently, the second user notices a slightly longer (one-second) delay in response time.

As more users connect and requests begin to queue up, the bottleneck becomes more pronounced. The server will slow down, and there will be some unhappy users.

The point at which server load increases and response time becomes unacceptable is when you've reached the number of users Exchange can support given the hardware.

Three variables exist that affect response time:

- User requests
- Number of users on one server
- Capacity of server hardware

As the number of user requests increases, so does response time. The same relationship is true for users per server. Hardware capacity has the opposite relationship: As it increases, so does its capability to handle more users and requests, which results in decreased response time.

The next section shows you how to make your operation more efficient by tuning existing resources and planning for your users' demands.

Using Exchange's Performance Tuning Tools

Three tools exist that can help you tune your server, reduce response time, and make your operation more efficient.

- *Performance Optimizer.* This tool ships with Exchange and optimizes a server's configuration (for example, threads for the information store or the MTA) after asking a series of usage questions—for example, the total number of users. It also analyzes hard drive space and performance to recommend placement of databases and logs. This tool is the easiest to use and can be run immediately after Exchange's setup.

- *Performance Monitor.* This handy utility ships with Windows NT Server and provides several graphical views on Exchange and the way that it utilizes hardware resources. During installation of the Exchange Administrator program, predefined monitors are added to the desktop window.
- *LoadSim.* This program ships with Exchange and can generate the load of hundreds of virtual clients from one physical computer. You can specify the type of user, such as light (handling perhaps 10 messages a day) or too heavy (handling more than 50 messages plus attachments). LoadSim determines the possible response time given your current server hardware and software configuration.

NOTE For best results, use LoadSim after employing Performance Optimizer and Performance Monitor. ■

Using the Performance Optimizer

The Performance Optimizer automatically analyzes and optimizes key hardware for the best performance with Exchange.

The Optimizer first analyzes the server's logical drives. Then it determines the most effective location for the MTA, information store, directory, and transaction log files. Specifically, the Optimizer locates the logical drive with the quickest sequential access time and uses it for the transaction log files. It does this because the transaction logs are written sequentially for maximum performance. The Optimizer then locates the logical drive with the fastest random access and uses it for the server's particular role. For example, a dedicated backbone server moving messages to other sites reserves its swiftest random access drive for MTA files. A public folder-only server will use its hard drive for the public information store files.

Keep in mind that the Performance Optimizer can examine a drive down to only the logical, not the physical, level. If you have divided your physical hard drive into sections or if you have partitioned a RAID array into multiple logical drives, the Performance Optimizer cannot provide a drive configuration that will give you increased performance.

The Performance Optimizer also analyzes the total amount of physical RAM and determines the amount of memory needed for the directory and information store. You are also given the option of limiting the amount of RAM that Exchange uses. This is especially useful another application that is running on the server needs a sizable amount of RAM (such as SQL Server).

Although you can and should run the Performance Optimizer immediately after setup, you should consider running it again *after* you make any of the following changes:

- Adding or removing a connector.
- Changing a server's role within a site (for example, changing a backbone server to a public folder server).
- Changing or upgrading any major hardware component, such as RAM, CPU, hard drives, or network adapter. If you double the amount of memory in your Exchange server, the extra memory will not be recognized until you run Performance Optimizer.

- Migrating a large number of users from a non-Exchange system (Microsoft Mail, cc:Mail, and so on).

The Optimizer is especially useful in its capability to automatically move the various databases and work queues from one drive location to another while also changing any necessary Windows NT Registry values and Exchange values (for example, if drive space for the Public Folder database (PUB.EDB) becomes constrained and a new multi-gigabyte RAID is added). The Performance Optimizer can be configured to easily shift the PRIV.EDB to the new drive space and make all the necessary changes.

All Microsoft Exchange 5.5 servers should run the Performance Optimizer because the database engine has been significantly changed to better use large amounts of memory and multiple processors.

Using the Performance Monitor

An Exchange system should be structured so its resources are used efficiently and distributed fairly among the users. Performance Monitor (PerfMon) monitors specific system resources so you can meet your system structure goals.

Many times, you might be motivated to solve all problems the instant they appear. In fact, you might find your motivation dramatically increasing when users loudly display their unhappiness. To be prepared for such problems, you should review PerfMon before moving too quickly in one direction. You can do that by using the set of overview counters presented later in this chapter. These counters will keep you from plunging too quickly and deeply into a dilemma, only to discover that you've missed the problem. When your system is under a load you want to monitor, bring up all the overview counters in PerfMon. Then you can determine which resource is being overworked.

PerfMon is powerful enough to be used as a console that runs 24 hours a day and includes thresholds for the various key counters. If a threshold is broken, the monitor might send a net broadcast or spawn a pager process to let an administrator know that attention is needed. This type of scenario helps to proactively solve problems before they affect end users too greatly.

The following sections are presented in order of their influence on Exchange's performance. Within each section, each counter is listed in the format Object: Counter. This will help you locate the particular counter within the Performance Monitor.

NOTE You might be wondering what a good figure is for *Server*: Bytes Total/Sec or for *MSExchangeMTA*: Messages/Sec. The truth is that there is no simple answer because each network has far too many variables.

Next, you might wonder what the maximum values are. Again, there are no simple answers. For example, how could you find how fast your car can go? You can probably discover this by driving as fast as possible. But notice all the variables that will affect your maximum speed. Do you test drive the car up or down a hill, at sea level, or at 10,000 feet? Whether you test drive on a cold or a hot day will affect the result. For example, cold air is denser and provides a performance boost, especially for turbo and supercharged engines.

The best approach is to drive your system through many conditions until you get a feel for its normal ranges or personality. To assist you in this process, LoadSim creates a synthetic load of hundreds of users on your system. While running your simulation, crank up PerfMon to monitor the load. ■

Detecting Disk Subsystem Bottlenecks

With most Exchange systems, the disk subsystem has the most influence on performance.

The primary consideration with the disk subsystem is not its size but its ability to handle multiple random reads and writes quickly. For example, when Exchange users open their inboxes, the set of properties in the default folder view must be read for approximately the first 20 messages. If the property information is not in the cache, it must be read from the information store on disk. Likewise, a message transferred from one server to another must be written to disk in order for the receiving server to acknowledge its receipt. (This is a safety measure that prevents message loss during power outages.) Now imagine the read and write activity created by 300 heavy e-mail users on one server. Their combined requests would generate a multitude of random traffic on the disk subsystem.

CAUTION

Sometimes, you see extremely high %Disk Times and think that your disk subsystem is causing a bottleneck. However, you want to examine other overview counters before going in any one direction. For example, when available memory drops to critical levels, Windows NT begins to *page* (write unused data or code to the hard drive to make room for more active programs). In a case of extreme RAM resource starvation, your disk subsystem can be reading and writing furiously and appear to be bottlenecked. Looking at other general disk counters in PerfMon will validate this illusion.

However, when you examine both memory and disk subsystem counters, you'll notice that during prolonged memory paging, disk activity increases. The solution is to add more memory, not to increase your disk subsystem capacity.

If you suspect that the server's disk subsystem is forming a bottleneck that slows down user requests, examine the following Windows NT Performance Monitor counters:

- *Physical Disk:* % Disk Time

  Disk Time is the percentage of elapsed time that the selected disk drive is busy servicing read or write requests. In other words, this counter provides an indication of how busy your disk subsystem is over the time period you're measuring in PerfMon. A consistent average over 95% indicates significant disk activity.

- *Physical Disk:* Disk Queue Length

  This counter measures the number of requests that are waiting to use the disk subsystem. This counter should average less than two percent for good performance. Use the Disk Queue Length counter combined with the % Disk Time counter to get an exceptional overview of your disk subsystem's workload.

Both counters can monitor either your server's physically installed disk spindles or RAID bundles.

Addressing Disk Subsystem Bottlenecks

Once you have established that the disk subsystem is the bottleneck slowing down your Exchange system, you can implement the following solutions to resolve the problem.

Separating All Transaction Logs

Both the public and private information stores utilize a transaction log that is written sequentially to disk. If possible, place the logs into separate physical spindles, preferably with the private store on the fastest drive, with a dedicated controller on a FAT partition, if possible.

Installing Additional Hard Disks

You can separate Windows NT processes (for example paging file) and Exchange processes (for example message tracking logs) to enhance performance. You can also separate the public and private information stores' transaction logs to separate disks or arrays for even better performance.

Overall, if you have a RAID subsystem, installing more drives coupled with a large RAM cache on the RAID controller yields faster throughput.

Installing Faster Hard Disks and Drive Controllers

Choose a disk with the lowest seek time available (seek time is the time required to move the disk drive's heads from one track of data to another). The ratio of time spent seeking as opposed to time spent transferring data is usually 10 to 1.

Determine what type of transfers the controller card performs: 8-bit, 16-bit, 32-bit, or 64-bit transfers. The more bits in the transfer operation, the faster the controller moves data. Ultra-SCSI technology, available from several vendors, offers an excellent combination of these features. The best way to judge is to run your performance simulations by using the guidelines, counters, and utilities (such as LoadSim) outlined in this chapter. Short of performing a full-scale simulation, your best bet is to find white papers from independent testing firms that profile the latest technology.

Using RAID Disk Striping to Increase Performance

Use RAID 0 (disk striping) to increase overall capacity for random reads and writes. You will need at least two physical drives for RAID 0. Use RAID 5 (disk striping with parity) for slightly less performance but more fault tolerance. You will need at least three physical drives for RAID 5.

If you implement RAID at the hardware level, choose a controller card with a large (4 megabytes) on-board cache. Several vendors offer complete solutions of this type.

Minding Memory Requirements in Exchange

When Exchange runs, it keeps only portions of needed data, referred to as *pages*, in memory at any one time. When it needs a page of data that is not in RAM (page fault), Windows NT loads that page into physical memory from a peripheral device, which is usually the hard drive. The average instruction in memory executes in nanoseconds, which is one-billionth of a second, and hard drive seek and access times are in milliseconds. Therefore, Windows NT must run 100,000 times slower than normal to retrieve a page from disk.

Keep in mind that Exchange needs a minimum of 32MB of RAM, and experience has shown that 64MB is a much more realistic level, given all that a Windows NT server and Exchange need to do quickly in RAM.

Detecting Memory Bottlenecks

The best indicator of a memory bottleneck on Exchange Servers is the rate of *hard page faults*. Hard page faults occur when the application cannot find data that it needs in memory and must access the disk subsystem to retrieve it. This slows down the Exchange Server because the data must be taken from the disk subsystem, a process that is slower than retrieving the data from memory. Accessing the data from the disk subsystem also increases the load on the disk subsystem.

This is why adding more memory to the Exchange Server can solve some disk subsystem bottlenecks that affect performance. Examine the following Windows NT Performance Monitor counter to determine if the Exchange Server's memory is forming a bottleneck:

- *Overview counter—Memory:* Pages/Sec

  The Pages/Sec counter reports the number of pages read or written to a disk to resolve page faults. You can turn this on when your system is under a typical load. If this counter averages greater than five, a memory bottleneck is starting to form, and your disk subsystem is beginning to take a beating.

Addressing Memory Bottlenecks

If you determine that the memory on the Exchange Server is forming a bottleneck, you can implement the following solutions to resolve the situation.

Adding Memory

You will want to add more memory until paging stops or occurs minimally. Afterward, be sure to run Performance Optimizer to adjust Exchange's memory caches.

Using Multiple Paging Files

If your disk subsystem supports concurrent I/O requests, using multiple paging files usually improves system performance. Be sure to place the paging file on your fastest hard drive, and then experiment with separating Windows NT's paging file from Exchange's transaction log files.

Removing Unnecessary Services

Disable any unneeded Windows NT services, protocols, and device drivers. Even idle components consume some memory and contribute to general system overhead.

The next section discusses performance issues related to your network infrastructure.

Detecting Network Bottlenecks

A network, by its heterogeneous nature, is full of potential performance bottlenecks. A company full of servers and clients talking in different protocols can often cause poor performance from Exchange. The following sections offer guidelines for detecting poor network performance with Exchange and suggestions to help you improve it.

When a network bottleneck forms, one of the following three scenarios can result:

- *Server overload.* The server doesn't respond to users' requests within a reasonable time given its current capacity. Sometimes this is due to an overload of another resource, such as the disk subsystem.
- *Network overload.* The network doesn't respond within a reasonable time because the load of the users' requests has exceeded the capacity of the physical medium. In other words, the network has run out of Net Available Bandwidth (NAB).

  Although the counters presented in the following section should indicate when the network or a specific link is overloaded, you will want to use Microsoft's SMS product or a packet sniffer to be certain.
- *Network corruption.* The network is periodically transmitting corrupt data. This puts an excessive load on both the server and the network because each bad transmission requires a retransmission.

Detecting Client Side Bottlenecks

The following counters are available to clients running Windows NT:

NWLink: Bytes Total/Sec (IPX/SPX)

Network Interface: Bytes Total/Sec (TCP/IP)

NetBEUI: Bytes Total/Sec

If you want to measure a client's workload, use the appropriate counter for your protocol. When your overview counters are generally idle but your network counters are high, you can usually infer that your network has a bottleneck on the client end. This means that your client is doing most of its work gabbing with the network.

In addition to the counters listed previously, the following counter also gives you an indication of how much load a particular client is placing on the network:

- *Redirector:* Network Errors/Sec

  This counts serious network errors between the redirector and one or more servers. It applies to any protocol running on the client station, and it shows if you have a network corruption problem. Each error is logged in detail in Windows NT's Event Log. This counter should normally be zero.

Detecting Server Side Bottlenecks

The following counters detect server side bottlenecks:

- *Server:* Bytes Total/Sec

  This counter measures most of the meaningful server activity and provides an insight into the server's load. It also provides an insight into how much load this server is contributing to the network's overall load.

- *Server:* Sessions Errored Out

  This counter measures the number of client sessions that are closed due to unexpected network errors. If this counter increases for one server, you might have a faulty network card. If the counter increases for several servers, examine the LAN infrastructure itself, including routers, hubs, bridges, physical cabling, and connections, to determine whether you have a more serious network corruption issue. This counter should normally be zero.

The following sections include suggestions that will improve network performance among your Exchange servers.

Addressing Network Bottlenecks

Once you have identified that the network is forming a bottleneck that's slowing down Exchange client-to-server response times, you can implement the following solutions to resolve the problem.

Applying Faster Hardware on Heavy Traffic Links

For the most leverage, you should apply hardware upgrades to machines generating the most traffic, as well as servers on the heaviest traffic links. This will provide a system-wide balance for your Exchange environment.

You can use a combination of the counters mentioned in the previous sections to determine which machine is generating traffic. A product such as Network Monitor (included as a tool with Microsoft SMS) or a standard network *sniffer* can determine which network links experience the greatest load.

Segmenting Your Network

If the Server: Bytes Total/Sec or corresponding client counter begins to reach the maximum bandwidth of the network link to which your server is connected, you should consider segmenting your network. On an ethernet segment, this value is approximately 1.2 megabits per second, including the overhead of the network.

Matching the Network Card to the System Bus

If your client or server has a 32-bit or 64-bit bus, use a 32-bit or 64-bit adapter card. Overall, you should use the fastest network card and matching bus available. Bus Master devices offer the best solution because they have their own intelligence and offload processing from the CPU.

Increasing Your Bandwidth

If you determine that your network is overloaded, increase its bandwidth by upgrading to faster network link technology, such as Fast Ethernet, FDDI, or ATM.

Detecting Processor Bottlenecks

Exchange is tightly integrated with Windows NT. Therefore, it can take full advantage of a more advanced processor or multiple processors. You should eliminate all other possible bottlenecks before investigating the processor. You can detect a processor bottleneck by monitoring the following counters:

- *Processor:* % Processor Time
- *System:* Processor Queue Length

If the % Processor Time exceeds 90% consistently on single processor systems or if it exceeds 50% on multiprocessor systems, the processor is possibly a bottleneck. Furthermore, if the Processor Queue Length often exceeds 2, the processor could be a bottleneck. However, this is not always true. Other devices on the server, such as memory, could form a bottleneck, which in turn increases the amount of processor use.

Addressing Processor Bottlenecks

Once you identify that the processor is truly the bottleneck affecting performance on your Exchange Server, you can implement one of the following solutions to resolve the problem.

Upgrading Your Processor

You can upgrade to the fastest processor available. Having done that, you can add additional processors if your hardware supports symmetrical multiprocessing. Keep in mind that Windows NT supports Power PC and Alpha as well as Intel processors.

Overall, adding another CPU typically gives a better performance increase than upgrading to a faster single processor does. The reason is that the multithreaded design of all Microsoft BackOffice products enables superior performance in a multiple processor environment.

For example, a server with two 90MHz CPUs outperforms a server with a single 200MHz CPU because Windows NT's symmetric multiprocessor (SMP) functions allow many more threads to be active.

Using Off-Peak Scheduling for the Processor

You might also consider scheduling processor-intensive activities during off-peak hours. Such processor-intensive functions might include generating the Offline Address Book, updating the routing table, or creating and sending storage limit warnings to users.

Detecting System Bus Bottlenecks

If you have a Pentium or Pentium Pro system, use the p5ctrs from the Windows NT Resource Kit to detect any bus bottlenecks. You'll have to take an extra step of running pperf to configure which of these Pentium counters you want to see:

Pentium: Bus Utilization (clks/sec)

Pentium: % Code Cache misses

Pentium: % Data Cache misses

> **CAUTION**
>
> Keep in mind that any counter or utility from the Windows NT Resource Kit has not been regression tested by Microsoft and is explicitly not supported by any area of Microsoft (including through the Web and Microsoft-monitored newsgroups). It is strongly recommended you test in an isolated lab environment before releasing into production.

If you see high bus utilization for your system and a high percentage of code and data cache misses, your bus may be forming a bottleneck.

Addressing System Bus Bottlenecks

Having identified the system bus as the bottleneck, you can implement the following solutions to resolve the problem.

Using Larger CPU Caches

If there are a lot of cache misses, upgrade to the next largest or the largest L2 cache available.

Using Off-Peak Scheduling for the Processor

As for processor bottlenecks, you might consider scheduling processor-intensive activities during off-peak hours. Such processor-intensive functions might include generating the Offline Address Book, updating the routing table, or creating and sending storage limit warnings to users.

Also, investigate and relocate any non-Exchange services that can be executed on a separate machine.

Exchange-Specific Counters

NOTE The following Exchange counters are available in PerfMon after you have installed Exchange. ■

The counters described in this section provide Exchange-specific monitoring information. If you are just beginning with Exchange or are new to monitoring, stick to the preceding hardware-specific counters. They provide an accurate high-level view. When you are ready to drill down on specific Exchange components, however, use the counters outlined here for detailed bottleneck detection.

Trend Counters

For best results, track trend counters with Performance Monitor's log. This allows you to average out the day-to-day spikes that can lead you down the wrong road. This average also sets a baseline of typical loads for your server.

Of course, you're also welcome to view these counters for an immediate snapshot of your server, but bear in mind that the numbers will be fairly meaningless unless you have a baseline to measure against. You should use the following Windows NT Performance Monitor counters when analyzing the usage trend on Exchange servers:

- *MSExchangeMTA:* Messages/Sec

  Messages/Sec monitors the number of messages the MTA sends and receives every second. In other words, it measures the traffic generated by message flow. This is a quick way to focus on message traffic sent to other servers. For more specific information on message traffic, refer to the message tracking logs.

- *MSExchangeMTA:* Messages Bytes/Sec

  Similar to the preceding counter, this counts the sums of the number of bytes in each message the MTA sends and receives each second. In other words, it reports the amount of message traffic measured in bytes.

- *MSExchangeISPublic:* Messages Submitted/Min and Message Recipients Delivered/Min

  These counters measure the rate of messages being submitted and delivered to the public store. Keep in mind that the delivered counter will generally be higher because messages often have multiple recipients.

- *MSExchangeISPrivate:* Messages Submitted/Min and Message Recipients Delivered/Min

  These counters measure the rate of messages being submitted and delivered to the public store. Keep in mind that the delivered counter will generally be higher because messages often have multiple recipients.

- *MSExchangeDS:* Reads/Sec

  This counter measures the amount of traffic generated by directory synchronization.

Service Time Counters

For best results, you should also track these counters with Performance Monitor's log. However, these counters are better suited for on-the-spot monitoring and evaluation, especially those counters that should be zero for the best throughput.

The following are service time counters. They tell you if the components are keeping up with the submitted load. The queues may be non-zero at peak traffic times, but they shouldn't stay there consistently, especially during slow times.

- *MSExchangeIS Private:* Send Queue Size
- *MSExchangeIS Public:* Send Queue Size
- *MSExchangeMTA*: Work Queue Length

The following counters indicate how long it takes the store to deliver messages:

- *MSExchangeIS Private:* Average Time for Delivery
- *MSExchangeIS Public:* Average Time for Delivery

Optimizing Dedicated Exchange Servers

This section is for advanced Exchange administrators who want to divide Exchange's functionality onto separate servers for even better performance and improved redundancy. Each server's hardware will be used differently depending on the dedicated role it's fulfilling for Exchange. After determining which hardware resource will be in demand, use the monitoring information and recommendations mentioned earlier to optimize the server for its role.

Optimizing Messaging Servers

Exchange servers that just facilitate user requests spend most of their time accessing the information store (IS) log and database. Because these two components have different personalities, you should create a disk environment that is tailored for maximum throughput for the appropriate IS need.

The IS log is stored on the hard drive, so use the fastest hard drive possible. Because the log is written sequentially, consider isolating it on a dedicated drive or even a dedicated cached controller and drive.

The IS database should also be on the fastest hard drive possible. Choose one with the lowest possible seek time because the database is accessed randomly. For best results, combine drives with low seek times in a RAID-5 array. Typically, the controller will have an on-board cache. The striping should speed up things considerably.

Besides the disk, the next most common bottleneck on dedicated user servers is the CPU. Use the processor counters and recommendations outlined earlier in this chapter to detect and eliminate any such bottlenecks.

The next most important things to monitor are network and memory resources. Again, use the counters and recommendations provided earlier.

Optimizing Connector Servers

A dedicated connector server uses one of Exchange's connectors (X.400, cc:Mail, IMS, site, or cc:Mail) to interface with other messaging platforms. Typically, the server will also serve non-Exchange clients using POP3, HTTP, NNTP and so on.

The key Exchange component in action is the MTA. Like the IS database, it uses the hard drive in a non-sequential (random) manner. You can use the IS database recommendation for disk bottlenecks on a connector server.

The next resource to monitor is the network interface. Review the network bottleneck section in this chapter. If any WAN links are involved, review Chapter 5, paying particular attention to the network links section to ensure that your WAN is adequate.

Finally, you'll want to look at the CPU. Connector servers can perform an extraordinary amount of message translation when talking to non-Exchange messaging systems. This translation tends to be CPU-intensive at times, so examine your processor counters and take the most appropriate action.

Optimizing Public Folder Servers

You'll have a more difficult time discovering the cause of bottlenecks on dedicated public folder servers. Because a public folder is so versatile, its usage and resulting load on hardware resources varies across a wide spectrum. For example, one company may use the folders to distribute a department status each week even though there isn't any posting of replies back into the folder. This kind of use is much different from a company that pulls and pushes gigabytes of newsgroups using Exchange's NNTP functionality.

The best approach here is to use the general purpose PerfMon counters to get an overview for your particular company. You may want to track these counters over time to ensure that your on-the-spot checks aren't missing the big picture. When you have discovered the hardware resource that's consistently bottlenecked on average, you can step in to alleviate things.

Typically, if your company is a heavy public folder user, you'll want to consider splitting the IS public database and logs to separate disks. Specifically, if it does more reading from the folders than writing, tune your disk subsystem for the IS database (non-sequential disk access). For heavy writing, focus on the IS logs (sequential disk access). Typically, companies with a strong appetite for using NNTP for Internet newsgroups will fall into the latter category.

CAUTION

Because each client must obtain the public folder hierarchy from a public information store, you need to take care when creating a dedicated public folder server. If you dedicate public folder servers, the server will reply to clients, which requires the public folder hierarchy and public folder contents. This creates load on the public folder servers and network. Maintaining a public folder store on private servers enables the client to retrieve the hierarchical tree information from his or her local server. This increases performance because the requests for the public folder hierarchy are distributed to multiple servers.

Optimizing Servers with Shared Roles

In smaller shops, Exchange often shares the server's resources with other non-Exchange functions (logon validation, SQL, print serving). If dedicating Exchange isn't an option, use the set of PerfMon overview counters to profile your particular system and determine how your particular mix is affecting the server. If you're planning to deploy Exchange to a server with other responsibilities (for example, a Primary Domain Controller), take the time to use LoadSim to determine if the server's current hardware will handle the additional load from Exchange.

Real World Answers to "How Many Users Can Exchange Support?"

Microsoft has provided a tool called LoadSim that applies the load of users against an Exchange Server. This tool is extremely valuable when trying to determine how many users a server can support or where a bottleneck resides. LoadSim is configurable to match the type of users in your organization, which means you can validate the Exchange hardware prior to it being used in production.

LoadSim can help you measure response times by using an artificially generated server load. LoadSim can also measure "user acceptability" by weighting certain actions that are perceived as more important by the user (for example, weighing opening versus sending). Most users expect mail to open quickly, but are comfortable with a slight delay when sending.

Calculating Acceptable Server Response Times

LoadSim measures two items with respect to an Exchange server: response time and "acceptability." To measure response time, LoadSim uses the 95th percentile. If the 95th percentile for a set of actions is one second, 95 percent of the response times are at or below one second. Only five percent (one in twenty) of the response times exceeded one second. To compare, the maximum response time is the 100th percentile (in other words, 100 percent of the response times are at or below the maximum).

To measure acceptability, LoadSim places a heavier weight on simulated actions that are perceived as more important to a real user. For example, most users expect quick responses when opening or deleting messages. They aren't, however, as affected by a small delay when sending mail. The actual actions and weights are categorized in Table 24.1.

Table 24.1 LoadSim's Weighted Values

Action	Weight
Read	10
Delete	2
Send	1
Reply	1
Reply All	1
Forward	1
Move	1

NOTE LsLog is a LoadSim tool that enables you to change the default percentile (95) and the weighted values for any actions. For more information, refer to the LoadSim documentation and online help.

To arrive at the final number, LoadSim multiplies each percentile value by the corresponding weight. Then LoadSim adds the results and divides by the sum of all weights. This final number is referred to as the score; it represents the response time experienced by a simulated user.

The following list includes client requirements and recommendations that might make your LoadSim experience more productive:

- The test clients should have Windows NT 3.51 or later, a Pentium 60MHz chip or faster, at least 32 MB of RAM, and a paging file of 100MB or more. If you want to simulate 200 or more users on one client, you'll need at least 64MB of RAM.
- Avoid simulating more than 300 users per client. The DLLs responsible for client-to-server communication will fail to scale, and your test results will not be realistic. In other words, the response time for 500 simulated clients will not be accurate for 500 actual clients on separate machines.
- For best results, you should allow six hours per simulation to gather enough data for reliable, reproducible results. Only analyze the last four hours of the simulation. This enables the server to stabilize after all simulated users have logged on. Of course, you are free to develop your own standards. However, remember to allow enough testing time, especially when simulating fewer than 100 users.
- Run your initial tests on an isolated network that removes real-world traffic. Then, after gathering enough lab data, you might want to run some tests with a network load on the wire to determine whether your environment's network load will affect response time.

- LoadSim cannot perfectly simulate the network traffic of real users. Although 200 LoadSim users create 200 logical server connections, there is only one network card and physical wire. Therefore, simulated network overhead (as measured by PerfMon) will be lower compared to a system using separate client machines.
- LoadSim doesn't simulate all Exchange features, such as rules and PST-based users. Review the LoadSim documentation for a complete updated list of simulated tasks.

LoadSim isn't a perfect simulation of your environment. Its numbers are only good estimates. Despite this, you will still find LoadSim's data extremely useful.

Capacity Planning with LoadSim

At the time of this writing, the author team for this book had the most current code base of Exchange 5.5 (RC1). Unfortunately, it had not been fully optimized for accurate testing. Thus any LoadSim scores would be extremely distorted and would not reflect real-world findings.

When Microsoft releases a fully optimized beta version or the final version, an errata will be posted on the Que Web site with the test statistics and a graph illustrating simulated users and their response times. You can find this and other updates at **www.mcp.com**.

CHAPTER 25

Maintaining Exchange

In this chapter

After you plan and lay out your Exchange organization, the next step will be to establish the maintenance strategy for your organization. No matter how solid your design and implementation of the Exchange architecture, some tasks must be performed daily to maintain optimum performance and smooth operation.

This section will assist you in performing the routine tasks that will prevent messaging errors, fine-tune performance, and recover lost data when the worst happens.

Relocating Server Recipients

During normal Exchange operation, there will be times when recipients created on one Exchange server need to be transferred to another. Some common circumstances for relocating recipients include:

- *Internal reorganization.* A user moves to a department in the company that is serviced by a different Exchange server.
- *The Exchange server is down.* The server must be taken offline for an extended period of time.
- *Performance optimization.* After reviewing usage, you decide that for better performance, you need to switch a user's home server (or site).

Distribution lists and custom recipients are server-independent objects. They belong to a site as a whole, not to a specific Exchange server and therefore, they do not need to be transferred among servers in a site.

Mailboxes are the most common types of recipients. Moving a mailbox also transfers its entire private information store contents (including attachments) to the destination server.

Because the Exchange information store uses intelligent storage techniques for handling attachments addressed to multiple recipients on the same server, additional space is required to split these files. Consider the following example.

User A and User B on server GARLAND01 both receive a message with a 1MB file attachment. The total storage space used on GARLAND01 to hold this file is 1MB. Both users are referencing the same instance of the file.

Suppose you transfer User A to server GARLAND05. The user's entire mailbox and its message contents and attachments are moved to GARLAND05's private information store. This means the 1MB file now exists on both servers.

To move mailboxes to another server in the same site, follow these steps:

1. Using the Exchange Administrator program, select and expand the desired site and server. You can find the servers within a site by expanding the Configuration container and then the Servers container. Then highlight the Server Recipients container.
2. Select the mailboxes you want to relocate. To select a series of continuous items, press and hold Shift and click the first and last items; to select a series of discontinuous items, press and hold Ctrl and click each item.

3. When all desired mailboxes are highlighted, select Move Mailbox from the Administrator program's Tools menu. The dialog box shown in Figure 25.1 appears.

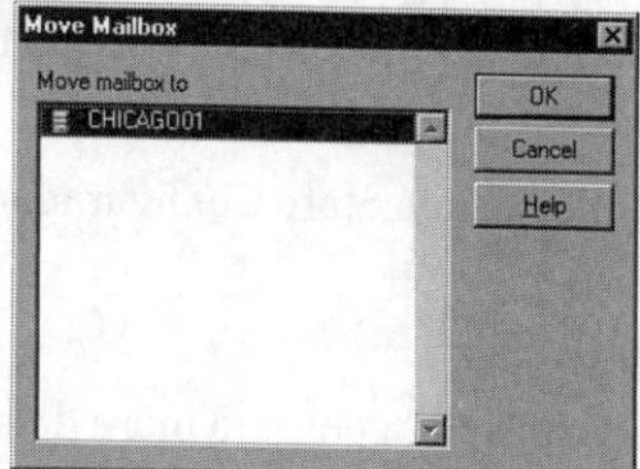

FIG. 25.1
Select the destination server in the Move Mailbox dialog box.

4. Select the destination server from the Move Mailbox To list. Click OK, and the mailboxes will be transferred immediately.
5. View the destination server's recipient container to confirm that the mailboxes now exist on the new server. Messages that are in transit to a mailbox when it is moved to another server will be delayed until the recipient's routing information is properly updated. Then the message will be sent to the new home server of the recipient.

To transfer a mailbox to a different site or recipient container, you must use the Import/Export utility provided in the Exchange Administrator program's Tools menu.

NOTE There is currently no automated method for moving users from one site or recipient container to another. The user's mail could be moved to a personal folder on the user's local desktop or file server home directory while a new mail account is created in the new site or recipient container. The mail could then be placed back on the server in the new mailbox. If you want to use the same mailbox address, follow the steps just given for saving the user's mail, and then export the user using the Directory Export process. Then delete the mailbox in the existing site or recipient container and import the user to the new location. You will need to manually edit the exported data file to correctly import the user into the appropriate container and to allow auto-creation of the new e-mail addresses associated with the new Exchange site. ■

Replicating Public Folders

Normally you will accommodate a wide number of public folder users by creating replicas of folders across your organization. Then, according to the replication schedule, the folders will update each other with changes.

To create a public folder replica, use the following instructions:

1. Using the Exchange Administrator program, select the site where the public folders reside.
2. Select the Recipients container for that site.

NOTE Select Hidden Recipients from the View menu if your public folders are hidden in the Administrator program display window.

3. Select the public folder you want to replicate and open its properties sheet to begin replication configuration.

For more information, see Chapter 15, "Information Store Configuration."

Public Folder Replicas

Chapter 16, "Creating and Configuring Recipients," goes into more detail about configuring all aspects of the public folder recipient type. The following steps show you how to make changes to the Replicas properties sheet for a public folder.

1. Select the Replicas tab of the public folder's properties sheet. The page shown in Figure 25.2 appears.

   The Servers display lists all Exchange servers in the site that's selected in the Site pull-down menu found in the lower-left corner.

   The Replicate Folders To display lists the Exchange servers currently selected as destinations for folder replicas.

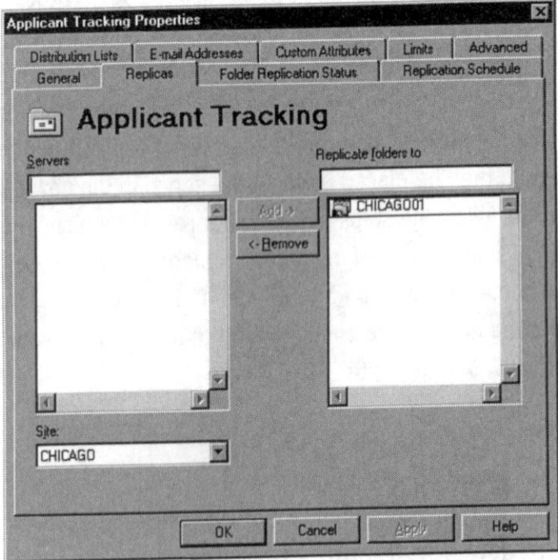

FIG. 25.2 Select the destination server for this public folder.

2. In the Site pull-down menu located in the lower-left corner, select a site from your organization.
3. Select or type the name of the destination Exchange server within that site. Click Add.
4. To remove a destination server, select it from the list on the right and click Remove.
5. Click Apply to set these properties and continue changing properties. If you are satisfied with all settings, click OK to return to the Administrator program.

CAUTION

Do not replicate the Offline Address Book public folder to any other server in your site. There must be only one instance of that folder in each site. Use caution when replicating any Address Book views that have been customized as well.

Moving a Public Folder with the Exchange or Outlook Client Software

The Exchange or Outlook Client (on Windows or Windows NT) can be used to move public folders. If you decide that for browsing purposes or restructuring needs the current hierarchy of Public Folders needs to be redesigned, you can do that only from a capable client.

You must have sufficient permissions on a specific folder in order to move it to a new location. Assuming you have the necessary permissions, move a public folder with the client software by following these steps:

1. Expand the Public Folders object from the client display window. (Using the Outlook Client, you may need to activate the Folder View first to see Public Folders.)
2. Locate the public folder you want to move.
3. Click and drag it to its new location. You will see a progress box as the information store data is relocated.

Moving a public folder via the client in this manner is not the same as replicating. The contents of the folder are actually physically moved. If the target folder is on a server in a remote site, the contents will be copied via the client PC to the remote server. This could be very time-intensive, depending on the amount of content in the folder being moved.

NOTE It is not possible to move Public Folders using the Exchange Administrator program. All moves of this manner can be made only from a capable Exchange client.

Creating Mailbox Templates

A principle part of Exchange maintenance will be adding and deleting mailbox users. When adding a large group of recipients, you can avoid having to enter similar information (such as department or address) by using a mailbox template. You create a template mailbox by creating a dummy mailbox account (one not intended to receive messages) whose detail content you can copy when creating new users.

To create a mailbox template, do the following:

1. Using the Exchange Administrator program, select a home site for this template mailbox in your organization.

2. Select New Mailbox from the Administrator program's File menu, and the New Mailbox properties sheet appears.
3. Give the new mailbox a Display name that will help you identify it as a template. (for example, Import Template 1).
4. Enter all additional mailbox attributes that you want to include in the new group of mailboxes, such as department name, city, state, fax numbers, and so on.
5. Do not assign the new account association a Windows NT account in order to prevent anyone from trying to use the account for mail purposes.

Check the Hide from Address Book option on the Advanced tab of the mailbox template's properties sheet to prevent it from receiving mail. Then you'll need to temporarily make it visible when you want to use it to import new users (unless you want all your newly created mailboxes to be hidden as well).

To use your template when creating a new user mailbox, follow this procedure:

1. Using the Exchange Administrator program, select the home server where you want the new mailbox to be created.
2. If the template mailbox is hidden, select Hidden Recipients from the Administrator program's View menu and deselect the Hide from Address Book option. Then select the Mailbox Template as previously defined.
3. Select Duplicate from the Exchange Administrator program's File menu.
4. Enter the relevant user information for the new mailbox, such as name, phone numbers, and so on.

By using the Directory Import option from the Tools menu, you can create a large number of mailboxes with basic information using a template just like the mailbox that was created in the previous steps.

If you need to create or modify many users at once, you can use the Directory Import feature of the Exchange Administrator program to import a list of users you have created or previously exported. To test this technique, export a list of your current users. Then, using the same file format, develop your new user list and import that user list. Pay careful attention to the format of the file and note the attributes of each user.

A tool for creating and modifying Import and Export "headers" is available in the Exchange Resource Kit, which you can download from the Exchange Web site.

Performing Information Store Maintenance

The *information store* is the central storage facility for all Exchange messaging data. The information store is made up of the private information store and the public information store. An information store can consume considerable disk space, depending on the size of your organization and the distribution of users per Exchange server. Of course with the massively increased database capacity of Exchange 5.5, these limits and sizes can be very large.

The following are important things to note when maintaining the information stores:

- *Private Information Store Properties: Mailbox Resources.* View mailbox storage usage.
- *Public Information Store: Public Folder Resources.* View public folder storage usage.
- *Exchange Server: Information Store Maintenance Properties Sheet.* Schedule hard drive optimizing for an Exchange server's information store.

Exchange 5.0/5.5 offers a few new "shortcuts" over the original Exchange 4.0 in order to allow the user to quickly access these status screens from the left pane of the Administrator program without having to drill down through to the properties sheet as noted above. See the additional information that follows about these options.

Private Information Store Properties

The Private Information Store Properties dialog box allows you to view the physical resources used by each mailbox on a particular server. This lets you evaluate hard disk space usage and determine storage limits.

First, select the private information store from a server within your site, as outlined in these steps:

1. Navigate to your desired site with the Exchange Administrator program and expand its container.
2. Expand the Configuration container of the selected site. All the site configuration objects appear in right pane of the Administrator program window.
3. Open the Servers container. A list of Exchange servers in your site appears.
4. Click the server name for the private information store you want to configure. The list of server objects appears in the right pane of the Exchange Administrator program window (see Figure 25.3).
5. Click the Private Information Store object to open its properties sheet.

Viewing the Physical Resources Used by the Exchange Mailboxes The Mailbox Resources page allows you to view the physical resources (such as hard disk storage space) used by the Exchange mailboxes on a server. It consists of one main display window that shows the mailboxes on the current server. The window is divided into columns of information. You can customize the columns both by the information shown and by their widths on the screen.

NOTE A mailbox will be displayed in this window only after the first time a user logs on to it. If the mailbox has never been used, it will not appear on the Mailbox Resources properties sheet.

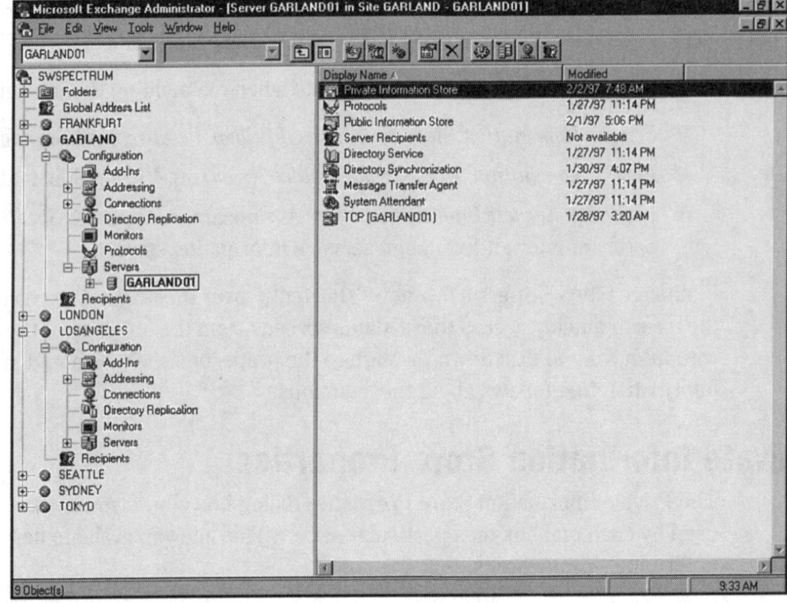

FIG. 25.3 Select the Private Information Store object from among all the other server objects.

There are two ways to view Mailbox Resources. These steps outline the first method:

1. Highlight the Private Information Store Container in the left pane of the Administrator window. Then choose Properties from the File menu. A new window appears on the screen.
2. Select the Mailbox Resources tab of the Private Information Store properties sheet. The page shown in Figure 25.4 appears. The display window shows all the mailboxes on this server that have been used at least once.

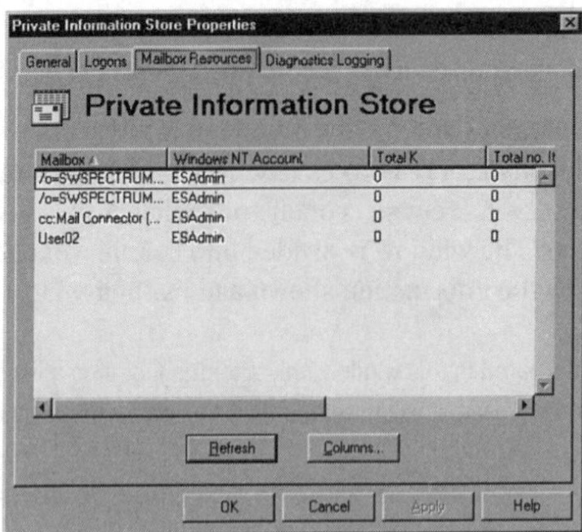

FIG. 25.4 Monitoring mailbox resources.

NOTE The Exchange System Attendant and the Exchange service account are always listed in this window. ■

3. Click the Refresh button to update the display window with the latest information.
4. Click the Columns button to edit which columns are displayed and their widths in pixels. (See the list following these steps for a description of the column headings and what type of information each one can display.)
5. Click Apply to set these properties and continue changing properties. When you are satisfied with all settings, click OK to return to the Administrator program.

Columns define what type of information is displayed in the standard dialog box. Default columns are preconfigured to display the most commonly needed information. Optional columns provide more detailed information that may be useful for troubleshooting errors. The following is a list of default columns:

- *Mailbox.* The Exchange Administrator program's object display name for this mailbox.
- *Windows NT Account.* The Windows NT account of the user currently logged in to this mailbox.
- *Total K.* The total amount of disk storage space (in kilobytes) taken up by the contents of this user's mailbox (this value includes any message attachments).
- *Deleted Items K.* The total amount of disk storage space (in kilobytes) taken up by the contents of the user's Deleted Items box.
- *Storage Limits.* Any storage limits imposed on the mailbox (such as Prohibit Send).
- *Total Number Items.* The sum of all messages and attachments stored in a mailbox.
- *Last Logon Time.* The last time a user logged in to this mailbox.
- *Last Logoff Time.* The last time a user logged off from this mailbox.

The following is a list of the optional columns you can display in the dialog box:

- *Full Mailbox Directory Name.* The entire X.400 e-mail address for this mailbox.
- *Total Number Associated Messages.* The sum of stored views and deferred action messages (messages scheduled to be sent/processed at a later time) in this mailbox.

The second way to view Mailbox Resources is to view them from the Exchange hierarchy (see Figure 25.5).

To access the Mailbox Resources information from the Exchange hierarchy, follow the instruction below:

1. Navigate to your desired site with the Exchange Administrator program.
2. Click the small plus sign adjacent to the Configuration container of the selected site to further expand the hierarchy in the left pane.
3. Expand the Servers container in the left pane, and a list of Exchange servers in your site appears.

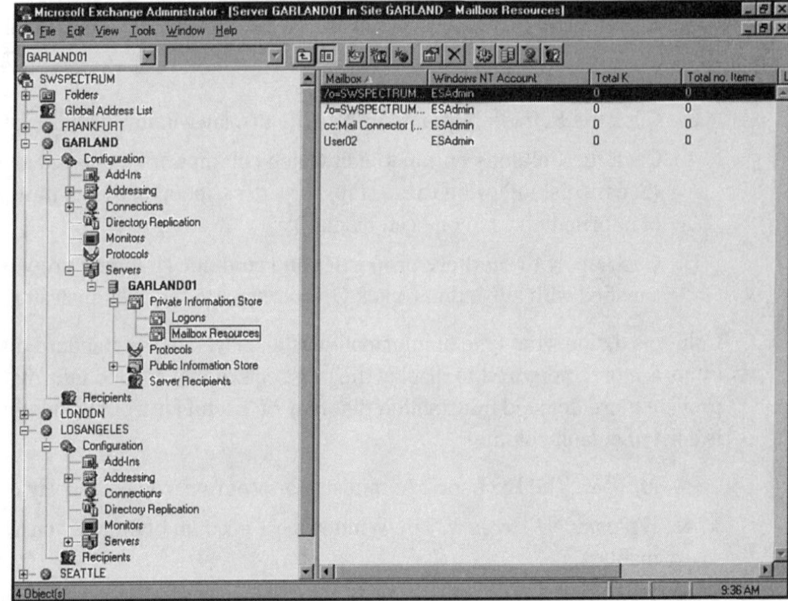

FIG. 25.5
Mailbox Resources information view.

4. Click to expand the server name on which the private information store you want to configure is located.
5. The displayed server objects now visible in the left pane of the Exchange Administrator program window are identical in name and function to similar objects displayed in the right pane. Selecting properties of either the private information store or public information store displays the same data.
6. Expand the Private Information Store item in the left pane. Then click the Mailbox Resources object, and the status information appears in the right pane. You can add to the default columns shown in the right pane by using the View menu and the Columns command.

Public Information Store Properties

The Public Information Store Properties dialog box enables you to view the physical resources (such as hard disk storage space) used by the folders held in an Exchange public information store. It consists of one main display window that shows the public folders on the current server. The window is subdivided into various columns of information. You can customize the columns both by the information shown and by their widths on the screen.

The Schedule+ Free/Busy Information and the Offline Address Book are, in essence, public folders as well and are listed in the Public Folder Resources properties sheet.

Viewing the Public Information Store Properties From the Public Folder Resources page, you can monitor the amount of system resources that are exhausted by the use of public folders on your system.

There are two ways to view the properties of the public information store. The first is to select the public information store from a server within your site as outlined in these steps:

1. Navigate to your desired site with the Exchange Administrator program.
2. Click the Configuration container of the selected site. All the site configuration objects appear in the right pane of the Administrator program window.
3. Open the Servers container, and a list of Exchange servers in your site appears.
4. Click the server name on which the public information store you want to configure is stored. The list of server objects appears in the right pane of the Exchange Administrator program window.
5. Highlight the Public Information Store item and select Properties from the File menu. Select the Public Folder Resources tab of the Public Information Store properties sheet. The page shown in Figure 25.6 appears. The display window shows all the public folders on this server, including those replicated from other servers.

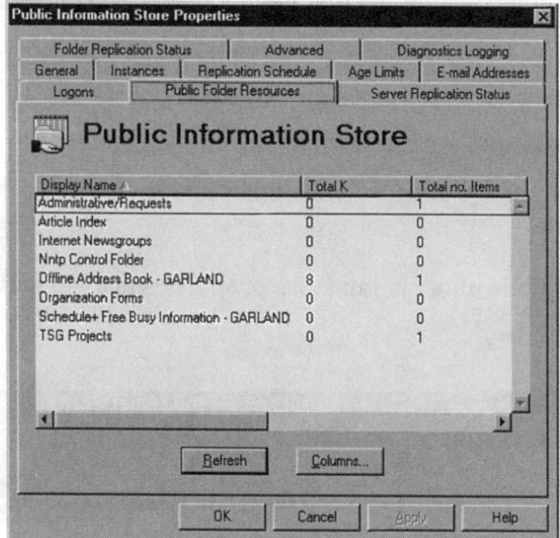

FIG. 25.6 View resources utilized by each public folder on this server.

6. Click the Refresh button to update the display window with the latest information.
7. Click the Columns button to edit which columns are displayed and their widths in pixels. See the list following these steps for a description of the column headings and what type of information each one can display.
8. Click Apply to set these properties and continue changing properties. If you are satisfied with all settings, click OK to return to the Administrator program.

Columns define what type of information is displayed in the standard dialog box. Default columns are preconfigured to display the most commonly needed information. Optional columns provide more detailed information that may be useful for troubleshooting errors. The following is a list of default columns:

- *Display Name.* The Exchange Administrator program's object display name for this public folder.
- *Total K.* The total amount of disk storage space (in kilobytes) taken up by the contents of this public folder (this value includes any message attachments).
- *Total Number Items.* The sum of all messages and attachments stored in a mailbox.
- *Deleted Items K.* The total amount of disk space (in kilobytes) occupied by deleted items for this public folder.
- *Created.* The date and time this folder was created.
- *Last Access Time.* The last time a user logged in to this public folder.
- *number of Owners.* The number of users designated as Owners of this public folder (see the section on defining roles for a public folder).
- *number of Contacts.* The number of users designated as contacts for this public folder (see the section on defining roles for a public folder).

The following is a list of optional columns that can be used to display additional information about server resources.

- *Folder.* Folder name where messages are stored.
- *Folder Path.* The system file path to where this folder is stored.
- *Total Number Associated Messages.* The sum of folder views and deferred action messages.

The second way to view public information store properties is to view them from the Exchange hierarchy (see Figure 25.7).

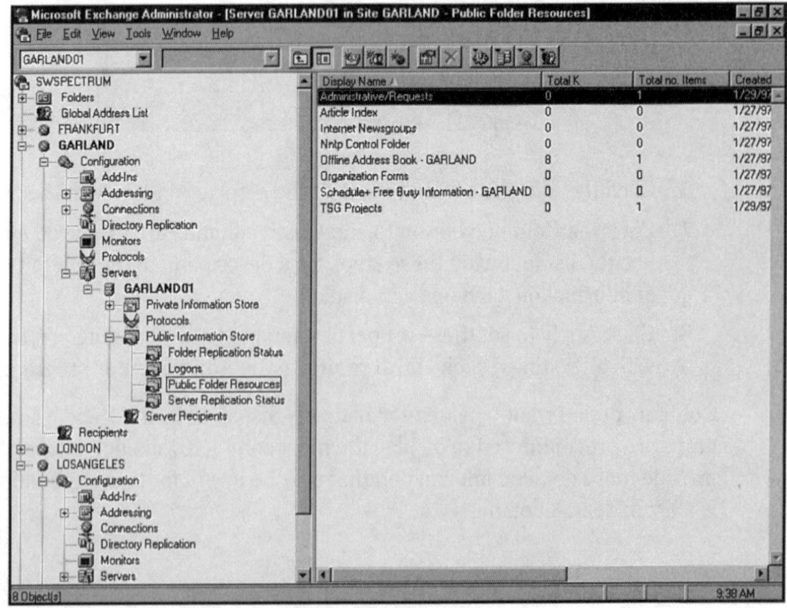

FIG. 25.7 Public Folder Resources information view.

To access the Public Folder Resources information using this new method, follow these steps:

1. Navigate to your desired site with the Exchange Administrator program.
2. Click the small plus sign adjacent to the Configuration container of the selected site to further expand the hierarchy in the left pane.
3. Expand the Servers container in the left pane, and a list of Exchange servers in your site appears.
4. Click and expand the server name on which the public information store you want to configure is located.
5. The displayed server objects now visible in the left pane of the Exchange Administrator program window are identical in name and function to similar objects displayed in the right pane. Selecting properties of either the private information store or public information store displays the same data.
6. Expand the Public Information Store item in the left pane. Then click the Public Folder Resources object, and the status information appears in the right pane. You can add to the default columns shown in the right pane by using the View menu and the Columns command.

Defragmenting and Compacting Information Stores Offline

Exchange automatically addresses most defragmentation and compaction issues, but there are times when a manual execution is desired or required. This involves using the Exchange EDBUTIL utility to defragment and optimize disk space allocation for an information store. It is important that you schedule this procedure at a time when message traffic is low or even nonexistent, because it involves stopping the information store service entirely.

NOTE Software Spectrum has noted that on Exchange servers with the Internet Mail Service installed handling SMTP mail (inbound or outbound), excessive amounts of "white space" in the PRIV.EDB are created as SMTP messages are processed. The automated database clean-up processes do not seem to adequately reduce this fragmented white space. Thus, you should perform a manual defragmentation periodically, depending on the amount and size of SMTP messages handled. The space recovery can be dramatic! One example decreased the size of a 1GB PRIV.EDB to less than 20MB using the EDBUTIL defrag option. ■

The following command-line entry will defragment and compact the PRIV.EDB file (Exchange Private Information Store) and automatically create a backup file. The EDBUTIL actually performs its work on the backup file, and once its work is satisfactorily completed, EDBUTIL renames the backup to replace the original. This method minimizes possible further corruption and introduction of errors into the current production file. Note, however, that you will need enough disk space to hold both your current EDB file and the backup. (It is possible to copy the file to an alternate location on the network.)

Here is an example command that includes a backup:

```
edbutil /d /ispriv
```

In this command, */ispriv* indicates that the work is to be performed on the private information store.

The following steps outline the general procedure for compacting the information store:

1. Open the Windows NT services Control Panel and stop the Exchange Information Store service (MSEXCHANGEIS).
2. Open a Windows NT command prompt window (or use the Run command from the Program Manager's File menu).
3. Enter the EDBUTIL command using the following syntax:

   ```
   EDBUTIL [/d] [/information store type]
   ```

   The [/d] indicates that switch options are present. See Table 25.1 for a list of available switch options for the EDBUTIL command.
4. Press Enter (or click OK if you're using the File, Run command from Program Manager) to start compacting.

NOTE Compacting a large information store could take a reasonably extended amount of time. So make sure to plan for downtime accordingly.

5. After the compacting process finishes, restart the information store service.
6. To test the information store for proper functioning, log in to it with an Exchange client and try to view messages or connect to a public folder.
7. If the information store is functional, you can remove the backup (.bak) file.

NOTE While the information store service is stopped, all message transfer attempts to the store are refused. Also, server mailbox users will not be able to open the store through their client.

Table 25.1 EDBUTIL.EXE Switch Options

Option	Description
/ds	Directory.
/ispriv	Private information store.
/ispub	Public information store.
/b	Backup. Makes a backup of the original file in the specified location.
/r	Defragment and repair. Defragments the database as usual, but if errors occur, it attempts to correct the problem or removes the error. The end result is a problem-free database—but essential data may be missing.

Option	Description
/c	Performs a read-only database consistency check without making a copy. It does not repair or affect the database; it simply creates a report.
/t*filename*	Renames the newly compacted database with a specified filename.

Maintaining Message Transfer Agents

Each Message Transfer Agent (MTA) in a site uses the routing table to calculate delivery paths for each message. Whenever a change is made that affects routing (for example, modifying address spaces for a connector), it will not take effect until the site routing table has been rebuilt.

Normally, the routing table is rebuilt once per day unless the Routing Calculation Schedule has been modified. For more information on changing the Routing Calculation Schedule, see Chapter 3, "Exchange's Integrated Server Components." You can also choose to rebuild the table manually, this way:

1. Highlight the server to which you had made routing changes. In the right pane, highlight the Messaging Transfer Agent and select Properties from the File menu. Select the General property page of the Message Transfer Agent property pages. The property page in Figure 25.8 appears.
2. Click the Recalculate Routing button to begin rebuilding the routing table.
3. Click OK to return to the administrator program.

The MTA retrieves updated routing information from the routing table every 15 minutes. Therefore, it could take up to 15 minutes for routing updates to be used by the MTA. In some cases, it is advantageous to stop and then restart the MTA server to force a "re-read" of the routing table and thus a rerouting of messages in the MTA work queues.

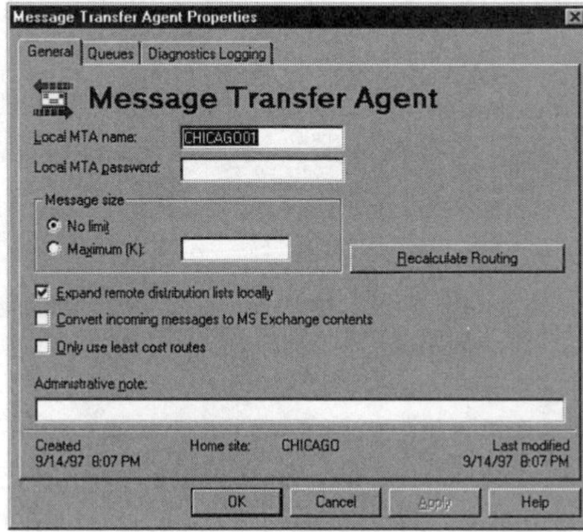

FIG. 25.8
Use the General Message Transfer Agent Properties page to recalculate MTA routing.

MTA Message Queues

The Queues Property page lists messages awaiting delivery by the MTA. There are two primary windows in this property page. The Queue name window shows which queue you are currently viewing and the Message list box displays the messages in that queue. From this, you can view details about a specific message in the queue, change its priority for delivery, or delete it entirely.

Within the Message list window are three columns that contain information about a particular message:

- Originator: The original sender of the message
- Submit time: The time the message entered the queue
- Size: The size of the message in kilobytes

To configure the Queues property page, perform the following steps:

1. Highlight the server that you want to monitor from the hierarchy in the left pane. In the right pane, highlight the Messaging Transfer Agent and select Properties from the File menu (or double click). Select the Queues Property page from the Message Transfer Agent property pages. The Queues Property page in Figure 25.9 appears.
2. Use the Queue name drop-down menu to select which message queue to display. There are queues for the private and public information stores and any installed gateways.

FIG. 25.9 The message queue. It is blank because all pending messages have been delivered.

NOTE The Internet Mail connector and Microsoft Mail connector have additional queues that can also be accessed through their respective property pages. ■

3. Select a message and click Details to view additional information about it.

   The additional message information includes message originator, submit time, message size, and priority. This button is dimmed if no messages are in the queue.

4. Click the Refresh button to update the message list window with the latest list of messages in the MTA queue.
5. Click Priority to display the message's priority.

   Change the priority of a message if desired. It can be low, medium, or high. Messages are sent in order of this priority. A message's priority is set when a message is created, but can be adjusted for the purposes of this queue by changing values here.
6. Select a message and click Delete to remove a message from the MTA queue.
7. Click Apply to set these properties and continue with other properties. If you are done with all settings, click OK to return to the administrator program.

When dealing with MTA queue dialog boxes (or any other Exchange queue box), the messages you see on the list are a "snap shot" of all queued messages at one point in time. To get a more dynamic view or to "catch" a message as it passes through the queue, you must continually press the Refresh button to get the latest updates. In some cases, it might be easier to increase the level of diagnostic logging and monitor the Windows NT Event Logs.

MTA Diagnostic Logging

Logging falls mainly in the realm of troubleshooting and is discussed in Chapter 28, "Troubleshooting Exchange with Diagnostic Tools." MTA logs can perhaps be used for other purposes, such as billing and accounting for number of messages transferred by person or department if desired.

> **CAUTION**
>
> Increasing diagnostic logging levels on very active servers can result in huge log file sizes in a very short amount of time and dramatically reduce disk performance.

Maintaining Microsoft Mail Connector

The Microsoft Mail Connector has its own temporary message store called the Microsoft Mail Connector post office. This is sometimes referred to as the "Shadow Post Office." The Microsoft Mail Connector maintains its own message queue property page from which to monitor message queue status.

To open the Microsoft Mail Connector message queue window, do the following:

1. Navigate through the administrator program to the site desired, open the Configuration Container, then locate and open the Microsoft Mail Connector within the Connectors container to view its property pages.
2. Select the Connections tab (see Figure 25.10).

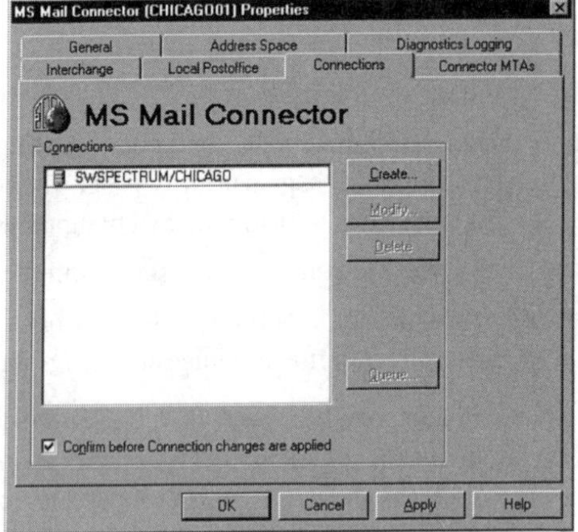

FIG. 25.10
View Connections.

3. Select from the Connections window the Microsoft Mail connection you wish to monitor.
4. Click the Queue button. The Microsoft Mail Connector message queue property page appears.
5. Select a sort order for the messages by clicking one of the categories on the top line of the Queued Messages window (see Figure 25.11).

   Information displayed in the queue:

From	The original message sender
Subject	The data on the message's subject line
Message ID	The message identifier
Date/Time	The time when the messaged entered the queue

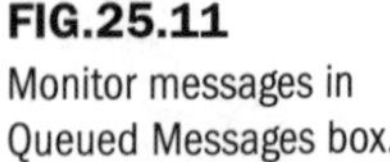

FIG.25.11
Monitor messages in Queued Messages box.

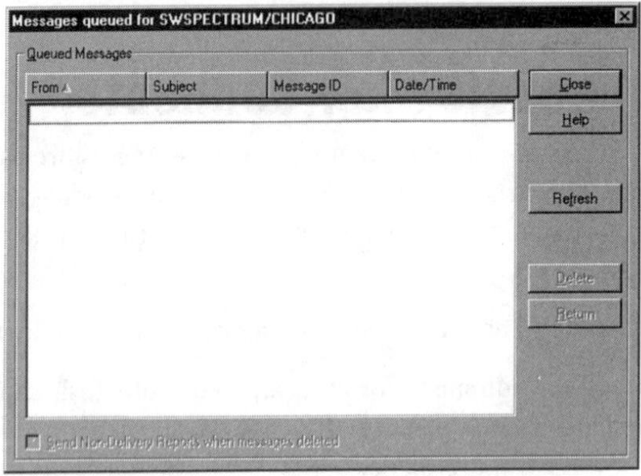

6. To remove a message, select it and then click Delete.

   If `Send Non-Delivery Reports` when messages deleted is checked, the original sender will be notified if his or her message was deleted from the queue. If it is clear, no notification will be sent when a message is deleted.

7. To return a message to its original sender, select it and then click Return.
8. Click Close to return to the Microsoft Mail Connector Connections property page. Then, click OK to return to the administrator program.

NOTE As in the MTA queues property page, the view of queued messages is static. To update the display you must click the Refresh button. ■

Maintaining Directories

There are two components to each directory object saved in a server's information store: the object itself and a corresponding entry in the directory. Consistency adjustment corrects errors arising by mismatched directory information. This feature will either add or delete a directory entry to match the existence or absence of information store data.

The property page allows you to control at what point these inconsistencies are to be corrected. Figure 25.12 shows the Advanced tab of the Server Properties page where you configure directory inconsistency adjustment.

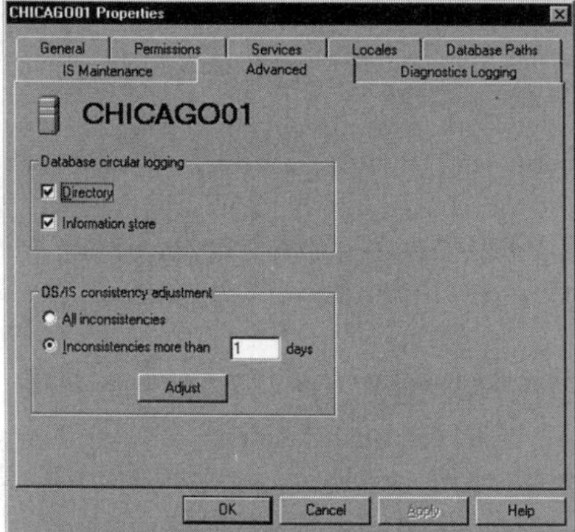

FIG. 25.12 This property page lets you adjust directory inconsistencies.

Select either `All inconsistencies` to correct them immediately or select `Inconsistencies more than X number of days` and enter the time an inconsistency can exist before it is automatically corrected.

Understanding Knowledge Consistency

Knowledge consistency for the local server is its awareness of other Exchange servers within a site and at other sites within your organization. The knowledge consistency operation is run automatically approximately every 15 minutes. If Exchange servers or sites were added and the local server's directory was not aware of those changes (for example, the local server was down during that time), then you may not want to wait for the automatic checking and do it manually.

Suppose Exchange server CHICAGO01 is brought down for two hours for a memory upgrade. During the time of the upgrade, a new server, CHICAGO08, is added to the site. When CHICAGO01 is restored to proper functioning, it will not be aware of the existence of the new server until the full knowledge consistency cycle is run at the end of the day. Knowing this, the administrator for CHICAGO01 runs the knowledge consistency cycle manually from the Directory Service property pages to make CHICAGO01 aware of the new server's existence. (See Chapter 3, "Exchange's Integrated Server Components," for additional detail on server properties.)

Resynchronizing Replicated Directory Information

If a directory inconsistency is detected when checking manually, it is a good idea to manually execute all processes related to correcting inconsistencies. Figure 25.13 shows the property page for the Directory Service. By using the following sequence, you can correct knowledge inconsistencies:

1. Check knowledge consistency from the directory service property pages and detect the error.
2. Manually update directory replication within the site by running Update Now also from the Directory Service property pages.
3. It might also be a good idea to open the Message Transfer Agent properties for this server and click Recalculate Routing from the General property page.

Although this sequence is optional and will be automatically executed within a 24-hour period, performing the tasks immediately will reduce the possibility of conflicts or errors.

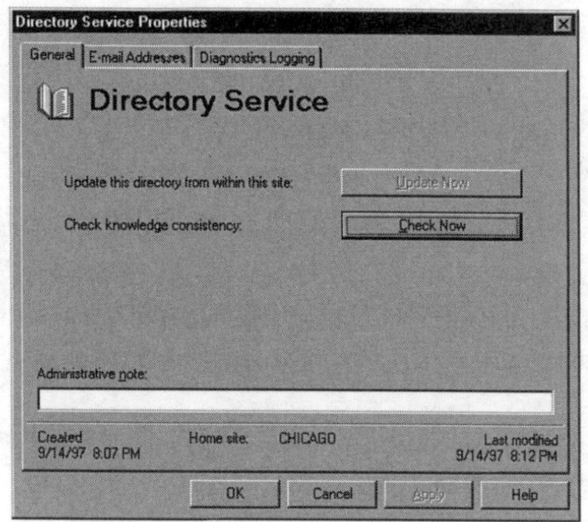

FIG. 25.13
This property page lets you adjust knowledge inconsistencies

Defragmenting and Compacting Directory Information

Much like the information store, the Exchange directory can benefit greatly from offline defragmentation and compacting. The Exchange directory service continually performs online compacting during its normal operation, but a dedicated, periodic, offline compacting will provide a more significant increase in performance. Not only will directory access speed improve after compacting, but also hard disk space wasted through inefficient storage will be freed for use. Offline directory defragmentation and compacting requires stopping the Exchange Directory and Directory Synchronization services.

The following command-line entry will compact the `DIR.EDB` file (Exchange Directory database) and automatically back up the original to a file named `DIR.BAK`. As with the aforementioned use of EDBUITL with the `PRIV.EDB` and `PUB.EDB`, there must be sufficient disk space available to make a complete copy of the current `DIR.EDB`. Here is an example command:

```
EDBUTIL /d /ds
```

where /ds notes that the process is to run against the directory.

The procedure for compacting a directory is as follows:

1. Open the Windows NT services control panel and stop the Exchange Directory service (MSEXCHANGEDSA) and the Directory Synchronization service (MSEXCHANGEDXA).
2. Open a Windows NT command prompt window (or use the Run command from the Program Manager File menu).

3. Enter the EDBUTIL command using the following syntax

```
EDBUTIL [/d] [/information store type]
```

where /d indicates that switch options are present. Please refer to Table 25.1 for the appropriate switch options.

4. Press Enter (or click OK if using the Run command from the Program Manager) to start compacting.

NOTE Compacting a large directory file could take a large amount of time, so make sure to plan accordingly. For a thousand users, for example, this process will possibly take an hour. ■

5. After the compacting process finishes, restart the Exchange Directory and Directory Synchronization services.
6. Test the directory for proper functioning by accessing into the local address list with an Exchange client.
7. If the directory is functional, you may proceed to remove the backup (.bak) files.

Working with Directory Event Logs

Part of maintaining a healthy Exchange Organization is working with the Windows NT Event Log. It is important to keep track of Event Log sizes (to set upper size limits and expiration dates for log entries) so as to not let the Event Log become too large, but it should be allowed to grow large enough to hold many days worth of log entries. The two Directory Services to watch are these:

- MSExchangeDS: The directory service and directory replication process
- MSExchangeDX: Directory Synchronization

Logging levels for each service are set in the Diagnostic Logging property page. See Chapter 28, "Troubleshooting Exchange with Diagnostic Tools," for tips on using the Diagnostic Logging property pages for each service.

Backing Up Your Exchange Server

Probably the most important maintenance procedure for an Exchange organization is backup of information store and directory information. Few things on a user's computer are as important to him or her as their email. Implementing a good backup strategy is well worth the effort. This section will provide a general conceptual guide to Exchange backup. For more detail in using the Exchange Backup utility, refer to your Exchange server documentation or the documentation of your Exchange "aware" Windows NT backup solution.

Windows NT provides built-in tape backup and restore utilities that are supplemented by extensions installed with Exchange server. These utilities provide the basics for an adequate

Exchange backup, but a full-featured backup software package would provide additional functionality and versatility. Note that the Windows NT Backup program has remained essentially unchanged in ability and features from early Windows NT 3.5 days, so usage of a newer tool is strongly recommended.

This section describes backup and restore procedures directly relevant to maintaining Exchange information. For full Windows NT server backups, refer to your Windows NT or third-party backup software documentation.

The version of Backup included with Exchange is aware of the servers in your Exchange Organization and allows you to do backups for a single server, server group, sites, or even an entire organization if necessary.

The main Exchange information you will want to back up is located in the following paths:

\EXCHSRVR\MDBDATA

and

\EXCHSRVR\DSADATA

Important Exchange files to be backed up are as follows:

- Information store databases: SYSTEM.EDB, PRIV.EDB, PUB.EDB
- Information store logs: EDB.LOG
- Directory database: SYSTEM.EDB (separate from the information store SYSTEM.EDB file), DIR.EDB
- Directory logs: EDB.LOG (separate from the information store EDB.LOG files)

When restoring lost data, the log files are played back to reconstitute the databases to the point of the last backup.

A proper Exchange aware backup sequence can be completed without any downtime of the server, but performance is affected for connected users. As backup is performed, the transaction logs associated with the main information databases of Exchange (DIR, PRIV, and PUB) are reset to reflect that a backup has been made.

If a "non-Exchange aware" backup tool is used, the Exchange services will need to be stopped in order to release file locks on open files and databases. Once backup is complete, the transaction log files will need to be manually reset.

NOTE Microsoft has provided a very detailed "White Paper" on backup and disaster recovery giving detailed steps to recover a server or an individual's mailbox from backup. Search the Exchange Web site for a recent version.

CHAPTER 26

Monitoring Your Organization

In this chapter

Monitoring is the art of watching over your Exchange organization to identify and correct malfunctions before they become serious problems. An Exchange system consists fundamentally of Windows NT servers and links between them. Included with Microsoft Exchange server are two monitoring tools that service both components; they will be your eyes 24 hours a day to alert you when something goes wrong:

- Link monitor: Tests messaging connections between Exchange servers in your organization.
- Server monitor: Tests the status of Windows NT services on designated Exchange server.

Chapter 25, "Monitoring Exchange," goes into more detail about how to use monitors to diagnose problems.

The following terms are pertinent to using Exchange monitoring tools:

- Polling interval: The amount of time between system tests (time between ping messages sent or time between checking system service status)
- Warning state: A condition indicating that there is a potential problem with a server or messaging link
- Alert state: A condition indicating that a serious problem exists within the server or messaging link
- Escalation path: The list of people, in order of notification priority, who receive alerts from a monitor
- Notification: The process of alerting a system administrator (SA) that a specific server or messaging link is functioning abnormally

Creating a Link Monitor

As an Exchange administrator, there are two fundamental ways in which you can be notified of a downed messaging link:

- You will receive an e-mail from a user who complains that when he tried to send a message, it came back undelivered.
- You can configure a link monitor to continuously watch that specific messaging connections are active and to detect unusual delays in message transmissions.

Link monitors watch for successful message connections between two points in an Exchange organization. They also can be configured to test connections to foreign messaging systems. Link monitors accomplish this by sending out a test message, called a ***ping message***, and timing the round trip of that message.

A link monitor sends a ping message to test messaging connections. At the polling interval, a ping message is sent to every Exchange server and foreign system listed on the link monitor's servers' property page.

To create a new link monitor, follow this procedure:

1. In the Exchange administrator program, select a site in your organization.
2. Open the Configuration container within the selected site.
3. Select the Monitors container; the right administrator program display window will show all the existing monitors (both link and server) in this site (see Figure 26.1).

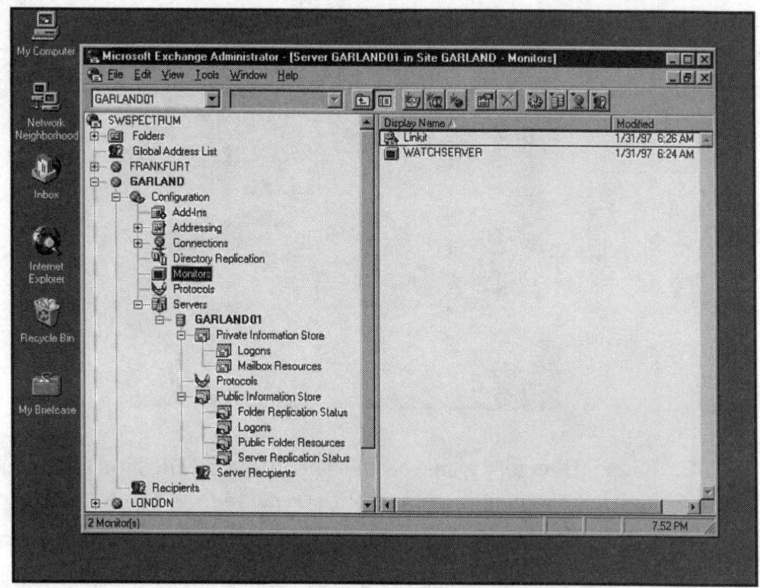

FIG. 26.1
The Monitors container shows all monitors in the selected site. In our example, monitors can be made and executed anywhere in the organization with proper permissions.

4. Select New Other, and then select Link Monitor. The Link Monitor property pages appear.

The link monitor has several property pages which enable the following options:

- General: Name the monitor, set the polling interval, and optionally select a log file location.
- Notification: Specify how and to whom warning and alert messages are sent.
- Servers: Specify the local and remote Exchange servers and foreign messaging systems that will receive ping messages.
- Recipients: Configure ping messages to foreign messaging systems.
- Bounce: Enter time delay before a server enters a warning or alert state due to a non-returned ping message.

These pages are described in more detail in the following sections.

The General Page

The General page enables you to name the monitor, set the polling interval, and optionally select a log file location. Use the following procedure to configure the link monitor:

1. Select the General tab of the Link Monitor property page. The property page shown in Figure 26.2 appears.

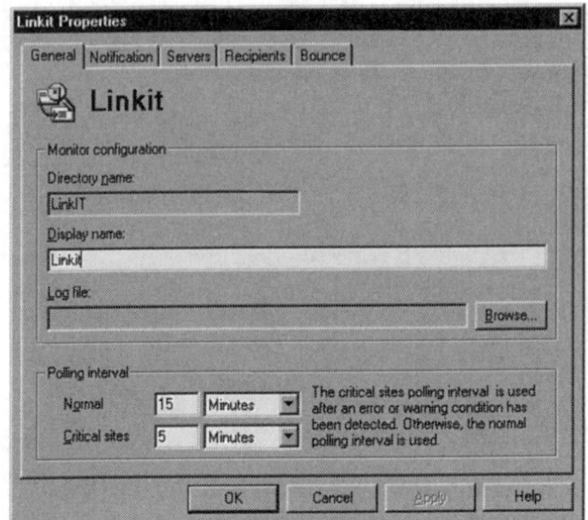

FIG. 26.2 The Link Monitor property page enables you to define a polling interval for this monitor.

2. Enter a Directory Name for this link monitor. (The directory name cannot be changed for a link monitor after it has been created.)
3. Enter a Display Name as you want it to be shown in the administrator display window.
4. The Log File window shows the file name of where monitor logs are being stored. Click Browse to select the file name and location.

NOTE Logging for link monitor activity is optional, so you need not specify a Log File location. ■

5. In the Polling Interval window, enter the units and time interval for Normal operation.
6. In the Polling Interval window, enter the units and time interval for Critical Sites.
7. Click Apply to set these properties and continue with other properties. When you are done with all settings, click OK to return to the administrator program.

The Notification Page

The Notification property page enables you to configure what happens when abnormal message link functioning is detected by a server monitor. There are three main types of notification:

- Launch a process: Loads an external application. This option is often used in conjunction with paging software.
- Mail message: Automatically sends an e-mail message to a selected recipient, describing the situation.

- Windows NT Alert: Uses the Windows NT Messenger service to notify a certain user or group of users.

The Notification property page is primarily one main display window list where all notification objects are displayed (see Figure 26.3). By default, this window is blank, and no notification is specific.

FIG. 26.3
The Link Monitor Notification property page shows whom to contact in case of malfunctions.

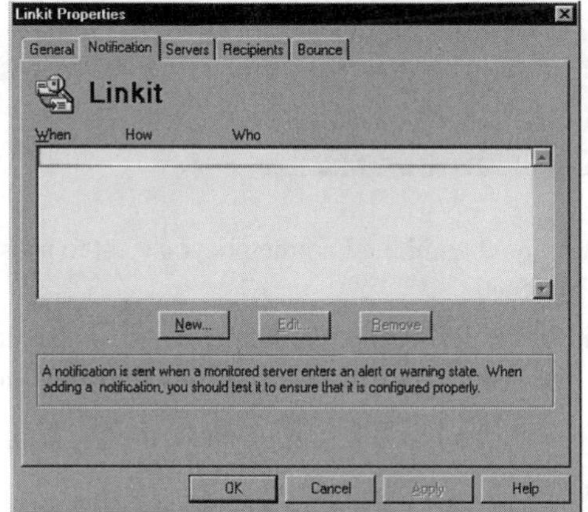

Click New to define a new notification object. Select the type of notification (see Figure 26.4).

FIG. 26.4
Select a Notification Type.

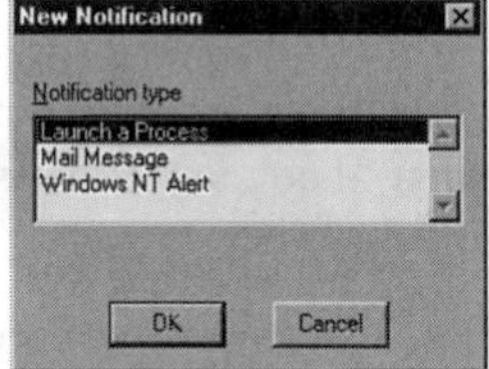

Launching a Notification Process Configuring an external notification application is as easy as choosing the application and setting the time delay for notification. You must configure that external process for the specific type of notification it provides (see Figure 26.5). All Exchange does is launch the process and pass along any additional required parameters.

To configure the Launch Process Notification properties, do the following:

1. In the Time Delay box, enter a numeric value and the time units (seconds, minutes, hours) from the pull-down menu.
2. Clear the Alert Only checkbox if you want this notification process to occur when the server is in a warning state as well. Otherwise, the notification process will only launch in an alert state after the time delay is exceeded.
3. Click the File button and navigate your directory hierarchy to locate the process you want to launch in this notification. The Launch Process box will display this file once selected.

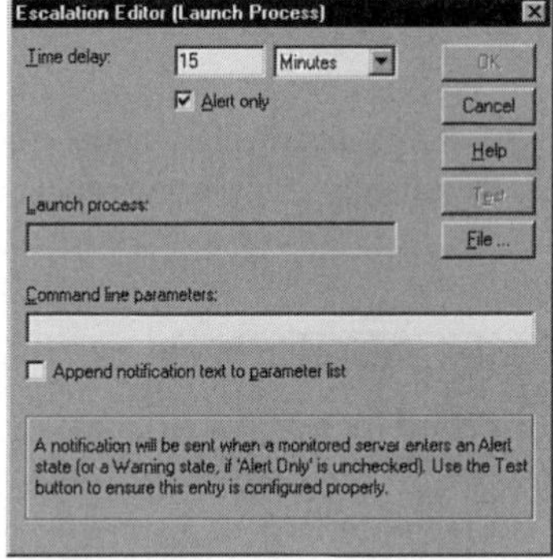

FIG. 26.5
Configure the parameters for the notification process.

4. Enter any additional Command-Line Parameters you want to pass to the notification process once it is launched.
5. Select the Append Notification Text to Parameter List checkbox in order to attach the actual notification text to the command-line parameters during the process launch.

NOTE If the external notification application is already configured, you can now use the Test button to verify a property is functioning.

6. Click OK to complete these settings and return to the Notification property page.

You can change a notification by selecting it from the Notification list and clicking Edit. You can delete a notification by selecting it from the list and clicking Remove.

Using Mail Message Notification Mail notification will alert an administrator via e-mail that a server has entered an alert state (or a warning state) due to excessive delays between message returns.

To configure Mail Message Notification properties, follow the procedure detailed in the list following Figure 26.6.

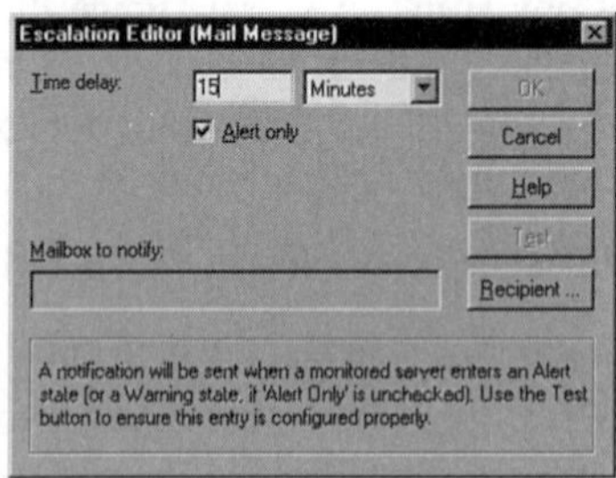

FIG. 26.6
Configure mail message Notification properties.

1. In the Time Delay box, enter a numeric value and the time units (seconds, minutes, hours) from the pull-down menu.

2. Clear the Alert Only checkbox if you want this notification process to occur when the server is in a warning state as well. Otherwise, the notification mail message will be sent in an alert state only after the time delay has been exceeded.
3. Click the Recipient button and navigate the Exchange address lists to select a recipient for the mail notification.
4. Click the Test button to verify proper notification functioning. Check the destination address to verify message delivery.
5. Click OK to complete these settings and return to the Notification property page.

Using Windows NT Alerts Notification by Windows NT Alert (see Figure 26.7) is useful only if the recipient computer is turned on and a user is logged on to it. These alerts are transmitted via the Windows NT Message service and are displayed on-screen to a user.

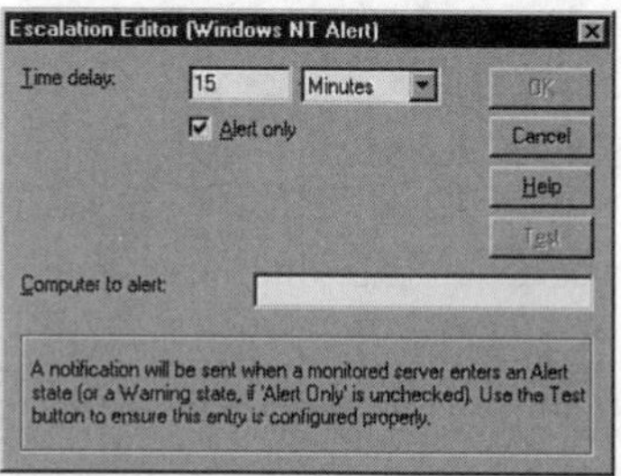

FIG. 26.7
Define Windows NT Alert parameters.

To configure notification properties for Windows NT Alert, follow these steps:

1. In the Time Delay box, enter a numeric value and the time units (seconds, minutes, hours) from the pull-down menu.
2. Clear the Alert Only checkbox if you want this notification process to occur when the server is in a warning state as well. Otherwise, the alert message will be sent in an alert state only after the time delay has been exceeded.
3. Enter the name of the Computer to Alert in the box provided. Use the Windows NT server name (Exchange server name) for that computer.
4. Click the Test button to verify proper notification functioning. Check the destination computer to verify alert message delivery.
5. Click OK to complete these settings and return to the Notification property page.

The Servers Page

The Servers property page enables you to determine to which Exchange servers the link monitor will send ping messages. Follow these steps:

1. Select the Servers property page from the Link Monitor property page. The property page shown in Figure 26.8 appears.

   The left display window lists the Microsoft Exchange server in the site selected in the lower-left pull-down menu.

The right display window shows which servers will receive ping messages from this server.

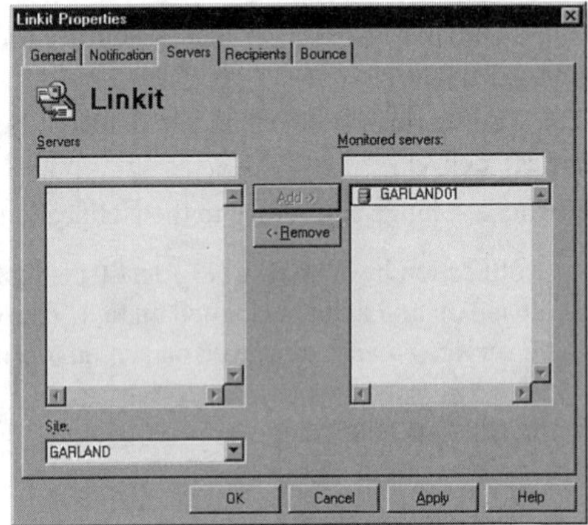

FIG. 26.8 Select which Exchange servers will receive ping messages.

2. Use the Site pull-down menu to select a site in your organization. The servers in that site will be listed in the left display window.
3. Select an Exchange server from the Servers window and click Add to enable monitoring for it.
4. To stop monitoring, click a server from the right display window and click Remove.
5. Click Apply to set these properties and continue with other properties. When you are done with all settings, click OK to return to the administrator program.

The Recipients Page

The Recipients property page enables you to configure ping message recipients in foreign messaging systems. At each polling interval, selected foreign recipients will receive a ping message. You must configure each recipient as a custom recipient in the Exchange administrator program. The link monitor will look at the returned ping message subject line for confirmation of message integrity. Alternatively, you can have the link monitor look at the returned message's body.

For link monitoring, ping messages must be returned by a foreign system. You must write a script that will return the ping message. Another common solution is to send a message to a nonexistent address on that system; the system then returns the nondeliverable message to the link monitor.

NOTE Some systems do not automatically return messages sent to nonexistent addresses; they redirect them into a default mailbox. Make sure the foreign system is configured to bounce back messages sent to nonexistent addresses.

Create a separate container to hold the custom recipients created for foreign system link monitoring. Also, set the Hide from Address Book option for each recipient, so that others in your organization will not accidentally send messages to the custom recipients.

1. Select the Recipients tab from the link monitor property pages. The Recipients property page appears.
2. In the left display window, click Modify and select the custom recipients you have created to get ping messages from this link monitor. The monitor will check the subject line of the returned message for confirmation of link status.
3. In the right display window, click Modify and select the custom recipients you have created to get ping messages from this link monitor. The monitor will check the body text of the returned message for confirmation of link status. Use this option when sending ping messages to a nonexistent address (when the subject line is not normally preserved).
4. Click Apply to set these properties and continue with other properties. When you are done with all settings, click OK to return to the administrator program.

The Bounce Page

The Bounce property page allows you the maximum allowable round-trips before a server enters a warning or alert state.

CAUTION

If you have created redundant paths to other Exchange sites or foreign messaging systems, the link monitor will not inform you that the primary link is down if the secondary link returns the ping message prior to the server entering an alert state.

To define bounce times, follow this procedure:

1. Select the Bounce tab from the Link Monitor property pages. The property page shown in Figure 26.9 appears.
2. Enter a number and select the time units (seconds, minutes, or hours) to wait for a return message before entering a warning state. The default time is 30 minutes.
3. Enter a number and select the time units (seconds, minutes, or hours) to wait for a return message before entering an alert state. The default time is 60 minutes.
4. Click Apply to set these properties and continue with other properties. When you are done with all settings, click OK to return to the administrator program.

After configuring all Link Monitor property pages, you must start the link monitor for it to carry out its functions. See the section "Starting and Using a Monitor" later in this chapter.

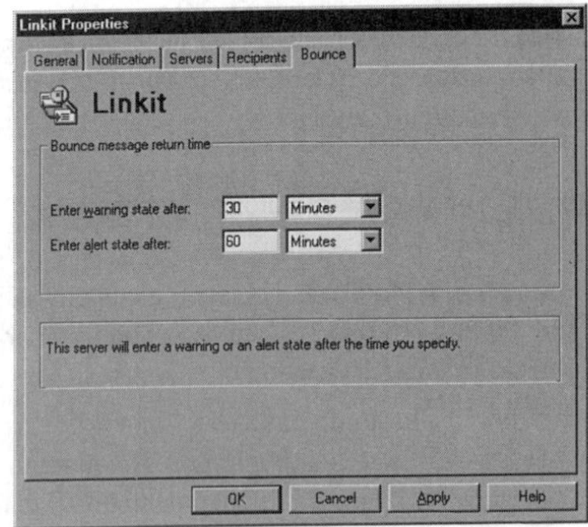

FIG. 26.9
Use this page to define threshold time before entering warning and alert states.

Creating a Server Monitor

A server monitor watches a selected list of Windows NT services for proper functioning. At each polling interval, the server monitor checks to see that the server is running by connecting to that server via a remote procedure call. The server's status is displayed in the server monitor's display window. You can also control (start, stop, or pause) services via the server monitor display window.

Additionally, these monitors can be used to monitor services that are not directly pertinent to Exchange if desired.

To create a new server monitor, follow this procedure:

1. In the Exchange administrator program, select a site in your organization.
2. Open the Configuration container within the selected site.
3. Select the Monitors container. The right administrator program display window will show all the existing monitors (both link and server) in this site.
4. Select New, Other, then select Server Monitor. The Server Monitor property pages appear.

The server monitor has several property pages, which enable the following options:

- General: Give the monitor a display name, set the polling interval, and select a log file location.
- Notification: Select alert type and delay times.
- Servers: Select which servers to monitor.

The Services Page

The Services property page shown on Figure 26.12 enables you to define which services a Microsoft Exchange server monitor will check. It is identical to the page found on the Server Monitor Servers page. The top display window shows all services currently installed on this

Windows NT server; the bottom display window shows the monitored services. Follow this procedure:

1. Select a service from the top window and click Add to add it to the list of Monitored Services.
2. Select a service from the bottom window and click Remove to take it off the list of Monitored Services.
3. Click Default to return to the basic services selected by Exchange Server.
4. Click None to remove all services from the monitored lists.

- Actions: Define procedure executed in case of malfunction.
- Clock: Set acceptable variations between system clocks.

If your organization includes several people who need to be notified of servers' malfunction, you must create separate server monitors. Also, if you want to set a different polling interval for a specific group of servers, you must create unique server monitors.

The General Page

The General property page allows you to name the server monitor, determine the polling interval, and determine the location for a log file, if one is desired.

To configure general settings for the server monitor, follow this procedure:

1. Select the General tab of the Server Monitor property pages. The property page shown in Figure 26.10 appears.

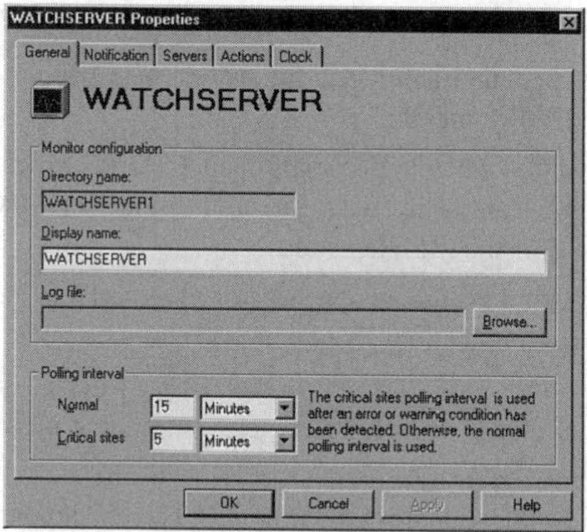

FIG. 26.10 Name this monitor and set its polling interval.

2. Enter a Directory Name for this server monitor. (The directory name cannot be changed for a server monitor after it has been created.)
3. Enter a Display Name as you want it to be shown in the administrator display window.
4. The Log File window shows the file name where monitor logs are being stored. Click Browse to select the file name and location.

5. In the Polling Interval window, enter the units and time interval for Normal operation.
6. In the Polling Interval window, enter the units and time interval for Critical Sites.
7. Click Apply to set these properties and continue with other properties. When you are done with all settings, click OK to return to the administrator program.

The Notification Page

The Notification property page enables you to configure what happens when a server monitor detects abnormal functioning. There are three main types of notification:

- Launch a process: Loads an external application. (This option is often used in conjunction with paging software.)
- Mail message: Automatically sends an e-mail message to a selected recipient describing the situation.
- Windows NT Alert: Uses the Windows NT Messenger service to notify a certain user or group of users.

The Notification property page is primarily one main display window in which all notification objects are displayed. By default, this property page is blank.

Click New to define a new notification object. Select the type of notification.

Launching a Notification Process Configuring an external notification application is as easy as choosing the application and setting the time delay for notification. You must configure that external process for the specific type of notification it provides. All Exchange does is launch the process and pass along any additional required parameters.

To configure Launch Process Notification properties, follow this procedure:

1. In the Time Delay box, enter a numeric value and the time units (seconds, minutes, or hours) from the pull-down menu.
2. Clear the Alert Only checkbox if you want this notification process to occur when the server is in a warning state. Otherwise, the notification process will only launch in an alert state after the time delay is exceeded.
3. Click the File button and navigate your directory hierarchy to locate the process you want to launch in this notification. The Launch Process box will display this file when it is selected.
4. Enter any additional command-line parameters you want to pass along to the notification process after it is launched.
5. Select the Append Notification Text to Parameter List checkbox in order to attach the actual notification text to the above command-line parameters during the process launch.

NOTE If the external notification application is already configured, you may now use the Test button to verify a property is functioning.

6. Click OK to complete these settings and return to the Notification property page.

You can change a notification by selecting it from the Notification list and clicking Edit. You can delete a notification by selecting it from the list and clicking Remove.

Using Mail Message Notification Mail message notification will alert an administrator via e-mail that a server has entered an alert state (or warning state as well, if desired).

To configure Mail Notification properties, follow this procedure:

1. In the Time Delay box, enter a numeric value and the time units (seconds, minutes, or hours) from the pull-down menu.
2. Clear the Alert Only checkbox if you want this notification process to occur when the server is in a warning state. Otherwise, the notification mail message will be sent in an alert state only after the time delay has been exceeded.
3. Click the Recipient button and navigate the Exchange address lists to select a recipient for the mail notification.
4. Click the Test button to verify proper notification functioning. Check the destination address to verify message delivery.
5. Click OK to complete these settings and return to the Notification property page.

Using Windows NT Alerts Notification by Windows NT Alert is useful only if the recipient computer is turned on and a user is logged on to it. These alerts are transmitted via the Windows NT Message service and are displayed on-screen to the specific user.

To configure notification properties for Windows NT Alert, follow these steps:

1. In the Time Delay box, enter a numeric value and the time units (seconds, minutes, or hours) from the pull-down menu.
2. Clear the Alert Only checkbox if you want this notification process to occur when the server is in a warning state. Otherwise, the alert message will be sent in an alert state only after the time delay has been exceeded.
3. Enter the name of the computer to alert in the box provided. Use the Windows NT server name (Exchange server name) for that computer.
4. Click the Test button to verify proper notification functioning. Check the destination computer to verify alert message delivery.
5. Click OK to complete these settings and return to the Notification property page.

The Servers Page

The Servers property page lets you determine what servers the server monitor is monitoring. Follow this procedure:

1. Select the Servers property page from the Server Monitor property page. Select the Server tab from the property page shown in Figure 26.11.

   The left display window lists the Microsoft Exchange server in the site selected in the lower-left pull-down menu.

   The right display window shows which servers are being monitored.

2. Use the Site pull-down menu to select a site in your organization. The servers in that site will be listed in the left display window.
3. Select an Exchange server from the Servers window, and click Add to enable monitoring for it.
4. To stop monitoring, click on a server from the right display window and click Remove.
5. To define specifically which services are monitored on each server, use the Services button. (See the procedure in the next section, "Configuring Monitored Services with the Server Monitor.")

You can determine specific services to be monitored for each selected Exchange server. By default, only the core Microsoft Exchange services (Directory, Information Store, and MTA) are configured for monitoring. Monitored services can also be configured on the property pages for each individual Exchange server.

FIG. 26.11
Select which servers this monitor will watch.

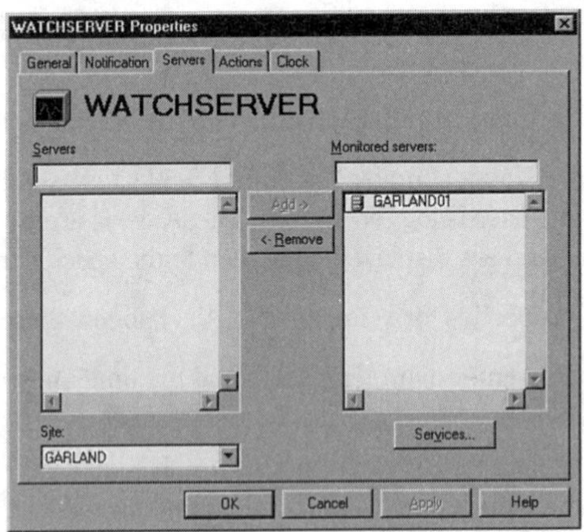

Configuring Monitored Services with the Server Monitor To configure monitored services with the server monitor, follow this procedure:

1. On the Servers tab of the Server monitor property pages, select a server to configure.

   Click the Services button. The dialog box shown in Figure 26.12 appears.

   The Installed Services window shows all the system services running on this Windows NT server.

   The Monitored Services window sho ws the system services currently being watched.

NOTE This dialog box is identical to the Services tab in an individual server's property pages.

2. Scroll through the list of installed Windows NT services and select which to monitor. Click Add.

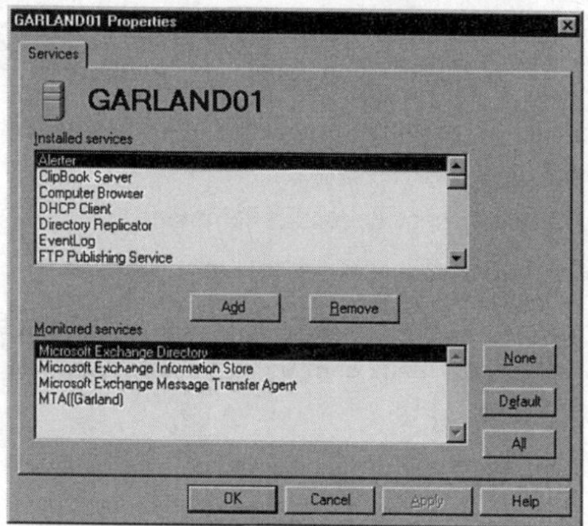

FIG. 26.12
Add or remove services to be monitored.

3. To remove a service from the Monitored Services list, select it and click Remove.
4. Click None to remove all services from the Monitored Services list.
5. Click Default to keep only the Microsoft Exchange Directory, Information Store, and MTA services on the monitored list.
6. Click All to include every Windows NT service in the Monitored Services window. (This is usually not a good idea, except under very special circumstances.)
7. Click Apply to set these properties and continue with other properties. When you are done with all settings, click OK to return to the Server Monitor's Servers property page.

Configuring Monitored Services from Exchange Server Property Pages To open Server property pages, follow this procedure:

1. Navigate to your desired site with the Exchange administrator program.
2. Click the Configuration container of the selected site. All the site configuration objects appear in the administrator program's right window.
3. Open the Servers container. A list of Exchange servers in your site will be listed.
4. Click the name of the server on which the Private Information Store you want to configure is located. The list of server objects is visible on the right display window of the Microsoft Exchange administrator program.
5. Open its property pages by selecting Properties from the administrator program file menu or by pressing Alt+Enter.
6. Select the Services tab.

The Actions Page

Use the Actions property page to define what steps are to be taken when a monitored service ceases to function. By default, no action is taken when a service goes down (except notification). Settings on this dialog box apply to all Exchange servers selected on the Servers property page. If you want to define different actions for other servers, you must create additional server monitors. There are three action choices to configure:

- Take no action: Literally, do nothing in response to a stopped service. (Normal notification functions will still occur.)
- Restart the service: Initiate a service restart command.
- Restart the computer: Initiate a server restart command.

First attempt actions are executed the first time a service is polled and found to be in a warning or alert state. The second attempt is made after the second time, and subsequent attempts are made any time after the first two.

To configure Actions, follow this procedure:

1. Select the Actions tab from the Server Monitor property pages. The property page shown in Figure 26.13 will appear.

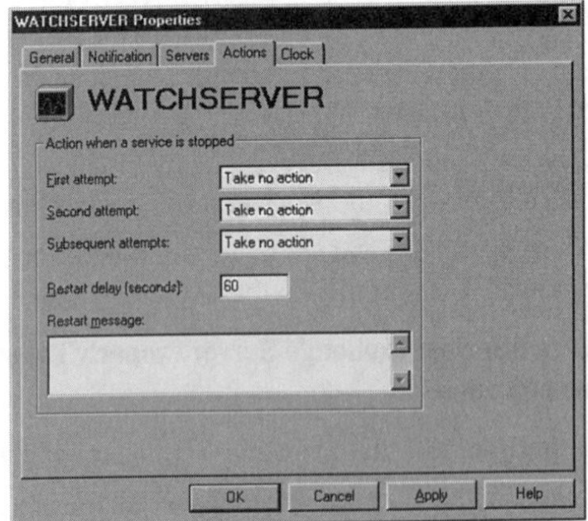

FIG. 26.13 Define what actions the server monitor should take upon detecting a service malfunction.

NOTE Actions defined in this property page are performed in addition to any notification action. ■

2. Use the pull-down menu next to First attempt to select an appropriate action. By default, Take No Action is chosen.
3. Use the pull-down menu next to Second attempt to select an appropriate action. By default, Take No Action is chosen.
4. Use the pull-down menu next to Subsequent attempts to select an appropriate action. By default, Take No Action is chosen.
5. Enter a Restart Delay (in seconds) to designate the amount of time that the server will wait before initiating a restart command. By default, this value is 60 seconds.
6. Type Restart Message that will be displayed by the server when a restart server action is initiated.

7. Click Apply to set these properties and continue with other properties. If you are done with all settings, click OK to return to the administrator program.

The Clock Page

The Clock property page configures system clock monitoring. Proper system clock synchronization is essential to running an efficient Exchange organization. Because so many connectors, gateways, and general maintenance processes depend on system-clock–based schedules, an incorrect time setting could create many problems. The monitoring computer will generate an alert if both computers' system clocks are off by a predetermined number of seconds.

To set clock monitoring, follow this procedure:

1. Select the Clock tab of the Server Monitor property pages. The dialog box shown in Figure 26.14 appears.

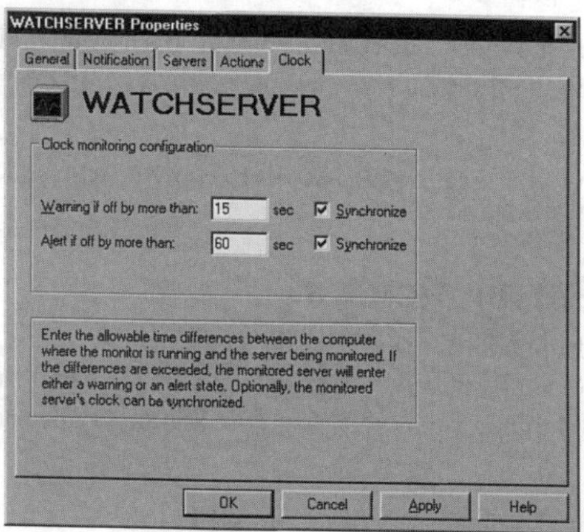

FIG. 26.14 Make sure clocks in your organization are properly synchronized.

2. In Warning If Off by More Than, type the maximum amount of time (in seconds) in which the two clocks can differ before entering a warning state.
3. In Alert If Off by More Than, type the maximum amount of time (in seconds) in which the two clocks can differ before entering an alert state.
4. Clear the Synchronize (Synchronize) checkboxes to prevent the clock from adjusting to the monitoring computer's clock. By default, this option is selected.
5. Click Apply to set these properties and continue with other properties. When you are done with all settings, click OK to return to the administrator program.

Starting and Using a Monitor

After creating a monitor, you must start it in order for it to perform its functions. You can start a monitor manually from the administrator program or automatically from the command line. The monitor's window must be open (or minimized at all times) when it is running.

Automatically Starting a Server Monitor

You can configure a server monitor for automatic startup by creating a program item for it in the Program Manager Startup group. The following sequence automatically starts the administrator program and designated monitors when you log on to Windows NT:

1. In the Windows NT Program Manager, open the Startup program group.
2. Select New from the Program Manager File menu.
3. Select Program Item from the New Program Object dialog box. Click OK.
4. Enter a description for this startup item.
5. Enter a command line following the format **`path\admin.exe /m[sitename]\monitorname\server`**

   An example command-line entry follows:

   ```
   E:\exchange\bin\admin.exe /mGARLAND\WATCHSERVER\GARLAND01
   ```

   Optionally, multiple monitors can be started with this command-line entry by adding an extra `/m` and identifying the monitor.

   An example follows:

   ```
   E:\exchange\bin\admin.exe /mGARLAND\WATCHSERVER\GARLAND01 /
   mGARLAND\LinkIT\GARLAND01
   ```

Manually Starting a Server Monitor

You can start a monitor from another server in the organization. In the following examples the monitors were constructed and started at the Garland site. Note that the monitors exist in Los Angeles as well. To start a monitor manually from the administrator program, follow this procedure:

1. Using the Exchange administrator program, select the site at which the desired server monitor resides.
2. Open the Configuration container for the selected site.
3. Click on the Monitors container for this site. The right administrator display window will show all the monitors you have created at your site (whether started or not).
4. Select the server monitor of your choice. From the administrator program Tools menu, select Start Monitor (see Figure 26.15).
5. In the Connect to Server dialog box, select which server to connect to as a home server. Click OK to start the monitor. The server monitor's display window appears.

NOTE You must connect to a specific server in order to execute server-based operations, such as sending mail.

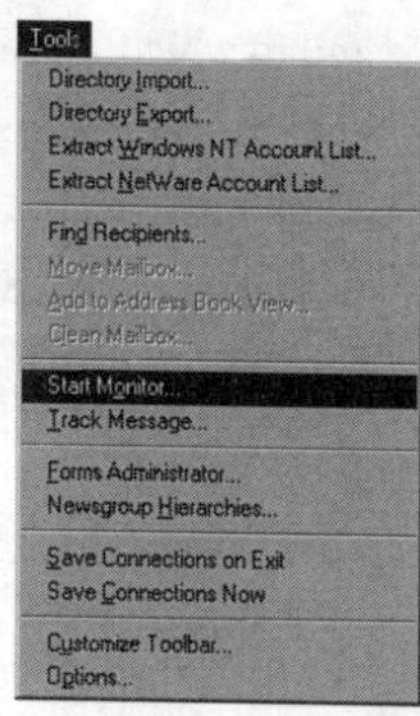

FIG. 26.15
The administrator program's Start Monitor command.

Using Monitor Status Windows

Monitor status windows are the portals through which you view the current condition of monitored links and servers. The status windows periodically update and display data on their operation. With enough strategically placed monitors, you can get an overall feel of your organization's messaging conditions from a single machine in your enterprise.

Reading the Link Monitor Window

The Link Monitor window displays the condition of monitored links; each line in the display represents one link. You can sort the display using the Column Heading buttons. You can also change the width of the columns to make the display easier to read (see Figure 26.16).

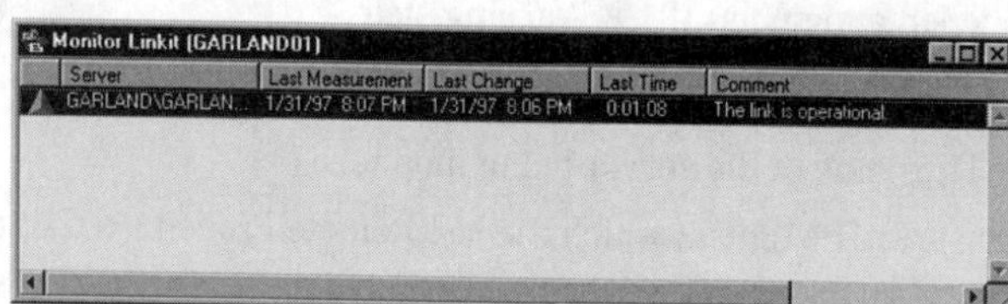

FIG. 26.16
A functioning Link Monitor window.

The columns indicate the following things:

- Icon: Visual representation of the link's status

Up	Link is operational.
Down	Link is not operational.
Exclamation point	Warning state.
Question mark	Link is not yet monitored.

- Server: The Server that sent the ping message and to which it is expected to return
- Last Measurement: The time at which the last ping message was sent
- Last Change: The time at which the status of the link changed
- Last Time: The round-trip time of the last ping message sent from the sending server
- Comment: A description of the monitored link condition

Reading the Server Monitor Window

The Server Monitor window displays one line for each server being monitored. The status icon reflects the status of all server components. If any component is down, the server is considered to be down (see Figure 26.17).

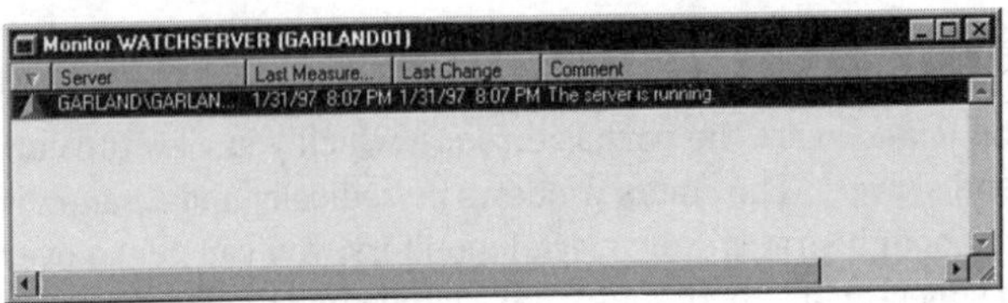

FIG. 26.17 A functioning Server Monitor window.

The columns indicate the following things:

- Icon: Visual representation of a server's status

Up	Server is operational.
Down	Server is not operational.
Exclamation point (!)	Warning state.
Question mark (?)	Server is not yet monitored.

- Server: The name of the server being monitored
- Last measure: The time at which the last Remote Procedure Call (RPC) was sent to test the status of Windows NT services
- Last change: The time at which the condition of service on a server changed

Double-clicking a status message in either a link or server monitor will bring up property pages with status information. See Chapter 28, "Troubleshooting Exchange with Diagnostic Tools," for an explanation of these property pages.

Stopping a Monitor for Maintenance

When bringing an Exchange server down for maintenance, consider the effects on monitors watching the server. Any server monitors will notice the halted services, initiate notifications, and enter an alert state. Any link monitors watching messaging connections through this server will enter alert mode and send out applicable notifications as well.

To prevent these problems, you can put a server into *maintenance mode*. When a monitor polls a server in this mode, it knows not to go through the normal alert and warning routines.

The command to specify a maintenance mode for a server is as follows:

```
ADMIN /t
```

After this command is executed, each monitor learns of the server's maintenance status at the next server poll. Keep in mind each monitor's polling interval to be sure that all monitors are notified before you bring a server down.

The command can be modified with these additional switches:

`-n`	Halts notification processes on a monitor, but keeps monitor-initiated repairs
`-r`	Keeps monitor-initiated notifications, but halts repair processes on a monitor
`-nr`	Halts both notification and repair processes
`-t`	Resets the monitor to normal mode

To confirm that a monitor has received a maintenance notification, open a link or a server entry in the monitor and select its Maintenance property page. The checkboxes will reveal this information.

Using SNMP to Monitor and Troubleshoot

If your system supports *SNMP (Simple Network Management Protocol)*, you can use SNMP to monitor and support your Exchange organization.

Microsoft Exchange Server complies with RFC 1566, which defines industry standards for Management Information Base for SNMP Mail and Directory Management, otherwise known as *MADMAN MIB*.

By making Windows NT Performance Monitor counters available for MIB objects, Microsoft Exchange supports SNMP.

All counters accessed by the Exchange MTA and the Internet Mail Service can be accessed by SNMP, which surpasses the requirements of RFC 1566.

Table 26.1 identifies the MIB objects defined in RFC 1566 and their corresponding Exchange Server counters.

Table 26.1 MIB Objects and Exchange Server Counters

MIB Object	MSExchangeIMC Counter	MSExchangeMTA Counter
MTAReceivedMessages	Inbound Messages Total	Inbound Messages Total
MTAStoredMessages	Total Messages Queued	Work Queue Length
MTATransmittedMessages	Outbound Messages Total	Outbound Messages Total
MTAReceivedVolume	Inbound Bytes Total	Inbound Bytes Total
MTAStoredVolume	Total Bytes Queued	Work Bytes Queued

continues

Table 26.1 Continued

MIB Object	MSExchangeIMC Counter	MSExchangeMTA Counter
MTATransmittedVolume	Outbound Bytes Total	Outbound Bytes Total
MTAReceivedRecipients	Total Recipients Inbound	Total Recipients Inbound
MTAStoredRecipients	Total Recipients Queued	Total Recipients Queued
MTATransmittedRecipients	Total Recipients Outbound	Total Recipients Outbound
MTALoopsDetected	Total Loops Detected	Total Loops Detected

Table 26.2 lists the MIB group objects and their related MTA Connections counters.

Table 26.2 MIB Objects and MTA Connections Counters

MIB Object	MSExchangeMTA Connections Counter
MTAGroupReceivedMessages	Inbound Messages Total
MTAGroupRejectedMessages	Inbound Rejected Total
MTAGroupStoredMessages	Queue Length
MTAGroupTransmittedMessages	Outbound Messages Total
MTAGroupReceivedVolume	Inbound Bytes Total
MTAGroupStoredVolume	Queued Bytes
MTAGroupTransmittedVolume	Outbound Bytes Total
MTAGroupReceivedRecipients	Total Recipients Inbound
MTAGroupStoredRecipients	Total Recipients Queue
DMTAGroupTransmittedRecipients	Total Recipients Outbound
MTAGroupOldestMessageStored	Oldest Message Queued (seconds)
MTAGroupInboundAssociations	Current Inbound Associations
MTAGroupOutboundAssociations	Current Outbound Associations
MTAGroupLastInboundActivity	Last Inbound Association (seconds)
MTAGroupLastOutboundActivity	Last Outbound Association (seconds)
MTAGroupScheduledRetry	Next Association Retry (seconds)

By accessing the MIBs in the mib.bin file, the Windows NT Server SNMP agent can respond to SNMP requests. To enable Exchange Server to support SNMP, you must install the MIB for the Microsoft Exchange Server computer (exchange.mib) on your server in the mib.bin file.

A compiled version of Exchange.mib is provided by Microsoft Exchange Server, which is installed by running a batch file from the Exchange Server CD-ROM. The following section, "Using the Batch File," explains how to run this file. If extension MIBs on your server have been configured, you must use other tools to install Exchange.mib rather than the batch file. These other tools to install Exchange.mib are also found on the Exchange Server CD-ROM.

NOTE The Windows NT SNMP service must be installed prior to installing SNMP support for Exchange. To install the Windows NT SNMP service from Control Panel, choose Network. After you install the service, you must reinstall Windows NT Service Pack 3. ■

Using the Batch File

As mentioned in the preceding section, if you have not installed any MIBs on your server other than those included with Windows NT, you can run the batch file included on the Exchange Server CD-ROM. The batch file is located in the following directory:

SUPPORT\SNMP*platform*\INSTALL.BAT

Using Perf2mib.exe and Mibcc.exe

Microsoft Exchange Server provides tools for SNMP support. Perf2mib.exe compiles Performance Monitor counters into a new MIB for Exchange Server. Mibcc.exe recompiles the Perfmib.mib file created by Perf2mib.exe and creates a new mib.bin file. Use the following procedure to use Perf2mib.exe and Mibcc.exe:

1. Run the Per2mib.exe program from a command prompt to create the perfmib.mib and perfmib.ini files.
2. Run the Mibcc.exe command to create the Mib.bin.
3. Copy Perfmib.dll, Perfmib.ini, and Mib.bin to the system32 directory.
4. Run the regini.exe command to set up the registry with the values to support the performance MIB.
5. Restart the SNMP service by choosing Services from Control Panel.

MIB Viewing

Any SNMP version 1-compatible management console can view the Microsoft Exchange Server MIB. Your management console may need to load the MIB file for the object descriptions, which is available on the Exchange Server CD-ROM. You can also use the SNMPUTIL utility, available with the Windows NT Resource Kit, to view a MIB. ●

CHAPTER 27

Exchange Security

In this chapter

Exchange relies on the C2-level security included within Windows NT for a portion of its structure. C2-level security is a U.S. Department of Defense rating. It provides for discretionary access control (users, groups, and so on), object reuse protection (protecting deleted data), mandatory logon, and auditing of security-related events. Windows NT can provide user authentication, resource access, and auditing. Each of these areas is described in this chapter. Exchange increases security with digital signatures and message encryption.

Understanding Windows NT Authentication

Every user, process, and service is required to enter a unique login name and password to gain access to the system. The operating system's interactive two-step security process of checking the login name with the password is known as *authentication*.

Microsoft Exchange Server enables the operating system to ascertain the identity and handle the validation of users and processes. The identity is the username and the validation is the user password. The operating system then will establish the security context, which explains and controls what kind of access will be granted to the user or process.

When a user or process logs in to the Windows NT server, there is no need for any other usernames or passwords to achieve access to Microsoft Exchange Server. This feature is unlike other types of message-system security features.

For example, suppose that a LAN Administrator on a Novell NetWare 3.1x is located on Server1 and the Microsoft Mail 3.x post offices and utilities are located on Server2. The administrator is required to enter a username and password for initial access to Server1. An additional username and password is needed for access to the directory structure on Server2. Moreover, a third username and password is needed to finally access the Admin program. Other message systems, such as Lotus cc:Mail, have similar security policies.

Defining Windows NT Domain Architecture

Each user or resource within a single location, such as the Microsoft Exchange Server, is a member of a particular *domain*. A domain is either a single Microsoft Windows NT server or multiple Windows NT servers that use the same security scheme and user-account database. Only one username and password is required to recognize, authenticate, and establish a connection to all the Windows NT servers and their resources in the domain.

Multiple domains or separate domain remote sites can connect by way of a trust relationship. This connection between the domains enables users on one domain to access resources within the other domain. When the domains are in a trusted relationship, one domain (*trusting domain*) trusts the other (*trusted domain*). Any user located in the trusted domain can gain access to objects within the other domain.

For example, a user at Software Spectrum located in Garland who logs on to Domain A wants access to a resource on Domain B. Because Domain B, located in Los Angeles, has a trusted relationship with Domain A, the Domain B resources are available to this user. This situation is known as *passthrough authentication*, which allows having only one user account on one domain and the capability to access resources on the other.

Understanding the Types of Windows NT Accounts

Windows NT accounts are the principal structure upon which authentication is based. Accounts consist of two main elements: the user ID and the associated password. These two fundamental bits of information provide the key to access various services. Two main types of Windows NT accounts exist:

- User Accounts
- Service Accounts

User Accounts

Single and multiple user accounts can be associated with a Microsoft Exchange Server mailbox. The user attempting to establish a connection with a Microsoft Exchange server must be located within the same domain as the Microsoft Exchange server to which the user is trying to connect. If the user and the Microsoft Exchange server are located on different domains, the domains must be in a trusted relationship.

As another example, a user on Domain A at Software Spectrum in Garland wants to acquire access to a Microsoft Exchange server located on Domain B in Los Angeles, but in this case, Domain A and Domain B do not have a trusted relationship. The user on Domain A cannot establish a connection with the Microsoft Exchange server located on Domain B.

Service Accounts

On the Microsoft Windows NT server, an assortment of services is initiated when the system goes through its startup process. The Microsoft Exchange Server information store service and MTA established connections are good examples of services that run on a Microsoft Windows NT Server. These services, through a user account known as a service account, log on to the system and start up automatically.

The service account is an important feature to Microsoft Exchange Server. Create this account before beginning the installation of Microsoft Exchange Server. This account affects the installation of and communication establishment between other Microsoft Exchange servers. When you install and join a new Microsoft Exchange server to a site with an existing Microsoft Exchange server, the service account is requested to complete the installation. The service account must be the same on all servers within a site. Without this account, Microsoft Exchange servers in the same site will not be able to communicate with each other. If a site extends over multiple domains, only one service account is needed, provided that a trust relationship exists between domains.

Understanding Windows NT Access Control

When a user logs on to a Microsoft Windows NT Server, the security features of the operating system look to the security context (covered previously in this chapter) for information determining the permissions to access specific network resources. A ***permission*** controls access to individual objects located in the system that use specific authorization information. Each object is different and, consequently, has different levels of permissions.

The following list shows the variety of permissions to control access that Microsoft Exchange Server offers:

- Mailbox
- Public Folder
- Directory
- Group

Each of the permissions is discussed in detail in following sections of this chapter.

Mailbox Permissions

The Administrator program is the application used to grant permissions to log on and gain access to a Microsoft Exchange Server mailbox. One mailbox can have either one or multiple user accounts with the user permission set for it.

Microsoft Exchange Server reviews all user accounts for the user permission when a logon is attempted. After the review completes, it verifies whether or not the user attempting to log on has this permission.

Public Folder Permissions

Using the Microsoft Exchange Client, the owner of a public folder can grant permission to the following areas to access it:

- Mailboxes
- Distribution lists
- Public folders

As stated previously, different objects have different levels of permissions. The owner of a public folder can grant others the following permissions:

- Create items
- Read items
- Edit items
- Delete items

The public folder, similar to other Windows NT resources, reviews the user accounts for permissions for this resource. Then the folder verifies that the object trying to access it has the appropriate permissions.

As an example, Software Spectrum has created two differing distribution lists within a Financial public folder on the Microsoft Exchange Server Accounting and Accounting Managers. The permissions can be modified on the Financial public folder so that members of the Accounting group have Read Access, and the Accounting Managers may have Read and Write permissions.

Applying Directory Permissions

Applying permissions to directories is different than applying permissions to public folders. With directories, the permissions are granted directly to the user's account database. Within the Administrator application, although all users can see the directory listed, unless the users have the correct permissions, they cannot view the data inside the directory. A good example of a directory permission is *Add Child.* With this permission on the Recipient Container, a user can create mailboxes.

Roles are another way of making administrative tasks easier. *Roles* consist of built-in groups of certain kinds of similar permissions. For example, the following list shows the built-in permissions for the Admin role:

- Add Child
- Modify user attributes
- Delete
- Logon

Applying Windows NT Groups and Permissions

Sets of user accounts with similar network resource needs can be placed into a *group.* This action simplifies the administrative task of adding permissions to individual users. If a group named MIS is created, all members of this group automatically have the permissions that are granted to the group, and these permissions are applied to the individual user. Any user accounts that are created after the group was created, or existing users who become additional members of this group, will have the same group permissions applied. Likewise, if the permissions of the group are modified, all members of the group will have their permissions changed. Microsoft Windows NT Server offers built-in *local* and *global groups* with the capability to also create local and global groups. When possible, a good recommendation is to use groups. Using groups diminishes the amount of time spent dealing with administrative tasks.

Local Groups Only the domain where the *local group* exists will contain the definition of resource permissions for this group. Additionally, no matter which domain the local group is located in, permissions can be granted only to that particular domain's resources. Local groups may contain the following:

- Other users
- Global groups from the same domain
- Users from trusted domains
- Global groups from trusted domains

NOTE Local groups cannot contain other local groups from the same domain. ■

Global Groups Groups that can use resources within other domains are known as *global groups*. Global groups consist of a group of user accounts that was given access to permissions and rights for the following:

- The global group's own domain
- Servers and clients of the domain
- Any trusting domains

Global groups also can be members of local domain groups.

In essence, the creation of global groups allows sets of users from within a particular domain and the available use of network resources, from both inside and outside the domain.

Using Windows NT Auditing Capabilities

Microsoft Windows NT has built-in auditing capabilities that allow the operating system to track events that occur within the system to detect security breaches. This tracking is an advantage for the Microsoft Exchange Server system. As discussed previously, the operating system handles the identity and validation of users for Microsoft Exchange Server. Moreover, the Microsoft Windows NT Server operating system can be modified to audit the Microsoft Exchange Server event services and directory objects. These events show up in the Windows NT event log.

NOTE Microsoft Exchange Server administrators do not require permissions to administer to the Microsoft Windows NT Server. ■

Introduction to Data Encryption

Microsoft Exchange Server provides confidentiality by encrypting the destined message. When the message is sent, the data-encryption security feature scrambles the message. If you viewed the message in this scrambled state, it would resemble a bunch of random alphanumeric characters. When the message is received at its destination, it is decrypted and put back together in the original format.

Microsoft Exchange Server supports the following two standards to complete this security task:

- CAST encryption algorithms
- Data Encryption Standard (DES)

NOTE The Data Encryption Standard (DES) is available with Microsoft Windows NT Server software in Canada and the United States. ■

When a user chooses Secure Message with Encryption from the toolbar, all of the recipients' certificates are retrieved from the directory. Next, a bulk encryption key is created to encrypt the message. Finally, the user's public encryption key is extracted from the certificate and placed in a *lockbox*. This action prevents the encryption key from being used while the encrypted message is in transit. The lockbox and the encryption key are then sent to the recipient.

When the recipient receives and opens the message, the encryption key is used to decrypt the lockbox, and the bulk encryption key from within the lockbox is used to decrypt the message. See Figure 27.1.

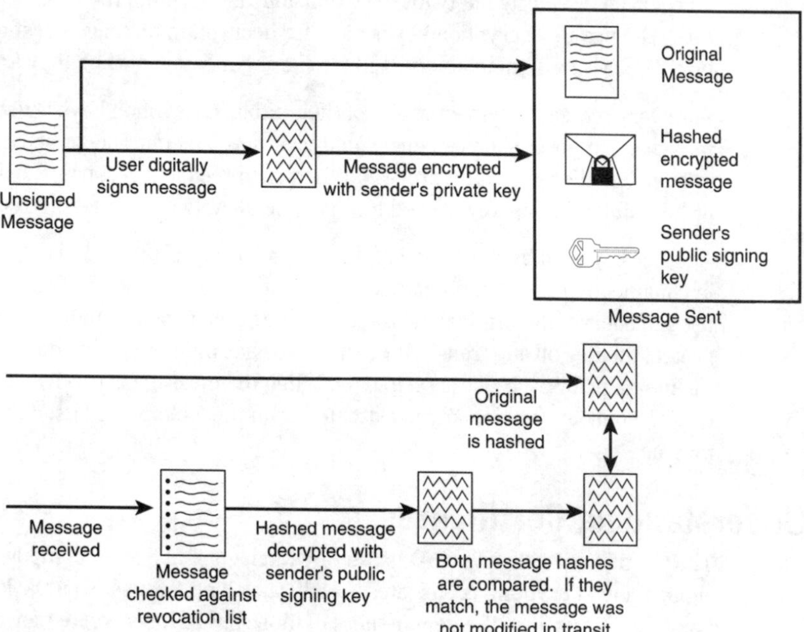

FIG. 27.1
Sending and receiving an encrypted message.

Using Exchange's Advanced Security

As mentioned previously, Exchange uses several of Windows NT's built-in C2-level security features. To augment this security, Exchange adds digital signatures and message encryption. To enable these advanced security features, you must designate one server within your organization that manages a special security database. This server is known as the Key Management (KM) Server. Before discussing how the KM Server works with digital signatures and message encryption, make sure that you understand keys, tokens, certificates, and Exchange's revocation list.

Understanding Keys

Each mailbox created within Microsoft Exchange Server is given two pairs of electronic keys. One key pair, used for signing and verifying actions, is created by the Microsoft Exchange Client. The other pair, used for encrypting and decrypting operations, is generated by the KM Server. The *private key* is known only by the user, and a public key is known by the public (it can be accessed by other mail users). This key type of security features is known as *public/private key technology*, a data-encryption industry standard.

The Microsoft Exchange Client, located on the user's local hard disk, stores the private keys in an encrypted security file (with the extension .EPF), within the client's local directory structure. The private encryption key is used for decrypting messages destined for the user's mailbox. The private signing key is used for signing messages when they are sent.

For every message recipient, each of their public encryption keys is used when the original message composer sends an encrypted message. The multiple public encryption keys are used to complete the encryption process. When each recipient receives the encrypted message, his or her public signing key is used to verify the identity of the message sender or composer.

Another key used by the Microsoft Exchange Server is the *bulk encryption key*. This key is used in conjunction with both the public and private encryption keys. The bulk encryption key is used to encrypt the original message. The key then is placed into a *lockbox*, where it is kept to protect the key during transit. If the message has multiple recipients, a lockbox is attached to the message for each of the recipients. When the message is received at the recipient's location, the bulk encryption key is extracted from the lockbox and used to decrypt the original message.

Understanding Certificates

The Certificate Authority (CA) is the Key Management Server component that generates signing and encrypting certificates. Certificates bind the user's public key to the user's mailbox. The CA certifies the genuineness of those public keys created for users. Users have two kinds of certificates: an encryption certificate and a signing certificate. The *encryption certificate* is an attribute of the mailbox and contains the user's public encryption key. The signing certificate is contained in the user's security file on the local hard disk drive. It holds the user's public signing key.

Microsoft Exchange supports the industry standard X.509v3 certificate type. Certificates that conform to the X.509v3 standard contain detailed identification information about the certificate-holder, including the type of business the certificate-holder operates and the number of years in business. Such detailed information prevents someone from masquerading as a stock broker, for example.

Because it supports the X.509v3 standard, Exchange Server will accept certificates that have been issued by certificate authorities such as VeriSign or the Certificate Server included with Internet Information Server 4.0. Likewise, by using Certificate Trust Lists, clients can trust X.509 certificates issued by these certificate authorities.

NOTE Support for X.509v3 certificates will be included in the first service pack. ■

The certificate also contains the following information:

- A unique serial number, generated by the CA for each certificate
- The CA's directory name (DN)
- The user's directory name (DN)
- The expiration date of the user's public key
- The holder's identifying information: name, organization, address, and so on

Exchange also supports the revocation of security certificates. This action permanently deactivates the security certificate for a mailbox. This should be done only when you are absolutely sure that you do not need to recover the security keys in the future. When the security certificate is revoked for a mailbox, anyone attempting to open an encrypted message previously sent from this mailbox is prompted with a warning, informing him or her that the message was secured with a revoked security certificate.

The revocation list contains the serial number and expiration date of all revoked certificates. This ensures that the revoked user's mail account cannot be used by unauthorized personnel. The user then can be reconfigured for advanced security and another certificate issued. Reconfiguration will issue another token and another certificate serial number and expiration date.

You may want to consider revoking advanced security when the following situations exist:

- Users feel their security was compromised because it appears that someone is signing messages on their behalf or because someone has gained access to their security files and passwords.

  For example, a Software Spectrum salesperson's laptop was stolen in the field. You should revoke this salesperson's certificate to ensure that this person's security certificates are in the relocation list. Then you should reconfigure the user for Exchange's advanced security, generating a new security certificate for the user.
- An employee leaves your organization, and you want to ensure that the digital signatures and encrypted messages from this user are identified as invalid.

All revoked certificates originate in the KM Server database and are distributed to all the clients. Each client caches the original list and receives a daily update from the KM Server. For performance reasons, revoke users judiciously. When a message reaches its recipient and the signature is verified, it must be checked against the list before the message can be decrypted. The more certificates are contained in the list, the more the advanced security and performance of the client will degrade.

Understanding Tokens

When a mail administrator activates advanced security for a user, a temporary security *token* is generated. This random eight-digit code not only enables digital signing and data encryption, but also can be recovered if lost. The token should be loaded on the local workstation. Tokens are used only once, to secure a connection with the KM server and complete the advanced security setup for Microsoft Exchange Server advanced security users.

Understanding Key Management Server

One Microsoft Exchange Server integrated component is the Key Management Server, which is the central point for advanced security within the system. The Key Management Server provides the following services:

- Certifies public signing and encryption keys
- Creates public and private encryption keys
- Maintains backups of private encryption keys and public signing keys
- Generates tokens
- Maintains the original copy of the revocation list

All private encryption keys, public signing keys, and the revocation list are stored in the key management database. For additional security, the KM Server database itself is encrypted.

Each user that you want to use advanced security must be configured after the KM Server is configured. The users are given a temporary token to allow access to the KM Server so that the advanced security features setup can be completed.

When the Key Management Server is properly set up and advanced security is activated, users can take advantage of Exchange's digital signatures and message encryption.

Understanding Digital Signatures

Microsoft Exchange Server provides *End-to-End Authentication* and *Data Integrity* through the use of Digital Signatures, which are based on a user's signing keys. Two processes, signing and verifying, are involved.

When a message is to be sent, the sender selects Digitally Sign Message. It then will have a "signature" placed on it. The signature, or signing key, claims that the message was derived from the indicated source. The name on the header is matched with the sender's name. This matching prevents forgeries. Before the recipient can receive the message, the destination verifies the signature on the message.

After the message is signed, it is transformed to *message hashes*, which are a unique representation of a message. Moreover, the hashes are then encrypted. The original message and the encrypted hash message are then sent with the signing certificate to the destination. The signing certificate contains the sender's signing key.

When the message reaches its recipient, the message is verified when user chooses Read Digital Signature from the toolbar. First, the sender's certificate is checked against the revocation list. If it is on the list, the recipient is notified that this user was revoked from the system. Next, the original message is hashed as the encrypted hash message is decrypted. These two messages, both in hashed states, now can be compared to each other. If the hashes don't match, the message has been modified in transit and the user is notified. This feature allows for built-in data integrity verification. See Figure 27.2 for an illustration of how messages are sent and received by using digital signatures.

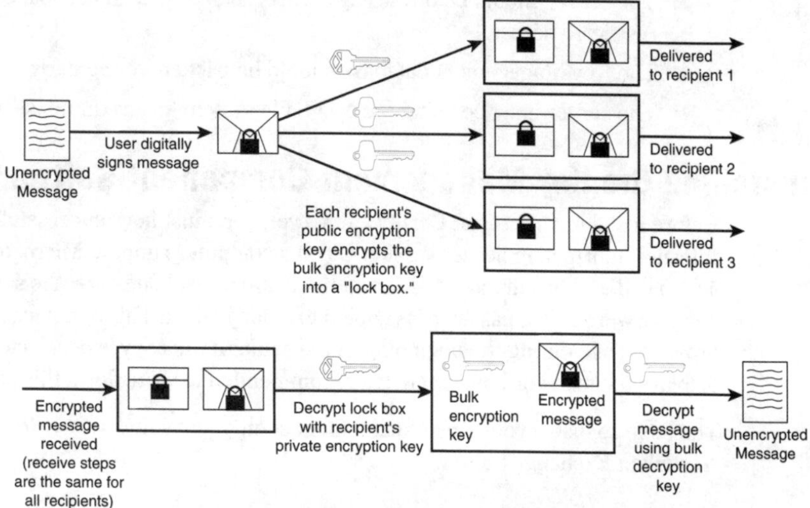

FIG. 27.2
Sending and receiving a message with a digital signature.

Understanding Key Management Server

The Key Management Server, which is a component of Microsoft Exchange Server, is the central point for advanced security. The following steps show what is involved to set up and maintain Microsoft Exchange Server advanced security:

- Selecting the server to manage the key management database
- Installing the Key Management component software and enabling individual users to take advantage of advanced security features
- Configuring remote sites to use advanced security
- Verifying that the Key Management component is functioning correctly
- Viewing security logs for errors or attempted breaches, and periodically clearing the logs of unneeded information
- Backing up and maintaining the key management database

Selecting the Server to Manage the Key Management Database

Only one Microsoft Windows NT Server in the organization that is running Microsoft Exchange Server can become the Key Management Server (KM Server) and manage the Key Management advanced security database. Having multiple KM Servers can cause authentication and encryption errors. When deciding which Microsoft Exchange Server to use as the KM Server, keep the following important points in mind:

- Advanced security administration can be done only from within the site where the KM Server is located.
- The server should be physically secure, such as placed in a locked room or area with restricted access.
- The Key Management database should be backed up regularly.
- The server must be using the NTFS file system for maximum security.

Installing the Key Management Component Software

Before installing Microsoft Certificate Server, you must have successfully installed Microsoft Internet Information Server version 4.0 on a computer running Microsoft Windows NT version 4.0. In order to install the Key Management component software, the setup process asks for two passwords. One password is copied to a floppy disk. This option can be deselected on the property page during the beginning of the setup. If the copy is deselected, the setup process displays the password onscreen. It's recommended to write down this password.

The steps to install your Key Management component software are described in Chapter 6, "Installing Exchange Server."

NOTE At the time of this writing, the author team had the most current release of the Exchange 5.5 Release Candidate 1. Unfortunately, Key Management Server (KM) was not included. In the final release of Exchange 5.5, KM could load as part of the initial installation of Exchange. When the information becomes available, the authors will post it as errata on Que's Web site at `www.mcp.com`. ■

Starting the Key Management Server Service

The Key Management Server Service must be started to enable and configure advanced security for individual users. Follow these steps:

NOTE If a KM Server Startup Floppy Disk wasn't created, the password that was displayed onscreen during the setup process must be input within the startup parameters for the KM Server service. To do this, go into Control Panel, Services and highlight the KM Server service. Choose Startup and enter the password in the Log on As section.

Important: Please write this password down somewhere. This password cannot be changed without reinstalling the component. This password is needed by the KM Server Service to start up. This is the password that would otherwise be placed on the floppy disk. ■

1. Log on to Microsoft Windows NT Server as administrator.
2. Select Control Panel, and then Services.
3. Locate the Key Management Server service entry, highlight it, and click the Start button. Refer to the preceding Note regarding diskless KM Server setups.

4. After displaying a message about starting the services, the Key Management Service status changes to Started.
5. Close the Services applet and exit Control Panel.

Changing Your Advanced Security Administrative Password

The Key Management Server requires an Advanced Security Administrator's password to modify any security-related items. This password is separate from any other passwords, which were explained in previous chapters. This password is specific for security-related administrative tasks.

If this is a new install or if the advanced security password has never been changed, take the following steps:

1. Launch the Microsoft Exchange Server Administrator program.
2. Connect to a Microsoft Exchange server.
3. Click the Configuration container.
4. Choose the Encryption object and open its property pages.
5. Click the Security tab.
6. Choose Key Management Administrators.
7. Enter the Advanced Security Administrator password.

NOTE If the password has never been changed for any reason, the default password is `password`. ■

8. Click Change Password, type the old password into the Old Password box, and then type your new password in the New Password box. You are then asked to verify the new password.
9. Click OK to save the changes.

Enabling Advanced Security Features for Individual Users

To allow users to digitally sign and encrypt messages, advanced security must be enabled for each recipient. With the KM Server in production, after the advanced security setup process for a user is initiated, an RPC call is made to the KM Server, which generates and returns a token.

Using Person-to-Person Key Exchange

Exchange 5.0 clients can individually exchange security keys and certificates, even between different organizations. This allows them to exchange signed and encrypted messages, even over the Internet. In previous versions, this function was limited to other Exchange users inside your organization.

Before you can send someone encrypted keys, or verify their digital signature, you must first obtain a trusted copy of their "public security keys." For users inside your organization, these keys are stored in the Global Address List for easy access. Exchange users outside of your organization must send you their public keys that can then be stored in your Personal Address Book for future use.

To send public security keys to a user in another organization, follow these steps:

1. Click Tools.
2. Choose Options and then Security.
3. Click the Send Security Keys button. A special e-form will be launched, which has details from your Global Address Book entry automatically filled out.
4. Type the Internet e-mail address of the person you want to send your keys to.
5. Click Send. The e-form will be sent through the Internet to the recipient whose name you typed.

On the receiving end:

1. The recipient opens the e-form in their Exchange client.
2. Click the ADD to PAB button. This creates an entry in their personal address book, including the sender's public security keys.

They can now verify the sender's digital signature and send encrypted mail. In turn, they can also send you their public security keys to enable full two-way secure e-mail.

Both the sender and receiver have a VERIFY SECURITY KEYS button on their e-form. This button provides a way for the receiver to ensure that the public keys the person sent are in fact the same public keys received. If you call the sender on the phone and ask him to click the VERIFY SECURITY KEYS button on the form sent (in the Sent Mail folder), he can read you the numbers from his screen, which form a unique "fingerprint" that identifies his keys. The receiver can do the same on the copy of the keys received. If the numbers match, you can be sure that the keys were not tampered with while traveling over the public Internet.

Configuring Remote Sites to Use Advanced Security

Users located in remote sites cannot be directly set up for advanced security because the KM Server uses RPC calls, but the users still can be set up for advanced security in an indirect manner. The Key Management Administrator can enter the names of the users located at remote sites from a site that contains the KM Server. The tokens are generated for the individual users in the same manner that users located in the local site are generated. Then, the tokens must be securely transferred to the individual users for final setup of the client. Such transfers of token information are done "out of band" by a phone call, fax, or alternative means of communication.

Verifying that the Key Management Component Is Functioning Correctly

The Microsoft Windows NT Server logs information about the Key Management Server in the applications Event Viewer, which includes information regarding the KM Server functions and duties. If the option is used when launching the KM Server (this is done under the Control Panel, Services icon, within the Startup Parameters option), the events also will be shown in the KM Server command box.

1. Navigate to Administrative Tools.
2. Launch the Event Viewer.
3. From the Log menu, choose Applications.

All log information regarding the Key Management Server that is being recorded in the Event Viewer is identified by an MSexchangeKM entry in the source column.

Viewing Security Logs for Errors or Attempted Breaches

Events that are generated by the Key Management Server are related to granting and revoking of permissions, security violations, and the internal operation of the KM Server. All events logged can be viewed in the Event Viewer.

Backing Up and Maintaining the Key Management Database

All advanced security data is stored in the SECURITY\MGRENT folder. This directory structure should be backed up on a regular basis. Any Microsoft Windows NT-compatible backup application can be used to archive the advanced security directory structure.

The two services that must be running at the start time of the backup are the Information Store service and Directory service.

S/MIME

Microsoft Exchange Server 5.5 supports the S/MIME specification for secure electronic messaging. S/MIME was codeveloped in 1995 by several software vendors and makes it easy to secure messages from prying eyes. Using S/MIME requires an S/MIME-aware client like Outlook Express or Netscape Communicator.

NOTE Support for S/MIME will be included in the first service pack.

CHAPTER 28

Troubleshooting Exchange with Diagnostic Tools

In this chapter

Exchange Server is an intricate product that consists of many components, so it is important in any pilot or installation that you set aside enough time for planning and installation. Many tools exist that can help you plan and analyze an Exchange Server installation. This chapter familiarizes you with some of the tools Exchange provides for diagnosing and troubleshooting various components of Exchange within your organization.

Tracking Exchange Messages

Tracking a message through an Exchange system can be a powerful way of finding link malfunctions. Message tracking can assist support professionals in pinpointing the exact servers or links at fault. It can also be used to determine the quality of service of the Exchange system in areas such as performance, round trips between two servers, alternate route setup, and usage and reliability issues such as lost mail. Exchange provides tools to follow a message through its journey to verify transmissions at certain points of your organization. Here are some common uses for Exchange message tracking:

- Analyzing a message's path through the system to test for proper routing
- Determine the time delay for messages to pass through each connector in their path
- Finding mail that was not appropriately delivered (also called "lost" mail)

All message tracking information is stored by the system attendant on each server when tracking is enabled. The Exchange Server component that actually writes the entries to the log file is the System Attendant.

The location of this log is:

driveletter:\EXCHSRVR\TRACKING.LOG

Tracking logs are kept for an entire day and a new log is created the next day. Tracking must be enabled on each component through which the message flows occur.

For example, to track a message to a remote site connected via the Internet, you would need to enable MTA tracking on both Exchange sites and the Internet mail connector used at each site.

Enabling Message Tracking

Message tracking is a powerful tool to debug any problems with the Exchange System. Following is a discussion of how to enable Message Tracking on various Exchange components:

- *Message Transfer Agent*—To enable tracking for every MTA in a site, select the Enable Message Tracking check box on the MTA Site Configuration General property page.
- *Information Store*—To enable tracking for every information store in a site, click the Enable Message Tracking check box on the Information Store Site Configuration General property page.
- *Microsoft Mail Connector*—To enable tracking for a Microsoft Mail Post Office connector, click the Enable Message Tracking check box on the MS Mail Connector

Interchange property page. You must enable tracking individually for each MS Mail connector in each site.

- *Internet Mail Connector*—To enable tracking for an Internet Mail Connector, click the Enable Message Tracking check box on the Internet Mail Connector Internet Mail property page. You must enable tracking individually for each Internet Mail Connector in each site.

Using Exchange Administrator Tracking Tools

Message tracking allows support professionals to view, sort, and filter the information collected by each server or the messages sent, received, and delivered by the server. Here is how you would use the Message tracking tools from the Exchange administrator program (see Figure 28.1):

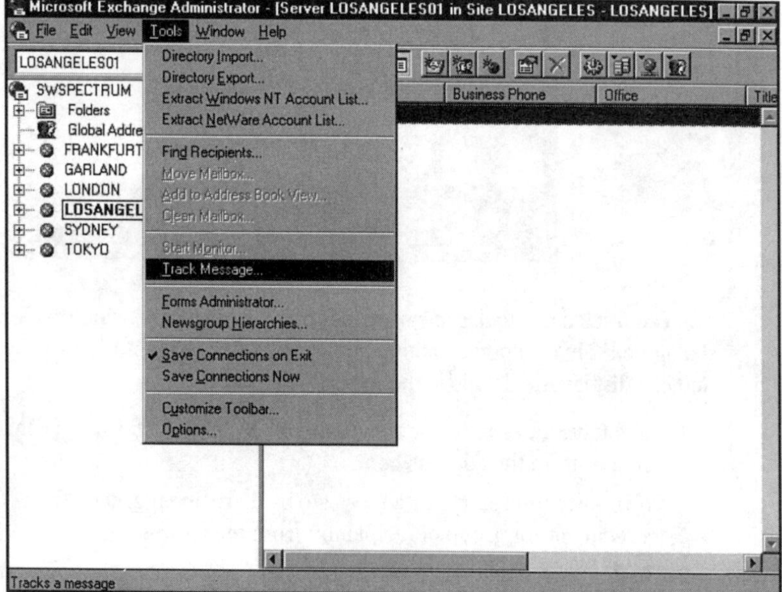

FIG. 28.1
Open the tracking tools from the Exchange Administrator program.

1. Choose Tools, Track Message from the administrator program menu. The Connect to Server dialog box appears.
2. Choose a server in your site to connect to. Preferably, connect to a server with either the sender or recipient of the message you want to track in its address list. The Select Message to Track dialog box appears.
3. In the Select Message to Track dialog box, find the message you want to track. You are given the option to search for messages either by sender or recipients. (In this search tool, the sender or recipients must be listed in the address lists available to this Exchange server.)

If the recipients you need are not listed in the address book, or if you already have a Message ID to use for tracking, click cancel on this page and proceed to the advanced search page (see the Select Message to Track dialog box in Figure 28.2).

FIG. 28.2
Search for message either via sender or recipients (must be visible in the address book).

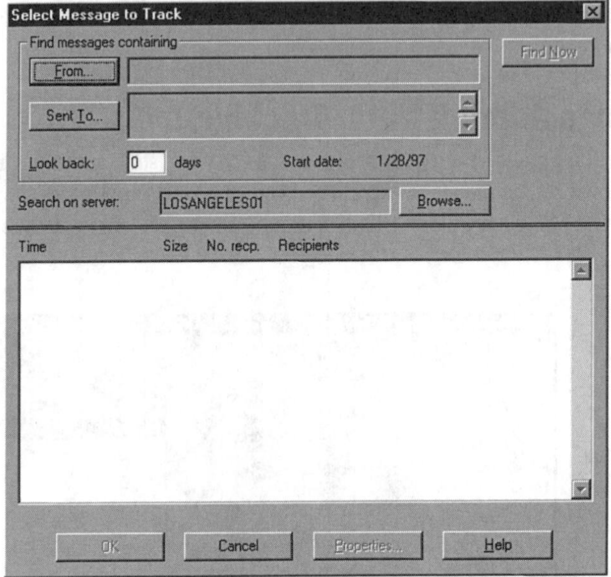

You can track a particular message identified in Step 3 by using the Select Message to Track dialog box. This dialog box allows you to search for a message by either sender or recipient and can display the details of the message:

1. If you want to search for a message by its sender, click the From button and select a sender from the address book.

   If you want to search for a message by its recipients, click the Sent To button and select a recipient (or group of recipients) from the address book.
2. In the Look Back box, enter the number of previous days you want to search for messages. Keep in mind that message tracking must have been enabled on those days for a log to have been created.
3. To connect to a different Exchange server, use the Browse button.
4. When all of your parameters are set, click the Find Now button. All tracking logs for the number of days selected will be searched sequentially. The results are displayed in the bottom window (see Figure 28.3).
5. Select a found message from the list and click Properties to view further property details about it (see Figure 28.4). Click Close when you are done viewing the message's details to return to the Select Message to Track dialog box.
6. Click OK to return to the Message Tracking Center dialog box.

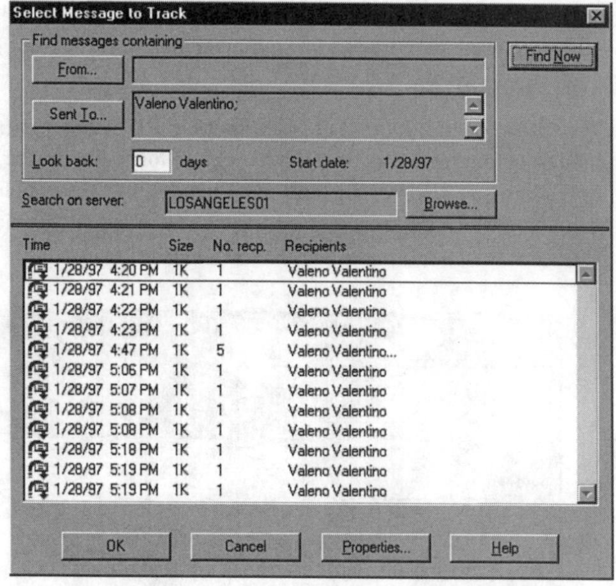

FIG. 28.3
A successful search displays the message matching your criteria in the bottom display window.

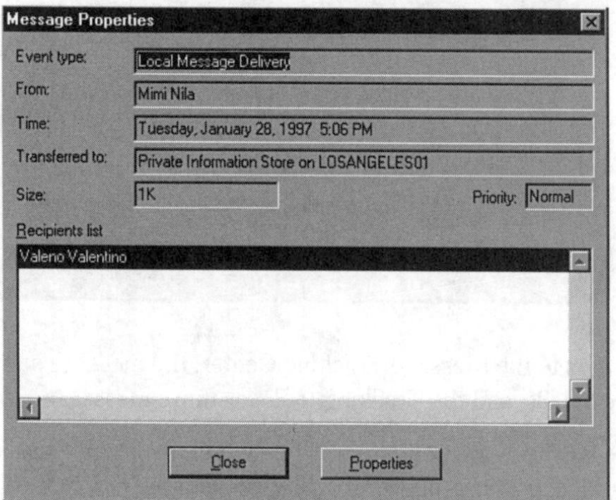

FIG. 28.4
The Message Properties dialog box shows you unique information about the messages your search found.

In the Message Tracking Center dialog box (see Figure 28.5), the Message ID field is now filled in with the appropriate information from the selected message and the Track button is now available.

Using the Message Tracking Center

The Message Tracking Center windows can trace a message (that is found in the search windows from the previous steps) through its path. It executes searches on all the message logs of the Exchange servers that handled it. This includes from the point it originated on an Exchange server (or entered the network through a connector or gateway) to the point it was delivered (or left the network).

Clicking the Track button in the Message Tracking Center dialog box (see Figure 28.5) performs the actual track on the message and fills in the information in the Tracking History box. The Tracking History box displays the steps taken in the process of delivering the message, including the action performed and the Exchange Server involved. A message's Tracking History is the sequence of steps taken to reach a destination.

FIG. 28.5
The Message Tracking Center lets you search for a message in various ways, then trace its route once it is found.

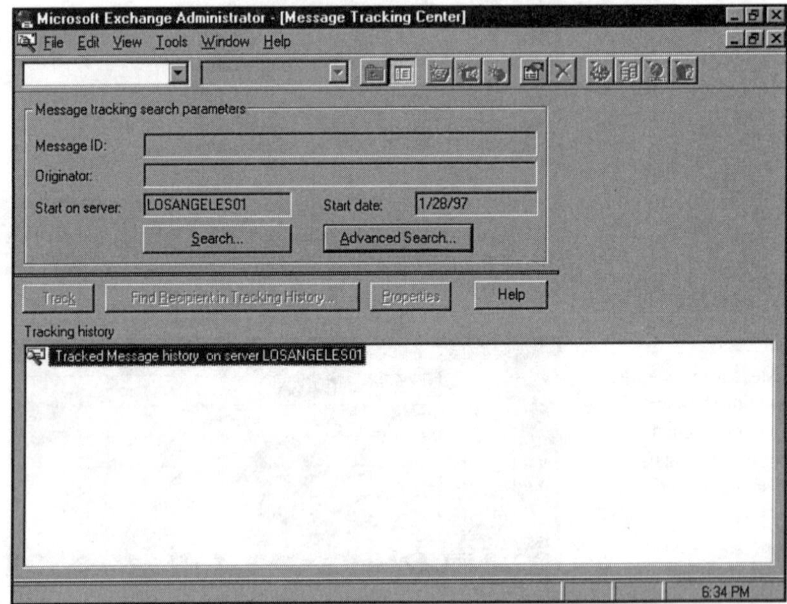

There are two parts to the Message Tracking Center: the message search utilities that also display message details, and the Tracking tools for those messages.

Once a message has been tracked, two additional buttons become available in the Message Tracking Center dialog. What follows is a discussion of the first button, which can search for messages and display message details:

1. The Message Tracking Search Parameters window displays the current message resulting from the search (blank if none). Click Search to bring up the Select a Message to Track dialog box (see previous page).
2. Click Advanced Search to find a message based on different parameters. The dialog box in Figure 28.6 appears.

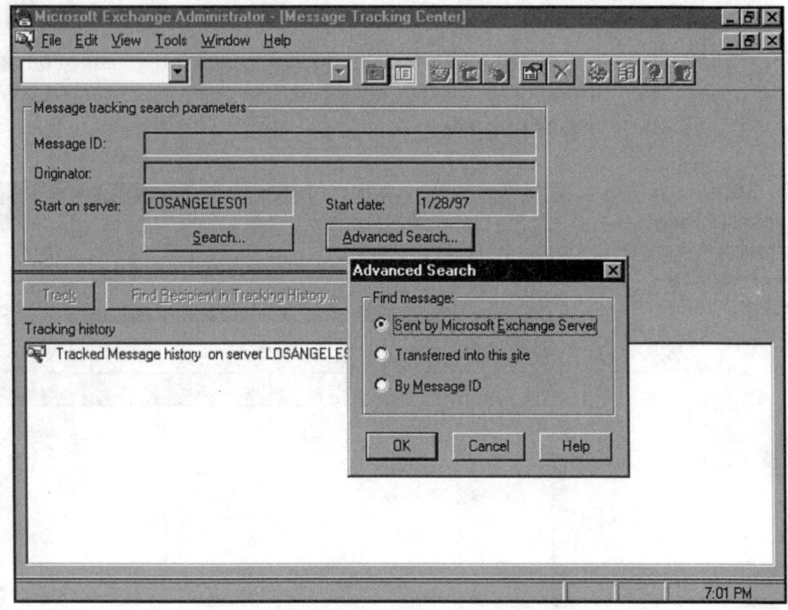

FIG. 28.6
Search for a message using more advanced parameters.

Sent by Exchange Server Selecting Sent by Exchange Server from the Advanced Search dialog box brings up the Select System Message to Track dialog box (see Figure 28.7), which helps you find messages originating from core Exchange components. Typically, these are warning and status messages from the Exchange server to an administrator:

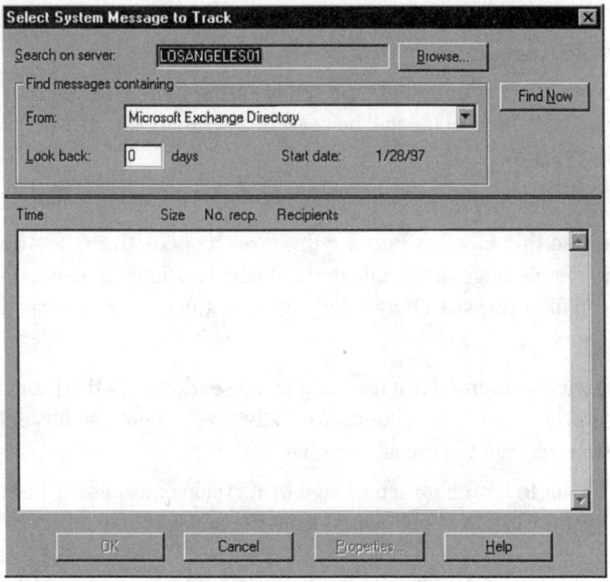

FIG. 28.7
The Select System Message to Track dialog box helps you find messages from core Exchange components.

1. To search on a different Exchange server, use the Browse button (see Figure 28.8).
2. Use the From drop-down menu to choose which Exchange component (Directory, Information Store, System Attendant, Directory Synchronization Agent) to scan for as the message originator.

FIG. 28.8
Select an Exchange component that could have originated the message.

3. In the Look Back box, enter the number of previous days you want to search for messages. Keep in mind that message tracking must have been enabled on those days for a log to have been created.
4. When all of your parameters are set, click the Find Now button. All tracking logs for the number of days selected will be searched sequentially. The results are displayed in the bottom window.
5. Click OK to accept the found messages and return to the Message Tracking Center.

Transferred into this Site Choosing this search option from the Advanced Dialog Box lets you search for a message that originated outside your Exchange organization (see Figure 28.9). You can filter this search by selecting the connector or gateway that a message passed through to enter the system:

1. If you want to search for a message by its sender, click the From button and select a sender from the address book. Normally, you will not use this option if the sender is not a custom recipient in the address list.

   If you want to search for a message by its recipients, click the Sent To button and select a recipient (or group of recipients) from the address book.

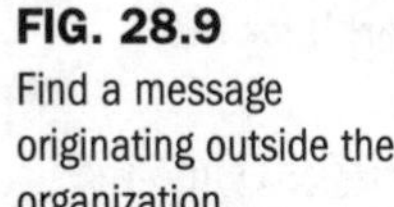

FIG. 28.9
Find a message originating outside the organization.

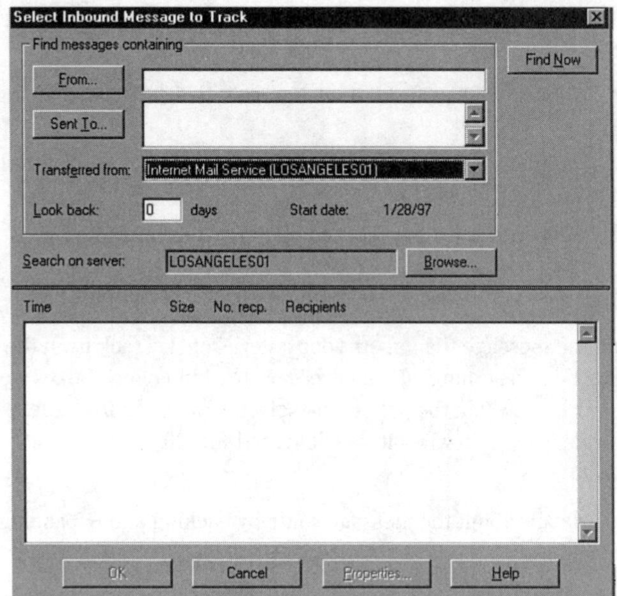

2. Use the Transferred From drop-down menu to select a connector in your site as the inbound gateway for the message you are searching for.
3. In the Look Back box, enter the number of previous days you want to search for messages. Keep in mind that message tracking must have been enabled on those days for a log to have been created.
4. To connect to a different Exchange server use the Browse button.
5. When all of your parameters are set, click the Find Now button. All tracking logs for the number of days selected will be searched sequentially. The results are displayed in the bottom window.
6. Click OK to accept the found messages and return to the Message Tracking Center.

By Message ID If you know the message ID for a particular message, you can find it by selecting this option. A message ID can be found in various Exchange logs, message queues, and also in the Exchange client (see Figure 28.10):

FIG. 28.10
Search for a message by its Exchange Message ID.

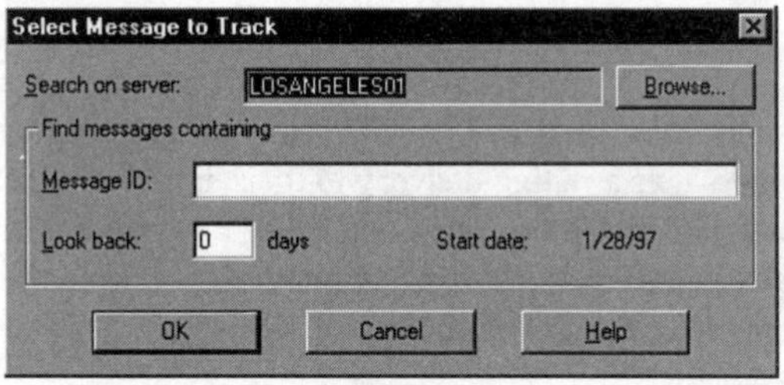

1. Click Browse to select an Exchange server on your site on which to search for the message.
2. Type (or paste if you've copied the message ID from a log file) the message ID into the Message ID text box.
3. Enter a number of days to Look Back into a log file. Start Date will display the first day to start looking for a message.
4. Click OK to search for the selected message and return to the Message Tracking Center.

Tracking a Message

After finding the message that meets your criteria, click Track from the Message Tracking Center dialog box. Assuming all the necessary tracking check boxes were activated, the display window will show you the path of the selected message from the first instant it entered the Exchange organization, to when it was delivered (or left the organization through a connector or gateway).

You can view details about the message route by clicking and expanding the message view in the display window.

Additional Exchange Core Component Troubleshooting Tools

Following is a discussion of some of the Core Troubleshooting Tools to diagnose problems with MS Exchange. These are: MTACHECK and ISInteg.

MTACheck is a support tool that assists the administrators in diagnosing the MTA queues. *ISInteg* is a support tool run on an offline information store that checks the consistency of the information store.

If the MTA queues become corrupt or unable to process a message, it is possible for the MTA to be unable to start. In these situations, a utility called MTACHECK.EXE, which can be found in the \exchsrvr\bin directory, can be used to repair the problem.

MTACHECK.EXE will check the consistency of the MTA queues, check the integrity of all objects, and if necessary, delete corrupt objects. Under most circumstances, the MTACHECK.EXE program will resolve any issues with a problematic MTA.

Using MTACHECK

A message transfer agent uses message queues to store messages. The queues are in essence databases that store messages awaiting delivery to their intended destinations. Occasionally, parts of these databases can become corrupt and cause message transfer errors. MTACHECK scans the queue database for damaged objects, removes them from the queue, and then rebuilds the message queue for correct operation.

MTACHECK can be used primarily in two types of situations:

- Routine tests of MTA queue databases for message integrity.
- Troubleshooting an MTA that has spontaneously stopped and will not properly restart. Running MTACHECK may clear the problem and enable the MTA to restart.

MTACHECK places removed data in a directory called MTACHECK.OUT. The MTACHECK.OUT directory is created in the path:

\EXCHSRVR\MTADATA\MTACHECK.OUT

The data files are created in that directory and given the name: DB*.DAT. MTACHECK creates one file for each damaged piece of data removed.

CAUTION

When removing damaged message files from the queue, MTACHECK may remove messages that cannot be recovered.

MTACHECK is run from the Windows NT command line of the Exchange server you want to scan. The executable is located in the directory:

driveletter:\EXCHSRVR\BIN\MTACHECK.EXE

First, you must manually stop the Message Transfer Agent Service before running this utility (MTACHECK will remind you if you forget). Then, delete the current contents of the MTACHECK.OUT directory. If it is the first time MTACHECK is run, the MTACHECK.OUT is not yet in existence.

NOTE The MTACHECK.OUT directory is automatically created when MTACHECK.EXE is run. ■

Use the following procedure to run MTACHECK on an Exchange server:

1. Stop the Message Transfer Agent service.
2. Remove or delete the contents of the MTACHECK.OUT directory.
3. Run MTACHECK.EXE from the Windows NT command line.
4. Analyze the results and restart the MTA service when appropriate.

Use these optional switches to modify the MTACHECK execution:

/v starts verbose display. Displays progress messages more frequently and in more detail.

/f filename saves progress messages to the specified filename.

/rd stands for Repair Database. This can be a very useful tool when data integrity is in danger.

/rp stands for Repair Postoffice. This switch is similar to rd but it specializes repairing corrupted postoffices. This option is used specifically to repair the database which can be used to save critical data if, in fact, it can be saved. This can repair user data, mailboxes, addresses.

MTACHECK /v /f MTACHECK.LOG is an example of a command that uses both of these switches. It enables the verbose status display, and it stores that display in a file called MTACHECK.LOG.

Using ISINTEG

The ISINTEG utility performs diagnostic and repair functions on the Exchange Information Store databases. This is a function similar to that performed by the MTACHECK utility.

Situations that would warrant use of this utility are:

- The Information Store service will not start properly.
- After recovering an information store database with software other than the built-in Windows NT backup utility

There are three main modes of operation for the ISINTEG:

- *Test Mode*—Runs diagnostic scan of the Information Store databases to detect errors.
- *Test Mode and Fix*—Runs the same diagnostics as normal, but proceeds to fix whatever it can in the process.
- *Patch Mode*—Used when recovering an information store database with a software other than the built-in Windows NT backup utility.

ISINSTEG is run from the Windows NT command line of the Exchange server you want to scan. The executable is located in the directory:

driveletter:\EXCHSRVR\BIN\ISINTEG.EXE

Use these optional switches to modify the ISINTEG execution:

-? Displays this options list

-pri Runs diagnostics on the private information store; by default, this is the test that will run

-pub Runs diagnostics on the public information store

-fix Runs diagnostics and corrects any errors that it can (also called Check & Correct)

-verbose Displays more detailed diagnostic information

-l (filename) Stores log information under a different file name; by default, INISTEG.PRI and INISTEG.PUB are the log files

-test testname,... Runs a specific ISINTEG test; all available tests can be viewed with the -? Switch

Using Diagnostic Logging

Diagnostic logging is a tool that lets you zero in on messaging problems that plague your system. These logging settings are set in the Diagnostic Logging property page for each component. Diagnostics are logged into the Windows NT event logs, which can then be viewed with the NT Event Viewer.

The following Exchange components have a diagnostic logging property page for their pertinent system services:

- Directory Service
- Directory Synchronization
- Internet Mail Connector
- Information store (both public and private)
- cc:Mail Connection
- Microsoft Mail Connector (including the MSMI)
- Message Transfer Agent
- IMAP4, NNTP, and POP3 Protocols

The Diagnostic Logging property page for each Exchange server shows a unified list of that server's logging settings. To view this property page, highlight the server you want to view and choose Properties from the File menu.

Subcomponents and Categories

Categories are the various functions of each Exchange service. You specify various levels of logging on a per-category basis. Different categories within a service (or subcomponent of that service) can be logged separately to track a problem to a specific function.

Some services (for example, the Information store) also have subcomponents. Subcomponents are logging subdivisions beneath each Exchange service. Each Subcomponent also has a set of categories that can be logged individually.

For example, the Information Store service (MSExchangeIS) has four subcomponents. Each subcomponent (System, Public, Private, and Internet Protocols) pertains to roles of that service. Each subcomponent also has a set of categories pertaining to its specific functioning. You would set a logging level for each category depending on the type of problem you are encountering (see Figure 28.11).

NOTE You can log the access of NNTP, IMAP4, and POP3 clients to the Information Stores. ■

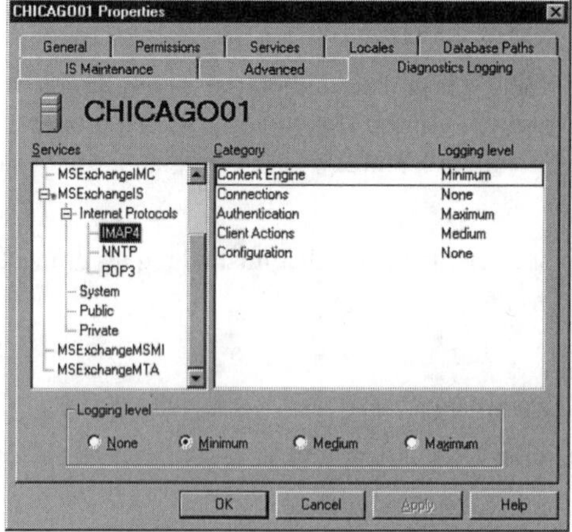

FIG. 28.11
Diagnostic logging settings on a specific server.

Logging Levels

Each Exchange component enables you to set various levels of logging. These levels determine what type and how critical an event must be before it is recorded. Every logging level includes events from the level above it. The following are the logging levels available for all Exchange components:

None (level 0): Log only critical events or error events. By default, this is set for every Exchange component.

Minimum (level 1): Log only very-high-level events.

Medium (level 2): Log important sequences of events.

Maximum (level 3): Log everything. This will log the complete operation of the service and even include certain lines of code from a service. Use only when you have narrowed the problem down to a couple of categories.

The level numbers pertain to what Windows NT defines the event to be.

Your decision to change logging levels should be based on tracking down a problem to a particular service and category. If you have a suspicion that a certain component is the culprit for a certain error, then start increasing logging levels gradually for a fewer number of categories.

For example, say that you are not properly receiving Internet mail anymore, yet all other types of messaging data are delivered without any problems. This would naturally suggest that you should increase the logging levels on all the categories of the Internet Mail Connector and not initially on the MTA or Information store. Then you proceed to narrow down the list of categories and increase the logging levels as you get closer to the source of the problem.

NOTE Use the high logging levels (maximum and medium) sparingly and only when you have narrowed down the problem to a few categories. These settings generate a large amount of events and tend to fill logging space quickly. ■

Using Windows NT Event Viewer

For review, an *event* is any notable incident within the Windows NT operating environment. Critical events will trigger an immediate on-screen notification to the administrator. However, the more run-of-the-mill events are only logged. These need not necessarily be errors, just occurrences worth recording. Windows NT logs three main types of events:

- *System events*—Status of system services and other system operations
- *Security events*—logons and permission auditing
- *Application events*—operational errors

The logging levels set for each Exchange component determine which events are actually logged.

Keep in mind that Event Viewer is a general-purpose diagnostic tool. Many of the errors generated for Exchange are sometimes vague to provide a solid solution. You should use the other tools in this chapter to gather information before taking any troubleshooting action.

PART IV

The Exchange Client

CHAPTER 29

Installing and Configuring Outlook

In this chapter

Outlook is your personal information manager. Outlook enhances the features available in the Exchange Client and Schedule+. Not only can you manage your messages and appointments under Outlook, but you also can keep track of your activities, contacts, and documents. Outlook doesn't stop there, however. In your Exchange organization, you can set up Outlook to share information with others and enable others to manage your information as well. This chapter covers how to get Outlook up and running.

Preparing to Install Outlook

Before running the setup program, consider a few questions that affect your client installation strategy. The questions are as follows:

- Do you want your installation to be server-based, or do you want all the executables to reside on the client?
- Do you want to install from the CD or over the network?
- Would you like the administrator to preconfigure client options or have the users choose their own settings?

The answers to these questions determines your approach to setting up Outlook. This chapter discusses each of the preceding installation and configuration issues, so that the answers to the questions are clearer.

Installing through an Installation Share

An installation share enables you to run the setup files directly off a hard drive without using a CD-ROM. You can locate an installation point to run setup on a server or on the local machine. After loading all the files, you then, in the case of a file server, share the directory with an appropriate title.

Follow these steps to install Outlook using an installation share:

1. You first need to copy the Outlook source file from the CD-ROM onto your hard drive.
2. To run an installation from the server, find the SETUP.EXE file and execute it.
3. The setup application runs as normal from that point.

With a server-based installation, all users use a server-based copy of Outlook. There are advantages and disadvantages in this scenario:

- *Pros*—You can perform fewer configurations on the clients. You can maintain all settings on the server. More change control over the installations.
- *Cons*—You have more LAN traffic. Each time a user loads Outlook, it must run across the network. Users may see a dramatic decrease in performance. Outlook cannot function while the server or network is down. Outlook does not take advantage of the client/server model efficiently.

Outlook System Requirements

Cross-Platform usability is greatly enhanced in Microsoft Outlook version 8.03, which ships with Exchange 5.5. New additions are a 16-bit version for Windows 3.x and a MacOS version (System 7.6 or higher). The following are the minimum requirements for your computer to run Outlook.

Hardware:

- 486 or higher processor
- 8MB of RAM for Windows 95, 16MB of RAM for Windows NT
- 24MB of hard disk space for Outlook files, 31MB required for a typical installation
- VGA or higher-resolution video adapter
- Mouse or compatible pointing device

Operating System:

- Windows 3.x
- Apple Macintosh (system 7.6 or higher)
- Windows 95
- Windows NT Workstation 3.51 Service Pack 5
- Windows NT Workstation 4.0 Service Pack 2

Saving Your Personalized Information

You can configure Outlook to use the personalized files you have under the following clients: Exchange Client in Windows 95, Windows Messaging in Windows NT, or the updated Exchange Client from Exchange Server 4.0.

In the following list, you find the default extensions for a user's personal files.

- *.PST* The file where all your personal folders and messages are stored.
- *.PAB* The file where all your Personal Address Book entries are stored.
- *.SCD* The file where all your Schedule+ information is stored.

NOTE If you are upgrading your client from Microsoft Mail 3.x, you need to save your *.MMF and *.SCH files. These files contain your mail folders, messages, and Schedule+ information. They are used to migrate all your information into Outlook ■

Installing Outlook

The entire install or setup process is very easy. All you have to do is follow the instructions in the dialog boxes. Ample help and various tips are available as you follow the setup screens.

The first step in the Microsoft Outlook procedure is to select the directory or folder into which you want the client to be installed (see Figure 29.1). You can either go with the default, which is C:\Program Files\Microsoft Office, or you may change that by choosing Change Folder.

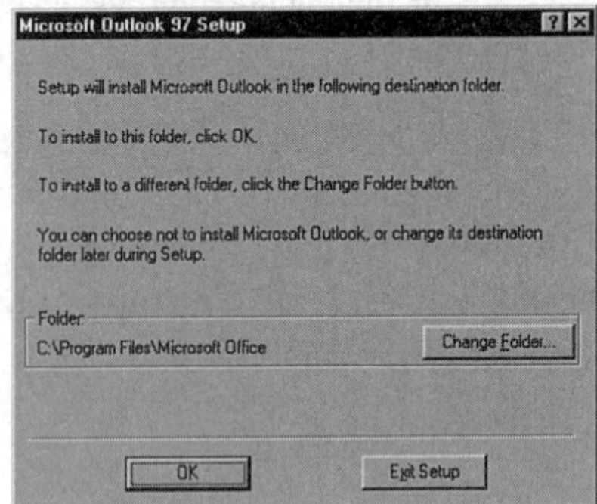

FIG. 29.1 Select the Destination Folder in which to store your messages.

At the next screen you are presented with two choices (see Figure 29.2):

- *Typical* takes the most commonly used settings and installs them.
- *Custom* gives you the opportunity to pick and choose the components you require.

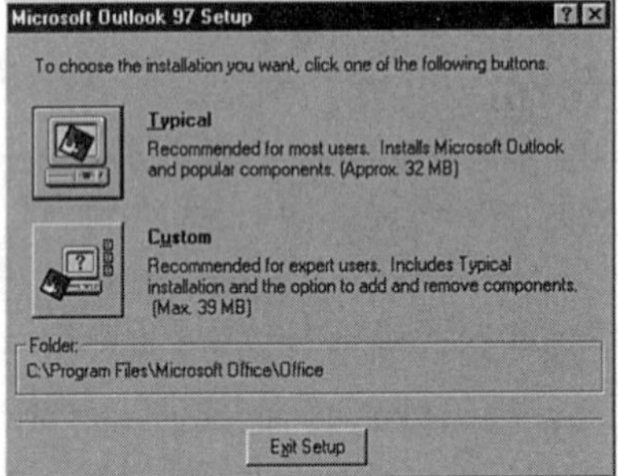

FIG. 29.2 Choose the type of Outlook setup.

Choose the installation method that fits your needs. If you are the adventurous sort and want to see all the options available, go down the custom path. This option enables you to pick only the options that fit your requirements.

Table 29.1 Typical Outlook Installation

Option	Installed?
Microsoft Outlook Program Files	Yes
Office Assistant	Yes
Microsoft Exchange Server Support	Yes
Visuals for Forms Design	No

Option	**Installed?**
Find Fast	Yes
Holidays and Forms	Yes
Lotus Organizer Converters	No
Microsoft Outlook Help	Yes
Schedule+ Support Files	Yes
MS Info	Yes
Spelling Checker	Yes

At this point you have the following two options (see Figure 29.3):

- *Change Option* enables you to view and choose the options within the highlighted choice.
- *Select All* does just what it says; it picks all the available options.

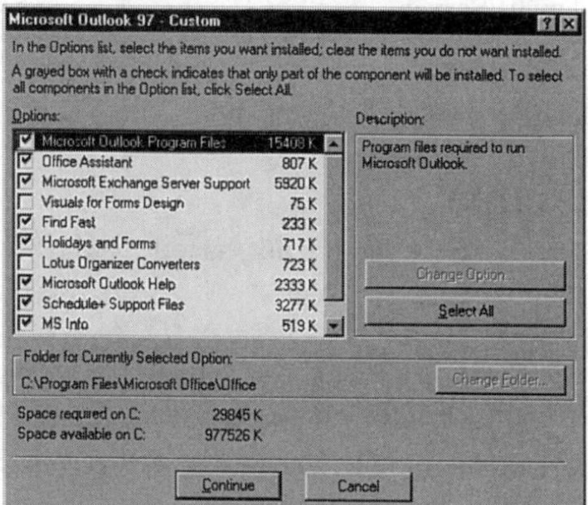

FIG. 29.3
Outlook Options available during setup.

At this screen you can specify what components of Outlook you want to load.

After you have made all the selections you want to use during setup, you can choose Continue to install the Outlook files. At this point you see the setup progress bar and the various screens introducing the latest features. When you see the Completed Suf?essfully screen (see Figure 29.4), click OK, and you return to your desktop display.

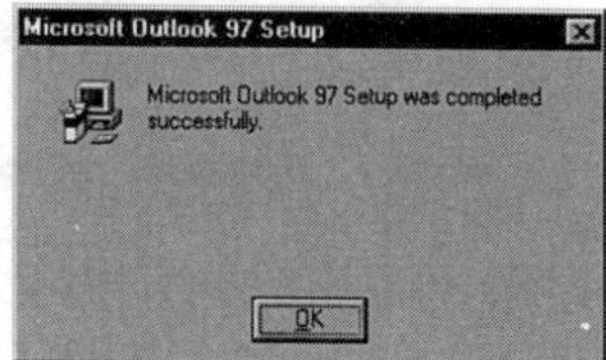

FIG. 29.4
Click OK.

Configuring Outlook

Now that you installed Outlook, you need to configure the program to work with your messaging environment. Start by installing some of the most common services to see how you configure the services. If you have any other Messaging Application Programming Interface (MAPI)-compliant messaging services, the configuration is essentially the same.

Knowing Your Messaging Services

Before you start configuring Outlook, take a few minutes to inventory what messaging services you want to access. Due to Outlook's many capabilities, you can receive messages from many sources other than the Exchange Server. You can also choose:

- Internet Mail (POP3 Server)
- Microsoft Fax
- Netscape Internet Transport
- Lotus Notes Mail
- Microsoft Network Online Service
- CompuServe Online Service
- Other MAPI-Compliant Mail Packages

Creating Your Outlook Profile

Your profile tells Outlook what services you will use, as well as where your personal files are located.

Before starting Outlook, you need to set up your profile. Follow these steps:

1. From Control Panel, double-click the Mail icon.
2. Choose Add to configure a new profile. The next screen you see is the Setup Wizard dialog box (see Figure 29.5).
3. Place check marks next to the information services you want to use. You also have the choice of manually configuring the information services. This option enables you to answer questions in a non-wizard style manner. The preferred method is to check the boxes and press the Next button. In this example, you select Exchange Server and Internet Mail.
4. In the next screen, you must enter a profile name. You should choose a name other than MS Exchange Settings. After you enter a profile name, click Next (see Figure 29.6).
5. Enter the name of your Exchange Server. You do not have to enter the normal backslashes.
6. Enter the Mailbox Name. This is set up on the Exchange Server and is usually either a common name or a company standard.

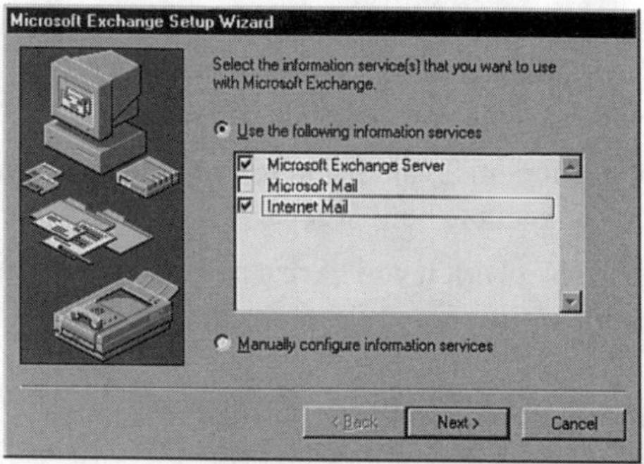

FIG. 29.5 Information services available to add to your profile.

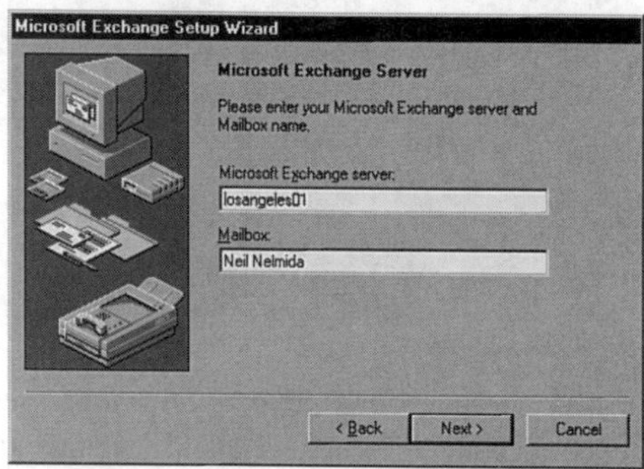

FIG. 29.6 Fields to enter your Exchange server and mailbox name.

7. You are now asked whether you will travel with this computer (see Figure 29.7). Your options are:
   - *Yes*—The setup program prompts you to choose whether you want to connect or work offline when you launch Outlook.
   - *No*—If you use a computer that normally is connected to a network, answering No bypasses some of the offline, mail-related issues.

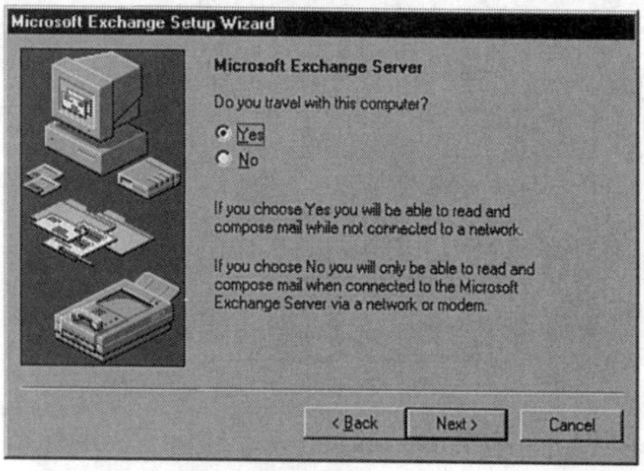

FIG. 29.7 Will you be working offline?

8. If at the last screen you chose Yes, you travel with this computer, you are then asked how you plan to connect to the Internet Mail server (see Figure 29.8). The best way to answer this question is to consider your normal mode of usage:
   - *Modem*—Choose Modem if you dial in from home or are on the road a lot and use your modem to connect to your server.
   - *Network*—Choose Network if you have a network interface card in your mobile computer, and this is the way you connect to your server while in the office.

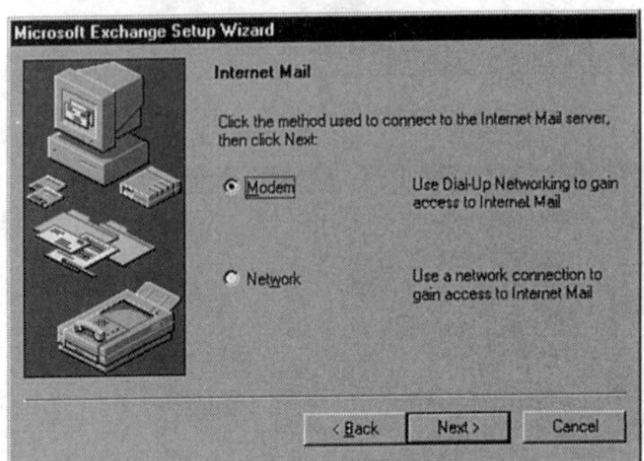

FIG. 29.8
Are you going to be using Dial Up Networking?

When you select Modem for your access method to the Internet mail server, the setup program offers you the choice of connections. If you have Dial Up Connections already defined, the Wizard enables you to choose from a drop-down list box. If you don't have predefined Dial Up Connections, or if you want to use another existing Dial Up Connection, choose New. This enables you to create a new connection profile.

The next screen asks you to enter the name or IP address of your Internet Mail server (see Figure 29.9). This is the server on which you have an Internet- or SMTP-style mail account.

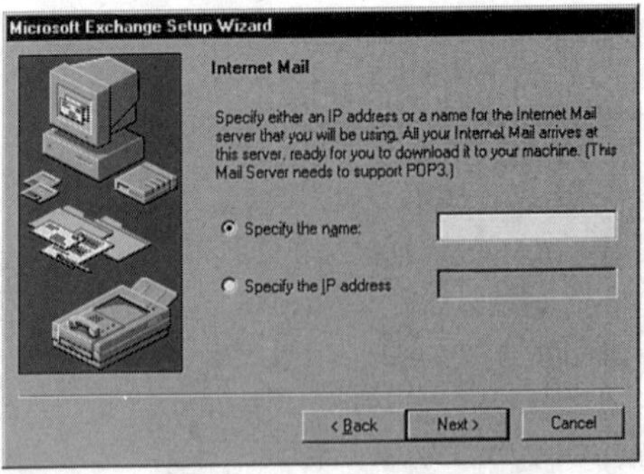

FIG. 29.9
Enter the name or IP address for the Internet Mail server.

The server from which you want to receive your Internet mail needs to support POP3 mail. This is a standard that enables other servers to interface and receive mail as a proxy service.

The next screen gives you the option of either choosing Off-line or Automatic.

- *Off-line*— Uses the Remote Mail feature of Outlook. This feature enables you to view the headers and sizes of messages before downloading them.

NOTE This option is especially nice when you are on the road with a slow modem, and someone sends you a 10MB PowerPoint presentation. ■

- *Automatic*—Downloads all incoming messages (regardless of size) and sends all outgoing mail. This method is fine if you have a fast modem and adequate space.

The next screen asks you to enter your account and name (see Figure 29.10). Your email address is either the account or alias defined on the POP3 server. This is in the normal Internet mail format of *username@domain*. Your name may already be entered from a previous setup or you may enter it now.

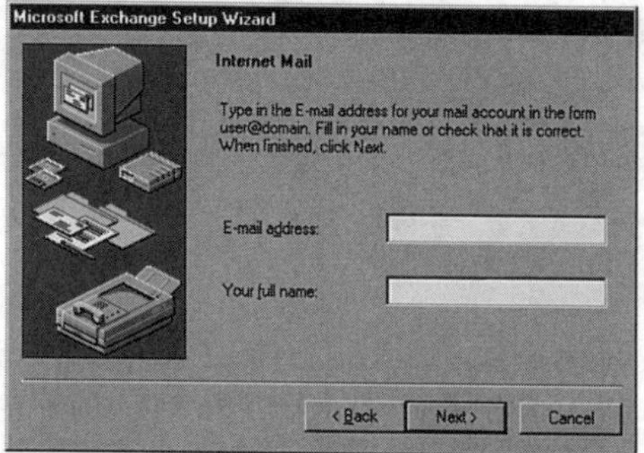

FIG. 29.10
This screen holds your Internet mail account information.

NOTE The name you enter displays as the sender on all your Internet mail, so put in a nickname if that is what you prefer. ■

Now you are at the point of entering your actual Internet mail account information. The Mailbox name is the account on the POP3 server. The Password is the password for this account (see Figure 29.11).

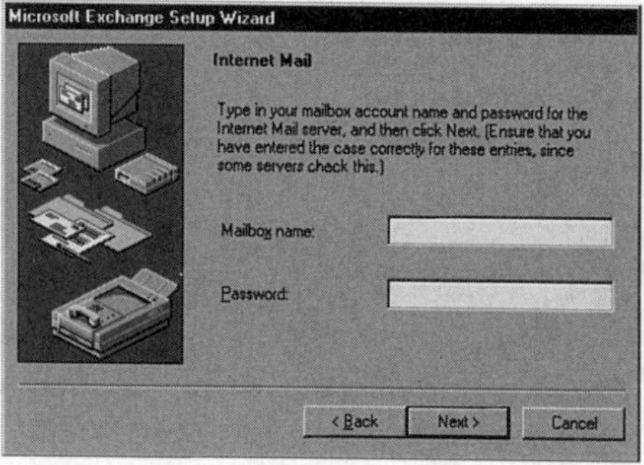

FIG. 29.11
Your Internet mail (POP) account information.

NOTE Ensure that you enter the account name and password correctly (including case-sensitivity) because most POP3 servers are located on UNIX servers. The UNIX operating system is case-sensitive in all fields. ■

Now you are given the chance of either using a preexisting Personal Address Book or creating a new one (see Figure 29.12). You can enter the path to your old Personal Address Book if you have one, or you can Browse for it. If you do not have a Personal Address Book, as is the case in a new install, you can choose Next and the setup program creates a Personal Address Book for you in the default location.

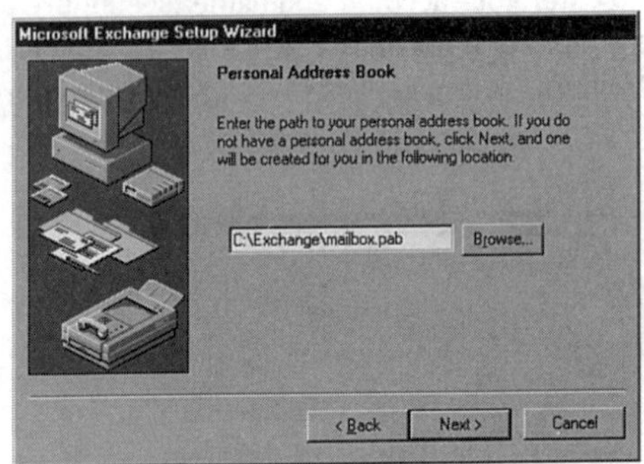

FIG. 29.12 Enter name for Personal Address Book.

NOTE If you want to keep your Personal Address Book in another directory, you may enter it here. This is a good idea if you store all data files in a certain place for backup or security reasons. It is also a good idea to change the default name of the file; *username*.PAB for example. ■

The next-to-the-last screen enables you to specify whether you want Outlook to start up when you first log on to your computer.

Congratulations! You made it to the wrap-up screen (see Figure 29.13). All that remains now is to select Finish. You may use Outlook with all the services you selected and configured.

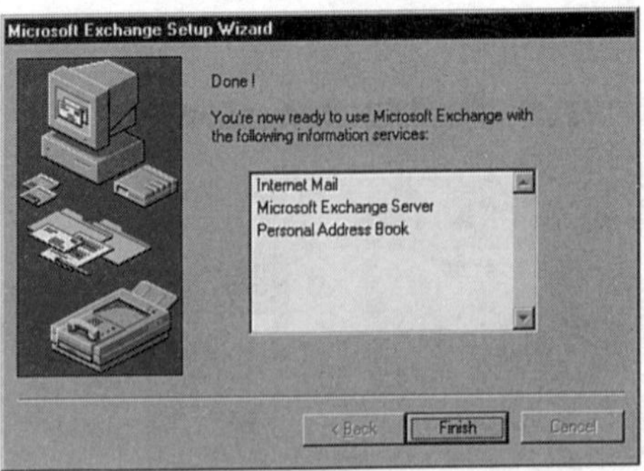

FIG. 29.13 This screen lists all your Information Services for this profile.

You are now ready to run Outlook. All you have to do is double-click your Outlook icon, and you are on your way to utilizing the full power of this versatile tool.

Configuring Offline Folders

If you expect to use Outlook while you are away from your local network, you need to configure an offline folder on your local hard drive. You must create this folder, essentially a replica of your server mailbox, before you can work offline. To create an offline folder:

1. From Control Panel, double-click the Mail icon.
2. Select the profile you want to configure with the offline folder.
3. Under the Services tab, select Microsoft Exchange Server, and then click Properties.
4. Under the Advanced tab, click Offline Folder File Settings.
5. In the File box, type in the path and name of the offline folder. Make sure that the extension for the folder is .OST (see Figure 29.14). When you finish, click OK.

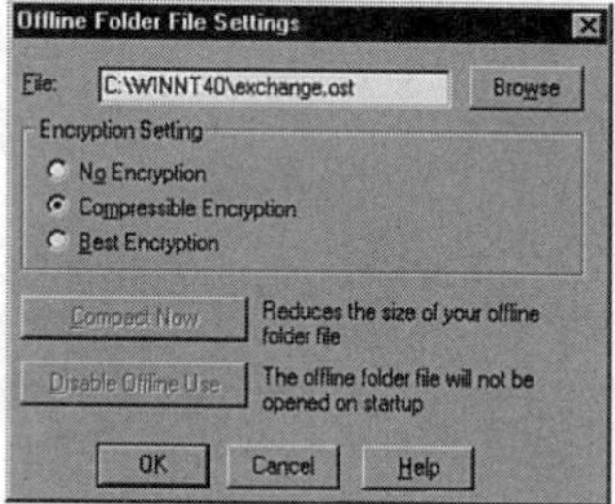

FIG. 29.14
Enter filename for an offline folder.

6. You may be notified that the file does not exist. Click Yes to create the new folder.
7. Save the changes made to the profile by clicking OK in the Microsoft Exchange Server window and clicking OK in your Profile Properties window.

Now you have an .OST file on your machine that can be synchronized with your server store. You are able to work offline, view, and edit your mail, as well as compose new messages. You can also synchronize all this activity the next time you are online ●

CHAPTER 30

Using Outlook

In this chapter

This chapter covers the basic features of Outlook. Whether you are using Outlook just as an e-mail client or as the tool to organize your company, you will find Outlook very powerful, but surprisingly easy to use. Furthermore, if you are familiar with using the Exchange Client and Schedule+, you will find that Outlook has integrated these functions into one nicely organized package.

Configuring Outlook Views

The Outlook screen contains two main windows (see Figure 30.1). The left window is the Outlook Bar that looks like a vertical toolbar with icons to your favorite items sorted in Outlook groups. The right window is called the Information Viewer. When you choose an icon from the Outlook Bar, the contents of that folder are displayed here.

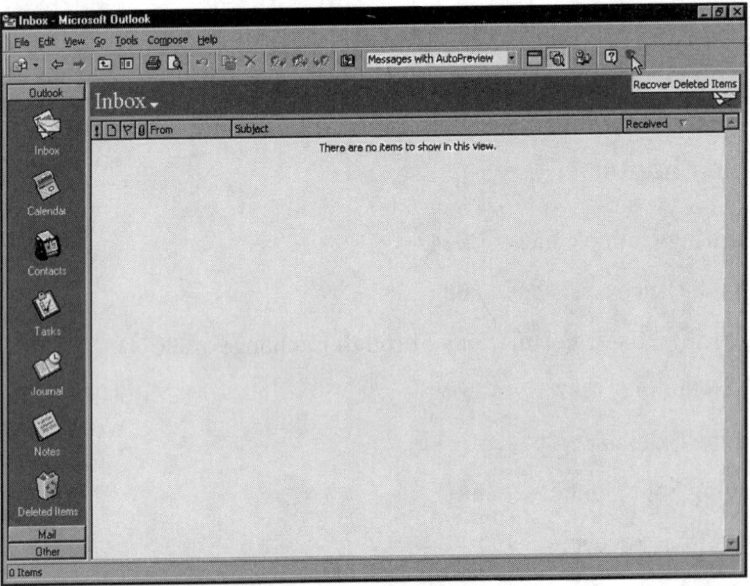

FIG. 30.1
The Outlook main view.

When you first run Outlook, you will find three default groups on the Outlook Bar: the Outlook Group, the Mail Group, and the Other Group. In Tables 30.1, 30.2, and 30.3, you will see which folders have been created in each group.

The Outlook Group has the set of folders that are the main features of Outlook (see Table 30.1).

Table 30.1 Outlook Group

Icon	What You Can Do
Universal Inbox	View the contents of your Inbox folder.
Calendar	View your calendar. The calendar can be viewed in Day, Week, or Month format.
Contacts	View the contact list in the Address Card view and other predefined views.
Tasks	Open your tasks list. Here you can view details such as the person to whom a task was assigned, whether the task is active or overdue, and more.
Journal	Open your Journal. You can manually add Journal entries or view entries grouped in various ways. Contact activities like e-mail, faxes, meeting requests, phone calls, and usage of Microsoft Office documents can be automatically tracked.
Notes	You can post small, miscellaneous notes in the Notes folder. Works like regular sticky notes.

The Mail Group contains the set of folders pertaining to e-mail (see Table 30.2).

Table 30.2 Mail Group

Icon	What You Can Do
Inbox	View your incoming mail.
Sent Items	View copies of outgoing mail.
Outbox	View outgoing mail waiting to be picked up.
Deleted Items	View mail and other items waiting to be deleted.

The Other Group is a group of folders that help you navigate around your computer system (see Table 30.3). This group is similar to Windows Explorer in Windows 95 and NT 4.0.

Table 30.3 Other Group

Icon	Action
My Computer	Accesses your computer's hard drives, floppy drives, mapped network drives, folders, and other files on your computer.
My Documents	Opens your folder for documents created using Microsoft Office and other Microsoft products.
Favorites	Displays your shortcuts to Internet links and other items.

Using the Office Assistant

When you open Outlook for the first time, you will see the Office Assistant (see Figure 30.2). The Office Assistant is an animated character that is helpful in several ways. It can search for an answer to any questions you may have about Outlook. Also, it can provide shortcuts that you may not be aware of or recommendations on how to make your work a little easier. You can hide the Office Assistant by clicking the X in the toolbar above it. You can display the Office Assistant by clicking the Office Assistant button on the toolbar.

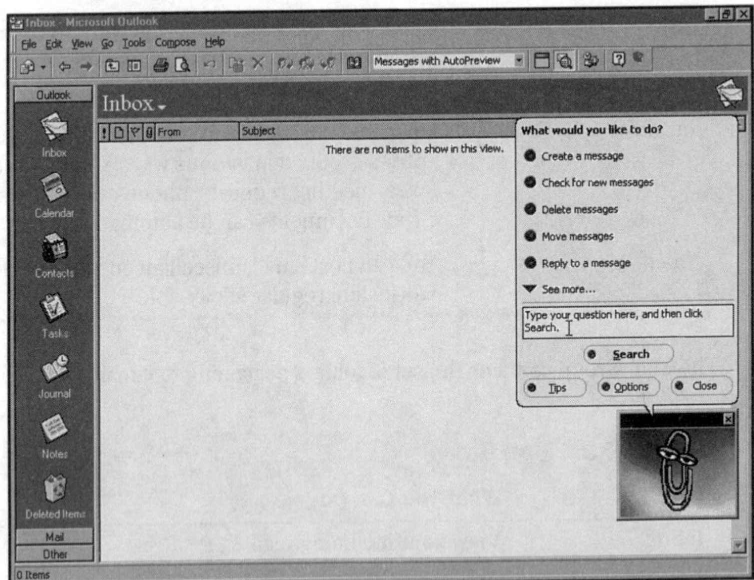

FIG. 30.2
The Office Assistant.

Configuring Folder Permissions Through Exchange

One of the best features in Outlook, when used in an Exchange organization, is the capability to set view permissions for your main Outlook folders: Inbox, Calendar, Contacts, Tasks, Journal, and Notes. With this capability, Outlook moves from being a standalone product to a powerful information manager for you and your organization. However, you don't need to be worried that someone else could be monitoring your Outlook folders. Initially, all of these folders can only be viewed by you, the mailbox owner.

By setting the proper permissions, you unlock a world of possibilities. You can allow others to view your schedule only to see when you are free or busy, or you can delegate authority to others to manage your schedule and other Outlook features as well. Figure 30.3 shows the Permission page.

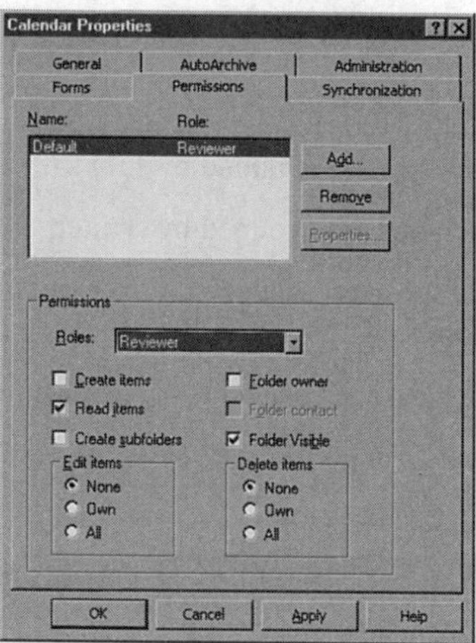

FIG. 30.3
The Permissions page on the Calendar folder properties page.

Using the Inbox

The Inbox folder is the most important feature in Outlook for helping you communicate with others. From here, you can send and receive electronic messages. These messages can be as simple as a memo or as complex as a formatted message with attachments or electronic forms. In the Inbox, you can sort your messages either manually or automatically. This is great for users who are tired of clutter and want to impose some structure and organization on their inbox.

A great place to start is understanding the types of views available to you...before your inbox gets completely out of hand. You can adjust these views as needed to make your inbox attractive and functional for you (see Figure 30.4).

Table 30.4 lists the predefined views and describes how your messages are displayed in each view.

Table 30.4 Inbox Views

View	Display Results
Messages	A list of messages.
Messages with AutoPreview	A list of messages with a preview of the first three lines of each message.
By Message Flag	Grouped by message flag.
Last Seven Days	Only those messages received during the past seven days are shown.
Flagged for Next Seven Days	Only those messages flagged for follow-up during the next seven days are shown.

continues

Table 30.4 Continued

View	Display Results
By Conversation Topic	Messages are grouped by subject.
By Sender	Messages are grouped by sender.
Unread Messages	Only those messages that have not been read yet are shown.
Sent To	The message recipients are shown rather than the sender.
Message Timeline	Icons arranged by date sent on a timeline are shown.

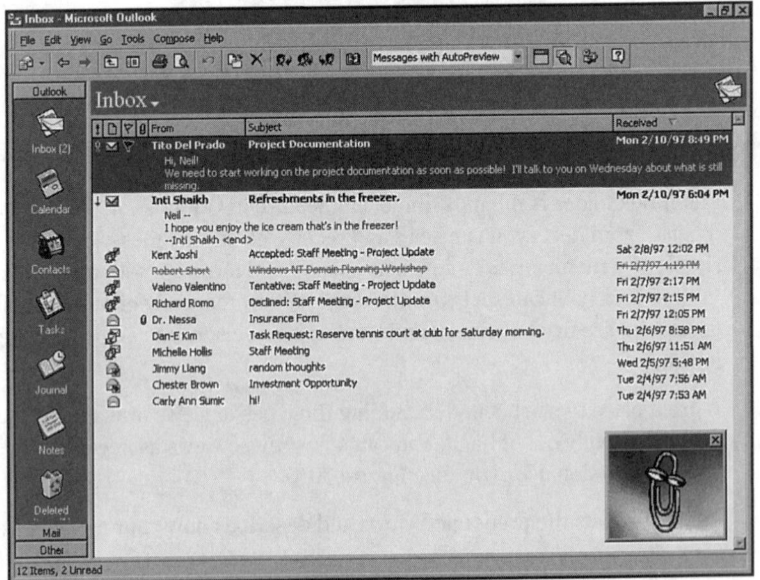

FIG. 30.4 Various messages in your inbox.

Creating Messages

In Outlook, you can start creating a new message in a number of ways. The screen that appears while composing messages is actually a mail form (see Figure 30.5). This form is a guide to help you get your message out to the appropriate recipient (person).

You can start a new mail message in a variety of ways. One way has already been described. Also, typing Ctrl+Shift+M from anywhere in Outlook will bring up a new mail form. A third method is to right-click the Information Viewer and choose New Mail Message from the menu. All other Outlook folders have the same set of shortcuts to open a new item.

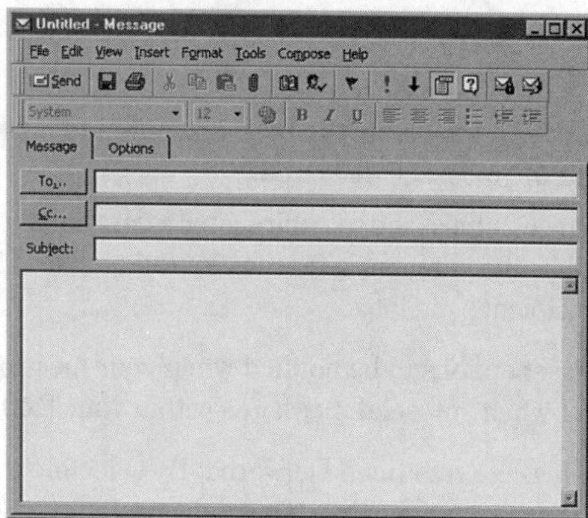

FIG. 30.5
The message page of the mail form.

NOTE A message needs only a valid name or distribution list in the To, Cc, or Bcc box for it to be deliverable. All other fields are optional.

The following sections will help you understand how to create and track your message. After you have configured all of the options, you can send the message by clicking the Send button on the toolbar or typing Ctrl+Enter.

Configuring Information Under the Message Tab of Your Message You have many options to configure before sending out a message. First, you need to decide who will get your message. You can type into the To name field or click the button and select one from the address book.

TIP By default, the Bcc field is not shown when you compose a message. You can activate (or view) it by selecting the item from the View menu.

In the Subject box, you can type in a subject for this message.

In the Message Area, you can start creating your message. Outlook supports rich text, so your message text can range from plain black text to something creative with color, different fonts, and attachments.

NOTE It is helpful to know what type of e-mail system and client your recipients are using. By default, Outlook uses RTF (rich text format). If your recipients cannot handle this type of format, you may need to keep your messages in plain text format. If you don't, what you may consider hard work and creativity will show up as garbage to the recipient of your message.

The Options Page In Outlook you can control many characteristics of your message. Under the Options page, you can set various details about your message.

General Options The General Options section helps you set notifications about your message. You can alert the recipient of the importance of your message. You can also control any replies you are expecting from the recipient about your message.

Delivery Options You can set options on when to deliver a message and how that message is handled after a particular day:

- Do Not Deliver Before: You can create the message now and have it wait for the actual day and time you want the message delivered.
- Expires After: You can set a message to expire after a certain day and time. This is great for messages that will be meaningless after the expiration date. The message will then be "grayed out" in the recipient's mailbox.

Tracking Options You can set options to be notified when your message was delivered and read. This option works best when you send messages within your Exchange organization:

- Tell Me When This Message Has Been Delivered: By selecting this option, you will receive a message that your message has been delivered.
- Tell Me When This Message Has Been Read: You will receive a message when this message has been read by the recipient.

Message Flag In Outlook, you can enhance a message by inserting a message flag. Suppose you really want to stress the importance of the message before the recipient reads through the whole message: A message flag can do exactly that. A flag appears in the recipient's inbox, and a brief description of the reason for the flag appears under the message page when the recipient opens the message. You can add your own flag to any messages you send out by clicking the message flag button on the toolbar. In the Flag Message dialog box, you can use the predefined flags or type in your own flag. You can also set a date and time that the message should be acted on.

Reading Messages

In Outlook, reading and sorting messages can be an overwhelming task if you don't manage your inbox efficiently. Messages that appear in your inbox may not be ordinary messages. Some messages have higher importance than others. Some may need special attention and require you to respond immediately to an appointment, meeting, or task request. Other messages may be important to you because they are responses to requests you sent out previously. You have many tools available in inbox to help you keep track of all these events.

You can open a message by double-clicking the message you want to read. Depending on the message options set by the sender, you may see a note about the message in the gray comment area above the message header.

Responding to Messages If you need to take further action on a message, you have three options:

- Reply: You can reply only to the sender of the message. This is helpful if you want to keep your response private from other recipients that have this message.

- Reply to All: If you choose Reply to All, your response is sent to everyone in the To and Cc line.
- Forward: You can send the current message to someone else without notifying the sender.

In all of these options, you can still edit the message as if you were creating a new message. Responding to a message saves you the hassle of typing in the correct e-mail address.

Sorting Messages: Arrow or Groups You can sort messages in many ways, depending on what you feel is most useful to you. You have two options on how to organize your messages.

Arrow When you choose to sort messages by field, an arrow appears after you click the field heading. Messages can be sorted in ascending or descending order. In a text field, such as the Subject field, an ascending sort (the up arrow) sorts information from A to Z. A descending sort (the down arrow) will sort from Z to A. In a field such as the Received field, the up arrow indicates messages sorted from oldest message to newest message. The down arrow indicates messages sorted from newest to oldest.

Groups You can sort your messages by groups in two ways:

1. Under the View menu, click the Group By box.
2. Drag the column header to the Drag a Column Header Here to Group By That Column box.

Using the Calendar

When you open Calendar for the first time, you see three sections in your Information view: your schedule for the current day, called the *Appointment area*; a calendar with a view of the current month and next month, called the *Date Navigator*; and your taskpad (see Figure 30.6). You can adjust the current view in several ways. You can change the width of your schedule for the current day by dragging the vertical bar that separates it from the other two sections to the left or right. By moving this bar, you increase or decrease the number of calendar months you can see, and you adjust the size of your taskpad. You can also move the horizontal bar above the taskpad to change the overall view.

Adding an Appointment to Your Calendar

In the Appointment area, you can instantly type in an appointment, without going into detail:

1. In the Appointment area, click the start time of your appointment.
2. Type in a short description of the appointment.
3. Drag the bottom bar for the appointment to the approximate ending time for it, then press Enter to set the appointment.

After you have set the appointment, you see a couple of default settings. The appointment is marked as Busy, represented by the blue bar. Also, a bell appears in your appointment, indicating that you will be reminded 15 minutes before the start of it.

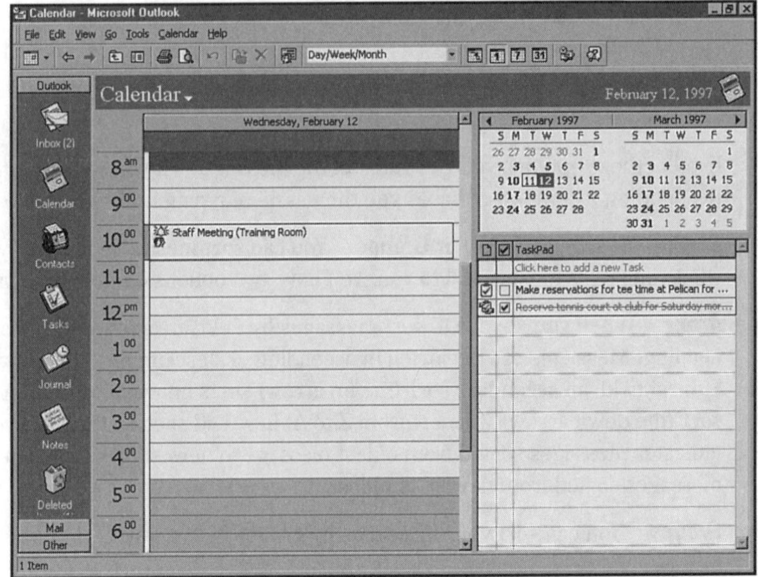

FIG. 30.6
The Calendar main view.

Adding a Detailed Appointment to Your Calendar

In Outlook, appointments can be more detailed and involve more than just a quick reminder to yourself of something that needs to be completed at a particular time. You may need to schedule a meeting with associates in your Exchange organization. Calendar will help you set a meeting time, send out requests to all attendees involved, and allocate resources that are required for the meeting.

Here is a step-by-step example of creating a detailed appointment:

1. Open your calendar.
2. Choose New Appointment from the Calendar menu (see Figure 30.7).
3. In the Subject text box, enter the topic for this appointment. When you are finished setting up the whole appointment, it will be saved as that subject.
4. In the Location text box, enter the location for the appointment. The drop-down list box will be available to you if you have set other appointments and want to use a previous location.
5. In the Start Time text boxes, enter the date and time of the appointment. Repeat this step for the End Time text boxes. If the appointment runs through the whole day, select the All Day Event option.
6. If you want to be reminded of the appointment, set the amount of time prior to the start of the appointment in the box next to Reminder. If you do not need a reminder, deselect the check box next to Reminder.

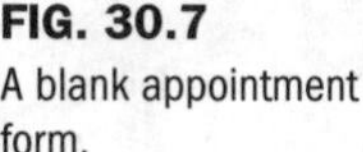

FIG. 30.7
A blank appointment form.

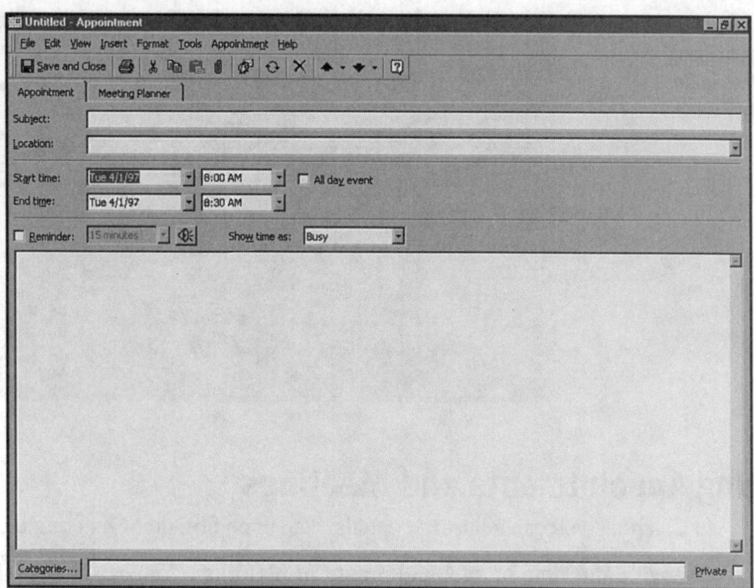

7. In the Show Time As box, use the drop-down list box to set your availability through the duration of the appointment. This choice affects the colored bar next to the appointment in the Information Viewer and is also reflected in the Free/Busy time in Meeting Planner.
8. The final section is the Notes area, where you can enter any miscellaneous notes for the appointment.

At this point, you have just finished setting up a detailed appointment. If your appointment involves only yourself, you can click Save and Close to complete the steps. However, if your appointment requires the attendance of your associates or a resource such as a conference room, you need to notify all parties involved.

Organizing a Meeting

This section guides you through setting up a meeting with other people in your company:

1. Create or open an existing appointment.
2. Click the Meeting Planner tab.
3. Under the Meeting Planner page, notice that your name is the first required attendee in the All Attendees box. To start adding attendees or resources, select Invite Others. This displays the Select Attendees and Resources dialog box.
4. From here, you have three options to configure: Required Attendees, Optional Attendees, and Resources. After you have configured all of the necessary options, click OK. This returns you to the Meeting Planner page.
5. You can now see an updated list of all attendees and their availability (see Figure 30.8).

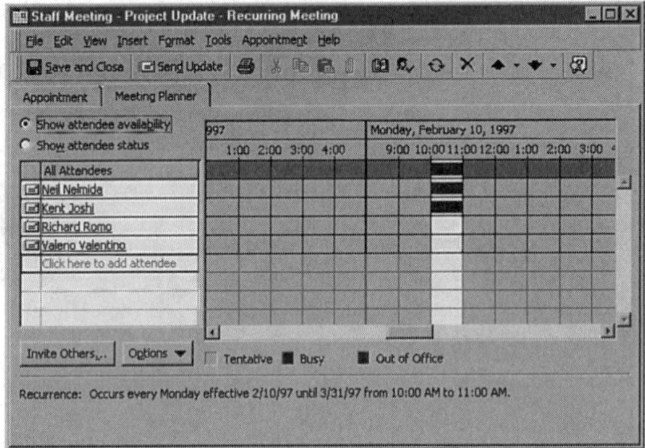

FIG. 30.8 Viewing meeting attendees under Meeting Planner.

Editing Appointments and Meetings

In Calendar, you can adjust the details of an appointment or meeting quite easily.

Changing the Time of an Appointment or Meeting You can change the starting and ending times of a meeting or appointment in various ways. In the Appointment area, you can drag the horizontal bar of either the starting time or ending time, or both, to the updated times. A second method is to double-click the appointment and change the time directly on the appropriate time box.

Moving an Appointment or Meeting If your appointment or meeting needs to be moved to a different day, you have two options available.

- First, you can drag-and-drop the appointment or meeting to the correct day. Make sure that the appointment or meeting appears in the Appointment area. Next, make sure the date that you want to move it to appears in the Date Navigator. Finally, you can click and hold down the appointment and drag it to the appropriate date in the Date Navigator.
- The second method is to double-click the appointment or meeting and change the date directly on the appropriate time box.

Recurring Appointments Recurring or regularly scheduled appointments can be set automatically. Using the Recurrence feature, you can plan your schedule more efficiently (see Figure 30.9).

On the toolbar, click the Recurrence button. You can also select Recurrence from the Appointment menu. In the Appointment Recurrence dialog box, you need to complete all of the required information for the recurrence to be set correctly.

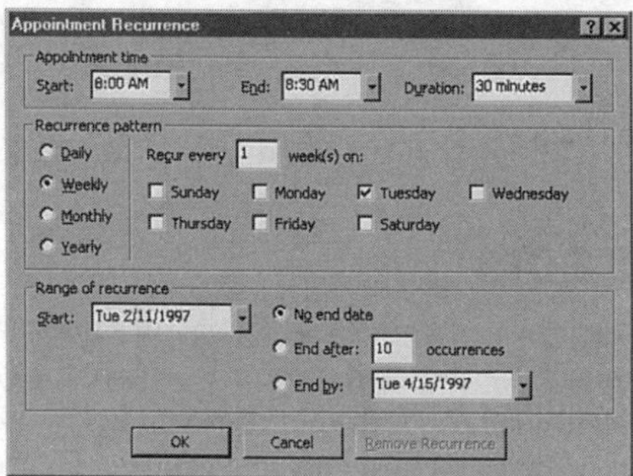

FIG. 30.9 Configuring the Appointment Recurrence dialog box.

- Appointment Time section: You need to type in the starting and ending times. Be sure to verify that the information in the Duration box is correct. You can set an appointment that lasts for more than one day.
- Recurrence Pattern section: You can set various options pertaining to the frequency of the recurrence.
- Range of Recurrence section: Set the start and end dates for the recurrence.

Adding Events

You can add special events such as a convention or anniversary to your calendar. The difference between an event and an appointment is that an event lasts the whole day.

Time Zone Issues

If your Exchange organization spans multiple time zones, there are a few things to consider when dealing with your calendar.

Setting Up Meetings over Different Time Zones Suppose you are in Los Angeles and you need to set up a conference call with someone in your Exchange organization in New York. You want to make sure that callers in both locations have the correct time information about that meeting. Outlook and the Exchange Server work together in getting meeting times correct. If the meeting is set for 9 a.m. Pacific time in Los Angeles, the meeting time should and will appear as 12 p.m. eastern standard time in New York.

Traveling in Multiple Time Zones Suppose you are traveling with your computer and your destination is in a different time zone. Outlook has a special feature to handle moving to a different time zone. The following steps demonstrate how to use this feature:

1. From the Tools menu, click Options.
2. Under the Options dialog box, click the Calendar tab.
3. To adjust the time zone, click the Time Zone button.
4. You will see the current time zone that you are in. You can add an additional time zone by selecting Show an Additional Time Zone and adjusting the time zone displayed.

5. When you choose the Swap Time Zones button, the additional time zone will be your current time zone.
6. Click OK to accept the changes.

Managing Your Contacts

The Contacts folder in Outlook provides a great way for you to store and organize all of the information you have about your associates and friends. It is more than a personal address book; it helps you track activities you have with your contact. Plus, you can define a view of contacts who are the most productive and meaningful to you (see Figure 30.10).

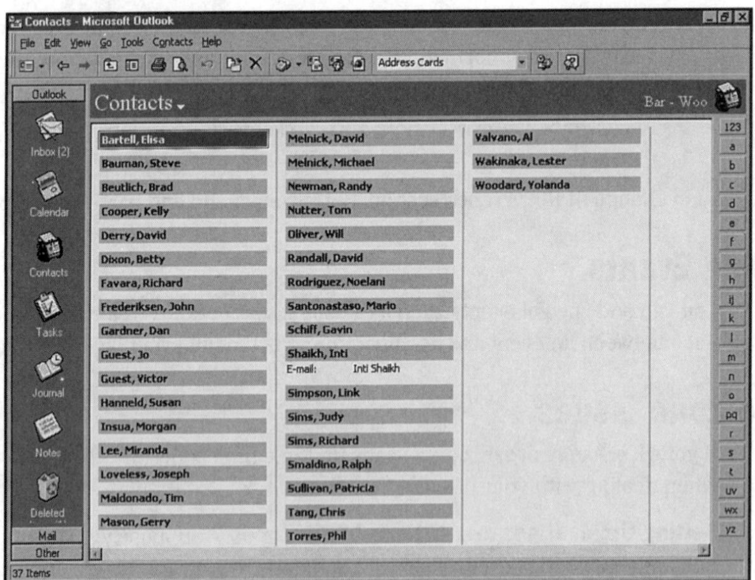

FIG. 30.10
The Contacts main view.

Adding Contacts

To add a contact, click Contacts on the toolbar and click New Contact. The Contact dialog box has four tabs under which you can add information about your contact: General, Details, Journal, and All Fields (see Figure 30.11).

The General Page Under the General page, you can type in some common information about your contact.

In the Full Name box, you can type in the name of your contact. You can also click the Full Name button to add more details about your contact's name such as Title and Suffix.

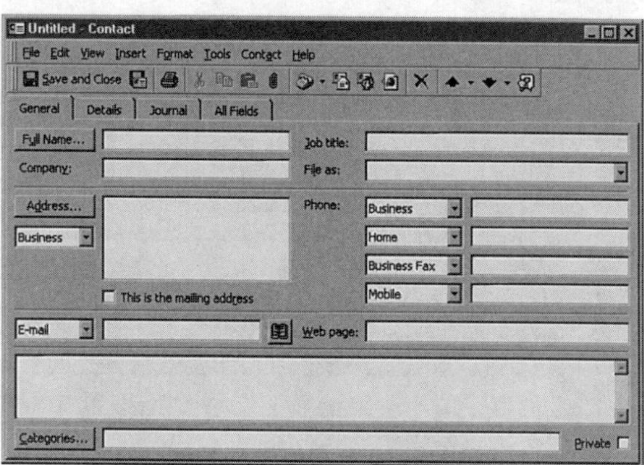

FIG. 30.11
Filling out the Contacts form.

If your contact works for a particular company, you can enter it in the Company box, along with the position that person holds in the company in the Job Title box. This information can be useful if you plan on grouping your contacts by company. Also, this affects the File As box, because you will have more options available to file your contact.

In the Address text box, you can type in the business, home, or other address of your contact. You have the option to fill in the address in greater detail for your contact, just as you can when you click the Full Name button.

In the Phone text boxes you can enter and save, up to four phone numbers for your contact. Also, you can specify what type of phone number each one represents, such as business, fax, home, cellular, pager, and so on.

If your contact is available through the Internet, by e-mail or a Web page, you can also save that information on the Contact dialog box.

Finally, you have the common features found throughout Outlook, such as a Notes area, the capability to put your contact in certain predefined categories, and the capability to store your contact as "private," hiding details of your contact from those who have access to your contacts.

The Details Page Under the Details page, you have the option to add extra information about your contact such as department, office, profession, assistant's name, manager's name, birthday, anniversary, nickname, and spouse's name (see Figure 30.12).

The Journal Page Under the Journal page, you can start recording journal entries for your contact and view particular entries made for your contact (see Figure 30.13).

The All Fields Page Under the All Fields page, you have the ability to add even more information about your contact (see Figure 30.14). You can select from many fields and even add a few of your own.

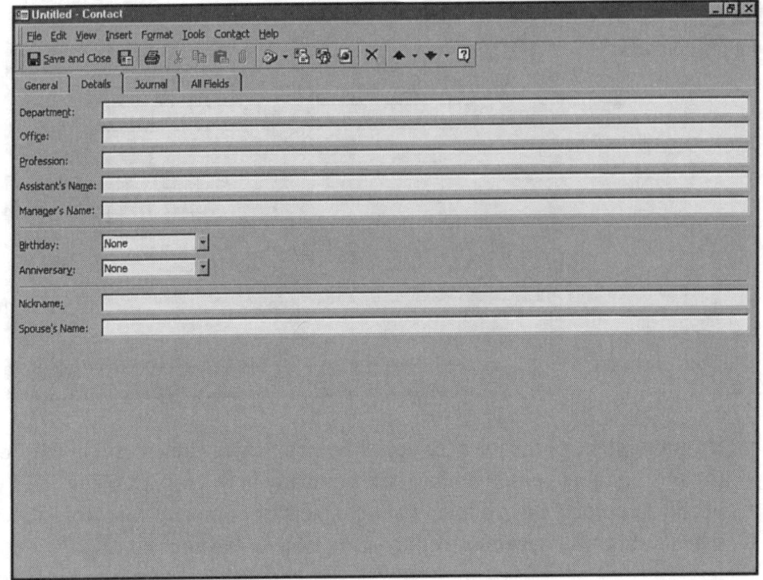

FIG. 30.12 Viewing the Details page.

After you have configured all of the important and useful information for yourself, be sure to click Save and Close to finish adding in your new contact.

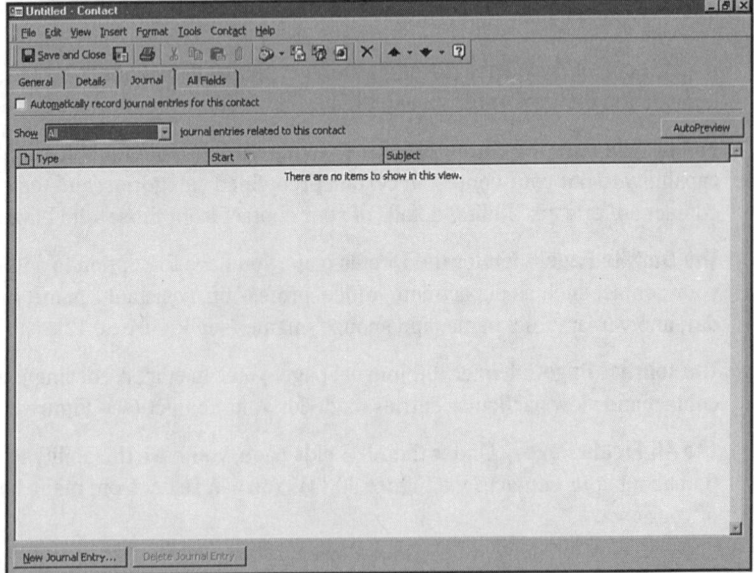

FIG. 30.13 Viewing all journal entries for your contact.

Viewing Contacts

Now that you have entered the appropriate information about your contact, you need to start organizing your contacts in such a way that you can find them when you need them.

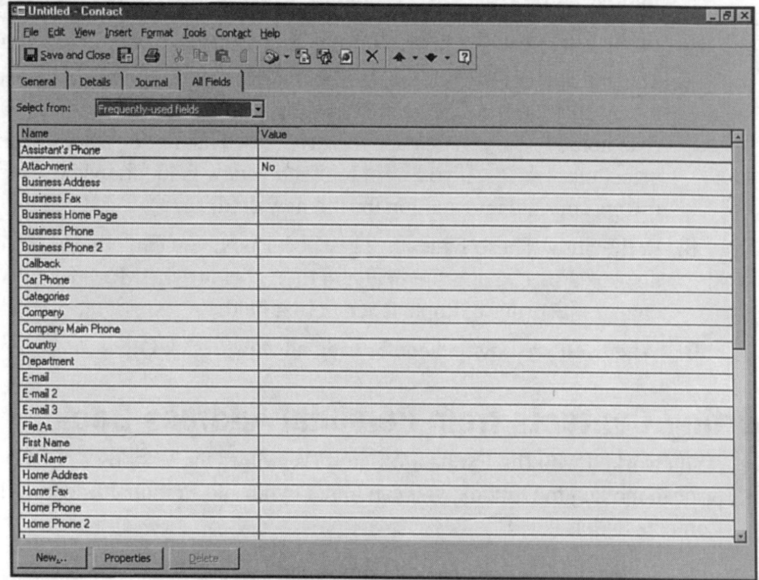

FIG. 30.14
A display of available fields for your contacts.

Table 30.5 displays a list of predefined views to see your contacts' information.

Table 30.5 Contacts

View	Display Results
Address Cards	Individual cards with primary mailing address and important phone numbers such as business, home, and fax.
Detailed Address Cards	Same as Address Cards, with secondary points of contact.
Phone List	Table that includes business, fax, home, and mobile numbers.
By Category	Grouped by category and sorted by contact name.
By Company	Grouped by company with job details.
By Location	Grouped by country.

Suppose you want to change the way you view your contacts. You may need to see information that is not set in the default views available. The following steps guide you through defining a view that is more useful.

1. In the View Menu, click Define Views.
2. In the Define Views for Contacts dialog box, click New.

3. In the Name of New View box, enter the name of this new view.
4. In the Type of View box, choose the type of display in which you want to see this new view.
5. In the Can Be Used On box, choose who and when this view can be displayed.
6. In the View Settings dialog box, click Fields to adjust the fields for the new view.
7. You can add fields from the Available Fields list to the Show These Fields in This Order list by clicking the desired field and then clicking Add. If a field is not displayed ín the Available Fields, you can use the drop-down list under Select Available Fields From to select more fields. If you want to create a new field, choose the New Field button type in the appropriate information for the new field.
8. In the Show These Fields In This Order box, you can change the order of the fields displayed by clicking the field and then clicking the Move Up or Move Down button, to change the order of importance of that field.
9. When you are finished configuring all views, click OK.

Importing Contacts from Personal Address Book

If you worked with the Exchange Client (Windows 95, Windows NT 4.0, Exchange Client 4.0) prior to moving to Outlook, you can import your old Personal Address Book into your new Contacts folder.

1. Under the File menu, click Import and Export.
2. In the Import and Export Wizard dialog box, highlight Import from Schedule+ or Another Program or File, and click Next (see Figure 30.15).
3. In the box under Select File Type to Import From, click Personal Address Book and then click Next.
4. In the box under Select Destination Folder, click Contacts and then click Next.
5. Click Finish to start importing data.

Deleted Item Recovery

Deleted Item Recovery is one of the new Exchange Server 5.5 enhancements that Outlook 8.03 was designed to deliver. This feature takes message deletion from a two-stage process to a three-stage process and puts additional control in the hands of the user. This section examines the steps involved in using this new functionality.

Figure 30.16 shows a Deleted Items folder with two items in it. These items are normally emptied upon exit or may be emptied manually if a user is cleaning house.

In Figure 30.17, the items are deleted and the folder is empty. Figure 30.18 shows the Recover Deleted Items button at the far right of the toolbar.

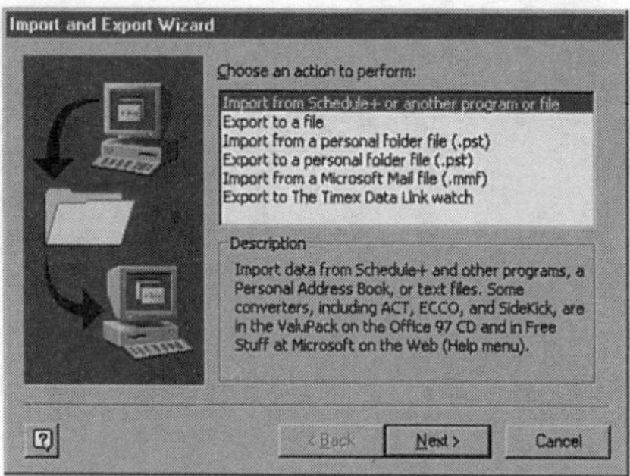

FIG. 30.15
The Import and Export Wizard dialog box.

Clicking the button brings up the Recover Deleted Items window (Figure 30.19), from which you can select multiple items and click Recover Selected Items. The items are then returned to your Deleted Items folder from which you can use them again.

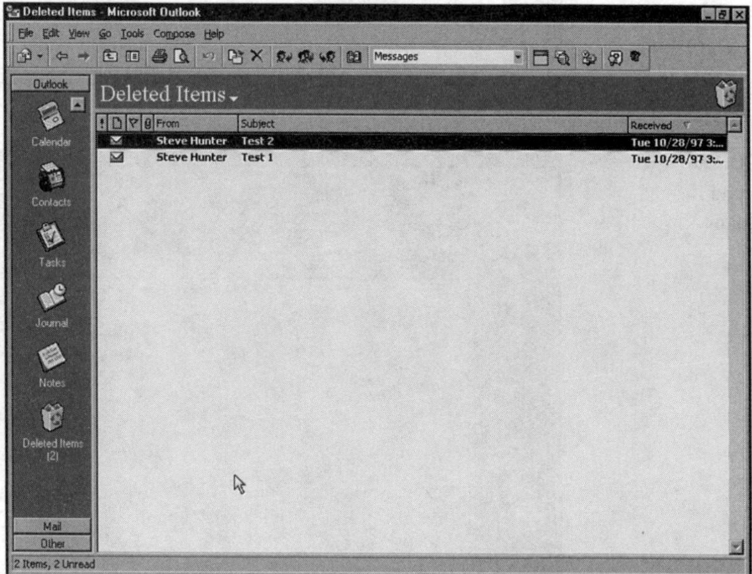

FIG. 30.16
The messages in the Deleted Items folder.

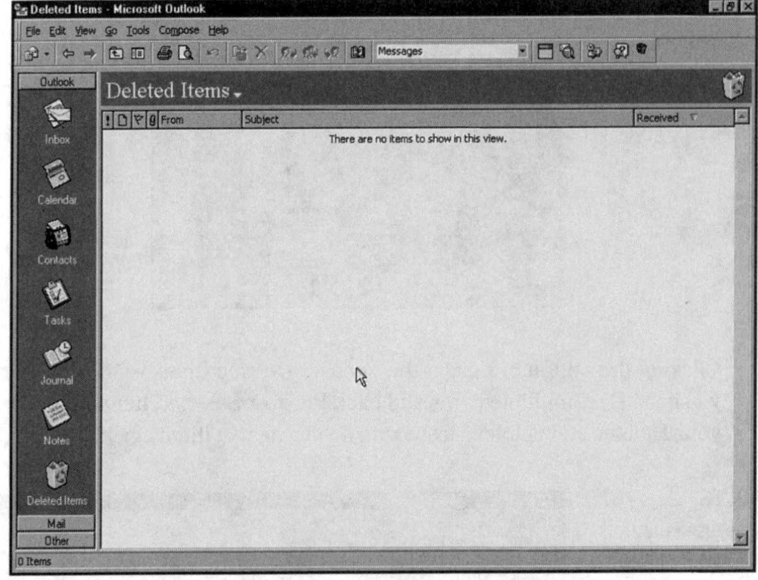

FIG. 30.17
The messages have been deleted.

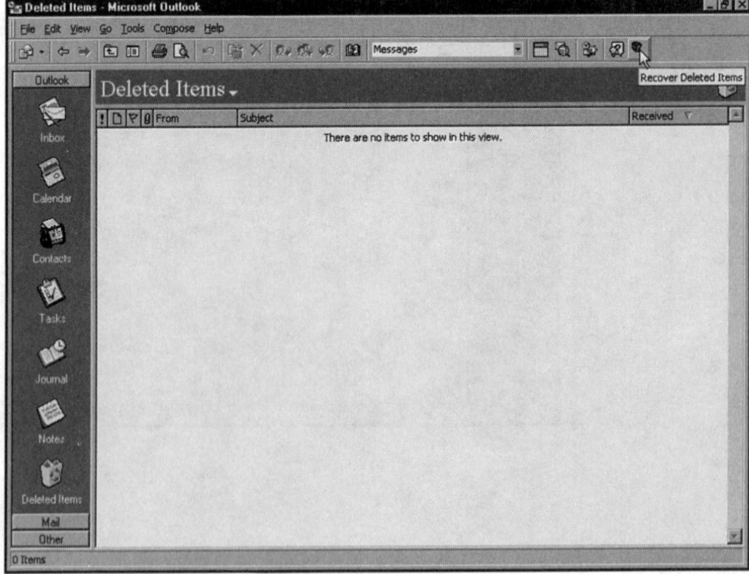

FIG. 30.18
The Recover Deleted Items button.

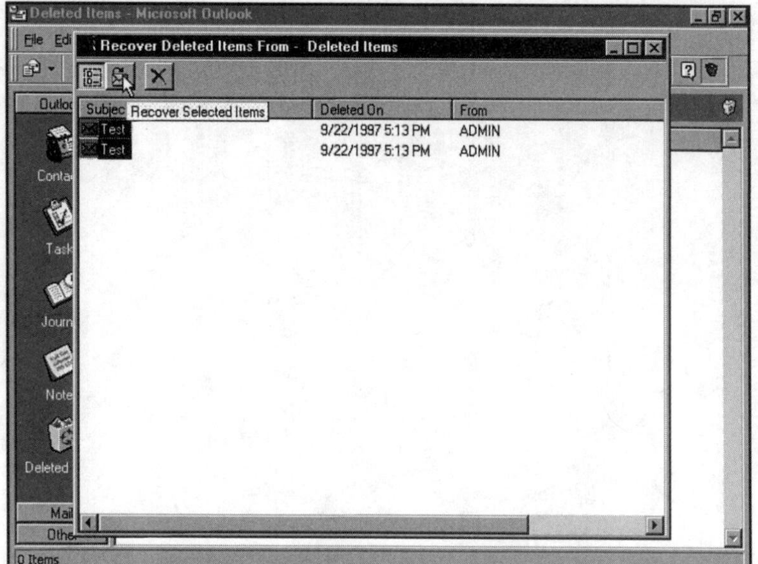

FIG. 30.19
The Recover Deleted Items window.

CHAPTER 31

Using Advanced Outlook Features

In this chapter

By now, this book has discussed Outlook in terms of being a replacement for the Microsoft Exchange Client and Schedule+. But Outlook doesn't stop there. It has other features to help you manage your activities and get through your schedule without a hitch. Some updates to previously available features and big changes to HTML access are new for Outlook 8.03.

Utilizing Auto Assistants

Auto Assistants help you manage your incoming mail by handling messages as they arrive in your Inbox. Auto Assistants check to see if the message meets specific conditions, and perform actions such as responding, filing, and routing items. There are two Auto Assistants:

- Inbox Assistant—Manages the mail coming into your Inbox on a daily basis
- Out of Office Assistant—Manages your mail when you are out of the office

Both Assistants essentially function in a similar manner. They're configured to accomplish tasks based on rules. Each rule is applied to incoming mail and consists of two parts: conditions and actions.

All rules are processed on the Microsoft Exchange Server, which enables the Assistant to continue running even if you have not started Outlook. If the rule's actions can be performed without user intervention, the rule is completed entirely in the Microsoft Exchange mailbox. Examples of this are moving a message into a specific folder or deleting messages with certain keywords. Remember that personal folders reside on your client.

NOTE If you set up more than one rule, they are performed in the order listed. Also, you need to be connected to your Exchange Server before you can add rules or edit them. ■

Using Remote Mail

You can use Remote Mail to view the headers of new items in your server Inbox. You then select specific items to transfer to your offline Inbox. Because you download only the items you specify, this method can be faster than synchronizing your offline Inbox, which downloads all new items. For users that regularly receive large amounts of mail, these added levels of control are very desirable since a single attachment in a message could take an hour or more to download across a modem connection. When synchronizing offline folders, you have no flow control and are required to wait until all mail is delivered before working with individual messages.

You can also use Remote Mail to send mail you compose while offline. While working offline, it is important that your computer and your Exchange configuration can authenticate your Outlook client with your NT Domain and user account. Before attempting to automatically connect with Outlook, check your dial-up and login options under the properties of your profile's Exchange Server service. Under the Dial-up Networking page, you must have the correct login information.

Managing Projects with Tasks

In Outlook, tasks can help you manage your daily responsibilities as well as keep track of all of your future due dates on projects (see Figure 31.1).

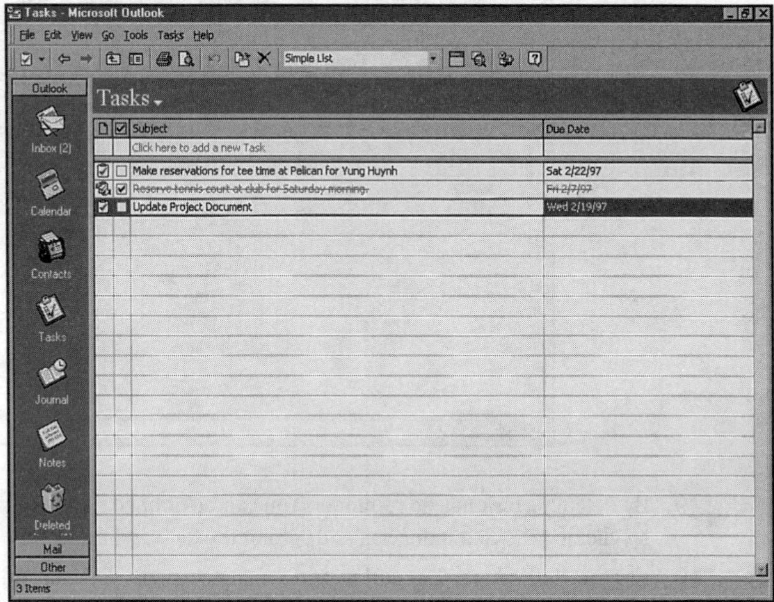

FIG. 31.1
Simple List view of Tasks.

Creating a New Task

The following steps help you create a new task:

1. Open Tasks from the Outlook Bar.
2. On the Standard toolbar, click the New Task icon to open a new task form.
3. On the Task page, you have several options to configure before saving the new task (see Figure 31.2).
4. In the Subject box, type a description of the task you need to complete.
5. In the Due Date section, you have two options:
   - If the task has no due date, choose None.
   - If the task has a due date, use the drop-down menu in the Due box to pick the due date. If you want to record the start date of the task, enter that date in the Start box.
6. In the Status box, use the drop-down menu to choose the current status of the task.
7. In the Priority box, set the priority of the task from Low to High.
8. In the % Complete box, enter the percentage of the task completed at this time.

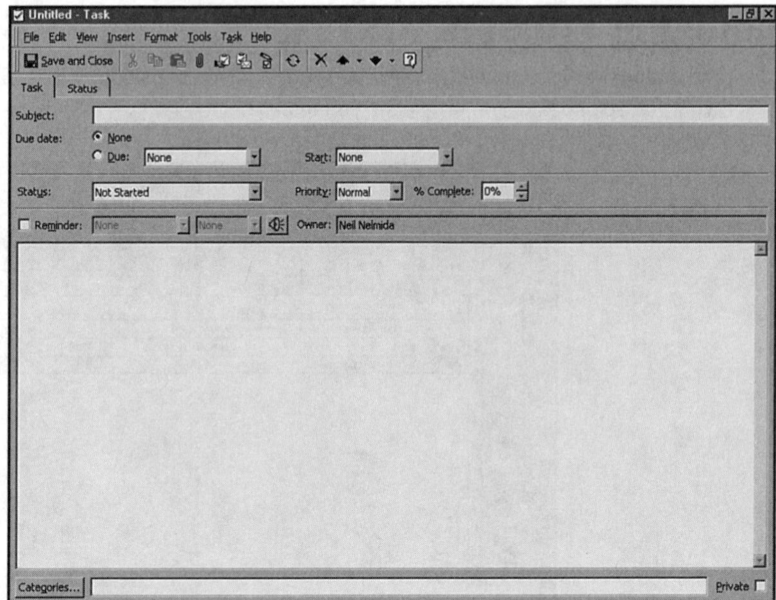

FIG. 31.2
Configuring information in the task form.

9. By default, a task has no reminder. You can be notified that your task is still incomplete by clicking the Reminder box and setting the date and time of the reminder.
10. For the Notes Area, Categories, and Private sections, you can add information similar to the appointment and contacts forms.
11. The Status page is where you save information such as Date Completed, Total Work, Actual Work, Mileage, Billing Information, Contacts, and Companies.
12. When you are finished with the Tasks details, click Save and then click Close.

Editing

You can edit tasks in many ways. You can double-click a task to edit the whole task at once. Another method is to utilize the various views available to you. You can edit a task in the Detailed List view, for example, by clicking the column you need to change and type over that information. In a column such as the Due Date, you can click the box and a drop-down menu with the Date Navigator appears.

Assigning Tasks to Others

You can assign a task to others in your organization if the person to whom you are assigning that task agrees to complete the task. When you try to assign a task, you must fill out a Task Request. This is similar to creating a new task for yourself, but you need to configure a few options before sending the request.

1. Under the Tasks menu, click New Task Request.
2. You will notice a few changes from the regular task form (see Figure 31.3).

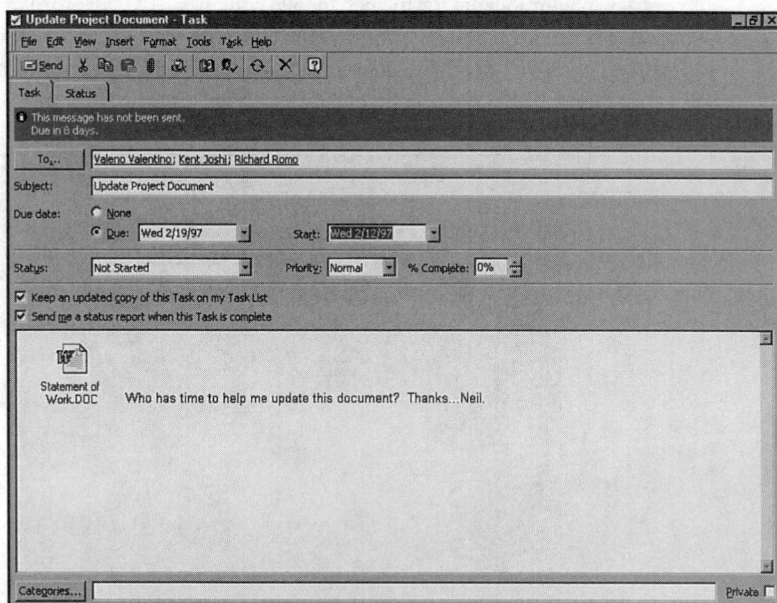

FIG. 31.3 A Task Request form ready to be sent.

3. In order for you to send this request, you must assign this task to at least one person. Enter that name in the To box. This is similar to addressing an e-mail message.
4. Notice that the Reminder box is missing, but is replaced with two other options: Keep an Updated Copy of this Task on My Task List and Send Me a Status Report When This Task Is Complete. You can choose how you want to be informed of the progress of the assigned task.
5. The rest of the New Task Request is the same as New Task.
6. When you are finished, click Send to send the task request.

Recurring Tasks

You create a recurring task the same way you create a recurring appointment. Some examples of a recurring task include filling out a time sheet or backing up your server. You can automatically set these tasks in your task list. All you need to do is create or open a task, click the Recurrence button on the toolbar, and set the recurrence pattern for your task.

Dragging a Task to Your Calendar

One of the many features in Outlook is being able to drag a task from your task list to your calendar. This is a great way to remind yourself that you need to block out some time in your day to complete a task. Once a task is on your calendar, you can edit it like any other appointment.

Using the Journal

In Outlook, you can keep a record of your daily activities in your journal, and you can manually add entries in your journal for miscellaneous activities. A key feature of Outlook is the ability to automatically record your activities that involve your contacts or any Microsoft documents that you worked on. If you need to locate a document or recall a meeting with a contact, the journal can be the best tool to help organize your work (see Figure 31.4).

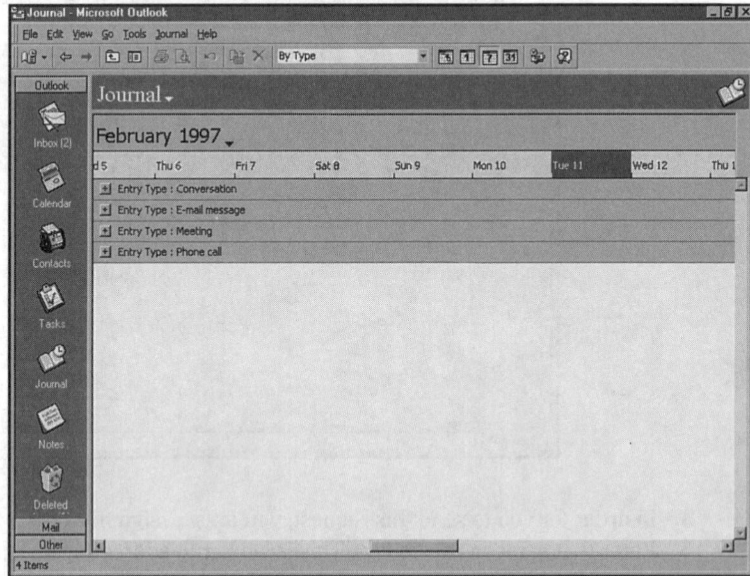

FIG. 31.4
Viewing journal entries by type.

Creating a Journal Entry

You can start recording a journal by following these steps:

1. Open Journal from the Outlook bar.
2. On the Standard toolbar, click the Journal icon to open a new journal entry (see Figure 31.5).
3. In the Subject box, enter the subject of this entry.
4. In the Entry Type box, use the drop-down menu to choose the action performed for this entry.
5. In the Contact box, enter the name of the contact. You can add the company name in the Company box.
6. In the Start Time section, you can enter the date and time.
7. In the Duration box, you can enter the amount of time spent on this subject.
8. The Notes Area, Categories, and Private boxes can be filled in the same way you filled out an appointment.

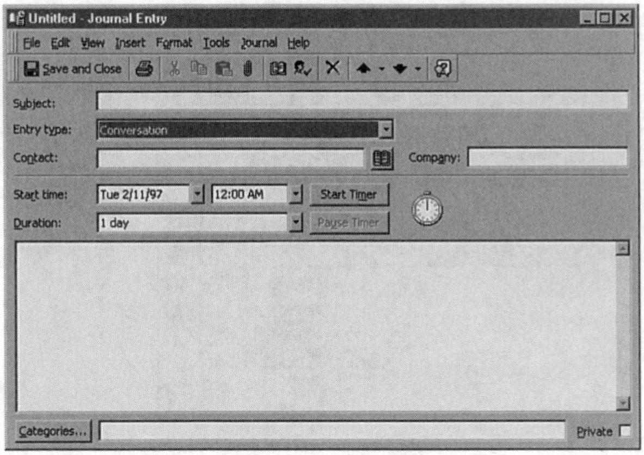

FIG. 31.5
Creating a new journal entry.

Using the Timer

The timer is available in Journal to keep track of the actual time the journal entry was open. This is useful if you want to keep track of the time spent in a meeting or on the phone.

Another feature in Outlook that will help you fill out a journal entry needing to be timed is the AutoDate feature. Outlook can convert text descriptions, such as today, to the current date and noon to 12:00 p.m. Outlook can also decipher holidays, such as New Year's Day and Independence Day.

The following example uses the AutoDate feature along with Journal to keep track of the actual minutes spent on an activity:

1. Create a new journal entry.
2. If the day is not correct in the Start time box, you can enter Today. This will automatically bring up the correct date.
3. In the box where the time is displayed, type Now. The current time will be displayed.
4. In the Duration box, type 0 for 0 minutes time elapsed.
5. Click Start Timer. The timer will run, and the time box will update every minute.
6. Click Pause Timer to stop the timer.
7. You can fill out the rest of the journal entry and click Save and then click Close to save it.

Setting Journal Options

In Outlook, you can select which items can be automatically recorded in your journal. These items include contacts, Outlook items that involve contacts, and Microsoft products. To set an automatic journal entry, follow this procedure:

1. Under the Tools menu, click Options.
2. In the Options menu, select the Journal tab (see Figure 31.6).

FIG. 31.6
Configuring items and contacts to be automatically recorded in Journal.

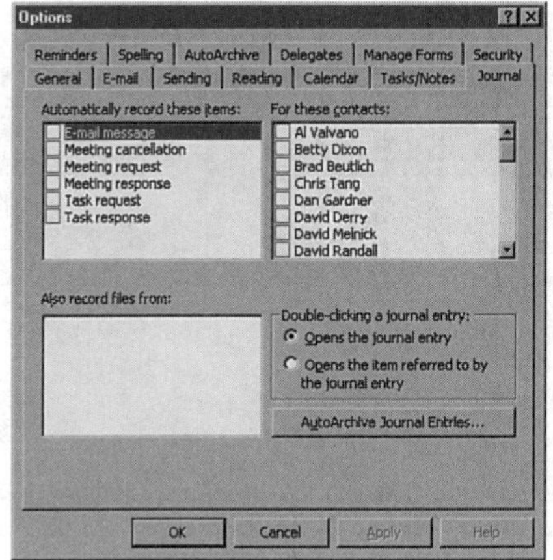

3. In the box under Automatically Record These Items, click the items you want automatically recorded for the contacts that you will choose.
4. In the box under For These Contacts, select the contacts you want to record in Journal.
5. In the box under Also Record Files From, select the Microsoft products you want to record in Journal.
6. Click AutoArchive Journal Entries if you want to set the options for automatically archiving your journal entries after a specific duration (see Figure 31.7).

FIG. 31.7
Setting the amount of time to elapse before archiving Journal entries.

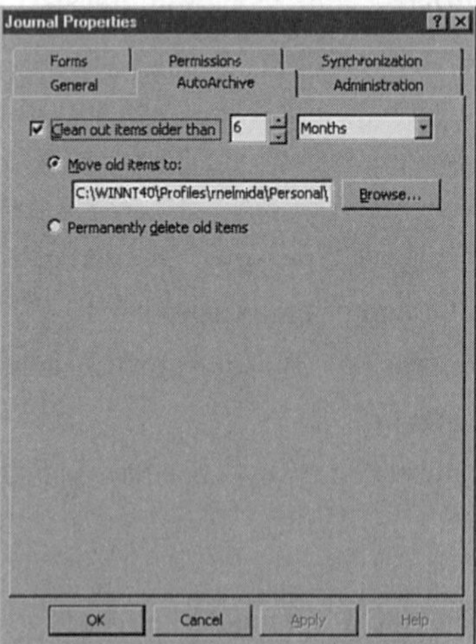

Using Notes

Notes can be very useful in helping you remember things. Just like the popular paper sticky notes, you can use Notes in Outlook to write down reminders for yourself, just as you would with paper.

To work with Notes in Outlook, click the Notes button on the Outlook bar (see Figure 31.8). To create a new note, select Note and then click New Note. You also can press Ctrl+Shift+N from anywhere within Outlook instead. The Notes Information Viewer opens. You can now type in any quick reminders, questions, or ideas. The note displays over whichever part of Outlook you are currently in. Type your comments in the note and press Escape. Outlook automatically saves the note in your Notes folder. Next time you bring up Notes, your message will appear.

FIG. 31.8
Sample notes in Notes folder.

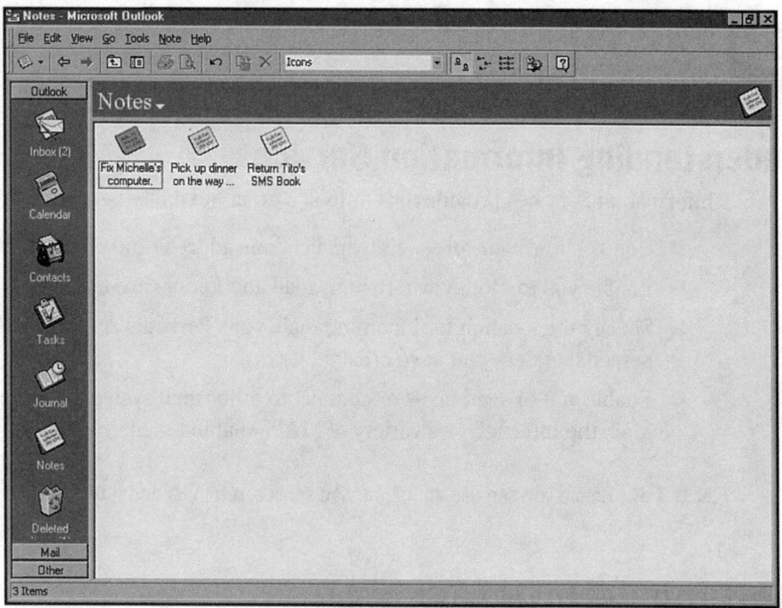

Notes are yellow by default, but you can change the color to blue, green, pink, or white to color code your messages. To change the color of your note, right-click the note you want to change. To change the color of a new note, click the icon at the top left corner of the note, choose Color in the menu, and select the new color from the list displayed.

Profiles and Information Services

Outlook is very flexible and can be used by more than one person or possess multiple configurations per user. This is accomplished with Profiles. Outlook can also be used to access multiple sources of information. This option is configured through a feature called Information Services.

Introduction to Profiles

Generally, the profile you create during installation is the only profile you will need, unless one of these situations occurs:

- More than one person uses the same computer. Each person should have a profile to keep mail private and secure.
- You need to work with a different set of services. You can create an additional profile with those custom services.

NOTE You can start Outlook with the default profile you have specified. You can also be prompted to select a profile each time you start Outlook. ■

TIP Being prompted to select a profile is a good idea when you use multiple profiles, or when there are multiple users per computer.

Understanding Information Services

Information Services provide for Outlook's great flexibility because they do the following:

- Control how your messaging applications address and route your mail.
- Enable you to modify where your mail and folders are stored.
- Specify the location for incoming mail, your Personal Address Book, and any sets of personal folders you have created.
- Enable you to send faxes or connect to other mail systems such as Exchange, Microsoft Mail, the Internet, or a variety of MAPI-enabled mail systems.

NOTE Before you can use an information service, you must add it to an active profile. ■

Working with Delegates

In Outlook, you can set up delegates to manage resources such as conference rooms, office equipment, and so on. These resources can be managed manually (making the delegate fully responsible for their availability) or automatically, depending on your organization's requirements. Since a resource cannot respond to any requests for its use, you can establish a delegate to take care of booking the resource for a particular meeting. To create a delegate, perform the following steps:

1. Open Outlook using the profile set up for the resource account.
2. Under the Tools menu, click Options.
3. In the Options dialog box, click the Delegates tab.
4. Click Add to assign a delegate to the resource account.

5. In the Add Users dialog box, choose a delegate and then click OK.
6. The Delegate Permissions dialog box appears and you can set up any additional permissions for the user.
7. Click OK when you are finished. This brings you back to the Delegates page.
8. In the Delegates page, click Send Meeting Requests and Responses Only to My Delegates, Not to Me checkbox.
9. Click OK to save these settings for the new delegate.

At this point, all meeting requests involving this resource are automatically forwarded to the delegate.

You can also set up the resource account to be booked on a first-come, first-served basis. This would fully automate the process of booking a resource. To override any advanced bookings, however, you need to contact the delegate or the administrator since they are the only ones with access to the resource account.

1. Open Outlook with the profile set up for the resource account.
2. Under the Tools menu, click Options.
3. In the Options dialog box, click the E-mail tab.
4. In the Settings for Automatic Processing of Mail section, make sure the Process Requests and Responses on Arrival checkbox is selected.
5. In the Options dialog box, click the Calendar tab.
6. Under the Calendar tab, click the Advanced Scheduling tab.
7. In the Processing of Meeting Requests section, select the options that need to be handled automatically.
8. After selecting the appropriate options, click OK.

Working with Public Folders Offline

If your Exchange organization uses public folders, you can work with some or all of these folders while you are offline. This feature is very useful for organizations that keep documents on the server. This enables users who work with offline folders to be continuously updated with information that is added to public folders. Also, this is a great way for you to make changes to documents while you are offline, and have those changes automatically updated when you connect online.

Under public folders, you will find a folder called Favorites. Store all the public folders you want to view offline here. To add these folders, follow these steps:

1. Under Public Folders, open All Public Folders.
2. Select the folder you want available when you are offline.
3. Under the File menu, choose Folder and click Add to Public Folder Favorites.

4. In the Add to Favorites dialog box, you can change the name of the folder. After choosing a name for this folder, click Add.
5. Under Public Folder Favorites, choose the folder you just added.
6. Under the File menu, choose Folder and click Properties
7. In the Properties dialog box, click the Synchronization tab.
8. In the This Folder Is Available box, click When Offline or Online.
9. Click OK to confirm that this folder is now available to you offline.

Web Outlook View

Outlook Web Access is an enhanced feature of Exchange Server 5.5. This feature is greatly improved from the Active Server component of 5.0 for users needing to attach to the server without having to use the full-featured Outlook client. Outlook Web Access is very practical for someone who wants to use a computer with Internet access to quickly and efficiently check e-mail. Your organization can also utilize Outlook Web Access on computers that cannot run the Outlook client and need an alternative to attaching to the Exchange Server for secure access to mailboxes and public folders, such as UNIX or Macintosh clients.

Messaging with Outlook Web Access

In Outlook Web Access, you can access your mailbox on the Exchange Server to send messages and read messages in your Inbox. Contact your administrator for details on how to log on to your Exchange Server from your Web browser. Once you pass the security set up by your network administrator, you receive the login screen (see Figure 31.9).

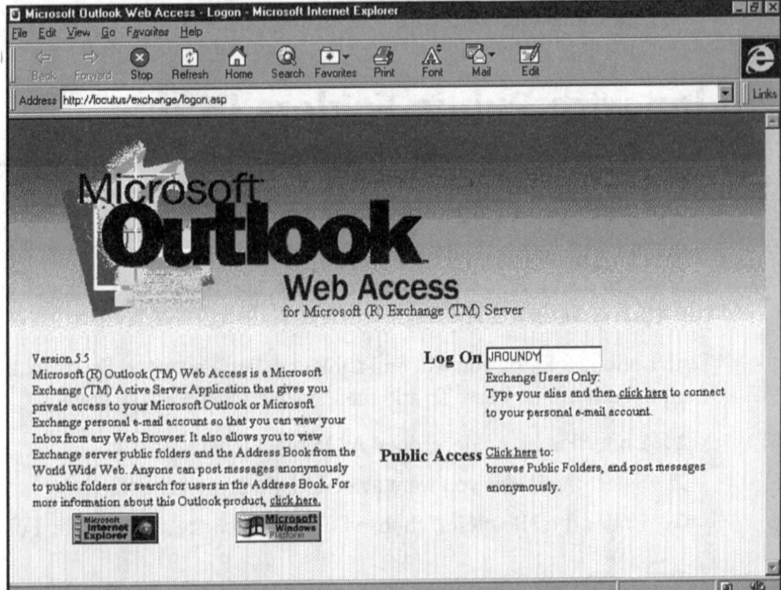

FIG. 31.9
User login to mailbox in Web Outlook view.

After successfully logging in to your mailbox, you see the current contents of your Inbox through Outlook Web Access (see Figure 31.10).

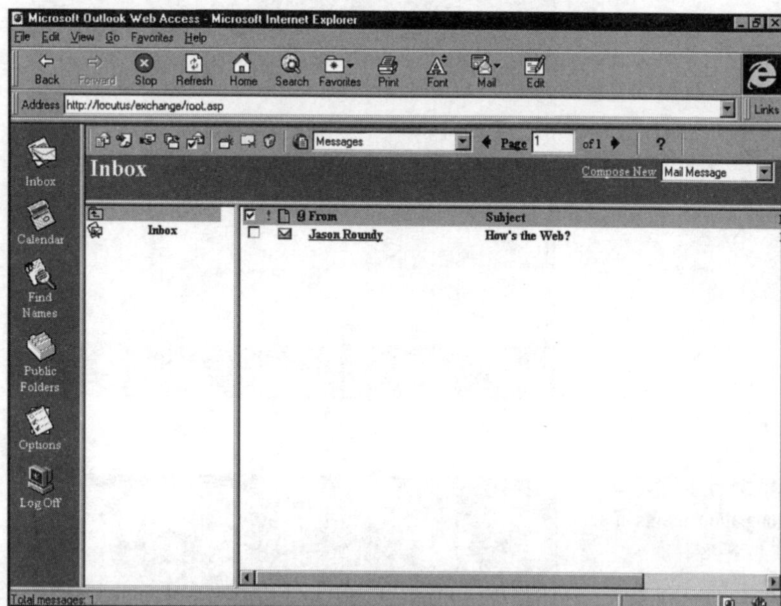

FIG. 31.10 Viewing the Inbox in Web Outlook view.

Creating Messages In the Inbox of Outlook Web Access, click Send New Message. A New Message form appears, which is similar to the Mail form in Outlook (see Figure 31.11). You have several options to configure before sending the message:

- To: This box contains a list of the main recipients of your message.
- Cc: Enter the recipients that need a carbon copy of the message.

NOTE When you enter a name in either of the above boxes, you can type in the Display Name of the recipient in your Exchange organization or the SMTP/Internet address for all other recipients.

- Subject: You can add a brief description of your message here.
- Message: Type in your full text message here.
- Attachments: These are files you want to send with your message (see Figure 31.12).

On the Attachments page, type a path to the files you want to attach to your message. On the Options page, configure read and delivery receipts and the use of BCCs (see Figure 31.13).

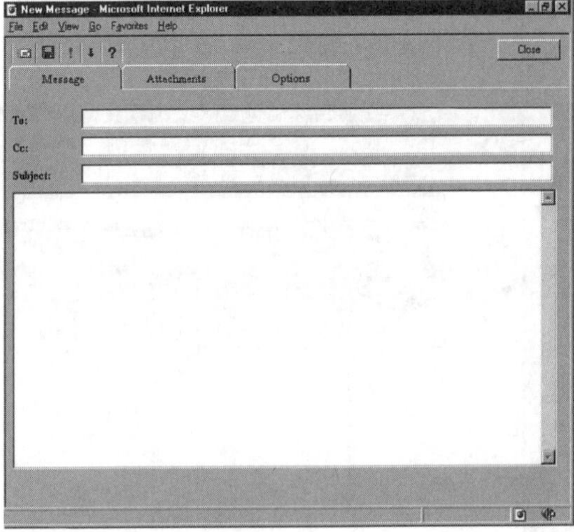

FIG. 31.11
New Message form.

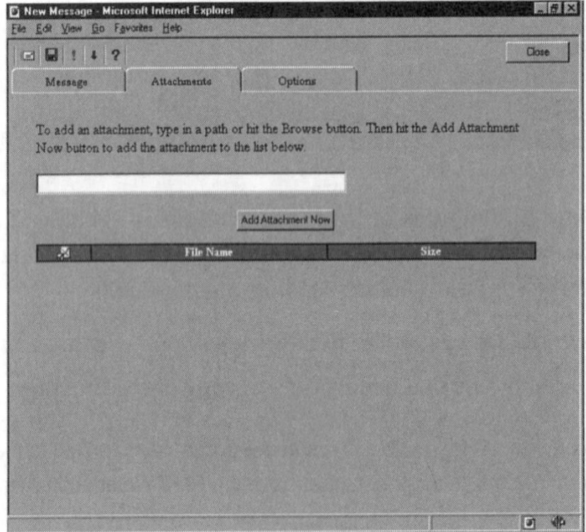

FIG. 31.12
Setting attachments in your message.

When you are finished filling out the form, you can send or cancel it.

Reading Messages You can open a message in your Inbox by clicking the sender in the From column (see Figure 31.14). After reading the message, you have several options to further handle this message:

- Reply: When you choose this option, you send a reply to only the sender of the original message.
- Reply to All: This option is similar to Reply, but the reply is sent to all recipients who received this message.

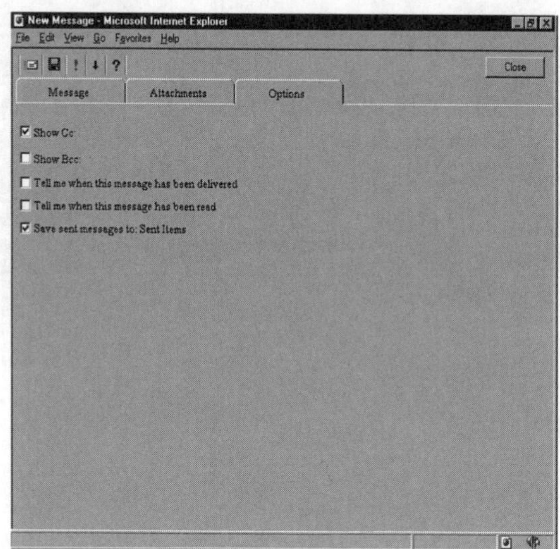

FIG. 31.13
Configuring options for read & delivery receipts and the use of BCCs.

- Reply to Folder: This option enables you to post your response to a folder.
- Forward: You can forward this message to another recipient.
- Move to Folder: You can move the current message to any folder available to you on the Exchange Server. You need to choose a folder and then verify that you want to move the message to that folder.
- Delete: This option deletes the message from your Inbox.
- Previous: This option takes you to the previous message in your Inbox.
- Next: This option takes you to the next message in your Inbox.
- Help: Enables you to access online help

Public Folders

You can access public folders as easily as your mailbox after you log in to your Exchange Server over Outlook Web Access. Once the server has authenticated you, you can start posting and reading items stored in the public folders (see Figure 31.15). The following sections provide a basic guide for you to manipulate public folders.

Post New Item From Outlook Web Access, you can post a new item to a public folder. First you need to select the correct public folder to which you want to post information (see Figure 31.16).

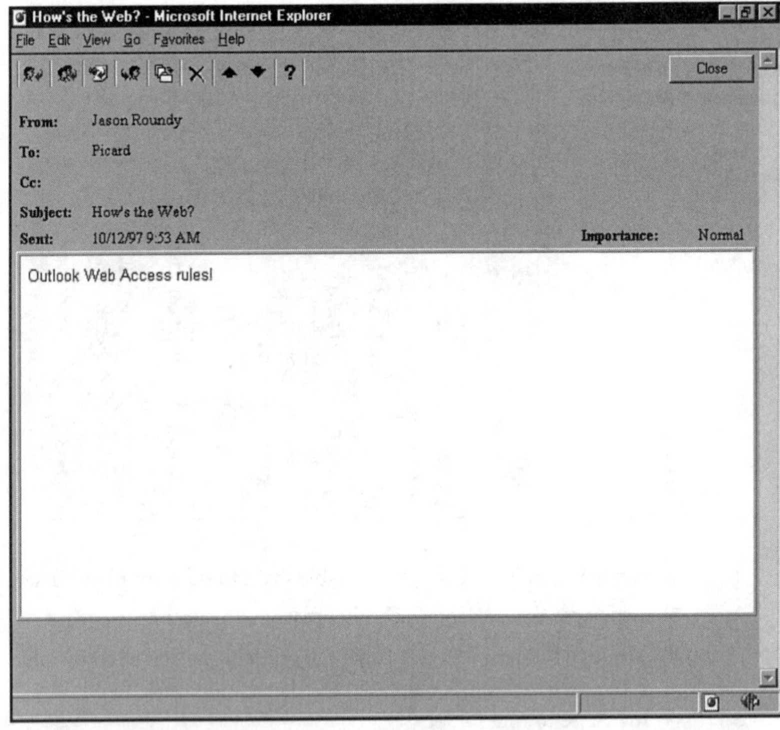

FIG. 31.14
Reading a message in your Inbox.

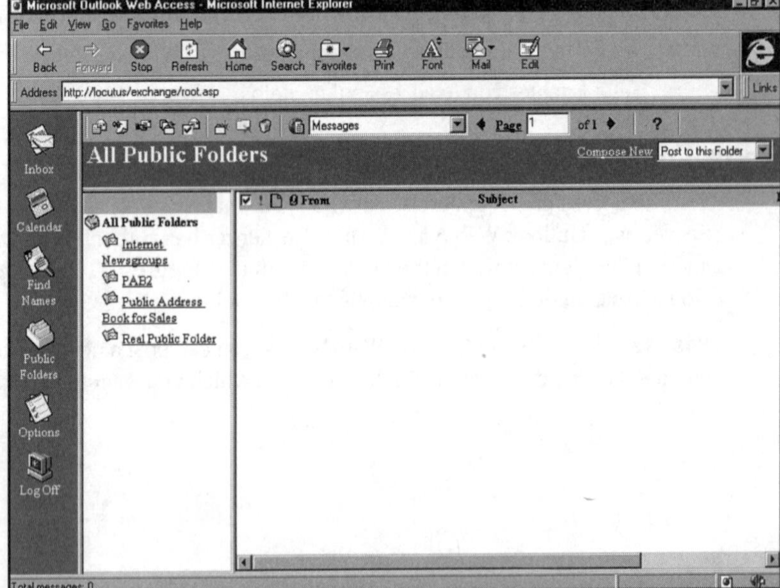

FIG. 31.15
Public folders viewed through Outlook Web Access.

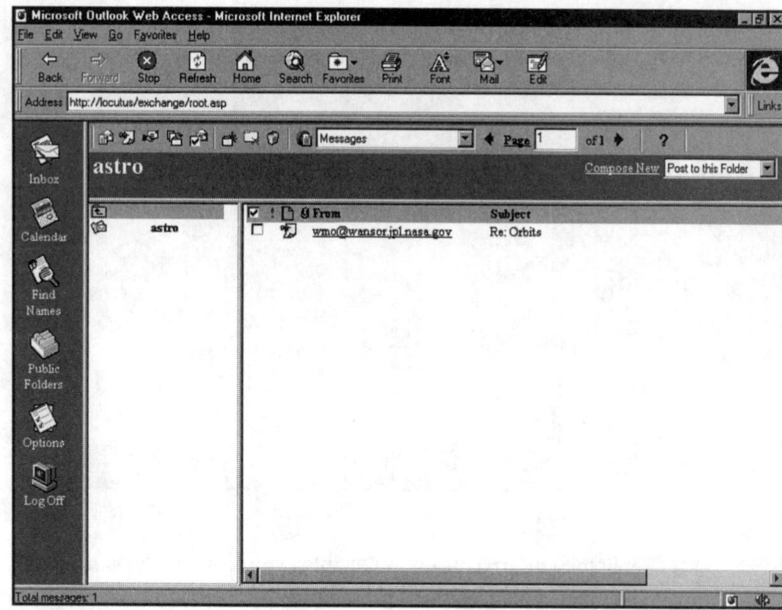

FIG. 31.16
Viewing posted messages in a public folder.

Then in the Action Area of the Outlook Web Access, click Post New Item. A New Post form appears, and you have several options to configure before finally posting the item in the public folder (see Figure 31.17).

- Keywords: You can add keywords to your post to help others determine whether your post is of some interest.
- Subject: This is a brief description about your post.
- Message: This is the body of the post. It contains the information you want to announce to the audience of this public folder.
- Attachments: This page functions exactly as it does for a new message.
- Importance: You can set the importance of your post as Low, Normal, or High by using the buttons in the toolbar.
- Post: Select this option when you are ready to post your information to the public folder.

Reading and Responding to Posts Posting information to a public folder is only part of what you can do over a Web browser. You can also read and respond to posts. To start reading posts, you need to select one from a public folder that interests you. After reading that post, you have three options to handle it and possibly continue the discussion.

- Reply to Folder: This option enables you to post a reply to the post you just read. When you click this option, a Post form appears with copy of the old post in the Message Box. You can edit your reply and set the same options as a new post. Be sure to click Post to post the reply in the public folder.

New Post - Microsoft Internet Explorer
File Edit View Go Favorites Help
Close
Message
Attachments
Post To
astro
Conversation
Keywords
Subject

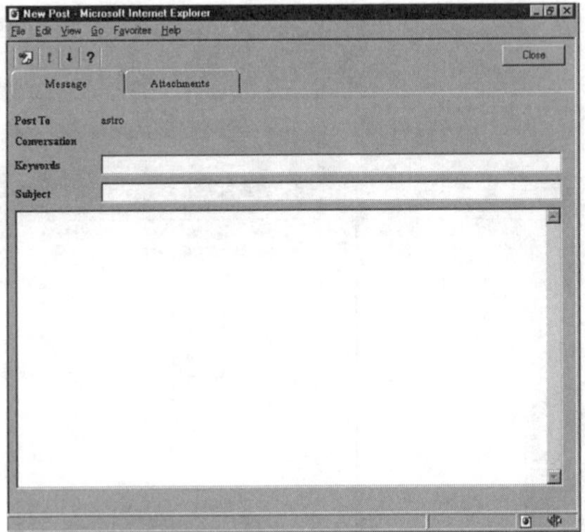

FIG. 31.17
The New Post form.

- Reply to Sender: This option enables you to send a new message to the author of the post. Since you are creating a new message, you can also send a copy of this post to other recipients.
- Forward: You can forward this post to another recipient.

Find Names

The Find Names option enables you to search the Exchange Address Book. You can get detailed information about someone in your organization by typing in any information you know about that person. The available fields include Display Name, First Name, Last Name, Title, Alias Name, Company, Department, Office, and City (see Figure 31.18).

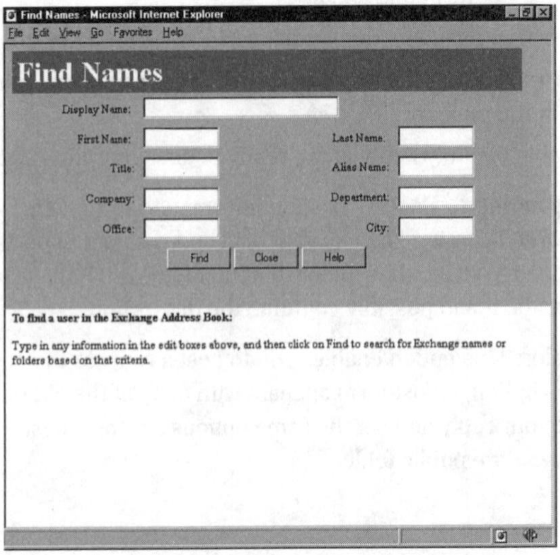

Find Names - Microsoft Internet Explorer
File Edit View Go Favorites Help
Find Names
Display Name:
First Name:
Last Name:
Title:
Alias Name:
Company:
Department:
Office:
City:
Find
Close
Help
To find a user in the Exchange Address Book:
Type in any information in the edit boxes above, and then click on Find to search for Exchange names or folders based on that criteria.

FIG. 31.18
Using Find Names.

After typing in that information, click Find, and if there are matches to the request, a list appears. You can then select the name to get more information about that person (see Figure 31.19).

FIG. 31.19
Viewing the Exchange Address Book.

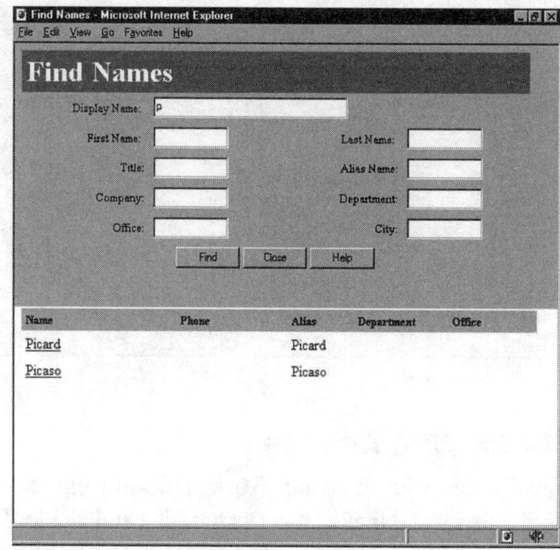

Options

Under Options in the Navigation Bar, you can set your Out of Office Assistant. You can indicate that you are In the Office, or you can select Out of the Office and have replies with a text message sent to each sender (see Figure 31.20). You can also reset your time zone and configure some aspects of the calendaring functionality (see Figure 31.21).

FIG. 31.20
Out of Office Assistant options.

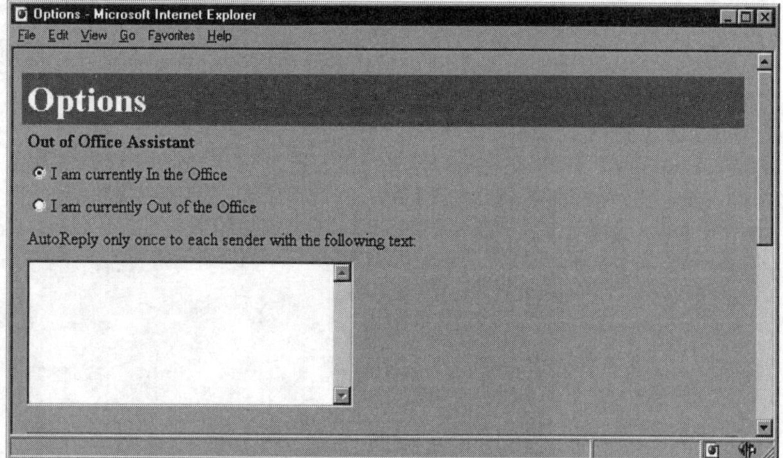

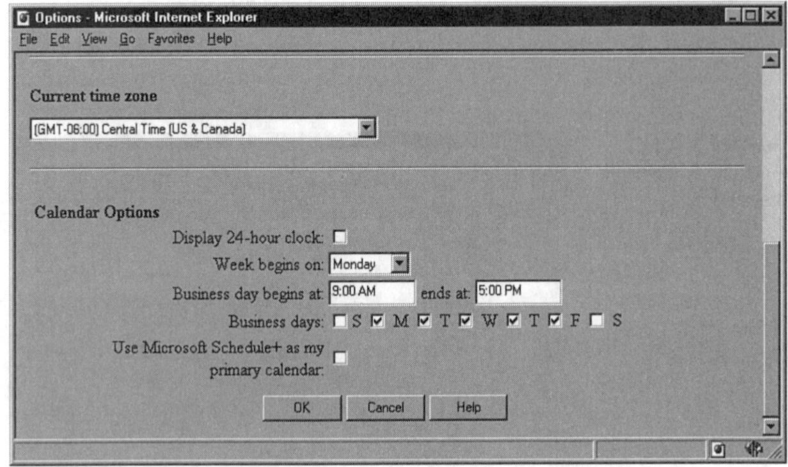

FIG. 31.21
Current time zone and Calendar options.

Calendaring in Outlook Web Access

Calendaring functionality, new with Exchange 5.5, significantly enhances the web-based solution for local and mobile users and makes it very attractive and viable. The initial Calendar view is in Figure 31.22. One of the great features is the continuity with the actual Outlook client interface. This will be familiar to Outlook users and intuitive to new users accessing Exchange services.

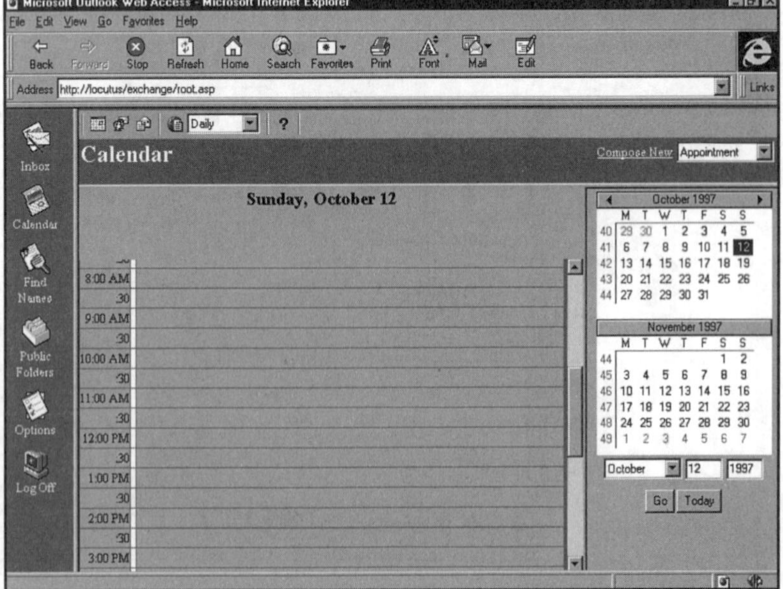

FIG. 31.22
Calendar view in Outlook Web Access.

In Figure 31.23, notice the striking similarity with the New Appointment screens in the Outlook client. Some features are exactly the same as they are in the client, such as the Meeting Planner page (see Figure 31.24). Others are offered in a new venue, such as the Recurrence features (see Figure 31.25), but allow for much of the same functionality. Again, attachments and options work as they do when you create a new message.

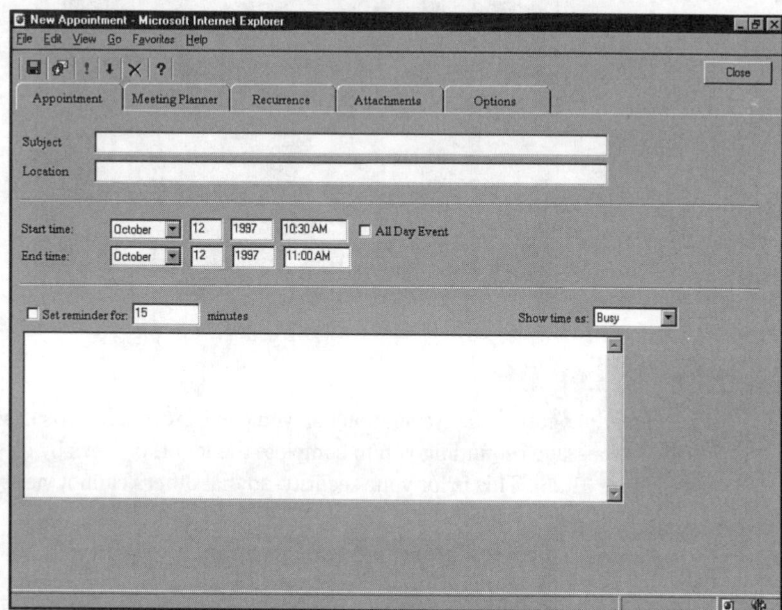

FIG. 31.23
The New Appointment screen in Outlook Web Access.

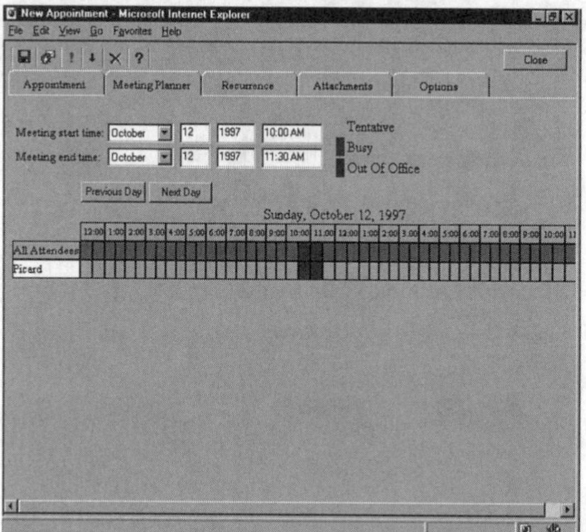

FIG. 31.24
The Meeting Planner page.

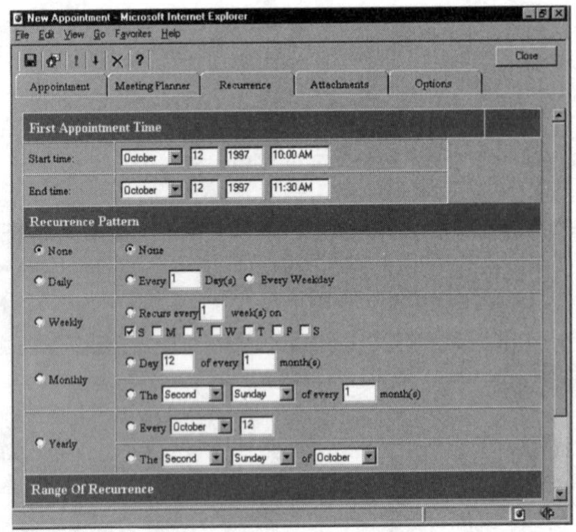

FIG. 31.25
Use the Recurrence page for new appointments in Outlook Web Access.

Selecting to Log Off

By selecting Logoff in the Navigation bar, you can log off of Microsoft Exchange. You will receive a message reminding you to complete the logoff process by closing the Web browser (see Figure 31.26). This is for your security, so that others cannot view your mailbox.

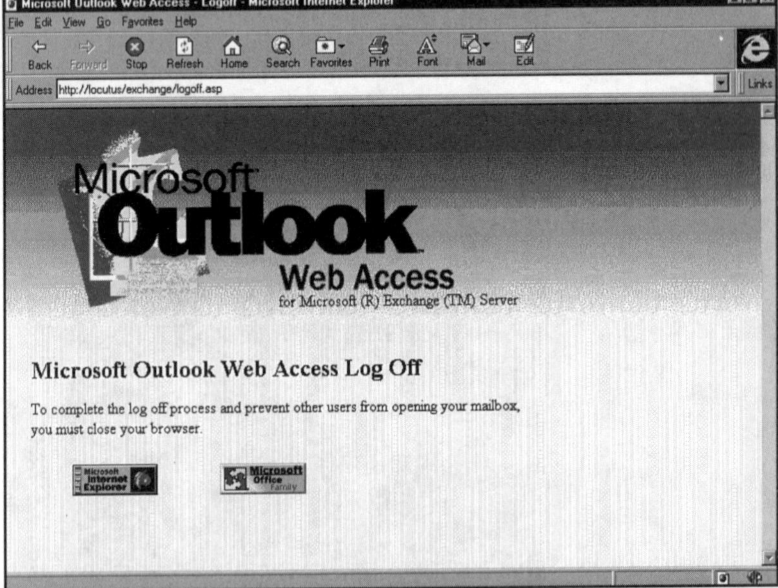

FIG. 31.26
Logoff message in Outlook Web Access.

PART V

Third-Party Integration and Application Development

CHAPTER 32

Leveraging Your Investment in the Exchange Platform

In this chapter

By now, we have discussed all the core functions of Exchange provided in the shipped version. Although Microsoft has an extensive array of features built into the application, it cannot deliver all the features that end users need in their environment.

Companies today are looking to derive greater benefit from their investments in messaging infrastructures. As the global market becomes a reality, organizations must find ways of reducing or maintaining operational costs and total cost of ownership (of the IT infrastructure) while improving productivity and customer satisfaction. One way to accomplish this is to provide business solutions that leverage current infrastructure investments. Exchange Server is an application that also serves the role of a platform. That is, Exchange must be leveraged as a platform on top of which organizations can deploy third-party or in-house applications and services. This will ensure that organizations obtain a solid return on investment (ROI) on their investment in Exchange Server.

Third-party developers are essential resources in the deployment of Exchange in your environment. You saw that Exchange is more than just a messaging system. Exchange is an application framework. Third-party developers can extend the framework to provide a wide array of solutions on top of your core Exchange architecture.

Using Workflow Technologies to Extend Exchange

The segment of groupware that automates business processes is called workflow. *Workflow* is an enabling technology that lets businesses streamline their processes for greater efficiencies. The lack of reliable, cost-efficient solutions built on pervasive infrastructures has stifled adoption of workflow technologies. Workflow is a sequence of actions or steps used in business processes. Automated workflow applies technology (in this case, messaging technology) to the workflow process. Reliable messaging connectivity between all participants and interested parties is a fundamental prerequisite to a robust and reliable workflow infrastructure.

Workflow is defined differently by different people. For many, the terms *groupware* and *workflow* are interchangeable. The distinction is fuzzy at best. One must view groupware as an umbrella term that encompasses a broad range of group productivity applications such as group scheduling, information sharing, bulletin boards, discussion forums, and so on. Workflow applications are a segment of groupware applications.

Workflow applications can be classified into five segments:

- Ad-hoc Document and message routing such as resume review and voting
- Administrative Forms such as expense reports
- Queue-based applications such as electronic help desks
- Collaborative workflow such as home loan processing
- Production workflow such as insurance claims processing

Messaging serves as an ideal infrastructure for the first four of these segments. Highly repetitive, high-throughput, production workflow applications can leverage messaging for backboning and exception processing.

Exchange has the following capabilities, which makes it the ideal infrastructure to deploy workflow applications:

- Replicated, secure, extensible public folders that can serve as storage for workflow definitions and instances
- Container intelligence in public folders—Views, Filters, Folder Assistant
- Scaleable, extensible directory to serve as a roles database
- Form and behavior definition tools—EFD, Outlook Forms, VB Script
- Application coding languages—VB, VC
- Application Interface to Exchange services for workflow applications—MAPI

Additionally, workflow is composed of several other key technologies: e-mail, imaging, document management, and databases. The end result is that workflow should streamline business processes and reduce system costs by using workflow servers to perform tasks based on the business model (see Figure 32.1). These applications will be integrated with the Exchange client and will provide an agent running on the Exchange Server to process and manage the workflow.

FIG. 32.1
Workflow framework and technologies.

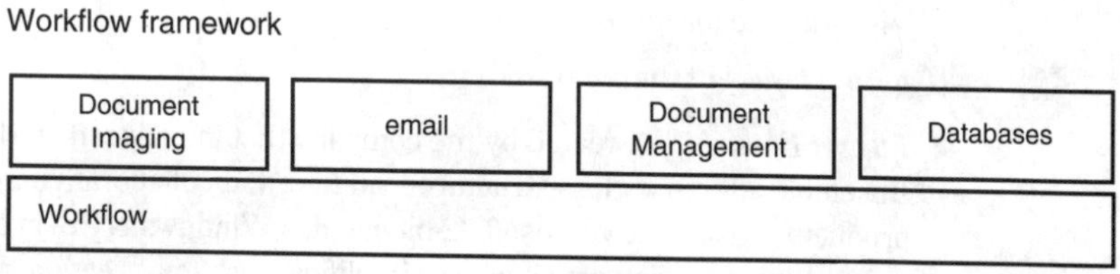

The following is a list of workflow technology solutions. Each product mentioned has a description of the components, as well as integration with Exchange. The products include Exchange client software integration and data routing to external database sources (see Figure 32.2).

- *KeyFile KeyFlow*—KeyFlow is among the first products to provide comprehensive functionality combined with ease of use that is seamlessly integrated with Exchange Server. The combination of KeyFlow workflow with Exchange Server enables global corporations to automate business processes, improve the efficiency of their organizations, and compete more effectively. All of this is provided at a truly affordable cost of ownership—far more economically than costly transaction-based workflow systems.

  Keyflow for Exchange Server provides a comprehensive suite of features and benefits for customers. A brief list of these features is given below:

  - Tightly integrated with Exchange
  - Graphical interface
  - Document attachments
  - Monitor running workflows
  - Production reporting
  - Conditional branching and looping

- Time-of-Day alerts
- Launch other workflows
- Exposed APIs

Visit this site for more information:

`http://www.keyfile.com`

- *Action Technologies*—Action promotes its Action Workflow System. Together with Microsoft, it is working on the Microsoft MAPI Workflow Framework. Action is a leader of the Workflow Coalition. This organization is promoting a common framework for workflow-enabled application. Action takes full advantage of Exchange's Groupware and Universal to provide an interface to the workflow of the business.

  Action uses Microsoft's Messaging Application Programming Interface (MAPI) and the inbox in the Exchange client to start workflows and then receive status reports via e-mail. The Action Workflow Manager Server triggers the appropriate business rules with respect to the business model. The Workflow Manager can populate a database with the information or route a request by way of e-mail to a subsequent recipient. This takes advantage of the existing network.

  Visit this site for more information:

  `http://www.actiontech.com`

- *FileNet Ensemble*—Created by the company that introduced workflow software, FileNet Ensemble addresses less-structured, ad hoc, and collaborative work. This client/server product for use on a Microsoft 32-bit client, a Windows NT Server, and a MAPI-compliant messaging architecture simplifies workflow creation, participation, and monitoring. You use a built-in process model to visually define the workflow, and then add details. Well-organized tab folders let you define criteria, such as the workflow item to route, the routing conditions, the participants, and their response options.

  Ensemble is fully integrated with Exchange, and this integration enables the storage of workflow-related messages in the Exchange Inbox and launches workflow-related tasks from the Inbox. Ensemble includes a workflow integrity checker (to verify the workflow's proper operation) and provides solid workflow auditing and monitoring for the cost of the product. Ensemble is a great tool for building workflow front ends. For example, you can link accounting applications to workflow-driven processes, such as requisitioning, travel and expense recording, time and billing, or budgeting. If developers need to develop more complex workflow solutions than Ensemble offers, they can add custom "agents" at any stage of the workflow.

  Visit this site for more information:

  `http://www.filenet.com`

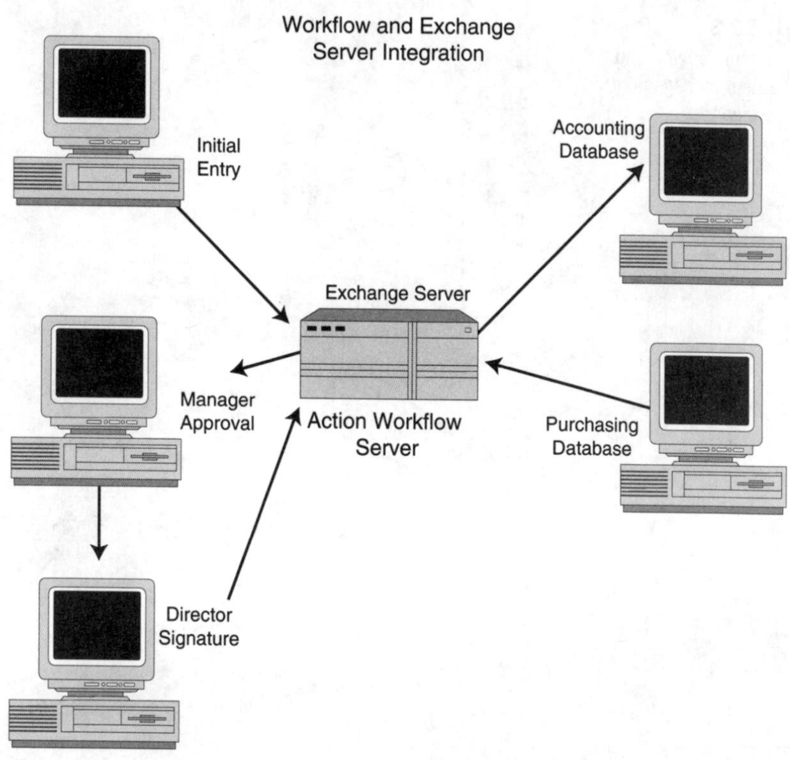

FIG. 32.2
Workflow business process.

Document Imaging and Management with Exchange

An important component for the development of workflow and collaborative systems and solutions is the capability to capture and manage the documents associated with a business process.

Document imaging is the capability to take an object, scan it, and store the image for later use on the computer system.

Document management is the capability to manage existing data or a newly created document in a variety of formats, including scanned images, audio and video files, word processing documents, spreadsheets, and so on. After the system has stored the object, the object is cataloged and managed for later use. This includes user-defined fields, object-file type conversions, version control, object indexing, and security permissions.

Both of these technologies are complementary and separate. Document imaging involves capturing the object from an external source: paper, fax, and so on. The image must be processed and stored. You then would store the image into a document management system, which could contain many different types of data objects (see Figure 32.3).

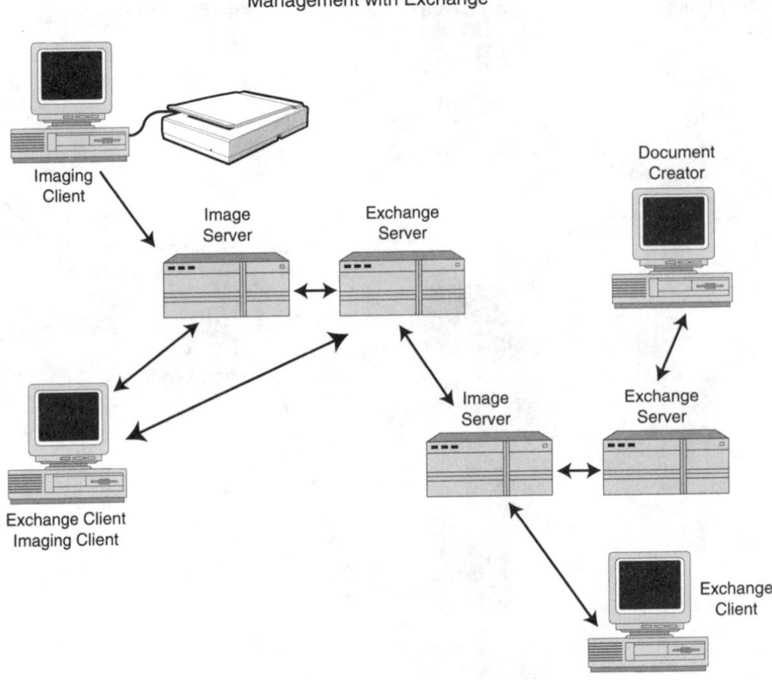

FIG. 32.3
Document imaging and document management with Exchange.

The following sections describe several document imaging and document management technology solutions. Each product mentioned has a description of the components as well as integration with Exchange. The products include Exchange client software integration and server connections to external image repositories.

- *FileNet's Watermark Enterprise Edition*—This is an NT-based imaging solution that tightly integrates with the Exchange client interface. Enterprise Edition image enables Exchange and other groupware applications. You can insert scanned documents, fax images, or even folders combining these images with other electronic document types to create custom solutions.

  Watermark Enterprise Edition can distribute scanned documents or faxes throughout the organization. This capability leverages the Exchange e-mail topology. Watermark provides the capability to e-mail a pointer into the storage system, to limit the amount of data transferred across the network, and to avoid duplicate copies.

  For more information:

  `http://www.filenet.com/watermark`

- *FrontOffice*— FrontOffice for Exchange is one of the first NT/Exchange-based products in the emerging groupware-based document management arena. Groupware-based DM systems can leverage groupware features like e-mail, routing, discussion databases, scheduling, electronic forms builders, and workflow. They can also integrate with other custom applications built on the groupware platform. As groupware systems add new features such as Windows NT and Internet integration, groupware-based DM systems can leverage them. FrontOffice for Exchange is a powerful tool for organizing, managing, and securing corporate documents across the entire enterprise and publishing to public folders, intranets, and the Internet. It can scale to support small workgroups or thousands of users. Exchange can also scale horizontally by implementing services on multiple servers or vertically by taking advantage of high-end features, such as SMP processors, to support huge numbers of users or volumes of documents. It utilizes a powerful three-tier architecture that streamlines processing between the client and the server.

FrontOffice for Exchange includes component technology such as ActiveX Controls, OLE Automation servers, and DCOM Network Communications. It integrates with your entire Microsoft BackOffice solution, builds upon the investments you have already made in that technology, and provides a complete set of administrative tools from within Microsoft BackOffice and Windows NT. Its native design enables FrontOffice for Exchange to automatically take advantage of extended functionality developed for Windows NT and Exchange.

Visit this site for more information:

`http://www.FrontOfficeTech.com`

- *PC Docs*—PC Docs provides a set of electronic tools for publishing documents and accessing the information through the Inbox in the Exchange client. An add-on product to DOCS Open, DOCS Interchange for Exchange, enables you to publish documents and document profiles stored in a DOCS Open library to existing public folders in Exchange. The DOCS Interchange Agent (a component of Interchange for Exchange) is responsible for distributing documents to Exchange folders and updating previously published documents as changes occur.

  DOCS Interchange for Exchange enhances collaboration among coworkers by enabling users to add discussion threads to published documents. Document authors can monitor these discussions in Exchange and, from an Exchange folder, access the associated documents in DOCS Open. As documents are revised, DOCS Interchange for Exchange automatically republishes the updated version to the Exchange folder.

  Visit this site for more information:

  `http://www.pcdocs.com`

Information Sharing

Information sharing is the capability to have group discussion forums with threaded conversations about a document, topic, or project. This capability is similar to an Internet News Group. Information sharing is one of the technologies that facilitates the implementation of groupware throughout organizations. The term groupware can encompass many technologies and human interaction paradigms. The information-sharing paradigm is defined as human interaction from one to many. In this way, a user can write to one place, and then many people can access and comment on the information. Exchange Server features permit organizations to easily implement groupware solutions (see Figure 32.4).

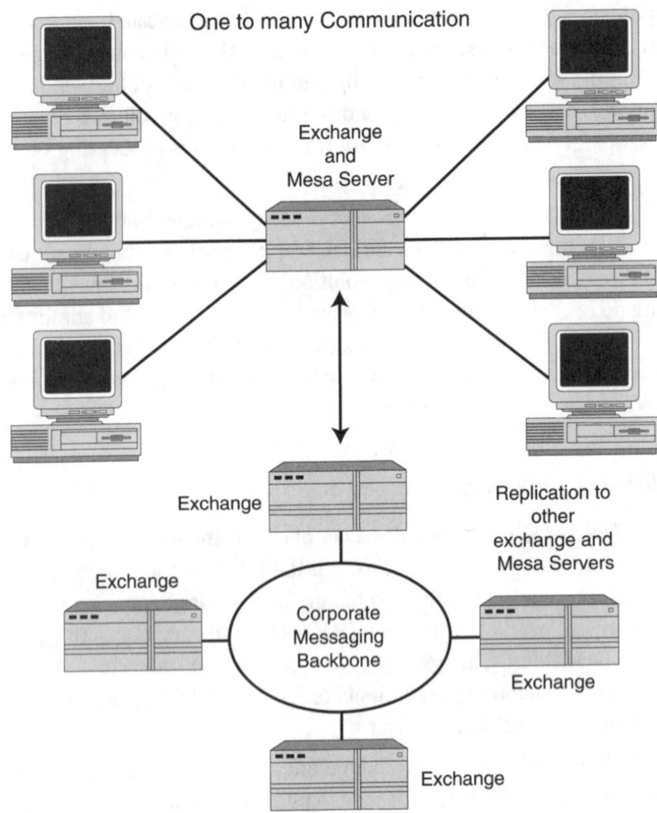

FIG. 32.4
Groupware: one-to-many communication.

- *Mesa*—Mesa has a product named Conference Plus. This application is an add-on to the Exchange client. Another folder appears in the Universal inbox in the Exchange client, representing the Conference Plus information store. After you click to open this folder, you can access the information with the threaded conversations.

  Mesa writes its information to the MAPI v1.0 Exchange data structure. Mesa was one of the first third-party developers that worked on Exchange solutions by using MAPI as the enabling interface. Mesa's MAPI Message store runs as another Exchange service, taking full advantage of the rich administration and replication tools.

  From the client, Mesa enables direct access to Conference Plus folders by way of the Exchange inbox as a root-level folder. Mesa then provides an Exchange Interchange that provides two-way replication between Conference Plus folders and Exchange Mesa message stores to address existing users of Mesa. Finally, a migration utility is included to assist with converting folders from Conference Plus to the Exchange MAPI message store architecture.

Mesa is currently working on an Exchange Interchange for Internet News Groups, Lotus Notes, and other interchanges as needed in the marketplace.

Visit this site for more information:

`http://www.mesa.com`

- *Verity*—topicTEAM for Exchange is an Exchange groupware application that enables distributed workgroups to track and share information—no matter where they are located or when they participate. A team moderator defines the group's goals and objectives, and creates the environment for the electronic conference. Team members can quickly and easily view and contribute to the discussion, promoting strong interaction and involvement from the entire group.

  Visit this site for more information:

  `http://www.verity.com`

Understanding Information Providers

Information providers leverage the content-driven focus of Exchange Server. Exchange can be leveraged as the foundation of an information retrieval and distribution system within organizations. This technology demonstrates the power of this client-server application framework.

Several companies provide intelligent agents running on the Exchange Server or client to retrieve information on a given subject (see Figure 32.5). This technology can parallel what is known as a "web crawler" on the Internet. These agents are given a specific topic and poll their respective information feeds.

This function is configured in a manner similar to other server-based rules on Exchange. The end user accesses the rules policy from the client workstation with the Exchange client and tells the agent what information to gather. At this point, the agent on the server (or client) executes the request and is not dependent on the client being connected. The agent returns the information and resources to the user.

- *Lexis/Nexis*—Lexis/Nexis is a leading provider of enhanced information services and management tools. The company's mission is to help legal, business, and government professionals collect, manage, and use information more productively. Lexis/Nexis is an information-service bureau with access to thousands of new sources of information daily for a broad range of topics.

  The user agent is configured to connect with Lexis/Nexis, execute the query, and return the "hit list" to the user. The user then can download the information that is needed. One of their products that integrates with Exchange is Tracker. Tracker searches across an index of 2,400 newspapers, with over 100,000 new articles each day. Users can customize

Tracker as needed to obtain specific information. Tracker gives professionals a competitive edge by providing a daily source of targeted, up-to-date information for decision making.

Visit this site for more information:

`http://www.lexis-nexis.com`

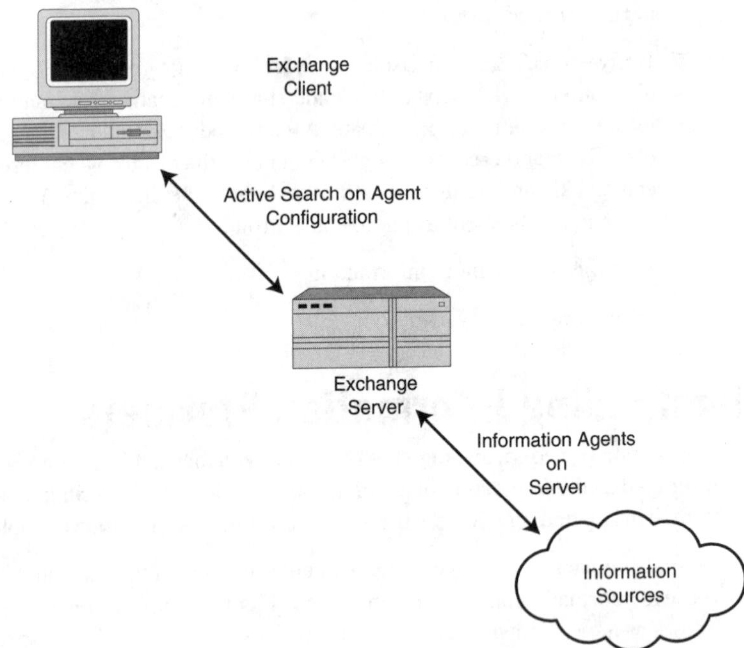

FIG. 32.5
Information providers for Exchange Server.

Communications Gateways and Connectors for Exchange

Connectors and gateways provide ways to integrate Exchange with legacy systems or to provide new functionality. These products provide wireless access to Exchange mail servers, connectivity to third-party messaging systems, integration with telephony functionality, faxing services, and paging services.

Communication Support for Exchange

Communications gateways and service providers for Exchange provide a mechanism for accessing the Exchange message stores by way of wireless networking protocols from a client PC or the technology to enable standards-based transmission of Exchange messages over X.400 and X.500 (see Figure 32.6).

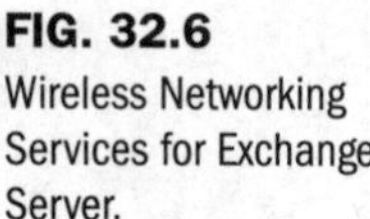

FIG. 32.6
Wireless Networking Services for Exchange Server.

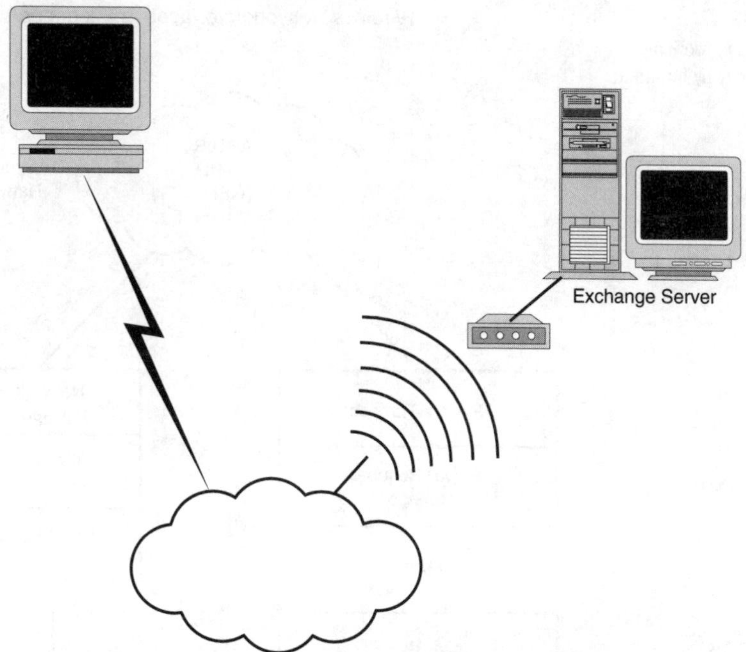

The process follows this scenario: A request is made from the mobile user on its PC with the Exchange inbox. The request is encapsulated in a message and transferred by way of the wireless network to a server-based agent. The agent then de-encapsulates the messages and performs the action dictated in the message. At this point, it communicates with the Exchange Server to send or retrieve mail, change a server-based rule, or perform another Exchange task.

The key standards for wireless technology are ARDIS, CDPD, GSM, and Inmarsat. The following list breaks down the technologies and service providers for wireless communication.

- *Inmarsat*—This is a standard satellite network provider with worldwide capability. Inmarsat is perhaps the largest provider worldwide, serving 50,000 users on land, on sea, and in the air. It provides both narrow-band and ISDN connections, and has worked closely with other wireless providers—AT&T, Vodafone, and Ardis—to create a set of standards for wireless networking. The goal was to split client and server functions from the network-layer transports.

  Inmarsat developed a solution to give the user a common interface to messaging (see Figure 32.7). It extends the MAPI interface with a wireless interface to provide ease of future development efforts over wireless networking. The technology is known as Inmarsat Wireless Messaging. The technology is composed of enhancements to the client, a middle-layer agent, and a server component. The technology integrates with other wireless networking standards—ARDIS, CDPD, and GSM.

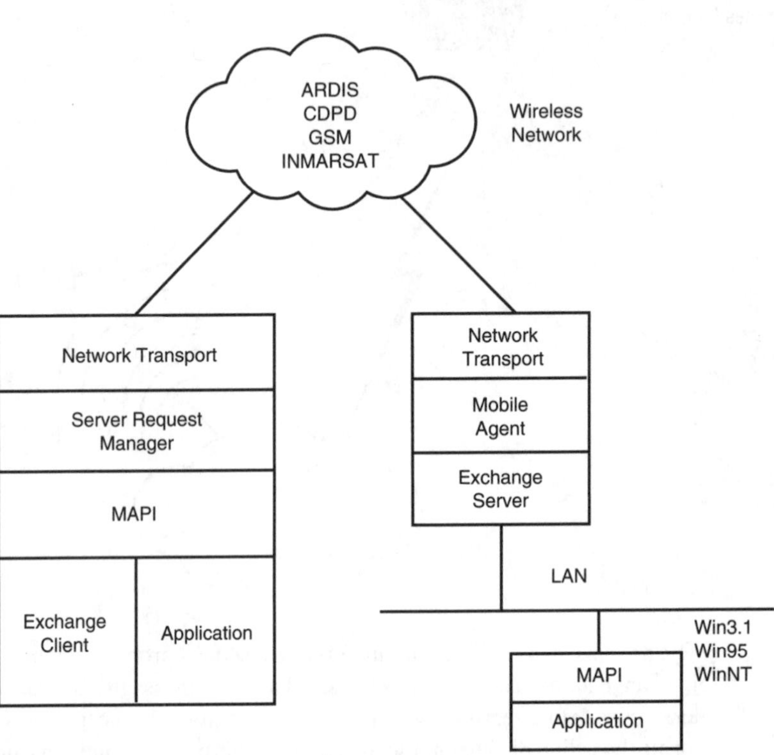

FIG. 32.7
Wireless networking technology by Inmarsat.

The key functionality of the user interface is the remote copy of message headers, remote copy of messages, remote deletion of messages, remote forwarding of messages, and remote configuration of user rules and filters. The server request manager interfaces with the Exchange Server. The purpose is to process client-side requests from the mobile agent. It performs this process by using standard MAPI transport providers.

Visit this site for more information:

`http://www.worldserver.pipex.com`

- *Vodafone Group*—Vodafone and Paragon Software have an Exchange Middleware messaging solution for wireless networking. Vodafone follows Inmarsat's wireless messaging technology to provide users with wireless access to Exchange around the world. Vodafone has 40 GSM roaming agreements to provide worldwide coverage. GSM is an organization that provides a standard for wireless communication, which is growing at the rate of 10,000 new customers each day. Based on the number of GSM agreements, Vodafone is a leader in wireless communication.

  Paragon provides Precis Link, which is a MAPI-based remote access standard for Exchange. Precis Link provides similar functionality to Inmarsat, with offline message processing, to include rules, filters, forwarding, and deleting.

Visit this site for more information:

`http://www.vodafone.co.uk`

- *AT&T*—AT&T wireless services provide wireless access into Exchange servers. AT&T relies on the communication standard, Cellular Digital Packet Data (CDPD). CDPD makes wireless data communication ready for end users. Currently, CDPD is deployed only in the United States. It's based on the TPC/IP protocol. This offers easy integration with existing infrastructures. CDPD offers transfer rates of up to 19.2 KBPS, enhanced security, and the capability to support voice and data. Forty-seven of the top fifty cities in the U.S. already have CDPD service available. AT&T's service hopes to provide a cost-effective solution for the workgroup model by allowing filed sales and support personnel to easily connect to resources.

  Similar to Inmarsat and Vodafone, AT&T enables users to download headers before retrieving messages, remotely administer rules and filters, and configure support for attachments. AT&T provides server-based agents to perform tasks for the client.

  Visit this site for more information:

  `http://www.attws.com/nohost/data`

- *Sprint*—Sprint provides Sprint Message Xchange (SMX) service for Exchange. SMX currently is used to link together various mail systems over Sprint's private network services. SMX now links Exchange LAN sites with other MS Mail, Lotus, and Exchange LAN sites. This method is effective to link LANs by outsourcing some of the messaging backbone to Sprint.

  Sprint's network extends to over 140 countries, which is a tremendous benefit if a company has both U.S. and European offices and wants to link together its Exchange LANs. Sprint acts as the messaging switch to support the connection, which is a huge cost savings to the companies because they can connect to Sprint in native Exchange formats without maintaining extra X.400 gateways. Sprint provides addressing templates for recipients on X.400, the Internet, fax, and telex.

  Visit this site for more information:

  `http://www.sprint.com`

Besides Sprint, several other value-added networking providers are working on supporting Exchange backbones. Services will provide companies with links from Exchange into legacy systems, Profs, All-in-One, and Officevision; into other LAN mail systems such as Lotus and cc:Mail; and into other forms of messaging—EDI, fax, telex, CompuServe, X.400, and the Internet. A good way to think about these public and private networks is as a way to out-source gateways and address/message conversion processes. By supporting native Exchange formats, the providers can allow easy integration from the corporate LANs into trading and business partners.

Gateway Support for Exchange

Gateways and connectors are used to extend Exchange into existing LAN-based mail systems or legacy host systems (see Figure 32.8). They also can provide new types of functionality, such as faxing and paging, to enhance messaging within the organization. With Exchange you can implement Exchange-specific connectors as well as leverage existing MS Mail gateways.

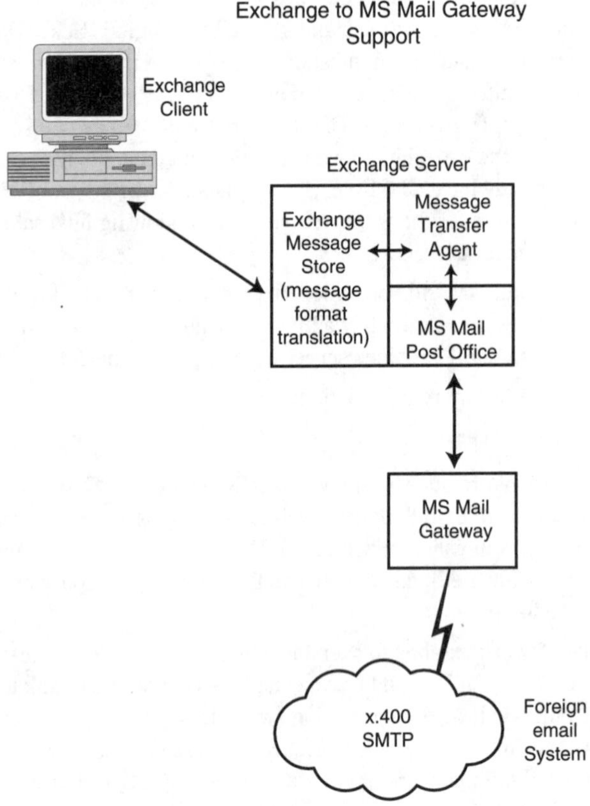

FIG. 32.8
The MS Mail gateways for Exchange Server.

The following is a list of gateways and connectors that can be used with Exchange:

- *Attachmate*—Attachmate is providing Profs and SNADS gateways for Exchange. These tools are used to extend Exchange into legacy SNA environments to link users with Profs and Officevision mail systems or use the SNA transport to communicate with other servers.

  The gateways are known as Zip! Office gateways for Exchange. These gateways enable users on VM/CMS host systems to share messages with Exchange clients (see Figure 32.10). The gateway routes messages and status reports between Exchange and the host systems. Host users can use Profs, CMS Notes, or CMS Reader to read and create messages. This gateway also is used for processing SENDFILE or PUCH requests from VM to the LAN.

  Exchange manages the in- and out-bound messages for the Zip gateway. Exchange stores the out-bound messages in its MTS Out folder. The Zip gateway polls this folder and, when it finds a message, processes the message. After the gateway has the message, it translates the message and attachment to be forwarded to the host system.

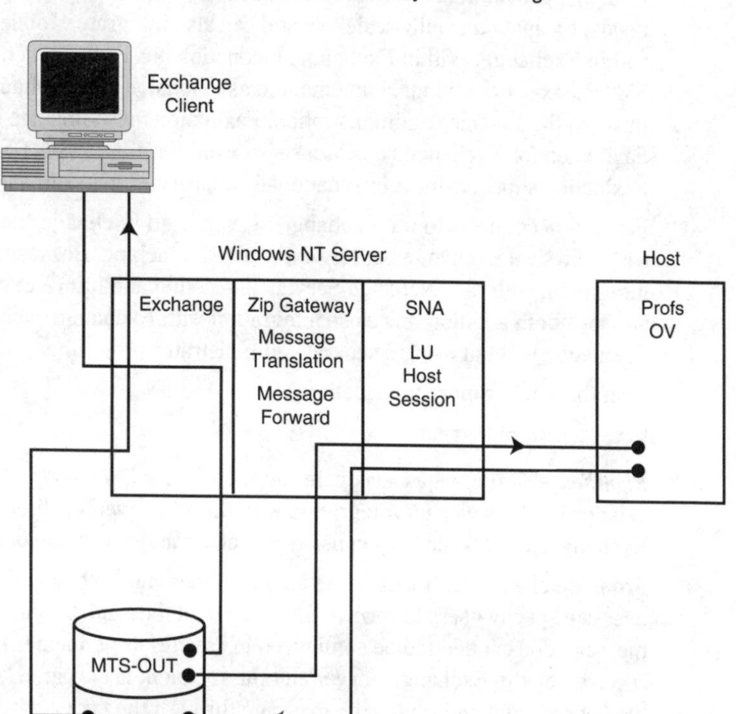

FIG. 32.9 ZIP! Office gateways for Exchange Server.

NOTE Due to message formats on the host systems, only one attachment can be sent in the body of a message. If multiple attachments must be sent to a host recipient, multiple messages must be used.

For more information:

`http://www.attachmate.com`

- *Fenestrae*—Faxination 3.0 for Exchange is a natively integrated fax solution specially designed for Exchange. It adds the power of sending and receiving faxes from, or within, Exchange, just like e-mail. Due to the true native integration, Faxination provides ease of use, ease of management, cost savings, and reliability. The cost of ownership is extremely low.

  Faxination for Exchange offers productivity enhancements and can actively control telecommunications costs by offering automatic “off-peak hour” scheduling and “least-cost routing” options. There is no need to install additional fax client software, provide additional end user training, or change workflow procedures. Faxination for Exchange is designed as a native Windows NT service. Faxination is available in English, German,

French, Spanish, Italian, Norwegian, Swedish, Finnish, and Danish. To suit your future needs, Faxination is fully scaleable and can also integrate Mobile messaging and Telex within Exchange. Within Exchange, Faxination is a Fax connector similar to X.400 and SMTP. Fax-specific items, implemented as extensions on Exchange, can be administered through the Exchange administration. Faxination fully supports Exchange 5.0. Faxination for Exchange runs as a service on the Windows NT Server or Workstation. Faxination supports most internationally approved ISDN and analog faxboards.

Faxination connects to the Exchange Server as an Exchange transport. It can run on the same physical Exchange Server or a separate machine. Because Faxination has native integration with the Exchange Server, all existing and future Exchange clients are fully supported. In addition this close integration with Exchange enables you to administer Faxination without using a separate administrator program.

Visit this site for more information:

`http://www.fenestrae.com`

- *RightFax*—RightFax has a fax gateway solution for Exchange. This gateway runs as a Windows NT service for integration with the Windows NT directory services and Exchange. The fax gateway consists of a client and server set of components.

  From the client, a user can create an e-mail message. When defining the recipients, the user can specify users to receive the same mail message by way of fax. (The mail message doesn't need to be configured in any different manner.) When the message is received by the Exchange Server and the recipient list is parsed, the server recognizes the fax recipient and routes the message through the fax gateway.

  On incoming faxes, RightFax supports DID lines for individual caller fax identifiers, which requires additional hardware to support phone-line trucks or direct connections to the phone systems coming in via T1 connections. One fax server can service over 700 DID lines. For a large organization, this capability enables every individual to have a direct fax line. When the fax server actually receives the incoming fax, it resolves the destination user recipient on the Exchange mail system by the DID identifier. The user receives faxes just as he or she does an e-mail message or other inbox applications.

  The RightFax client becomes integrated with the Exchange inbox on the desktop. This client has numerous advanced features, including support for DTMF, OCR, Imaging letterhead, signatures, voice prompting, group send options, delayed transmissions, and support for complex graphics. Additionally, you can send document attachments by way of fax without doing the conversion on the client PC. The conversion is handled by the server gateway.

  Visit this site for more information:

  `http://www.rightfax.com`

- *Ikon Office Solutions*—The Ikon Wireless Messaging Server (WMS) makes sending a page as easy as sending an e–mail message. Using the Wireless Messaging Server and Exchange, you can automatically send wireless messages and pages to any digital or alpha-numeric pager from the convenience of your desktop. You can even send wireless messages to PDAs or laptops with onboard paging cards or wireless modems.

One of the most powerful features uses Exchange's "Inbox" and "Out of Office" assistants to automatically forward messages from a workstation to an alphanumeric pager or a laptop with an onboard paging card or wireless modem. You can even create rules to forward e-mail messages that meet your specified criteria.

Another powerful feature is the ability to send a wireless message via the Internet. When the Wireless Messaging Server is installed in conjunction with the Exchange Internet Connector, both the wireless and Internet addresses are created at the same time. This enables users to send a wireless message from anywhere in the world.

Visit this site for more information:

`http://www.ikon.net/wms`

- *Octel*—Octel developed a framework for voice messaging on top of the Exchange platform. The Unified Messaging Strategy consists of using the e-mail backbone for Exchange to connect to PBX phone switches and route voice mail directly to the desktop in the Exchange client inbox (see Figure 32.10).

  Octel positions the phone systems as an extension to the messaging architecture of an organization. From within the inbox you may receive e-mail, faxes, documents, and now voice mail. Voice mail also can be accessed 24 hours a day by touch-tone phone. Voice mail has many of the same communication properties that e-mail uses. Voice-mail messages are stored and forwarded between users as needed. The messages also are routed by content or request.

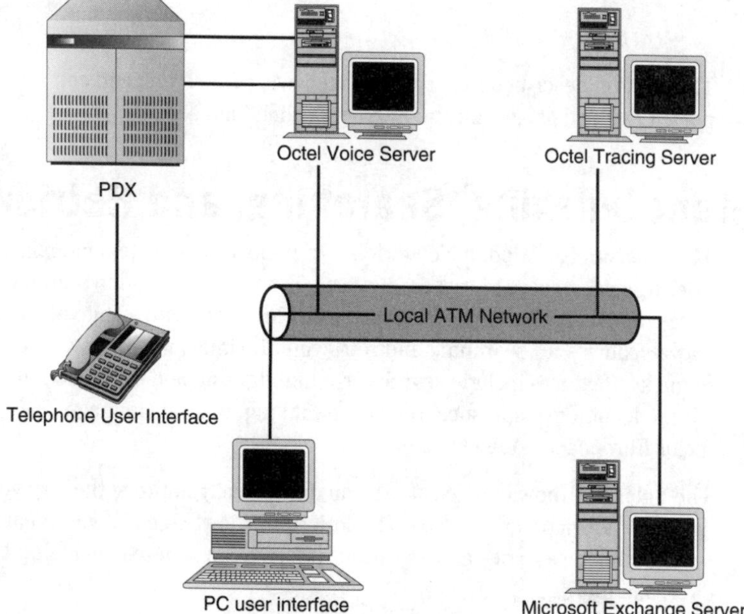

FIG. 32.10 Sample office configuration–Octel Voice-Mail gateway for Exchange Server.

The Octel server provides in- and out-bound voice functionality. It acts as a voice-mail gateway to external systems. The user can create a voice-mail message from the desktop and have Octel route the message to the destination to be played back for the user. This Octel system can take advantage of multimedia PCs but doesn't require them. If a user has sound capabilities on the PC, the voice-mail message can be played back from the PC. If the user doesn't have sound capabilities, when he or she opens the e-mail note that contains the Octel message, Octel dials the user's phone number from the PBX and plays the message back over the phone.

The key to this strategy is that Exchange and Windows NT will handle all the directory services for the enterprise. The Exchange account that originates from the Windows NT Domain account also will be used for the voice-mail system. A component of the user account includes the voice-mail system information. However, all the voice-mail data is stored inside the Exchange message in a compressed format. Octel also plans to include faxing as a functionality of this Unified Messaging Strategy.

The Octel server supports voice, fax, text-to-speech, and voice recognition. This includes support for DTMF, DID lines, PBX connectivity, and open computer-industry standards for customization. The server is based on Windows NT and takes full advantage of the user accounts, Windows NT registry, Event Log, performance monitor, and all other Windows NT management utilities. Octel provides additional management capabilities for the Octel server by way of Exchange's Administration utility and a separate administration application.

Visit this site for more information:

`http://www.octel.com`

This section described many of the gateways, connectors, and communication protocols supported by third parties for the Exchange client and server.

Content Indexing, Searching, and Retrieval

The Fulcrum Knowledge Network is a high-performance text-indexing and retrieval engine offering rapid access to vast amounts of corporate information stored in documents or databases. Fulcrum Knowledge Network provides users with a suite of advanced information retrieval features for searching and retrieving the information they need to build knowledge. Some key features include search-term highlighting and navigation to pinpoint information within documents, statistical relevance ranking, natural language searching, and support for major European and Asian languages.

The Fulcrum Knowledge Network can dramatically improve the way your organization manages its information resources. The Fulcrum Knowledge Network enables users to conduct single, unified searches across various information sources, including Exchange Server, web sites, and more.

Visit this site for more information:

`http://www.fulcrum.com`

Virus Protection Products

With the rapid pace at which new computer viruses are being created and spread, organizations must implement virus detection and cleaning tools. Virus infections, especially macro viruses, are particularly hard to eradicate because viruses can hide in old message attachments and public folders. The following section presents a subset of third-party products that provide this functionality for Exchange Server.

- *Cheyenne*—Cheyenne AntiVirus Agent for MS Exchange Server detects and cures viruses in documents attached to Exchange messages. The Agent works in real-time with Cheyenne InocuLAN, which is certified to detect most, if not all, viruses—including the rapidly spreading macro viruses. The AntiVirus Agent works on messaging servers, scanning all file attachments before they can be delivered to the desktop. Users can also perform scheduled scans of the Exchange system. Like all Cheyenne anti-virus products, the Exchange agent tightly integrates into Cheyenne's anti-virus system, making it easy to remotely manage and update your anti-virus soft vare.

  Key features include the following:

  - Support for Exchange 5.0 and previous versions
  - Scan and cure of attachments in Exchange E-mail and shared libraries
  - Notification of viruses by Exchange E-mail and other methods
  - Real-time and scheduled scan and cure

  Cheyenne's AntiVirus Agent for Exchange Server works in conjunction with Cheyenne's network anti-virus solution, InocuLAN. It scans for viruses in documents attached to messages while the messaging system is live and running, without impacting users. Infected files are automatically cured and users are notified directly through e-mail.

  Visit this site for more information:

  `http://www.cheyenne.com`

- *Trend Micro Inc.*—Trend Micro's ScanMail enables the administrator to manually scan for viruses in old files to ensure a clean start-up environment. Depending on how your Exchange Server is deployed, ScanMail can check Internet or Intranet e-mail attachments for viruses.

  ScanMail uses Trend's proprietary virus scanning engine, which incorporates both rule-based and pattern recognition technology to provide detection and removal capabilities for more than 8,000 known computer viruses. ScanMail will also incorporate MacroTrap, Trend's patent-pending generic macro virus scanning engine, which will detect and remove known and unknown macro viruses. Viruses that cannot be cleaned may be mailed to Trend Micro's Virus Hospital.

  ScanMail provides automatic web-based updating. The system administrator may also configure ScanMail to automatically update the pattern file weekly or monthly.

  Visit this site for more information:

  `http://www.trendmicro.com`

Various ISV Solutions

Several companies have developed third-party enhancements to Exchange. These enhancements include electronic forms, Visual Basic reporting, directory service providers, security, and more. The following products continue to describe additional ways to leverage an investment in Exchange.

- *Delrina*—Delrina offers its FormFlow electronic forms designer package for use with Exchange. The package offers forms and data routing, using the Exchange topology. This forms package offers database connectivity, multi-platform support, printing, and scalable architecture.

  Visit this site for more information:

  `http://www.delrina.com`

- *Crystal Reports*—Seagate's 101 Crystal Reports for BackOffice CD provides you with the information you need to create a cost-effective and efficiently managed Microsoft BackOffice solution. It turns the vast amount of data stored within the BackOffice environment into useful decision-making information.

  Seagate Software products provide the only way to report on information stored in Windows NT® Event Logs and Exchange Administrator Objects. Seagate Crystal Reports Professional and Seagate's 101 Crystal Reports for the BackOffice CD provide presentation quality reporting, including integrated graphing and distribution of reports via e-mail. With Seagate Crystal information you can add scheduling and automatic information sharing to your BackOffice reporting solution, including publishing of information to an Exchange Public Folder.

  It includes over 101 reports with data access DLLs for the Windows NT Event Logs, Exchange Public Folders, and Exchange Administrator Objects. Each report is ready-to-run. Simply click on the refresh button in Seagate Crystal Reports Professional or Seagate Crystal Info to refresh the report with your own data. You can customize the reports on the CD to add fields, graphs, and drilldown options.

  Visit this site for more information:

  `http://www.img.seagatesoftware.com/crystalreports/`

- *Nortel Entrust*—Northern Telecom's Entrust security technology provides the software-based encryption and digital signatures services. Security is important because it provides a wrapper around confidential or sensitive data. The content of the message is guaranteed by a digital signature. The digital signature ensures the identity of the sender.

  With Entrust's security in Exchange, Exchange can be used for electronic commerce, electronic transfer of funds, or database transactions. Nortel provides a solution for large-scale management of cryptographic keys. The automated key management is invisible to the end user, yet provides privacy into a distributed computing environment.

  Entrust provides support for RSA, DSA, DES, and CAST security algorithms.

Visit this site for more information:

`http://www.entrust.com`

- *Casahl Technology Inc.*—Replic-Action for Exchange 5.0. Replic-Action is a client/server-based data replication and migration tool that accesses, transforms, and synchronizes data between Exchange and back-end relational databases, legacy systems, and Lotus Notes. Replic-Action for Exchange is targeted at corporations that want to integrate or migrate their groupware tools and workflow processes into their existing IT environment to capitalize on and maximize the use of their existing data. Replic-Action for Exchange provides users with access to corporate data, even triggering workflow processes based on changes in corporate data, all within a single user interface—Exchange.

  Casahl's Replic-Action for Exchange 5.0 includes three major components: Composer, Server, and Server Manager. Composer is a GUI tool from which users can easily and visually create Replic-Action applications by simply following a user-friendly wizard—without programming. The Replic-Action Server runs as an operating system process to serve the Composer applications. Replic-Action Server Manager is an administrator application that enables users to monitor and configure multiple Replic-Action Servers.

  Visit this site for more information:

  `http://www.casahl.com`

We mentioned several third-party solutions for Exchange, But this list is by no means complete. Please contact Microsoft for continued updates to the list of ISV's developing third-party applications for Exchange at the following web page:

`http://www.microsoft.com/exchange`

For additional information on third-party products that leverage the Exchange infrastructure, visit the following web page:

`http://www.amrein.com/eworld.htm`

Consulting Solutions

Microsoft Consulting Services (MCS) is committed to assisting large customers to effectively design, deploy, and maintain all types of Exchange organizations. MCS also partners with Software Spectrum to conduct an Exchange Planning Workshop (EPW). More information on the EPW is presented in the following list.

In addition to Exchange consulting, MCS also offers:

- *Architecture and Design*—MCS provides solid architecture and design consulting using the Microsoft BackOffice family for your distributed computing environment.
- *Line-of-Business Application Design*—Drawing upon its own expertise as the world's leading software developer, MCS has designed, as well as managed, the development of mission-critical client/server applications for several large companies. Using the

Microsoft Solutions Framework (a proven methodology), all knowledge is transferred to fully empower your company.

- *Project Management*—MCS can also serve in a project management role. Here, MCS guides your team through the enterprise-wide projects providing quality control, team management, and knowledge transfer to all involved.
- *Enterprise Program Manager (EPM)*—The EPM program is designed for organizations that see value in a close, long-term relationship with MCS. A senior-level consultant would work on-site for typically a one-year commitment. This close relationship enables the consultant to fully understand your business and leverage MCS's expertise and resources to successfully design and deploy Microsoft technologies within your company.

For more information on Microsoft Consulting Services, visit this site:

`http://microsoft.com`

Software Spectrum-TSG has extensive experience in the implementation of messaging, collaborative, and workflow systems. We have performed these kinds of services for our Fortune 1000 customers throughout the world. By implementing our proven methodology, we ensure the successful completion of projects in a timely and cost-effective manner. The areas where we can assist our customers in regards to messaging and collaborative solutions include the following:

- Developing an enterprise-wide messaging architecture.
- Providing project management services.
- Implementing and deploying the messaging infrastructure and clients.
- Assisting the IT operations group in defining and documenting standard operational processes, such as:
  - Helping in the definition of staffing requirements.
  - Developing training programs for the administrative staff.
  - Developing, documenting, and implementing Exchange system monitoring, administrative, and maintenance procedures, disaster recovery procedures, and public folder policies and procedures.
  - Developing an Exchange Public Folder hierarchy to serve as a core component of information sharing and knowledge management systems within organizations.
- Performing business process re-engineering consulting services to automate existing processes through the use of Outlook forms and public folders. This can include the implementation of workflow through the use of products such as KeyFile's KeyFlow for Exchange.
- Providing Outlook forms development services.
- Implementing third-party solutions that integrate with Exchange Server to provide faxing services, document management services, and integration with telephony systems such as Octel's Unified Messenger.

Software Spectrum also offers consulting worldwide in the following focus technologies: networking, application development, Internet/Intranet Services, enterprise management (Microsoft's Systems Management Server), and of course, enterprise messaging.

For more information on the Exchange Planning Workshop, contact this site:

`http://www.softwarespectrum.com`

Phone: (800) 624-2033

For more information on consulting, contact the following site:

`http://www.softwarespectrum.com`

Phone: (800) 753-3266

CHAPTER 33

Developing Exchange Forms

In this chapter

This chapter introduces you to the world of making custom applications for Exchange and Outlook without prior programming experience. If you're already familiar with Windows and Visual Basic, you'll have a very easy time using the Forms Designer interface.

The Forms Designer lets you lay out all the different fields on your form, link them to messaging objects, and designate actions on events. Without any previous programming experience, you can create applications that will make your organization more productive. Many example applications are provided on the Exchange CD-ROM. You can use these pre-designed forms and modify them for your use.

The Forms Designer enables the creation of two types of forms:

- Stand-alone forms: These forms are not associated with any particular folder. They facilitate data input with the intent to send data to an individual or group of users. These applications include message-taking, office supply requisitions, and vacation requests.
- Folder forms: These forms facilitate the input of information into a public folder where permitted users can view it in an organized way. These applications include group discussions, bulletin boards, and enterprise-wide groupware databases. Filters can be applied to move data into subfolders, and views can be applied to group or soft information.

Among the potential custom applications you can create are *electronic forms*. In many organizations there are standard forms routed to specific individuals. Using the Forms Designer, you can create a travel request form, time-off request form, or office supply requisition. These applications take the work out of making simple requests. In addition, with the integration of *public folders*, the forms are easy to distribute throughout the organization. You no longer have to make sure that everyone has the most up-to-date form, and that they have enough copies. Distributing the forms electronically makes it easier for the user, and for the recipient who receives all the forms. The recipient can easily organize and process all the requests in the universal Inbox.

Another strong suit of the Forms Designer is to maximize the effectiveness of public folders. By designing an application, you can make it really easy to enter data into a public area. A great example of this use is for those organizations that post a lot of memos. Instead of printing out the memos and distributing them through the mailroom or by e-mail into everyone's Inbox, you can just create a public folder called Company Memos, and then write an application that lets the user enter the memo into some structured fields. Once the user executes the form, the memo is posted to an appropriate subfolder under the main Company Memos folder. The subfolder could be based on a field on your form that has a drop-down list of company departments. Everybody wins using this system. The mail room folks have less junk mail to route, the people in the copy room have less to copy (which saves toner), and most importantly, paper is saved, which is good for the environment.

Installation of the Exchange Forms Designer

As mentioned throughout this book, the Forms Designer is a *client application*. It is installed with Schedule+/ and the Exchange Client, as well as Outlook. You may not have installed it when you installed the other components, however. The following list is an installation procedure:

NOTE Before you install the Exchange Forms Designer on your workstation, please consider using 48MB–64MB of memory. This is especially needed for application development that uses the Visual Basic 16-bit program to extend your applications.

These recommendations directly affect the capability of your development environment. ■

1. From the Client CD-ROM, under either the Eng directory or the Frn directory, double-click the EfdSetup directory and choose Setup.
2. Choosing Complete/Custom from the menu, you see two options—Exchange Forms Designer and Sample Applications. This option gives you the option to install the Sample Applications. You may also choose Typical setup, which automatically installs the Forms Designer and the Sample Applications.
3. From the Complete/Custom window, choose Change Options.
4. In the Options box, select Forms Designer and Sample Applications and then choose OK.
5. Choose Continue.

If you had any previous version of the Forms Designer on your drive, Setup detects it and displays a screen asking you to reinstall, add/remove programs, or remove all. Any forms you create will not be overwritten by any new versions you may install.

Along with the application, all the different sources of help are installed. There are three different sources of help when you are designing applications: Cue Cards, Online Help, and Online Documentation.

These various sources of online help are a great supplement to this chapter. You will get the context-sensitive help you need, and at the same time you'll get more step-by-step tutorials to walk you through all the functions. The online manuals give you access at your fingertips.

Using Forms in Your Organization

Exchange's structure provides for many different uses of the containers in the hierarchy. You can design applications that leverage this flexibility.

Discussing Applications

In many organizations, several different teams work on different projects. As they get ideas, they usually send out an e-mail to all the people involved. As the weeks go by, everyone winds up with many e-mail and voice-mail messages that have no structure. Many are simply carbon copies, forwarded messages, or replies. Recipients usually must go back and sift through all the messages looking for information.

Some groups use a ***bulletin board*** or ***internal newsgroup*** to help centralize all the data. The only problem with this solution is that most e-mail packages that provide bulletin board capability have poor security. You can't control who can post, read, or modify. When using Usenet-style newsgroups, you can't control very easily who can read and post. You either would have to set up passwords or host entries for each machine to read or post. It isn't very easy or robust.

Using a custom Exchange application for discussion, you gain all the access control that is inherent in Exchange and NT Server. You can allow only members of the proper teams to access their information. In some cases, you would want to allow read-only access to people in other groups to promote team cooperation. Exchange's public folder structure is flexible enough to enable this.

Using a custom application can structure the data. The forms you create can contain certain fields, and information about threads. The capability to structure information in different views gives the user the ability to choose a report sorted by date, author, or subject. You can also use structure subjects if you want to keep discussions along a certain topic.

Some of the most common uses of discussion applications are customer-support databases, brainstorming applications where team members can input ideas as they come to them, frequently asked questions lists, and meeting summarization applications.

Referencing Repositories

Exchange serves as a great repository of documents and objects as well as e-mail. You can easily write applications that provide easy access to all your standard documents throughout the enterprise. Many organizations have several standard documents, such as policies and procedures manuals, style guides, and computer-usage guidelines. In addition, many organizations have standard Word document templates. These objects can be placed in an Exchange public folder and made available right on the user's desktop.

Explaining the Forms Environment

A few pieces of the Forms environment need to be explained in the scope of the large Exchange picture. These components consist of the following:

- Forms libraries
- Views
- Rules

- Permissions
- Items

Forms Libraries

When you create a form, you save and install it into a Folder Forms Library. The properties of the forms saved into a particular folder are dependent on the properties of the folder. This includes access permissions. When the user chooses New Form on the Tools menu in the Exchange Client, a list of forms available in the folder is presented.

The Global Forms Library The Global Forms Library houses all the forms you want to make available to everyone in the enterprise. These forms could include vacation-request forms, corporate memos, or telephone message forms.

The Folder Library Every folder, either public or private, has a forms library associated with it. You can save forms into one of your private folders, but they will only be shared with anyone to whom you have given access to your folders.

By putting forms into a public folder, you allow robust sharing based on the permissions of the folder, which are generally easy to change if the need arises. When new users are added to the Exchange system, their group memberships can determine to which public folders they have access.

Say you had a group called Directors, for example, that contained people at or above the level of director in your organization. You could create a folder that contained a form these users could fill out that would make it easy to enter product data sheets, and store them in a public folder so that all people at that level or above could view and modify them. The folder you set up has the permission properties set to enable only members of the NT group Directors to view and modify.

The Personal Forms Library This library is not shared with any other user. It contains the forms the person uses most often. If you have functions you perform every day and create a form to automate those tasks, you would place the form in your personal library. In addition, you can use these forms when working offline as long as your default information store resides on your local disk.

Views

Because forms reside in folders, it is pertinent to discuss folder views. Global views apply across all forms and folders, and folder views apply only to the selected form containing the view.

Think of views as the different reports generated off a database. In the old days, you had to write different report specifications to get the data you wanted presented in the order you wanted.

Views enable you to order information and present it to the user the way he or she would like to see it. When you establish a form, you create structured fields within it that lend themselves very nicely to the four kinds of views:

- Filtering: Using filtering gives you the ability to view only information that meets certain criteria. Let's go back to the Directors example. If you want, you can set a filter to display only product descriptions of a certain product line rather than the whole line.
- Sorting: This view enables you to sort on any field. In the example, you can easily sort by part number or department number. Even better, you can sort by director name, which lets you easily see which director was responsible for which products.
- Grouping: Grouping lets you use a hierarchical model such as the Windows Explorer in Windows 95 or the File Manager in Windows NT. You can click a certain title to expand or collapse the information. You can group the items by product line, and then filter down to more specific product information for each product in that particular line.
- Columns: You can format the data in your folder like a spreadsheet. This makes it very easy to read and very familiar to the majority of users. You can place all your fields in any order across the screen.

Views are created outside the form in the Exchange Client. Once you install a form into a Folder Form Library, all its fields are published to the library, enabling you to set up views easily later on in the Client.

Rules

Just as views are folder properties that apply to form, so are rules. Rules are a powerful feature in Exchange that enable you to control what happens to an item once it is submitted to a folder.

Many e-mail packages have this functionality in some form. In most cases, however, you must be logged in to your mail application for the rules to take effect. Also, most e-mail packages lack the ability to do this with bulletin board-type functionality.

With Exchange, an example of applying rules to a form entry would be that any item meeting certain criteria can be moved to a subfolder, e-mailed to someone else as a carbon copy, or even deleted.

This functionality gives you much more control over the organization of your data, and even helps reduce redundant entries. It cuts down on administration because everything is automatic once the rules are established. For more information on rules, see the section titled "Setting Folder Rules" later in this chapter.

Permissions

By establishing folder permissions, you control who has access to any of the forms contained in that folder's Library. You also control what the user can do in the folder. You can set options to allow read, write, and edit access. In addition, you can select pre-defined roles that enable the administrator to quickly establish a set of permissions for the user.

You can also delegate any user as an owner of a certain folder. This enables that user to give other users access permissions. This is analogous to Windows NT Server permissions that allow multiple users to be administrators for a certain domain. Giving someone else ownership permissions allows for multiple administrators and the delegation of responsibilities.

Items

An easy way to think of items is to think of database tables. In a database, tables consist of records, which consist of fields that have values. Exchange forms work the same way. Folders contain items that contain fields that have values. It's very straightforward. An item is like a record in a database.

Explaining the Form's Components

If you are familiar with Visual Basic at all, this section will be refresher material. If you've never used Visual Basic, this section will provide very important information that will aid you in understanding the form design process.

Visual Basic is mentioned because Exchange forms are Visual Basic Version 4 executable programs. They do not need to be run independently of Exchange, as the Exchange Client takes care of this process. Using forms is completely transparent to the user.

The Forms Designer serves as a front end to Visual Basic, so non-programmers can create robust applications using a simple tool without the advanced knowledge needed to use Visual Basic.

Using Visual Basic comes with some consequences. Non-Windows clients are not able to use Exchange forms because there is machine-executed code involved, and non-Windows platforms cannot run this code.

On the flip side, however, companies that have in-house Visual Basic expertise can build robust, enterprise-caliber applications that take full advantage of object linking and embedding, as well as SQL Server access. You could have an Exchange application, for example, that relies on the Global Address Book for addressing information, but at the same time writes fields to an SQL Server database somewhere on the network.

An Exchange form is made up of the following components:

- The Form Itself: The form's appearance and behavior are set through its properties that is discussed in the next section. You can use a form within a folder as a part of another application, or as a standalone application.

  The form itself acts as a shell that encases its components. It is at the top level of the hierarchical structure of the form.
- The Form Windows: Forms can contain multiple windows that are used for different functions. One window might contain addressing information, while another might be an output window. Windows enable you to keep the screen neat and logically organized by function. Keep this in mind as you design your forms.

By using multiple windows in the same form as opposed to multiple forms, you keep greater control. It is easier to pass information between windows than forms.

- The Window Fields: Each window presents information as fields. You determine which fields appear in which windows. You can either create new fields in each window or carry over field values from other windows in the same form.

  Fields are not limited to input and output: they also can be menus and toolbars. They can initiate actions by having events assigned to them. The field's actions are governed by its properties.

Setting Properties of Form Components

Setting a form's properties is the most daunting task facing the Form Designer. The application takes the desired effect through these properties. Properties sheets are the means by which the Forms Designer accomplishes its magic without the need for writing code. Depending on the properties of each object, certain actions bring about certain results.

As indicated by the title of the section, setting up the properties of each component is made easier because the properties are organized by Form, Window, and Field. The properties you can set for an item varies with the item:

- *Form Properties*: The general properties of forms consist of the display name, the icon the user will see, the version of the form, the item type associated with the form, and a brief description. In addition to the general properties, the event properties control what happens when a user takes a certain action on the form. If the user clicks a Submit button, for example, you could have the form display a configuration window showing the value of all the current fields.
- *Window Properties*: The general properties of a window are the name, tab order of the fields in the window, caption, and the WinHelp filename. You can also control resizing options, borders, and window colors with the format properties.
- *Field Properties*: In addition to the standard general properties such as field name, caption, and location, fields enable you to set initialization values. This enables you to set default values to all the fields in your window. If you have a radio button in your window, for example, you can set whether one button is the default, or no button is selected at all. Note that all these properties are discussed in greater detail when the design of a real form is discussed. Each property is explained in detail. What is important at this stage is that you get the feel for what needs to be done when designing a form.

Installing Forms

Upon the creation of a form, a form project file with an .EFP extension is created. It is very similar to a Visual Basic project file.

When you choose the Install command from the Forms Designer, several things happen that are transparent to you. The form files are taken by the installation routine and Visual Basic project files are created. This enables you to use these .MAK files and use them within Visual Basic 4 to extend your applications at a later time.

Once that happens, the form is compiled into an .EXE file, just as when you use the Make .EXE command from the File menu in Visual Basic. In addition, a configuration file with a .CFG extension is created. This is used by the forms library for installation.

After that step is completed, the form gets installed into the forms library of your choice. You will now be able to access your form from the folder you chose.

Planning Your Exchange Form

You now have all the information you'll need to create an application. The information in this section gives you a general overview of the steps to follow to create an application from beginning to end.

When designing a form, you should follow these simple steps:

- Define the purpose of the application. This sounds very obvious, but this simple step helps you stay focused. By determining what the form will do, you'll give yourself information that will aid in the design. If the application is a simple message-taking application that will be available to everyone in the organization, for example, you may want to keep the design very simple. You know that the form will most likely wind up in the Global Forms Library, so you might want to contact the administrator of the system to get permission to post it there.
- Define the fields. Defining the purpose of your form gives you a good basis for which fields you should include on the form. To continue the example from above, you might want to include the time the person called, his name, company, the message, and whether to return the call.

  It is a good idea to come up with a logical field structure, which will help you lay them out on the screen and decide whether you need more than one window.
- Create a folder for your application. You need to determine where your form will reside.
- Create the form. Using the Forms Designer, create the actual screen that will contain the fields. Drag and drop the objects onto the window on the form. This part of the Forms Designer feels very much like a drawing program. Make sure the form has a logical flow, and that all fields are appropriately marked.
- Set the properties of all objects. Once you create the form, you need to go back and set the properties of all the objects on your form, including the form itself. Although some people like to set the properties of each object when it is created, doing it in two steps enables people to collaborate on the layout and confirm all the field choices and names before moving forward.

- Install the form. Once you set properties on the objects on your form, you need to install it in order to test the functionality of the application. If the application spans multiple forms, be sure all the forms are installed in the folder. It's a good idea to keep the application in a personal folder so no one else can access it while it is being debugged and tested.
- Test the form. In order to make sure your form performs all the functions you intended and in the way you intended, you need to test the form extensively. Things to look for are whether the screen layout is correct, required fields are in fact required, and that button groups work properly.
- Design the views. As explained before, views let you order the data for your users. Once the form is installed, you need to establish the views that will better facilitate the purpose of the form. You can sort, group, filter, and make columns. Once you register your forms with the folder, users can access the views from the Exchange Client.
- Move or copy the form. Once the views are designed, and further testing is performed, you can move or copy the form into its final destination folder. In your first step, you knew who would be using the form, so you contacted the administrator to get permission to post the form into the proper public folder. You now use that permission and post the form. Planning ahead will save you a lot of time.
- Set folder properties. Now that the form is in a public place, you can set the properties that do such things as define a default view and whether or not the form is accessible. This is a good feature if you have not completely finished the testing process.
- Set permissions. As stated throughout this chapter, you can set the permissions of the public folder that houses your forms. If you only want certain users to access your applications, or want the form to be read only for certain people, you can set the permissions to reflect your wishes.
- Set folder rules. You can set rules to specify actions for incoming data based on conditions. You could use this feature to eliminate duplicate data, generate carbon copies to certain recipients automatically, or move data to subfolders.

You are now ready to create applications using the Microsoft Exchange Forms Designer. The next section goes into detail with a step-by-step tutorial. A sample form is created from scratch, showing you how the outline above helps you design custom applications.

Creating the Web Site Button Form

You are now ready to design a form from scratch. Try to follow the outline for designing forms as closely as possible.

Defining the Purpose

Many organizations that have World Wide Web sites on the Internet choose to advertise their sites on other servers. These companies must design forms that enable the technical staff to communicate effectively and quickly with the media department that purchases the space on others' web sites.

The form you're going to design facilitates that need. It makes it very easy to let the technical staff know exactly what's needed by the company housing the hypertext links.

Defining the Fields

The purpose of the form has been stated rather clearly, so move on to defining the fields you'll use on the form.

It is a good idea to collaborate with all the departments involved with the fields on the form at design time. They can provide a lot of key insights that will make the form much more useful to all the parties involved. For this form, the media, creative, and account departments need to be involved in the form-layout process.

The fields are shown in Table 33.1.

Table 33.1 Web Site Button Form Field Names and Descriptions

Name of Field	Purpose
To	Addressee on the technical staff
Date	Date the note was sent
Subject	User-definable subject field
Company	Company from whom you leased space
URL	Web site URL the button will reside on
OurURL	URL the button will point to
Size	Pixel size required by the company
StartDateEffective	Button start date
EndDateEffective	Button end date
Transport	Type of media required, if any
Address	E-mail address of company
Contact	Name of contact person
ContactPhone	Phone number of contact

This table is exactly what you should draw out before ever loading the Forms Designer. The field names are used later in the field properties definitions. The purposes of each field will also help you and your colleagues better design the form and add fields later.

Creating a Folder for Your Application

You now have to determine where your form will reside. For this application, just store the form in a Folder Forms Library. There's a person in the media department who coordinates all the web site space lease agreements and starts the routing of the form. She will use this form from a private folder. When troubleshooting the form, it is much safer to keep the form in a private folder until it is ready.

You don't need to do anything special to use your Folder Forms Library. The form-installation procedure does this for you. If you were using a public folder, you would have to obtain permission from the Exchange administrator to create the public folder and write items into it.

Creating the Form

You are now ready to launch the Forms Designer and start drawing out your form. This section goes through the procedure step by step. Figures are used to walk you through each step. Each figure is the result of the step before it. For example, step one will yield the figure immediately following it.

1. Double-click the Forms Designer icon. The Microsoft Exchange Forms Designer dialog box appears (see Figure 33.1).

You can use any of the sample forms provided to familiarize yourself with the different kinds of forms.

2. Choose the Form Template Wizard and click Next (see Figure 33.2).
3. Select To Another User (send) and click Next.
4. Select To Send info and click Next (see Figure 33.3).
5. Choose One Window and click Next (see Figure 33.4).
6. Type **Website Button Form** in the Name field, and **This form is used to send detailed information to the technical staff to expedite Web site media buys** in the Description field (see Figure 33.5).
7. Click Finish (see Figure 33.6).
8. Our form does not require a "cc" field. Click the middle of the field and press the DEL key.
9. We are now going to add the necessary fields to the form. First, select the Frame tool and click the right side of the form. A frame will be created that will house the StartDateEffective and EndDateEffective fields.
10. Now you'll create the text entry boxes for the fields that will go inside the frame. The frame is just an easy way to group fields. To create a text entry field, click the Entry Field tool and drop the fields inside the frame. Then resize the fields as necessary by dragging on the border when the arrows appear.

    There are a few ways to create multiple fields. You can either create each one separately, or you can create one, size it, and copy and paste it.

You can replace the word Caption with the text describing the field. Just click in the box with the text of the caption and type over it.

11. You now create a listbox containing the names of the companies you usually deal with when you buy space. You can always add new companies easily.

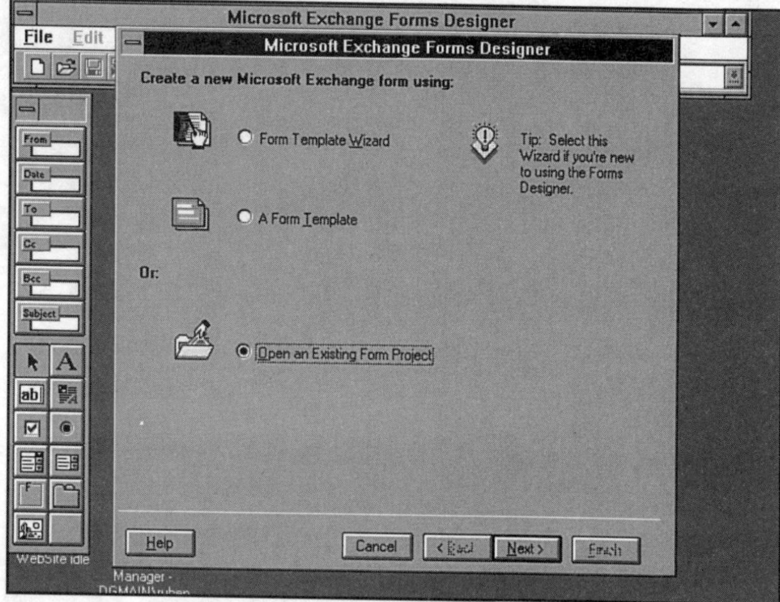

FIG. 33.1 You can use the Wizard, open a template, or use an existing application.

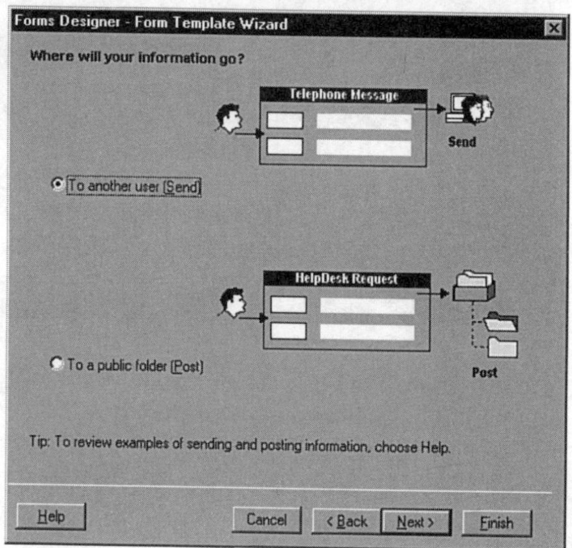

FIG. 33.2 The Wizard gives you the choice of using the form to send to another user or to post to a public folder.

FIG. 33.3
You can either use the form to send information, or let the user enter a response to an existing item.

Forms Designer - Form Template Wizard
How will your Send form be used?
To Send information.
Telephone Note
(While you were out)
To Send a Response.
Note: Choose this option to create a Response to a previously created Send form.
Company Picnic
Company Picnic
(Send)
(Response)
Tip: To review examples of using a Send or a Response form, choose Help.
Help
Cancel
< Back
Next >
Finish

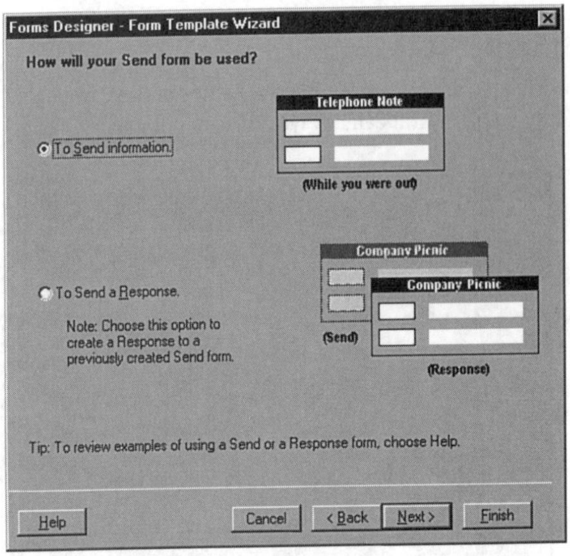

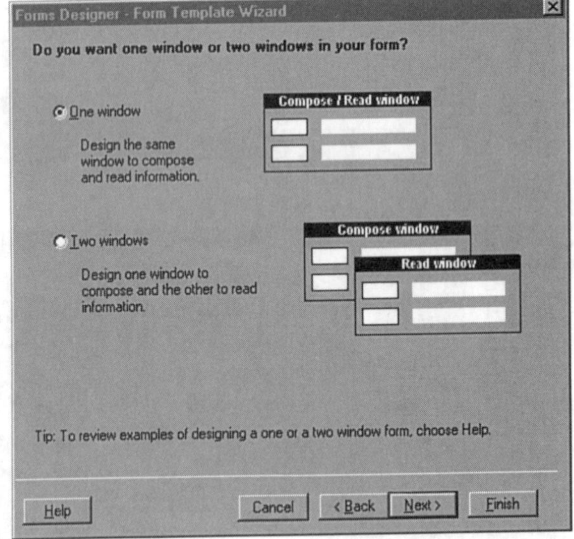

FIG. 33.4
The name and description given to the form determines how the user sees it in the Viewer.

Forms Designer - Form Template Wizard
Do you want one window or two windows in your form?
One window
Design the same window to compose and read information.
Compose / Read window
Two windows
Design one window to compose and the other to read information.
Compose window
Read window
Tip: To review examples of designing a one or a two window form, choose Help.
Help
Cancel
< Back
Next >
Finish

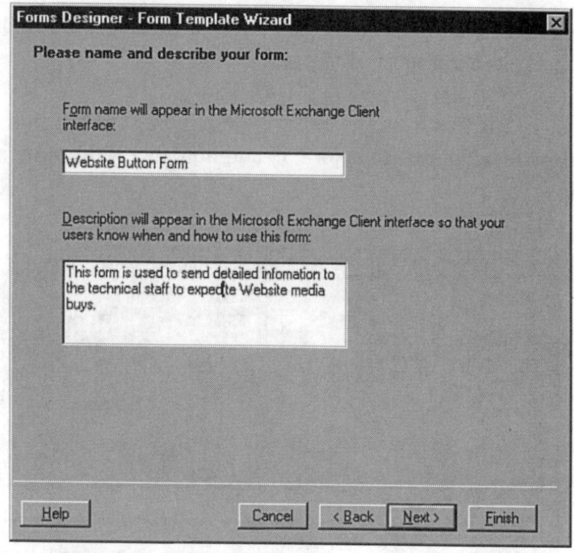

FIG. 33.5
The Finish screen of the Wizard shows you the next steps you'll need to take when designing your form.

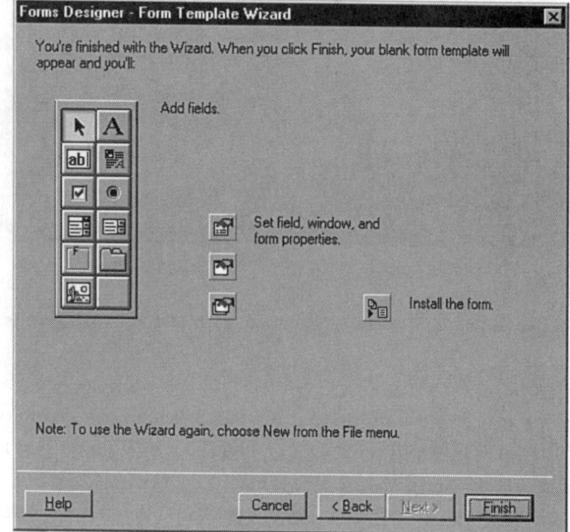

FIG. 33.6
Clicking Finish lays out the default fields onto the form and brings up the screen where you can add fields.

NOTE You could use an Entry Field for this field, but for this example, it is good to try to experiment with the different field types. ■

Select the Listbox tool from the toolbar. Drop it onto the left side of the form and size by using the same technique as before. In addition, type **Company** into the caption (see Figure 33.7).

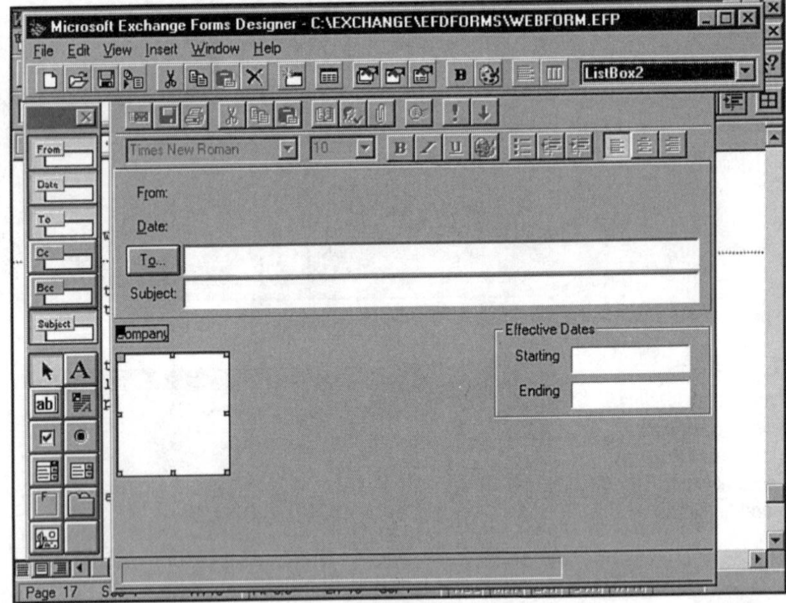

FIG. 33.7 You now have four elements on your form: a frame, two entry fields, and a listbox.

NOTE The items that appear in the listbox will be input later when setting properties for each field. ■

12. Next add three more entry fields that will sit between the frame on the right and the listbox on the left. They will contain the URL, OurURL, and Size fields.

It is a good idea to save your form at this point. Select Save from the File menu, give your form the name WEBFORM, and click OK.

13. Next you create the frame for the Transport field. This will consist of creating a frame with three radio buttons. The frame caption should read "Transport," and the three radio buttons should have the captions "America Online," "Compuserve," and "Internet," respectively.

    As a reminder, click within a caption to change the text and drag the edges of the box to resize. To move boxes around, click somewhere inside the box when the cursor is an arrow and drag the item around the form. If you are familiar with Windows applications, this should be familiar to you.

NOTE You'll notice that the listbox containing the company field has been extended. It is very easy to control the length of the box by dragging on the border. ■

14. You only need to create three more fields: entry fields that will hold the Address, Contact, and ContactPhone fields. They are shown in Figure 33.8.

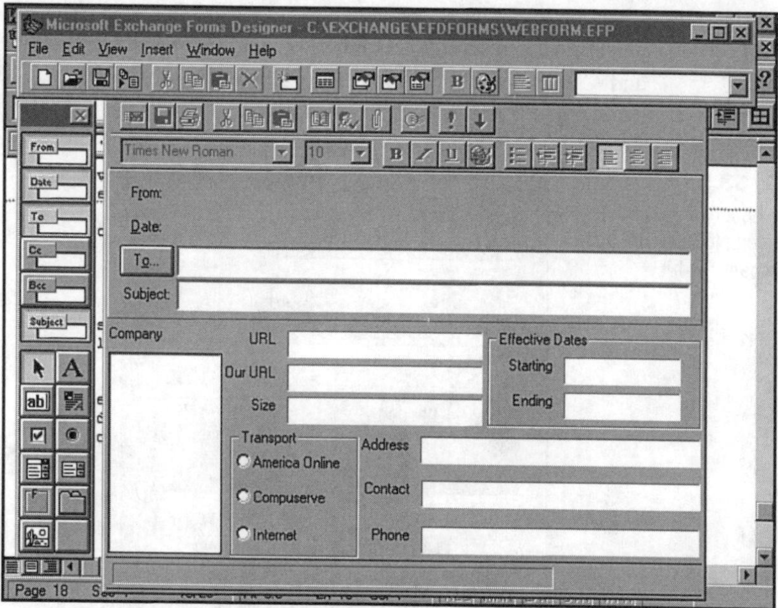

FIG. 33.8 The form is now completed.

Setting the Properties of All Objects

Now that the form has all the objects laid out on the screen, the next step is to make them actually perform functions, which is done through the use of properties.

Setting Form Field Properties First set the properties for all the fields on the form. The reason the fields come first is that each field is given a name in the properties field that makes it easier to reference when setting Window properties.

1. Double-click the Company field; the properties screen will appear as shown below. There are tabs of information: General, Format, and Initial Value.

You can select the field and press F4 instead of double-clicking the object. For fields in tight areas of the screen, this is the preferred method because double-clicking these areas sometimes yields strange results, such as the selection of text.

2. On the General tab, enter **Company** into the Reference Name field. The reference name is simply the variable name assigned to the field. You will use this when determining things such as tab order.

3. Check the Required check box (see Figure 33.9). This field is required because without a company name, the rest of the fields cannot be complete. The purpose you established earlier will aid you in determining whether a field is required or not.
4. Click the Format tab. This tab controls the font, alignment, appearance, and style of the field value and the caption. The formatting defaults are correct for your purposes for this application.
5. Click the Initial Value tab (see Figure 33.10). This tab differs for each kind of field. Since you are using a listbox, this tab gives you the opportunity to fill in the values in the list and select a default. Fill in the values according to Figure 33.9. These are the names of some popular web sites that sell advertising space.

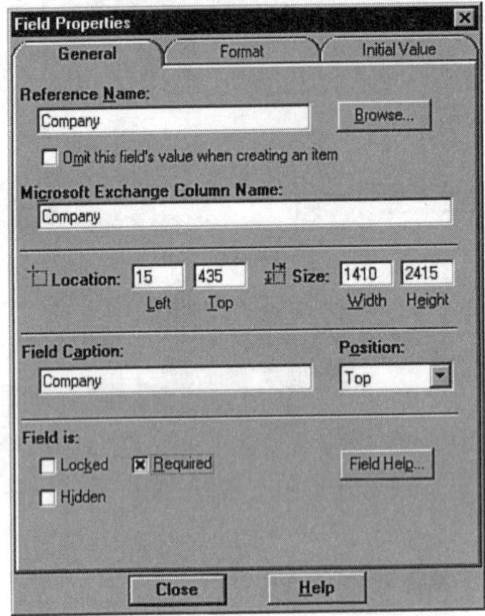

FIG. 33.9 The General Properties are complete for the Company field.

6. Click the Close button.
7. Move the pointer over the URL field and double-click.
8. On the General tab, type **URL** as the Reference Name (see Figure 33.11).
9. Check the Required check box.
10. Complete the procedures in steps 7 through 9 for all the fields remaining on the form. The Reference Name will match the Caption in the General tab of all the fields (excluding spaces).
11. Double-click the Internet radio button in the Transport frame.
12. Click the Initial Value tab.
13. Click the selected radio button.
14. Select Close.

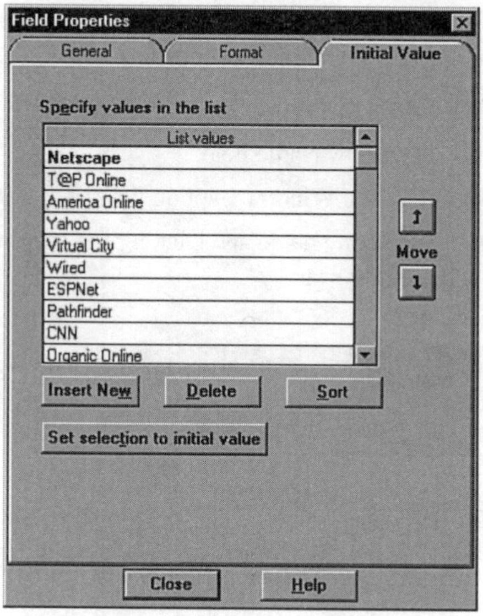

FIG. 33.10
Highlight any entry and click the Set selection to initial value button to make it the default.

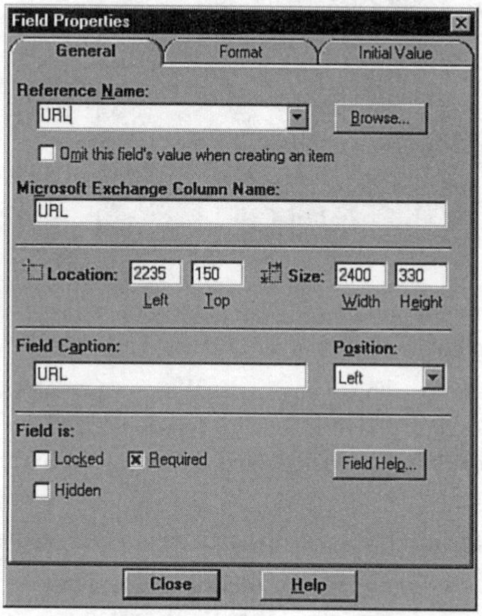

FIG. 33.11
The General tab contains the same information regardless of field type.

You've now completed all the form properties required for this form. You'll probably need to set other properties for other forms, and this example provides you with a good starting point.

Setting Window Properties Forms contain fields and windows. Just as fields have properties, so do windows. Follow these steps to set window properties:

1. Select Window Properties from the View menu.
2. Type **WebButton** into the Window Name field.
3. Type **Web Button Form** into the Window Caption field.
4. Establish the tab order by selecting fields and clicking the button marked. See Figure 33.12 for an example of the field order.

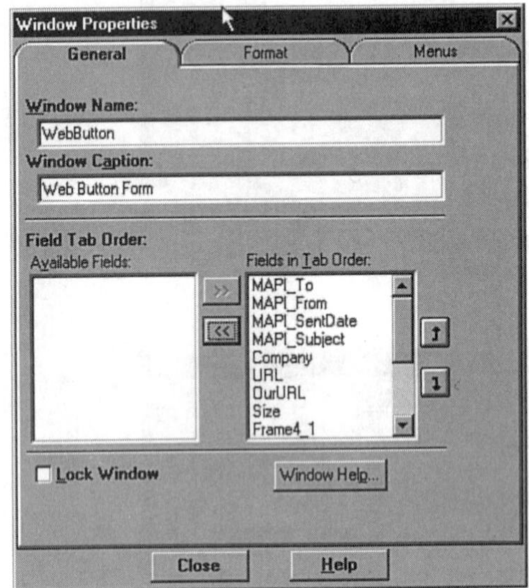

FIG. 33.12 The layout of the window is determined by its properties.

5. Click the Format tab (see Figure 33.13). This tab contains properties for window behavior. Background color, window icon, and title-bar icons are set using this tab.
6. Click the Formatting toolbar check box in the Window Options section. Since all the necessary fonts are configured for each field, you don't need the Formatting toolbar for this specific application. It has been removed to show you the variations you can make to a form. (You can leave.)
7. Change the Window Sizing Options drop-down box to Resizeable.
8. Click the Menus tab (see Figure 33.14). You can add and modify menu items here. For your form, you do not need to modify this at all. Refer to the online help and Microsoft documentation for more information on modifying menus.
9. Click the Close button.

The Window Properties have now been set. This is the second tier of properties you need to set for your form. This chapter now moves on to the third and final set of properties that control how the form itself interacts with the user.

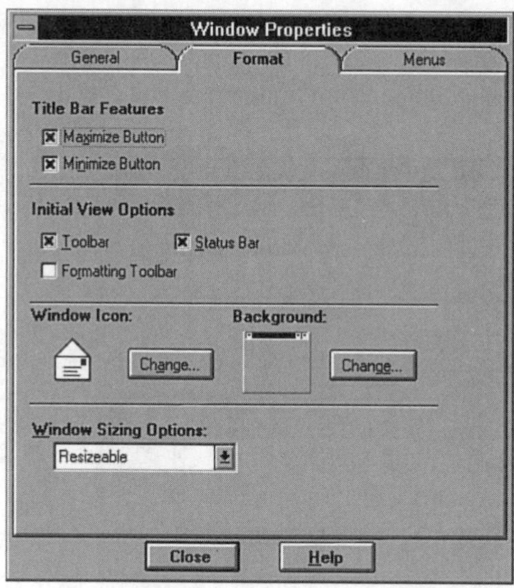

FIG. 33.13
Your Format properties are now complete.

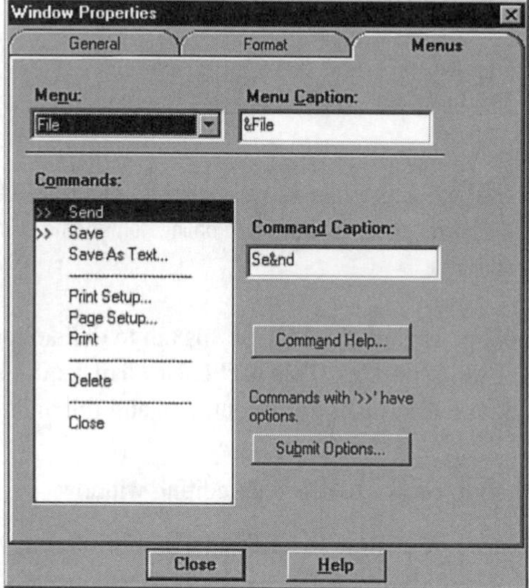

FIG. 33.14
The Menus tab gives you the opportunity to change the menus at the top of the screen.

Setting Form Properties You'll now set the form properties. Follow the step-by-step model, using the various figures to keep you on track:

1. Select Form Properties from the View menu.

You can also press Ctrl+F to get to the Form Properties.

This brings up the properties that define your form. As you can see, the General tab contains the Form Display Name and Description you entered in the wizard (see Figure 33.15). There are no other mandatory properties you need to set for this application.

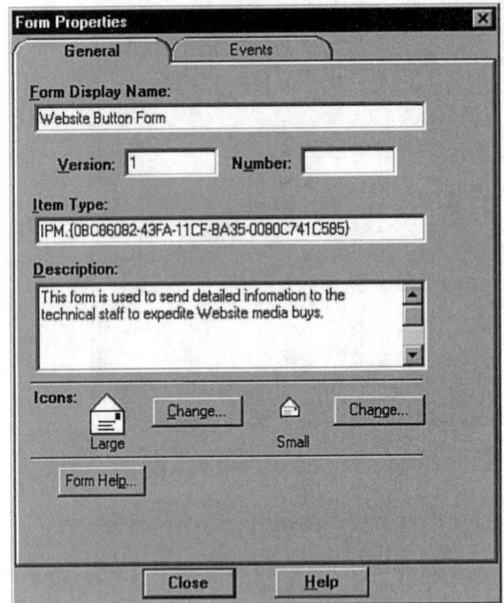

FIG. 33.15
Use the General tab to control how the user sees your form.

NOTE Although the icon and help settings are set here, they are not modified for this application. Please refer to the Microsoft documentation and online help for more information on setting up help for your applications. ■

2. Click the Events tab (see Figure 33.16). Use this tab to define how the form will react to different events the user generates. This particular form requires no modification of these properties. See the Microsoft documentation and the online help for a full description of these fields.
3. Click the Close button to return to the main editing window.

All the needed properties are now complete for this form. From here, you'll continue on with the list of steps that need to be followed when creating custom forms with Exchange.

Installing the Form

When you install a form, Visual Basic code is generated, and an executable file is generated that Exchange runs when someone calls the form. This code can be called up within Visual Basic later on to add more functionality to the form or application. Follow these steps to install the form:

1. In the Viewer, create a new private folder called **Web site Buttons** in your Mailbox container (see Figure 33.17).

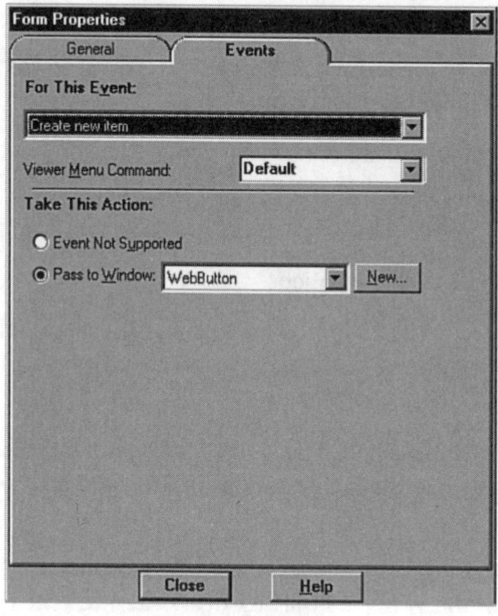

FIG. 33.16
The Events tab is used to control how the form will react when different events are triggered.

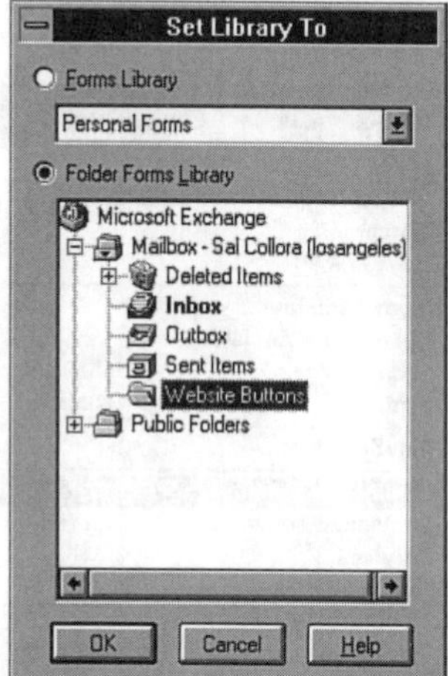

FIG. 33.17
The installation procedure does all the work for you. All you have to do is select where you want the form to reside.

2. Choose Install from the File menu. This initiates the process of calling Visual Basic and compiling the form. After the computer finishes all those steps, a prompt appears asking you where to install the form.
3. Click the Folder Forms Library radio button and select Web site Buttons from the list of folders. If the list doesn't appear, click the plus symbol to expand the tree of folders.
4. Click OK.

Testing the Form

You now need to run through the form to make sure everything works properly. This is really not a step-by-step process. Look for the following items:

- Required in the Field Properties are actually required to submit the form.
- Button groups let you select only one button.
- Form layout is correct.
- Fonts look appropriate at all resolutions.

To use the form, select New Web site Button Form from the Compose menu in the Viewer.

Designing the Views

The Column Name property of each field becomes very important when designing views. You can group, sort, and display information by any one of the column names you defined in the design phase.

The Web site Button form is used to send structured data to another user (see Figure 33.18). You've created a folder for the form, and will now design a view. When the user receives a Button Form in his or her Inbox, dragging into this folder will make the item conform to the default view. Follow these steps to design the views:

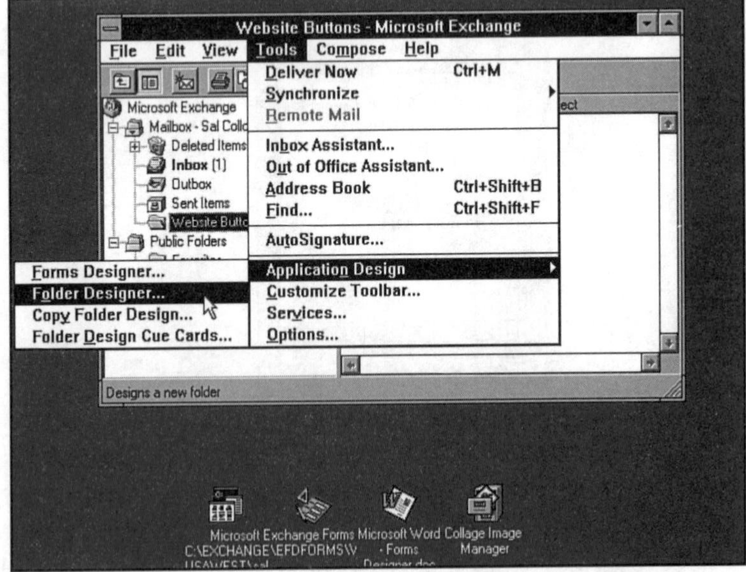

FIG. 33.18 Designing views is made easy by the Folder Designer.

1. From the Tools menu, choose Application Design, then Folder Designer.
2. Click the Views tab (see Figure 33.19).
3. Click the New button.

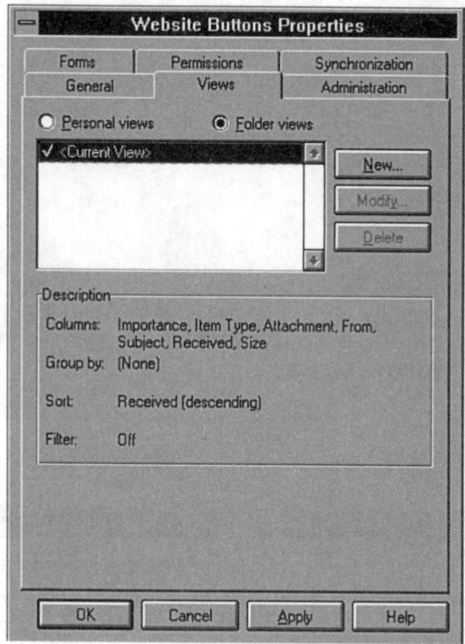

FIG. 33.19
The Views tab displays the views available and provides a textual description of each.

4. Type **by Company** in the View name box.
5. Click the Columns button.
6. Highlight each of the entries in the Show the Following list and click the Remove button so the list is empty.
7. Click Company in the Available Columns list and then click the Add button.
8. Click Transport in the Available Columns list and then click the Add button.
9. Highlight Transport in the Show the Following list and then click the Move Down button.
10. Click Address in the Available Columns list and then click the Add button.
11. Highlight Address in the Show the Following list and then click the Move Down button.
12. Click Sent in the Available Columns list and then click the Add button (see Figure 33.20).

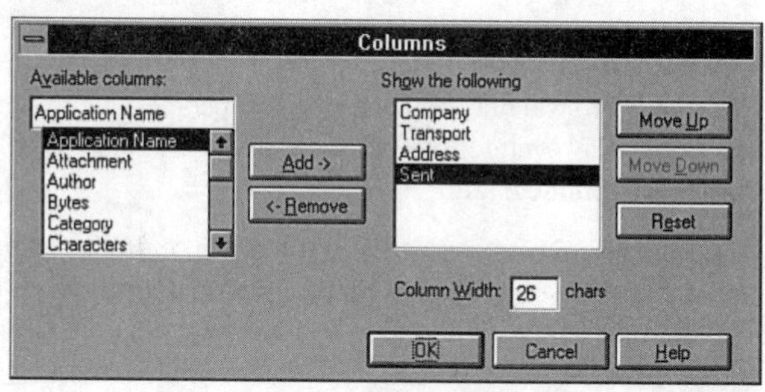

FIG. 33.20
The layout of the columns included in the view should look like this after steps 5–12 are completed.

13. Highlight Sent in the Show the Following list and then click the Move Down button.
14. Click OK.
15. Click Sort.
16. In the drop-down list, select Sent.
17. Click the Descending radio button.
18. Click OK.
19. Click OK.
20. Double-click the Company entry in the list check box. It is now the default view.
21. Click OK.

All the entries in this folder will now be displayed according to the view you created (see Figure 33.21).

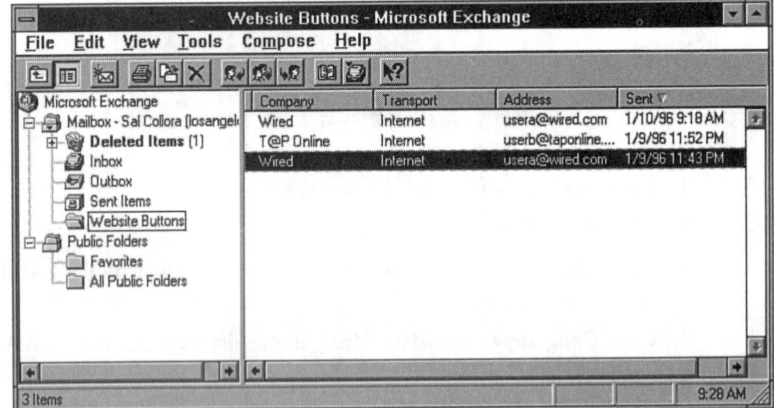

FIG. 33.21
Views determine how the items appear in the folder.

You have now completed all the necessary steps for the web site button form. The next steps are provided for demonstration only because this form is a send form, which is intended to simplify sending structured information to a particular user.

You can, however, make the public folder the recipient of the message. This would enable a centralized repository of all the Web site Button buys.

Copying or Moving the Form to a Public Folder

The Web site Button Form will only be used by a few people, so putting it into a public folder isn't really appropriate; however, for the purposes of illustration, you will go through the steps of copying a form into a public folder.

In some organizations, administration of these folders is centralized, and information policy prevents the administrator from giving users permission to manipulate public folders. The user must pass the folder on to the administrator, and have the administrator perform the following steps.

In some cases, however, a new public folder will be created, and permission will be granted to the user to manipulate the folder and its forms library. The following tutorial assumes you have all the proper permissions:

1. Select the Web site Button Form folder.
2. Choose Copy from the File menu.
3. In the Copy box, select the public folder into which you would like to copy the Web site Buttons form. In this case, it's the All Public Folders folder.
4. Click OK.

Setting the Folder Properties

Now that the form has been moved to a public folder, you must now follow these steps to set the properties for that folder:

1. Right-click the Web site Button folder and select Properties.
2. Select the Administration tab (see Figure 33.22).

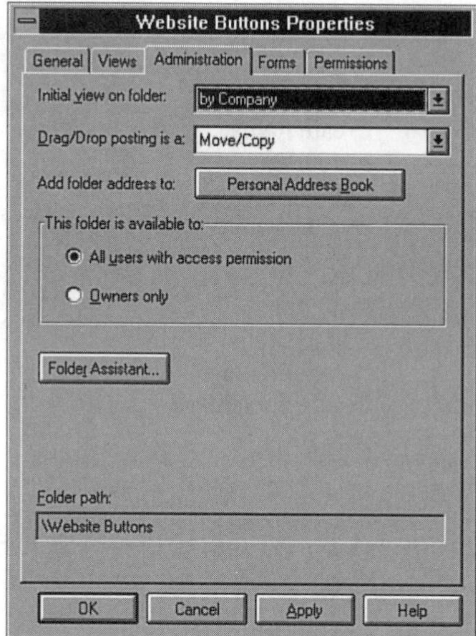

FIG. 33.22
The Administration tab should now be completed.

3. Select Company as the Initial view on folder. This will ensure that all items in that folder conform to the view we defined earlier.
4. Select Move/Copy in the Drag/Drop listbox.
5. Select the All users with permission radio button in the This folder is available to box.
6. Select the Forms tab.

7. Click the Only forms listed above radio button. This ensures that only the Web site button form will be allowed in this folder. This protects against someone putting in some other type of form, such as a Vacation/Absence form in the Web site Button folder.

Setting Folder Permissions

To set the folder permissions, follow these steps:

1. Click the Permissions tab (see Figure 33.23).
2. Click the Default user and change the Role to None. These are the properties for all users. Changing the Role to None means that users have no privileges in the folder. Table 33.2 lists all the roles and their associated permissions.

Table 33.2 Roles and Permissions

Role	Permission
Owner	All
Editor	Create Items Read Items Edit All Items Delete All Items
Author	Create Items Read Items Edit Own Items Delete Own Items
Publishing Editor	Create Items Read Items Edit All Items Delete All items Create Subfolders
Publishing Author	Create Items Read Items Edit Own Items Delete Own Items Create Subfolders
Reviewer	Create Items Read Items
Contributor	Create Items
None	No Permissions Granted
Custom	Enables you to set permissions that do not match a predefined role

3. Click the Add button.
4. Select the users you want to have access to your folder and click the Add button.
5. Change the role of each user you've added to Author. This allows them to Create and Read items in the folder. As you can see, each user can only edit and delete their own items.

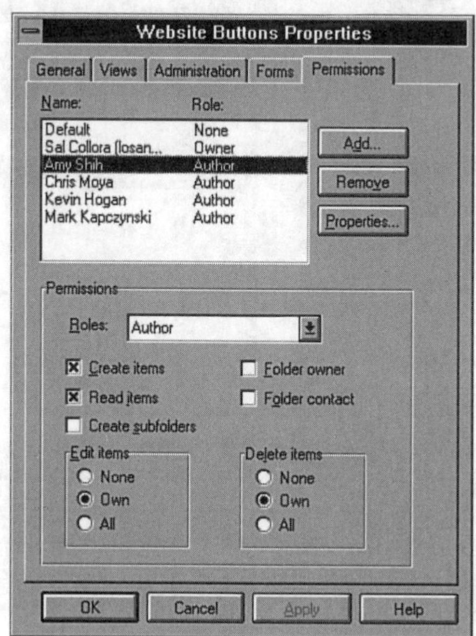

FIG. 33.23
The Permissions tab enables you to control who has access to your form and what operations each user can perform within the folder.

Setting Folder Rules

You can use rules for any folder, including the Inbox. Rules process incoming items by running them through a series of criteria. The rule itself is the action to take upon the meeting of those specified criteria.

Some organizations have people with certain contacts or specialties. You can set up rules to copy messages to certain users with those specialties.

You're going to set a rule that will forward all Web site Button requests for ESPNet to Ruben Perez because he processes all the ESPNet dealings. The user you choose obviously depends upon your own site. Follow these steps to set folder rules:

1. Right-click the Web site Button folder and select Properties.
2. Select the Administration tab.
3. Push the Folder Assistant button.
4. Click Add Rule.

5. Click the Advanced button.
6. Click the Folder: Web site Buttons radio button in the Show properties of group.
7. Select the Company check box.
8. Select the ESPNet listbox (see Figure 33.24).

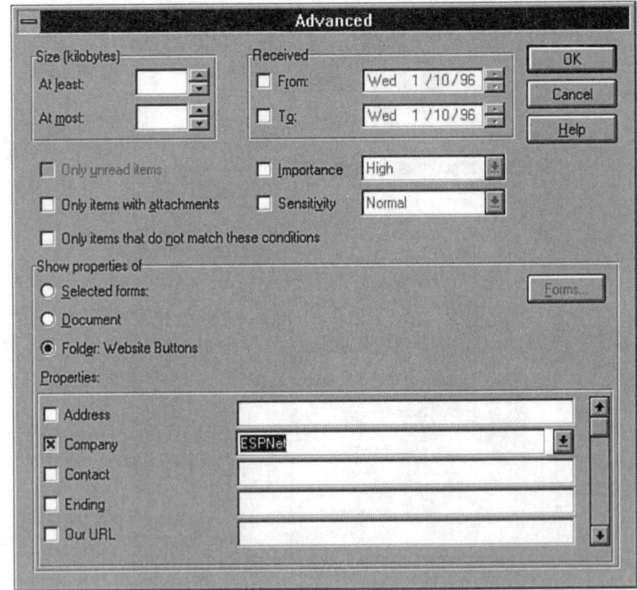

FIG. 33.24
In the Advanced properties, you select fields on the form as search criteria.

9. Click OK.
10. Click the Forward check box (see Figure 33.25).

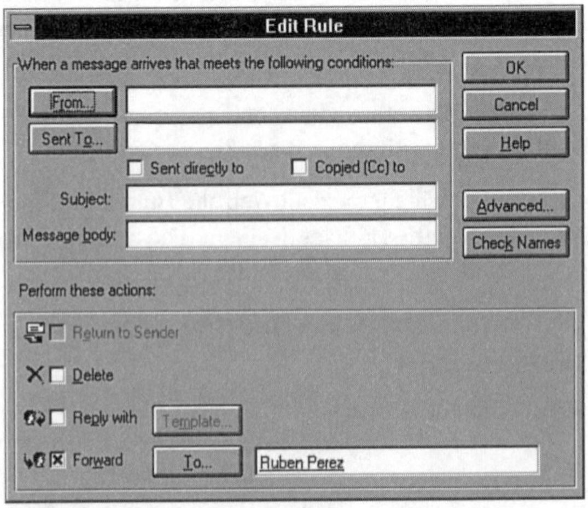

FIG. 33.25
You've now set up a complete rule. All ESPNet requests will be forwarded to the user you chose.

11. Click the To button.
12. Select the proper user from the list and click the To button.
13. Click OK.
14. Click OK (see Figure 33.26).
15. Click OK.

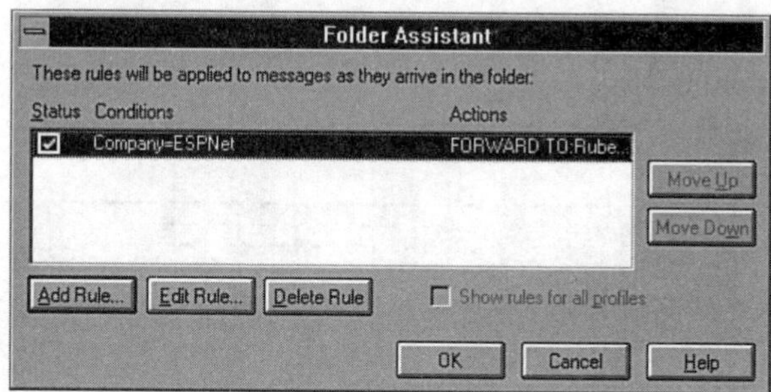

FIG. 33.26
The newly created rule is now added to the rule list in the Folder Assistant.

You've now completed all the steps in the folder design process. Your form now makes it a lot easier to expedite Web site Button requests. The purpose of using this type of application is to show you how you automate any kind of process.

The Exchange CD-ROM ships with many examples of common office forms. Using what you have learned here, you can go about modifying those for your own purposes.

Using Your Form

Now that you've created a new form and placed it in a public folder, accessing it and using it are a snap.

Address to a person by completing the following steps:

1. Select the Web site Buttons Folder.
2. From the Compose menu, choose New Web site Button Form. The forms appear on your screen.
3. Fill out all the required fields.
4. Click the To button.
5. Select a recipient and click the To button.
6. Click OK.
7. Click the Send icon.

Address to the Web site button Public Folder by completing the following steps:

1. Select the Web site Buttons Folder.
2. Right-click and select Properties.

3. Click the Administration tab.
4. Click the Personal Address Book button. This copies the name of the folder to your Personal Address Book so you can send an item to the folder.
5. Click OK.
6. From the Compose menu, choose New Web site Button Form. The form appears on your screen.
7. Fill out all the required fields.
8. Click the To button.
9. Select Personal Address Book from the Show Names from listbox (see Figure 33.27).

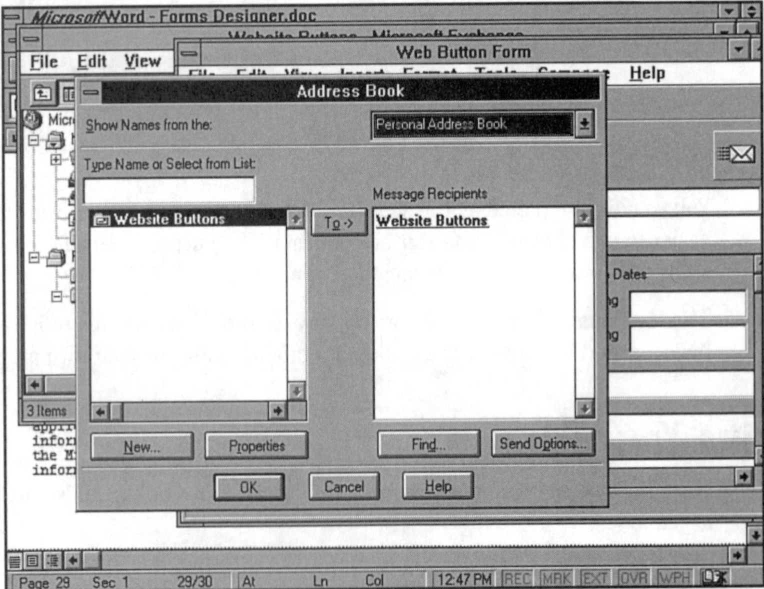

FIG. 33.27 The Web site Buttons folder is now in your Personal Address Book.

10. Select the Web site Buttons entry.
11. Click the To button.
12. Click OK.
13. Click the Send icon.

Extending Forms with Visual Basic

Since forms are Visual Basic applications, you can actually use Visual Basic to extend the functionality of forms beyond what the Forms Designer offers. The Forms Designer simply gives you a "No Programming" environment where you design very powerful applications without typing one line of code.

This section covers only a brief overview of what you need, what goes into using Visual Basic to modify applications, and why you would want to use Visual Basic to modify applications. You can refer to the Microsoft documentation and Visual Basic documentation for specifics on using Visual Basic for MAPI and OLE applications.

Anyone who wants to use VB to extend an application created with the Forms Designer should be very experienced with Visual Basic, as well as MAPI and OLE. Forms are 16-bit applications; therefore, you can only use the Visual Basic for Exchange that is installed when installing the Exchange Client and Forms Designer or 16-Bit Visual Basic 4.0.

Potential Uses of Visual Basic with Exchange Forms

You might be asking yourself, why would I want to use VB to extend forms? Here are just a few examples of how VB can improve your forms:

- You can use a form to enter data into external databases. If you have a form for ordering office supplies, for example, you can extend the form. Once the purchasing supervisor reviews the requisition and approves it, the data gets entered into a Microsoft SQL Server database automatically, and the purchase order is generated with the daily run.

  By using public folders, you can distribute the application throughout the Exchange network without actually copying the .EXE file on all the servers in your network for all your users to access. In addition, when the form is modified, all the users on the network get the most up-to-date version of the form automatically without the need to redistribute. All that is controlled by the synchronization within Exchange.
- You can include OLE controls in a form that can take data from OLE-compliant applications such as Excel. If you want your form to grab the latest data from a spreadsheet and paste it into the form, for example, you can write code that reads the contents of the OLE control into a file, and then reads the file into the form using OLE Messaging functions.

  You can use this function to send hourly time sheets to a user in native Excel format. The form can contain a blank Excel worksheet that has the header cells filled in with the days of the month, and you just fill data right into the worksheet. The recipient can then either cut, copy, and paste the data, or save it directly as an Excel file.

Modifying Applications

When you install a form using the Forms Designer, several files get created in a directory called <FORMNAME>.VB. These files are used when extending forms with Visual Basic (see Figure 33.28).

When using VB, only the <WINDOW NAME>.FRM files and the <FORM FILE>.CFG files are modified. Once you finish using Visual Basic to modify your form, you need to register all the new fields and properties in your form with Exchange. You will need to modify the .CFG file directly in Notepad or Wordpad to add all the objects and properties so they are recognized by Exchange.

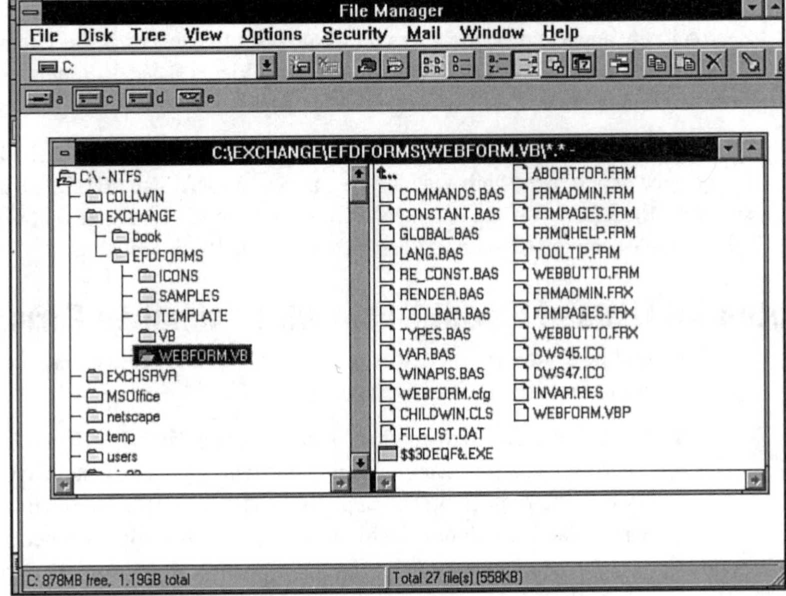

FIG. 33.28
The WEBFORM.VB directory contains all the files used by Visual Basic.

NOTE Before you can install the Forms Designer, the Exchange Microsoft client must be installed. In order to get the sample applications along with your installation, you can choose either Typical or Custom/Complete. Typical installs with most files. Custom/Complete enables you to choose whether to install the sample applications or not. When you choose either of these installations, you must reboot because system files will be changed during the installation system. ■

NOTE When using forms with an NTFS partition, you are not able to use the custom forms in Microsoft Exchange if you are running Windows NT 3.51 Server or a Workstation computer. To change this, you must alter a specific registry key that reads as follows:

HKEY_LOCAL_MACHINE\SYSTEM\CurrentControlSet\Control\FileSystem\NtfsDisable8dot3NameCreation = 0x1

To use custom forms, you must delete this key or set its value to 0. In a Windows NT 4.0 Workstation and Server environment, this particular registry key value is set to 0 by default. ■

When you are planning to design forms, decide on a home directory for your work to give you a sense of structure from the beginning. If you don't establish structure from the beginning, you won't know where the Forms Generator is keeping your files, which may lead to duplicate files in other directories all over your hard drive. When you pick a directory (such as c:\exchange\efdforms), the Electronic Forms Designer (EFD) starts to store all your information in that folder. This is especially helpful when you extend your forms with Visual Basic's 16-bit version. The 32-bit version of Visual Basic 4.0 is not currently compatible with EFD. When you install the form, you are finished. The EFD creates a folder with the same name as your efp file and a Visual Basic extension. Inside this folder is the Visual Basic Project file (VFP).

Creating the Personnel Profile Information Application

In the following pages you create an application using both Form Designer and Visual Basic's 16-bit version. This demonstrates a first look at extending your forms application with Visual Basic. Start the forms designer by clicking the Start button, Programs, and then the Microsoft Exchange Folder. Click the option for the Forms Designer to start it.

Creating the Personnel Information application may not cause your company's stock to rise, but it will teach you some useful tricks you can bring into the world of development using Microsoft Exchange's Development tools. In this section you take a look at using Send Forms in a folder, calling a hidden response form, using a rich edit field with the help of Visual Basic to enable file attachments in your form, and creating a custom response.

The Personnel Profile Information folder is a public folder that houses the forms you will create in this section. It also contains different views you will create and the result of the information collected by your Personnel Information Application. A sample view of items submitted to the Personnel Profile Information folder is shown in Figure 33.29.

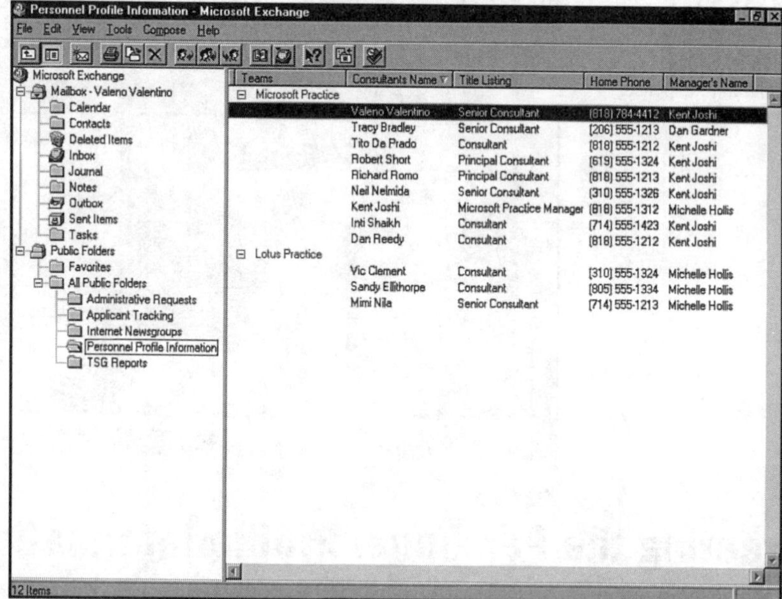

FIG. 33.29
Sample View of the Personnel Profile Information folder.

The Personnel Profile Information Request form's compose window, as shown in Figure 33.30, is used by a Manager to send a Personnel Information Request item to the user's Inbox. Its Read window is used by the members of the organization to read the request and open the Personnel Profile Information Response form.

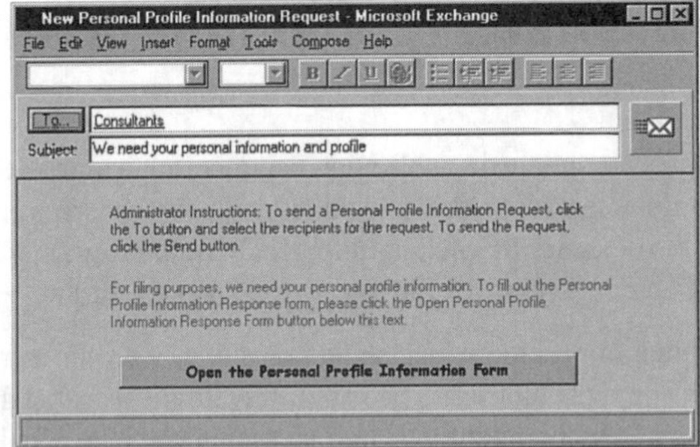

FIG. 33.30 Pre-addressing the Response form

The Personnel Profile Information Response form's Compose window, as shown in Figure 33.31, is pre-addressed to the Personnel Profile Information folder. When the user clicks the Send button, the item is automatically routed to that folder. The Read Window displays the information in the Personnel Profile Information Response item that the user submits to the Personnel Profile Information folder.

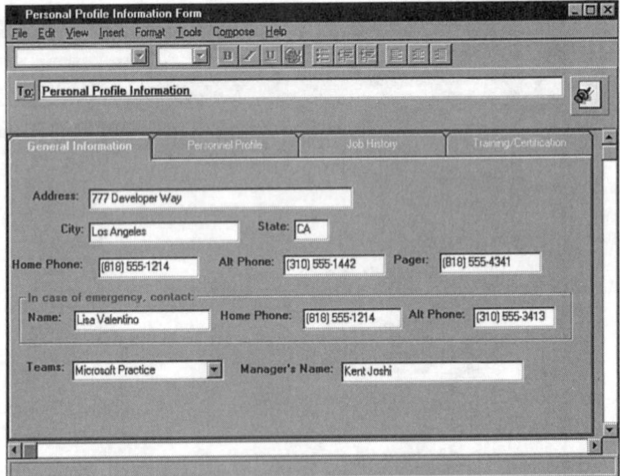

FIG. 33.31 Pre-addressing the Personnel Profile Information Response form.

Creating the Personnel Profile Information Folder

You must log in as yourself to begin. If you don't, your profile will not reflect the location of your mailbox. Next, you need to create a public folder for storing the Personnel Information items. Where you create this folder is really up to you, but to make this application available to everyone, you should use the All Public Folders folder as your starting point. To create the Personnel Information Folder, follow these steps:

1. In the set of public folders in the Microsoft Exchange Client, Select All Public Folders.
2. Choose New Folder from the File menu, and in the Folder Name box, type **Personnel Profile Information**.
3. Choose OK.

Restricting Folder Access

While you work on the folder, restrict access to the folder so that you can design it without being interrupted. To restrict access, follow these steps:

1. Select the Personnel Information folder and then choose Properties.
2. Select the Administration tab and then select the Owners Only option button, as shown in Figure 33.32.

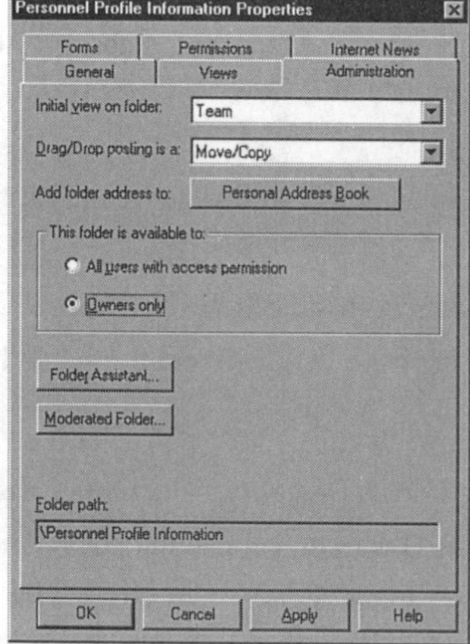

FIG. 33.32
Using the Administration tab to select the Owners Only option.

Don't choose OK yet. You're not finished with the Administration tab (the steps are completed in the following section).

Making the Folder Address Available

For this application, you will create a pre-addressed Response form. It's a lot like a pre-addressed envelope that you receive in the mail. In this case, the Response Information form is pre-addressed so that posting to the folder is automatic. You now learn how to pre-address a folder. Before you can pre-address a form to a folder, the folder's address must be available to the address book.

To add a folder address to your Personal Address Book, do the following:

1. In the Administration tab, click the Personnel Address Book button to add the folder address to your Personnel Address Book. Although you won't get any confirmation, the address is added to your Personnel Address Book. If you look down at the bottom of the Administration tab, you will see a backslash and the name of your folder in the folder path area.
2. Choose OK to return to the Microsoft Exchange Client.

Creating the Personnel Profile Information Request Form

The Forms Designer provides several generic pre-designed templates for you to begin using immediately.

To get started with the Personnel Profile Information Request form, use the SNDR2WND.EFP template. This is a two-window Send form similar to the one you would use to send messages. It has To, From, and Subject fields, such as a standard mail message. Although you can use the Form Template Wizard to choose a template, it is faster to choose a template directly from the list of the File Directory dialog box.

Before you open any files, create an application directory to house your files for this application.

1. Change directories to the following path: C:\EXCHANGE\EFDFORMS.
2. Create two subfolders. Call the first one PQINFO and the second PPINFO.

To open and use the SNDR2WND.EFP template, follow these steps:

1. From the opening screen of the Forms Designer, select the *A Form Template*.

   If you are already running Forms Designer, choose File, Open from the menu bar.
2. This is a read-only file, so in order to edit it you must save it with another name in the PQINFO subfolder. In the Exchange\Efdforms\Template folder, select the SNDR2WND.EFP file.
3. Click File from the menu and choose Save As.
4. Navigate through the directory structure to C:\EXCHANGE\EFDFORMS\PQINFO.
5. In the filename box type **pqinfo**.

Designing the Compose Window

Figure 33.33 displays how the form looks when it is selected from the Compose menu. To run the Personnel Profile Information Request Form, choose new Personnel Profile Information Request from the Compose menu.

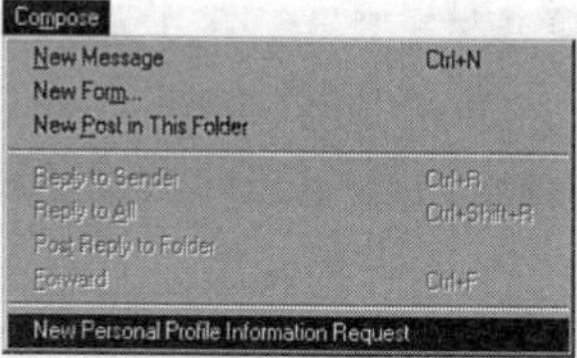

FIG. 33.33
Displays how the form will look when it is selected from the Compose menu.

The Personnel Profile Information Request window, shown in Figure 33.34, is great for anyone who needs profile/personal information from a user or group of users in the company. You can use Figure 33.34 as a model to help customize this form.

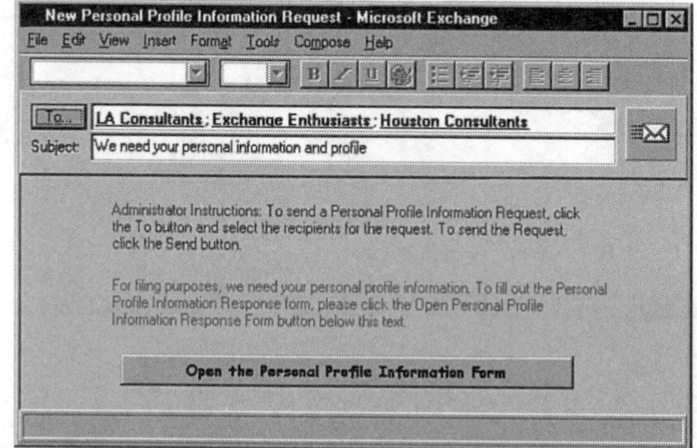

FIG. 33.34
Shows you how the Personnel Profile Information Request form looks in its final state.

Setting the Window Properties for the Compose Window

When you start designing forms, you must always consider who will be using your form and how. On many occasions the Compose window is different from the Read window. You use the Personnel Profile Information form to request information in a Compose window. The end users see a form that looks similar to the one you sent, but they see only who sent the form to them and the date and time that it was sent. The Request form in the Read window should include brief instructions to inform the recipient how to fill out the form.

Designing the Read Window

At run-time, the Read window of the form appears when the user double-clicks a Personnel Profile Information Request item in the user's Inbox. The Read window displays the Personnel Profile Information Request form and your instructions. Figure 33.35 shows you an example of what the user sees in his Inbox.

Setting the Initial Value for the Subject Field

As a courtesy to the user, you can set the initial value to display in the Subject field of the Read window.

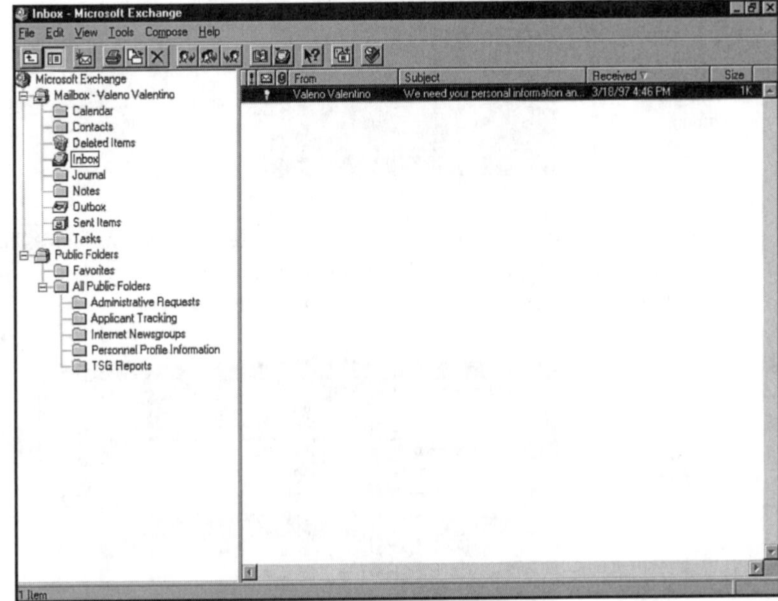

FIG. 33.35
An example of what the user will see in his Inbox when the Personnel Profile Information Request item has been delivered to him.

To set the initial value of the Subject field, follow these steps:

1. Double-click the Subject field to view field properties and then select the Initial value tab.
2. In the Subject box, type **We need your Personnel Profile Information**.
3. Choose close.

The title bar of the Form window can also be defined in the Window Properties dialog box. As a general rule, it should begin with New, followed by the name of the form (see Figure 33.36).

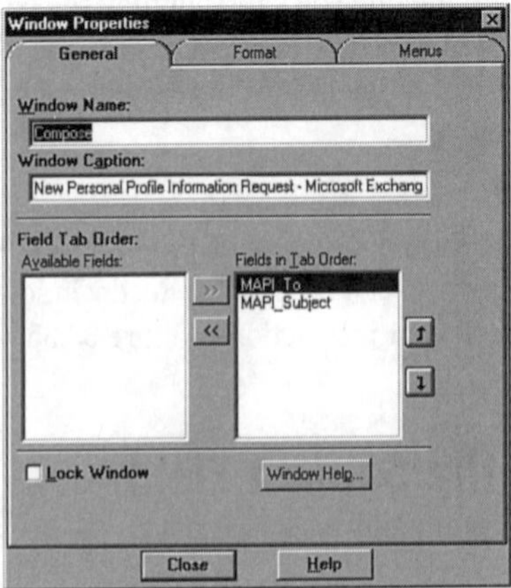

FIG. 33.36
Defining the title bar of the form.

To set the window caption, follow these steps:

1. Click View from the menu and select Window Properties.
2. In the General tab, change the Window caption to read "New Personnel Profile Information Request."
3. Click the Close button.

Copying User Instructions Label Field to the Compose Window

In general practice, I usually create the information for the Compose Window first, and then I copy that to the Read window. Refer to Figure 33.30 for an example of text to use as user and Administrator instructions.

To copy the user instructions, use the following steps:

1. Click the user instructions label field.
2. Select Edit from the menu and choose Copy.
3. Select Window from the menu and choose Read.
4. Once again select Edit from the menu and choose Paste.

NOTE You add the Open Personnel Profile Information Form command button later in Visual Basic. ■

After opening the Read window, remove the unnecessary fields from the form. You can do this by selecting them and pressing the Delete key on your keyboard.

To remove the To and Cc fields from the Read window, select each one and press the Delete key on your keyboard. Now you can paste and re-position the user label field.

Resizing the Read Window

The Read window re-sizes just as any other window—just be sure you leave enough room for the button made later in Visual Basic.

Setting the Window Properties for the Read Window

The window caption is the only property to set in the Window Properties dialog box. To set the window caption, follow these steps:

1. Select View from the menu and click Window Properties.
2. Click the General tab and then change the window caption to read Personnel Profile Information Request. Then choose Close.

Setting the Form Properties for the Read Window

In the General tab of the Form Properties dialog box, change the display name and the item type for the form. To set the forms general properties, follow these steps:

1. Select View from the menu and click Form Properties.
2. In the General tab, change the settings to reflect the settings in Table 33.3.

Table 33.3 Setting Form Properties

Property	Setting
Form Display Name	Personnel Profile Information Request
Version	1.00
Number	PINFO7.1
Item Type	IPM.PersonnelProfileInformationRequest
Description	Send requests for Personnel and profile information in your company

Selecting Events for the Request Form

The most common event is the Create New Item event. Select View from the menu and click Forms properties. Then click the Events tab—you should see something similar to Figure 33.37.

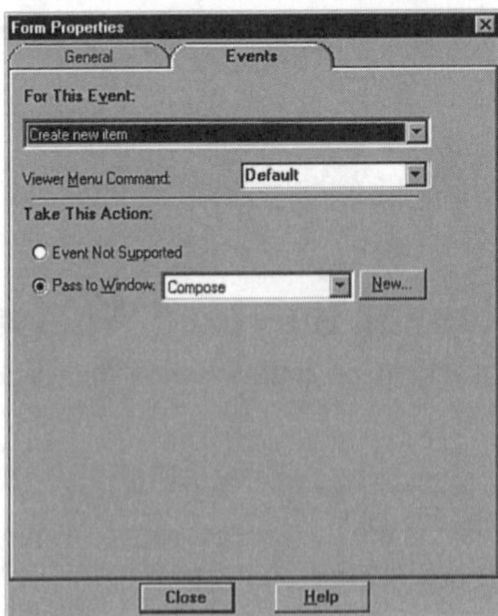

FIG. 33.37
Viewing the Create New Item event.

Every time the New Personnel Profile Information Request is chosen from the menu, the Create New Item event executes. This event creates a new instance of The Personnel Profile Information Request form. In other words, the Compose version of the Request form appears when the New Personnel Profile Information Request is chosen from the Compose menu. Figure 33.38 illustrates a new instance of the Personnel Profile Information item.

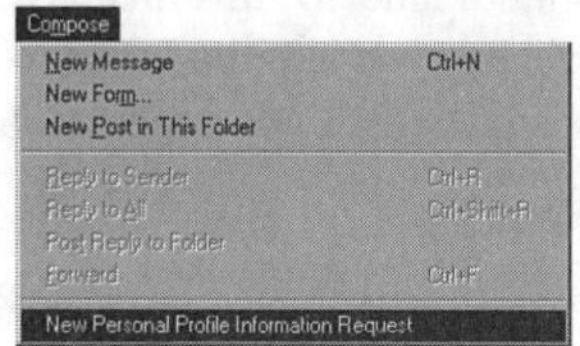

FIG. 33.38 Viewing the new instance of the Personnel Profile Information Request item from the Compose menu.

Creating a Custom Response

The first time people start working with custom responses, they ask themselves, "Why do I need two forms?" The Read version of the request form is a request from you to the end user for information you need from him/her. On this form is a button that enables the end user to open another form so they can enter the information you requested and return the form to the Personnel Profile folder for review.

You still must set up a Custom Response event to launch the Personnel Profile Information form. This creates a new Compose menu item each time it executes. To do this use the Forms Properties events tab as shown in Figure 33.39:

1. Open the Form Properties Events tab.
2. Choose Custom Response 1 in the For This Event field.
3. Select the Create Response radio button.
4. Browse to select the Response form(PQINFO.EFP). Accept the default Response Form Item Type.

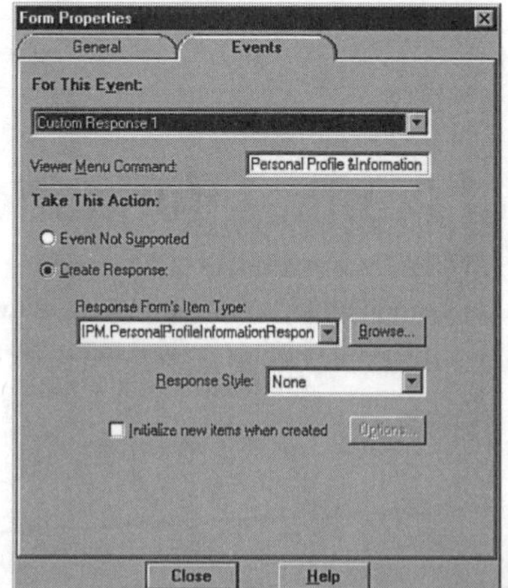

FIG. 33.39 Viewing a Custom Response already created in the Forms Properties window.

Saving and Installing the Form

The Forms Designer gives you a start in the design of forms, but the limited toolbox doesn't offer much depth. Most of the shortcomings of the Forms Designer can be easily overcome with Visual Basic or Visual C++. Before you can extend the functionality with Visual Basic, you must first install the form into the Personnel Profile Information folder. When you install this form, the Visual Basic code is created for it automatically; this means a Visual Basic Project file and a .CFG file are created. The .CFG file will be used later by Inbox to install the Visual Basic Executable so that the form with the new Visual Basic Code can run from the Inbox.

To install the Request Form, follow these steps:

1. Click the File menu and select install. If your file has not been saved before or changes are detected, the Forms Designer displays a message box informing you that changes to your form will be saved before continuing.
2. When the Folder Library appears, click Personnel Profile Information folder, as shown in Figure 33.40
3. Click OK.

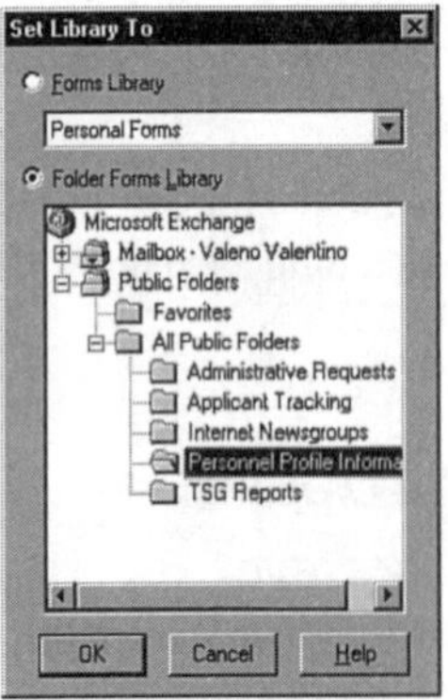

FIG. 33.40 Installing the Request form in the Personnel Profile Information folder.

NOTE Always save the files with a name that relates to the contents of the file and is easy to remember. ■

Creating the Personnel Profile Information Form

To get started with the Personnel Profile Information form, you can use the SNDR2WND.EFP template. This is a two-window send form used for creating response items. This file however is read-only, so you must rename it before you can use it. The name I will be using throughout this chapter is ppinfo.

To open and use the SNDR2WND.EFP template, follow these steps:

1. Select File from the menu and choose Open.
2. This is a read-only file, so in order to edit it you must save it with another name in the PPINFO subfolder. In the Exchange\Efdforms\Template folder, select the SNDR2WND.EFP file.
3. Click File from the menu and choose Save As.
4. Navigate through the directory structure to C:\EXCHANGE\EFDFORMS\PPINFO.
5. In the filename box type **ppinfo**.

To remove the cc and Subject fields, select them and press Delete.

From the toolbox, select the Tab control and click your form. Resize the Tab control to fill the contents panel. To fill the reference name fields, name the tabs by double clicking each one. The names I have chosen are as follows:

Personnel Profile

Job History

Training/Certification

Adding Fields to the Compose Window of the Response Form

Using the Designer toolbox, place the following fields on each respective tab, as illustrated in Figures 33.41–33.44 (see Tables 33.4–33.7).

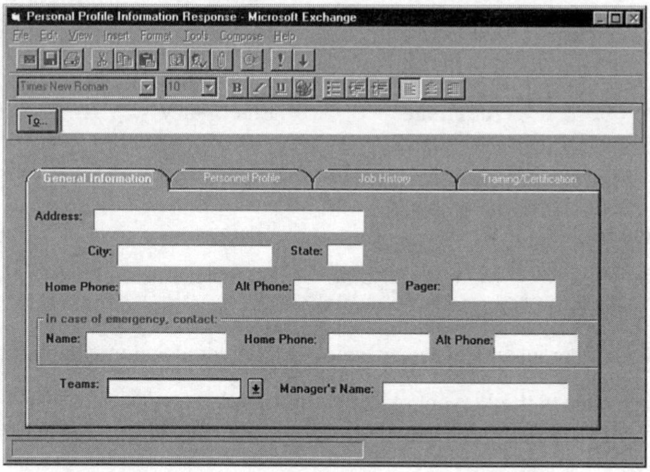

FIG. 33.41
The first tab and the fields it contains.

Table 33.4 Fields on the first tab

Type of Field	Caption	Reference Name	Column Name
Entry	Address:	Address	Address
Entry	City:	City	City
Entry	Home Phone:	HomePhone	HomePhone
Entry	Alt Phone:	AltPhone	AltPhone
Entry	Pager:	Pager	Pager
Entry	In case of emergency,contact:	Frame1	Frame1
Entry	Name: ContactName	Emergency	Emergency Contact Name
Entry	Home Phone: HomePhone	Emergency HomePhone	Emergency
Entry	Alt Phone: AltPhone	Emergency	Emergency AltPhone
ComboBox	Teams:	Teams	Teams
Entry	Manager's Name:	Manager's Name	Manager's Name

In addition to or instead of a user typing in a Personal Statement, she can attach relevant files.

To attach a file to the Personnel Profile Information form, select Insert from the Menu and click file. The file automatically finds the RichEntry field with the MAPI_Body_Custom type.

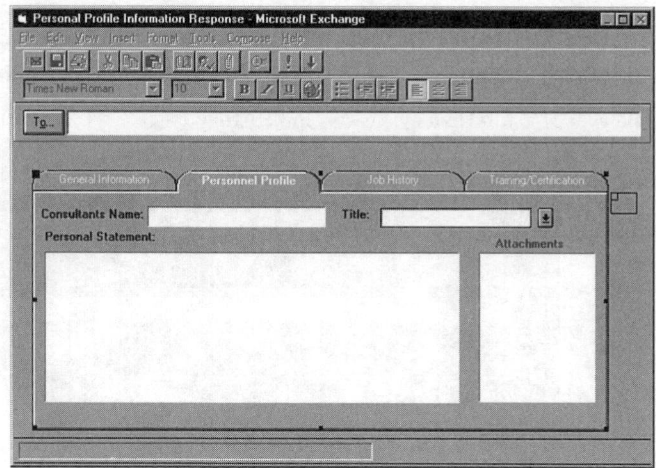

FIG. 33.42
The second tab and the fields it contains.

Table 33.5 Fields on the second tab

Type of Field	Caption	Reference Name	Column Name
Entry	Consultant's Name:	Consultants Name	Consultants Name
ComboBox	Title:	Title Listing	Title
Entry	Personnel Statement	Personnel Statement	Personnel Statement
RichEntry	Attachments:	Attachments	Attachments

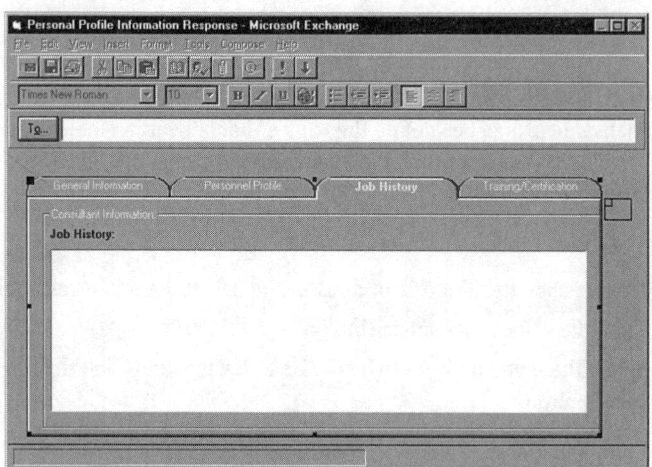

FIG. 33.43
The third tab and the fields it contains.

Table 33.6 Fields on the third tab

Type of Field	Caption	Reference Name	Column Name
RichEntry	Job History:	Job History	Job History

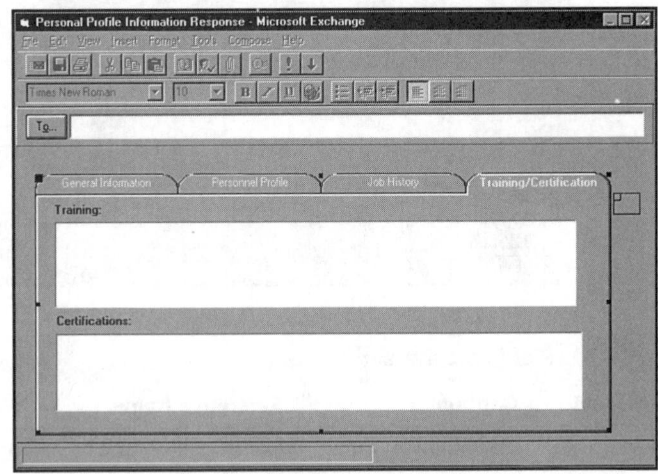

FIG. 33.44 The fourth tab and the fields it contains.

Table 33.7 Fields on the fourth tab

Type of Field	Caption	Reference Name	Column Name
RichEntry	Training:	Training	Training
RichEntry	Certifications:	Certifications	Certifications

Setting the Initial Value of the Teams Field

The initial value properties define the values that appear in a field at run-time. In this case, define the initial values for the Team ComboBox on the first tab. You can also choose a default value to appear at run-time.

To set the initial value for the ComboBox field, follow these steps:

1. Double-click the Teams ComboBox and select the initial value tab.
2. Type the values that appear in Figure 33.45.
3. Select the field you want to be the default value and click the Set selection to initial value button.

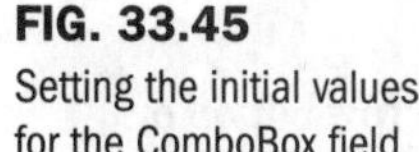

FIG. 33.45
Setting the initial values for the ComboBox field

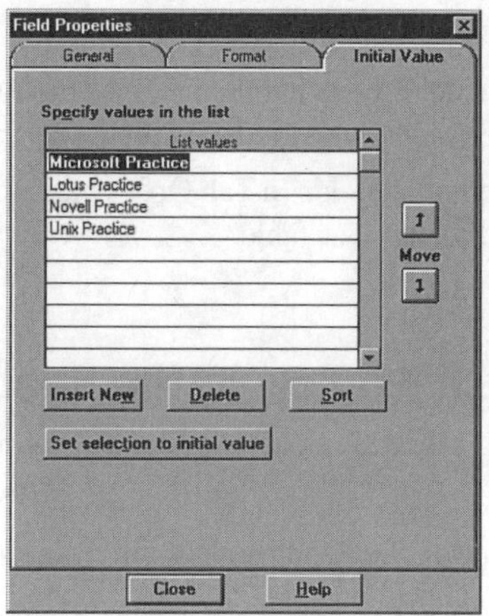

Pre-addressing the Response Form

As stated earlier, a pre-addressed form is like an envelope with a return address. You pre-address this form by setting the initial value of the To field to the Personnel Profile Information folder.

To predate the form, follow these steps:

1. Double-click the To field.
2. In the Initial Value tab, choose To and then choose Personnel Address Book from the Show Names From The: drop-down box.
3. Select the Personnel Profile Information folder. Choose To and then choose OK.
4. Choose Close to return to the Forms Designer.

Setting the Window Properties for the Response Compose Window

Now set the window caption and the field tab order. The window caption appears in the title bar of the window. The field tab order is a property that controls the order in which the windows fields gain focus as the user presses the Tab key.

To set the Window Caption, complete the following steps:

1. From the View menu, click Window Properties.
2. In the Window Caption box in the General tab, change the current caption to Personnel Profile Information Response.

To set the tab order, complete the following steps:

1. Select the field in the Available fields box, and then choose the Add arrow button or double-click the field to add the field to the Fields In Tab Order box.

   Leave MAPI-To as the first tab in the Fields In Tab Order box. Add the rest of the fields in the order they are listed in the previous table.
2. Choose Close.

Copying Fields in the Compose Window to the Read Window

You can save design time by copying everything you have done so far in the Compose Window to the Read Window.

To copy fields in the Compose window to the Read window, follow these steps:

1. Select the Tab Control by clicking in an empty space anywhere on the Tab Control.
2. Choose Copy from the toolbar.
3. From the Window Menu select Read, and then choose Paste from the toolbar.

Setting Window Properties for the Response Read Window

In the Window Properties dialog box, repeat the same procedures as were performed in the Compose Window to set the tab order and window caption name properties.

NOTE Leave the pre-assigned MAPI fields set, and then order your fields in the same order of the Compose Window. ■

Setting Form Properties for the Response Read Window

Now you can name the form and give it a unique item type that matches the item type you specified for the Custom Response 1 event in the Request form.

To set the form display name, follow these steps:

1. On the Main window toolbar, click the Form Properties button.
2. In the Form Display Name box inside the General tab, type **Personnel Profile Information Response**.

To set the version, number and item type, follow these steps:

1. In the Version box, change the number to 1.00.
2. In the Number box, type **PINFO7.2**.
3. In the Item Type box, change the item type to IPM.PersonnelProfileInformationResponse.

To set the form description, follow these steps:

1. In the Description box, type **Use this form to fill out and send Personnel profile and emergency information to the Personnel Profile Information folder.**
2. Choose Close.

Saving and Installing the Response Form

As stated earlier, when you choose install from the File menu in Forms Designer, the Forms Designer tells you it will save the form before it installs it (unless it is already saved). After a moment, the Folder Library appears. This enables you to save your form in a particular folder (such as the Personnel Profile Information folder).

NOTE Always save the files with a name that is logical, descriptive, and easy to remember.

Creating the By Team View

The By Team view indicates which practice(s) the consultant is a member of.

The By Team view consists of the following fields: Teams, Consultant's Name, Title Listing, Home Phone, and Manager's Name. The view groups these fields by team and sorts items in ascending order by Consultant's Name.

To create the By Team View, follow these steps:

1. In the Exchange Client, select the properties for the Personnel Profile Information folder.
2. Find the Views tab and choose New.
3. Be sure to Remove any fields from the Show the following columns box, so that it is empty when you start to add fields.
4. In the Available Columns box, select Teams and Consultant's Name and then double-click them separately.
5. Set the column width of the fields as follows:

   Teams 36

   Consultant's Name 36
6. Choose OK.
7. In the Group Items By drop-down box, select teams, choose OK, and then choose OK again.

Setting Permissions

In the Permissions tab, you define different levels of security for your folder.

To set permissions, select the Permissions tab in the Personnel Profile Information Properties dialog box. Then set permissions according to the following table.

Sometimes you might want to restrict users to only the items you want them to interact with. Figure 33.46 shows how to limit the forms a folder displays.

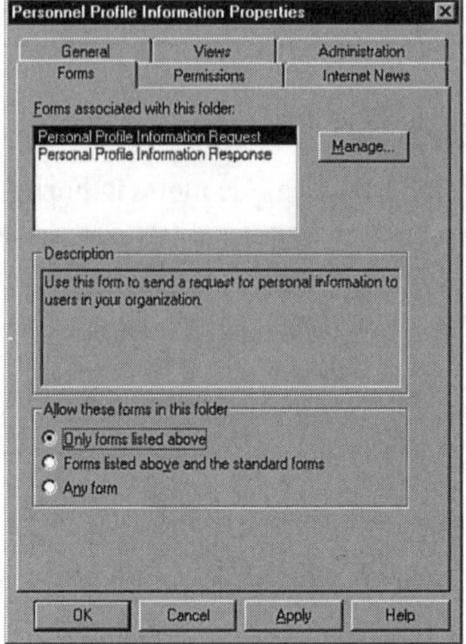

FIG. 33.46
Limiting the forms a folder displays.

To restrict the types of items, follow these steps:

1. Select the Personnel Profile Information folder and then choose Properties from the File menu.
2. In the Properties dialog box, select the Forms tab.
3. Select the Only Forms Listed Above option button, and then choose OK.

Testing the Application

The time has come to test the application. Once you are satisfied that it's working correctly, you can enhance its usability by giving it some extended capabilities in Visual Basic.

To test the Request form in the Personnel Profile Information folder, follow these steps:

1. Select the Personnel Profile Information folder.
2. From the Compose menu, choose New Personnel Profile Information Request. The Request form's Compose window appears.
3. In the To box, type your name and then press Ctrl+K to resolve the address. Then click the Send Button.
4. Select the Inbox and double-click your new mail. The form will install (if it hasn't been installed on your computer before) and display the read version of the Request form.

To test the Response form, follow these steps:

1. Select the Personnel Profile Information folder.

2. From the Compose menu, choose New Personnel Profile Information Response. The Response form appears.
3. Fill out the appropriate information. Then click the Post button located at the top right of the Response form. This action will post the form to the Personnel Profile Information folder.
4. Select the Personnel Profile Information folder and then make sure the view is set to teams. Click the plus symbol next to the appropriate team and then double-click the consultant's name. This action displays the form with the information you requested. Tab through it and make sure it is correct. Because it is posted in the Personnel Profile Information folder, the information can always be changed.

Adding a Button to the Form with Visual Basic

To modify a form generated using the Forms Designer, you must use the Visual Basic that comes with the Microsoft Exchange Client or the 16-bit compiler of Visual Basic version 4.0 or later.

To add a command button to the Compose Window, follow these steps:

1. In Visual Basic, choose Open Project from the File menu.
2. Select the pqinfo.vbp file, which is located in the directory path you created earlier in this chapter to house all project files for this application.
3. The directory name will be **PQINFO.vb**. Here is an example: C:\EXCHANGE\EFDFORMS\PQINFO.VB\pqinfo.vbp.
4. After the project has been loaded, double-click the COMPOSE.FRM from the Project window.

To add the Command button to the form, follow these steps:

1. If the toolbox is not visible, select toolbox from the View menu.
2. Click the Command button and then add it to the Compose form.
3. While the Command Button is still selected, press the F4 key on your keyboard. This opens the Properties dialog box. Set the Command button's Caption property to Open &Personnel Profile Information Response Form. Then set the Enabled property to False.

Cleaning up the Form Window

When the Forms Designer generates Visual Basic code for the form, it seems to scramble the components in the Compose and Read windows. Fortunately, the generated code contains several procedures that arrange these components in the window at run-time. To clean up the window, the first thing you should do is enlarge the window. Then hide the scroll bars by dragging them to the edges of the window. Next hide the status bar by setting the Align property for the Status Bar Control to 0 –None. Now drag the status bar out of your work area as you did the scroll bars.

Increasing the Canvas Size

The Form window canvas consists of a large picture control (Canvas_Ctrl) inside a much smaller canvas control (CanvasParent). To resize the canvas, follow these steps:

1. Before you can select the CanvasParent control to resize it, you must first reposition the Canvas Ctrl inside the CanvasParent, as shown in Figure 33.47.

FIG. 33.47
Increasing the size of the Canvas Ctrl.

2. Select the CanvasParent control, and then resize it until it looks like Figure 33.48

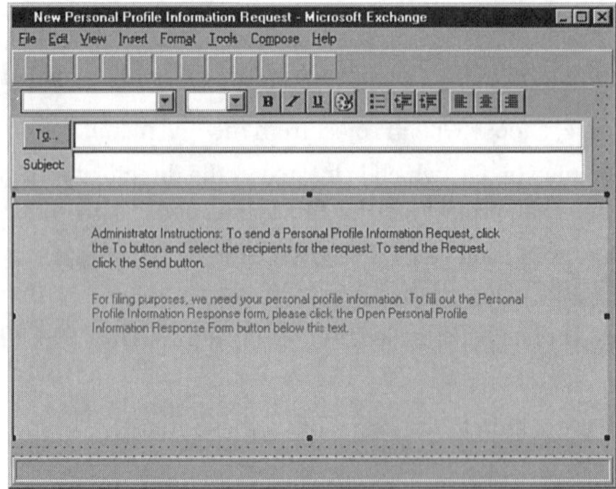

FIG. 33.48
Visual representation of how the CanvasParent control should look after resizing.

Adding Code to the Command Button

To add code to the Command button, double-click the Command button, and add the code as shown to the button-click procedure.

```
***begin code listingPrivate Sub Command1_Click()
    Call menComposeCustomResponse_Click(0)
End Sub
```

This code calls the Click procedure for the Custom Response command and passes it an Index value of 0. This is the same value that the Custom Response menu command passes to the procedure. In the number system, when you count from 0 to 9, you have actually counted 10 numbers. The zero you passed in the menComposeCustomResponse Sub procedure represents the Custom Response 1 event you set up in the Forms Designer earlier in this chapter. If we were to pass a 1 to this procedure, this would represent the Custom Response 2 event.

Copying Command Button and Code Contents to the READ.FRM

To copy the Command button and code contents to the READ.FRM, complete the following steps:

1. Right-click the Command button and choose Copy.
2. Return to the Project window and double-click READ.FRM. Repeat the steps to clean up this form as explained in the "Cleaning up the Form Window" section.
3. Select READ.FRM and paste the Command button on the form.
4. Double-click the Command button and insert the same code you inserted earlier in the Command button on the COMPOSE.FRM.
5. Save this project by selecting Save Project from the File menu of Visual Basic.

Making an .EXE File

When you create a new executable (.EXE) file, you incorporate the changes that were made in Visual Basic. When you see the odd name of the executable that is generated, your first reaction will be to change it to something more readable. My advice is to leave it as is. When the Forms Designer creates an .EXE file for the form, it also creates a .CFG file. If you were to change the name of the executable created by Visual Basic, you would have to update all the references made to it in the .CFG file. Frankly, it is more trouble than it is worth at this point.

Reinstalling the Personnel Information Request Form

When changes are made to a form in Visual Basic, you must use the Forms Manager in the Microsoft Exchange Client to install the form. Remember, only the person who created the folder can make these types of changes.

To reinstall the Personnel Information Request form, follow these steps:

1. In the Microsoft Exchange Client, select the Personnel Profile Information folder.
2. From the File menu, choose Properties and then select the Forms tab.
3. Choose the Manage button and then click the Install button.
4. Double-click the pqinfo.cfg file, which is located in the pqinfo.vb directory. If you are asked to overwrite an existing executable, choose Yes.

To check and see if you have the right form, select the Personnel Profile Information folder and select the request form from the menu.

Outlook Forms Development

This section introduces you to the art of making custom Outlook applications without prior programming experience. If you're already familiar with Windows and Visual Basic or Visual Basic Script, you should have an easy time using the Outlook Forms Designer.

Outlook Forms Designer

The Outlook Forms Designer enables you to lay out all the different fields on your form, link them to Outlook objects, and designate actions on events. Without any previous programming experience, you can create applications that will make your organization more productive. Many example applications are provided for you when you load Outlook from the Microsoft Office 97 Resource CD. You can also use the pre-designed forms that are built into Outlook and modify them for your use.

The Outlook Forms Designer enables the creation of two types of forms:

- *Standalone Outlook forms*—These forms are not associated with any particular folder. They facilitate the input of information with the intent to send it to an individual or group of users. These applications include message-taking, office supply requisitions, and vacation requests.
- *Folder Outlook forms*—These forms facilitate the input of information into a public folder where permitted users can view the information in an organized way. These applications include group discussions, bulletin boards, and enterprise-wide groupware databases. Filters can be applied to move data into subfolders, and views can be applied to group or sort information.

Outlook Form Categories

Before developing a new form, you need to decide which type of message is being created. In the Outlook environment there are three basic categories of forms:

- Message: A Message form is used as a starting point that lets users send information to another user, distribution list, or folder.
- Post: A Post form is used as a starting point for building forms that enable users to post, open, and respond to information in a personal or public folder.
- Office Document: An Office Document form is used as a starting point for building forms that have a Word, PowerPoint, or Microsoft Excel document embedded in them.

The Message form can be used as a starting point for building forms that enable users to send information to other users, distribution lists, or other folders. Good examples of this concept are a Vacation Request form and a While You Were Away form.

The Post form is good for centralizing e-mail responses and submitting items directly to the active folder. Examples of this are Product Idea Applications and Technical User-Groups.

Office Document forms are essentially office documents wrapped in either a Message or Post form. You can create Office Document forms to send documents to other users and to post documents in a folder. Examples of the Office Document forms are Expense Reports and Purchase Requests. Both of these sample applications are included with Outlook.

Modifying Built-in Forms

Modifying a form that already exists allows you the luxury of not having to start from scratch. You can now build upon the functionality provided by a built-in form. To modify a built-in form, follow these steps:

1. Select the folder where your Application will be stored.
2. Select Choose form from the Compose menu.
3. Select the Application form that is best for the application you have in mind.
4. Select Tools from the menu of the running forms and select Design Outlook Form.

You are now in Design mode for that particular form. The tabs you see are called pages. To begin designing, simply click the tab of your choice.

There are two methods you can use to place fields on your form. First, you can select the category of the fields you want, select a field, and then drag it to the page. If you don't find a field that fulfills your requirements, you can create your own and then drag the newly formed field to your page. After you position the field on the page, you can resize it.

The second method you can use to place a field on a form involves the use of the Control toolbox. This option is located on the Form menu of the form you currently have in Design mode.

Creating a Custom Form

The Calendar, Contacts, Journal, and Tasks are built-in Forms you can modify. These built-in Forms provide a basis from which you can create your design strategy.

The following example shows you how easy it is to design a simple form. The first step is to create a folder to house the application:

1. Right-click your Inbox and choose Create Subfolder.
2. In the name box, type **Tech Solutions** and click OK.
3. Select the Tech Solutions folder you just created. At this time, you can type a description for the folder and create a shortcut on the Outlook bar.
4. Click Compose from the menu and then select Choose Template.
5. Select the Post it template.
6. From the Tools menu of the Post Template, select Design Outlook Form.
7. Click the (P.2) tab and then select Form from the menu. Choose Rename Page type **Discussions** for the Tab Page Control.

After you create the folder in which to store the application, you can add some fields to the Page Control by completing the following steps:

1. Click the Control toolBox and drag the combo box control to your Page Control, named Discussions.
2. Click the Label Control and drag that to the form, resizing it as necessary. The caption for the Label Control should be Topics of Interest.
3. Right-click the Combo Control and choose Properties.
4. Click the New button and type **txtTopics of Interest** in the name field.
5. Type **SMS, Exchange, SQL Server, IIS,** and **Active Server Pages** in the Possible values box (these titles should all be separated by a comma). Click OK.

Publishing the Form

When you publish a form, you make it available to everyone that has permission to the Tech Solutions folder. When a user selects the Tech Solutions Folder, he or she can then invoke a new instance of the form by selecting it from the Compose menu.

Follow these steps to publish the form:

1. Select File from the menu and choose Publish Form As. Make sure that the name of your form is displayed next to the Publish In area.
2. In the forms name area, type **Technical Discussion Form** and click OK.

Whereas the first part of this chapter gives a quick overview about how to customize forms in Outlook, the remainder of the chapter explores accessing Exchange objects through a web browser by using IIS, VBScript, and Active Server Pages.

Exporting Your Forms and Outlook Applications

In the Exchange Forms Designer, I had many more files to keep track of if I wanted to successfully move the files necessary to run my application to a standalone computer.

In Outlook, however, you can export your applications to a .pst or .fdm file, which in turn can be imported back into Outlook, running on a standalone workstation.

Form Views

You set up views in Outlook the same way as in the Exchange Development Platform. The only difference is that instead of selecting the folder, choose Properties and select the View tab to create a view. You now select View from the Outlook menu bar and select Define Views.

If your organization is using Exchange and Outlook Clients, you should select the Automatically generate Microsoft Exchange views check box. This option generates Microsoft Exchange view for the folder so that views created in Outlook can be seen by Microsoft Exchange Clients. The rest is pretty much the same. ●

CHAPTER 34

Taking Exchange to the Web

In this chapter

The world revolves around information, and messaging vehicles make it quicker and easier to send, retrieve, and act upon information. In the center of the Information age is the Internet with E-mail and the World Wide Web. Microsoft's BackOffice entries that meet the challenges of the Information age are Exchange Server and Internet Information Server. The glue that adheres these two infrastructure building blocks is Active Server Pages (ASP). This chapter demonstrates how to leverage the power of Exchange Server with the ease of access provided through Internet Information Server via Active Server Pages.

Understanding the Active Server Platform

The Active Server term was coined in 1996 to categorize the technologies being released with BackOffice that enable tighter integration and exposure to custom development. It is no surprise that the integration model revolved around the Common Object Model (COM) and the ability to drive the services of the BackOffice components using development tools such as Visual Basic, Visual C++, and Visual J++. Each BackOffice component, including Exchange Server, has COM objects that enable a developer to harness the vertical power of the component and produce a horizontal business solution. Figure 34.1 provides a visual depiction of the BackOffice components and where they fit into the Active Server platform.

FIG. 34.1
BackOffice and the Active Server Platform.

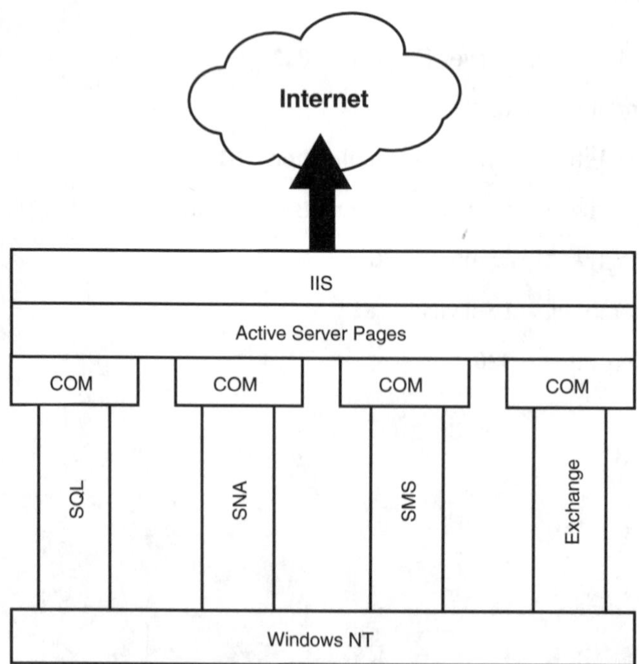

As you can see in Figure 34.1, Window NT Server is the foundation for the Active Server platform and is required to run any of the BackOffice applications. Each vertical pillar of the Active Server platform—SQL Server, SNA Server, Systems Management Server, and Exchange

Server—provide unique services to the Active Server platform. SQL Server provides for data storage using a relational database. SNA Server provides access to legacy data that is resident on mini or mainframe computers. Systems Management Server is used to manage an enterprise's desktop population. Also, Exchange Server provides enterprise-wide messaging.

Each of the pillars is capped with a layer that enables a developer to create applications that automate common tasks within the vertical application or extract information from the vertical application. This layer is the public COM layer, which provides a set of clearly defined methods and properties that enable the developer to manipulate the vertical application.

The COM layer's methods and properties are controlled using a development tool such as Visual C++, Visual J++, or Visual Basic. Visual Basic is the most commonly used development tool for developing active server applications. A derivative of Visual Basic is *VBScript*. VBScript is the most commonly used scripting language for Active Server Page development.

Active Server Pages can be developed using any ASCII text editor, HTML editor, or word processor. Most developers, however, would prefer to develop using an interactive developing environment, such as Front Page '97 or Visual InterDev. These two development tools provide the most robust environment for Active Server Page development. The key to making Active Server Pages run is simple: Just enclose the VBScript that is to run at the server within the HTML tags of "<%" and "%>" and save the file with an extension of ".ASP". Well, maybe it is *not* that easy, and a further explanation of the coding syntax is provided later in this chapter, but the .ASP file extension is important.

NOTE An alternative to using the <% and %> HTML special tags is to use the <SCRIPT LANGUAGE="VBScript" RunAt=Server> and </SCRIPT> HTML tags to encapsulate scripting code that is to be run on the web server. ■

The .ASP file extension is important because all files with this identifier are preprocessed by the Internet Information Server via an Internet Server Application Programming Interface (ISAPI) extension. The .ASP file extension is associated with the ISAPI extension, ASP.DLL. ASP.DLL interprets and processes the VBScript code within the Active Sever Page file. The results of the Active Server Page preprocess is HTML code that will be interpreted by the client's web browser.

The browser receives the results of a request made to an Active Server Page that uses the Active Server platform to provide informative and timely dynamic content to the user. An example of how Exchange can be used to provide active content is provided later in this chapter.

Laying the Foundation

Before active content can be developed and published, you must ensure that you have a properly laid foundation. Windows NT Server and Internet Information (IIS) server are the backbone for hosting Active Server Pages, but you need to make sure that you have the correct versions running before you begin to develop.

Windows NT Server 4.0 is the base component needed to host active server content. IIS 3.0 is the Internet web server that makes it possible to host Active Server Pages. Active Server Pages have an advantage over CGI or other technologies because of the simplified process of providing dynamic web content using the technologies of COM and a scripting language such as VBScript.

The Internet Information Server accompanies the Windows NT Server CD or can be downloaded from the Microsoft web site at backoffice.microsoft.com if you have enough patience or bandwidth. Active Server Pages require Internet Information Server 3.0 and Windows NT Server 4.0 with a minimum of Service Pack 2. Instructions for applying the service packs are provided on the CD or in the download files.

NOTE At the time this chapter was written, Windows NT 4.0 Service Pack 4 had just been released. All examples in this chapter were developed under Windows NT Service Pack 3. ■

Following the installation of Windows NT Server 4.0, Internet Information Server 3.0, and the appropriate server packs, you can verify that Active Server Pages have been installed by reviewing two Registry entries. The entries are found under HKEY_LOCAL_MACHINE/SYSTEM/CurrentControlSet/Services/W3SVC/Parameters/Script Map. The entries should have a value name of .ASA and .ASP associated with data value c:\[Windows NT directory]\system32\inetsrv\ASP\ASP.dll. Check to make sure ASP.dll resides in the directory specified in the Registry data value.

When installing Active Server Pages from the service pack, you are given the option to install the Adventure Works sample Active Server Page application, Active Server Page examples, and documentation. I would highly recommend expending the necessary hard drive space to accommodate these excellent resources.

Once you have verified that Active Server Pages process components have been installed on your server, run a quick test by launching the Adventure Works demo application at `http://[your` web server]/AdvWorks/ or one of the sample pages found at `http://[your` web server]/ASPSamp. This assumes you heeded the recommendation to install the samples with your installations of IIS 3.0. If not, proceed with this chapter and you'll create your own test Active Server Page.

Preparing IIS for Active Server Page Application

Once all the service packs have been installed and you've tested to ensure Active Server Pages processing has been installed, you're ready to prepare Internet Information Server for a new Active Server Pages application.

Each Active Server Pages application must reside in its own directory at the web server. A directory and its subdirectories specify the global boundaries of the Active Server Pages application. To draw a correlation between a compiled application and an Active Server Pages application, the compiled application is bound within the address space created by the compiled executable, .EXE. The Active Server Pages application's "address space" is relative to requests made of Active Server Pages within a web site directory.

In order to set up an Active Server Pages application address space, you must configure an Internet Information Server directory. To configure new application directories where all the files necessary for your Active Server application will reside, follow these steps:

1. Create a directory on the web server or a network share that will be used to store the web pages for the Active Server Pages application.

NOTE If the pages are stored on a network, the web server must be able to access the files across the LAN to fulfill the user's request. ■

2. From the Start button, select Programs and click Microsoft Information Server.
3. Click Internet Server Manager.
4. The WWW service should have a state of Running. If not, start the service by highlighting the computer name and clicking the Start Service button on the toolbar (see Figure 34.2).
5. Click the Directory tab and then click the Add button (see Figure 34.3).

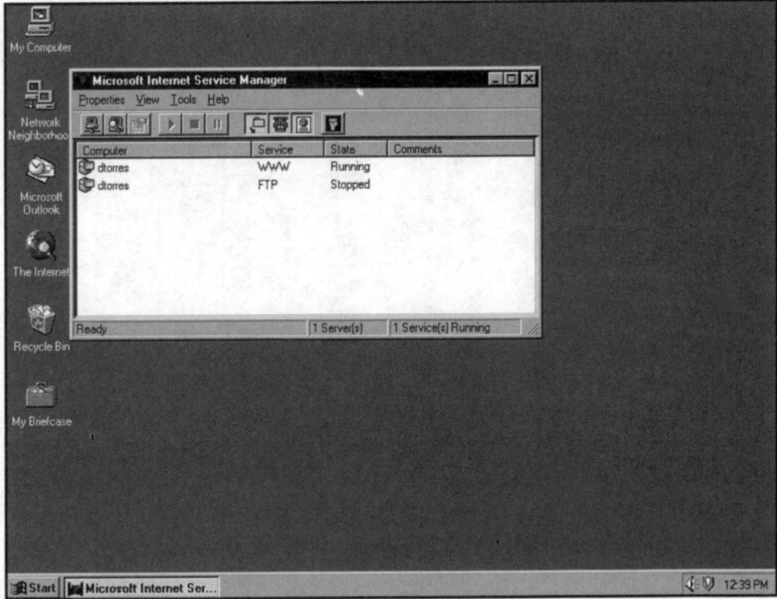

FIG. 34.2
The Microsoft Internet Service Manager.

6. Click the Add button—this will bring up the Directory Properties dialog box.
7. Click the Browse button to navigate to the directory created in step one, or type the UNC path or physical path to the created directory.

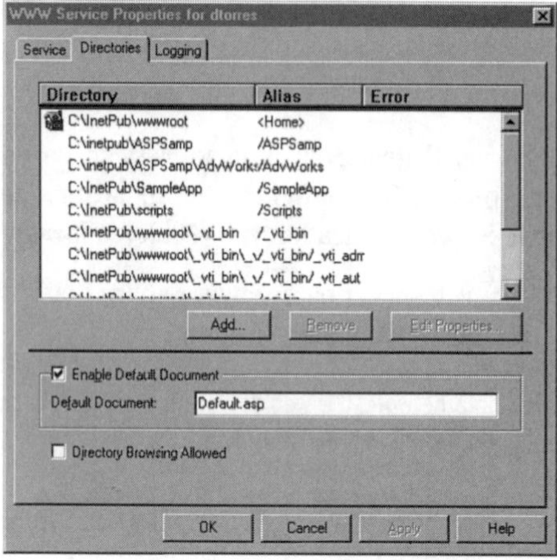

FIG. 34.3 The WWW Service Property's Directories tab.

8. Give the new Virtual Directory an alias name by typing an application title in the Alias text box. The alias name must have a forward slash in front of it so the browser can interpret it correctly (see Figure 34.4).
9. Select both Read and Execute Access for the directory (see Figure 34.4).

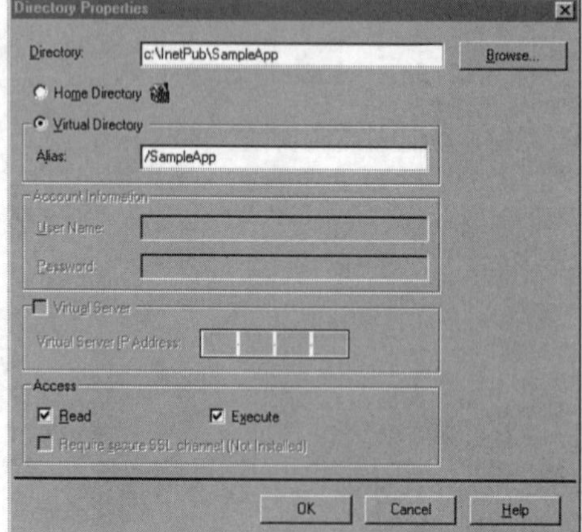

FIG. 34.4 WWW Service Properties focusing on the Directories Properties dialog box.

10. Click OK to add the new Active Server Pages directory to the web site.
11. Click OK on the WWW Service Properties dialog box.
12. Close the Microsoft Internet Service Manager application.

You are now ready to begin the development of an Active Server Pages application. The following sections in this chapter further discuss Active Server Pages development and guide you through the development of a simple Active Server Pages application using Exchange Server's public COM interface.

Introduction to Active Server Pages Using VBScript

Remember the days when you had to code CGI applications, Perl scripts, or even ISAPI extensions to get anything dynamic out of your web site? It wasn't that long ago, maybe all of two years, but it seems that way now that we have Active Server Pages.

The next few sections outline how Active Server Pages enable you to create dynamic content as easily as creating applications with Visual Basic. So throw away the "C" compiler and jump onboard the ASP train.

Working with VBScript

Visual Basic (VB) has been the darling of the information technology industry since 1993. With several major revisions and improvements, it has become the language of choice for the development of corporate client-server applications. VB has captivated millions of developers as being the first "object-style" language for the masses. VB gave birth to a whole industry that built reusable components using the Visual Basic Extension (VBX) and OLE Control Extension (OCX) programming models.

With the ground swell of support for Visual Basic in the development community, Microsoft developed a version of VB called Visual Basic for Applications (VBA), which has become the common scripting language in all the Microsoft Office desktop applications. VBA is a subset of the functionality available in VB, replacing WordBasic and Excel's macro language to enable users to learn one scripting language to automate tasks and construct applications based on Microsoft's office productivity tools.

Since Microsoft already had a loyal following with the VB language, it was natural for it to continue to use the VB pyridine when it came to scripting languages for web applications. VBScript, like VBA, is a subset of the functionality available in VB. VBScript can be used at the client browser, assuming that the browser is Microsoft Internet Explorer 3.x or later, or within Active Server Pages in the context of Internet Information System version 3.x or later.

With the ability to use VBScript at both the web browser and web server, you obtain the ability to manipulate publicly exposed COM interfaces in the development of web-based applications. On the client side, these COM objects are known as ActiveX controls. On the server side, these COM objects are known as Active Server objects. The examples that follow concentrate on the development of Active Server Pages that utilize VBScript to manipulate the Active Messaging library of objects provided with Exchange Server to create HTML pages that are returned to the web browser. Because results of an Active Server Page request is HTML code, it does not matter which web browser or operating system the client is using, as long as it properly interprets standard HTML 3.x web pages.

Many companies today struggle with cross platform client-server application development issues. Active Server Pages provides an alternative in the development of these applications. Multi-tiered application development is now underway in many corporations using VBScript as the glue that holds the server-based vertical data services to business rule components and the presentation on the web browser. The web browser becomes the host for "thin client" applications that utilize the Internet/Intranet to provide location independence and harness the power of the "big iron" multiprocessors (multi-megabyte, mass-storage servers that are proliferating themselves within corporations today).

Using Active Server Page Applications

Microsoft has begun to develop more and more Active Server Pages applications as tools for managing and using the BackOffice applications. The first of these Active Server Pages applications was the Internet Service administrator. The web-based version of the Internet Service administrator tool works in much the same way as its compiled counterpart. This gave web masters the ability to manage their web sites remotely via a web browser.

This trend continued with Web-based tools for the management of Windows NT Servers and in Exchange 5.0 Service Pack 1. Then Microsoft introduced one of the first Active Server Page applications for the end user, Outlook Web Access. Outlook Web Access is similar to its Office 97 counterpart, but is completely web based as an Active Server Pages application. Does the Microsoft Outlook Web Access client meet all of your personal information management needs? Your answer is most likely yes, Microsoft has worked hard to provide a client that is feature rich and easy to use at the same time. If the answer was no, you can make modifications easily to Outlook Web Access to tailor it to your company, and at the same time introduce the client to as many platforms as possible. Microsoft has taken a very large step in providing tools and technologies that leverage the Active Server platform and provide access cross-platform via the Internet. This chapter previously discussed the preparation necessary to begin an Active Server Pages application by outlining the proper installation of Windows NT Server and Internet Information Server and adding an Active Server Pages application directory to the web server. For development, however, Internet Information Server doesn't have to be used. Peer Web Server 3.0 for Windows NT Workstation 4.0 and Personal Web Server for Windows 95 can also be used as a development testing ground.

To take our first step in the development of Active Server Pages applications, you need to start with the basics. The first application will be the same application that every other programming textbook uses, the "Hello World" example. The example below assumes that you've created an Active Server Pages directory as outlined previously on the web server called \SampleApp. The following steps outline the syntax needed for your first Active Server Pages applet:

1. Open up your favorite text editor and enter the following HTML code. This HTML code is the basic requirement for any HTML page:

```
<HTML>
<HEAD>
<TITLE>Hello World!</TITLE>
</HEAD>
<BODY>
<!-- This is where we'll insert our VBScript -->
</BODY>
</HTML>
```

2. Replace the line of code at the "<!--" tag with VBScript code that is to run at the server by enclosing it with the <% and %> HTML tags:

```
<% Response.Write("Hello World!")%>
```

NOTE Active Server Pages applications have several unique intrinsic objects that are used to create instances of Active Server objects, respond to requests, and access application variables. The `Application`, `Server`, `Session`, `Request`, and `Response` objects are documented in the Active Server Pages Roadmap documentation that accompanies IIS 3.0. ■

3. Save the file in the directory associated with /SampleApp as HelloWorld.ASP.
4. Open your web browser and request `http://[your` web server]/SampleApp/HelloWorld.ASP. The results should be as those found in Figure 34.5.

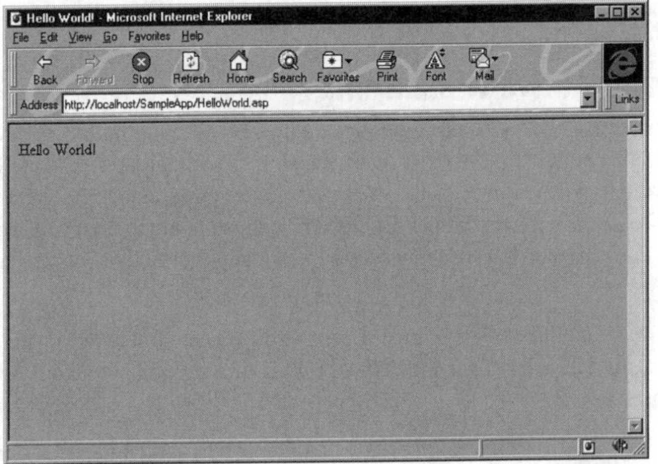

FIG. 34.5
Results of Hello World ASP applet.

5. Now open the source file received by the browser. With Internet Explorer, this is accomplished by right-clicking on the body of the page and selecting View Source. The following is what the browser received from the web server:

```
<HTML>
<HEAD>
<TITLE>Hello World!</TITLE>
</HEAD>
<BODY>
Hello World!
</BODY>
</HTML>
```

6. Notice that the web server has replaced the Active Server Pages code with HTML text using VBScript code added in step 2.

Now that you have created your first Active Server Pages application, you are ready for a more complex and interesting example. In the next section, you will create an Active Server Page that utilizes the Active Messaging technology for Exchange Server.

Understanding Active Messaging

Now that you have a basic understanding of what Active Server Pages are, you can explore one step further with Active Messaging, which enables you to take advantage of the Messaging and Collaborative capabilities of Exchange Server. Active Messaging enables you to write Active Server Applications that can read and send mail, access public folders, and access the messaging directory through a web browser. The Active Messaging object libraries and included files are provided by Microsoft to jump start your development efforts by providing a foundation for messaging and groupware application development that is available to multiple client operating system platforms. All the processing that occurs happens at the server. This is why the client web browser becomes agnostic to what platform it is on.

Working with Active Messaging

The concept of Active Messaging is not a new messaging model; however, it provides scripting capabilities built upon the existing messaging model of MAPI. To take full advantage of Active Messaging, during the installation of Exchange Server select the option for installing the Outlook Web Access Components. By installing these components, you are immediately capable of connecting to your Exchange server by requesting an Active Server Page through your Web browser.

Key areas that must be discussed if you wish to create full-featured web applications include Messaging Libraries. There are two libraries you can utilize to build Active Server Pages applications:

- The Active Messaging Library enables you to send and receive mail.
- The Active Messaging Rendering Library is used to render the Active Messaging objects and HTML information.

These libraries can be called from Visual Basic, VBScript, JavaScript, Java, and any application that supports Visual Basic for Applications (VBA). To utilize the libraries, you should have a good familiarity with Visual Basic and an understanding of MAPI.

Like any application development project that involves objects, when you develop applications for Exchange, you need to know its properties and methods. For example, if you are accessing the `Recipient` object, there are various *properties* that are addressable, such as `Address`, `Class`, `ID`, `Name`, and `Session`, which enable you to either enter or read information on specific details about the object in question. There are corresponding *methods* that are available for each object, such as `Delete`, `IsNameAs`, and `Resolve`. These methods are the actual means of how to accomplish the task on the property.

When approaching Active Messaging, you also must understand that because MAPI is still the primary interface, a MAPI session must be established for access. The Microsoft Exchange Client default timeout is sixty minutes for authenticated users. The pages included with Exchange provide an example of Active Server Pages scripts on which you can base your development for custom Login screens and mailboxes. The easiest way to understand how to utilize the features of Active Messaging is to walk through an example. The following exercise shows you how Active Messaging can utilize your Web browser to query and display information from your Exchange Server's global address list. As is true with many other development environments, you must rely on libraries to add extra functionality. These libraries include functions that can be called by your program as needed. These and other libraries are automatically installed in the C:\ExchSrvr\WebData directory as part of the Exchange Server installation.

Following an Active Server Page Example

Our Active Server Pages code example is intended to explain the major points to be aware of when developing an Active Server Pages application that interacts with Exchange Server. For a more in depth survey of Active Server Pages applications using Active Messaging, review the sample applications found on Microsoft's web site at `www.microsoft.com/technet/appfarm`. This web site has a number of Active Server Pages example applications that will provide a wealth of information on the many uses of Exchange Server on the web.

NOTE The initial invocation of an Active Messaging application executes Global.ASA. This file is supplied with the Outlook Web Access installation, and invokes the base Active Server objects to access the services within Exchange Server. Make sure to copy this file into your Active Server Page application directory when developing an application that interacts with Exchange Server. ■

Begin your Active Server Page by referencing the standard Exchange Server, including files provided with the Outlook Web Access installation:

```
<!--#include file='constant.inc' -->
<!--#include file='session.inc' -->
<!--#include file='getrend.inc' -->
```

Within Global.ASA, an instance of the Message Rendering object is created and stored within an Application variable. Application variables are shared amongst users accessing the Active Server Pages application. This reduces the overhead required to create and delete objects each time an Active Server Page is requested. In the code that follows, the local variable `objRenderApp` is set with a reference to the object stored in the Application variable named `bstrRenderApp`:

```
<% set objRenderApp = Application( bstrRenderApp ) %>
```

After a reference to the Message Rendering object is established, properties can be set and queried and methods can be executed. In the code that follows, if the property ConfigParameter("Publish GAL") and the Session variable of `bstrAuthenticated` are set to "False," then an error is reported:

```
<%
If objRenderApp.ConfigParameter("Publish GAL") = False And
➥Session(bstrAuthenticated) = False Then
  ReportErrorClose errPageDisabled
  Response.End
End If
%>
```

The following code once again accesses the Message Rendering object's ConfigParameter to determine the publishing limit for the Global Address List (GAL).

This Active Server Page is executed as a result of an HTML form being completed and submitted. Data from the form is retrieved from the requesting form using the Active Server Pages intrinsic `Request` object. This object contains the collection of the elements within the requesting form. These elements will be used later to create a filter for listing addresses from the GAL. The final line of code in this section establishes a new Hierarchy object that will be used in the next section of code:

```
<%
    nPubLimit = objRenderApp.ConfigParameter("Publish GAL Limit")
     If CStr(nPubLimit) = "" Then
          nPubLimit = 9999
     End If
     If nPubLimit > 0 Then
          strDisplayName = Request.Form("DN")
          strFirstName = Request.Form("FN")
          strLastName = Request.Form("LN")
          strTitle = Request.Form("TL")
          strAlias = Request.Form("AN")
          strCompany = Request.Form("CP")
          strDepartment = Request.Form("DP")
          strOffice = Request.Form("OF")
          strCity = Request.Form("CY")
          Set Hierarchy = objOMSession.AddressLists
     EndIf
%>
```

The `Hierarchy` object created above is tested to determine if it exists. If it does not exist, an error is reported. If it is valid, processing continues by validating the entries in the Hierarchy collection. Additional error checking is provided to ensure that the address list is valid. Finally, in this section you will create an `Address Entry Filter` object, which is populated in the next section of code (see Listing 34.1).

Listing 34.1 An Address Entry Filter Object

```
<%
     If Hierarchy Is Nothing Then
          ReportError1 errAddrBookInvalid
     End If
     For i = 1 to  Hierarchy.Count
          Set objAddressList = Hierarchy.Item(i)
          If objAddressList.Fields(ActMsgPR_DISPLAY_TYPE) = ActMsgDT_GLOBAL then
               Err.Clear
               Exit For
          End If
     Next
     If objAddressList Is Nothing Then
           ReportError1 errAddrBookInvalid
     End If
     Set objAddrEntries = objAddressList.AddressEntries
```

```
    If objAddrEntries Is Nothing or Err.Number <> 0 Then
        ReportError1 errAddrBookInvalid
    End If
    Set objAEFilter = objAddrEntries.Filter
    If objAEFilter Is Nothing or Err.Number <> 0 Then
        ReportError1 errAddrBookInvalid
    End If
%>
```

In the following section of code (see Listing 34.2), filter object is populated with the variables received from the requesting query form. The information from the querying form is used to reduce the scope of the addresses returned and rendered for the web browser.

Listing 34.2 Populating the Filter Object

```
<%
        objAEFilter.Or = False
        If strDisplayName <> "" Then
            objAEFilter.Fields.Add ActMsgPR_DISPLAY_NAME, strDisplayName
        End If
        If strFirstName <> "" Then
            objAEFilter.Fields.Add ActMsgPR_GIVEN_NAME, strFirstName
        End If
        If strLastName <> "" Then
            objAEFilter.Fields.Add ActMsgPR_SURNAME, strLastName
        End If
        If strTitle <> "" Then
            objAEFilter.Fields.Add ActMsgPR_TITLE, strTitle
        End If
        If strAlias <> "" Then
            objAEFilter.Fields.Add ActMsgPR_ACCOUNT, strAlias
        End If
        If strCompany <> "" Then
            objAEFilter.Fields.Add ActMsgPR_COMPANY_NAME, strCompany
        End If
            If strDepartment <> "" Then
            objAEFilter.Fields.Add ActMsgPR_DEPARTMENT_NAME, strDepartment
        End If
        If strOffice <> "" Then
            objAEFilter.Fields.Add ActMsgPR_OFFICE_LOCATION, strOffice
        End If
        If strCity <> "" Then
            objAEFilter.Fields.Add ActMsgPR_LOCALITY, strCity
        End If
%>
```

The final section of code (see Listing 34.3) produces the actual HTML page based on the query submitted by the user. The `GetAddressContainerRender` function is found in the GETREND.INC include file, which you registered at the beginning of the application. The `GetAddressContainerRender` creates an object that produces the HTML page that is returned to the user's web browser.

Listing 34.3 Producing the Actual HTML Page

```
<%
        Set objRender = GetAddressContainerRenderer
        objRender.RowsPerPage = objAddrEntries.Count
        objRender.DataSource = objAddrEntries
        objRender.Render 1, 1, 0, Response
%>
```

Our example above demonstrated some of the aspects of using the Active Messaging objects and libraries provided by Microsoft within an Active Server Pages code. The Microsoft Outlook Web Access application is a wonderful example of a feature-rich Active Server Pages application, but even it may not meet the messaging needs of your organization. If your organization has unique messaging requirements, the tools are available to create very robust web-enabled applications using Active Messaging.

Working with Remote Data Services

Up to this point, the book has strictly dealt with web-enabling Exchange Server using Active Server Pages. Active Server Pages provide for cross platform compatibility in your web messaging applications. But when feature-rich functionality is more important than cross-platform compatibility and you have the luxury of dictating a web browser, there are alternatives. Microsoft has developed a technology called Remote Data Services (RDS), which enables a client web page to invoke methods and proprieties of Active Server objects that reside at the web server.

Remote Data Services consists of two parts: client-side ActiveX controls and a server-side ISAPI extension. These two components provide the communication plumbing and data marshalling between the client's web page and business rule objects on the web server.

The primary functionality of Remote Data Services is to access relational data that is accessible via a web server. A secondary function of Remote Data Service is the capability to invoke custom business objects that perform business rule processing on the server and return responses back to the client's web page. This is where we can hook into Exchange Server to produce very robust web applications.

For additional information concerning Remote Data Services, please refer to `www.microsoft.com/data/rds`. At Microsoft's web site you can download the client and server files, review system requirements, and investigate the technology's documentation.

Utilizing Remote Data Services, a web page may make any number of method calls to a business rule object that resides on a web server. The web server does not even have to be the web server where the web pages are hosted. Thus, three-tiered and multi-tiered web applications become a reality. Figure 34.6 visually depicts a three-tiered architecture using the Remote Data Services to interact with Exchange Server.

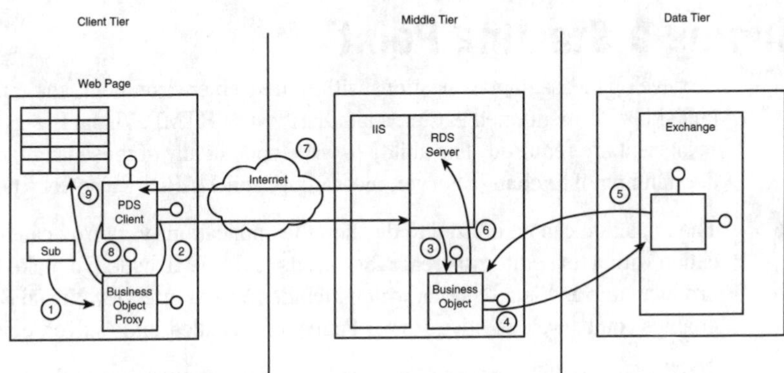

FIG. 34.6
A web-based, three-tiered application.

Using Figure 34.6, the following is a description of the data flow between the client browser, middle-tiered business object, and the information stored within Exchange Server.

1. Using VBScript within a client web page, a request is made to create an instance of a business rule object that resides on the web server. A proxy of the object on the web server is created at the client. Once the proxy has been created, the client can invoke the methods of the business object.
2. The method request is packaged by the client-side Remote Data Service using a special MIME type and transmitted to the web server.
3. The web server receives the request, unpacks it, invokes the business rule object, and executes the requested method.
4. The business rule object then invokes the exposed methods of Exchange Server.
5. Exchange Server responds to the business rule object's request, and returns the requested information or issues response code.
6. The business rule object in turn creates a response for the client web page, which is passed through the Remote Data Service server-side component.
7. Remote Data Service server-side component packages up the response into a special MIME time and returns the response back to the client's web browser.
8. The Remote Data Services client-side service unpacks the response and notifies the client web page of the results.
9. VBScript code within the client web page is executed and presents the results back to the user.

The subject of Remote Data Services or Universal Data Access is a book unto its own. This section was intended to whet the appetite of a developer to investigate the multitude of possibilities available to a web client using Remote Data Services.

Finding a Starting Point

To develop messaging applications within the web environment, you must acquire some important skills. As mentioned earlier, a familiarity with HTML, Visual Basic, VBScript, Java, and JavaScript are required. The ability to write code in any of these languages and a working understanding of Exchange Server, messaging, and MAPI are also very helpful.

The tools that can be utilized to develop the applications vary. You can develop the entire application with a text editor to create the scripts and HTML code. To make life easier on yourself, a product such as Visual Studio, which includes Visual InterDev, Visual Basic, and Visual J++ enables you to create Active Server Pages, HTML files, and ActiveX objects is invaluable.

You'll also find that there are a number of resources available on the Internet, several of which have been mentioned in this chapter. As always, Microsoft provides invaluable information via their web sites (**www.microsoft.com, backoffice.microsoft.com, www.microsoft.com/msdn, www.microsoft.com/workshop**) on updates, code examples, add-ons, and betas. It also contains many technical articles and white papers on the various development skills mentioned previously, as well as news and discussion groups specifically for Active Server Pages.

NOTE One of the most comprehensive web sites available besides **www.microsoft.com** for information relating to Active Server Pages can be found at **www.genusa.com/asp**. This site has a very complete FAQ, tutorial, and software library, and is an excellent resource for Active Server Page development. ■

Index

A

B

C

D

E

F

G

H

I

M

N

O

P

Q

R

S

X

Z

Complete and Return this Card for a *FREE* Computer Book Catalo

Thank you for purchasing this book! You have purchased a superior computer book writte expressly for your needs. To continue to provide the kind of up-to-date, pertinent coverage you've come to expect from us, we need to hear from you. Please take a minute to comple and return this self-addressed, postage-paid form. In return, we'll send you a free catalog o all our computer books on topics ranging from word processing to programming and the internet.

Mrs. ☐ Ms. ☐ Dr. ☐

irst) ☐☐☐☐☐☐☐☐☐☐☐ (M.I.) ☐ (last) ☐☐☐☐☐☐☐☐☐☐☐☐☐☐

State ☐☐ Zip ☐☐☐☐☐ ☐☐☐☐

Fax ☐☐☐ ☐☐☐ ☐☐☐☐

y Name

ddress

e check at least (3) influencing factors for
ıasing this book.

- back cover information on book ☐
- approach to the content ☐
- eness of content ☐
- s reputation ☐
- r's reputation ☐
- ver design or layout ☐
- table of contents of book ☐
- book ☐
- effects, graphics, illustrations ☐
- lease specify): ___ ☐

did you first learn about this book?

- Macmillan Computer Publishing catalog ☐
- nended by store personnel ☐
- book on bookshelf at store ☐
- nended by a friend ☐
- d advertisement in the mail ☐
- advertisement in: ___ ☐
- ok review in: ___ ☐
- lease specify): ___ ☐

many computer books have you
ıased in the last six months?

- ok only ☐ 3 to 5 books ☐
- ☐ More than 5 ☐

4. Where did you purchase this book?

- Bookstore ☐
- Computer Store ☐
- Consumer Electronics Store ☐
- Department Store ☐
- Office Club ☐
- Warehouse Club ☐
- Mail Order ☐
- Direct from Publisher ☐
- Internet site ☐
- Other (Please specify): ___ ☐

5. How long have you been using a computer?

- ☐ Less than 6 months
- ☐ 6 months to a year
- ☐ 1 to 3 years
- ☐ More than 3 years

6. What is your level of experience with personal computers and with the subject of this book?

	With PCs	With subject of book
New	☐	☐
Casual	☐	☐
Accomplished	☐	☐
Expert	☐	☐

Source Code ISBN: 0-7897-1503-1

Which of the following best describes your job title?

dministrative Assistant .... ☐
oordinator .... ☐
anager/Supervisor .... ☐
rector .... ☐
ce President .... ☐
esident/CEO/COO .... ☐
wyer/Doctor/Medical Professional .... ☐
acher/Educator/Trainer .... ☐
gineer/Technician .... ☐
onsultant .... ☐
ot employed/Student/Retired .... ☐
her (Please specify): ________ ☐

Which of the following best describes the area of the company your job title falls under?

ccounting .... ☐
gineering .... ☐
anufacturing .... ☐
erations .... ☐
arketing .... ☐
les .... ☐
her (Please specify): ________ ☐

9. What is your age?

Under 20 ....
21-29 ....
30-39 ....
40-49 ....
50-59 ....
60-over ....

10. Are you:

Male ....
Female ....

11. Which computer publications do you read regularly? (Please list)

____

mments: ________________

Fold here and scotch-t

NO POSTAGE
NECESSARY
IF MAILED
IN THE
UNITED STATE

BUSINESS REPLY MAIL

FIRST-CLASS MAIL PERMIT NO. 9918 INDIANAPOLIS IN

POSTAGE WILL BE PAID BY THE ADDRESSEE

ATTN MARKETING
MACMILLAN COMPUTER PUBLISHING
MACMILLAN PUBLISHING USA
201 W 103RD ST
INDIANAPOLIS IN 46290-9042

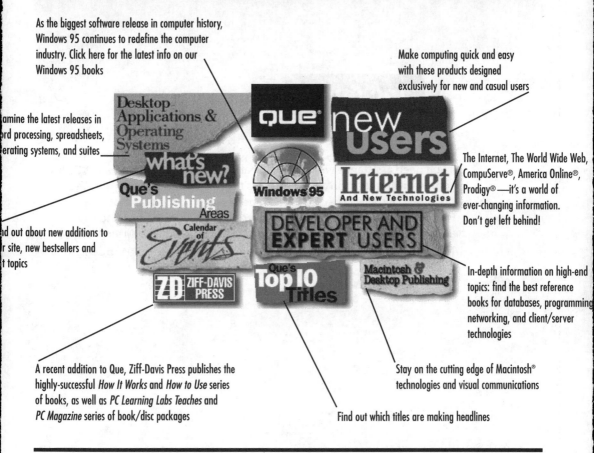

Technical Support:

If you need assistance with the information in this book or with a CD/Disk accompanying the book, please access the Knowledge Base on our Web site at http://www.superlibrary.com/general/support. Our most Frequently Asked Questions are answered there. If you do not find the answer to your questions on our Web site, you may contact Macmillan Technical Support (317) 581-3833 or e-mail us at support@mcp.com.